the Unofficial Guide® to Las Vegas

1998

Also available from Macmillan Travel:

the Unofficial Guide® to Las Vegas

1998

Bob Sehlinger

Macmillan • USA

In memory of Dan Wallace, a Gamblin' Man

Every effort has been made to ensure the accuracy of information throughout this book. Bear in mind, however, that prices, schedules, etc., are constantly changing. Readers should always verify information before making final plans.

Macmillan Travel
A Simon & Schuster Macmillan Company
1633 Broadway
New York, NY 10019-6785

Produced by Menasha Ridge Press
Design by Barbara E. Williams

MACMILLAN is a registered trademark of Macmillan, Inc.
UNOFFICIAL GUIDE is a registered trademark of Simon & Schuster, Inc.

ISBN 0-02-862037-2

ISSN 1064-5640

Manufactured in the United States of America

10 9 8 7 6 5 4 3 2 1

1998 Edition

CONTENTS

ACKNOWLEDGMENTS

The people of Las Vegas love their city and spare no effort to assist a writer trying to dig beneath the facade of flashing neon. It is important to them to communicate that Las Vegas is a city with depth, diversity, and substance. "Don't just write about our casinos," they demand, "take the time to get to know us."

We made every effort to do just that, enabled each step of the way by some of the most sincere and energetic folks a writer could hope to encounter. Myram Borders of the Las Vegas News Bureau provided us access to anyone we wanted to see, from casino general managers to vice cops. Cam Usher of the Las Vegas Convention and Visitors Authority also spared no effort in offering assistance and contacts.

Restaurant critic Muriel Stevens ate her way through dozens of new restaurants but drew the line when it came to buffet duty. Bonnie Parrish stayed up late and worked hard to gather information on Las Vegas night life. Jim McDonald of the Las Vegas Police Department shared his experiences and offered valuable suggestions for staying out of trouble. Jack Sheehan evaluated Las Vegas golf courses, and forest ranger Debbie Savage assisted us in developing material on wilderness recreation.

Purple Hearts to our field research team, who chowed down on every buffet and $2 steak in town, checked in and out of countless hotels, visited tourist attractions, and stood for hours in show lines:

Mike Jones	K'-Lynne Cotton	Nicole Jones	Marty Newey
Julie Newey	Holly Brown	Shirley Gutke	Dan Cotton
Joan Burns	Lee Wiseman	Molly Burns	Leslie Cummins
Grace Walton	Sean Ross		

Much gratitude to Chris Crochetière, Julie Allred, Holly Brown, Grace Walton, Brian Taylor, Ann Cassar, and Clay White, the pros who somehow turned all this effort into a book.

On a Plane to Las Vegas

I never wanted to go to Las Vegas. I'm not much of a gambler and have always thought of Las Vegas as a city dedicated to separating folks from their money. As it happens, however, I have some involvement with industries that hold conventions and trade shows there. For some years I was able to persuade others to go in my place. Eventually, of course, it came my turn to go, and I found myself aboard a Delta jumbo jet on my first trip to Las Vegas.

Listening to the banter of those around me, I became aware that my fellow passengers were divided into two distinct camps. Some obviously thought themselves on a nonstop flight to nirvana and could not have been happier. Too excited to remain seated, they danced up and down the aisles clapping one another on the back in anticipation. The other passengers, by contrast, groused and grumbled, swore under their breath, and wore expressions suggesting a steady diet of lemons. These people, as despondent as Willie Nelson en route to a tax audit, lamented their bad luck and cursed those who had made a trip to such a place necessary.

To my surprise, I thoroughly enjoyed Las Vegas. I had a great time without gambling and have been back many times with never a bad experience. The people are friendly, the food is good, hotels are a bargain, it's an easy town to get around in, and there is plenty to do (24 hours a day, if you are so inclined).

It's hard to say why so many folks have such strong feelings about Las Vegas (even those who have never been there). Among our research team we had people willing to put their kids in boarding school for a chance to go, while others begged off to have root canal surgery or prune their begonias. A third group wanted to go very badly but maintained the pretense of total indifference. They reminded me of people who own five TVs yet profess never to watch television; they clearly had not mustered the courage to come out of the closet.

What I discovered during my first and subsequent visits is that the nongambling public doesn't know very much about Las Vegas. Many people cannot see beyond the gambling, cannot see that there could possibly be anything of value in Las Vegas for nongamblers or those only marginally interested in gambling.

When you ask these people to describe their ideal vacation, they wax eloquent about lazy days relaxing in the sun, playing golf, enjoying the luxury of resort hotels, eating in fine restaurants, sight-seeing, shopping, and going to the theater. Outdoor types speak no less enthusiastically about fishing, boating, hiking, and, in the winter, skiing. As it happens, Las Vegas offers all of these diversions and probably at the lowest prices available anywhere. Gambling is just the tip of the iceberg in Las Vegas, but it's all many people can see.

Las Vegas is, of course, about gambling, but there's much more. Las Vegas has sunny, mild weather two-thirds of the year, some of the finest hotels and restaurants in the world, the most diversified celebrity and production show entertainment to be found, unique shopping, internationally renowned golf courses, and numerous attractions. For the outdoor enthusiast, Red Rock Canyon National Conservation Area, Lake Mead National Recreation Area, and Toiyabe National Forest offer some of the most exotic and beautiful wilderness resources in North America.

This guide is designed for those who want to go to Las Vegas and for those who *have* to go to Las Vegas. If you are a recreational gambler and/or enthusiastic vacationer, we will help you pour champagne over the iceberg. We will show you ways to have more fun, make the most of your time, and spend less money. If you are one of the skeptics, unwilling spouses or companions of gamblers, business travelers, or people who think they would rather be someplace else, we will help you discover the nine-tenths of the Las Vegas iceberg that is hidden. We will demonstrate that you can have the time of your life in this friendly city and never bet that first nickel.

Looking Back, Looking Ahead

As construction of new casinos and hotels continued unabated through 1997, the number of guest rooms in Las Vegas nudged the 100,000 mark. New casinos opened during the year included the Spanish-themed Sunset Station in Green Valley and the Orleans (on Tropicana just west of the Strip) with a New Orleans/Cajun/Bayou theme. Also, Main Street Station, closed for several years, reopened downtown under the management of the Boyd group.

Circus Circus began development of its "Master Plan Mile," at the south end of the Strip. When completed, a 3,800-room South Sea island theme resort will occupy the old Hacienda site and will be adjoined by a nongaming Four Seasons luxury hotel with 400 rooms. A second phase of development will include "Project Z," an 8,000-room hotel-casino of undetermined theme, and a 2,000-unit timeshare, retail, and office complex on the east side of the Strip. All told, the Master Plan Mile will encompass 23,000 rooms, including existing rooms in the Excalibur and Luxor.

Ground was broken in 1997 for Paris, a Parisian-themed property that will erect a 50-story Eiffel Tower and an Arc de Triomphe to attract attention to its 3,000 rooms and casino. Paris will be yet another Hilton hotel, joining the Flamingo, Bally's, and the Las Vegas Hilton. Meanwhile, across the Strip, work continues apace on Bellagio, the Mirage-owned luxury casino scheduled for opening in late 1998. Moving north on the Strip, work has begun on the Venetian, a 6,000-room super-resort to be erected on the site of the recently demolished Sands.

Work will begin soon on a new 1,000-room tower and casino expansion for New York–New York, the newest currently operating hotel on the Strip. The new tower will be erected on the site of La Quinta Inn next door. Caesars Palace, already in the midst of major expansion, has announced plans for a new retail, restaurant, and entertainment complex to be called Caesars Maximus. Among other things, the complex will feature chariot races held in the middle of a mock Roman hill town. No tourists will be fed to the lions in Caesars Roman hill town: that, after all, is what the casino is for.

Other major expansions and renovations are virtually epidemic, with whole makeovers at the Aladdin, Harrah's, Desert Inn, and Sahara, and major projects at the Las Vegas Hilton and MGM-Grand. In addition to the foregoing, renovations have recently been completed at the Rio, Luxor, Flamingo, Arizona Charlie's, Las Vegas Club, Showboat, and Fitzgeralds.

As significant as the building boom on the Strip is, what's not happening is any aggressive and workable plan to tackle the Strip's horrendous traffic problem. Adding 10,000 Strip hotel rooms a year is great if guests arrive by parachute or bicycle. If you have the crazy notion of accessing your hotel by cab, bus, or car, you will find that the congestion loosens up a bit around 3 a.m.

Of the recently opened new casinos, New York–New York and Monte Carlo logged good first years while the Stratosphere struggled, scaled back, and ultimately reorganized. Debbie Reynolds' Hollywood Hotel and Casino is in need of $5 million in improvements to stay afloat. The future of Bourbon Street, already without a casino for more than a year, is likewise iffy. In a war of the giants, Hilton tried to acquire ITT-Sheraton (Desert Inn and Caesars Palace) in a hostile takeover. Fallout from this move has thus far postponed the Planet Hollywood Hotel-Casino project and caused the Desert Inn to be put up for sale.

In a rare combination of commercial development and historic preservation, millionaire Bart Maybie has purchased the Moulin Rouge, which opened in the 1950s as the first racially integrated hotel-casino in Las Vegas. Maybie plans to restore the Moulin Rouge, preserving as much of its architecture and decor as possible. A onetime late-night hangout for such stars as Sammy Davis Jr. and Frank Sinatra, the Moulin Rouge is located at 900 West Bonanza Road.

Las Vegas's average room rate has continued its upward spiral. Increased room inventory coupled with lackluster profits in the casinos, however, are putting pressure on room rates to level off or decline. In the summer of 1997, some amazing room deals were offered. And, as always, the second- and third-tier casinos still offer excellent values in the room-rate department. Besides, compared to the expense of visiting Walt Disney World or staying overnight in a New York, Chicago, or San Francisco hotel, even the new midrange hotels are a bargain.

In dining, theme and upscale chain or franchise restaurants continue to be the rage, as do brew pubs. The theme joints are trendy and expensive; many have an attitude, but you can dine surrounded by rock and roll, sports, Motown, movie star, motorcycle, or nautical memorabilia (among others) while you scarf down your $12 burger. If you usually go to Disney World for your vacation, you will love the theme restaurants: they all make you wait in a long line for the privilege of eating mediocre, overpriced food. The brew pubs, in our estimation, are a happier development. They brew some nice beer (mostly ales), the food is better (and usually cheaper), and the service is friendlier than at the theme dining spots.

Finally, in a radical effort to stop the aging process, the Riviera has had the seven dancers known as the "Crazy Girls" bronzed. The life-size, 1,540-pound statue, celebrating the 10th anniversary of the Crazy Girl adult show at the Riviera, depicts the ladies from the rear in their traditional thong bikinis. No ifs or ands, just butts. Passersby are impressed. What, after all, can top the Statue of Liberty, an exploding volcano, or a pirate battle? Answer: the Riviera's seven moons.

About This Guide

■ How Come "Unofficial"? ■

Most "official" guides to Las Vegas tout the well-known sights, promote the local casinos, restaurants, and hotels indiscriminately, and leave out a lot of good stuff. This guide is different.

Instead of pandering to the tourist industry, we'll tell you if a well-known restaurant's mediocre food is not worth the wait. We'll complain loudly about overpriced hotel rooms that aren't convenient to the places you want to be, and we'll guide you away from the crowds and congestion for a break now and then.

We sent in a team of evaluators who toured the casinos and popular attractions, reviewed the production shows, ate in the area's best restaurants, performed critical evaluations of its hotels, and visited the best nightclubs. If a restaurant serves bad food or a show is not worth the admission price, we can say so—and, in the process, hopefully make your visit more fun, efficient, and economical.

■ Creating a Guidebook ■

We got into the guidebook business because we were unhappy with the way travel guides make the reader work to get any usable information. Wouldn't it be nice, we thought, if we were to make guides that are easy to use?

Most guidebooks are compilations of lists. This is true regardless of whether the information is presented in list form or artfully distributed through pages of prose. There is insufficient detail in a list, and prose can present tedious helpings of nonessential or marginally useful information. Not enough wheat, so to speak, for nourishment in one instance, and too much chaff in the other. Either way, these types of guides provide little more than departure points from which readers initiate their own quests.

Many guides are readable and well researched, but they tend to be difficult to use. To select a hotel, for example, a reader must study several pages of descriptions with only the boldface hotel names breaking up large blocks of text. Because each description essentially deals with the same variables, it is difficult to recall what was said concerning a particular hotel.

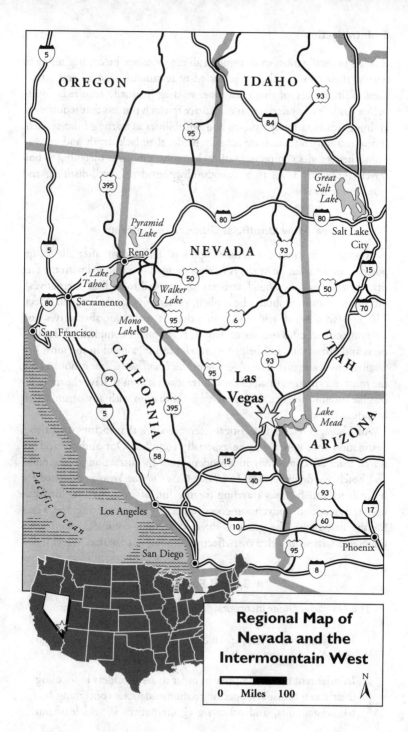

Regional Map of Nevada and the Intermountain West

0   Miles   100

N

Readers generally must work through all the write-ups before beginning to narrow their choices. The presentation of restaurants, shows, and attractions is similar except that even more reading is usually required. To use such a guide is to undertake an exhaustive research process that requires examining nearly as many options and possibilities as starting from scratch. If any recommendations are actually made, they lack depth and conviction. These guides compound rather than solve problems by failing to boil travelers' choices down to a thoughtfully considered, well-distilled, and manageable few.

■ How Unofficial Guides Are Different ■

Readers care about the author's opinion. The author, after all, *is* supposed to know what he or she is talking about. This, coupled with the fact that the traveler wants quick answers (as opposed to endless alternatives), dictates that authors should be explicit, prescriptive, and above all, direct. The *Unofficial Guide* tries to do just that. It spells out alternatives and recommends specific courses of action. It simplifies complicated destinations and attractions and helps the traveler feel in control in the most unfamiliar environments. The objective of the *Unofficial Guide* is not to have the most information or all of the information; it aims to have the most accessible, useful information, unbiased by affiliation with any organization or industry.

An *Unofficial Guide* is a critical reference work that focuses on a travel destination that appears to be especially complex. Our authors and research team are completely independent from the attractions, restaurants, and hotels we describe. *The Unofficial Guide to Las Vegas* is designed for individuals and families traveling for the fun of it, as well as for business travelers and convention-goers, especially those visiting Las Vegas for the first time. The guide is directed at value-conscious, consumer-oriented adults who seek a cost-effective, though not Spartan, travel style.

■ Special Features ■

The *Unofficial Guide* incorporates the following special features:

1. Its organization relates specifically to where travelers want to go and what they want to do.

2. Its orientation is prescriptive in order to assist readers in focusing their travel decisions. Specific recommendations concerning hotels, restaurants, and other travel alternatives should leave no

doubt as to the author's opinion. The responsibility for research and distillation is accepted by the author, as appropriate, rather than delegated to the reader.

3. The information presented is easily accessible, in a logical and user-friendly framework.

4. The Hotel Information Chart appendix eliminates the need for exhaustive reading in order to compare hotels.

5. A detailed table of contents and a comprehensive index ensure easy reference and cross-reference.

6. The *Unofficial Guide* provides in-depth descriptions of popular destinations and activities, with more abbreviated descriptions of less popular destinations and activities. Information of questionable value has been omitted to make room for more pertinent, universally valuable data.

■ How This Guide Was Researched and Written ■

While much has been written about Las Vegas, very little has been evaluative. Some guides practically regurgitate the hotels' and casinos' own promotional material. In preparing this work, we took nothing for granted. Each casino, hotel, restaurant, show, and attraction was visited at different times throughout the year by a team of trained observers. They conducted detailed evaluations and rated each property and entertainment according to formal, pretested rating criteria. Interviews were conducted to determine what tourists of all ages enjoyed most *and least* during their Las Vegas visit.

While our observers are independent and impartial, they do not claim to have special expertise. Like you, they visited Las Vegas as tourists or business travelers, noting their satisfaction or dissatisfaction.

The primary difference between the average tourist and the trained evaluator is the evaluator's skills in organization, preparation, and observation. The trained evaluator is responsible for much more than simply observing and cataloging. While the average tourist is being entertained by the magic of *Siegfried & Roy*, for instance, the professional is rating the performance in terms of theme, pace, continuity, and originality. The evaluator also checks out the physical arrangements: Is the sound system clear and audible without being overpowering? Is seating adequate? Can everyone in the audience clearly see the staging area? And what about the performers: Are they competent and professional; are they compelling and engaging? Does the performance begin and end on time? Does the show contain the features described in the hotel's promotional literature? These and many other considerations figure prominently in the rating of any staged performance. Observer teams used detailed checklists to analyze casinos, attractions, hotel rooms, buffets, and restaurants. Finally, evaluator ratings and observations were integrated with tourist reactions and the opinions of patrons for a comprehensive quality profile of each feature and service.

In compiling this guide, we recognize that tourists' ages, backgrounds, and interests will strongly influence their taste in Las Vegas offerings and will account for a preference for one show or casino over another. Our sole objective is to provide the reader with sufficient description, critical evaluation, and pertinent data to make knowledgeable decisions according to individual tastes.

■ Letters, Comments, and Questions from Readers ■

We expect to learn from our mistakes, as well as from the input of our readers, and to improve with each book and edition. Many of those who use the *Unofficial Guides* write to us to ask questions, make comments, or share their own discoveries and lessons learned in Las Vegas. We appreciate all such input, both positive and critical, and encourage our readers to continue writing. Readers' comments and observations will be frequently incorporated in revised editions of the *Unofficial Guide* and will contribute immeasurably to its improvement.

How to Write the Author:

Bob Sehlinger
The Unofficial Guide to Las Vegas
P.O. Box 43059
Birmingham, AL 35243

When you write, be sure to put your return address on your letter as well as on the envelope—sometimes envelopes and letters get separated. And remember, our work takes us out of the office for long periods of time, so forgive us if our response is delayed.

Reader Survey

At the back of this guide you will find a short questionnaire that you can use to express opinions concerning your Las Vegas visit. Clip the questionnaire out along the dotted line and mail it to the above address.

How Information Is Organized:
By Subject and by Geographic Zones

To give you fast access to information about the *best* of Las Vegas, we've organized material in several formats.

Hotels Because most people visiting Las Vegas stay in one hotel for the duration of their trip, we have summarized our coverage of hotels in charts, maps, ratings, and rankings that allow you to quickly focus your decision-making process. We do not go on page after page describing lobbies and rooms which, in the final analysis, sound much the same. Instead, we concentrate on the specific variables that differentiate one hotel from another: location, size, room quality, services, amenities, and cost.

Restaurants We provide a lot of detail when it comes to restaurants. Since you will probably eat a dozen or more restaurant meals during your stay, and since not even *you* can predict what you might be in the mood for on Saturday night, we provide detailed profiles of the best restaurants in Las Vegas.

Entertainment and Night Life Visitors frequently try several different shows or nightspots during their stay. Because shows and nightspots, like restaurants, are usually selected spontaneously after arriving in Las Vegas, we believe detailed descriptions are warranted. All continuously running stage shows, as well as celebrity showrooms, are profiled and reviewed in the entertainment section of this guide. The best nightspots and lounges in Las Vegas are profiled alphabetically under night life in the same section (see pages 216–231).

Geographic Zones Though it's easy to get around in Las Vegas, you may not have a car or the inclination to venture far from your hotel. To help you locate the best restaurants, shows, nightspots, and attractions convenient to where you are staying, we have divided the city into geographic zones:

- Zone 1   The Las Vegas Strip and Environs
- Zone 2   Downtown Las Vegas
- Zone 3   Southwest Las Vegas
- Zone 4   North Las Vegas
- Zone 5   Southeast Las Vegas and the Boulder Highway

All profiles of hotels, restaurants, and nightspots include zone numbers. For example, if you are staying at the Golden Nugget and are interested in Italian restaurants within walking distance, scanning the restaurant profiles for restaurants in Zone 2 (downtown) will provide you with the best choices.

Comfort Zones   Because every Las Vegas hotel-casino has its own personality and attracts a very specific type of customer, we have created a profile for each property that describes the casino's patrons (demographically) and gives you a sense of how it might feel to spend time there. The purpose of the comfort zone section is to help you find the hotel-casino where you will feel most welcome and at home. Comfort zone descriptions begin on page 90.

Las Vegas
Touring Zones

Miles

0   N   2

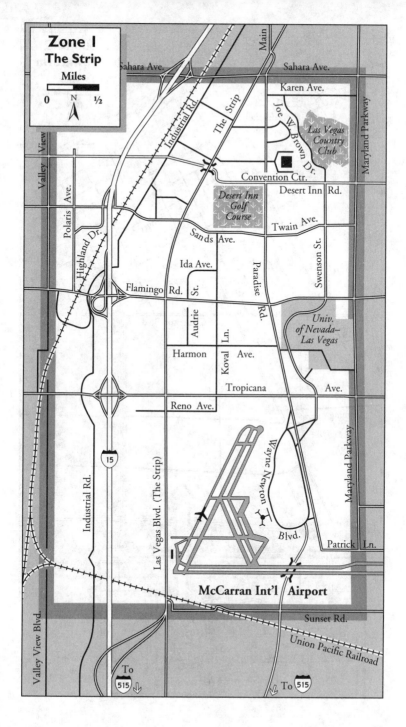

Zone 1
The Strip

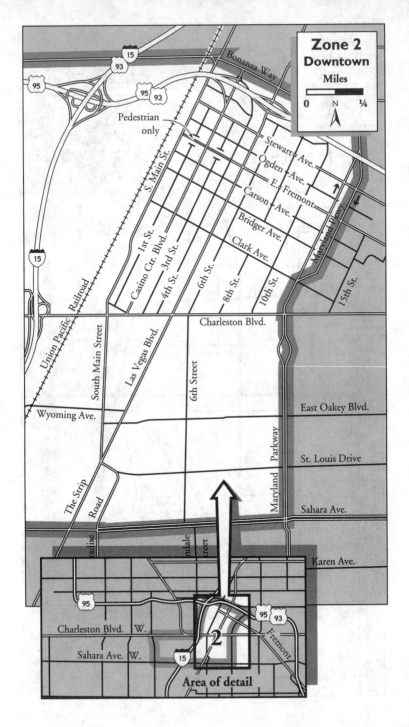

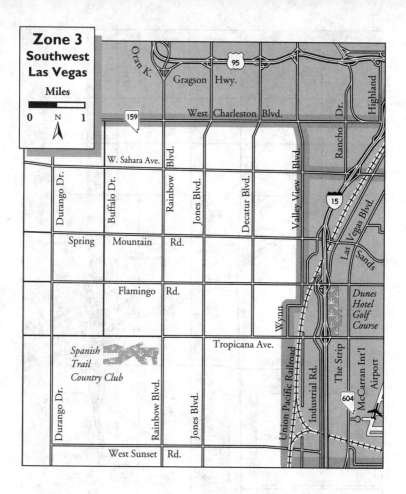

Zone 3
Southwest
Las Vegas

Miles

0   N   1

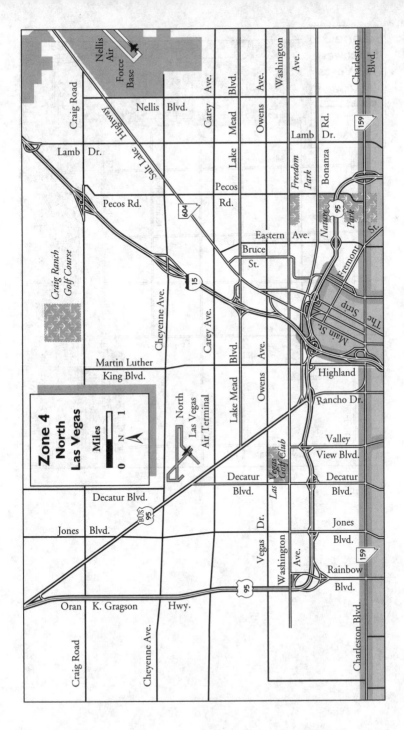

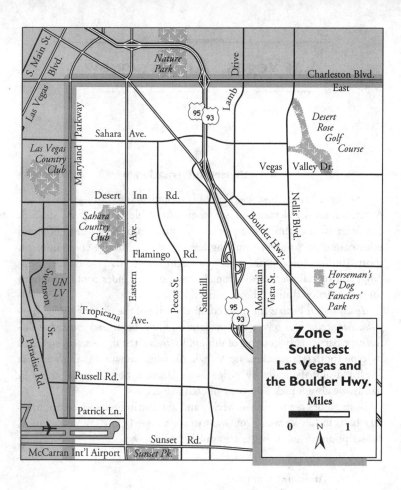

Zone 5
Southeast
Las Vegas and
the Boulder Hwy.

Miles

0   N   1

Las Vegas: An Overview

Las Vegas has the best selection of complimentary visitor guides of any American tourist destination we know. Available at the front desk or concierge table at almost every hotel, the guides provide a wealth of useful information on gaming, gambling lessons, shows, lounge entertainment, sports, buffets, meal-deals, tours and sight-seeing, transportation, shopping, and special events. Additionally, most of the guides contain coupons for discounts on dining, shows, attractions, and tours.

Today in Las Vegas is the most comprehensive of the visitor guides. *Tourguide Magazine* is also very comprehensive, but is organized somewhat differently, particularly in terms of dining. In *Today*, restaurants are organized by type (buffets, brunches, steak, Italian), while restaurants in *Tourguide* are listed alphabetically by host casino. Because both formats come in handy, we always pick up a copy of each magazine.

Both guides are published weekly and are distributed on a complimentary basis in Las Vegas. If you want to see a copy before you leave home, subscriptions or single issues are available as follows:

Today in Las Vegas
Lycoria Publishing Company
3625 Pecos McCleod Drive, Suite 14
Las Vegas, NV 89121
(702) 385-2737

Tourguide Magazine of Las Vegas
4440 South Arville Street, Suite 12
Las Vegas, NV 89103
(702) 221-5000

Other weeklies are *Showbiz Magazine*, published by the *Las Vegas Sun* newspaper, and *What's On in Las Vegas*. Both have much of the same information discussed above plus feature articles and weekly television listings. *Showbiz* and *What's On* are generally distributed gratis to hotel guest rooms.

The *Las Vegas Advisor* is a 12-page monthly newsletter containing some of the most useful consumer information available on gaming, dining, and entertainment, as well as taking advantage of deals on rooms, drinks, shows, and meals. With no advertising or promotional content, the newsletter serves its readers with objective, prescriptive, no-nonsense advice, presented with a sense of humor. At a subscription rate of $50 a year, the *Las Vegas Advisor* is the best investment you can make if you plan to spend four or more days in Las Vegas each year. If you are a one-time visitor but wish to avail yourself of all this wisdom, single copies of the *Las Vegas Advisor* can be purchased at the Gambler's Book Club store at 630 South 11th Street, (702) 382-7555. For additional information, write:

> *Las Vegas Advisor*
> Huntington Press
> 3687 South Procyon Avenue
> Suite A
> Las Vegas, NV 89103
> (702) 252-0655
> (800) 244-2224

Las Vegas and the Internet

The explosive growth of Las Vegas is not only physical, it's also virtual. Last year at this time, Las Vegas casinos had a minimal presence on the World Wide Web; this year, there are too many sites to list. The following are the best places to go on the Web to launch yourself into Las Vegas cyberspace. Use the directories to surf the many individual sites.

The (almost) Ultimate Guide to Las Vegas Internet Addresses is found at http://www.infi.net/vegas.

For the largest selection of Las Vegas casinos on the Web, go to http://intermind.net, then hit Hotels & Casinos.

An extensive site aimed at people relocating to Las Vegas or interested in investing in Las Vegas real estate is at http://www.lasvegasnexus.com/relocation/.

Other Las Vegas on-ramps include:

> http://www.vegas.com/vegas/
> http://www.earthlink.net/~chatterbox/
> http://www.pcap.com/lvindex.htm.

■ When to Go to Las Vegas ■

The best time to go to Las Vegas is in the spring or fall, when the weather is pleasant. If you plan to spend most of your time indoors, it

LAS VEGAS WEATHER AND DRESS CHART

Month	Average a.m. Temp.	Average p.m. Temp.	Pools O=Open	Recommended Attire
January	57	32		Coats and jackets are a must.
February	50	37		Dress warmly: jackets and sweaters.
March	69	42	/O	Sweaters for days, but a jacket at night.
April	78	50	O	Still cool at night—bring a jacket.
May	88	50	O	Sweater for evening, but days are warm.
June	99	68	O	Days hot and evenings are moderate.
July	105	75	O	Bathing suits.
August	102	73	O	Dress for the heat—spend time at a pool!
September	95	65	O	Days warm, sweater for evening.
October	81	53	O/	Bring a jacket or sweater for p.m.
November	67	40		Sweaters and jackets, coats for night.
December	58	34		Coats and jackets a must: dress warm!

doesn't matter what time of year you choose; if you intend to golf, play tennis, run, hike, bike, or boat, try to go in March, April, early May, October, November, or early December.

Because spring and fall are the nicest times of year, they are also the most popular. The best time of year for special deals and bargain room rates is in December (after the National Finals Rodeo and excluding the week between Christmas and New Year's), January, and during the scorching months of the summer, particularly July and August.

Weather in December, January, and February can vary incredibly. While high winds, cold, rain, and even snow are not unheard-of, chances are better than even that temperatures will be mild and the sun will shine. Though the weather is less dependable than in spring or fall, the winter months are generally pleasant and are well suited to outdoor activities. For instance, we talked to people who in late February water-skied on Lake Mead in the morning and snow-skied the same afternoon at Lee Canyon up in the mountains. Though the weather is iffy, the winter months provide an unbeatable combination of good value and choice of activities. From mid-May through mid-September, however, the heat is blistering. During these months it's best to follow the example of the gambler and the lizard—stay indoors or under a rock.

Crowd Avoidance

In general, weekends are busy and weekdays are slower. The exceptions are holiday periods and when large conventions or special events are being held. Most Las Vegas hotels have a lower guest room rate for weekdays than for weekends. For a stress-free arrival at the airport; good availability of rental cars; and a quick, easy hotel check-in, try to arrive Monday afternoon through Thursday morning (Tuesday and Wednesday are best).

Las Vegas hosts huge conventions and special events (rodeos, prize fights) that tie up hotels, restaurants, transportation, showrooms, and traffic for a week at a time. If you are interested in the convention or event, fine. In case you prefer to schedule your visit at a time when things are a little less frantic, we provide a calendar listing the larger citywide conventions and regularly scheduled events to help you avoid the crowds. Note that two or three medium-sized conventions meeting at the same time can impact Las Vegas as much as one big citywide event.

Because conventions of over 12,000 attendees can cause problems for the lone vacationer, the following list will help you plan your vacation dates. Included are the convention date, the number of people expected to attend, and the convention location (with hotel headquarters, if known at the time of publication).

Convention and Special Events Calendar

Dates	Convention/Event	Number of Attendees	Location/HQ
1997			
Oct 6–9	National Funeral Directors Association	12,000	Conv Ctr/Hilton
Oct 13–16	Packaging Machinery Manufacturers	10,000	Sands Expo/Mirage
Oct 14–17	World Gaming Congress	20,000	Hilton
Oct 19–22	National Frozen Food Association	3,000	Bally's
Oct 19–22	American Trucking Association	2,500	Hilton
Oct 21–23	California Rental Association	3,500	Conv Ctr/Hilton
Oct 23–25	National Tire Dealers & Retreaders Association	10,000	Conv Ctr
Oct 24–26	Lighting Dimensions International	10,000	Sands Expo/Hilton
Oct 24–Nov 1	International Foundation for Telemetering	3,000	Riviera
Oct 31–Nov 3	Automotive Parts Rebuilders Association	6,000	Hilton
Nov 4–7	Specialty Equipment Market Association	60,000	Conv Ctr/Hilton
Nov 17–21	Softbank Comdex, Inc.	190,000	Conv Ctr/Various
Dec 3–5	Professional Rodeo Cowboys Association	10,000	Riviera
Dec 5–7	National Autobody Congress & Expo	16,000	Conv Ctr/Various
Dec 12–16	American Vocational Association	10,000	Conv Ctr/Hilton
1998			
Jan 8–11	Consumer Electronics Show	100,000	Conv Ctr
Jan 18–21	GiftSource West Las Vegas	10,000	Sands Expo/TBA
Jan 18–21	Souvenir Super Show	50,000	Sands Expo/TBA
Jan 19–21	Nightclub and Bar Convention and Trade Show	10,000	Bally's

Convention and Special Events Calendar (continued)

Dates	Convention/Event	Number of Attendees	Location/HQ
Jan 19–22	Club Managers Association of America	3,400	Conv Ctr/Hilton
Jan 27–30	Shooting Hunting Outdoor Trade Show and Convention	35,000	Conv Ctr/Hilton
Feb 8–11	National Roofing Contractors Association	8,000	Conv Ctr/Hilton
Feb 8–11	Western Shoe Associates	25,000	Sands Expo
Feb 10–12	National Grocers Association	5,000	Conv Ctr/Bally's
Feb 18–21	Men's Apparel Guild in California (MAGIC)	70,000	Conv Ctr
Feb 22–26	Associated Surplus Dealers	50,000	Sands Expo/Hilton
Mar 2–6	Ski Industries of America	28,000	Conv Ctr/Various
Mar 9–12	National Postal Forum	6,300	Hilton
Mar 12–14	National Truck Equipment Association	4,000	Conv Ctr/TBA
Mar 17–19	National Association of Pizza Operators	12,000	Conv Ctr/MGM Grand
Mar 23–25	Association for Computer Operations Management	3,500	Conv Ctr/Bally's
Mar 23–25	American Home Sewing and Craft Association	3,000	Bally's
Mar 24–26	Pacific Equipment and Technology Expo	5,000	Conv Ctr
Mar 26–28	World Class Network	12,000	Conv Ctr/Hilton
Apr 16–19	National Science Teachers Association	15,000	Conv Ctr/Hilton
Apr 22–24	International Wireless Communications Expo	8,000	Conv Ctr/Hilton
Apr 25–29	National Systems Contractors Association	6,000	Conv Ctr/Hilton
Apr 27–29	National Art Materials Trade Association	4,000	Conv Ctr/Hilton
May 4–8	Networld+Interop	60,000	Conv Ctr
May 6–8	FutureShow	3,000	Bally's
June 7–10	Daughters of the Nile	5,000	Bally's

Convention and Special Events Calendar (continued)

Dates	Convention/Event	Number of Attendees	Location/HQ
June 10–13	International Silk Flower Show	10,000	Conv Ctr/Hilton
June 18–20	National Apartment Association	5,000	Conv Ctr/Hilton
June 20–23	GiftSource West Las Vegas	10,000	Sands Expo/TBA
June 21–23	Karel Exposition Management	5,000	Sands Expo
June 22–25	U.S. Junior Chamber of Commerce	5,500	Conv Ctr/MGM Grand/Bally's
July 20–23	National Conference of State Legislators	7,000	Conv Ctr
July 27–31	National Association of Letter Carriers	16,000	Conv Ctr/Hilton
July 31– Aug 7	Improved Benevolent Protective Order of Elks	16,000	Cashman Field Ctr/Bally's
Aug 6–9	Beauty and Barber Supply Institute	16,000	Conv Ctr/Hilton
Aug 12–23	American Accounting Association	5,000	Bally's
Aug 16–20	Associated Surplus Dealers	32,000	Sands Expo/Various
Aug 27–30	Western Shoe Associates	25,000	Sands Expo
Sept 14–16	American Public Works Association	11,000	Conv Ctr/TBA
Sept 22–25	World Gaming Congress and Expo	22,000	Conv Ctr/Hilton
Oct 4–7	International Foundation of Employee Benefit Plans	10,000	TBA
Oct 6–8	International Sanitary Supply Association	10,000	Conv Ctr/Hilton
Oct 19–21	National Electrical Contractors Association	8,000	Conv Ctr/Hilton
Oct 19–21	National Business Aircraft Association	20,000	Conv Ctr
Nov 3–6	Specialty Equipment Market Association	60,000	Conv Ctr/Various
Nov 16–19	SoftBank Comdex	190,000	Conv Ctr/Various

Convention and Special Events Calendar (continued)

Dates	Convention/Event	Number of Attendees	Location/HQ
Dec 6–9	Entomological Society of America/American Phytopathological Society	5,150	Hilton
Dec 14–16	National Ground Water Association	5,000	Conv Ctr/Hilton

Arriving and Getting Oriented

If you drive, you will have to travel through the desert to reach Las Vegas. Make sure your car is in good shape. Check your spare tire and toss a couple gallons of water in the trunk, just in case. Once en route, pay attention to your fuel and temperature gauges.

Virtually all commercial air traffic into Las Vegas uses McCarran International Airport. At McCarran, a well-designed facility with good, clear signs, you will have no problem finding your way from the gate to the baggage claim area, though it is often a long walk. Fast baggage handling is not the airport's strongest suit, so don't be surprised if you have to wait a long time on your checked luggage. If you are renting a car from a rental company with a counter at the airport, you can easily complete the paperwork before your checked baggage arrives. Once you have picked up your bags, you will have to produce the baggage claim check before you're allowed to exit the building.

If you do not intend to rent a car, getting from the airport to your hotel is no problem. Limousine services are available starting at $3.50 one-way and $8 round-trip for a shuttle. Sedans and "stretch" jobs range from about $25 to $33 one-way. Cabs are also available. The fare to Las Vegas Strip locations ranges from $7 to $15 one-way plus tip. One-way taxi fares to downtown run about $15 to $20. The limo service counters are located in the hall just outside the baggage claim area. Cabs are at the curb.

If you rent a car, you will need to catch your rental company's courtesy vehicle at the middle curb of the authorized vehicle lanes. These lanes are located at ground level between the baggage claim building and the main terminal.

If someone is picking you up in their car, you should proceed on ground level to the opposite side of the baggage claim building (away from the main terminal) to the baggage claim/arrivals curb. If the person picking you up wants to park and meet you, the best place to hook up is on the ground level of the baggage claim building near the car rental counters where the escalators descend from the main terminal.

There are now two ways to exit the airport by car. You can depart via the old route, Swenson Street, which runs north-south roughly paralleling the Strip; or you can hop on the new spur of Interstate 515. Dipping south

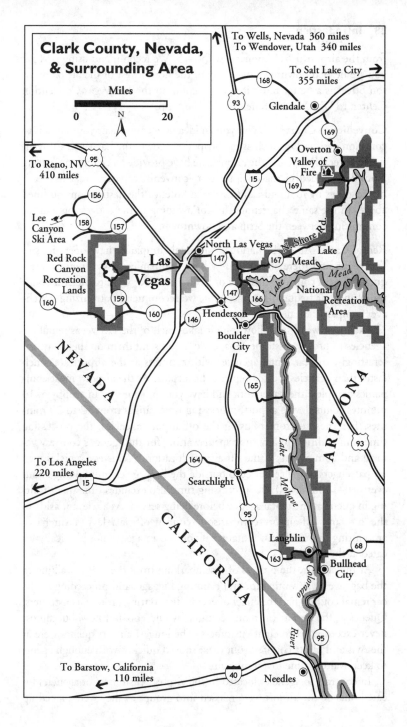

Clark County, Nevada, & Surrounding Area

Miles

0   N   20

To Wells, Nevada 360 miles
To Wendover, Utah 340 miles

To Salt Lake City
355 miles

168

93

Glendale

169

Overton
Valley of
Fire

15

169

To Reno, NV
410 miles

95

156

Lee
Canyon
Ski Area

158

157

North Las Vegas

147

N. Shore Rd.

167

Lake
Mead

Red Rock
Canyon
Recreation
Lands

Las
Vegas

147

166

Lake

Lake

Mead

National
Recreation
Area

159

160

160

146

Henderson

Boulder
City

NEVADA

165

ARIZONA

93

To Los Angeles
220 miles

164

15

Searchlight

95

Lake

Mohave

CALIFORNIA

Laughlin

68

163

Bullhead
City

Colorado

95

To Barstow, California
110 miles

40

Needles

River

from the airport, I-515 connects with I-15. We recommend using I-515 if you are headed downtown or to any of the hotels west of the Strip. Swenson Street is a better route if you are going to the Las Vegas Convention Center, to UNLV, or to hotels east of the Strip.

Convenience Chart   To give you an idea how convenient your hotel is to common destinations such as the Strip, downtown, the Las Vegas Convention Center, UNLV, and the airport, we have provided a chapter on getting around. Included in that chapter is a "convenience chart" that lists estimated times by foot and cab from each hotel to the destinations outlined above. In the same chapter are tips for avoiding traffic congestion and for commuting between the Strip and downtown.

Rental Cars   All of the national car rental companies have operations in Las Vegas, and there are also a few local companies. If you rent cars frequently in the course of business or leisure travel, or want to pick up bonus miles on your frequent-flyer account, we recommend patronizing whichever company you normally use.

Each year we observe how long it takes each of the Las Vegas rental car agencies to process customers' paperwork and send them on their way. Interestingly, the car rental agencies with counters at the airport are much faster than agencies located outside the airport. At the airport, most companies complete the paperwork and have you on your way in a zippy 5–10 minutes. Outside the airport, processing time ranges from 12 to 20 minutes. For those customers using the off-airport agencies, the processing time is in addition to any time spent waiting for the agency's courtesy vehicle and commuting to the off-airport location. (Courtesy vehicles pick up passengers at the center curb outside the baggage claim building about every 10–15 minutes.) The processing time also excludes time spent waiting in queue at the rental agency before being served. As a relevant aside to the on- and off-airport comparison, county officials levy a surcharge amounting to 8% of your rental fee if you use an agency not physically located at the airport.

At the airport, the process of disembarking from the plane, walking to the baggage area, waiting for and claiming luggage, and proceeding to the car rental counter had the effect of evenly distributing car rental customers. Queues at the airport car rental counters would ebb and flow, but almost never exceeded six to eight customers. The longest airport queues were at the Avis and Hertz counters, but these moved quickly, with enough agents to keep waiting time to a minimum.

In contrast to agencies located in the airport, customers of agencies located outside the airport were massed into groups as they were picked up

by the shuttle buses. Therefore, instead of arriving in a more or less continuous, manageable flow (as at the airport), customers of off-airport agencies
frequently descended in veritable platoons. Alamo generally had enough
agents to handle the crunch, but Payless, Thrifty, and Value were often
overwhelmed.

In the dollar and cents department, prices fluctuate so much from week
to week that it's anyone's guess who will offer the best deal during your
visit. Our advice is to have your travel agent check rates at all of the rental
agencies for the dates in question. Rental car companies list their most
competitive rates on the airline computer systems that travel agents use.
Also, rental companies will give you better service when they are account-
able to two persons: you and your travel agent, who is a potential source of
additional business.

Be aware that Las Vegas is a feast-or-famine city when it comes to rental
car availability. On many weekends, or when a citywide convention is in
town, it may be impossible to get a rental car unless you reserved way in
advance. If, on the other hand, you come to town when business is slow,
the rental agencies will practically give you a car. We have been able to rent
from the most expensive companies for as little as $18 a day under these
circumstances. If you are certain that you are visiting during a slow time,
reserve a car in advance to cover yourself and then, on arrival, ask each
rental company to quote you its best price. If you can beat the price on
your reserved car, go for it.

When you (or your travel agent) call to reserve a rental car, ask for the
smallest, least expensive car in the company's inventory, even if you ultimately intend to rent a larger vehicle. Chances are better than even that

Rental Car Agencies	
At the Terminal	*Off-Airport*
Savmor	Practical
Holiday	Resort
Budget	Alamo
Ace	Ladki International
Hertz	Value
Dollar	USave Auto Rental
National	Thrifty
Avis	Enterprise
	US RentCar

you will be upgraded without charge when you arrive. If not, rental agencies frequently offer on-site upgrade incentives that beat any deals you can make in advance. Always compare daily and weekly rates.

If you decline insurance coverage on the rental car because of protection provided by your credit card, be aware that the coverage provided by the credit card is secondary to your regular auto insurance policy. In most situations the credit card coverage only reimburses you the deductible on your regular policy. Also be aware that some car rental contracts require that you drive the car only in Nevada. If you, like many tourists, visit Hoover Dam or trek out to the Grand Canyon, you will cross into Arizona. Another item to check in advance, if applicable, is whether your rental agency charges for additional drivers.

When you rent your car, make sure you understand the implications of bringing it back empty of fuel. Some companies will charge $3 or more per gallon if they have to fill the tank on return. We returned a car to Alamo with between a third and a half tank of gas remaining and were charged $36, the same as if we had coasted in with a completely empty tank. Also, beware of signs at the car rental counters reading "Gas Today—$1.05 per gallon" or some such. That price usually applies to the gas already in the car when you rent it, not the price per gallon of a fill-up should you return the car empty. The price per gallon for a fill-up on return will be somewhere in the fine print of your rental contract.

Another rental car problem we encountered involved a pinhead-sized chip on the windshield. Understanding the fine print of rental car contracts, and because we always decline the insurance offered by the agencies, we inspect our cars thoroughly for any damage before accepting the car and leaving the lot. In this instance, as always, we inspected the car thoroughly and did not notice any windshield flaws. When we returned the car after three days, we were requested to remain at the counter to complete an "accident report." Insisting that we were unaware of any damage, we requested that the car be retrieved for our inspection. Still unable to find the alleged damage, we asked the counter agent to identify it for us. The agent responsible for the accident report then had to scrutinize the windshield for half a minute before she could find the mark, even though she knew its exact location from the employee who checked the car in. The conclusion to be drawn here is that if you decline coverage, the rental agency may hold you responsible for even the tiniest damage, damage so slight that you may never notice it. Before you leave the lot, inspect your rental car with care, scrutinizing every inch, and have the agency record anything you find. This will not inhibit them from charging you for damage sustained while the car is in your possession, but at least you will have the peace of mind of knowing that they are not putting one over on you.

Finally, some rental companies will charge you for "loss of use" if you have an accident that takes the car out of rental inventory. Since some car insurance policies do not pay loss-of-use charges, check your coverage with your insurance agent before you rent.

Public Transportation   Las Vegas's Citizen's Area Transit (CAT) provides reliable bus service at reasonable rates. Although one-way fares along the Strip are $1.50, one-way fares in residential areas are only $1. Children age 5 and under ride all routes for free, and children ages 6–18, seniors, and handicapped persons ride all routes for 50 cents, with valid identification.

Commonly Used Public Transportation Routes				
	Round-trip from/to	Hours of Operation	Frequency of Service	Fare
Citizen's Area Transit Bus # 301	Vacation Village/ Downtown Transportation Center	24 hours	Every 15 minutes	$1.50
Citizen's Area Transit Bus # 302 (Strip Express) Northbound	Vacation Village/ Downtown Transportation Center	5:00 a.m.– 12:00 a.m.	Every 20 minutes	$1.50
Citizen's Area Transit Bus # 302 (Strip Express) Southbound	Downtown Transportation Center/Vacation Village	6:00 p.m.– 12:30 a.m.	Every 20 minutes	$1.50
Citizen's Area Transit Bus # 303	Vacation Village/ Las Vegas Factory Outlet Stores	5:35 a.m.– 12:05 a.m.	Once an hour	$1.50
Las Vegas Strip Trolley Route 1	Luxor/ Stratosphere	9:30 a.m.– 2:00 a.m.	Every 20 minutes	$1.30
Las Vegas Strip Trolley Route 2	Stratosphere/ Plaza	9:30 a.m.– 2:00 a.m.	Every 25 minutes	$1.30
Bally's/MGM Grand Monorail	Bally's/ MGM Grand	8:00 a.m.– 12:00 a.m.	Every 15 minutes	free

All public transportation requires exact fare. Transfers are free on all routes but must be used within one hour of issue. All CAT buses are equipped with wheelchair lifts and bicycle racks, both of which are provided at no extra charge. Handicapped persons requiring door-to-door service should call ahead for reservations. For general route and fare information, to request a schedule through the mail, or to make reservations for door-to-door service, call (702) 228-7433.

The Las Vegas Strip Trolley Company is privately owned and provides transportation along the Strip and between the Strip and downtown. These buses are styled to look like San Francisco cable cars, and they cost a little less than CAT buses.

Bally's and MGM Grand are connected by a monorail, which is free of charge and handicapped accessible.

■ Las Vegas Customs and Protocol ■

In a town where the most bizarre behavior imaginable is routinely tolerated, it is ironic that so many visitors obsess over what constitutes proper protocol. This mentality stems mainly from the myriad customs peculiar to gaming and the *perceived* glamour of the city itself. First-timers attach a great deal of importance to "fitting in." What makes this task difficult, at least in part, is that half of the people they are trying to fit in with are first-timers too.

The only hard rules for being accepted downtown or on the Strip are to have a shirt on your back, shoes on your feet, some manner of clothing below the waist, and a little money in your pocket. Concerning the latter, there is no maximum. The operational minimum is bus fare back to wherever you came from.

This notwithstanding, there are three basic areas in which Las Vegas first-timers tend to feel especially insecure:

Gambling   The various oddities of gaming protocol are described under the respective casino games in the chapter on gambling. Understand, however, that despite appearances, gambling is very informal. While it is intelligent not to play a game because you do not know how, it is unwarranted to abstain because you are uncertain of the protocol. What little protocol exists (things like holding your cards above the table and keeping your hands away from your bet once play has begun) has evolved to protect the house and honest players from cheats. Dealers (a generic term for those who conduct table games) are not under orders to be unfriendly, silent, or rigid. Observe a game that interests you before you sit down. Assure yourself that the dealer is personable and polite. Never play in a casino where the staff is surly or cold; life's too short.

Eating in Gourmet Restaurants   These are mostly meat and potatoes places with fancy names, so there is no real reason to be intimidated. Men will feel more comfortable in a sport coat, but ties are optional. Women turn up in everything from slacks and blouses to evening wear. When you sit down, a whole platoon of waiters will attend you. Do not remove your napkin from the table. In gourmet rooms, only the waiters are allowed to place napkins in the laps of patrons. After the ceremonial placement of the napkin, the senior waiter will speak. When he concludes, you may order cocktails, consider the menu, sip your water, or engage in conversation. If there are women in your party, their menus will not have prices listed. If your party is totally comprised of women, a menu with prices listed will be given to the woman who looks the oldest. When you are ready to order, even if you only want a steak and fries, do not speak until the waiter has had an opportunity to recite in French from the menu. To really please your waiters, order something that can be prepared tableside with dramatic flames and explosions. If your waiters seem stuffy or aloof, ask them to grind peppercorns or parmesan cheese on something. This will usually loosen them up.

There will be enough utensils on the table to perform a cesarean section. Because these items are considered expendable, use a different utensil for each dish, surrendering it to the waiter along with the empty plate at the end of the course. If there are small yellow sculptures on the table, they are probably butter.

Tipping   Because half the resident population of Las Vegas are service providers in the tourist industry, there is no scarcity of people to tip. From the day you arrive until the day you depart, you will be interacting with redcaps, porters, cabbies, valet parking attendants, bellmen, waiters, maitre d's, dealers, bartenders, keno runners, housekeeping personnel, room service, and others.

Tipping is an issue that makes some travelers very uncomfortable. How much? When? To whom? Not leaving a tip when one is customary makes you feel inexperienced. Not knowing how much to tip makes you feel vulnerable and out of control. Is the tip you normally leave at home appropriate in Las Vegas?

The most important thing to bear in mind is that a tip is not automatic, nor is it an obligation. A tip is a reward for good service. The following suggestions are based on traditional practices in Las Vegas:

Porters and Redcaps   A dollar a bag.

Cab Drivers   A lot depends on the service and the courtesy. If the fare is less than $8, give the cabbie the change and $1. On a $4.50 fare, in other words, give him the fifty cents change plus a buck. If the fare is more than $8, give the cabbie the change and $2. If you are asking the cabbie to take you only a block or two, the fare will be small, but your tip should be large ($3–5) to make up for his wait in line and to partially compensate him for missing a better-paying fare. Add an extra dollar to your tip if the cabbie does a lot of luggage handling.

Valet Parking   Two dollars is correct if the valet is courteous and demonstrates some hustle. A dollar will do if the service is just OK. Only pay when you check your car out, not when you leave it. Because valet attendants pool their tips, both of the individuals who assist you (coming and going) will be taken care of.

Bellmen   When a bellman greets you at your car with one of those rolling carts and handles all of your bags, $5 is about right. The more of your luggage that you carry, of course, the less you should tip. Sometimes bellmen who handle only a small bag or two will put on a real performance when showing you your room. I had a bellman in one Strip hotel walk into my room, crank up the air conditioner, turn on the television, throw open the blinds, flick on all the lights, flush the commode, and test the water pressure in the tub. Give me a break. I tipped the same as if he had simply opened the door and put my luggage in the room.

Waiters   Whether in a coffee shop, a gourmet room, or ordering from room service, the standard gratuity for acceptable service is 15% of the total tab, before sales tax. At a buffet or brunch where you serve yourself, it is customary to leave $1–2 for the folks who bring your drinks.

Cocktail Waiters/Bartenders   Here you tip by the round. For two people, $1 a round; for more than two people, $2 a round. For a large group, use your judgment: Is everyone drinking beer, or is the order long and complicated? In casinos where drinks are sometimes on the house, it is considered good form to tip the server $1 per round or per every couple of rounds.

Dealers and Slot Attendants   If you are winning, it is a nice gesture to tip the dealer or place a small bet for him. How much depends on your winnings and on your level of play. With slot attendants, tip when they perform a specific service (like turning you on to a loose machine), or when you hit a jackpot. In general, unless other services are also rendered, it is not customary to tip change makers or cashiers.

Keno Runners   Tip if you have a winner or if the runner really provides fast, efficient service. How much to tip will vary with your winnings and with your level of play.

Showroom Maitre d's, Captains, and Servers   There is more to this than you might expect. If you are planning to take in a show, see our suggestions for tipping in the chapter on entertainment.

Hotel Maids   On checking out, leave $1–2 for each day you stayed, providing the service was good.

How to Look and Sound Like a Las Vegas Old-Timer   If you wish to appear as if you are a real Las Vegas veteran, there are several affectations that will give you credibility:

- Never refer to Las Vegas as "Vegas."

- Wear a UNLV shirt or jacket at all times, even in bed.

- Comment often and disparagingly about traffic on the Strip.

- Be able to give directions to the rest rooms at the Riviera.

- Never say "Hilton" when referring to the Flamingo.

■ **Does Anyone Know What's Going on at Home?** ■
(Does Anyone Really Care?)

If you are more interested in what you are missing at home than what is going on in Las Vegas, Las Vegas International News Stand at 3900 Paradise Road stocks Sunday papers from most major cities. To find out whether Las Vegas International News Stand stocks your favorite newspaper, call (702) 796-9901.

Las Vegas as a Family Destination

Every year the publisher sends me around to promote the *Unofficial Guide* on radio and television, and every year I am asked the same question: Is Las Vegas a good place for a family vacation?

Objectively speaking, Las Vegas is a great place for a family vacation. Food and lodging are a bargain, and there are an extraordinary number of things, from swimming at Wet 'n Wild to rafting through the Black Canyon on the Colorado River, that the entire family can enjoy together. If you take your kids to Las Vegas *and forget gambling*, Las Vegas compares favorably with every family tourist destination in the United States. The rub, of course, is that gambling in Las Vegas is pretty hard to ignore.

The marketing gurus, as you may have observed, are trying mightily to recast the town's image and to position Las Vegas as a family destination. The strategy will no doubt attract some parents already drawn to gambling but previously unwilling to allocate family vacation time to a Las Vegas trip. Excepting these relatively few families, however, it will take a lot more than hype to convince most parents that Las Vegas is a suitable destination for a family vacation.

For years, Las Vegas has been touted as a place to *get away* from your kids. For family tourism to succeed in Las Vegas, that characterization has to be changed, or at least minimized. Next, and much more unlikely, gambling must be relegated to a position of secondary importance. There is gambling on cruise ships, for example, but gambling is not the primary reason people go on cruises. Las Vegas, similarly, cannot develop as a bona fide family destination until something supersedes gambling as the main draw. Not very likely. The MGM Grand Adventures Theme Park and Grand Slam Canyon (Circus Circus) represent a start, but they are only a fraction of what Las Vegas will require to achieve critical mass as a family vacation venue.

To legitimately appeal to the family travel market, the city must consider the real needs of children and parents. Instead of banishing children to midway and electronic games arcades, hotels need to offer substantive, educational, supervised programs or "camps" for children. Once again, the MGM Grand (following the lead of the Las Vegas Hilton) is breaking some new ground in this area. Additionally, and equally important, Las Vegas must target and sell the family tourist trade in nontraditional geographic markets. Though Southern California is Las Vegas's largest and most lucrative market, is it reasonable to expect families with Disneyland, Sea World, and Universal Studios in their backyard to travel to Las Vegas to visit a theme park?

■ **Taking Your Children to Las Vegas Today** ■

Las Vegas today is a fairly adult tourist destination. As a city (including the surrounding area), however, it has a lot to offer children. What this essentially means is that the Strip and downtown have not been developed with children in mind, but if you are willing to make the effort to venture away from the gambling areas there are a lot of fun and wholesome things for families to do. As a rule, however, people do not go to Las Vegas to be continually absent from the casinos.

Persons under 21 are not allowed to gamble, nor are they allowed to hang around while *you* gamble. If you are gambling, your children have to be somewhere else. On the Strip and downtown, the choices are limited. True, most Las Vegas hotels have nice swimming pools, but Las Vegas summer days are too hot to stay out for long. While golf and tennis are possibilities, court or green fees are routinely charged, and you still must contend with limitations imposed by the desert climate.

After a short time, you will discover that the current options for your children's recreation and amusement are as follows:

1. You can simply allow your children to hang out. Given this alternative, the kids will swim a little, watch some TV, eat as much as their (or your) funds allow, throw water balloons out of any hotel window that has not been hermetically sealed, and cruise up and down the Strip (or Fremont Street) on foot, ducking in and out of souvenir stores and casinos.

2. If your children are a mature ten or older, you can turn them loose at the MGM Grand Adventures Theme Park, at the Grand Slam Canyon theme park at Circus Circus, or at the Wet 'n Wild swimming park. At the MGM Grand Adventures, they will find enough to keep them busy for five or so hours. As for the other parks, however, the kids will probably cut bait and go cruising after two hours of Grand Slam and about four hours of Wet 'n Wild.

3. You can hire a baby-sitter to come to your hotel room and tend your children. This works out pretty much like option 1 without the water balloons and the cruising.

4. You can abandon the casino (or whatever else you had in mind) and "do things" with your kids. Swimming and eating (as always) will figure prominently into the plan, as will excursions to places

that have engaged the children's curiosity. You can bet that your kids will want to go to the MGM Grand Adventures Theme Park, to Grand Slam Canyon, and probably to the Wet 'n Wild swimming park. The white tigers, dolphins, and exploding volcano at the Mirage are big hits with kids, as are the naval battle at Treasure Island, the high-tech attractions at the Luxor, and the Stratosphere Tower. The Excalibur offers a sort of movie/ride in which you feel as if you are riding a real roller coaster. Caesars Palace, in a similar vein, offers Omnimax, short movies projected on a five-story screen. New York–New York features a real roller coaster. If you have two children and do a fifth of all this stuff in one day, you will spend $80–250 for the four of you, not counting meals and transportation.

If you have a car there are lots of great, inexpensive places to go—enough to keep you busy for days. We recommend Red Rock Canyon and Hoover Dam for sure. On the way to Hoover Dam, you can stop for a tour of the Ethel M. Chocolate Factory. On the way back, you can watch marshmallows being made at Kidd's Marshmallow Factory.

A great half-day excursion (during the spring and fall) is a guided raft trip through the Black Canyon on the Colorado River. This can easily be combined with a visit to Hoover Dam. Trips to the Valley of Fire State Park (driving, biking, hiking) are also recommended during the more temperate seasons.

Around Las Vegas there are a number of real museums and museum-cum–tourist attractions. The Lied Discovery Children's Museum (just north of downtown) is worthwhile, affordable, and a big favorite with kids 14 years and younger. While you are in the neighborhood, try the Natural History Museum directly across the street.

5. You can pay someone else to take your kids on excursions. Some in-room sitters (bonded and from reputable agencies) will take your kids around as long as you foot the bill. For recommendations, check with the concierge or front desk of your hotel. Another option, if your kids are over age 12, is to pack them off on a guided tour, advertised by the handful in the various local visitor magazines.

Hotels That Solicit Family Business

The MGM Grand does not expressly pursue family clientele, though it is difficult to avoid with a theme park on the property. Likewise, the Luxor is positioned as an adult property, but it has a number of attractions that rank high with kids. Circus Circus and the Excalibur actively seek the family trade with carnival game midways where children and adults can try to win stuffed animals, foam rubber dice, and other oddities. A great setup for the casinos, the midways turn a nice profit while innocuously introducing the youngsters to games of chance. In addition, Circus Circus operates the Grand Slam Canyon theme park and offers free circus acts each evening, starring top-notch talent, including aerialists (flying trapeze). The Excalibur provides family-oriented production shows, as well as impromptu magic, puppet, and comedy shows in its second-floor Medieval Village. Both hotels offer reasonably priced rooms and inexpensive food and drink. The Excalibur has the better swimming pool of the two, but Circus Circus offers the nicer guest rooms (Excalibur bathrooms are equipped with a shower only—i.e., no tub).

Parents traveling with children are welcome at all of the larger hotels, though certain hotels are better equipped to deal with children than others. If your children are water puppies and can enjoy being in a swimming pool all day, the Flamingo, Monte Carlo, MGM Grand, Mirage, Rio, Tropicana, Caesars Palace, and Treasure Island have the nicest pools in town. The Las Vegas Hilton, Hard Rock Hotel, Sahara, and Desert Inn, among others, also have excellent swimming facilities.

If your kids are older and into sports, the Desert Inn and MGM Grand, along with Caesars Palace, the Las Vegas Hilton, and Bally's, offer the most variety. During the warmer months you can't beat the Santa Fe, with its hockey-sized ice-skating rink (open all year) and huge bowling complex.

When it comes to childcare and special programs, the MGM Grand, Sunset Station, and Gold Coast provide the only service in town.

Tours and Excursions

For the most part, the various bus sight-seeing tours available in Las Vegas offer two things: transportation and drivers who know where they're going. In our opinion, if you have a car and can read a map, you will save both money and hassle by going on your own.

Special Events

There is almost always something fun going on in Las Vegas outside of gambling. Among other things, there are minor league baseball, rodeos, concerts, UNLV basketball and football, and, of course, movies. If you are traveling with children, it's worth the effort to pick up a local newspaper and check out what's going on.

PART ONE

Lodging and Casinos

Where to Stay: Basic Choices

■ The Las Vegas Strip and Downtown ■

From a visitor's perspective, Las Vegas is more or less a small town and fairly easy to get around in. Most of the major hotels and casinos are located in two areas: downtown and on Las Vegas Boulevard, known as the Strip.

The downtown hotels and casinos are often characterized as older and smaller than those on the Strip. While this is true in a general sense, there are both large and elegant hotels downtown. What really differentiates downtown is the incredible concentration of casinos and hotels in a relatively small area. Along Fremont Street, downtown's main thoroughfare, the casinos present a continuous, dazzling galaxy of neon and twinkling lights for more than four city blocks. Known as Glitter Gulch, these several dozen gambling emporiums are sandwiched together in colorful profusion in an area barely larger than a parking lot at a good-sized shopping mall.

Contrast in the size, style, elegance, and presentation of the downtown casinos provides a varied mix, combining extravagant luxury and cosmopolitan sophistication with an Old West boom-town decadence. Though not directly comparable, downtown Las Vegas has the feel of New Orleans's Bourbon Street: alluring, exotic, wicked, sultry, foreign, and above all, diverse. It is a place where cowboy, businessman, showgirl, and retiree mix easily. And like Bourbon Street, it is all accessible on foot.

If downtown is the French Quarter of Las Vegas, then the Strip is Plantation Row. Here, huge resort hotel-casinos sprawl like estates along a four-mile section of Las Vegas Boulevard, South. Each hotel is a vacation destination unto itself, with casino, hotel, restaurants, pools, spas, landscaped grounds, and even golf courses. While the downtown casinos are fused into a vibrant, integrated whole, the huge hotels on the Strip demand individual recognition.

While the Strip is literally a specific length of Las Vegas Boulevard, South, a larger area is usually included when discussing hotels, casinos, restaurants, and attractions. East and parallel to the Strip is Paradise Road, where the Las Vegas Convention Center and several hotels are located. Also included in the Strip area are hotels and casinos located on streets intersecting Las Vegas Boulevard, as well as properties positioned to the immediate west of the Strip (on the far side of I-15).

Choosing a Hotel

The variables that figure most prominently in choosing a hotel are price, location, your itinerary, and your quality requirements. Downtown, on Boulder Highway, on the Strip, and elsewhere in Las Vegas, there is a wide selection of lodging with myriad combinations of price and value. Given this, your main criteria for selecting a hotel should be its location and your itinerary.

The Strip vs. Downtown for Leisure Travelers

Though there are some excellent hotels on the Boulder Highway and elsewhere around town, the choice for most vacation travelers is whether to stay downtown or on (or near) the Strip. Downtown offers a good choice of hotels, restaurants, and gambling but only a limited choice of entertainment, and fewer amenities such as swimming pools and spas. There are no golf courses and only four tennis courts downtown. If you have a car, the Strip is a 8- to 15-minute commute from downtown via I-15. If you do not have a car, public transportation from downtown to the Strip is as efficient as Las Vegas traffic allows and quite affordable.

If you stay on the Strip, you are more likely to need a car or require some sort of transportation. There are more hotels to choose from on the Strip, but they are spread over a much wider area and are often (but not always) pricier than downtown. On the Strip, one has a sense of space and elbowroom, as many of the hotels are constructed on a grand scale. The selection of entertainment is both varied and extensive on the Strip, and Strip recreational facilities rival those of the world's leading resorts.

Downtown is a multicultural, multilingual melting pot with an adventurous, raw, robust feel. Everything in this part of town seems intense and concentrated, an endless blur of action, movement, and light. Diversity and history conspire in lending vitality and excitement to this older part of

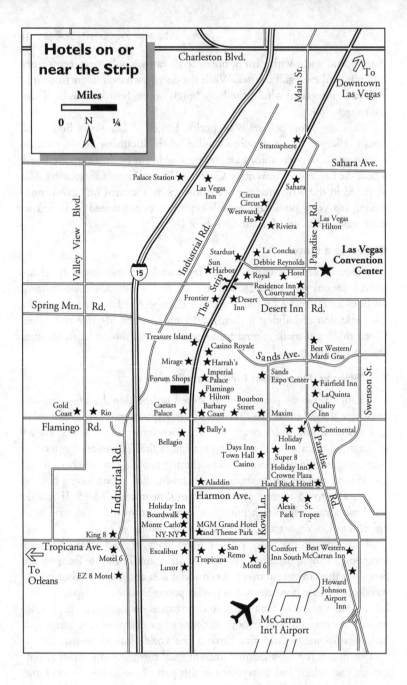

Hotels on or near the Strip

Miles

0   N   ¼

Charleston Blvd.

To Downtown Las Vegas

Main St.

Stratosphere ★

Sahara Ave.

Palace Station ★   ★
                    Las Vegas Inn   Sahara ★

                Circus Circus ★
                Westward Ho ★   Las Vegas Hilton
                        ★ Riviera

Valley View Blvd.

I-15

Industrial Rd.

The Strip

Stardust ★   ★ La Concha
Sun Harbor ★   Debbie Reynolds   Las Vegas Convention Center ★
            Royal ★   Hotel ★
            Residence Inn ★
            ★ Courtyard

Paradise Rd.

Spring Mtn. Rd.   Frontier ★   ★ Desert Inn   Desert Inn Rd.

Treasure Island ★
            ★ Casino Royale   Best Western/ Mardi Gras ★
Mirage ★   ★ Harrah's   Sands Ave.
            Imperial Palace
Forum Shops ■   Flamingo Hilton ★   Sands Expo Center   ★ Fairfield Inn
        Caesars Palace ★   Barbary   Bourbon   ★ LaQuinta
Gold Coast ★   ★ Rio   Coast ★   Street   Maxim ★   Quality Inn ★

Flamingo Rd.   ★ Bally's   ★ ★   ★ Continental

        Bellagio ★   Days Inn   Holiday Inn ★
                Town Hall   Super 8 ★
                Casino ★   Holiday Inn ★
                        Crowne Plaza
            ★ Aladdin   Hard Rock Hotel ★

Industrial Rd.   Harmon Ave.   Koval Ln.   Alexis   St.
                        Park   Tropez
        Holiday Inn
        Boardwalk ★   Paradise Rd.
        Monte Carlo ★   MGM Grand Hotel
        NY-NY ★   and Theme Park ★
King 8 ★   Comfort   Best Western
Tropicana Ave.   Excalibur ★   ★ San   Inn South   McCarran Inn
    Motel 6   Remo   ★
To Orleans   Luxor ★   Tropicana   Motel 6   Howard Johnson Airport Inn ★
    EZ 8 Motel ★

                    McCarran Int'l Airport

Swenson St.

42

Las Vegas, an essence more tangible and real than the monumental, plastic themes and fantasies of many large Strip establishments.

Though downtown caters to every class of clientele, it is less formal and, with exceptions, more of a working man's gambling town. Here the truck driver and welder gamble alongside the secretary, the realtor, and the rancher. The Strip, likewise, runs the gamut but tends to attract more high rollers, middle-class suburbanites, and business travelers going to conventions.

The Fremont Street Experience

For years, downtown casinos watched from the sidelines as Strip hotels turned into veritable tourist attractions. There was nothing downtown, for example, to rival the exploding volcano at the Mirage, the theme parks at Circus Circus and the MGM Grand, the pirate battle at Treasure Island, or the view from the Stratosphere Tower. As gambling revenue dwindled and more customers defected to the Strip, downtown casino owners finally got serious about mounting a counterattack.

The counterattack, known as the Fremont Street Experience, was launched at the end of 1995. Its basic purpose was to transform downtown into an ongoing event, a continuous party, a happening. Fremont Street through the heart of Glitter Gulch was forever closed to vehicular traffic and turned into a park with terraces, street musicians, and landscaping. An aesthetically pleasing environment, Las Vegas–style, the project united all of the casinos in a sort of diverse gambling mall.

Transformative events on the ground aside, however, the main draw of the Fremont Street Experience is up in the air. Four blocks of Fremont Street are covered by a 1,400-foot-long, 90-foot-high "space frame"— an enormous, vaulted geodesic matrix. This futuristic structure totally canopies Fremont Street. In addition to providing nominal shade from the blistering sun, the space frame serves as the stage for a nighttime attraction that has definitely improved downtown's fortune. Set into the inner surface of the space frame are 2.1 million tiny lights, which come to life in a computer-driven, multisensory show. The small lights are augmented by 40 speakers on each block, booming symphonic sound in syncopation with the lights.

That the Fremont Street Experience turns downtown Las Vegas into a unique urban theater is beyond dispute. What remains to be seen is whether visitors, the vast majority of whom lodge on the Strip, will continue to venture downtown to enjoy the show. This writer's guess is that they will want to but may not because of Las Vegas's increasingly horrendous traffic.

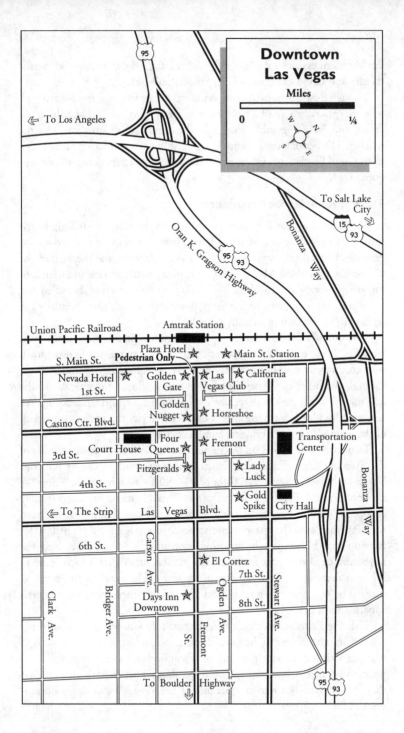

Downtown Las Vegas

Miles

0   1/4

To Los Angeles

95

To Salt Lake City

15
93

Oran K. Gragson Highway

95
93

Bonanza Way

Union Pacific Railroad

Amtrak Station

Plaza Hotel

Pedestrian Only

Main St. Station

S. Main St.

Nevada Hotel

Golden Gate

Las Vegas Club

California

1st St.

Golden Nugget

Horseshoe

Casino Ctr. Blvd.

Court House

Four Queens

Fremont

Transportation Center

3rd St.

Fitzgeralds

Lady Luck

4th St.

Gold Spike

City Hall

To The Strip

Las   Vegas   Blvd.

6th St.

Carson Ave.

El Cortez

7th St.

Bridger Ave.

Days Inn Downtown

Ogden Ave.

8th St.

Stewart Ave.

Bonanza Way

Clark Ave.

Fremont St.

To Boulder Highway

95
93

We at the *Unofficial Guide* enjoy and appreciate downtown Las Vegas, and all of us hope that the Fremont Street Experience will continue to have a beneficial effect. We are amazed and appalled, however, by the city's general lack of commitment to improving its infrastructure, particularly the traffic situation. The market, in terms of aggregate numbers of gamblers, is undeniably located out on the Strip. To create an attraction sufficiently compelling to lure this market downtown is to fight only half the battle. The other half of the battle is to make it easy for all those folks on the Strip to get downtown, and on this front the war is being lost.

If You Visit Las Vegas on Business

If you are going to Las Vegas for a trade show or convention, you will want to lodge as close as possible to the meeting site, ideally within easy walking distance. Many Strip hotel-casinos, including the Riviera, Stardust, Flamingo, Las Vegas Hilton, MGM Grand, Treasure Island, Tropicana, Sahara, Mirage, Desert Inn, Caesars Palace, Harrah's, and Bally's, host meetings of from 100 to 2,000 attendees, offer lodging for citywide shows and conventions held at the Las Vegas Convention Center, and have good track records with business travelers.

Our maps should provide some assistance in determining which hotels and motels are situated near your meeting site.

Because most large meetings and trade shows are headquartered at the Convention Center or on the Strip, lodging on the Strip is more convenient than staying downtown. Citywide conventions often provide a shuttle service from the major hotels to the Las Vegas Convention Center, and, of course, cabs are available too. Las Vegas traffic is a mess, however, particularly in the late afternoon, and there are a finite number of cabs. The best bet, if you can swing it, is either to stay in the convention's host hotel or within walking distance. One alternative to staying near your meeting site is to find a good deal on a room elsewhere around town and commute to your meeting in a rental car. Often the savings on the room will pay for the transportation.

Large Hotel-Casinos vs. Small Hotels and Motels

Lodging properties in Las Vegas range from tiny motels with a dozen rooms to colossal hotel-casino-resort complexes of 5,000 rooms. As you might expect, there are advantages and drawbacks to staying in either a large or small hotel. Determining which size is better for you depends on how you plan to spend your time in Las Vegas.

If your leisure or business itinerary calls for a car and a lot of coming and going, the big hotels can be a real pain. At the Luxor, Excalibur, and

Las Vegas Hilton, for example, it can take as long as 15 minutes to get from your room to your car if you use the self-parking lot. A young couple staying at the Las Vegas Hilton left their hotel room 40 minutes prior to their show reservations at the Mirage. After trooping to their van in the Hilton's distant self-parking lot, the couple discovered they had forgotten their show tickets. By the time the husband ran back to their room to retrieve the tickets and returned to the van, only five minutes remained to drive to the Mirage, park, and find the showroom. As it turned out, they missed the first 15 minutes of the performance.

Many other large hotels have multistory, self-parking garages that require lengthy and dizzying drives up and down ramps. If you plan to use the car frequently and do not want to deal with the hassle of remote parking lots, big garages, or the tipping associated with valet parking, we recommend that you stay in a smaller hotel or motel that provides quick and convenient access to your car.

Quiet and tranquility can also be reasons for choosing a smaller hotel. Many Las Vegas visitors object to passing through a casino whenever they go to or leave their room. Staying in a smaller property without a casino permits an escape from the flashing lights, the never-ending clanking of coins, and the unremitting, frenetic pace of an around-the-clock gambling town. While they may not be as exciting, smaller hotels tend to be more restful and homelike.

The ease and simplicity of checking in and out of smaller properties has its own appeal. To be able to check in or pay your bill without standing in a line, or to unload and load the car directly and conveniently, all significantly diminish the stress of arriving and departing. When we visited the registration lobby of the MGM Grand on a Friday afternoon, for example, it reminded us of Kennedy International Airport shut down by a winter storm. Guests were stacked dozens deep in the check-in queues. Others, having abandoned any hope of registering in the near future, slept curled up around their luggage or sat reading on the floor. The whole lobby was awash in suitcases, hanging bags, and people milling about. Though hotel size and check-in efficiency are not always inversely related, the sight of a registration lobby fitted out like the queuing area of Disneyland's Jungle Cruise should be enough to make a sane person think twice.

Along similar lines, a large hotel does not ensure more comfortable or more luxurious accommodations. In Las Vegas there are exceptionally posh and well-designed rooms in both large and small hotels, just as there are threadbare and poorly designed rooms in properties of every size. A large establishment does, however, usually ensure a superior range of amenities, including on-site entertainment, room service, spas or exercise rooms, concierge services, bell services, valet parking, meeting rooms, baby-sitting, shoe shining, dry cleaning, shopping, 24-hour restaurants, copy and fax services, check cashing, and, of course, gambling.

If you plan to do most of your touring on foot or are attending a convention, a large hotel in a good location has its advantages. There will be a variety of restaurants, entertainment, shopping, and recreation close at hand. In case you are a night owl, you will be able to eat or drink at any hour, and there will always be lots going on. Many showrooms offer 11 p.m. or midnight shows, and quite a few hotels (Sam's Town, Showboat, Gold Coast, Orleans, Santa Fe, Arizona Charlie's) have 24-hour bowling.

For visitors who wish to immerse themselves in the atmosphere of Las Vegas, to live in the fast lane, and to be where the action is, a large hotel is recommended. These people feel they are missing something unless they stay in a large hotel-casino. For them, it is important to know that the excitement is only an elevator ride away.

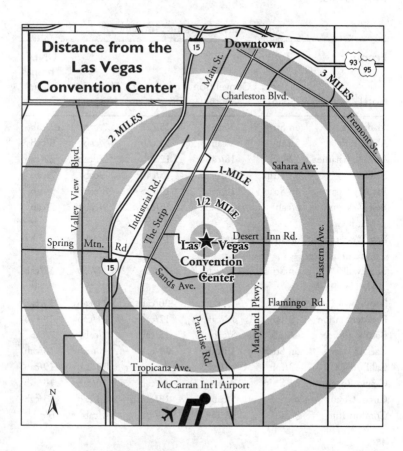

Getting Around:
Location and Convenience

The following chart will give you a feel for how convenient specific hotels and motels are to common Las Vegas destinations. Both walking and cab commuting times are figured on the conservative side. You should be able to do a little better than the times indicated, particularly by cab, unless you are traveling during rush hour or attempting to navigate the Strip on a weekend evening.

Commuting Time in Minutes					
From:	**To:**				UNLV Thomas
Hotel	Las Vegas Strip	Convention Center	Downtown	McCarran Airport	& Mack Center
Aladdin	on Strip	9/cab	15/cab	7/cab	7/cab
Alexis Park	5/cab	8/cab	15/cab	5/cab	6/cab
Arizona Charlie's	12/cab	18/cab	12/cab	20/cab	22/cab
Bally's	on Strip	8/cab	15/cab	7/cab	7/cab
Barbary Coast	on Strip	10/cab	15/cab	8/cab	9/cab
Best Western Mardi Gras	6/cab	10/walk	15/cab	9/cab	7/cab
Best Western McCarran Inn	6/cab	9/cab	15/cab	4/cab	7/cab
Boardwalk Holiday Inn	on Strip	12/cab	15/cab	11/cab	12/cab
Boomtown	10/cab	17/cab	20/cab	11/cab	15/cab
Boulder Station	19/cab	18/cab	12/cab	21/cab	20/cab
Bourbon Street	4/walk	8/cab	15/cab	7/cab	7/cab
Caesars Palace	on Strip	10/cab	12/cab	10/cab	10/cab
California	13/cab	15/cab	downtown	19/cab	19/cab
Casino Royale	on Strip	9/cab	14/cab	10/cab	10/cab
Circus Circus	on Strip	5/cab	13/cab	14/cab	13/cab
Comfort Inn	3/cab	9/cab	15/cab	4/cab	6/cab

Commuting Time in Minutes (continued)

From: Hotel	To: Las Vegas Strip	Convention Center	Downtown	McCarran Airport	UNLV Thomas & Mack Center
Continental	4/cab	5/cab	15/cab	6/cab	5/cab
Courtyard	4/cab	5/walk	15/cab	9/cab	8/cab
Debbie Reynolds Hollywood Hotel	6/walk	7/walk	15/cab	10/cab	9/cab
Desert Inn	on Strip	5/cab	15/cab	9/cab	9/cab
El Cortez	11/cab	15/cab	6/walk	16/cab	17/cab
Excalibur	on Strip	13/cab	14/cab	7/cab	8/cab
E-Z 8 Motel	4/cab	9/cab	12/cab	9/cab	10/cab
Fairfield Inn	5/cab	5/cab	15/cab	9/cab	8/cab
Fiesta Hotel	18/cab	18/cab	10/cab	22/cab	22/cab
Fitzgeralds	14/cab	15/cab	downtown	17/cab	17/cab
Flamingo Hilton	on Strip	9/cab	13/cab	8/cab	8/cab
Four Queens	15/cab	15/cab	downtown	19/cab	17/cab
Fremont	15/cab	15/cab	downtown	19/cab	17/cab
Frontier	on Strip	8/cab	13/cab	11/cab	10/cab
Gold Coast	4/cab	13/cab	14/cab	10/cab	10/cab
Gold Spike	14/cab	15/cab	4/walk	18/cab	17/cab
Golden Gate	14/cab	15/cab	downtown	19/cab	18/cab
Golden Nugget	14/cab	15/cab	downtown	18/cab	19/cab
Hard Rock Hotel	4/cab	6/cab	15/cab	6/cab	6/cab
Harrah's	on Strip	9/cab	15/cab	10/cab	10/cab
Holiday Inn Emerald Springs	4/cab	8/cab	15/cab	7/cab	7/cab
Holiday Inn Crowne Plaza	5/cab	5/cab	14/cab	8/cab	6/cab
Horseshoe	14/cab	15/cab	downtown	19/cab	19/cab
Howard Johnson	4/cab	14/cab	14/cab	9/cab	11/cab
Howard Johnson Airport	5/cab	7/cab	15/cab	3/cab	5/cab
Imperial Palace	on Strip	9/cab	15/cab	10/cab	10/cab
King 8	4/cab	13/cab	14/cab	8/cab	10/cab
Lady Luck	14/cab	15/cab	3/walk	19/cab	18/cab
Las Vegas Club	14/cab	15/cab	downtown	19/cab	18/cab
Las Vegas Hilton	5/cab	5/walk	13/cab	10/cab	8/cab
Luxor	on Strip	13/cab	15/cab	8/cab	10/cab

Commuting Time in Minutes (continued)

From: Hotel	To: Las Vegas Strip	Convention Center	Downtown	McCarran Airport	UNLV Thomas & Mack Center
Main Street Station	14/cab	15/cab	downtown	19/cab	19/cab
Maxim	4/walk	8/cab	15/cab	7/cab	7/cab
MGM Grand	on Strip	12/cab	15/cab	9/cab	9/cab
Mirage	on Strip	11/cab	15/cab	11/cab	10/cab
Monte Carlo	on Strip	12/cab	15/cab	11/cab	12/cab
Motel 6 (Tropicana)	3/cab	12/cab	15/cab	6/cab	8/cab
Nevada Hotel	14/cab	15/cab	downtown	19/cab	18/cab
Nevada Palace	21/cab	26/cab	21/cab	19/cab	18/cab
New York– New York	on Strip	12/cab	15/cab	11/cab	12/cab
Orleans	4/cab	15/cab	14/cab	11/cab	11/cab
Palace Station	5/cab	10/cab	10/cab	14/cab	15/cab
Plaza Hotel	14/cab	15/cab	downtown	19/cab	18/cab
Quality Inn	5/walk	8/cab	15/cab	8/cab	8/cab
Residence Inn	4/cab	6/cab	15/cab	12/cab	12/cab
Rio	5/cab	14/cab	13/cab	10/cab	10/cab
Riviera	on Strip	4/cab	14/cab	11/cab	10/cab
Royal Hotel	3/walk	5/cab	14/cab	13/cab	11/cab
Sahara	on Strip	4/cab	13/cab	13/cab	11/cab
St. Tropez	5/cab	6/cab	15/cab	7/cab	6/cab
Sam's Town	20/cab	25/cab	20/cab	18/cab	17/cab
San Remo	5/walk	11/cab	15/cab	6/cab	8/cab
Sante Fe	27/cab	30/cab	23/cab	33/cab	36/cab
Showboat	19/cab	18/cab	12/cab	21/cab	20/cab
Stardust	on Strip	4/cab	13/cab	12/cab	10/cab
Stratosphere	3/cab	7/cab	9/cab	14/cab	14/cab
Sunrise Suites	19/cab	24/cab	19/cab	17/cab	16/cab
Sunset Station	15/cab	17/cab	19/cab	14/cab	13/cab
Texas Station	17/cab	16/cab	13/cab	22/cab	22/cab
Treasure Island	on Strip	11/cab	14/cab	11/cab	10/cab
Tropicana	on Strip	11/cab	15/cab	6/cab	9/cab
Vacation Village	8/cab	18/cab	18/cab	8/cab	12/cab
Westward Ho	on Strip	5/cab	15/cab	13/cab	12/cab

Commuting to Downtown from the Strip

Commuting from the Strip to downtown is a snap on I-15. From the Strip you can get on or off I-15 at Tropicana Avenue, Flamingo Road, Spring Mountain Road, or Sahara Avenue. Once on I-15 heading north, stay in the right lane and follow the signs for downtown and US 95 South. If you exit onto Casino Center Boulevard, you will be right in the middle of downtown with several large parking garages conveniently at hand. Driving time to downtown varies from about 14 minutes from the south end of the Strip (I-15 via Tropicana Avenue) to about 6 minutes from the north end (I-15 via Sahara Avenue).

Commuting to the Strip from Downtown

If you are heading to the Strip from downtown, you can pick up US 95 (and then I-15) by going north on either Fourth Street or Las Vegas Boulevard. Driving time from downtown to the Strip takes 6–14 minutes, depending on where you are going on the Strip.

What's in an Address?

■ Downtown ■

The heart of the downtown casino area is Fremont Street between Fourth Street (on the east) and Main Street (on the west). Hotel-casinos situated along this quarter-mile four-block stretch known as Glitter Gulch, include the Plaza Hotel, Golden Gate, Las Vegas Club, Binion's Horseshoe, Golden Nugget, Sam Boyd's Fremont, Four Queens, and Fitzgeralds. Parallel to Fremont and one block north is Ogden Avenue, where the California, Lady Luck, and the Gold Spike are located. Main Street Station, which reopened in 1997, is situated on Main Street at the intersection of Ogden.

All of the downtown hotel-casinos are centrally positioned and convenient to the action, with the exception of the El Cortez, which sits three blocks to the east. While there is a tremendous difference in quality and price among the downtown properties, the locations of all the hotels (except the El Cortez) are excellent. When you stay downtown, everything is within a five-minute walk. By way of comparison, on the Strip it takes longer to walk from the entrance of Caesars Palace to the entrance of the Mirage, next door, than to cover the whole four blocks of the casino center downtown.

■ The Strip ■

While location is not a major concern when choosing from among the downtown hotels, it is of paramount importance when selecting a hotel on the Strip.

I once received a promotional flyer from a Las Vegas casino proudly proclaiming that it was located "right on the Strip." It supported the claim with a color photo showing its marquee and those of several other casinos in a neat row with their neon ablaze. What recipients of this advertisement (except those familiar with Las Vegas) never would have guessed was that the photo had been taken with a special lens that eliminated all sense of distance between the casinos. While the advertised casino appeared to be next door to the other casinos in the picture, it was in reality almost a mile away.

A common variation on the same pitch, but without the photo, is "Stay Right on the Las Vegas Strip at Half the Price." Once again, the promoter is attempting to deceive by taking advantage of the recipient's ignorance of Strip geography. As it happens, the Las Vegas Strip (Las Vegas Boulevard, South) starts southwest of the airport and runs all the way downtown, a distance of about seven miles. Only the four-mile section between the former Hacienda site and the Stratosphere contains the large casinos and other attractions of interest to visitors. South of the Hacienda site "on the Strip" is the airport boundary and some nice desert. North of the Stratosphere en route to downtown, the Strip runs through a recently resurgent commercial area sprinkled with wedding chapels, fast-food restaurants, and small motels.

The Best Locations on the Strip

Beware of hotels and motels claiming to be on the Strip but not located between the old Hacienda site and the Stratosphere. They might be nice properties, but chances are you will be disappointed with the location.

If you stay on the Strip, you want to be somewhere in the Hacienda to Stratosphere stretch, and even there, some sections are much more desirable than others. The old Hacienda site basically anchors the south end of the Strip, about a quarter mile from the Luxor, its closest neighbor. Likewise, at the other end, the Stratosphere and the Sahara are somewhat isolated. In between, there are distinct clusters of hotels and casinos.

Strip Cluster 1: The Cluster of the Giants   At the intersection of the Strip (Las Vegas Boulevard, South) and Tropicana Avenue are five of the world's largest hotels. The MGM Grand Hotel is the largest hotel in the United States. Diagonally across the intersection from the MGM Grand is the Excalibur, the third largest hotel in the United States. The other two corners of the intersection are occupied by New York–New York and the Tropicana. Nearby to the south is the Luxor (second largest) and to the north is the Holiday Inn Boardwalk and Monte Carlo (all on the Strip). The San Remo is situated on Tropicana across from the MGM Grand. From the intersection of the Strip and Tropicana, it is a half-mile walk south to the old Hacienda site or about the same distance north to the Aladdin. The next cluster of major hotels and casinos is at the intersection of Flamingo Road, one mile north. With the opening of New York–New York and the Monte Carlo in 1996, Strip Cluster 1 challenged the status, at least in terms of appeal and diversity, of Strip Cluster 2. Progress always has its dark side, however. Here it is the phenomenal increase of traffic and congestion on East Tropicana Avenue as it approaches the Strip.

Strip Cluster 2: The Grand Cluster   From Flamingo Road to Spring Mountain Road (also called Sands Avenue, and farther east, Twain Avenue) is the greatest numerical concentration of major hotels and casinos on the Strip. If you wish to stay on the Strip and prefer to walk wherever you go, this is the best location. At Flamingo Road and Las Vegas Boulevard are Bally's, Caesars Palace, Barbary Coast, and Bellagio (opening in Fall 1998). Heading east on Flamingo are Bourbon Street and Maxim. Toward town on the Strip are the Flamingo, O'Shea's, Imperial Palace, Mirage, Harrah's, Casino Royale, and Treasure Island. Also located in this cluster is the Forum Shops, Las Vegas's most unique shopping venue. A leisure traveler could stay a week in this section (without ever getting in a car or cab) and not run out of interesting sights, good restaurants, or good entertainment. On the negative side, for those with cars, traffic congestion at the intersection of the Strip and Flamingo Road is the worst in the city.

Strip Cluster 3   Another nice section of the Strip is from Spring Mountain Road up to the Frontier and the Desert Inn. This cluster, located pretty much in the center of the Strip, is distinguished by its easy access. The Desert Inn and the Frontier can each be reached by two different roads. Visitors who prefer a major hotel on the Strip but want to avoid the daily traffic snarls could not ask for a more convenient location. Though the Desert Inn and the Frontier (across the street) are about a quarter mile from the nearest cluster of casinos in either direction, both are situated within a four-minute walk of Fashion Show Mall, one of the most interesting and diversified upscale shopping centers in the United States. There are also some very good restaurants in this section, including Chin's in the mall, Monte Carlo at the Desert Inn, and Margarita's at the Frontier. Finally, this cluster is a 4-minute cab ride (or a 16-minute walk) from the Las Vegas Convention Center. On the downside, the Desert Inn is in the throes of an ambitious expansion, and the Frontier has been crippled by an interminable feud with the local Culinary Workers Union.

Strip Cluster 4   The next cluster up the Strip is between Convention Center Drive and Riviera Boulevard. Arrayed along a stretch just over a half mile long are the Stardust, Westward Ho, Slots of Fun, Silver City, Royal Hotel, Riviera, and Circus Circus with its Grand Slam Canyon theme park. Great for people-watching and enjoying the lights, this area contains the third largest concentration of major hotels and casinos. Casinos and hotels in this cluster are considerably less upscale than those in the "grand cluster" but offer acceptable selections for dining and entertainment, as well as close proximity to the Las Vegas Convention Center. Traffic along this section of the Strip is also woefully congested.

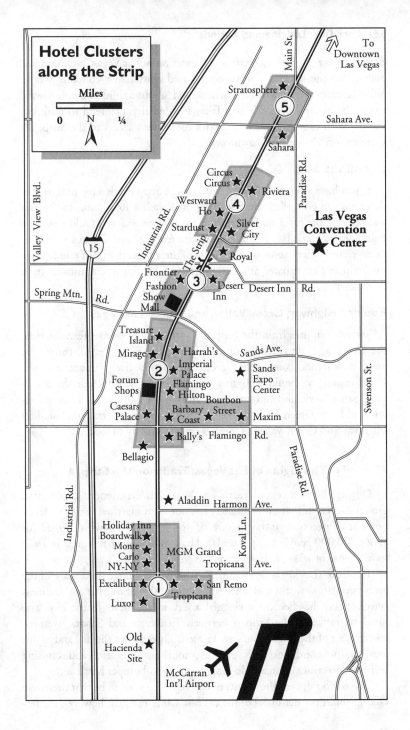

Hotel Clusters along the Strip

Miles

0   N   ¼

To Downtown Las Vegas

Main St.

Stratosphere ★ **5**

Sahara Ave.

Sahara ★

Circus Circus ★

Westward Ho ★ **4** Riviera ★

Silver City ★

Stardust ★

Royal ★

The Strip

Industrial Rd.

Las Vegas Convention Center ★

Paradise Rd.

Frontier ★

Fashion Show Mall

Desert Inn

3 Desert Inn Rd.

Spring Mtn. Rd.

Valley View Blvd.

15

Treasure Island ★

Harrah's ★

Sands Ave.

Mirage ★

Imperial Palace ★

2 Flamingo ★

Sands Expo Center

Swenson St.

Forum Shops

Hilton ★

Bourbon Street ★

Caesars Palace ★

Barbary Coast ★

Maxim

Bally's ★ Flamingo Rd.

Paradise Rd.

Bellagio ★

Aladdin ★ Harmon Ave.

Holiday Inn ★

Industrial Rd.

Boardwalk ★

Monte Carlo ★

Koval Ln.

NY-NY ★

MGM Grand ★

Tropicana Ave.

Excalibur ★ **1** ★ San Remo ★

Luxor ★ Tropicana

Old Hacienda Site ★

McCarran Int'l Airport

55

Strip Cluster 5   Finally, near the intersection of Las Vegas Boulevard and Sahara Avenue there is a relatively isolated cluster that contains Wet 'n Wild (a water theme park), the Sahara, and, about a third of a mile toward town, the Stratosphere. Though fairly isolated if you intend to walk, for visitors with cars this cluster provides convenient access to the Strip, the Convention Center, and downtown.

Just off the Strip

If you have a car, and if being right on the Strip is not a big deal to you, there are some excellent hotel-casinos on Paradise Road, and to the east and west of the Strip on intersecting roads. The Rio and Gold Coast on Flamingo Road, Palace Station on Sahara Avenue, and Orleans on Tropicana Avenue offer exceptional value; they are all less than half a mile from the Strip and are situated at access ramps to I-15, five to ten minutes from downtown.

Boulder Highway, Green Valley, and North Las Vegas

Twenty minutes from the Strip in North Las Vegas are Texas Station, the Fiesta, and, on the edge of civilization, the Santa Fe. All three have good restaurants, comfortable guest rooms, and lively, upbeat themes. Hotel-casinos on Boulder Highway southeast of Town include the Showboat, Sam's Town, and Nevada Palace. Also to the southeast is the new Sunset Station in Green Valley. Like the North Las Vegas trio, the Boulder Highway and Green Valley properties cater primarily to locals.

■ The Lights of Las Vegas: Traffic on the Strip ■

During the past several years, Las Vegas has experienced exponential growth—growth that unfortunately has not been matched with the development of necessary infrastructure. If you imagine a town designed for about 300,000 people being inundated by a million or so refugees, you will have a sense of what's happening in Las Vegas.

The Strip (Las Vegas Boulevard, South), where a huge percentage of the local population works and where more than 80% of tourists and business travelers stay, has become a clogged artery in the heart of the city. The heaviest traffic on the Strip is between Tropicana and Sahara Avenues, where most of the larger hotels are located. Throughout the day and night, local traffic combines with gawking tourists, shoppers, and cruising teenagers to create a three-mile-long, bumper-to-bumper bottleneck.

When folks discuss the "lights of Las Vegas," it used to be that they were talking about the marquees of the casinos. More recently, however, the reference is to the long, multifunctional traffic lights found at virtually every intersection on the Strip. These lights, which flash a different signal for every possible turn and direction, combine with an ever-increasing number of vehicles to ensure that nobody goes anywhere very fast. Also affected are the major traffic arteries that cross the Strip east to west; the worst snarls occur at the intersection of the Strip and Flamingo Avenue.

Strip traffic is the Achilles heel of the current Las Vegas development boom. It is sheer lunacy to believe you can plop a litter of megahotels on the Strip without compounding an already horrific traffic situation. While city government and the hospitality industry dance around the issue, traffic gets worse and worse. Approximately 33,000 hotel rooms were added along the Strip from 1993 through 1997, and about 20,000 more are scheduled to come on line by 2000. Clearly, an elevated train or some other form of fast, efficient public transportation is needed, but the city leaders and the hoteliers are now so far behind the curve that nothing is likely to save the Strip from massive gridlock.

Sneak Routes

Fortunately, most of the large hotels located along this section of the Strip have back entrances that allow you to avoid the insanity of the main drag. Industrial Road and I-15 run parallel to the Strip on the west side, providing backdoor access to hotels situated on the west side of Las Vegas Boulevard. Paradise Road and Koval Lane run parallel to the Strip on the east side.

Sneak Routes for Hotels on the West Side of the Strip
The Stratosphere's self-park garage is located off Baltimore Street, which connects to the Strip.
Circus Circus, Westward Ho, the *Stardust*, and *Caesars Palace* (on the west side of the Strip) can be reached via Industrial Road.
The Frontier has an entrance off Fashion Show Drive, which connects to both Industrial Road and Spring Mountain Road.
The Mirage and *Treasure Island* are accessible by taking Industrial Road or I-15 and then turning east on Spring Mountain Road.
New York–New York can be reached via Tropicana.
The Holiday Inn Boardwalk and the *Monte Carlo* must be accessed from the Strip.

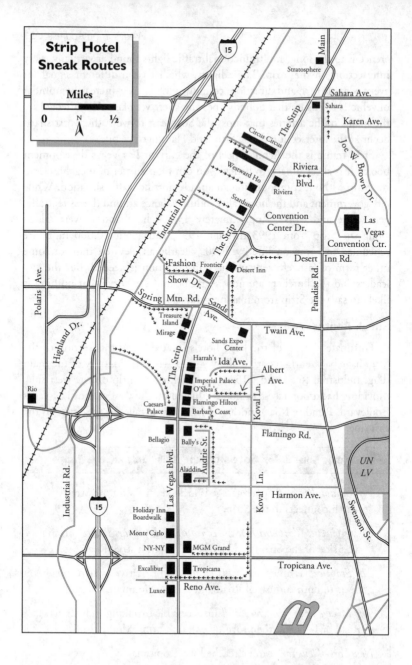

Strip Hotel
Sneak Routes

Miles

0   N   ½

Main

Stratosphere

Sahara Ave.

Sahara

Karen Ave.

The Strip

Joe W. Brown Dr.

Circus Circus

Westward Ho

Riviera
Blvd.

Riviera

Stardust

The Strip

Industrial Rd.

Convention
Center Dr.

Las
Vegas
Convention Ctr.

Desert
Inn Rd.

Fashion
Show Dr.

Frontier

Desert Inn

Paradise Rd.

Spring Mtn. Rd.

Sands
Ave.

Twain Ave.

Treasure
Island

Mirage

Sands Expo
Center

Harrah's

Ida Ave.

Albert
Ave.

Imperial Palace

O'Shea's

Flamingo Hilton

Barbary Coast

Koval Ln.

Caesars
Palace

The Strip

Rio

Polaris Ave.

Highland Dr.

Bellagio

Bally's

Audrie St.

Flamingo Rd.

Aladdin

Las Vegas Blvd.

Koval Ln.

Harmon Ave.

UN
LV

Holiday Inn
Boardwalk

Monte Carlo

NY-NY

MGM Grand

Swenson St.

Excalibur

Tropicana

Tropicana Ave.

Industrial Rd.

Luxor

Reno Ave.

Sneak Routes for Hotels on the West Side of the Strip (cont'd)

The Excalibur and the *Luxor* can be reached by turning south off Tropicana onto Koval Lane and then turning right onto Reno Avenue. Reno Avenue intersects the Strip at a traffic light, allowing you to cross to the Excalibur and the Luxor.

Sneak Routes for Hotels on the East Side of the Strip

The Sahara has an entrance on Paradise Road.

The Riviera can be reached by turning west on Riviera Boulevard from Paradise.

The Desert Inn has an entrance on Twain Avenue. For most of 1998, however, Desert Inn traffic will be disrupted by construction projects. Until these projects are complete, it may be necessary to access the Desert Inn via the Strip.

Harrah's Las Vegas, the *Imperial Palace, O'Shea's,* and the *Flamingo Hilton* each have a back entrance off Audrie Street, a small thoroughfare branching off Flamingo Road. Audrie Street can also be reached by turning west on Albert or Ida Avenues from Koval Lane.

The Barbary Coast is the only major hotel on the east side of the Strip that is truly stuck. If you want to go to the Barbary Coast, park somewhere else and walk over. Don't even think about arriving at or departing from the Barbary Coast's parking lot between 3:30 p.m. and 8 p.m.

Bally's and the *Aladdin* can be reached by turning north off Harmon Avenue onto an isolated section of Audrie Street. Be forewarned that while it is possible to sneak *into* Bally's, the only way *out* is on the Strip in a highly congested area. Also, expect some confusion and congestion in Bally's south parking lot as construction on the new Paris hotel-casino proceeds next door.

The MGM Grand is accessible by heading west (toward the Strip) on Tropicana Avenue or by turning west off Koval Lane.

The Tropicana is accessible by turning south off Tropicana onto Koval Lane and then turning right onto Reno Avenue.

■ Please Pardon Our Dust ■

The competitive climate among hotel-casinos in Las Vegas is so charged that almost every major property is undertaking some sort of renovation or expansion. Although hotels strive mightily to minimize noise and inconvenience to their guests, there's really no way to throw up a new 30-story hotel tower without raising a little dust. To preclude any unpleasant surprises, we list below the hotel-casinos that we know will be involved in major construction projects during the fourth quarter of 1997 and most of 1998. Because more projects will be scheduled after this guide goes to press, we strongly recommend that you call about on-site or nearby construction at any Las Vegas hotel before you make your reservation.

Hotel-Casinos with Ongoing or Nearby Construction Projects	
Aladdin	Project on-site
Bally's	Project next door and across the street
Caesars Palace	Project on-site
Casino Royale	Project next door
Desert Inn	Project on-site
Luxor	Project next door
MGM Grand	Project on-site
Monte Carlo	Project next door
New York–New York	Project on-site
Orleans	Project on-site
Riviera	Project on-site
Sahara	Project on-site
Treasure Island	Project across the street

Room Reservations:

Getting a Good Room, Getting a Good Deal

Because Las Vegas is so popular for short weekend getaways, weekend occupancy averages an astounding 96% of capacity for hotels and 86% of capacity for motels. Weekday occupancy for hotels is a respectable 86%, and for motels, 63%. What these figures mean, among other things, is that you want to nail down your lodging reservations before you leave home.

Also, consider that these occupancy percentages are averages. When a large convention is in town, or when Las Vegas hosts a championship prizefight, the National Finals Rodeo, or any other major event, rooms become hard to find. If you are heading to Las Vegas purely for fun and relaxation, you may want to avoid going when the town is packed. For more information about dates to avoid, see pages 22–25.

■ The Wacky World of Las Vegas ■
Hotel Reservations

Though there are almost 100,000 hotel rooms in Las Vegas, getting one is not always a simple proposition. In the large hotel-casinos there are often five or more separate departments that have responsibility for room allocation and sales. Of the total number of rooms in any given hotel, a number are at the disposal of the casino; some are administered by the reservations department at the front desk; some are allocated to independent wholesalers for group and individual travel packages; others are blocked for special events (fights, Super Bowl weekend, etc.); and still others are at the disposal of the sales and marketing department for meetings, conventions, wedding parties, and other special groups. Hotels that are part of a large chain (ITT Sheraton, Holiday Inn, Hilton, etc.) have some additional rooms administered by their national reservations systems.

At most hotels, department heads meet each week and review all the room allocations. If rooms blocked for a special event, say a golf tournament, are not selling, some of those rooms will be redistributed to other departments. Since special events and large conventions are scheduled far in advance, the decision makers have significant lead time. In most hotels, a major reallocation of rooms takes place 40–50 days prior to the dates for which the rooms are blocked, with minor reallocations made right up to the event in question.

If you call the reservations number at the hotel of your choice and are informed that no rooms are available for the dates you've requested, it does not mean the hotel is sold out. What it does mean is that the front desk has no more rooms remaining in their allocation. It is a fairly safe assumption that all the rooms in a hotel have not been reserved for guests. The casino will usually hold back some rooms for high rollers, the sales department may have some rooms reserved for participants in deals they are negotiating, and some rooms will be in the hands of tour wholesalers or blocked for a citywide convention. If any of these remaining rooms are not committed by a certain date, they will be reallocated. So a second call to the reservations department may get you the room that was unavailable when you called two weeks earlier.

■ Getting the Best Deal on a Room ■

Compared to that in other destinations, lodging in Las Vegas is so inexpensive that the following cost-cutting strategies may seem gratuitous. If you are accustomed to paying $120 a night for a hotel room, you can afford almost any hotel in town, and you may not be inclined to wade through all the options listed below to save $20 or $30 a night. If, on the other hand, you would like to obtain top value for your dollar, read on.

Beating Rack Rates

The benchmark for making cost comparisons is always the hotel's standard rate, or rack rate. This is what you would pay if, space available, you just walked in off the street and rented a room. In a way, the rack rate is analogous to an airline's standard coach fare. It represents a straight, nondiscounted room rate. In Las Vegas, you assume that the rack rate is the most you should have to pay and that with a little effort you ought to be able to do better.

To learn the standard room rate, call room reservations at the hotel(s) of your choice. Do not be surprised if there are several standard rates, one for each type of room in the hotel. Have the reservationist explain the difference in the types of rooms available in each price bracket. Also ask the hotel which, of the described class of rooms, you would get if you came on a wholesaler, tour operator, or airline tour package. This information will allow you to make meaningful comparisons among various packages and rates.

The Season

December and January are roller-coaster months for Las Vegas. In December, town is empty except for National Finals Rodeo week in early December and Christmas/New Year's week. Similarly, in January, town is packed during the Consumer Electronics Show and the Super Bowl weekend, and pretty much dead the rest of the time. During the slow parts of these months, most of the hotels offer amazing deals on lodging. Also, hotels sometimes offer reduced rates in July and August. While the list below stands up pretty well as a general guide, one type of deal or package might beat another for a specific hotel or time of year.

Sorting Out the Sellers and the Options

To book a room in a particular hotel for any given date, there are so many different in-house departments, as well as outside tour operators and wholesalers selling rooms, that it is almost impossible to find out who is offering the best deal. This is not because the various deals are so hard to compare but, rather, because it is so difficult to identify all the sellers.

Though it is only a rough approximation, here is a list of the types of rates and packages available, ranked from the best to the worst value.

Room Rates and Packages	Sold or Administered by
1. Gambler's rate	Casino or hotel
2. December, January, and summer specials	Hotel room reservations or marketing department
3. Wholesaler packages	Independent wholesalers
4. Tour operator packages	Tour operators
5. Reservation service discounts	Independent wholesalers and consolidators
6. Half-price programs	Half-price program operators
7. Commercial airline packages	Commercial airlines
8. Hotel packages	Hotel sales and marketing
9. Corporate rate	Hotel room reservations
10. Hotel standard room rate	Hotel room reservations
11. Convention rate	Convention sponsor

The room rate ranking is subject to some interpretation. A gambler's rate may, at first glance, seem to be the least expensive lodging option available, next to a complimentary room. If, however, the amount of money a guest is obligated to wager (and potentially lose) is factored in, the gambler's rate might be by far the most expensive.

Complimentary and Discounted Rooms for Gamblers

Most Las Vegas visitors are at least peripherally aware that casinos provide complimentary or greatly discounted rooms to gamblers. It is not unusual, therefore, for a business traveler, a low-stakes gambler, or a nongambling tourist to attempt to take advantage of these deals. What they quickly discover is that the casino has very definite expectations of any guest whose stay is wholly or partially subsidized by the house. If you only want a gambler's discount on a room, they will ask what game(s) you intend to play, the amount of your average bet, how many hours a day you usually gamble, where (at which casinos) you have played before, and how much gambling money you will have available on this trip. They may also request that you make an application for credit or provide personal information about your occupation, income, and bank account.

If you manage to bluff your way into a comp or discounted room, you can bet that your gambling (or lack thereof) will be closely monitored after you arrive. If you fail to give the casino an acceptable amount of action, you will probably be charged the nondiscounted room rate when you check out.

Even for those who expect to do a fair amount of gambling, a comp or discounted room can be a mixed blessing. By accepting the casino's hospitality, you incur a certain obligation (the more they give you, the bigger the obligation). You will be expected to do most (if not all) of your gambling in the casino where you are staying, and you will also be expected to play a certain number of hours each day. If this was your intention all along, great. On the other hand, if you thought you would like to try several casinos or take a day and run over to Hoover Dam, you may be painting yourself into a corner.

Taking Advantage of Special Deals

When you call, always ask the reservationist if the hotel has any package deals or specials. If you plan to gamble, be sure to ask about "gambling sprees" or other gaming specials. If you do not anticipate gambling enough to qualify for a gambling package, ask about other types of deals. If the reservationist is not knowledgeable, don't conclude that the hotel offers no packages or special deals of its own. Instead, have the reservationist transfer your call to the sales and marketing department and ask them.

If you have a lot of lead time before your trip, write or call the hotel and ask about joining their slot club. Though only a few hotels will send you a membership application, inquiring about the slot club will get you categorized as a gambler on the hotel's mailing list. Once in Las Vegas, sign up for the slot clubs of hotel-casinos that you like. This will ensure that you receive notification of special deals that you can take advantage of on subsequent visits. Also, being a member of a hotel's slot club can also come in handy when rooms are scarce. Once, trying to book a room, we were told the hotel was sold out. When we mentioned that we had a slot card, the reservationist miraculously found us a room. If you are a slot club member, it is often better to phone the slot club member services desk instead of the hotel reservations desk.

Having shopped the hotel for deals, start checking out tour operator and wholesaler packages advertised in your local newspaper, and compare what you find to packages offered in the Sunday edition of the *Los Angeles Times*. Next, check out packages offered by the airline tour services (American Airlines Fly-Away, Delta Vacations, etc.). When working with the airline tour services, always ask if they have any special deals going on with particular hotels.

Take the better deals and packages you discover, regardless of the source, and discuss them with a travel agent. Explain which one(s) you favor and ask if he or she can do any better. After your travel agent researches the options, review the whole shooting match and select the deal that best fits your schedule, requirements, and budget.

Since Las Vegas room rates are among the most reasonable in the country, you may not want to go to all of this effort. If you are working with a restricted budget, or plan to visit Las Vegas once or more each year, it is probably worth the hassle to check the rate and package options. If, conversely, you are used to paying $65–125 a night for a hotel room, you may prefer to choose a hotel and leave it to your travel agent to get you the best deal available.

Timing Is Everything

Timing is everything when booking a guest room in Las Vegas. If a particular hotel has only a few rooms to sell for a specific date, it will often bounce up the rate for those rooms as high as it thinks the market will bear. Conversely, if the hotel has many rooms available for a certain date, it will lower the rate accordingly. The practice remains operative all year, although the likelihood of hotels having a lot of rooms available is obviously greater during "off-peak" periods. As an example, we checked rates at an upscale nongaming hotel during two weeks in October. Depending on the specific dates, the rate for the suite in question ranged from $75 (an incredible bargain) to $200 (significantly overpriced) per night.

Which day of the week you check in can also save or cost you some money. At some hotels a standard room runs 20% less if you check in on a Monday through Thursday (even though you may stay through the weekend). If you check into the same room on a weekend, your rate will be higher and will not change if you keep your room into the following week. A more common practice is for the hotel to charge a lower rate during the week and a higher rate on the weekend.

Helping Your Travel Agent to Help You

A travel agent friend told me once, "Las Vegas is our least favorite destination." What she meant, essentially, is that travel agents cannot make much money selling trips to Las Vegas. Air fares to Las Vegas are among the lowest in the country, and hotel rooms frequently go for less than $50 a night. On top of this, the average stay in Las Vegas is short. To a travel agent this adds up to a lot of work with little potential for a worthwhile commission. Because an agent derives only a small return for booking travel to Las Vegas, there isn't much incentive for the travel agent to become product knowledgeable.

Except for a handful of agents who sell Las Vegas travel in volume (usually in Las Vegas's primary markets), there are comparatively few travel agents who know much about Las Vegas. This lack of information translates into travelers not getting reservations at their preferred hotel, paying more than is necessary, or being placed in out-of-the-way or otherwise undesirable lodging.

When you call your travel agent, ask if he or she has been to Las Vegas. Firsthand experience means everything. If the answer is no, either find another agent or be prepared to give your travel agent a lot of direction. Do not accept any recommendations at face value. Check out the location and rates of any suggested hotel and make certain that the hotel is suited to your itinerary.

Because travel agents tend to be unfamiliar with Las Vegas, your agent may try to plug you into a tour operator's or wholesaler's preset package. This essentially allows the travel agent to set up your whole trip with a single phone call and still collect an 8–10% commission. The problem with this scenario is that most agents will place 90% of their Las Vegas business with only one or two wholesalers or tour operators. In other words, path of least resistance for them, and not much choice for you.

Often, travel agents will use wholesalers who run packages in conjunction with airlines, like Delta's Vacations or American's Fly-Away Vacations. Because of the wholesaler's exclusive relationship with the carrier, these trips are very easy for travel agents to book. However, they will probably be more expensive than a package offered by a high-volume wholesaler, who works with a number of airlines in a primary Las Vegas market.

To help your travel agent get you the best possible deal, do the following:

1. Determine where you want to stay in Las Vegas (the Strip, downtown, Boulder Highway, etc.), and if possible choose a specific hotel. This can be accomplished by reviewing the hotel information provided in this guide and by writing or calling hotels that interest you.

2. Check out the Las Vegas travel ads in the Sunday travel section of your local newspaper and compare them to ads running in the newspapers of one of Las Vegas's key markets (i.e., Los Angeles, San Diego, Phoenix, Chicago). See if you can find some packages that fit your plans and that include a hotel you like.

3. Call the wholesalers or tour operators whose ads you have collected. Ask any questions you might have concerning their packages, but do not book your trip with them directly.

4. Tell your travel agent about the packages you find and ask if he or she can get you something better. The packages in the paper will serve as a benchmark against which to compare alternatives proposed by your travel agent.

5. Choose from among the options uncovered by you and your travel agent. No matter which option you elect, have your travel agent book it. Even if you go with one of the packages in the newspaper, it will probably be commissionable (at no additional cost to you) and will provide the agent some return on the time invested on your behalf. Also, as a travel professional, your agent should be able to verify the quality and integrity of the package.

No Room at the Inn (Maybe)   If you are having trouble getting a reservation at the hotel of your choice, let your travel agent assist you. As discussed, the agent might be able to find a package with a wholesaler or tour operator that bypasses the hotel reservations department. If this does not work, he or she can call the sales and marketing department of the hotel and ask them, as a favor, to find you a room. Most hotel sales reps will make a special effort to accommodate travel agents, particularly travel agents who write a lot of Las Vegas business. Do not be shy or reluctant about asking your travel agent to make a special call on your behalf. This is common practice in the travel industry and affords the agent an opportunity to renew contacts in the hotel's sales department.

If your travel agent cannot get you a room through a personal appeal to the sales department and does not know which tour operators and wholesalers package the hotel you want, have the agent call hotel room reservations and:

1. Identify him- or herself as a travel agent.

2. Inquire about room availability for your required dates; something might have opened up since their (or your) last call.

3. If the reservationist reports that there are still no rooms available, have your travel agent ask for the reservations manager.

4. When the reservations manager comes on the line, have your agent identify him- or herself and ask whether the hotel is holding any space for wholesalers. If the answer is yes, have your agent request the wholesalers' names and phone numbers. This is information the reservations manager will not ordinarily divulge to an individual but will release to your travel agent. Armed with the names and numbers of wholesalers holding space, your agent can start calling the listed wholesalers to find you a package or a room.

No Room at the Inn (for Real)   More frequently than you would imagine, Las Vegas hotels overbook their rooms. This happens when guests do not check out on time, when important casino customers arrive on short notice, and when the various departments handling room allocations get their signals crossed. When this occurs, guests who arrive holding reservations are told that their reservations have been canceled.

To protect yourself, always guarantee your first night with a major credit card (even if you do not plan to arrive late), send a deposit if required, and insist on a written confirmation of your reservation. When you arrive and check in, have your written confirmation handy.

Precautions notwithstanding, the hotel still might have canceled your reservation. When a hotel is overbooked, for whatever reason, it will take care of its serious gambling customers first, its prospective gambling customers (leisure travelers) second, and business travelers last. If you are informed that you have no room, demand that the hotel honor your reservation by finding you a room or by securing you a room at another convenient hotel. Should the desk clerk balk at doing this, demand to see the reservations manager. If the reservations manager stonewalls, go to the hotel's general manager. Whatever you do, do not leave until the issue has been resolved to your satisfaction.

Hotels understand their obligation to honor a confirmed reservation, but they often fail to take responsibility unless you hold their feet to the fire. We have seen convention-goers, stunned by the news that they have no room, simply turn around and walk out. Wrong. The hotel owns the problem, not you. You should not have to shop for another room. The hotel that confirmed your reservation should find you a room comparable to or better than the one you reserved, and for the same rate.

■ Where the Deals Are ■

Hotel room marketing and sales is confusing even to travel professionals. Sellers, particularly the middlemen, or wholesalers are known by a numbing array of different and frequently ill-defined terms. Furthermore, roles overlap, making it difficult to know who specifically is providing a given service. Below we try to sort all of this out for you and encourage you to slog through it. Understanding the system will make you a savvy consumer and will enable you to get the best deals regardless of your destination.

Tour Operators and Wholesalers

Las Vegas hotels have always had a hard time filling their rooms from Sunday through Thursday. On the weekends, when thousands of visitors arrive from Southern California, Phoenix, and Salt Lake, the town comes alive. But on Sunday evening, as the last of the Los Angelenos retreat over the horizon line, Las Vegas lapses into the doldrums. The Las Vegas Convention and Visitors Authority, along with hotel sales departments, seek to fill the rooms on weekday nights by bringing meetings, conventions, and trade shows to town. While collectively they are very successful, on many weekdays there remain a lot of empty hotel rooms.

Recognizing that an empty hotel room is a liability, various travel entrepreneurs have stepped into the breach, volunteering to sell rooms for the hotels and casinos. These entrepreneurs, who call themselves tour operators, inbound travel brokers, travel wholesalers, travel packagers, or receptive operators, require as a quid pro quo that the hotels provide them a certain number of rooms at a significantly reduced nightly rate, which they in turn resell at a profit. As this arrangement extends the sales outreach of the hotels, and as the rooms might otherwise go unoccupied, the hotels are only too happy to cooperate with this group of independent sales agents. Though a variety of programs have been developed to sell the rooms, most are marketed as part of group and individual travel packages.

This development has been beneficial both to the tourist and the hotel. Predicated on volume, some of the room discount is generally passed along to consumers as an incentive to come to Las Vegas during the week or, alternatively, to stay in town beyond the weekend. Wholesalers have made such a positive contribution to the Las Vegas hotel occupancy rate that rooms are now made available to them for weekends as well as weekdays.

By purchasing your room through a tour operator or wholesaler, you may be able to obtain a room at the hotel of your choice for considerably less than if you went through the hotel's reservations department. The hotel commits rooms to the wholesaler at a specific deep discount, usually 18–30% or more off the standard quoted rate, but makes no effort to control the price the wholesaler offers to his customers.

Wholesalers holding space at a hotel for a specific block of time must surrender that space back to the hotel if the rooms are not sold by a certain date, usually 7–14 days in advance. Since the wholesaler's performance and credibility is determined by the number of rooms filled in a given hotel, the wholesaler is always reluctant to give rooms back. The situation is similar to when the biology department at a university approaches the end of the year without having spent all of its allocated budget. The department head reasons that if the remaining funds are not spent (and the surplus is returned to the university), the university might reduce his budget for the forthcoming year. Tour wholesalers depend on the hotels for their inventory. The more rooms the hotels allocate, the more inventory they have to sell. If a wholesaler keeps returning rooms unsold, it is logical to predict that the hotel will respond by making fewer rooms available in the future. Therefore, the wholesaler would rather sell rooms at a bargain price than give them back to the hotel unsold.

Taking Advantage of Tour Operator and Travel Wholesaler Deals
There are several ways for you to tap into the tour operator and wholesaler market. First, check the travel sections of your Sunday paper for travel packages or tours to Las Vegas. Because Las Vegas hotels work with tour operators and wholesalers from all over the country, there will undoubtedly be someone in your city or region running packages to Las Vegas. Packages generally consist of room, transportation (bus or air), and often other features such as rental cars, shows, etc. Sometimes the consumer can buy the package for any dates desired; other times the operator or wholesaler will specify the dates. In either event, if a particular package fits your needs, you

Tour Operators and Travel Wholesalers

Some of the following businesses will deal directly with consumers while others will not. Concerning the latter, have your travel agent call for you.

A & P Tours
East McKeesport,
Pennsylvania
(412) 351-4800
(Deals directly with
consumers)

Adventure Vacations
Hunt Valley, Maryland
(410) 785-3500

American Travel
Kansas City, Kansas
(913) 384-DEAL or
(800) 827-7997
(Deals directly with
consumers)

America West Vacations
Tempe, Arizona
(800) 356-6611
(Deals directly with
consumers)

Funjet Vacations
Des Moines, Iowa
(515) 278-9690

Funjet Vacations
Milwaukee, Wisconsin
(800) 558-3050

Hamilton, Miller, Hudson
& Fayne
Southfield, Michigan
(810) 827-4050

Kingdom Tours
Plains, Pennsylvania
(800) 626-8747

Mile High Tours
Denver, Colorado
(303) 758-8246 or
(800) 777-TOUR
(Deals directly with
consumers)

MLT Vacations
Minnetonka, Minnesota
(612) 474-2540 or
(800) 328-0025
(Deals directly with
consumers)

Premier Vacations
Honolulu, Hawaii
(808) 596-0030

Sunmakers
Seattle, Washington
(800) 841-4321
(Deals directly with
consumers)

Sunquest Vacations
Toronto, Ontario
(416) 485-1700

Sunquest Vacations West
Richmond, British
Columbia
(604) 273-9465

(or your travel agent) can book it directly by calling the phone number listed in the ad.

If you cannot find any worthwhile Las Vegas packages advertised in your local paper, go to a good newsstand and buy a Sunday paper, preferably from Los Angeles, but alternatively from San Diego, Phoenix, Salt Lake City, Denver, or Chicago. These cities are hot markets for Las Vegas, and their newspapers will almost always have a nice selection of packages advertised. Because the competition among tour operators and wholesalers in these cities is so great, you will often find deals that beat the socks off anything offered in your part of the country.

Find a package that you like and call for information. Do not be surprised, however, if the advertised package is not wholly available to you. If you live, say, in Nashville, Tennessee, a tour operator or wholesaler in Los Angeles may not be able to package your round-trip air or bus to Las Vegas. This is because tour operators and wholesalers usually work with bus and air carriers on a contractual basis, limiting the transportation they sell to round trips originating from their market area. In other words, they can take care of your transportation if you are flying from Southern California but most likely will not have a contract with an airline that permits them to fly you from Nashville. What they sometimes do, however, and what they will be delighted to do if they are sitting on some unsold rooms, is sell you the "land only" part of the package. This means you buy the room and on-site amenities (car, shows, etc.), if any, but will take care of your own travel arrangements.

Buying the "land only" part of a package can save big bucks since the wholesaler always has more flexibility in discounting the "land" part of the package than in discounting the round-trip transportation component. One of the sweetest deals in travel is to purchase the "land only" part of a package at a time when the airlines are running a promotion. We combined a two-for-one air special from Delta with a "land only" package from a wholesaler and chalked up a savings of 65% over separate quoted rates and a 22% savings over the full air/land package offered by the wholesaler.

Half-Price Programs

The larger discounts on rooms in nongaming properties (hotels without casinos), in Las Vegas or anywhere else, are available through half-price hotel programs, often called travel clubs. Program operators contract with an individual hotel to provide rooms at a deep discount, usually 50% off rack rate, on a "space available" basis. In practice, space available generally means that you can reserve a room at the discounted rate whenever the hotel expects to be at less than 80% occupancy. A little calendar sleuthing to help you avoid citywide conventions and special events will increase the chances of choosing a time for your visit when the discounts are available.

Most half-price programs charge an annual membership fee or directory subscription charge of $25 to $125. Once enrolled, you are mailed a membership card and a directory listing all the hotels participating in the program. Examining the directory, you will notice immediately that there are a lot of restrictions and exceptions. Some hotels, for instance, "black out" certain dates or times of year. Others may only offer the discount on certain days of the week or require you to stay a certain number of nights. Still others may offer a much smaller discount than 50% off rack rate.

Some programs specialize in domestic travel, some in international travel, and some specialize in both. The more established operators offer members up to 4,000 hotels to choose from in the United States. All of the programs have a heavy concentration of hotels in California and Florida, and most have a very limited selection of participating properties in New York City or Boston. Offerings in other cities and regions of the United States vary considerably. The programs with the largest selection of hotels in Las Vegas are Encore, Travel America at Half Price (Entertainment Publications), International Travel Card, and Quest.

One problem with half-price programs is that not all hotels offer a full 50% discount. Another slippery problem is the base rate against which the discount is applied. Some hotels figure the discount on an exaggerated rack rate that nobody would ever have to pay. A few participating hotels may deduct the discount from a supposed "superior" or "upgraded" room rate, even though the room you get is the hotel's standard accommodation. Though the facts can be hard to pin down, the majority of participating properties base discounts on the published rate in the *Hotel & Travel Index* (a quarterly reference work used by travel agents) and work within the spirit of their agreement with the program operator. As a rule, if you travel several times a year, you will more than pay for your program membership in room rate savings.

Half-Price Programs	
Encore	(800) 638-0930
Entertainment Publications	(800) 285-5525
International Travel Card	(800) 342-0558
Quest	(800) 638-9819

A noteworthy addendum to this discussion is that deeply discounted rooms through half-price programs are not commissionable to travel agents. In practical terms this means that you must ordinarily make your own inquiry calls and reservations. If you travel frequently, however, and run a lot of business through your travel agent, he or she will probably do your legwork, lack of commission notwithstanding.

Players Club

The most visible discount travel club selling Las Vegas is the Players Club. The Players Club advertises savings of 25–60% on lodging, cruises, shows, and dining. In addition to Las Vegas, Players Club also sells Atlantic City, Lake Tahoe, Reno, the Caribbean, Hawaii, Mexico, and five cruise lines.

Players Club costs $144 (plus $6 handling fee) a year for membership. In Las Vegas, Players Club uses Bally's, San Remo, the Flamingo Hilton, the Las Vegas Hilton, the Luxor, the Aladdin, the Holiday Inn Boardwalk, and the Stardust. The Club also offers a three-month no-risk guarantee during which you can cancel your membership and receive a full refund of all fees.

An extremely determined person who knows Las Vegas can probably find a deal that beats Players Club but will have to invest a lot of time for a package only marginally less expensive. By joining Players Club, we were able to secure rooms in hotels that were otherwise sold out and to realize discounts of 18–45%. Since discounts apply to weekends and weekdays, as well as any length of stay, Players Club can be a real godsend for anyone traveling to Las Vegas to attend a convention or trade show. The savings we describe above are based on discounting standard rates quoted by the hotel. If you figure the percentage discount on convention rates, you can save in excess of 60%.

Savings on shows ranged as high as 50%, though most discounts in this category were in the 25% range. A nice extra, however, is that Players Club membership allows you "Invited Guest" privileges at participating shows, which means no waiting in show lines. Savings of up to 25% on meals applies only to designated restaurants, but there are some pretty decent restaurants on the list.

Though Players Club also offers discount air fares, we were able to beat their prices pretty regularly, but only with nonrefundable advance purchase tickets. If you purchase air travel from Players Club, you will pay a little more ($20–55) but will gain the advantage of canceling your reservations with only a nominal penalty.

Dealing with Players Club agents for tickets and reservations has so far been quick and efficient. To date we have not been subjected to the dreaded "hold button from hell." As the club's membership pushes 125,000, however, we remain alert to any decline in service.

If you are interested in Players Club, you can call (800) 275-6600. When you call, an operator will take your name, address, and phone number. Later an aggressive telemarketer will call you back and try to sign you and your credit card up over the phone. If you ask for membership information, they will likewise try to respond over the phone. State that you do not have time to listen to an oral sales presentation, and insist that a complete written description of the club be mailed to you. Incidentally, if you join and later decide to cancel, Players Club will honor their money-back guarantee without any hassle.

Reservation Services

When wholesalers and consolidators deal directly with the public, they frequently represent themselves as "reservation services." When you call, you can ask for a rate quote for a particular hotel, or alternatively, ask for their best available deal in the area where you prefer to stay. If there is a maximum amount you are willing to pay, say so. Chances are the service will find something that will work for you, even if they have to shave a dollar or two off their own profit.

The discount available (if any) from a reservation service depends on whether the service functions as a consolidator or a wholesaler. Consolidators are strictly sales agents who do not own or control the room inventory they are trying to sell. Discounts offered by consolidators are determined by the hotels with rooms to fill. Consolidator discounts vary enormously depending on how desperate the hotel is to unload the rooms. When you deal with a room reservation service that operates as a consolidator, you pay for your room as usual when you check out of the hotel.

Reservation Services	
Hotel Reservations Network	(800) 96-HOTEL
City Wide Reservations	(800) 733-6644
RMC Travel Center	(800) 782-2674 or (800) 245-5738
Accommodations Express	(800) 444-7666

Wholesalers, as we discussed above, have long-standing contracts with hotels that allow the wholesaler to purchase rooms at an established deep discount. Some wholesalers hold purchase options on blocks of rooms while others actually pay for rooms and own the inventory. Because a wholesaler controls the room inventory, it can offer whatever discount it pleases consistent with current demand. In practice, most wholesaler reservation-service discounts fall in the 10–40% range. When you reserve a room with a reservation service that operates as a wholesaler, you must usually pay for your entire stay in advance with your credit card. The service then sends you a written confirmation and usually a voucher (indicating prepayment) for you to present at the hotel.

Our experience has been that the reservation services are more useful in finding rooms in Las Vegas when availability is scarce than in obtaining deep discounts. Calling the hotels ourselves, we were often able to beat the reservation services' rates when rooms were generally available. When the city was booked, however, and we could not find a room by calling the hotels ourselves, the reservation services could almost always get us a room at a fair price.

Hotel-Sponsored Packages

In addition to selling rooms through tour operators, consolidators, and wholesalers, most hotels periodically offer exceptional deals of their own. Sometimes the packages are specialized, as with the Desert Inn's golf packages, or are only offered at certain times of the year, for instance, December and January. Promotion of hotel specials tends to be limited to the hotel's primary markets, which for most properties is Southern California, Arizona, Utah, Colorado, Hawaii, and the Midwest. If you live in other parts of the country, you can take advantage of the packages but probably will not see them advertised in your local newspaper.

Some of the hotel packages are unbelievable deals. Once, for instance, Maxim offered three nights' free lodging, no strings attached, to any adult from Texas; and the Stardust ran a $32 special that included a room, a show, and a buffet for two people. Look for the hotel specials in Southern California newspapers, or call the hotel and ask.

An important point regarding hotel specials is that the hotel reservationists do not usually inform you of existing specials or offer them to you. In other words, *you have to ask.*

Exit Information Guide

A company called EIG (Exit Information Guide) publishes a book of discount coupons for bargain rates at hotels throughout California and

Nevada. These books are available free of charge in many restaurants and motels along the main interstate highways. Since most folks make reservations prior to leaving home, picking up the coupon book en route does not help much. For $3 ($5 Canadian), however, EIG will mail you a copy (third class) before you make your reservations. Properties listed in the guide for Las Vegas are generally smaller, nongaming hotels. If you call and use a credit card, EIG will send the guide first class for an additional charge. Write or call:

Exit Information Guide
4205 NW Sixth Street
Gainesville, FL 32609
(904) 371-3948

■ How to Evaluate a Travel Package ■

Hundreds of Las Vegas package trips and vacations are offered to the public each year. Almost all include round-trip transportation to Las Vegas and lodging. Sometimes room tax, transportation from the airport, a rental car, shows, meals, welcome parties, and/or souvenirs are also included.

In general, because the Las Vegas market is so competitive, packages to Las Vegas are among the best travel values available. Las Vegas competes head-to-head with Atlantic City for Eastern travelers and with Reno, Lake Tahoe, Laughlin, and other Nevada destinations for Western visitors. Within Las Vegas, downtown competes with the Strip, and individual hotels go one-on-one to improve their share of the market. In addition to the fierce competition for the destination traveler, the extraordinary profitability of gambling also works in the consumer's behalf to keep Las Vegas travel economical. In almost every hotel, amazing values in dining and lodging are used to lure visitors to the casino.

Packages should be a win/win proposition for both the buyer and the seller. The buyer (or travel agent) only has to make one phone call and deal with a single salesperson to set up the whole trip: transportation, lodging, rental car, show admissions, and even golf, tennis, and sight-seeing. The seller, likewise, only has to deal with the buyer one time, eliminating the need for separate sales, confirmations, and billings. In addition to streamlining selling, processing, and administration, some packagers also buy air fares in bulk on contract like a broker playing the commodities market. Buying or guaranteeing a large number of air fares in advance allows the packager to buy them at a significant savings from posted fares. The same practice is also applied to hotel rooms. Because selling packaged trips is an efficient way of doing business, and the packager can often buy individual components (air fare, lodging) in bulk at a discount, savings in operating expenses realized by the seller are sometimes passed on to the buyer. So the package is not only convenient but an exceptional value. In any event, that is the way it is supposed to work.

In practice, the seller occasionally realizes all of the economies and passes none of the savings along to the buyer. In some instances, packages are loaded with extras that cost the packager next to nothing but run the retail price of the package sky-high. While this is not as common with Las Vegas packages as those to other destinations, it occurs frequently enough to warrant some comparison shopping.

When considering a package, choose one that includes features you are sure to use. Whether you use all the features or not, you will most certainly pay for them. Second, if cost is of greater concern than convenience, make a few phone calls and see what the package would cost if you booked its individual components (air fare, lodging, rental car) on your own. If the package price is less than the à la carte cost, the package is a good deal. If the costs are about the same, the package is probably worth it for the convenience.

An Example　A business associate of mine was looking at a package his travel agent found with American Airlines Fly-Away Vacations. The package included round-trip air (on American) from Chicago, three nights' lodging (Thursday, Friday, Saturday) at the Mirage, and airport transfers (transportation to and from the airport). The package price, tax included, was $460 each for him and his wife, or $920 altogether.

By checking the Mirage and a number of airlines, he discovered the following:

Same room at the Mirage, two people to a room, for three nights with room tax included	$414
Transportation to and from the airport (for two)	14
Subtotal	$428

Subtracting the $428 (lodging and airport transfers) subtotal from the cost of American's package total of $920, he determined that the air portion of the package was worth $492 ($920 – $428 = $492). If he could fly himself and his wife to Las Vegas for less than $492, he would be better off turning down the package.

Scouting around, the lowest fare he could find was $278 on Continental with an advance purchase ticket. This piece of information completed his analysis as follows:

Option A American Fly-Away package for two	$920
Option B Booking his own air and lodging:	
Lodging, including tax	$414
Air on Continental for two ($278 × 2)	556
Transportation to and from hotel	14
Total	$984

For Business Travelers

■ **Convention Rates: How the System Works** ■

Business travelers, particularly those attending trade shows or conventions, are almost always charged more for their rooms than leisure travelers. For big meetings, called citywide conventions, huge numbers of rooms are blocked in hotels all over town. These rooms are reserved for visitors attending the meeting in question and are usually requested and coordinated by the meeting's sponsoring organization in cooperation with the Las Vegas Convention and Visitors Authority.

Individual hotels negotiate a nightly rate with the convention sponsor, who then frequently sells the rooms through a central reservations system of its own. Since the hotels would rather have gamblers or leisure travelers than people attending conventions (who usually have limited time to gamble), the negotiated price tends to be high, often $10–50 per night above the rack rate.

Meeting sponsors, of course, blame convention rates on the hotels. Meanwhile the hotels maintain a stoic silence, not wishing to alienate meeting organizers. Following the publication of an earlier edition of this guide, the publisher received the following irate letter from a major convention sponsor:

> "Mr. Sehlinger writes that the convention sponsors often charge what they think the market will bear. Therefore, if the convention-goer gets gouged on a room, it is the doing of the convention sponsor, not the hotel. This statement is completely false and misleading and puts [convention sponsors] in a false light. [Our organization] does not make any profit on hotel rooms. . . . The general practice is to charge our members exactly what the hotel charges us. Each member pays his or her own hotel bill when leaving Las Vegas, and [we] receive no commission, kickback, or other payment from the hotel."

To be fair, convention sponsors should be given some credit simply for having their meeting in Las Vegas. Even considering the inflated convention rates, meeting attendees will pay 20–60% less in Las Vegas for comparable lodging than in other major convention cities. As for the rest, well, let's take a look.

Sam Walton taught the average American that someone purchasing a large quantity of a particular item should be able to obtain a better price (per item) than a person buying only one or two. If anyone just walking in off the street can buy a single hotel room for $50, why then must a convention sponsor, negotiating for 900 rooms for 5 nights in the same hotel (4,500 room-nights in hotel jargon), settle for a rate of $60 per night?

Many Las Vegas hotels take a hardline negotiating position with meeting sponsors because (1) every room occupied by a convention-goer is one less room available for gamblers, and (2) they figure that most business travelers are on expense accounts. In addition, timing is a critical factor in negotiating room rates. The hotels do not want business travelers occupying rooms on weekends or during the more popular times of the year. Convention sponsors who want to schedule a meeting during high season (when hotels fill their rooms no matter what) can expect to pay premium rates. In addition, and regardless of the time of year, many hotels routinely charge stiff prices to convention-goers as a sort of insurance against lost opportunity. "What if we block our rooms for a trade show one year in advance," a sales manager asked, "and then a championship prizefight is scheduled for that week? We would lose big-time."

A spokesman for the Las Vegas Convention and Visitors Authority indicated that the higher room rates for conventioneers are not unreasonable given a hotel's commitment to the sponsor to hold rooms in reserve. But reserved rooms, or room blocks as they are called, fragment a hotel's inventory of available rooms, and often make it harder, not easier, to get a room in a particular hotel. The bottom line is that convention-goers pay a premium price for the benefit of having rooms reserved for their meeting—rooms that would always be cheaper, and often easier to reserve, if the sponsor had not reserved them in the first place. For a major, citywide convention, it is not unusual for attendees to collectively pay in excess of $1 million for the peace of mind of having rooms reserved.

Whether room blocking is really necessary is an interesting question. The Las Vegas Convention and Visitors Authority works with convention sponsors to ensure that there is never more than one citywide meeting in town at a time and to make sure that sponsors do not schedule their conventions at a time when Las Vegas hotels are otherwise normally sold out (National Finals Rodeo week, Super Bowl weekend, New Year's, and so on). Unfortunately for meeting planners, some major events (prizefights, tennis matches) are occasionally scheduled in Las Vegas on short notice. If a meeting planner does not block rooms and a big fight is announced for the week the meeting is in town, the attendees may be unable to find a room. This is such a nightmare to convention sponsors that they cave in to exorbitant convention rates rather than risk not having rooms. The actual likelihood of a major event being scheduled at the same time as a large convention is small, though the specter of this worst-case scenario is a powerful weapon in the bargaining arsenal of the hotels.

On balance, meeting sponsors negate their volume-buying clout by scheduling meetings during the more popular times of year or, alternatively, by caving in to the hotels' "opportunity cost" room pricing. Conversely, hotels play unfairly on the sponsor's fear of not having enough rooms, and they charge premium rates to cover improbable, ill-defined opportunity losses. Is there collusion here? Probably not. The more likely conclusion is that both hotels and sponsors have become comfortable with an inflexible negotiating environment, but one that permits meeting sponsors to distribute the unreasonable charges pro rata to their attendees.

Working through the Maze

If you attempt to bypass the sponsoring organization and go directly through the hotel, the hotel will either refer you to the convention's central reservations number or quote you the same high price. Even if you do not identify yourself as a convention-goer, the hotel will figure it out by the dates you request. In most instances, even if you lie and insist that you are not attending the convention in question, the hotel will make you pay the higher rate or claim to be sold out.

By way of example, we tried to get reservations at the Riviera for a major trade show in the spring, a citywide convention that draws about 30,000 attendees. The show runs six days plus one day for setting up, or seven days total, Saturday through Friday. Though this example involves the Riviera, we encountered the same scenario at every hotel we called.

When we phoned reservations at the Riviera and gave them our dates, they immediately asked if we would be attending a convention or trade show. When we answered in the affirmative, they gave us the official sponsor's central reservations phone number in New York. We called the sponsor and learned that a single room at the Riviera (one person in one room) booked through them would cost $91 per night including room tax. The same room (we found from other sources) booked directly through the Riviera would cost $80 with tax included.

We called the Riviera back and asked for the same dates, this time disavowing any association with the trade show, and were rebuffed. Obviously skeptical of our story, the hotel informed us that they were sold out for the days we requested. Unconvinced that the hotel was fully booked, we had two different members of our research team call. One attempted to make reservations from Wednesday *of the preceding week* through Tuesday of the trade show week, while our second caller requested a room from Wednesday of the trade show week through the following Tuesday. These respective sets of dates, we reasoned, would differ sufficiently from the show dates to convince the Riviera that we were not conventioneers. In each case we were able to make reservations for the dates desired at the $80-per-night rate.

It should be stressed that a hotel treats the convention's sponsoring organization much like a wholesaler who reserves rooms in a block for a negotiated price. What the convention, in turn, charges its attendees is out of the hotel's control. Once a hotel and convention sponsor come to terms, the hotel either refers all inquiries about reservations to the sponsor or accepts bookings at whatever nightly rate the sponsor determines. Since hotels do not want to get in the way of their convention sponsors (who are very powerful customers) or, alternatively, have convention attendees buying up rooms intended for other nonconvention customers, the hotel reservations department carefully screens any request for a room during a convention period.

Strategies for Beating Convention Rates

There are several strategies for getting around convention rates:

1. Buy a package from a tour operator or a wholesaler This tactic makes it unnecessary to deal with the convention's central reservations office or with an individual hotel's reservations department. Many packages allow you to buy extra days at a special discounted room rate if the package dates do not coincide perfectly with your meeting dates.

Packages that use air charter services operate on a fixed, inflexible schedule. As a rule these packages run three nights (depart Thursday, return Sunday; or depart Friday, return Monday) or four nights (depart Monday, return Friday; or depart Sunday, return Thursday). Two-night, five-night, and seven-night charter packages can also be found. Charter air packages offer greater savings, but usually less flexibility, than packages that use commercial carriers.

Since the Riviera would not give us their standard rate for the trade show dates, our remaining alternatives were to either find a package or book through the sponsor's central reservations. We wanted to travel from Birmingham, Alabama, and stay at the Riviera for the seven nights of the show. For one person, the options were as follows:

Option A: Reservations through show's official sponsor

Riviera for seven nights at $91 per night (tax included)	$637
plus round-trip air fare from Birmingham, Alabama	344

Total	$981

Option B: Charter package

Riviera for seven nights, all taxes, round-trip direct flights, two breakfasts, two dinner buffets, and three shows

Total	$798

Option C: Airline tour service's package

American's Fly-Away Vacations offered round-trip air fare, seven nights' lodging, taxes included, to the Riviera for $789 but were sold out for the required dates when we called six weeks in advance. They were able to offer the same package for the Las Vegas Hilton at $873. The Las Vegas Hilton is within easy walking distance of both the Riviera and the Convention Center.

Total	$789 or $873

Delta Vacations do not use the Riviera but had a package with round-trip air fare and seven nights' lodging, all taxes included, available for the desired dates at two hotels *not* within walking distance of the Riviera or the Las Vegas Convention Center:

Flamingo Hilton	$769
Harrah's	$879

United's Vacation Planning Center, whose wholesaler is Funway Holidays, had a package with round-trip air fare, seven nights' lodging at the Riviera, taxes, and airport transfers available for the dates of the show.

Total	$851

If you are able to beat the convention rate by booking a package or getting a room from a wholesaler, don't blow your cover when you check in. If you walk up to the registration desk in a business suit and a convention ID badge, the hotel will void your package and charge you the full convention rate. If you are supposed to be a tourist, act like one, particularly when you check in and check out.

2. Find a hotel that does not participate in the convention room blocks Many of the downtown, North Las Vegas, and Boulder Highway hotels, as well as a few of the Strip hotels, do not make rooms available in blocks for conventions. If you wish to avoid convention rates, obtain a list of your convention's "official" hotels from the sponsoring organization and match it against the hotels listed in this guide. Any hotel listed in this book that does not appear on the list supplied by the meeting sponsors is not participating in blocking rooms for your convention. This means you can deal with the nonparticipating hotels directly and should be able to get their regular rate.

Most citywide trade shows and conventions are held at the Las Vegas Convention Center. Of all the nonparticipating hotels, only Circus Circus and Westward Ho are within a 15-minute walk. If you stay at any of the other hotels, you will have to commute to the Convention Center by shuttle, cab, or car.

3. Reserve late Thirty to sixty days prior to the opening of a citywide convention or show, the front desk room reservations staff in a given hotel will take over the management of rooms reserved for the meeting from the hotel's sales and marketing department. "Room Res," in conjunction with the general manager, is responsible for making sure that the hotel is running at peak capacity for the dates of the show. The general manager has the authority to lower the room rate from the price negotiated with the

Strip Hotels That Rarely Participate in Room Blocks		
Circus Circus	Luxor	Westward Ho
Excalibur	MGM Grand	

Downtown Hotels That Seldom Participate in Room Blocks		
Binion's Horseshoe	Fitzgeralds	Lady Luck
California	Four Queens	
El Cortez	Fremont	

sponsor. If rooms are not being booked for the convention in accordance with the hotel's expectations, the general manager will often lower the rate for attendees and, at the same time, return a number of reserved rooms to general inventory for sale to the public. A convention-goer who books a room at the last minute might obtain a lower rate than an attendee who booked early through the sponsor's central housing service. Practically speaking, however, do not expect to find rooms available at the convention headquarters hotel or at most of the hotels within easy walking distance. As a rule of thumb, the farther from the Convention Center or headquarters a hotel is, the better the chances of finding a discounted room at the last minute.

■ The Las Vegas Convention Center ■

The Las Vegas Convention Center is the second largest convention and trade show facility in the United States. Much of the 1.3 million square feet of exhibit space is in one building. Divided into five halls, the building houses the largest single-floor exhibit area in North America. Trade shows that crowd facilities in Washington, San Francisco, and New York fit with ease on this one floor of the immense Las Vegas complex. In addition to the exhibit area, the Center has 85,200 square feet in lobby and public areas, a kitchen that can cater a banquet for 12,000 people, and 89 meeting rooms. Serving as headquarters for shows and conventions drawing as many as 225,000 delegates, the Convention Center is located on Paradise Road, one block off the Las Vegas Strip and three miles from the airport.

For both exhibitors and attendees, the Las Vegas Convention Center is an excellent site for a meeting or trade show. Large and small exhibitors can locate and access their exhibit sites with a minimum of effort. Numerous loading docks and huge bay doors make loading and unloading quick and simple for large displays arriving by truck. Smaller displays transported in vans and cars are unloaded on the north side of the main hall and can be carried or wheeled directly to the exhibit area without climbing stairs or using elevators. The exhibit areas and meeting rooms are well marked and easy to find.

The Las Vegas Convention and Visitors Authority also operates Cashman Field Center, home of Las Vegas's AAA baseball team. In addition to a baseball stadium, the Center contains a 2,000-seat theater and 100,000 square feet of meeting and exhibit space. For more information, call (702) 892-0711.

Lodging within Walking Distance of the Las Vegas Convention Center

While participants in citywide conventions lodge all over town, a few hotels are within easy walking distance of the Convention Center. Next door, and closest, is the huge Las Vegas Hilton, with over 3,100 rooms. The Hilton routinely serves as headquarters for meetings and shows in the Convention Center and provides, if needed, an additional 247,000 square feet of exhibit, ballroom, banquet, special event, and meeting room space. Many smaller conventions conduct all their meetings, including exhibits, at the Hilton. The walk from the lobby of the Hilton to the Convention Center is about five minutes for most people.

A long half a block away (to its rear entrance) is the 2,100-room Riviera Hotel. Like the Las Vegas Hilton, the Riviera is often the headquarters for large shows and meetings at the Convention Center. With 105,000 square feet of meeting and banquet space, the Riviera, like the Hilton, hosts entire meetings and provides supplemental facilities for events at the Convention Center. The walk from the rear (eastern) entrance of the Riviera to the Convention Center takes about ten minutes.

Parking at the Las Vegas Convention Center

In all, there are about 4,000 parking spaces, with about one-third of the spaces in front off Paradise Road and the remainder off East Desert Inn Road. The front lot, because of its visibility, is usually packed. The lots off

Other Hotels within a 20-Minute Walk of the Convention Center		
Circus Circus	3,741 rooms	15-minute walk
Debbie Reynolds Hollywood Hotel	192 rooms	7-minute walk
Desert Inn	715 rooms	18-minute walk
Frontier	988 rooms	20-minute walk
La Concha	352 rooms	15-minute walk
Las Vegas Courtyard (Marriott)	149 rooms	6-minute walk
Mardi Gras Inn (Best Western)	314 suites	12-minute walk
Residence Inn (Marriott)	192 suites	7-minute walk
Royal Hotel	220 rooms	12-minute walk
Stardust	2,500 rooms	15-minute walk

East Desert Inn Road on the south side of the Convention Center are less well known and usually have space available.

Though access to the exhibit floor varies from meeting to meeting, attendees are often required to enter through the Convention Center's main entrance off Paradise Road. In this situation, convention-goers using the East Desert Inn parking lots must hike around the south side of the complex in order to reach the front door, a seven- to ten-minute walk. For other meetings, properly credentialed attendees (i.e., those with registration badges) are permitted to enter the exhibit halls by one of several doors along the south side of the Convention Center. As a rule, getting out is not as hard as getting in, and attendees are usually permitted to exit through the south-side doors.

Cabs and Shuttles to the Convention Center

Large, citywide conventions often provide complimentary bus service from major hotels to the Convention Center. If you are staying at a smaller hotel and wish to use the shuttle bus, walk to the nearest large hotel on the shuttle route. Though cabs are plentiful and efficient in Las Vegas, they are sometimes in short supply at convention or trade show daily opening and closing times. Public transportation, CAT buses ($1.50) and the Las Vegas Strip Trolley ($1.30), is also available from the larger hotels. Exact fare is required.

Your best bet is to stay within walking distance of the Convention Center. If you end up staying too far away to walk, a car is usually less hassle than depending on cabs and shuttle buses.

Lunch Alternatives for Convention and Trade Show Attendees

The Convention Center food service provides a better than average lunch and snack selection. As at most convention centers, however, prices are high. Outside of the Convention Center, but within walking distance, are the buffet and coffee shop at the Hilton, and Nippon, a Japanese restaurant and sushi bar (a ten-minute walk). The better restaurants at the Las Vegas Hilton are not open for lunch.

The restaurants mentioned above provide decent food and fast service but are bustling eateries not particularly conducive to a quiet business lunch. At 3900 Paradise Road, however, there is a small shopping center (only three minutes from the Convention Center by cab) that has several quiet, high-quality ethnic restaurants. Shalimar, a good Indian restaurant, offers a lunch buffet. Across the parking lot are Yolie's, a Brazilian steak house, and its neighbor Beijing, one of the city's better Chinese restaurants. Also located in the shopping center are a sandwich shop and Cafe Milano, a decent Italian restaurant.

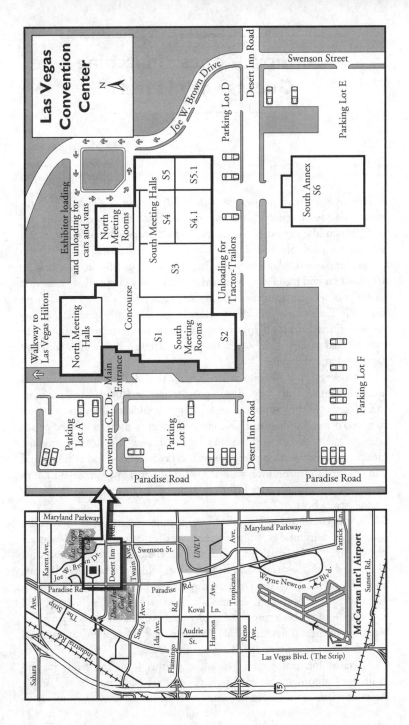

Comfort Zones: Matching Guests with Hotels

I have a good friend, a single woman of 32, who, in search of a little romance, decided to take a Caribbean cruise. Thinking that one cruise was pretty much like any other, she signed up for a cruise without doing much shopping around. She ended up on a boat full of retired married folks who played bingo or bridge every evening and were usually in the sack by 10:30. My friend mistakenly assumed, as have many others, that cruises are basically homogeneous products. In fact, nothing could be farther from the truth. Each cruise provides a tailored experience to a specific and narrowly defined market. If my friend had done her homework, she could have booked passage on a boat full of young, single people and danced and romanced into the night.

In Las Vegas, it is likewise easy to assume that all the hotels and casinos are fairly similar. True, they all have guest rooms, restaurants, and the same mix of games in the casino, but each property molds its offerings to appeal to a well-defined audience. This concerted effort to please a specific population of guests creates what we call a "comfort zone." If you are among the group a hotel strives to please, you will feel comfortable and at home and will have much in common with the other guests. However, if you fail to determine the comfort zone before you go, you may end up like my friend: on the wrong boat.

Visitors come to Las Vegas either to vacation and play or to attend a meeting or convention. While these reasons for coming to Las Vegas are not mutually exclusive, there is a marked difference between a recreational visitor and a business traveler. The vacationer is likely to be older (45 years and up), retired, and from the Midwest, Southern California, Arizona, Colorado, or Hawaii. The business traveler is younger on average and comes from just about anywhere. Individual hotels and casinos pay close attention to these differences and customize their atmosphere, dining, and entertainment to satisfy a specific type of traveler.

Harrah's, for example, targets older visitors from the Midwest and Southern California. The hotel buffets and restaurants serve basic, simple American entrees in ample portions, and the hotel's show features traditional entertainment in a clean, tasteful presentation. The California Hotel, downtown, targets Hawaiians and maintains a specialty food store and restaurants that supply their clientele with favorite snacks and dishes from the islands.

On the Boulder Highway, Sam's Town is geared toward cowboys and retired travelers. It has both a huge Western-wear retail outlet and an RV park. Entertainment at Sam's Town consists of bowling and country-western dancing. Circus Circus on the Strip likewise attracts the RV crowd (with its own RV park) but also offers large, low-priced rooms, buffets, free circus acts, and an amusement park to lure families. The Las Vegas Hilton, next door to the Convention Center, goes the extra mile to make business travelers feel at home.

Some hotels are posh and exclusive, while others are more Spartan and intended to appeal to younger or more frugal visitors. Each property, however, from its lounge entertainment to its guest room decor or the dishes served in its restaurants, is packaged with a certain type of guest in mind.

Because Las Vegas is basically a very informal town, you will not feel as out of place as my friend did on her cruise if you happen to end up in the wrong hotel. In any given property there is a fairly broad range of clientele. There always will be hotels where you experience a greater comfort level than at others, however. In a place as different as Las Vegas, that added comfort can sometimes mean a lot.

Democracy in the Casinos

While Las Vegas hotels and casinos continue to be characterized as appealing to "high rollers" or "grinds," the distinction has become increasingly blurred. High rollers, of course, are wealthy visitors who come to gamble in earnest, while grinds are less affluent folks who grudgingly bet their money a nickel or quarter at a time. For many years, the slot machine was symbolic of the grinds. Unable to join the action of the high-stakes "table games," these blue-collar gamblers would sit for hours pumping the arms of the slots. More recently, however, the slots are the symbol of casino profitability, contributing anywhere from 40 to 100% of a given casino's bottom line.

The popularity of the slot machine among gamblers of all types has democratized the casino. The casinos recognize that the silver-haired lady at the quarter slots is an extremely valuable customer and that it is good business to forgo the impression of exclusivity in order to make her comfortable. In Las Vegas there are casinos that maintain the illusion of an upper-crust clientele while quietly practicing an egalitarianism that belies any such pretense. By virtue of its economic clout, the slot machine has broadened the comfort zone of the stuffiest casinos and made Las Vegas a friendlier, more pleasant (albeit noisier) place.

The Feel of the Place

Las Vegas's hotel-casinos have distinctly individual personalities. While all casinos contain slot machines, craps tables, and roulette wheels, the feel of each particular place is unique, a product of the combined characteristics of management, patrons, and physical plant. This feel, or personality, determines a hotel-casino's comfort zone, the peculiar ambiance that makes one guest feel totally at home while another runs for the exit.

The Author's Bias Openly Admitted   As you read the hotel-casino descriptions that follow, you will perhaps intuit that the author is a little claustrophobic. I do not understand why so many casinos are dark, noisy, and confining; they are more like submarines than places of recreation. Why, I'd like to know, isn't there a casino in a nice, rooftop atrium where you can watch the sun set and the birds fly over? Is there a reason why we should be blinded by blinking lights or deafened by clanking coins in gloomy tunnels upholstered with red Naugahyde?

Apparently there is some casino marketing theory which postulates that customers will gamble longer and more aggressively if their circadian rhythms are disturbed, their natural clocks unplugged. Zoos confuse nocturnal animals this way to make them rummage around when they should be sleeping. Casino customers, like these animals, are never supposed to know if it is day or night. This is patently ridiculous, of course, unlike bats and lemurs, almost every gambler has a watch or can tell what time it is by the type of food on the buffet.

Why do I worry about this, you ask? Isn't doubling down on any two cards and resplitting pairs in blackjack more important than how low the ceiling is? Maybe to you, my friend, but not to me. I want to gamble where I can breathe, stand up straight, and not smell the person playing at the next machine. I'd like for my pupils to be the same size for more than three consecutive seconds, and I'd like to be able to conduct a conversation without using a megaphone. I'd even like to know whether or not it's raining outside. And while I'm aware that it is perfectly possible to play craps in an alley, that's not why I go to Las Vegas. We've got plenty of alleys at home.

This is not to imply that I gamble in the departure concourse at the airport but to warn you about my natural bias against hotels and casinos that feel like velveteen U-boats. If, in the following descriptions, I talk about "ceiling height" a lot, I hope you will understand.

Hotels with Casinos

How to Avoid Reading the Hotel-Casino Descriptions If you don't care how a place "feels" but just want to know whether it has room service and tennis courts, or when check-out time is, you can skip to the alphabetically arranged Hotel Information Chart in an appendix at the back of the book.

Aladdin

Over the years the Aladdin has changed ownership many times, resulting in an eclectic, constantly changing identity. As in cooking, where too many cooks invariably serve up a bland dish, so it goes with the Aladdin, where each new owner tacks on a wing or changes the upholstery or removes the wall art inherited from a predecessor. The Aladdin is the operational definition of a mixed metaphor. Yet at the same time it is friendly and habitable. The casino is large enough to allow for some elbowroom and plush enough to be comfortable. Guest rooms at the Aladdin are quite nice. During 1998, the Aladdin will continue its extensive renovation and expansion intended to make it competitive with the Monte Carlo, its ritzy neighbor across the Strip.

With a good location, a fine production show, a large theater for special events, adequate restaurants, and comfortable rooms, the Aladdin somehow integrates its multiple personalities. Middle-income leisure travelers from Southern California and Asia, as well as some convention attendees, make up the Aladdin's usual clientele. As the renovation is completed, and particularly with new British minority ownership, look for the Aladdin to target the upscale European market.

Arizona Charlie's

Patronized primarily by locals, Arizona Charlie's is a working man's casino with a Southwestern ranch flavor. Everything here is informal, a sort of shirtsleeves place. And it's busy. There is an energy, a three-ring circus feel of much going on at once—lots of slots, some table games, a big bowling complex, a sports book,* burgers and beer, and a lounge that often fea-

---

* A sports book is a casino facility, sometimes simple, often elaborate, where wagers are taken on sporting events.

tures big-name (OK, medium-name) entertainment. Recent improvements, including some new and very nice hotel rooms, have made Arizona Charlie's much more appealing to out-of-towners.

Bally's

A complete resort, Bally's is blessed with exceptional restaurants, one of the better buffets in Las Vegas, and *the* best Sunday champagne brunch. Entertainment likewise is top-quality, with an outstanding production show and a celebrity headliner room. Guest rooms are large and comfortable, and the hotel, although quite spread out, is easy to find your way around in. Amenities include a health club and spa and a large, diversified shopping arcade.

The casino is immense, open, and elegantly modern—sophisticated in a formal, understated way, like a tuxedo. Active without being claustrophobic, and classy without being stiff, Bally's captures the style of Continental casinos without sacrificing American informality.

Bally's caters to meetings and conventions and is one of the few hotels where you will not feel out of place in a business suit. Guests are frequently under 40 here and come from all over, but particularly Southern California, Chicago, and elsewhere in the Midwest. Bally's also has a loyal Spanish-speaking clientele.

Demonstrating legitimate concern about the traffic congestion on the Strip, Bally's joined with the MGM Grand in constructing a monorail that connects Bally's with the MGM Grand Hotel and theme park. It is the hope of Bally's and the MGM Grand that the city continue the initiative, extending the monorail the length of the Strip and perhaps even downtown. In a separate project, Bally's has built a series of moving walkways to transport guests from Las Vegas Boulevard into the casino. In a Las Vegas first, Bally's also offers moving walkways *out* of the casino. Maybe this is the only way, short of a forklift, that Bally's could get the bulk loaders out of the buffet. Caesars Palace also has a moving walkway, but it only goes one way: in.

Barbary Coast

The Barbary Coast is an elegant casino for real gamblers. Appointed in dark wood embellished with murals in stained glass, this medium-sized hotel-casino serves a loyal clientele of locals and serious gamblers. With the feel of an exclusive and tasteful gentleman's club, the Barbary Coast's offerings are straightforward and simple. Table games still reign supreme in the casino, and the gourmet restaurant, Michael's, is regarded by many locals as the most dependable in town. There is no showroom, no swimming pool, no sauna or whirlpool, and most hotel rooms (decorated in a San Francisco-turn-of-the-century style) are reserved for regular customers.

Boardwalk Holiday Inn

The Boardwalk, though completely upgraded, remains a modest casino by Las Vegas standards. Blessed with a good location next to the Monte Carlo, the Boardwalk is a jumping-off place for guests heading to more imposing surroundings up and down the Strip. Acquired in 1994 by Holiday Inn, the casino has been expanded and rebuilt from scratch with a light, airy, Coney Island–boardwalk theme. Though all table games are represented, the emphasis is definitely on slots. A new hotel tower offers guest rooms that live up to the Holiday Inn standard. On the down side, dining is limited to counter service and a small coffee shop. Because the only entrance to the Boardwalk is via the Strip, auto accessibility is also a problem. Owing to the Holiday Inn connection, guests at the Boardwalk run the gamut.

Boomtown

Located southwest of Las Vegas at the Blue Diamond Road exit off I-15, Boomtown opened in 1994 with a nicely executed Old West mining-town theme. The casino is visually interesting, with rough-hewn beams, mine tunnels, overhead mine car tracks, and a sizable array of prospecting and mining artifacts. The buffet is better than average, as is the coffee shop. The lounge features country music and dancing. Ten minutes from the Strip, Boomtown is in a great position to snag Southern Californians. Boomtown also targets the RV crowd with a large, full-service RV park.

Boulder Station

Boulder Station is a clone of Palace Station, sharing its railroad theme and emphasis on good food and lounge entertainment. Located on Boulder Highway not far from the Showboat, Boulder Station features a roomy casino with a Western town motif (more in the image of turn-of-the-century Denver than of Dodge City). Tastefully done, with much attention to detail, the casino includes one of the nicest sports books in Las Vegas. Thirty-three big-screen, high-resolution monitors make the Boulder Station sports book a superb place for spectators. Like its sister property, Boulder Station is an oasis for the hungry, with a great buffet, several good full-service restaurants, and possibly the best selection of fast food found in any casino. Guest rooms in the 1,000-room hotel tower are modest but comfortable, with good views. There is a swimming pool, but it is small and stark. Clientele consists primarily of locals and Southern Californians.

Comparing Boulder Station to Palace Station, we like the casino much better at Boulder Station but prefer the guest rooms at Palace Station's tower. The buffets and restaurants run pretty much a dead heat. Boulder Station is much less crowded and much easier to access by car.

Bourbon Street

Bourbon Street is known locally as an "overflow joint," a place where visitors end up when more popular hotels are sold out. The casino is dark, crowded, noisy, and smoky when it is open. For the past year or so the casino has been closed as its owners tried to sell the property. The hotel, however, continues to rent rooms that are nicer than Bourbon Street's public areas suggest.

Caesars Palace

Of Las Vegas's theme hotels and casinos, Caesars Palace was the first to fully realize its potential. As an exercise in whimsical fantasy and excess, Caesars's Roman theme has been executed with astounding artistry and attention to detail. Creating an atmosphere of informality in surroundings too pretentious to believe is hard to pull off, but that is exactly what Caesars Palace has done. Somehow the vaulted ceilings, classic statuary, and graceful arches accommodate the clanking of coins and the activity of the pits. Gambling at Caesars feels a little like pitching horseshoes in the Supreme Court, but incredibly, it works.

Caesars Palace provides two spacious and luxurious casinos, excellent restaurants, beautiful landscaping, top celebrity entertainment, exquisite guest rooms, and all of the services and amenities of a world-class resort. In addition to its showroom, Caesars offers Caesars Magical Empire, a dining and entertainment complex where small groups of guests enjoy intimate banqueting hosted by magicians and other entertainers. The adjoining Forum Shops, opened in 1992 and expanded in 1997, give Caesars Palace the distinction of offering the most unique themed shopping complex in the United States.

Our only gripe about Caesars is the fishtrap design of the entrance to the Forum Shops. If you walk in off the Strip to see what the Forum Shops are about, be prepared for a hike. You cannot exit through the entrance portal. Instead, you must hike all the way through the shopping complex, into the Caesars casino, and finally back to the Strip via an outdoor sidewalk. All told, it's about a 15-minute walk.

In 1997 Caesars embarked on a major expansion that includes a new

29-floor hotel tower with its own casino, as well as a 20,000-square-foot health spa and fitness center. Guest rooms in the new tower (floors five and up) offer some of the best views on the Strip. Outside there is an elaborate new "Roman bath" swimming complex with four large pools and two outdoor whirlpool spas. On the drawing board is Caesars Maximus, a shopping and entertainment complex set in an indoor replication of a Roman hill town. Ten stories high, two football fields long, and covered with a "projected sky" ceiling, Caesars Maximus will feature chariot racing. Check the paramutual board for your favorite team and driver.

Originally designed for high rollers, Caesars is now enjoyed by a broad range of clientele from the East, the Midwest, and Southern California. Popular with Asian and Hispanic visitors, Caesars also hosts small meetings and caters to the business traveler. Though a myth persists that Caesars's employees are as imperious as their surroundings, we find Caesars Palace to be a friendly, easygoing, albeit pricey place to play. As a tourist attraction in its own right, Caesars Palace should be on every visitor's must-see list.

California

The California is a pleasant downtown hotel-casino with excellent, moderately priced restaurants and a largely Hawaiian clientele. It is a friendly, mellow place to stay or gamble—unpretentious, but certainly comfortable. The casino rambles but, like most downtown casinos, does not allow much elbowroom. The decor is subdued and tasteful, with wood paneling and trim. The shops, menus, and services work to make visiting Pacific Islanders feel as much at home as visitors from Kansas City or Tampa. While some hotel-casinos are spectacles or happenings, the California is simply a nice, relaxed place to spend some time.

Casino Royale

Located across the Strip from the Mirage, the diminutive Casino Royale has just under 250 guest rooms. Small, accessible, and unpretentious, Casino Royale provides bargain lodging in the Strip's high-rent district. While the crowded and slot-heavy casino will make downtown gamblers feel right at home, the Casino Royale's best feature is its second-floor lounge and snack bar. The property's clientele runs the gamut from tour groups, to convention-goers on a tight budget, to folks who could not get rooms at other hotels on the block.

Circus Circus

Circus Circus was the first hotel on the Strip to actively pursue family trade. Children, young adults, retirees, and the novice (or modest) gambler are welcome here. The labyrinthine casino has low ceilings and is frenetic, loud, and always busy. Dollar blackjack and nickel slots abound. The circus theme, both exciting and wholesome at the same time, is extended to every conceivable detail of the hotel's physical plant and operation. Entertainment consists of live, top-quality circus acts (free) and a games midway. Bright reds, blues, oranges, and pinks (often in stripes) are everywhere, even in the recently redecorated hotel rooms. The constant flurry of activity, the veritable assault of noise, and the garish decor create an intense, jostling carnival feel. "Circus Circus," commented a droll local obstetrician, "is where we bring overdue expectant mothers to induce labor." We believe it.

Circus Circus has a very good steak house (the only escape from the circus theme); a huge, inexpensive buffet; an RV park; and a monorail shuttle that connects the property's two main buildings. And, to give credit for great innovation, Circus Circus was the first casino to set aside a nonsmoking gaming area. In 1993, Circus Circus launched Grand Slam Canyon, a desert-canyon-themed amusement park totally enclosed in a giant pink dome. Here guests can enjoy a roller coaster, a flume ride, robotic dinosaurs, and more. A detailed description of Grand Slam Canyon can be found in "Part Five: Shopping and Seeing the Sights" on page 341.

In 1997 Circus Circus opened a new hotel tower as well as a shopping and restaurant arcade adjoining Grand Slam Canyon. The new tower conforms to the circus theme but is decidedly less garish. If you worry about your room decor causing LSD flashbacks, ask for accommodations in the new tower or wait until early 1998 when the refurbishment of Circus Circus's remaining 2,700 guest rooms will be complete. As concerns the new restaurants, they provide Circus Circus with some much-needed alternatives to the steak house and the buffet.

Continental

The Hotel Continental is basically a blue-collar slot operation with table action on the side. Its dated decor is as bland as the hotel's food. The casino is L-shaped and wraps around a bar that is the Continental's best feature. Guests here are older (some are very old), but all seem to be content and satisfied.

Debbie Reynolds Hollywood Hotel and Casino

In 1993, Debbie Reynolds purchased and completely renovated the Paddlewheel Casino on Convention Center Drive. Reopened as Debbie Reynolds Hollywood Hotel and Casino, the property is unrecognizable from its Paddlewheel days. For starters, Reynolds threw out most of the casino and installed North America's only Hollywood Motion Picture Museum, featuring her own sizable collection of costumes, props, rare film clips, and other memorabilia. Another addition is a showroom, modeled after the Desert Inn's Crystal Room, where Reynolds performs regularly. In terms of amenities, the Hollywood Hotel offers two restaurants and a pool. Guest rooms are tastefully decorated and feature large televisions and floor-to-ceiling windows. Regular customers include Southern Californians as well as business travelers attending trade shows at the nearby Las Vegas Convention Center.

Desert Inn

The Desert Inn is arguably the most complete resort hotel in Las Vegas. In addition to having the area's best golf course, the Desert Inn also features tennis, an exceptional pool, a jogging track, and a complete spa and fitness center with supervised programs, including aerobics classes. Elegant, understated, without any theme, the Desert Inn has nothing to prove. Its tasteful guest rooms, fine restaurants, celebrity/production showroom, and totally renovated chandeliered casino make the Desert Inn the self-confident aristocrat of Las Vegas hotels. There aren't any casbahs, forums, barges, big tops, medieval villages, pirate ships, or sphinxes. There is only an island of efficient, quiet, informal luxury in a Las Vegas sea of excess.

The Desert Inn is a place to relax, to savor, to enjoy; it's expensive, but an exceptional value for the money. Tower guest rooms feature floor-to-ceiling windows and (along with Caesars Palace) the most luxurious bathrooms in Las Vegas. Monte Carlo (gourmet Continental) offers imaginative menus and consistently distinctive fare. Unlike that of other major Strip hotels, the Desert Inn's self-parking is close and convenient. The staff is friendly, knowledgeable, and responsive. Guests tend to be professionals, business travelers, and sportsmen. Popular with Southern Californians and Southwesterners, the Desert Inn also draws its clientele from Latin America and Asia, particularly Japan and Taiwan.

Construction of a new hotel tower and pool began in 1996 and will continue into 1998. Part of the renovation includes a complete external face-lift. The "new" Desert Inn will reflect the 1920s architecture of Palm Beach, California. Expect a bit of turmoil, noise, and disruption until the renovation and construction are completed.

El Cortez

Situated several blocks east of the central downtown casino area, El Cortez caters to seniors, motor coach tours, and blue-collar locals. The large, rambling casino is congested and bustling; the slots are the major draw. The oldest original casino in Las Vegas, El Cortez has the aesthetic appeal of a garment factory, with narrow aisles, low ceilings, and slot machines packed into every conceivable crevice. Food and drink are bargains, however, and the loose slots give patrons a lot of play for their money. Also, there is considerable Las Vegas history in El Cortez; one section of the original building appears just as it did when the casino opened in 1941. Guest rooms at El Cortez have been recently renovated. In addition to being quite nice, they are also an exceptional value.

Excalibur

The Excalibur is owned by Circus Circus Enterprises and is designed to attract an upscale family business. By combining a Knights of the Round-table theme, restaurants with giant portions, family-oriented entertainment, and moderate costs, the Excalibur "packs 'em in," especially on weekends. A Las Vegas rendition of a medieval realm, the Excalibur is over-sized, garish, and more in the image of Kmart than of King Arthur.

Situated on three levels, the Excalibur's restaurants and shops are integrated into a medieval village theme area on the top floor. On the lower floor is a midway-type games arcade, the Excalibur's showroom (where jousting tournaments are featured), and a combination movie/ride that simulates a roller coaster. The cavernous middle level contains the casino, a roomy and festive place with a '50s art deco decor, meant no doubt to approximate the best in Dark Ages interior design. The atmosphere is supposed to be courtly and regal but has more the feel of an aircraft hangar decorated by Ozzie and Harriet. To augment the reality of the medieval theme, the Excalibur tossed in Wild Bills Saloon and Steakhouse, which serves up country music along with big wads o' meat. Nobody seems too upset about trading in their knightly armor for a good pair of snakeskin boots. And so it goes.

The Excalibur is the third largest hotel in the United States (the MGM Grand and Luxor are larger), and it certainly features the world's largest hotel parking lot (so far removed from the entrance that trams are dispatched to haul in the patrons). If you can get past the parking lot commute, the plastic execution of its medieval theme, and the fact that guest rooms have showers only (no tubs), and you do not object to joining the masses, there is good value to be had at the Excalibur. The food is good and economically priced, as is the entertainment. The staff is friendly and accommodating, and you won't go deaf or blind, or become claustrophobic, in the casino. If you need a change of pace, a covered walkway connects the Excalibur with the Luxor next door, and a pedestrian bridge provides direct access to New York–New York and the Tropicana.

Fiesta

The Fiesta, which opened in 1994, was the first of several casinos to be situated at the intersection of Rancho Drive and Lake Mead Boulevard in North Las Vegas. With 100 guest rooms and a slot-packed 25,000-square-foot casino, the Fiesta features an Old Mexico theme. Entertainment offerings include a country dance hall. Restaurants specializing in Mexican and Southwestern food are the Fiesta's major draw. An excellent buffet features a mesquite grill. On Sunday there is a good Margarita Brunch. In 1997, the Fiesta finally got around to putting in a swimming pool. The Fiesta depends primarily on local clientele and competes fiercely with nearby Texas Station.

Fitzgeralds

Located downtown, Fitzgeralds anchors the east end of the Glitter Gulch section of Fremont Street. The casino is large and compartmentalized with gold press-metal ceilings, mirrored columns, and print carpet with little Irish hats. Completely renovated, the casino has largely abandoned its signature "luck of the Irish" theme. While the new look is more consistent with the clean, polished style pioneered by the Golden Nugget, Fitzgeralds has sacrificed much of its traditional warmth and coziness.

Rooms on the upper floors of the Fitz afford some of the best views in town, and corner rooms with jacuzzis are a great bargain. The Fitzgeralds's registered guests tend to be older travelers and retirees from the Midwest. In the casino, the crowd is a mixed bag of regulars and bargain hunters lured by ads for free gifts in the local visitor guides.

Flamingo Hilton

Built with gang money in the '40s and acquired by the Hilton Hotel chain in 1970, the Flamingo is a curious blend of Las Vegas hyperbole and corporate pragmatism. Once a tourist attraction in itself, this venerable hotel was the first super-resort on the Strip. Today, with its 3,642 rooms, 4 towers, and prime location, it is the centerpiece of the Strip's most prestigious block, surrounded by Bally's, the Barbary Coast, the Imperial Palace, Caesars Palace, Harrah's, and the Mirage. In 1995, the Flamingo renovated its guest rooms and added a stunning central swimming and garden complex complete with rock grottos and wildlife habitats. In 1997 the Flamingo's Strip facade was face-lifted and a large, comfortable sports book was opened in the inner casino.

Hilton, as you might expect, has curbed the excesses of the colorful previous owners and transformed the Flamingo from a Las Vegas exaggeration into a very dependable chain hotel. Flashier than the Las Vegas Hilton and Bally's (its sister properties), the Flamingo is also less formal, offering an ambiance comfortable to leisure and business traveler alike. The large, bustling casino retains the bright Miami pinks, magentas, and tangerines that established the Flamingo's identity more than four decades ago, but the hotel lobby, rooms, and services are standard Hilton. The Flamingo has consistent restaurants, a passable buffet, a fine production show, truly creative lounge entertainment, and one of the top swimming areas in town.

Thanks to the Hilton national reservations system, the hotel's clientele comes in all colors and sizes, and from all over the country (but especially Southern California). The Flamingo actively cultivates the Japanese market and also does a strong business with tour wholesalers. Because it has one of the most diverse customer bases of any Las Vegas hotel, the Flamingo likewise has a very broad comfort zone.

Four Queens

The Four Queens, situated in the heart of downtown, offers good food, recently renovated hotel rooms, possibly the best lounge entertainment in town, and a positively cheery casino. Joining its neighbor, the Golden Nugget, as a member of the "All Right to Be Bright Club," the Four Queens's casino has abandoned the standard brothel red in favor of a glistening, light decor offset by a tropical print carpet. The result, as at the Golden Nugget, is a gaming area that feels fun, upbeat, and even clean. Loyal Four Queens hotel guests tend to be middle-aged or older and come from Southern California, Texas, Hawaii, and the Midwest. The Four Queens also caters to the motor coach tour market. In the casino there is a mix of all ages and backgrounds. Locals love Hugo's Cellar restaurant and the Four Queens's top-quality lounge shows.

Fremont

Sam Boyd's Fremont is one of the landmarks of downtown Las Vegas. Acquired by the Boyd family in 1985, the Fremont offers good food, budget lodging, and a robust casino. Recently redecorated and considerably brightened up, the casino is noisy and crowded. The table games are roomily accommodated beneath a high ceiling ringed in neon, while the slots are crammed together along narrow aisles like turkeys on their way to market. Locals love the Fremont, as do Asians, Hawaiians, and the inevitable Southern Californians. The Fremont, like all Boyd properties, is friendly, informal, and comfortable.

Frontier

The Frontier is situated in the middle of the Strip, within easy walking distance of the Fashion Show Mall. Hotel guests come from Southern California; many of the rooms are sold by wholesalers. Upgraded in 1992 by the addition of a large block of minisuites and a spruced-up casino, the Frontier has established itself as a comfortable midmarket hotel. Two-room suites in the tower are spacious and a bargain. The large, rambling casino, decorated in the usual dark colors, is somewhat nondescript and does not feature any entertainment. This notwithstanding, the Frontier is a place that tourists and locals (particularly younger gamblers) like for its unpretentious feel.

With good restaurants, a tranquil pool and landscaped garden area, and tennis courts, the Frontier should be able to offer a balanced, high-quality vacation package. During our last two visits, unfortunately, the property was poorly maintained and service was uniformly terrible. On one occasion, as our hotel inspectors entered the casino, they were spit on by striking union pickets.

Gold Coast

The Gold Coast, located a half mile west of the Strip on Flamingo, is a favorite hangout for locals. A casual inspection of the Gold Coast reveals nothing unique: no fantasy theme, no special decor or atmosphere. But the Gold Coast does pay attention to detail and has the local market wired. The Gold Coast serves one of the best breakfast specials in town, provides lounge entertainment at all hours of the day, offers Western and ballroom dancing, and makes sure it has the locals' favorite kind of slots. To top things off, there is also a multiscreen movie complex and a huge bowling alley. Free transportation is provided throughout the day to the casino's sister property, the Barbary Coast, on the Strip.

Gold Spike

Situated downtown and about a four-minute walk from the heart of Fremont Street, the Gold Spike is basically a slot joint. Congested, loud, and smoky, with all the ambiance of a boiler room, the Gold Spike lures customers with nickel and even penny slots.

Golden Gate

Another downtown casino devoted primarily to slots, the Golden Gate is crowded and dingy but redeems itself in part by offering the best shrimp cocktail special in Las Vegas. Located on the western end of Glitter Gulch on Fremont Street, the Golden Gate has 106 budget hotel rooms.

Golden Nugget

The undisputed flagship of the downtown hotels and one of the most meticulously maintained and managed properties in Las Vegas, the Golden Nugget is located smack in the middle of Glitter Gulch. The hotel offers bright, cheery rooms with tropical decor, first-rate showroom and lounge entertainment, excellent restaurants, a large pool, a first-rate spa, a shopping arcade, and a workout room. The casino is clean and breezy with white enameled walls and white lights. The feel here is definitely upscale, though comfortable and informal. There is breathing room at the Golden Nugget, and an atmosphere that suggests a happy, more fun-filled approach to gambling.

If you stay or gamble at the Golden Nugget you are likely to meet people from New York, Dallas, Chicago, Los Angeles, and San Diego, as well as visitors from Taiwan, Hong Kong, and Japan. Younger travelers (28–39) like the Golden Nugget, as do older tourists and retirees, many of whom arrive on motor coach tours.

Hard Rock Hotel

Located off the Strip on Harmon near Paradise, the Hard Rock is billed as the world's first rock and roll hotel and casino. Like the adjoining Hard Rock Cafe, the hotel and domed casino are loaded to the gills with rock memorabilia and artifacts. Everywhere it's rock, rock, rock, from lounge music to the casino, which features piano-shaped roulette tables and chandeliers made from gold saxophones. The guest rooms, which offer a nice view, are surprisingly tasteful, with a Danish–modern European feel. The pool area likewise is comfortable and nicely designed. Other strengths include Mortoni's, a good Italian restaurant, and The Joint, Las Vegas's most intimate venue for live rock. Weaknesses, unexpectedly, include lounge entertainment (there usually isn't any). The Hard Rock Hotel targets baby boomers and younger folks from Southern California as well as from the Midwest and the big Northeastern cities.

Harrah's Las Vegas

Harrah's occupies the middle of the Strip's most prestigious block, and is within easy walking distance of Bally's, the Flamingo, the Mirage, Caesars Palace, and Treasure Island. Unpretentious and upbeat, Harrah's offers tasteful guest rooms as well as a beautiful showroom, a comedy club, above-average restaurants and buffet, pool, exercise room, and spa. The L-shaped casino is bright and roomy, and there is a feeling of lightheartedness and fun that is missing in far too many gambling halls. Best of all, the staff at Harrah's, from dealers to desk clerks, is exceptionally friendly and helpful. Though it is hard to imagine anyone not feeling comfortable at Harrah's, its clientele tends to be older visitors from the Midwest and Southern California, as well as business and convention travelers.

In 1996, Harrah's elected to forgo its highly successful riverboat theme for a new theme celebrating carnival and Mardi Gras. An ambitious expansion accompanied the retheming, including a new hotel tower and a totally new facade featuring two giant gold-leaf court jesters hefting a 10-ton, 22-foot-diameter globe. The casino has been enlarged by 30% and redecorated with brightly colored confetti-patterned carpet, ceiling murals, and jazzy fiber-optic lighting. Other additions include a renovated swimming area, a new bar/restaurant with an outdoor patio fronting the Strip, and Carnival Court, an outdoor plaza with fountains and street entertainment.

Horseshoe

The Horseshoe, or more correctly Binion's Horseshoe, is one of the anchors of Glitter Gulch. The casino is large and active, with row upon row of slots clanking noisily away under a suffocatingly low ceiling. The table games are less congested and are situated under an extended vertical space canopied by mirrors. With an Old West theme executed in the obligatory reds and lavenders, the Horseshoe is dark, but not dark enough to diminish the enthusiasm of the locals and "real gamblers" who hang out there. One of the city's top spots for poker and craps, the Horseshoe is famous for not having any maximum bet limitations. You can bet a million dollars on a single roll of the dice if you wish.

On the lower (basement) level, the Horseshoe has a late-night steak special that consistently ranks among the best in town. Also in the basement is one of the most pleasant bars in the city; it, too, is dark but for once is paneled in rich woods. Twenty or so stories up from the cellar is the Steak House restaurant and lounge, offering a great view of the city.

Imperial Palace

The Imperial Palace has a large, active casino lavishly executed in crystal and carved wood beams. There is a lovely swimming and sunbathing area complete with waterfall, and a Nautilus-equipped exercise room and spa. *Legends in Concert,* one of the hottest shows in Las Vegas, plays nightly at the Imperial Palace's showroom, and the on-site auto museum is a first-rate tourist attraction in its own right. No hotel in Las Vegas has a better location than the Imperial Palace.

Most of the guest rooms at the Imperial Palace are modern and of Holiday Inn–level quality. A few rooms, however, still await renovation. If you book the Imperial Palace, tell the reservations clerk that you do not want to be placed in one of the rooms with the old "brown and rust" decor. The food at the Imperial Palace is on a par with most neighboring hotels, and the Embers restaurant can hold its own with the top steak houses in town.

In a 1993 initiative, the Imperial Palace established the Strip's first medical clinic. Open 7 days a week, with physicians on call 24 hours a day, the clinic offers rapid-response medical care to any Las Vegas visitor in need. The staff is multilingual.

Lady Luck

The Lady Luck is located downtown a block north of Fremont Street. It offers nice rooms (or small suites) at a great price, and it has an excellent restaurant (the Burgundy Room), and a large, uncomplicated casino. Not afraid to be different, the Lady Luck is one of the few casinos anywhere to have wall-sized plate glass windows. If you are claustrophobic and looking for a casino where you won't feel cooped up, the Lady Luck might be your place. The staff is personable and the atmosphere informal. If you want variety, Glitter Gulch is a four-minute walk away.

The Lady Luck appeals to a diverse clientele, including Filipinos, Asian-Americans, Californians, motor coach tourists, and locals.

Las Vegas Club

The Las Vegas Club is a downtown hotel-casino with a sports theme. The corridor linking the casino with the Dugout Restaurant is a veritable sports museum and has dozens of vintage photos of boxing, baseball, and basketball legends. The casino itself, with its high, mirrored ceilings, is modest but feels uncrowded. It also has some of the most player-friendly blackjack rules around. Recently renovated guest rooms are quite nice and are also a great value for the dollar. The food is good and consistent. The Las Vegas Club draws from Hawaii and the Midwest but also does a big business with bus groups and seniors.

Las Vegas Hilton

Located next door to the Las Vegas Convention Center, the Hilton does more meeting, trade show, and convention business than any other hotel in town. There are days at the Hilton when it's rare to see someone not wearing a convention badge. As you might expect, the Hilton is accommodating but not glitzy and provides a comfortable, neutral environment for its business clientele.

A 10- to 12-minute walk from the Strip, the Hilton operates under the valid assumption that many of its guests may never leave the hotel during their Las Vegas stay (except to go to the Convention Center). Thus the Hilton is an oasis of self-sufficiency and boasts lounges, a huge pool, an exercise room, a shopping arcade, a buffet, and a coffee shop.

The Las Vegas Hilton has some of the best restaurants in town and features enough ethnic and culinary variety to keep most guests happy. The showroom at the Hilton hosts one of the newest, most different, and most action-packed production shows in town. In 1997, the Hilton premiered *Star Trek: The Experience,* an interactive video and virtual reality amusement center featuring a space-flight simulation ride.

The casino, like the hotel itself, is huge and tastefully businesslike in its presentation but by no means formal or intimidating. The Hilton sports book is the largest and most elegant in Las Vegas. If you can afford it, the Hilton is the most convenient place to stay in town if you are attending a trade show or convention at the Las Vegas Convention Center. If, however, you are in Las Vegas for pleasure, staying at the Hilton is like being in luxurious exile. Anywhere you go, you will need a cab or your own car. If you park in one of the Hilton's far-flung, self-parking lots, it will take you as long as 15 minutes to reach your car from your guest room.

Luxor

The Luxor is located on the Strip south of Tropicana Road next to the Excalibur. Representing Circus Circus Enterprises' most ambitious effort to attract a more upscale, less family-oriented clientele, the Luxor is among the more tasteful of Las Vegas's themed hotels. Though not originally believed to be on a par with the new Treasure Island and the MGM Grand, the Luxor may well be the most distinguished graduate of the much-publicized new hotels of 1993–94. While the MGM Grand and Treasure Island are respectively larger and more ostentatious, the Luxor demonstrates a creativity and architectural appeal unmatched by any hotel-casino on the Strip.

Rising 30 stories, the Luxor is a huge pyramid with guest rooms situated around the outside perimeter from base to apex. Guest room hallways circumscribe a hollow core containing the world's largest atrium. Inside the atrium, elevators rise at a 39° angle from the pyramid's corners to access the guest floors. While the perspective from inside the pyramid is stunning, it is easy to get disoriented. Stories about hotel guests wandering around in search of their rooms are legion. After reviewing many complaints from readers, we seriously recommend carrying a small pocket compass.

The Luxor's main entrance is from the Strip via a massive sphinx. From the sphinx, guests are diverted into small entryways designed to resemble the interior passages of an actual pyramid. From these tunnels, guests emerge into the dramatic openness of the Luxor's towering atrium. Rising imposingly within the atrium is an ancient Egyptian city, flanked incongruously on the left by a New York skyline. Around the inside base of the atrium flows a "River Nile."

Proceeding straight ahead at ground level from the main entrance brings you into the casino. Open and attractive, the 100,000-square-foot casino is tasteful by any standard.

One level below the casino and the main entrance is the Luxor's main showroom, a 1,100-seat arena.

One floor above the entry/casino level, on a mezzanine of sorts, is an array of structures representing the past, present, and future. Reaching high into the atrium, these dramatic buildings and monuments transform the atrium into a surrealistic vision, anachronistic yet powerful. The past is represented by an Egyptian temple and obelisk and the apparent excavation of an archeological dig. In stark contrast nearby, representing the present, is a New York skyscraper scene. Finally, across a plaza is a grouping of futuristic structures. Here you'll find two continuously running, gated (paid-admission) attractions designed by Douglas Trumbull, creator of the *Back to the Future* ride at Universal Studios Florida, and an Omnimax theater. In addition to the attractions, three restaurants, a huge electronic games arcade, and a collection of retail shops are located on this level.

Flanking the pyramid are two new hotel towers that were part of a $300 million expansion completed in 1997; the expansion also included a new health spa and fitness center, and additional meeting and conference space.

The biggest surprise of all (to anyone who has ever stayed in a Circus Circus property) are the Luxor's large, tasteful guest rooms. Decorated in an understated Egyptian motif with custom-made furniture, the standard guest rooms are among the most nicely appointed in town. The only disappointment is that many of the guest rooms do not have tubs. In all, the Luxor offers 4,427 guest rooms, making it the second largest hotel in Las Vegas.

The Luxor's large, attractive pool complex, surrounded by private cabanas, desperately needs some additional plants and trees. Self-parking is as much a problem at the Luxor as at most large properties. Valet parking is quick and efficient, however, and well worth the $1 or $2 tip. The Luxor is within a 5- to 12-minute walk of the Excalibur, the Tropicana, and the MGM Grand. A moving walkway connects the Luxor to the Excalibur.

Main Street Station

Situated on Main Street between Ogden and Stewart in downtown Las Vegas, Main Street Station originally opened in 1992 as a paid-admission nighttime entertainment complex with a casino on the side. Owned and managed by an Orlando, Florida, entrepreneur with no casino experience, it took Main Street Station less than a year to go belly-up. The property was acquired several years later by the Boyd Group, which used Main Street Station's hotel to accommodate overflow guests from the California across the street. In 1997, the Boyds reopened the casino, restaurants, and shops, adding a brew pub in the process.

The casino is one of the most unusual in town (thanks largely to the concept of the original owner), with the feel of a turn-of-the-century gentleman's club. Though not as splendid now as in its original incarnation, the casino still contains enough antiques, original art, and oddities to furnish a museum. With its refurbished guest rooms, brew pub, steak house, excellent buffet, and unusual casino, Main Street Station is both interesting and fun, adding some welcome diversity to the downtown hospitality mix.

Maxim

The Maxim is a medium-sized hotel-casino located across Flamingo Road from Bally's. The guest rooms have recently been renovated, and overall the Maxim is a nice property. The casino is modern but cramped, attractively decorated in earth tones with futuristic lighting fixtures. The hotel's restaurants and buffet are good values. Maxim picks up a lot of business from visitors attending meetings at Bally's and is a favorite of seniors because the whole property is so accessible. Other amenities include a modest showroom, a small shopping arcade, and a rooftop swimming pool.

MGM Grand Hotel, Casino, and Theme Park

When Steve Wynn opened the Mirage, he created a new standard for the Las Vegas hotel-casino by combining the amenities of a world-class resort with the excitement and visual appeal of a tourist attraction. For Wynn, however, at both the Mirage and his new Treasure Island, the attraction component is rendered in terms of nonparticipatory visual spectacle: at the Mirage, an exploding volcano, and at Treasure Island, a naval battle. The attraction is peripheral, no more or no less than a powerful and eye-popping way to generate traffic for the casino.

At Kirk Kerkorian's MGM Grand, the evolutionary combination of gambling resort and attraction has been carried to the next logical stage, the development of a theme park ostensibly, if not actually, on an equal footing with the casino. This elevation of a nongaming attraction to a position of such prominence signals the first significant tourism product diversification in Las Vegas since the dawn of the luxury resort hotel-casinos in the '50s. Make no mistake, the purpose of the theme park is to funnel patrons into the casino. What is different is that the theme park offers a recreation alternative intended to attract nongamblers as well as gamblers.

With the exception of Walt Disney World, the MGM Grand combines more facilities and recreational opportunities than any other resort in the

United States. It claims the distinction of being both the largest hotel in the United States (with 5,005 rooms) and the world's largest casino. Within the 112-acre complex, there is a 33-acre movie- and entertainment-themed amusement park; a 15,200-seat special-events arena; 158,000 square feet of convention space; an enormous swimming area; four tennis courts; a health spa; and a multilevel parking facility.

The MGM Grand is located on the northeast corner of Tropicana Avenue and the Strip. The Strip entrance passes beneath a 45-foot-tall MGM Lion atop a 25-foot pedestal, all surrounded by three immense digital displays. The lion entrance leads to a domed rotunda with table games and a Rain Forest Cafe, and from there to the MGM Grand's four huge casinos. The first is the Emerald City Casino, elaborating the theme of *The Wizard of Oz*. Next comes the Hollywood Casino, followed by the Monte Carlo Casino with a French Riviera atmosphere. Finally there is the Sports Casino, which includes the race and sports book. All of the casinos are roomy and plush, with high ceilings and a comfortable feeling of openness.

A second entrance, with a porte-cochere 15 lanes wide, serves vehicular traffic from Tropicana Avenue. For all practical purposes, this is the main entrance to the MGM Grand, permitting you to go directly to the hotel lobby and its 53 check-in windows without lugging your belongings through the casinos. Just beyond the registration area is the elevator core, with 35 elevators servicing 30 guest floors. If there is a problem with the design of the MGM Grand, it is that most of the theme-park pedestrian traffic also passes through this entrance, traversing the hotel public areas and casinos en route to the park.

Beyond the elevator core, a wide passageway leads toward the theme park. Situated along this passageway are five of the MGM Grand's eight distinct restaurants (not counting theme-park restaurants or fast food). Among the upscale restaurants are Tre Visi/La Scala, serving Italian cuisine; the Brown Derby, offering beef and seafood; Gatsby's, serving California-style French cuisine; Emeril's, offering Creole/Cajun dishes; Wolfgang Puck Cafe; and Dragon Court, a Chinese restaurant. More informal dining is available at the Coyote Cafe, featuring Southwestern cuisine. The MGM Grand has assembled an impressive team of chefs. The MGM Grand's buffet (disappointing), 24-hour café, and pizza kitchen adjoin the casinos between the porte-cochere and Lion entrances. For fast food there is a food court housing McDonald's, Mamma Ilardo's, and Hamada's Oriental Express.

There are two showrooms at the MGM Grand (exclusive of live entertainment in the theme park). The 630-seat Hollywood Theater features headliners, while the larger (1,700-seat) Grand Theater is home to a high-energy production show. Entertainment is also offered at the Catch a Rising Star comedy club, and in the casinos' four lounges. In addition, the MGM Grand's special-events arena can accommodate boxing, tournament tennis, rodeo, and basketball, as well as major exhibitions.

Amenities at the MGM Grand, not unexpectedly, are among the best in Las Vegas. The swimming complex is huge, with 23,000 square feet of pool laid out in a keyhole configuration. Other highlights of the complex include a sand beach, a poolside bar, and luxury cabanas. Adjoining the swimming area are a complete health club and spa and four lighted tennis courts. For those to whom recreation means pumping quarters into a machine, there is an extensive electronic games arcade supplemented by a "games of skill" midway.

A first at the MGM Grand is a youth center that provides supervised programs for children ages 3–12 of hotel guests both day and night. Activities are varied and include swimming, sports, learning programs, games, and outings. Unfortunately, the overall capacity of the youth center is small. Only 50 or so children can be accommodated in the center, with a maximum of 8 children participating in programs and field trips outside. Be sure to make reservations for the center two days in advance. The MGM Grand Adventures Theme Park features 10 major rides and attractions distributed throughout 8 themed areas. There are ten restaurants and fast-food outlets in the park as well as a dozen retail shops. The theme park is covered in "Part Five: Shopping and Seeing the Sights" on pages 336–340.

Guest rooms at the MGM Grand are comfortable, with large baths. Nicely appointed but not luxurious, standard guest rooms are decorated in *Casablanca, Gone with the Wind,* Hollywood, or *Wizard of Oz* themes. The wall art is a little bizarre in some of the rooms (Bert Lahr in his lion costume hanging over your bed, for example), but in general, the guest rooms are quite livable. Almost all of the rooms have a small sitting area positioned by a large window. Rooms on the higher floors have exceptional views. Part of the old MGM Marina Hotel was incorporated into the new MGM Grand. Rooms in the old structure have been renovated but are not comparable in size or quality to the new rooms.

The MGM Grand's biggest problem is weekend hotel registration and check-out. Management evidently underestimated the facilities and staff required to serve guests in a 5,000-plus-room hotel. Thus, almost every weekend, newly arriving guests inundate the check-in counter and pile up by the hundreds in waiting queues. If you want to stay at the MGM Grand, we recommend arriving before noon Friday and checking out as late as possible on Sunday. Given the problems the MGM Grand is experiencing, you shouldn't have any difficulty getting permission for a late check-out.

Drawing from a wide cross-section of the leisure market, the MGM Grand derives 80% of its business from individual travelers and tour and travel groups, with only 10% coming from trade show and convention attendees. The youth center, PG-rated showroom entertainment, and theme park make the MGM Grand a natural for families. Room rates in the $70–120 range make the MGM Grand accessible to a broad population. Geographically, the MGM Grand targets Southern California, Phoenix, Denver, Dallas, Houston, Chicago, and the Midwest.

Mirage

The Mirage has had an impact on the Las Vegas tourist industry that will be felt for years to come. By challenging all the old rules and setting new standards for design, ambiance, and entertainment, the Mirage precipitated the development of a class of super-hotels in Las Vegas, redefining the thematic appeal and hospitality standard of hotel-casinos in much the same way Disney did theme parks.

Exciting and compelling without being whimsical or silly, the Mirage has demonstrated that the public will respond enthusiastically to a well-executed concept. Blending the stateliness of marble with the exotic luxury of tropical greenery and the straightforward lines of polished bamboo, the Mirage has created a spectacular environment that artfully integrates casino, showroom, shopping, restaurants, and lounges. Both lavish and colorful, inviting and awe-inspiring, the Mirage has avoided cliché. Not designed to replicate a famous palace or be the hotel version of "Goofy Golf," the Mirage makes an original statement.

An atrium rain forest serves as a central hub from which guests can proceed to all areas of the hotel and casino. Behind the hotel's front desk, a 60-foot-long aquarium contains small sharks, stingrays, and colorful tropical fish. In the entranceway from Las Vegas Boulevard is a natural-habitat zoological display housing rare white Bengal tigers. Outside, instead of blinking neon, the Mirage has a 55-foot-tall erupting volcano that disrupts traffic on the Strip every half hour. There is also a live dolphin exhibit and a modern showroom that is among the most well designed and technologically advanced in Las Vegas.

The restaurants at the Mirage are special, especially Kokomo's, with its seafood specialties; the Northern Italian Ristorante Riva; and the creative California Pizza Kitchen. For bulk eaters, there is an ample and affordable buffet. Illusionists Siegfried and Roy are the headliners in the showroom. Their show takes Las Vegas entertainment (and prices) into the 21st century. Amenities at the Mirage include a stunning swimming and sunning complex with waterfalls, inlets, and an interconnected series of lagoons; a stylish shopping arcade; and a spa with exercise equipment and aerobics instruction. The casino is huge and magnificently appointed, yet informal, with its tropical motif and piped-in Jimmy Buffett music. Most guest rooms at the Mirage have been completely renovated and are now among the nicest in town.

Though registered guests pay premium prices (by Las Vegas standards) for the privilege of staying at the Mirage, the hotel is not an exclusive retreat of the wealthy. With its indoor jungle, live tigers and sharks, and traffic-snarling volcano, the Mirage is Clark County's top tourist attraction. Whether by foot, bus, trolley, cab, or bicycle, every Las Vegas visitor makes at least one pilgrimage. The Mirage has become the Strip's melting pot and hosts the most incredible variety of humanity imaginable. Visitors wander wide-eyed through the casino at all hours of the day and night.

Monte Carlo

Monte Carlo opened on June 21, 1996. Its 3,014 guest rooms rank Monte Carlo as the seventh largest hotel in Las Vegas (and therefore the country—eighth in the world). The megaresort is modeled after the Place du Casino in Monte Carlo, Monaco, with ornate arches and fountains, marble floors, and a Gothic glass registration area. If the Monte Carlo fails as a resort, the building will be a perfect place to relocate the Nevada State Capitol.

On the surface, it's yet another huge hotel in the Las Vegas Age of the Megaresort. But scratch the surface just a little and you glimpse the future of Monopoly-board Las Vegas and the gambling business in general. Monte Carlo is a joint venture between Mirage Resorts (which put up the land and a small amount of cash) and Circus Circus (which put up the rest of the cash and will run the joint), two of the largest casino competitors in the world. By combining their resources, Mirage and Circus were able to finance, design, and construct a monumental hotel-casino in record time (15 months from start to finish) and can operate it without taxing their individual infrastructures.

In addition, if you look at the west side of the Strip from Treasure Island to the old Hacienda site, you see that Mirage controls a mile of valuable frontage to the north of Monte Carlo (Bellagio, Mirage, and Treasure Island, with only Caesars Palace in between) and Circus Circus controls the mile to the south (Excalibur and Luxor with only New York–New York in between). Now imagine a Strip transportation system, such as a monorail, built jointly by Mirage and Circus à la MGM and Bally's: Monte Carlo, as the transfer point between the Mirage line and the Circus line, becomes the focus of a whole lot of traffic.

The guest rooms, traditionally furnished with marble entryways and French period wall art, are mid- to upper-priced (to compete with MGM Grand). There is an elaborate swimming complex with slides, a wave pool, and a man-made stream for floating. There is also an exceptional health and fitness center, an interesting shopping arcade, and a brew pub with live entertainment. The casino, about a football field long and similarly shaped, is capped with simulated skylights and domes. The showroom is designed especially for illusionist Lance Burton, who signed a long-term contract to perform there. Restaurants cover the usual bases, offering steak, Italian, and Chinese specialties respectively.

Compared to the powerful themes of New York–New York, Treasure Island, and the Luxor, the Monte Carlo's turn-of-the-century Monacan theme fails to stimulate much excitement or anticipation. Besides being beyond the tourist's frame of reference, the theme lacks any real visceral dimension. The word *grand* comes to mind, but more in the context of a federal courthouse or the New York Public Library. Simply put (and this may be a big plus), Monte Carlo is an attractive hotel-casino as opposed to a crowd-jammed tourist attraction.

New York–New York

Opening in December 1996, this architecturally imaginative hotel-casino sets a new standard for the realization of Las Vegas megaresort themes. It's a small joint by megaresort standards ("only" around 2,200 rooms), but the triumph is in the details. The guest rooms are in a series of distinct towers reminiscent of a mini–Big Apple skyline, including the Empire State, Chrysler, and Seagrams buildings. Though the buildings are connected, each offers a somewhat different decor and ambiance.

A half-size Statue of Liberty and a replica of Grand Central Station lead visitors to one entrance, while the Brooklyn Bridge beckons to another. The 1,000-seat theater is called Radio City Music Hall, and the interior of the property is broken into themed areas such as Greenwich Village, Wall Street, and Times Square.

The casino, one of the most visually interesting in Las Vegas, looks like an elaborate movie set. Table games and slots are sandwiched between buildings, shops, restaurants, and a jumble of city street facades.

The street scenes are well executed, conveying both a sense of urban style and tough grittiness. New York–New York sacrificed much of its visual impact, however, by not putting in an imitation sky. At Sunset Station, by way of contrast, the Spanish architecture is augmented significantly by vaulted ceilings, realistically lighted and painted with clouds. This sort of finishing touch could have done wonders for New York–New York.

Like its namesake, New York–New York is congested in the extreme, awash day and night with curious sight-seers. There are so many people just wandering around gawking that there's little room left for hotel guests and folks who actually came to gamble. Because aisles and indoor paths are far too narrow to accommodate the crowds, New York–New York succumbs periodically to a sort of pedestrian gridlock.

Manhattan rules, however, do not apply at New York–New York: It's OK here to make eye contact and decidedly rude to shove people out of the way to get where you want to go. If you find yourself longing for the thrill of a New York cab ride, go hop on the roller coaster. New York–New York's coaster is the fourth one on the Strip, but it's the only one where you can stand on the street and hear the riders scream.

Guest rooms at New York–New York approximate the Holiday Inn standard but are somewhat disappointing for a hotel with such a strong, resonant theme. Likewise, the swimming area and health and fitness center are just average. Full-service restaurants are a little better than average, offering both variety and quality, while counter-service fast food is quite interesting, if not altogether authentic New York. Our favorite feature of New York–New York is Hamilton's, a cozy piano bar with a balcony overlooking the casino.

Like Monte Carlo next door, New York–New York is also a joint venture; this one is between MGM Grand and Primadonna, which operates a trio of casinos at the California state line, 40 miles southwest of Las Vegas. New York–New York has acquired the adjacent property to the north and plans to build a 1,000-room hotel tower.

Nevada Palace

The Nevada Palace is a small, recently renovated Boulder Highway property patronized primarily by locals and by seniors who take advantage of its 168-space RV park. Pleasant, with a new pool, spa facilities, two decent restaurants, and fair room rates, the Nevada Palace is a friendly, less hectic alternative to staying downtown or on the Strip.

Orleans

Opened in 1997, Orleans is situated just west of I-15 on Tropicana Avenue and is owned by Coast Resorts, which also run the Barbary Coast and the Gold Coast. Marketed primarily to locals, Orleans has a New Orleans/bayou theme executed in a hulking cavern of a building. The casino is festive with bright carpets, high ceilings, a two-story replication of a French Quarter street flanking the table games, and a couple of nifty bars. Orleans has a showroom that is struggling to establish an identity and several restaurants that have little to do with the Louisiana theme. The buffet, which serves Creole/Cajun dishes, has come a long way but still needs some work. Upstairs, over the slots and buffet area, is a 70-lane bowling complex. An 840-room hotel tower completes the package.

Orleans struggled in its opening months, prompting the owners to add a New Orleans–style restaurant and nightclub, a 12-theater movie complex, a games arcade, and a child-care center.

Palace Station

Located four minutes off the Strip on West Sahara, Palace Station is a local favorite that is beginning to attract the attention of the tourists. With one of the top buffets in town, dependable (also popular and crowded) restaurants that continuously offer amazing specials, a tower of handsome guest rooms, good prices, and a location that permits access to both downtown and the Strip in less than ten minutes, Palace Station has arrived. Decorated in a railroad theme, the casino is large and busy and places heavy emphasis on the slots (which are supposedly loose—i.e., having a high rate of payoff). There is also first-rate lounge entertainment.

Plaza

The Plaza had the distinction of being the only hotel in Las Vegas with its own railroad station until Amtrak cut its service in 1996. Not too long ago, the hotel was run-down and about what you would expect for a downtown property attached to a train terminal. Recently, however, the Plaza renovated its tower rooms and now offers nice accommodations at very good prices. The only downtown hotel to provide on-site tennis, the Plaza also has one of only two downtown Las Vegas showrooms, featuring production shows and, periodically, live theater (invariably comedy). The property houses a domed restaurant with a view straight down the middle of Glitter Gulch and the Fremont Experience. The view (as opposed to the food) is the main attraction here. If you go, reserve a table by the window.

The casino's table gaming area is very pleasant, with its high, dark green ceiling punctuated by crystal chandeliers. Patrons include downtown walk-ins, attendees of small meetings and conventions, and Southern Californians.

Quality Inn and Key Largo Casino

The Quality Inn is a great compromise property. Though small, it has all the essentials (mini-casino, restaurant, gift shop, lounge, pool). The

Quality offers quiet and simplicity with most of the amenities of a large resort; a wet bar and a refrigerator are standard in every room. The Quality's crowning glory is a green and extraordinarily peaceful central courtyard and pool complex. Its location permits easy access to the Strip and the airport.

Rio

The Rio is one of Las Vegas's hidden treasures. Tastefully decorated in a Latin American carnival theme, the Rio offers resort luxury at local prices. The guest rooms (all plush suites) offer exceptional views and can be had for the price of a regular room at many other Las Vegas hotels. The combination of view, luxury, and price makes the Rio our first choice for couples on romantic getaways or honeymoons.

Located on Flamingo Road three minutes west of the Strip, the Rio also allows easy access to downtown via I-15. With excellent restaurants, a great buffet, high-energy entertainment, a huge new shopping arcade, a workout room, and an elaborate multipool swimming area, the Rio offers exceptional quality in every respect. Festive and bright without being tacky or overdone, the recently enlarged casino also offers a comfortable sports book.

In a phased expansion over the past four years, the Rio has tripled its guest room inventory, doubled the size of its swimming complex, quadrupled the number of its restaurants, and in the process turned into a true destination resort. In 1997, the Rio premiered Masquerade Village, a retail, restaurant, and specialty shopping venue that rings the casino. Masquerade Village is home to the "Masquerade in the Sky," a parade featuring floats and performers suspended from tracks high above the casino floor.

The Rio staff ranks very high in terms of hospitality, warmth, and an eagerness to please. The Rio is one of the few casinos to successfully target both locals and out-of-towners, particularly Southern Californians.

Riviera

Extending from the Strip halfway to Paradise Road (and the Las Vegas Convention Center), the Riviera is perfectly positioned to accommodate both leisure and business travelers. Though not at all isolated, the Riviera provides so much in the way of gambling, entertainment, and amenities that many guests never feel the need to leave the property. The Riviera has more showrooms (four) than any other hotel in Las Vegas and offers an unusually varied entertainment mix. These include a production show, a comedy club, a striptease show, a female impersonator show, celebrity entertainers, and lounge acts.

While some hotels may serve better food, there are few that offer more variety, especially to the informal diner. Guests on the move can choose from a number of fast-food restaurants in the Food Court or go for the Riviera's buffet. Upscale restaurants round out the package and supply ethnic diversity. As for amenities, the Riviera provides a spacious pool and sunbathing area, tennis courts, a shopping arcade, and a wedding chapel. Guest rooms, particularly in the towers, are more comfortable and luxurious than the hotel's public areas suggest.

The casino is huge (big enough to get lost in on the way to the rest room) and somewhat of a maze. There is always a lot of noise and light, and a busy, unremitting flurry of activity. Walk-in traffic mixes with convention-goers, retirees on "gambling sprees," and tourists on wholesaler packages. Asians, Asian-Americans, and Southern Californians also patronize the Riviera.

The expansion and renovation epidemic has finally hit the Riviera. During 1997–98, all of the guest rooms will be remodeled. The Riviera also plans to develop an entertainment complex and possibly a new hotel tower.

Sahara

The Sahara, sporting a Moroccan theme and undergoing an extensive renovation, is situated at the far north end of the Strip (toward downtown). A complex of many buildings and towers, the Sahara offers a casino, a convention hall, a showroom, a decent buffet, a shopping arcade, two upscale restaurants, and two swimming pools. The Sahara is a little remote for anyone who wants to walk, but if you have a car, it is nicely positioned in relation to the Strip, downtown, and the Convention Center.

The Sahara is comfortable, not flashy. If it has a distinctive personality, we're not sure what it is. Guest rooms are modern but not luxurious, and the casino, appointed in the predictable burgundies and reds, will be upgraded during the renovation. For the most part, the Sahara caters to businessmen attending meetings or conventions and to leisure travelers from Southern California and the Southwest.

Sam's Town

Located about 20 minutes east of the Strip on the Boulder Highway, Sam's Town is a long, rambling set of connected buildings with an Old West mining-town motif. In addition to the hotel and casino, there are a bowling alley, a very good buffet, one of Las Vegas's better Mexican eateries, a steak house, a great '50s-style diner, an RV park, and a huge outlet store for Western wear. The lounge features live country-western music and dancing and is popular with both locals and visitors.

A total of 650 new guest rooms were added in the summer of 1994, as well as a free-form pool, a sand volleyball court, and a spa. A new sports bar features pool, computerized golf, indoor half-court basketball, and TVs for the more sedentary. Joining the "let's be an attraction" movement, Sam's Town capped its renovation with an atrium featuring plants, trees, footpaths, waterfalls, and even a "mountain." A waterfall in the atrium is the site of a free but very well done fountains-and-light show (keep your eye on the robotic wolf). Frequent customers, besides the locals, include seniors and cowboys.

San Remo

The San Remo sits next door to the Tropicana and across Tropicana Avenue from the MGM Grand Hotel and Theme Park. Since it is close to the airport and the southern end of the Strip, the San Remo's traditional market has business travelers. With the addition of its new tower, however, the San Remo has more than doubled in size and begun to actively court Southern Californians, Southwestern leisure travelers, and the Japanese market.

The San Remo has a chandeliered casino, an OK restaurant, an average buffet, and a good sushi bar. Dark hardwood furniture contrasts pleasantly with light wallpaper and patterned accessories in the well-appointed guest rooms. A central courtyard and pool complete the package.

Santa Fe

The Santa Fe opened in 1991 and is located about 20 minutes northwest of Las Vegas, just off US 95. Like Sam's Town, the Rio, and the Showboat, the Santa Fe targets both locals and tourists. Bright and airy, with a warm Southwestern decor, the Santa Fe is one of the more livable hotel-casinos in Las Vegas.

The Santa Fe offers a spacious casino, a better-than-average buffet, and an all-purpose restaurant featuring steak, prime rib, and Mexican specialties. The Santa Fe doesn't have a showroom, but live entertainment is provided in the lounge. And though there isn't a pool, there is a bowling alley and, amazingly, a hockey-sized ice-skating rink. Guest rooms, also decorated in a Southwestern style, are exceptionally nice and a good value.

Showboat

The Showboat is located on the Boulder Highway not far from downtown and about 12 minutes from the Strip. To many of its local patrons, the Showboat is a huge bowling alley with a hotel and casino on the side. Not that there is anything dinky about the hotel or casino, but with over 100 lanes and inexpensive charges per game, it is the bowling complex that gives the Showboat its informal, sporty identity. The casino, which includes an elaborate and immense bingo parlor, is decorated in the style of a turn-of-the-century riverboat, with large murals and high ceilings. Though the casino is usually busy, there is little sensation of congestion or overcrowding. Restaurants at the Showboat offer a good value for the dollar, with an excellent buffet, coffee shop, and Italian eatery. Guest rooms were totally renovated in 1995. There is good lounge entertainment.

Stardust

Situated on the Strip at the intersection with Convention Center Drive, the Stardust caters to the tour and travel market, meeting and trade show attendees, and locals. With a location that affords easy access to the Riviera and Circus Circus, the Stardust is well placed for Strip action and is about a 15-minute walk from the Las Vegas Convention Center. A new high-rise tower with handsome guest rooms has doubled the number of rooms available at the Stardust, while new meeting facilities have elevated the property's status with business travelers. Amenities include a shopping arcade and a heated pool. The Stardust has consistent, high-quality restaurants such as William B's, which features some of Las Vegas's better prime rib.

The lounge entertainment is better than average at the Stardust, and the production show is excellent. The casino is vast and spread out but is otherwise unremarkable—i.e., another nice, big gambling emporium decorated in dark colors. If you fell asleep at the Stardust and woke up in the Riviera, Sahara, or Frontier, you would probably never know the difference.

Stratosphere

The Stratosphere Tower is the brainchild of Vegas World owner Bob Stupak, the quintessential Las Vegas maverick casino owner. Vegas World had been one of the last sole-proprietorship casinos in Las Vegas, but the lack of financing to complete the tower forced Stupak to sell 75% of his company to Lyle Berman and Grand Casinos of Minnesota and Mississippi (not to be confused with Las Vegas's MGM Grand). Stupak's original idea was to attach a tourist attraction (the tower) to Vegas World. Berman, however, realized that such a juxtaposition would be like locating the Washington Monument next to a Texaco station and insisted that Vegas World be bulldozed. The resort that has risen from the rubble happily combines Stupak's vision with Berman's taste.

The Stratosphere hotel-casino opened on April 30, 1996, and Las Vegas hasn't been the same since. At 1,149 feet, Stratosphere Tower is the tallest building west of the Mississippi—taller than the Eiffel Tower. It houses indoor and outdoor observation decks, a 360-seat revolving restaurant, four wedding chapels, and meeting rooms. The 360° view is breathtaking day (a life-size relief map of Las Vegas Valley and beyond) and night (the shimmering blaze of a billion bulbs).

Also at the top (hang on to your hats!) are two thrill rides. The world's highest roller coaster is also the world's slowest and shortest. It's a yawner, barely worth the 50 seconds of your time. However, if you try it, be sure to step out to the right! The other ride, however, a gravity/thrill experience called The Big Shot, is a monster: it rockets you straight up the tower's needle with a force of four g's, then drops you back down with no g's. And it all happens, mind you, at 1,000 feet in the air!

A second construction phase, including another 1,000 rooms, a pool and spa, a shopping mall, a Kids Quest daycare facility, several new restaurants, and a King Kong thrill ride that crawls 600 feet up and down the south leg of the tower (with you in King Kong's belly), was put on indefinite hold when the Stratosphere ran into major financial problems in 1997. Stay tuned.

During the prior four-year construction of the tower itself, politicos, pundits, and industry bigwigs pegged their hopes on the tower attraction to revitalize the northern end of the Strip, which has long needed some modernizing. So far, however, the only project progressing nearby is the expansion of the Sahara. The billion-dollar Starship Orion resort planned to replace the old El Rancho has been shelved. Two new resorts rumored to be in the works for the vacant lots on either side of the Sahara, and a small casino called Chicago–Chicago planned for the site now occupied by Holy Cow!, have failed to materialize.

Texas Station

Owned by Station Casinos who also own and operate Palace Station, Sunset Station, and Boulder Station, Texas Station has a single-story full-service casino with 60,000 square feet of gaming space, decorated with black carpet sporting cowboy designs such as gold, boots, ropes, revolvers, covered wagons, etc. The atmosphere is contemporary Western, a subtle blend of Texas ranch culture and Spanish architecture. This property offers seven restaurants, one of Las Vegas's best buffets, two bars, a dance hall called the Armadillo Honky Tonk, and a 12-screen theater showing first-run movies. Texas Station caters to locals and cowboys and is located at the intersection of Rancho Drive and Lake Mead Boulevard in North Las Vegas.

Treasure Island

Owned by Steve Wynn of Mirage and Golden Nugget fame, Treasure Island is one of three megacasino resorts to open during the fall of 1993 and the winter of 1994. Located on the southwest corner of the Strip at Spring Mountain Road, next door to the Mirage, Treasure Island is Caribbean in style, with a buccaneer theme. Though similar in amenities and services, Treasure Island targets a younger, more middle-class family clientele than the Mirage.

In the spirit of the Mirage, Treasure Island is an attraction as well as a hotel and casino. Crossing Buccaneer Bay from the Strip on a plank bridge, guests enter a pirate fort and seaside village reminiscent of Disney's Pirates of the Caribbean ride. Colorful and detailed, the village (which serves as the main entrance to the hotel and casino) is sandwiched between rocky cliffs and landscaped with palms. Every hour a British man-o'-war sails into the harbor and engages the pirate ship *Hispaniola* in a raging battle (firing over the heads of tourists on the bridge). Exceptional special effects, pyrotechnics, and a cast of almost 80 pirates and sailors ensure that any Strip traffic not snarled by the Mirage's volcano (next door) will most certainly be stopped dead by Treasure Island's sea battle.

Passing through the main sally port, you enter the commercial and residential area of Buccaneer Bay Village, complete with town square, shops, restaurants, and, of course, the casino. The casino continues the old Caribbean theme, with carved panels and whitewashed, beamed ceilings over a black carpet, punctuated with fuschia, sapphire blue, and emerald green. The overall impression is one of tropical comfort: exciting, but easy on the eye and spirit. In addition to the usual slots and table games, a comfortable sports book is provided.

The hotel lobby and public areas are likewise elaborate and detailed. The lobby bar, a sort of building within a building, is especially eye-catching. Here, incredibly, a patio framed by exotic arches and columns is lit by chandeliers made from cast plastic human bones. The Treasure Island publicity people are quick to point out, however, that the various skulls, femurs, and scapulas are "finished in gold so that they don't look gory."

Pirate's Walk, the main interior passageway, leads to a shopping arcade, a steak house, and the buffet, featuring Italian, American, and Chinese cuisine. Treasure Island's most upscale restaurant is the Buccaneer Bay Club overlooking the bay. Here you can enjoy a quiet, relaxing meal while watching the British and the pirates fire cannons at each other outside. Only in America.

Treasure Island amenities include a beautifully landscaped swimming area with slides, waterfalls, grottoes, and tranquil pools. The pirate theme gives way to luxury and practicality in the well-equipped health club and spa. Larger than that of the Mirage, the facility features weight machines, free weights, a variety of aerobic workout equipment, large whirlpools, steam rooms, and saunas.

Treasure Island is home to the extraordinary *Cirque du Soleil*, which performs in a new, custom-designed, 1,500-seat theater. For the kids there is Mutiny Bay, an 18,000-square-foot electronic games arcade.

Guest rooms at Treasure Island are situated in a Y-shaped, coral-colored tower that rises directly behind the pirate village. Decorated in soft, earth-tone colors, the rooms provide a restful retreat from the bustling casino. Additionally, the rooms feature large windows affording a good view of the Strip or (on the west side) of the mountains and sunset. The balconies that are visible in photos of Treasure Island are strictly decorative and cannot be accessed from the guest rooms. Self-parking is easier at Treasure Island than at most Strip hotels. Valet parking is fast and efficient. An elevated tram connects Treasure Island to the Mirage next door.

Tropicana

At the southern end of the Strip, the Tropicana sits across Las Vegas Boulevard from the Excalibur, and opposite the new MGM Grand on Tropicana Avenue. With its Paradise and Island Towers and 1,910 rooms, the Tropicana is one of the larger resort hotels in town. It offers a full range of services and amenities, including tennis, an exercise room, meeting and convention space, and a shopping arcade. The Tropicana is also home to one of Las Vegas's most celebrated swimming and sunbathing complexes. This facility, a convoluted system of lagoons and grottoes embellished with waterfalls and fountains, is less a "swimming pool" than a water park.

The Tropicana has four restaurants of merit that specialize, respectively, in steak and prime rib, Italian food, and Japanese teppan grill combinations. The champagne brunch at the Tropicana is among the top Sunday brunches in the city. Entertainment offerings consist of a comedy club, a long-running production show, and lounge acts. The Tropicana's casino is spectacular and bright, with multicolored floral carpeting and a stunning, 4,000-square-foot stained-glass canopy over the table games. Both festive and elegant, the Tropicana casino is an attraction in its own right and ranks as one of the city's most pleasant and exciting places to gamble, especially for table players.

Guest rooms are furnished in an exotic, tropical bamboo motif that (in some rooms) includes mirrors on the ceiling. Views from the upper rooms of both towers are among the best in town.

The Tropicana does a thriving business with the travel wholesalers and motor coach tours, and also aggressively targets the Japanese and Hispanic markets. In the casino you will find a more-youthful-than-average clientele, including a lot of guests from the nearby Excalibur enjoying the Trop's more luxurious and sophisticated style. The Tropicana's domestic market draws, not unexpectedly, from Southern California. It is particularly popular with slot players.

Vacation Village

To say that Vacation Village is on the Strip is stretching a point. Located south of the airport at the southern end of Las Vegas Boulevard, Vacation Village is the most remote property in town. It provides budget accommodations and basic amenities to Californians taking the southernmost exit from I-15 onto the Strip. Vacation Village offers a nice Southwestern-style casino, pool, buffet, and Mexican restaurant. Though Vacation Village is friendly and informal and welcomes the family trade, its isolation makes it an inconvenient place to stay unless, for some reason, you enjoy the desert.

Westward Ho

A sprawling motel next to the Stardust, the Westward Ho offers a slot-oriented casino decorated in the usual dark colors. There is lounge entertainment, a couple of pools, palatable but nondistinguished dining, good deals on drinks and snacks, and easy foot access to a number of nearby casinos.

Suite Hotels

Suites

The term *suite* in Las Vegas covers a broad range of accommodations. The vast majority of suites consist of a larger-than-average room with a conversation area (couch, chair, and coffee table) and a refrigerator added to the usual inventory of basic furnishings. In a two-room suite the conversation area is normally in a second room separate from the sleeping area. Two-room suites are not necessarily larger than one-room suites in terms of square footage but are more versatile. One-room and two-room suites are often available in Las Vegas for about the same rate as a standard hotel room.

Larger hotels, with or without casinos, usually offer roomier, more luxurious multiroom suites. Floor plans and rates for these premium suites can be obtained for the asking from the hotel sales and marketing department.

There are a number of suite hotels that do not have casinos. Patronized primarily by business travelers and nongamblers, these properties offer a quiet alternative to the glitz and frenetic pace of the casino hotels. Because there is no gambling to subsidize operations, however, suites at properties without casinos are usually (but not always) more expensive than suites at hotels with casinos.

While most hotels with casinos offer suites, only the Rio is an all-suite property. The basic suite is a plush, one-room affair with wet bar and sitting area but no kitchen facilities. The Rio, located on Flamingo Road just west of the I-15 interchange, sometimes makes its suites available at less than $110 per night and is one of the best lodging values in town.

Suite Hotels without Casinos

Alexis Park

The Alexis Park is the best known of the Las Vegas one- and two-room suite properties. Expensive, and therefore relatively exclusive, the Alexis offers most of the amenities of a large resort hotel, including a lovely pool, lighted tennis courts, and an exercise room. Pegasus, a Continental restaurant at the Alexis, has been rated in past years by Mobil and others (though not by us) as the best gourmet restaurant in Las Vegas. Suites are upscale and plush, with a Southwestern decor. The hotel's staff are extremely friendly and not at all pretentious. Alexis Park's clientele includes executive-level business travelers and a good number of Southern California yuppies.

Holiday Inn Crowne Plaza

Located on Paradise Road, the Plaza Suites is four minutes by cab to both the Strip and the Las Vegas Convention Center. There is a pool and a café, and an excellent selection of ethnic restaurants are located within easy striking distance. Suites are mostly of the two-room variety and are nicely, but not luxuriously, appointed.

Holiday Inn Emerald Springs

The Holiday Inn, formerly the Emerald Springs Inn, two blocks east of the Strip on Flamingo Road, is a newer property offering moderately priced one- and two-room suites. Featuring pink stucco, marble, and large fountains both inside and out, the lobby, common areas, and rooms are tranquil and sedate by Las Vegas standards. The Veranda Cafe is the in-house coffee shop and serves a breakfast buffet. There is a lounge, heated pool, and spa.

Mardi Gras Inn (Best Western)

The Mardi Gras offers spartan suites at good rates. Quiet, with a well-manicured courtyard and a pool, the Mardi Gras is only a short walk from the Las Vegas Convention Center. There is a coffee shop on the property, and a number of good restaurants are less than half a mile away. Though a sign in front of the property advertises a casino, there is only a small collection of slot machines.

Residence Inn

Located across from the Las Vegas Convention Center, the Residence Inn by Marriott offers comfortable one- and two-bedroom suites with full kitchens. Patronized primarily by business travelers on extended stays, the Residence Inn provides a more homelike atmosphere than most other suite properties. While there is no restaurant at the hotel, there is an excellent selection within a half-mile radius. Amenities include a pool, jacuzzis, and a coin laundry.

St. Tropez

The St. Tropez offers beautifully decorated one- and two-room suites at rates often less than $100 per night. Adjoining a small shopping mall, the St. Tropez provides a restaurant, a lounge, a heated pool, a fitness center, VCRs in the suites, and a complimentary buffet breakfast. The St. Tropez is within five minutes of the Strip and the airport, and about seven minutes from the Convention Center. Most guests are upscale business and convention travelers.

Las Vegas Motels

Because they must compete with the huge hotel-casinos, many Las Vegas motels offer great rates or provide special amenities such as a complimentary breakfast. Like the resorts, motels often have a very specific clientele. La Quinta Motor Inn, for instance, caters to government employees while the Best Western on Craig Road primarily serves folks visiting Nellis Air Force Base.

For the most part, national motel chains are well represented in Las Vegas. Best Western, with five motels, has the strongest presence. Travelodge follows closely with four motels—two in prime Strip locations, one downtown, and one on Sierra Avenue. Days Inn, Super 8, and Holiday Inn each have three properties; Comfort Inn, Motel 6, and Rodeway each have one location. Marriott also operates the Residence Inn (an all-suite property) and the Marriott Courtyard.

We have included enough chain and independent motels in the following ratings and rankings section to give you a sense of how these properties compare with hotel-casinos and all-suite hotels. Because chain hotels are known entities to most travelers, no descriptions are provided beyond the room quality ratings and summary charts. After all, a Comfort Inn in Las Vegas is pretty much like a Comfort Inn in Louisville, and we are all aware by now that Motel 6 leaves the light on for you.

All this aside, there are a couple of specific recommendations we would like to make:

If You Need to Be Close to the Airport:
Best Western McCarran Inn, 4970 Paradise Road   (702) 798-5530

If You Need to Be Close to Nellis Air Force Base:
Best Western Nellis Motor Inn, 5330 E. Craig Road   (702) 643-6111

Hotel/Motel Toll-Free Reservation Lines	
Best Western	(800) 528-1234 Continental U.S. & Canada (800) 528-2222 TDD
Comfort Inns	(800) 228-5150 Continental U.S.
Courtyard by Marriott	(800) 321-2211 Continental U.S.
Days Inn	(800) 325-2525 Continental U.S.
Fairfield Inn by Marriott	(800) 228-2800 Continental U.S.
Hilton	(800) 445-8667 Continental U.S. (800) 368-1133 TDD
Holiday Inns	(800) 465-4329 Continental U.S. & Canada
Howard Johnson	(800) 654-2000 Continental U.S. & Canada (800) 654-8442 TDD
Quality Inns	(800) 228-5151 Continental U.S. & Canada
Ramada Inns	(800) 272-6232 Continental U.S. (800) 228-3232 TDD
Residence Inn by Marriott	(800) 331-3131 Continental U.S.
Rodeway Inns	(800) 228-2000 Continental U.S. & Canada
Super 8 Motels	(800) 843-1991 Continental U.S. & Canada
Travelodge	(800) 255-3050 Continental U.S. & Canada

Hotel-Casinos and Motels:
Rated and Ranked

■ What's in a Room? ■

Except for cleanliness, state of repair, and decor, most travelers do not pay much attention to hotel rooms. There is, of course, a discernible standard of quality and luxury that differentiates Motel 6 from Holiday Inn, Holiday Inn from Marriott, and so on. In general, however, hotel guests fail to appreciate that some rooms are better engineered than others.

Contrary to what you might suppose, designing a hotel room is (or should be) a lot more complex than picking a bedspread to match the carpet and drapes. Making the room usable to its occupants is an art, a planning discipline that combines both form and function.

Decor and taste are important, certainly. No one wants to spend several days in a room where the decor is dated, garish, or even ugly. But beyond the decor, there are variables that determine how "livable" a hotel room is. In Las Vegas, for example, we have seen some beautifully appointed rooms that are simply not well designed for human habitation. The next time you stay in a hotel, pay attention to the details and design elements of your room. Even more than decor, these are the things that will make you feel comfortable and at home.

It takes the *Unofficial Guide* researchers about 40 minutes to inspect a hotel room. Here are a few of the things we check that you may want to start paying attention to:

Room Size   While some smaller rooms are cozy and well designed, a large and uncluttered room is generally preferable, especially for a stay of more than three days.

Temperature Control, Ventilation, and Odor   The guest should be able to control the temperature of the room. The best system, because it's so quiet, is central heating and air conditioning, controlled by the room's own thermostat. The next best system is a room module heater and air conditioner, preferably controlled by an automatic thermostat, but usually by manually operated button controls. The worst system is central heating and air without any sort of room thermostat or guest control.

The vast majority of hotel rooms have windows or balcony doors that have been permanently secured shut. Though there are some legitimate safety and liability issues involved, we prefer windows and balcony doors that can be opened to admit fresh air. Hotel rooms should be odor-free and smoke-free and not feel stuffy or damp.

Room Security Better rooms have locks that require a plastic card instead of the traditional lock and key. Card and slot systems allow the hotel, essentially, to change the combination or entry code of the lock with each new guest who uses the room. A burglar who has somehow acquired a room key to a conventional lock can afford to wait until the situation is right before using the key to gain access. Not so with a card and slot system. Though larger hotels and hotel chains with lock and key systems usually rotate their locks once each year, they remain vulnerable to hotel thieves much of the time. Many smaller or independent properties rarely rotate their locks.

In addition to the entry lock system, the door should have a deadbolt, and preferably a chain that can be locked from the inside. A chain by itself is not sufficient. Doors should also have a peephole. Windows and balcony doors, if any, should have secure locks.

Safety Every room should have a fire or smoke alarm, clear fire instructions, and preferably a sprinkler system. Bathtubs should have a nonskid surface, and shower stalls should have doors that either open outward or slide side-to-side. Bathroom electrical outlets should be high on the wall and not too close to the sink. Balconies should have sturdy, high rails.

Noise Most travelers have occasionally been kept awake by the television, partying, or amorous activities of people in the next room, or by traffic on the street outside. Better hotels are designed with noise control in mind. Wall and ceiling construction are substantial, effectively screening routine noise. Carpets and drapes, in addition to being decorative, also absorb and muffle sounds. Mattresses mounted on stable platforms or sturdy bed frames do not squeak even when challenged by the most passionate and acrobatic lovers. Televisions enclosed in cabinets, and with volume governors, rarely disturb guests in adjacent rooms.

In better hotels, the air conditioning and heating system is well maintained and operates without noise or vibration. Likewise, plumbing is quiet and positioned away from the sleeping area. Doors to the hall, and to adjoining rooms, are thick and well fitted to better keep out noise.

Darkness Control Ever been in a hotel room where the curtains would not quite come together in the middle? In Las Vegas, where many visitors stay up way into the wee hours, it's important to have a dark, quiet room where you can sleep late without the morning sun blasting you out of bed.

Thick, lined curtains that close completely in the center and extend beyond the dimensions of the window or door frame are required. In a well-planned room, the curtains, shades, or blinds should almost totally block light at any time of day.

Lighting   Poor lighting is an extremely common problem in American hotel rooms. The lighting is usually adequate for dressing, relaxing, or watching television but not for reading or working. Lighting needs to be bright over tables and desks and alongside couches or easy chairs. Since so many people read in bed, there should be a separate light for each person. A room with two queen beds should have an individual light for four people. Better bedside reading lights illuminate a small area so that if you want to sleep and someone else prefers to stay up and read, you will not be bothered by the light. The worst situation by far is a single lamp on a table between beds. In each bed, only the person next to the lamp will have sufficient light to read. This deficiency is often compounded by light bulbs of insufficient wattage.

In addition, closet areas should be well lit, and there should be a switch near the door that turns on lights in the room when you enter. A seldom seen, but desirable, feature is a bedside console that allows a guest to control all or most lights in the room from bed.

Furnishings   At bare minimum, the bed(s) must be firm. Pillows should be made with nonallergenic fillers and, in addition to the sheets and spread, a blanket should be provided. Bedclothes should be laundered with a fabric softener and changed daily. Better hotels usually provide extra blankets and pillows in the room or on request, and sometimes use a second topsheet between the blanket and the spread.

There should be a dresser large enough to hold clothes for two people during a five-day stay. A small table with two chairs, or a desk with a chair, should be provided. The room should be equipped with a luggage rack and a three-quarter- to full-length mirror.

The television should be color and cable-connected and, ideally, should have a volume governor and remote control. It should be mounted on a swivel base and preferably enclosed in a cabinet. Local channels should be posted on the set and a local TV program guide should be supplied.

The telephone should be touchtone, conveniently situated for bedside use, and on it or nearby there should be easy-to-understand dialing instructions and a rate card. Local white and yellow pages should be provided. Better hotels have phones in the bath and equip room phones with long cords.

Well-designed hotel rooms usually have a plush armchair or a sleeper sofa for lounging and reading. Better headboards are padded for comfortable reading in bed, and there should be a nightstand or table on each side of the bed(s). Nice extras in any hotel room include a small refrigerator, a digital alarm clock, and a coffeemaker.

Bathroom   Two sinks are better than one, and you cannot have too much counter space. A sink outside the bath is a great convenience when two people are bathing and dressing at the same time. Sinks should have drains with stoppers.

Better bathrooms have both tub and shower with a nonslip bottom. Tub and shower controls should be easy to operate. Adjustable shower heads are preferred. The bath needs to be well lit and should have an exhaust fan and a guest-controlled bathroom heater. Towels should be large, soft, fluffy, and provided in generous quantities, as should hand towels and washcloths. There should be an electrical outlet for each sink, conveniently and safely placed.

Complimentary shampoo, conditioner, and lotion are a plus, as are robes and bathmats. Better hotels supply their bathrooms with tissues and extra toilet paper. Luxurious baths feature a phone, a hair dryer, sometimes a small television, or even a jacuzzi.

Vending   There should be complimentary ice and a drink machine on each floor. Welcome additions include a snack machine and a sundries (combs, toothpaste) machine. The latter are seldom found in large hotels that have 24-hour restaurants and shops.

■ Room Ratings ■

To separate properties according to the relative quality, tastefulness, state of repair, cleanliness, and size of their standard rooms, we have grouped the hotels and motels into classifications denoted by stars. Star ratings in this guide apply to Las Vegas properties only and do not necessarily correspond to ratings awarded by Mobil, AAA, or other travel critics. Because stars have little relevance when awarded in the absence of commonly recognized standards of comparison, we have tied our ratings to expected levels of quality established by specific American hotel corporations.

Star ratings apply to *room quality only* and describe the property's standard accommodations. For most hotels and motels, a "standard accommodation" is a hotel room with either one king bed or two queen beds. In an all-suite property, the standard accommodation is either a one- or two-room suite. In addition to standard accommodations, many hotels offer luxury rooms and special suites, which are not rated in this guide. Star ratings for rooms are assigned without regard to whether a property has a casino, restaurant(s), recreational facilities, entertainment, or other extras.

What the Ratings Mean		
★★★★★	*Superior Rooms*	Tasteful and luxurious by any standard
★★★★	*Extremely Nice Rooms*	What you would expect at a Hyatt Regency or Marriott
★★★	*Nice Rooms*	Holiday Inn or comparable quality
★★	*Adequate Rooms*	Clean, comfortable, and functional without frills—like a Motel 6
★	*Super Budget*	

In addition to stars (which delineate broad categories), we also employ a numerical rating system. Our rating scale is 0–100, with 100 as the best possible rating, and zero (0) as the worst. Numerical ratings are presented to show the difference we perceive between one property and another. Rooms at the Flamingo Hilton, the Frontier, and Palace Station, for instance, are all rated as ★★★½ (three and a half stars). In the supplemental numerical ratings, the Flamingo Hilton and the Frontier are rated 81 and 79, respectively, while Palace Station is rated 76. This means that within the three-and-a-half-star category, the Flamingo Hilton and the Frontier are comparable, and both have somewhat nicer rooms than Palace Station.

■ How the Hotels Compare ■

Here is a comparison of the hotel rooms in town. We've focused strictly on room quality and excluded any consideration of location, services, recreation, or amenities. In some instances, a one- or two-room suite can be had for the same price or less than that of a hotel room.

If you used an earlier edition of this guide, you will notice that many of the ratings and rankings have changed. These changes are occasioned by such positive developments as guest-room renovation, improved maintenance, and improved housekeeping. Failure to properly maintain guest rooms and poor housekeeping negatively affect the ratings. Finally, some ratings change as a result of enlarging our sample size. Because we cannot check every room in a hotel, we inspect a number of randomly chosen rooms. The more rooms we inspect in a particular hotel, the more representative our sample is of the property as a whole. Some of the ratings in this edition have changed as a result of extended sampling.

The guest rooms in many Las Vegas hotels vary in quality. In most hotels the better rooms are situated in high-rise structures known locally as "towers." More modest accommodations, called "garden rooms," are routinely found in one- and two-story outbuildings. It is important to understand that not all rooms in a particular hotel are the same. When you make inquiries or reservations, always define the type of room you are talking about.

Finally, before you begin to shop for a hotel, take a hard look at this letter we received from a couple in Hot Springs, Arkansas:

> We canceled our room reservations to follow the advice in your book [and reserved a hotel room highly ranked by the *Unofficial Guide*]. We wanted inexpensive, but clean and cheerful. We got inexpensive, but [also] dirty, grim, and depressing. I really felt disappointed in your advice and the room. It was the pits. That was the one real piece of information I needed from your book! The room spoiled the holiday for me aside from our touring.

Needless to say, this letter was as unsettling to us as the bad room was to our reader. Our integrity as travel journalists, after all, is based on the quality of the information we provide to our readers. Even with the best of intentions and the most conscientious research, however, we cannot inspect every room in every hotel. What we do, in statistical terms, is take a sample: we check out several rooms selected at random in each hotel and base our ratings and rankings on those rooms. The inspections are conducted anonymously and without the knowledge of the management. Although it would be unusual, it is certainly possible that the rooms we randomly inspect are not representative of the majority of rooms at a particular hotel. Another possibility is that the rooms we inspect in a given hotel are representative but that by bad luck a reader is assigned a room that is inferior. When we rechecked the hotel our reader disliked, we discovered that our rating was correctly representative, but that he and his wife had unfortunately been assigned to one of a small number of threadbare rooms scheduled for renovation.

The key to avoiding disappointment is to snoop around in advance. We recommend that you ask for a photo of a hotel's standard guest room before you book, or at least get a copy of the hotel's promotional brochure. Be forewarned, however, that some hotel chains use the same guest room photo in their promotional literature for all hotels in the chain; a specific guest room may not resemble the brochure photo. When you or your travel agent call, ask how old the property is and when your guest room was last renovated. If you arrive and are assigned a room inferior to that which you had been led to expect, demand to be moved to another room.

Cost estimates are based on the hotel's published rack rates for standard rooms, averaged between weekday and weekend prices. Each "$" represents $30. Thus a cost symbol of "$$$" means a room (or suite) at that hotel will cost about $90 a night.

How the Hotels Compare

Hotel	Star Rating	Quality Rating	Cost ($=$30)
Desert Inn	★★★★★	97	$$$$$+
Caesars Palace	★★★★★	96	$$$$$$$−
Alexis Park	★★★★½	94	$$$+
St. Tropez	★★★★½	93	$$$$$$−
Mirage	★★★★½	92	$$$$$$$$$−
Bally's	★★★★	88	$$$+
Las Vegas Hilton	★★★★	88	$$$$−
Rio	★★★★	88	$$$$$−
Golden Nugget	★★★★	87	$$$+
Hard Rock Hotel	★★★★	87	$$$$$−
Holiday Inn Crowne Plaza	★★★★	85	$$$$$−
MGM Grand	★★★★	85	$$$$$$+
Harrah's (Carnival tower rooms)	★★★★	83	$$$$$$$−
Residence Inn by Marriott	★★★★	83	$$$$−
Riviera	★★★½	82	$$$$−
Stratosphere	★★★½	82	$$$$−
Sunset Station	★★★½	82	$$$$−
Flamingo Hilton	★★★½	81	$$$$$−
Luxor	★★★½	81	$$$$$−
Orleans	★★★½	81	$$$+
Monte Carlo	★★★½	80	$$$$$−
Sam's Town	★★★½	80	$$$−
Treasure Island	★★★½	80	$$$$+
Courtyard by Marriott	★★★½	79	$$$+
Frontier	★★★½	79	$$+
Barbary Coast	★★★½	78	$$$−
Harrah's (Mardi Gras tower rooms)	★★★½	78	$$$$$$+
San Remo	★★★½	78	$$$$+
California	★★★½	77	$$+
Palace Station	★★★½	76	$$$$
Showboat	★★★½	76	$$$−
Stardust (tower rooms)	★★★½	76	$$$$$

How the Hotels Compare (cont'd)

Hotel	Star Rating	Quality Rating	Cost ($=$30)
Aladdin (tower rooms)	★★★½	75	$$$$+
Holiday Inn Emerald Springs	★★★½	75	$$$−
Arizona Charlie's (tower rooms)	★★★	74	$$−
Horseshoe	★★★	73	$$
Main Street Station	★★★	73	$$+
Comfort Inn South	★★★	72	$$$−
Santa Fe	★★★	72	$$+
Bourbon Street	★★★	71	$$+
Sunrise Suites	★★★	71	$$$−
Circus Circus (tower rooms)	★★★	70	$$$+
Holiday Inn Boardwalk	★★★	70	$$$+
Maxim	★★★	70	$$$−
Plaza	★★★	70	$$
Sahara	★★★	70	$$$−
Texas Station	★★★	70	$$$−
Debbie Reynolds Hollywood Hotel	★★★	69	$$$+
Las Vegas Club	★★★	69	$$−
New York–New York	★★★	69	$$$$$−
Tropicana	★★★	69	$$$$+
Best Western Mardi Gras Inn	★★★	67	$$$−
Boomtown	★★★	67	$$+
Boulder Station	★★★	67	$$$$−
Imperial Palace	★★★	67	$$$−
Lady Luck	★★★	67	$$$−
Days Inn Downtown	★★★	66	$$$−
Howard Johnson	★★★	66	$$$−
Excalibur	★★★	65	$$$$−
Sun Harbor Budget Suites (W. Tropicana)	★★★	65	$$+
La Quinta (Paradise Blvd.)	★★½	64	$$$−
Circus Circus (manor rooms)	★★½	63	$$$−
Nevada Palace	★★½	63	$$−
Quality Inn	★★½	63	$$$−
Aladdin (garden rooms)	★★½	62	$$$−
Fitzgerald's	★★½	62	$$$−
Best Western McCarran Inn	★★½	61	$$$−
Fiesta	★★½	61	$$$−
Four Queens	★★½	61	$$$$−

How the Hotels Compare (cont'd)

Hotel	Star Rating	Quality Rating	Cost ($=$30)
El Cortez	★★½	60	$+
Howard Johnson Airport	★★½	60	$$$–
Sam Boyd's Fremont	★★½	60	$$$–
Casino Royale	★★½	59	$$$–
Days Inn Town Hall	★★½	58	$$+
Stardust (garden rooms)	★★½	58	$$$–
Sun Harbor Budget Suites (Stardust Rd.)	★★½	58	$$+
Royal Hotel	★★½	57	$$+
Gold Coast	★★½	56	$$$$–
Continental	★★	54	$$$–
Arizona Charlie's (garden rooms)	★★	52	$+
Travelodge Las Vegas Inn	★★	49	$$–
Vacation Village	★★	49	$$$–
Super 8	★★	48	$$–
Westward Ho	★★	48	$$$–
King 8 Motel	★★	47	$$–
Motel 6	★★	47	$$+
Golden Gate	★½	45	$$+
La Concha	★½	45	$$–
E–Z 8 Motel	★½	39	$$–
Gold Spike	★	31	$–
Nevada Hotel	★	31	$$–

■ The Top 30 Best Deals in Las Vegas ■

Having listed the nicest rooms in town, let's reorder the list to rank the best combinations of quality and value in a room. As before, the rankings are made without consideration of location or the availability of restaurant(s), recreational facilities, entertainment, and/or amenities. Once again, each lodging property is awarded a value rating on a 0–100 scale. The higher the rating, the better the value.

A reader recently complained to us that he had booked one of our top-ranked rooms in terms of value and had been very disappointed in the room. We noticed that the room the reader occupied had a quality rating of ★★½. We would remind you that the value ratings are intended to give you some sense of value received for dollars spent. A ★★½ room at $30 may have the same value rating as a ★★★★ room at $85, but that does not mean the rooms will be of comparable quality. Regardless of whether it's a good deal or not, a ★★½ room is still a ★★½ room.

Listed below are the best room buys for the money, regardless of location or star classification, based on averaged rack rates. Note that sometimes a suite can cost less than a hotel room.

Hotel	Star Rating	Quality Rating	Cost ($=$30)
The Top 30 Best Deals in Las Vegas			
1 Arizona Charlie's (tower rooms)	★★★	74	$$−
2 El Cortez	★★½	60	$+
3 Frontier	★★★½	79	$$+
4 California	★★★½	77	$$+
5 Sam's Town	★★★½	80	$$$−
6 Horseshoe	★★★	73	$$
7 Las Vegas Club	★★★	69	$$−
8 Bally's	★★★★	88	$$$+
9 Golden Nugget	★★★★	87	$$$+
10 Plaza	★★★	70	$$
11 Main Street Station	★★★	73	$$+
12 Desert Inn	★★★★★	97	$$$$$+
13 Santa Fe	★★★	72	$$+
14 Bourbon Street	★★★	71	$$+
15 Alexis Park	★★★★½	94	$$$$$−
16 Las Vegas Hilton	★★★★	88	$$$$−
17 Barbary Coast	★★★½	78	$$$−
18 Showboat	★★★½	76	$$$−
19 Holiday Inn Emerald Springs	★★★½	75	$$$−
20 Orleans	★★★½	81	$$$+
21 Sunrise Suites	★★★	71	$$$−
22 Boomtown	★★★	67	$$+
23 Nevada Palace	★★½	63	$$−
24 Residence Inn by Marriott	★★★★	83	$$$$−
25 Courtyard by Marriott	★★★½	79	$$$+
26 Sun Harbor Budget Suites	★★★	65	$$+
27 Comfort Inn South	★★★	72	$$$−
28 Arizona Charlie's (garden rooms)	★★	52	$+
29 Stratosphere	★★★½	82	$$$$−
30 St. Tropez	★★★★½	93	$$$$$$−

Leisure, Recreation, and Services Rating of Hotel-Casinos

Many Las Vegas visitors only use their hotel rooms as a depository for luggage and a place to take a quick nap or shower. These folks are far more interested in what the hotel has to offer in terms of gambling, restaurants, live entertainment, services, and recreational pursuits.

Ranked below, in terms of the breadth and quality of their offerings, are Las Vegas hotels with full casinos. Using a weighted model, we have calculated a composite Leisure, Recreation, and Services Rating. The rating is designed to help you determine which properties provide the best overall vacation or leisure experience.

	LR&S Rating for Hotels with Full Casinos	
Rank	Hotel	Leisure, Recreation & Services Rating
1	Caesars Palace	99
2	Mirage	96
3	MGM Grand	95
4	Rio	93
5	Bally's	92
6	Stratosphere	91
7	Las Vegas Hilton	90
8	Flamingo Hilton	90
9	Treasure Island	89
10	Monte Carlo	88
11	Luxor	87
12	Harrah's	86
13	New York–New York	85
14	Desert Inn	85
15	Tropicana	84
16	Golden Nugget	83
17	Sunset Station	82
18	Hard Rock Hotel	82

LR&S Rating for Hotels with Full Casinos (cont'd)

Rank	Hotel	Leisure, Recreation & Services Rating
19	Imperial Palace	80
20	Riviera	80
21	Excalibur	78
22	Stardust	77
23	Sam's Town	76
24	Circus Circus	75
25	Texas Station	74
26	Palace Station	73
27	Aladdin	71
28	Showboat	68
29	Boulder Station	67
30	Fiesta	65
31	Sahara	64
32	Debbie Reynolds Hollywood Hotel	63
33	Santa Fe	63
34	Orleans	63
35	Main Street Station	63
36	Four Queens	62
37	Gold Coast	62
38	Lady Luck	61
39	Frontier	60
40	Boomtown	59
41	Maxim	58
42	Plaza	56
43	Barbary Coast	54
44	California	53
45	San Remo	51
46	Arizona Charlie's	50
47	Holiday Inn Boardwalk	50
48	Horseshoe	50
49	Las Vegas Club	49
50	Fitzgeralds	49
51	Sam Boyd's Fremont	48
52	Nevada Palace	45
53	King 8 Motel	43
54	Westward Ho	42
55	Casino Royale	38

LR&S Rating for Hotels with Full Casinos (cont'd)

Rank	Hotel	Leisure, Recreation & Services Rating
56	Continental	37
57	Vacation Village	36
58	Super 8	35
59	El Cortez	32
60	Golden Gate	20
61	Nevada Hotel	18
62	Gold Spike	17

Interpreting the LR&S Ratings

Room quality is not considered in the Leisure, Recreation, and Services Rating (LR&S). Therefore a hotel with ordinary rooms may attain a high LR&S score. A casino could have very ordinary guest rooms, for example, but score high in the LR&S rankings because it has a beautiful casino, excellent restaurants, a highly regarded buffet, shopping, and a good showroom.

Some hotels may score low because they offer little in the way of entertainment, recreation, or food service. If the property is somewhat isolated, like the Continental, Vacation Village, or El Cortez, these deficiencies pose serious problems. If, on the other hand, a hotel is situated in a prime location, the shortcomings hardly matter. The Barbary Coast does not have a showroom, but is within easy walking distance of showrooms at Caesars Palace, Bally's, the Mirage, Harrah's, the Imperial Palace, and the Flamingo. Likewise, the Four Queens, downtown, doesn't have a buffet but is within a three-minute walk of buffets at the Golden Nugget, Fremont, and Lady Luck.

Because the LR&S is a composite rating, its primary value is in identifying the properties that offer the highest quality and greatest variety of restaurants, diversions, and activities. The rating does not, however, indicate what those restaurants, diversions, or activities are. Caesars Palace and the Mirage have the highest LR&S ratings, but neither has a golf course. If you want to walk right out your door and tee off, you need to stay at the Desert Inn. Use the LR&S evaluations as a general guideline. When you have identified several properties that seem interesting, check the alphabetized profiles in the Hotel Information Chart appendix to make sure your preliminary selections offer the features that are important to you.

Percentage Value of LR&S Components

Weight	Subject of Evaluation
20%	**Casino:** Design, quality, gaming variety, aesthetic appeal, and atmosphere.
20%	**On-Site Restaurants:** Quality, variety, aesthetic appeal, and atmosphere.
10%	**Showroom, Lounge, and Entertainment:** Availability, variety, and quality of live shows, movies, and other entertainment.
10%	**Hotel Services:** Valet parking, concierge, room service, check-in and check-out efficiency.
8%	**Sports and Recreational Offerings:** Availability, variety, and quality of on-site sports and recreational activities, including golf, tennis, racquetball, bowling, ice skating, weight lifting, stationary cycling, aerobics, jogging, and swimming.
8%	**Swimming and Sunbathing Area:** Quality, size, aesthetic appeal, and atmosphere of the pool and surrounding area.
6%	**Spa Facilities:** Availability, variety, and quality of on-site spa services, such as steam room, sauna, whirlpool, facials, massage, dietary services.
6%	**Buffet:** Availability and quality of a daily-offered buffet.
6%	**Shopping:** Availability, quality, and variety of shopping.
6%	**Landscaping and Upkeep:** Cleanliness, state of repair, and aesthetic appeal of buildings, facilities, and grounds.
100%	Leisure, Recreation, and Services Rating (LR&S)

When Only the Best Will Do

The trouble with profiles, including ours, is that details and distinctions are sacrificed in the interest of brevity and information accessibility. For example, while dozens of properties are listed as having swimming pools, we've made no qualitative discriminations. In the alphabetized profiles, a pool is a pool. In actuality, of course, though most pools are quite basic and ordinary, a few (Mirage, Tropicana, Flamingo, Monte Carlo, MGM Grand, Treasure Island, and the Rio) are pretty spectacular. To distinguish the exceptional from the average, we provide the following:

Best Dining (Expense No Issue)

1. Caesars Palace
2. MGM Grand
3. Mirage
4. Rio
5. Las Vegas Hilton

Best Dining (for Great Value)

1. Palace Station
2. Rio
3. Texas Station
4. California
5. Sunset Station
6. Boulder Station
7. Excalibur
8. Fiesta
9. Main Street Station
10. Sam's Town

Best Buffets

1. Texas Station
2. Rio
3. Fiesta
4. Main Street Station
5. Boulder Station
6. Palace Station
7. Bally's
8. Mirage
9. Caesars Palace
10. Golden Nugget

Best Champagne Brunches

1. Bally's
2. MGM Grand
3. Tropicana
4. Circus, Circus
5. Boulder Station
6. Caesars Palace
7. Fiesta
8. Santa Fe

Most Romantic Hotel-Casinos

1. Rio
2. Caesars Palace
3. Mirage
4. Stratosphere
5. Luxor

Best Guest Room Baths

1. Desert Inn
2. Caesars Palace
3. Rio
4. MGM Grand

Best for Families with Children
(Listed Alphabetically)

Circus, Circus
Excalibur
MGM Grand
Mirage
Stratosphere

Best Views from Guest Rooms

1. Rio
2. Tropicana (towers)
3. Stratosphere (south view rooms)
4. Caesars Palace (new tower)
5. Palace Station (tower)
6. Hard Rock Hotel
7. Fitzgeralds
8. MGM Grand
9. Treasure Island
10. New York–New York

Most Interesting Casinos

1. Mirage
2. Caesars Palace
3. Sunset Station
4. New York–New York
5. Treasure Island
6. Monte Carlo
7. Rio
8. Main Street Station
9. MGM Grand
10. Hard Rock Hotel

Best for Shopping On-Site or within a Four-Minute Walk

1. Caesars Palace
2. Mirage
3. Treasure Island
4. Desert Inn
5. Frontier
6. Bally's

Best for Golf

Desert Inn

Best for Tennis

1. Desert Inn
2. MGM Grand
3. Bally's
4. Caesars Palace
5. Las Vegas Hilton
6. Flamingo

Best for Bowling

1. Showboat
2. Gold Coast
3. Sam's Town
4. Orleans
5. Santa Fe
6. Arizona Charlie's

Best for Jogging or Running

1. Desert Inn
2. Las Vegas Hilton

Best for Racquetball, Handball, & Squash

Caesars Palace

Best for Ice Skating

Santa Fe

Best Spas

1. Caesars Palace
2. Desert Inn
3. Mirage
4. Monte Carlo
5. Treasure Island
6. Luxor
7. Golden Nugget
8. MGM Grand

Best Swimming & Sunbathing

1. Mirage
2. Flamingo
3. Tropicana
4. Monte Carlo
5. Caesars Palace
6. Treasure Island
7. Hard Rock Hotel
8. Rio
9. MGM Grand
10. Las Vegas Hilton
11. Luxor
12. Alexis Park
13. St. Tropez
14. Frontier
15. Imperial Palace

Best for Weight Lifting, Nautilus, Stationary Cycling, Stair Machines, & Other Indoor Exercise Equipment

1. Mirage
2. Caesars Palace
3. Treasure Island
4. MGM Grand
5. Desert Inn
6. Monte Carlo
7. Luxor
8. Golden Nugget
9. Las Vegas Hilton
10. Bally's
11. Harrah's
12. Flamingo
13. Hard Rock Hotel
14. Imperial Palace

Putting the Ratings Together

To complete the picture (for hotels with casinos), we need to combine the Room Quality Rating; the Room Value Rating; and the Leisure, Recreation, and Services (LR&S) Rating to derive an Overall Rating. In the first edition of this guide, we weighted each of these ratings equally and averaged them to obtain the Overall Rating. Subsequently, our readers indicated that the atmosphere, amenities, and services of their hotel-casino were as important to them as the quality and value of their guest room. Given this appreciated input, we have developed a new calculation for the Overall Rating. In our new calculation, guest room considerations (quality and value) account for half of the Overall Rating, while the LR&S Rating (reflecting the quality of the casino, restaurants, shows, physical plant, and services) accounts for the remaining half.

	Overall Ratings			
Hotel	50% LR&S Rating	25% Quality Rating	25% Value Rating	100% Overall Rating
Caesars Palace	99	96	51	86
Bally's	92	88	70	85
Desert Inn	85	97	66	83
Las Vegas Hilton	90	88	64	83
Golden Nugget	83	87	74	82
Rio	93	88	50	81
Stratosphere	91	82	55	80
Mirage	96	92	34	79
MGM Grand	95	85	38	78
Sam's Town	76	80	78	78
Treasure Island	89	80	46	76
Flamingo Hilton	90	81	40	75
Hard Rock Hotel	82	87	44	74
Luxor	87	81	40	74
Monte Carlo	88	80	39	74
Sunset Station	82	82	51	74

Overall Ratings (cont'd)

Hotel	50% LR&S Rating	25% Quality Rating	25% Value Rating	100% Overall Rating
Riviera	80	82	51	73
Frontier	60	79	89	72
Harrah's (Carnival tower rooms)	86	83	33	72
Harrah's (Mardi Gras tower rooms)	86	78	30	70
Imperial Palace	80	67	47	69
Showboat	68	76	63	69
Arizona Charlie's (tower rooms)	50	74	97	68
Tropicana	84	69	34	68
Main Street Station	63	73	71	67
New York–New York	85	69	29	67
Orleans	63	81	60	67
Palace Station	73	76	47	67
Stardust (tower rooms)	77	76	37	67
Texas Station	74	70	50	67
California	53	77	81	66
Circus Circus (tower rooms)	75	70	45	66
Santa Fe	63	72	66	66
Aladdin (tower rooms)	71	75	44	65
Circus Circus (manor rooms)	75	63	42	64
Excalibur	78	65	34	64
Plaza	56	70	74	64
Barbary Coast	54	78	64	63
Stardust (garden rooms)	77	58	41	63
Horseshoe	50	73	77	62
Sahara	64	70	52	62
Aladdin (garden rooms)	71	62	38	61
Boomtown	59	67	60	61
Las Vegas Club	49	69	76	61
Boulder Station	67	67	39	60
Debbie Reynolds Hollywood Hotel	63	69	44	60
Lady Luck	61	67	47	59
Maxim	58	70	50	59
Fiesta	65	61	36	57
San Remo	51	78	44	56
El Cortez	32	60	90	54
Four Queens	62	61	29	54

Overall Ratings (cont'd)

Hotel	50% LR&S Rating	25% Quality Rating	25% Value Rating	100% Overall Rating
Holiday Inn Boardwalk	50	70	45	54
Nevada Palace	45	63	60	53
Arizona Charlie's (garden rooms)	50	52	57	52
Gold Coast	62	56	27	52
Fitzgerald's	49	62	38	50
Sam Boyd's Fremont	48	60	39	49
Casino Royale	38	59	36	43
King 8 Motel	43	47	36	42
Continental	37	54	30	40
Westward Ho	42	48	25	39
Super 8	35	48	34	38
Vacation Village	36	49	27	37
Golden Gate	20	45	20	26
Gold Spike	17	31	27	23
Nevada Hotel	18	31	13	20

PART TWO

Entertainment and Night Life

Las Vegas Shows and Entertainment

Las Vegas calls itself the "Entertainment Capital of the World." This is arguably true, particularly in terms of the sheer number of live entertainment productions staged daily. On any given day in Las Vegas a visitor can select from dozens of presentations, ranging from major production spectaculars to celebrity headliners, from comedy clubs to live music in lounges. The standard of professionalism and value for your entertainment dollar is very high. There is no other place where you can buy so much top-quality entertainment for so little money.

Most Las Vegas live entertainment offerings can be lumped into several broad categories:

Celebrity Headliners	Impersonator Shows
Long-Term Engagements	Comedy Clubs
Production Shows	Lounge Shows

Celebrity Headliners As the name implies, these are concerts or shows featuring big-name entertainers on a limited-engagement basis, usually one to four weeks, but sometimes for a one-night stand. Headliners are usually backed up by a medium-sized orchestra, and the stage sets and special production effects are kept simple. Performers such as Wayne Newton, Diana Ross, Tom Jones, Bill Cosby, and Joan Rivers play Las Vegas regularly. Some even work on a rotation with other performers, returning to the same showroom for several engagements each year. Other stars such as Dolly Parton play Las Vegas only occasionally, transforming each rare appearance into a truly special event. While there are exceptions, the super-stars are regularly found at the MGM Grand, Bally's, the Desert Inn, and Caesars Palace; sometimes at the Mirage and the Riviera; and occasionally at the Aladdin. Big-name performers in the city's top showrooms command premium admission prices of $25–90. Headliners of slightly lesser stature play at various other showrooms.

Long-Term Engagements   These are shows by the famous and once-famous who have come to Las Vegas to stay. Debbie Reynolds, for example, performs practically year-round at her own showroom at the Debbie Reynolds Hollywood Hotel.

Production Shows   These are continuously running, Broadway-style theatrical and musical productions. Cast sizes run from a dozen performers to well over a hundred, with costumes, sets, and special effects spanning a comparable range. Costing hundreds of thousands, if not millions, to produce, the shows feature chorus lines, elaborate choreography, and great spectacle. Usually playing twice a night, six or seven days a week, production shows often run for years.

Production shows generally have a central theme to which a more or less standard mix of choreography and variety acts (also called specialty acts) are added. Favorite central themes are magic/illusion—four such shows are currently running—and a "best of Broadway" theme, which figures prominently in five current shows. Making inroads is a Nashville/country music theme, which forms the basis for three current productions.

In the most common format, the show will open with an elaborate production number featuring dancers or ice skaters and, often, topless showgirls. As the presentation continues, variety acts alternate with either magic or musical numbers, depending on the theme. Variety acts frequently integrated into production shows include stand-up comics, jugglers, acrobats, balancing artists, ventriloquists, martial arts specialists, bola-swinging gauchos, and even archers. Even if magic is not the central theme of the show, a magician or illusionist is usually included among the variety acts. As a rule, the show closes with a spectacular finale showcasing the entire cast in some unimaginably colossal set, augmented by an impressive array of costuming, lighting, and special effects. Special effects figure prominently in Las Vegas production shows, and even more prominently in advertisements for Las Vegas production shows. Special effects are defined as "better than regular effects." Nobody knows what regular effects are.

Las Vegas puts its own distinctive imprint on all this entertainment, imparting a great deal of homogeneity and redundancy to the mix of productions. The quality of Las Vegas entertainment is quite high, even excellent, but most production shows seem to operate according to a formula that fosters a numbing sameness. Particularly pronounced in the magic/illusion shows and the Broadway-style musical productions, this sameness discourages sampling more than one show from each genre. While it is not totally accurate to say that "if you've seen one Las Vegas production or magic show, you've seen them all," the statement comes closer to the truth than one would hope.

In the magic/illusion shows, the current rage is to put unlikely creatures or objects into boxes and make them disappear. Some featured magicians repeat this sort of illusion more than a dozen times in a single performance, with nothing really changing except the size of the box and the object placed into it. Into these boxes go doves, ducks, turkeys, parrots, dwarfs, showgirls, lions, tigers, sheep dogs, jaguars, panthers, motorcycles (with riders), TV cameras (with cameramen), and even elephants. Sometimes the illusionist himself gets into a box and disappears, reappearing moments later in the audience. Generally the elephants and other animals never reappear. These box illusions are amazing the first time or two, but become less compelling after that. After they had seen all of the illusion shows in Las Vegas, our reviewers commented that they had witnessed the disappearance in a box of everything except Jerry Falwell. Food for thought.

The Broadway-style musical productions likewise lack differentiation, tending to merge after more than one sample into a great blur of bouncing bare breasts and fanciful, feathery costumes. It should be reiterated, however, that like the magic productions, most of the musicals are well done and extremely worthwhile. But like the magic productions, the musicals offer only slight variations of the same theme.

While they share a common format, production shows, regardless of theme, can be differentiated by the size of the cast and by the elaborateness of the production. Other discriminating factors include the creativity of the choreography, the attractiveness of the performers, the pace and continuity of the presentation, and its ability to build to a crescendo. Strength in these last-mentioned areas sometimes allows a relatively simple, lower-budget show such as *Country Tonite* (Aladdin) to provide a more satisfying evening of entertainment than a lavish, long-running spectacular like *Splash* (Riviera).

Impersonator Shows   These are usually long-running production shows, complete with dancers, which feature the impersonation of celebrities both living (Joan Rivers, Cher, Neil Diamond, Tina Turner, Madonna) and deceased (Marilyn Monroe, Elvis, Liberace, the Blues Brothers). In shows such as the Imperial Palace's *Legends in Concert*, the emphasis is on the detail and exactness of the impersonation. In general, men impersonate male stars and women impersonate female stars (as you might expect). *La Cage* at the Riviera, however, features males impersonating female celebrities.

Comedy Clubs   Stand-up comedy has long been a tradition in Las Vegas entertainment. With the success of comedy clubs around the country and the comedy club format on network and cable television, stand-up comedy in Las Vegas was elevated from lounges and production shows to its own specialized venue. Las Vegas comedy clubs are small- to medium-sized showrooms featuring anywhere from two to five comedians per show. As a rule, the shows change completely each week, with a new group of comics rotating in. Each showroom has its own source of talent, so there is no swapping of comics from club to club. Comedy clubs are one of the few Las Vegas entertainments that draw equally from both the tourist and local populations. While most production shows and many celebrity headliner shows are packaged for the over-40 market, comedy clubs represent a concession to youth. Most of the comics are young, and the humor is often raw and scatological, and almost always irreverent.

Lounge Entertainment   Many casinos offer exceptional entertainment at all hours of the day and night in their lounges. For the most part, the lounges feature musical groups. On a given day almost any type of music, from oldies rock to country to jazz to folk, can be found in Las Vegas lounges. Unlike the production and headliner showrooms and comedy clubs, no reservations are required to take advantage of lounge entertainment. If you like what you hear, just walk in. Sometimes there is a two-drink minimum for sitting in the lounge during a show, but just as often there are no restrictions at all. It is unlikely that you will be familiar with the lounge entertainers by name, but you can trust that they will be highly talented and very enjoyable. To find the type of music you prefer, consult one of the local visitor guides available free from the front desk or concierge at your hotel.

   Lounge entertainment is a great barometer of a particular casino's marketing program; bands are specifically chosen to attract a certain type of customer. In general, if you find a casino with lounge entertainment that suits your tastes, you will probably be comfortable lodging, dining, and gambling there also.

They Come and They Go

   Las Vegas shows come and go all the time. Sometimes a particular production will close in one Las Vegas showroom and open weeks later in another. Some shows actually pack up and take their presentations to other cities, usually Reno/Lake Tahoe or Atlantic City. Other shows, of course, close permanently. During the past couple of years, we have seen the following productions disappear from the Las Vegas scene:

Copacabana (Rio)	*Cabaret Circus* (Lady Luck)
Melinda (Lady Luck)	*Wild Things* (Dunes)
Luck Is a Lady (Lady Luck)	*Bare Essence* (Sands)
Nudes on Ice (Plaza)	*Swing, Swing, Swing* (Sands)
Lido de Paris (Stardust)	*Hanky Panky* (San Remo)
Showstopper (Desert Inn)	*Brazilia* (Rio)
Thriller (Aladdin)	*Marty Allen & Steve*
Tropical Heat (Rio)	*Rossi* (Vegas World)
Abracadabra (Aladdin)	*Forbidden Vegas* (Plaza)
Alakazaam (Aladdin)	*Hot Stuff* (Sands)
Playboy's Girls of Rock &	*Winds of the Gods* (Luxor)
Roll (Maxim)	*City Lites* (Flamingo)
Comedy Cabaret (Maxim)	*Nashville USA* (Boomtown)
Fire & Ice (Hacienda)	*Outrageous* (San Remo)
Keep Smilin' America (Holiday)	*Hell on Heels* (Maxim)
Rodney's Place (El Rancho)	

In the same period, *Spellbound* moved from Harrah's Lake Tahoe to Harrah's Las Vegas. *Boy-lesque* moved from the Sahara to the Stardust, then to the Plaza, back to the Sahara, and then to Debbie Reynolds' showroom. Melinda, of *Melinda & Her Follies Revue*, has bounced from the Landmark to the Sands, to the Sahara, back to the Sands, back again to the Sahara, to the Lady Luck, and then disappeared off the radar screen. The bottom line: it's hard to keep up with all this coming and going. Do not be surprised if some of the shows reviewed in this guide have bitten the dust before you arrive. Also do not be surprised if the enduring shows have changed.

Learn Who Is Playing before Leaving Home

The Las Vegas Convention and Visitors Authority publishes an entertainment calendar for all showrooms and many lounges. The brochure *Showguide,* organized alphabetically according to host hotel, tells who is playing, provides appearance dates, and lists information and reservation numbers. The *Showguide* can be obtained without charge by writing or calling:

Las Vegas Convention and Visitors Authority
Visitor Information Center
3150 Paradise Road
Las Vegas, NV 89109-9096
(702) 892-7576

Show Prices and Taxes

Admission prices for Las Vegas shows range from around $7 all the way up to $90 or more per person. If you go to a dinner show, dinner is extra. Usually show prices are quoted exclusive of entertainment and sales taxes. Also not included are server gratuities.

As recently as 1990, there was no such thing as a reserved seat at a Las Vegas show. If you wanted to see a show, you would make a reservation (usually by phone) and then arrive well in advance to be assigned a seat by the showroom maitre d'. Slipping the maitre d' a nice tip ensured a better seat. Typically, the price of the show included two drinks, and you would pay at your table after you were served. While this arrangement is still practiced in some showrooms, the prevailing trend is toward reserved seating. With reserved seating, you purchase your tickets at the casino box office (or by phone in advance with your credit card). As at a concert or a Broadway play, your seats are designated and pre-assigned at the time of purchase, and your section, aisle, and seat number will be printed on your ticket. When you arrive at the showroom, an usher will guide you to your assigned seat. Reserved seating, also known as "hard" or "box office" seating, sometimes includes drinks and sometimes does not.

A common package (once *the* most common package) is the cocktail show, where your admission usually includes the show and one or two drinks. If the quoted admission price for the cocktail show is $20 per person, your actual cost will be approximately as follows:

Cocktail show admission	$20.00
Entertainment and sales tax (17%)	3.40
Total (before gratuities)	$23.40

If there are two performances per night, the early show is often (but not always) more expensive than the late show. In addition, some shows add a "surcharge" on Saturdays and holidays. If you tip your server a couple of bucks and slip the maitre d' or captain some currency for a good seat (in a showroom without reserved seating), you can easily end up paying $27 or more for a $20 list-price show and $63 or more for a $50 list-price show.

Showrooms, like other Las Vegas hotel and casino operations, sometimes offer special deals. Sometimes free or discounted shows are offered with lodging packages. Likewise, coupons from complimentary local tourist magazines or casino funbooks (see page 257) provide discounts or "two for one" options. Since these specials come and go, your best bet is to inquire about currently operating deals and discounts when you call for show reservations. If you plan to lodge at a casino where there is a show you want to see, ask about room/show combination specials when you make your room reservations. When you arrive in Las Vegas, pick up copies of the many visitor magazines distributed in rental car agencies and at hotels. Scour the show ads for discount coupons.

■ How to Make Reservations for Las Vegas Shows ■

Almost all showrooms take phone reservations. The process is simple and straightforward. Either call, using the reservation numbers listed in this book, or have your hotel concierge call. Most shows will accept reservations at least one day, and often several days or even weeks, in advance.

Some shows, when you call for reservations, will take only your name and the number of people in your party. Under this arrangement, you will either pay at the box office on the day of the show or, alternatively, pay in the showroom after you are seated.

An increasing number of shows will allow you to prepurchase your admission on the phone using a credit card. If you prepay, you will have to pick up your tickets at the box office before the show.

The box office at the Mirage is the only Las Vegas box office that does not accept phone reservations (except for Mirage hotel guests).

Hotel Lobby Ticket Sales

For some reason many people do not trust the phone reservation system, though it works perfectly well. These folks often purchase show tickets at booths operated by independent tour brokers in the hotel lobbies, paying substantial booking and gratuity surcharges for the privilege of having a ticket. Upon arriving at the showroom they discover that the ticket does not guarantee a reserved seat. In fact, they learn that it offers nothing except a mechanism for prepayment (sometimes at an inflated price). Further, at several showrooms, the ticket purchased earlier must be exchanged for one of the showroom's own tickets, thus necessitating another wait in line. Finally, not all shows are available through the brokers.

In some casinos there are both independent operators selling tickets to shows all over town and (in another location in the same casino) a reservations and ticket booth for the shows that are playing at that specific casino. The official reservations/ticket booth will usually only sell tickets or make reservations for the casino's own shows and, unlike the independent operator, will not tack on any extra charges.

When you pay your admission before entering the showroom, be sure to ask whether drinks and gratuities are included.

Trying to See a Show without a Reservation or Ticket

On Sunday through Thursday, you have a fair shot at getting into most Las Vegas shows just by asking the maitre d' to seat you or by purchasing a ticket at the box office if reserved seats are sold.

On most Fridays and Saturdays, however, it is a different story. If you decide on the spur of the moment that you would like to see the show at the casino where you have been dining or gambling, do not wait in line at the entrance to the showroom to make your inquiry. Instead, go directly to the maitre d' or to one of the other show personnel at the entrance and ask if they have room for your party. In some instances you may be asked to join the end of the guest line or stand by while they check for no-shows or cancellations. An amazing percentage of the time you will be admitted. Superstar celebrity headliner shows and performances of *Siegfried & Roy, Cirque du Soleil's Mystere, Legends in Concert, EFX!,* and *King Arthur's Tournament* are generally the most difficult shows to see on an impromptu basis.

■ Dinner Shows vs. Cocktail Shows ■

For some early shows (7–8 p.m. show times) you will be able to choose between a cocktail show and a dinner show. Usually the show itself will begin at 7:45 or 8 p.m. If you decide to go for dinner, you will be expected to arrive for seating by 6 p.m. This early seating allows you to be fed and the table cleared before show time. If you elect to forgo dinner, your admission will usually include two drinks. For this less expensive cocktail show you will normally be required to arrive for seating an hour before show time. If you go the cocktail route at a show that serves dinner, be advised that the diners (who arrive about an hour earlier) often will be given the better seats. Shows that are scheduled for 9 p.m. or later are exclusively cocktail shows.

Some dinner shows represent good deals, others less so. At the Flamingo, for example, the additional cost of a chicken dinner over the

Typical Dinner Show Menu (prices may vary)

Flamingo Hilton—*The Great Radio City Music Hall Spectacular*
(prices are rounded and include tax and gratuities)

Cocktail show	$38–46
Dinner show with coq au vin	$46–54
Dinner show with salmon	$50–63
Dinner show with prime rib	$52–64
Dinner show with New York steak	$54–64

price of just the show with cocktails is only about $10. Be aware, however, that with all dinner shows, your drinks (if you have any) will be extra, and invariably expensive.

Food quality at dinner shows varies. In general it can be characterized as acceptable, but certainly not exceptional. What you are buying is limited-menu banquet service for 300–500 people. Whenever a hotel kitchen tries to feed that many people at once, it is at some cost in terms of the quality of the meal and the service.

King Arthur's Tournament at the Excalibur does not provide the cocktail option. At *King Arthur's* all shows automatically include dinner of Cornish hen with soup, potatoes, vegetable, dessert, and choice of nonalcoholic beverage at $30 per person, taxes and gratuities included. Likewise, *Caesars Magical Empire*, a fixed-price dinner attraction at Caesars Palace, does not offer a cocktail option. Both *King Arthur's Tournament* and *Caesars Magical Empire* are described in detail below.

Luau dinner shows have become popular in Las Vegas over the past couple of years. For the most part, the shows include a buffet dinner followed by Polynesian music and dancing. Discount coupons from local visitor magazines make luaus the bargain of the dinner show circuit.

The Riviera, Aladdin, Maxim, Tropicana, Stardust, and occasionally others offer show and dinner combos where you get dinner and a show for a special price, but where dinner is served in one of the casinos' restaurants instead of in the showrooms. The restaurants provide only coffee-shop ambiance, but the food is palatable and a good deal for the money. At the Maxim, the Riviera, and the Tropicana, the included meal is a buffet. At each casino you can eat either before or after the early show.

Early vs. Late Shows

If you attend a late show you will have time for a leisurely dinner prior to the performance. For those who prefer to eat late, the early show followed by dinner works best. Both shows are identical except that often the early show is covered and the late show is topless. On weekdays, late shows are usually more lightly attended. On weekends, particularly at the most popular shows, the opposite is often the case.

■ Practical Matters ■

What to Wear to the Show

While it is by no means required, guests tend to dress up a bit when they go to a show. For a performance in the main showrooms at Bally's, Caesars Palace, the Las Vegas or Flamingo Hiltons, the Desert Inn, the Tropicana, or the Mirage, gentlemen will feel more comfortable in a sport coat, with or without a necktie. At the Las Vegas Hilton and Bally's, where there is a lot of convention traffic, men would not be overdressed in a suit. Women generally wear suits, dresses, skirt and blouse/sweater combinations, and even semiformal attire.

Showrooms at the Luxor, the Stratosphere, Monte Carlo, New York–New York, Treasure Island, the MGM Grand, Harrah's, the Rio, the Maxim, the Riviera, the Sahara, and the Stardust are a bit less dressy (a sport coat is fine, but slacks and a sweater or a sport shirt are equally acceptable for men), while showrooms at the Aladdin, the Excalibur, the Imperial Palace, the Golden Nugget, and the Hard Rock are the least formal of all (come as you are). All of the comedy clubs are informal, though you would not feel out of place in a sport coat or, for women, a dress.

Getting to and from the Show

When you make your reservations, always ask what time you need to arrive for seating, and whether you should proceed directly to the showroom or stop first at the box office. Usually, if the show is a dinner show, you will need to arrive two hours before show time. This allows dinner to be served and the tables cleared before the show begins. If the show is a cocktail show (all late shows and most early shows), you are normally asked to arrive one hour before the curtain rises. If you are driving to another hotel for a show and do not wish to avail yourself of valet parking, be forewarned that many casinos' self-parking lots are quite distant from the showroom. Give yourself an extra ten minutes to park, walk to the casino, and find the showroom. If you decide to use valet parking, be advised that the valet service may be swamped immediately following the show.

Showrooms Where Self-Parking Is Easy and Convenient		
Hard Rock	San Remo	Debbie Reynolds
Holiday Inn	Desert Inn	Hollywood Hotel
Boardwalk	Orleans	Stratosphere

A show with a large seating capacity in one of the major casinos can make for some no-win situations when it comes to parking. At the Excalibur, the Luxor, the MGM Grand, and the Las Vegas Hilton, self-parking is either way off in the boonies or in a dizzying multistory garage, so your inclinations may be to use valet parking. After the show, however, 1,000 to 1,650 patrons head for home, inundating the valets, particularly after a late show. The problem is compounded for stadium events or for special concerts held in the Las Vegas Hilton's 9,000-seat Hilton Center. If you encounter these situations, your best bet is to use self-parking and give yourself some extra time, or use valet parking and plan to stick around the casino for a while after the show.

Invited Guests and Line Passes

Having arrived at the casino and found the showroom, you will normally join other show-goers waiting to be seated. If the showroom assigns reserved seats, the process is simple: just show your tickets to an usher and you will be directed to your seats. At showrooms without reserved seating, you will normally encounter two lines. One line, usually quite long, is where you will queue up unless you are an "Invited Guest." There is a separate line for these privileged folks which allows them to be seated without waiting in line or coming an hour early. Most invited guests are gamblers who are staying at that casino. Some have been provided with "comps" (complimentary admission) to the show. These are usually regular casino customers or high rollers. If you are giving the casino a lot of action, do not be shy about requesting a comp to the show.

Gamblers or casino hotel guests of more modest means are frequently given line passes. These guests pay the same price as anyone else for the show but are admitted without waiting via the Invited Guest line. To obtain a line pass, approach a floorman or pit boss (casino supervisory personnel are usually distinguished from dealers by their suits and ties) and explain that you have been doing a fair amount of gambling in their casino. Tell him or her that you have reservations for that evening's show and ask if you can have a line pass. Particularly if you ask on Sunday through Thursday, your chances of being accommodated are good.

If you are an invited guest under any circumstances, always arrive to be seated at least 30 minutes early.

Reservations, Tickets, and Maitre d' Seating

If, like most guests, you do not have a line pass, you will have to go through the process of entering the showroom and being seated. Many showrooms practice what is known as maitre d' seating. This means that, except in the case of certain invited guests, no seats are reserved. If you called previously and made a reservation, that will have been duly noted and the showroom will have your party listed on the reservations roster, but you will not actually be assigned a seat until you appear before the maitre d'. At some showrooms with maitre d' seating, you are asked to pay your waiter for everything (show, taxes, drinks, etc.) once you have been seated and served.

At the comedy clubs and an increasing number of major showrooms you will be directed to a booth variously labeled "Tickets," "Reservations," "Box Office," or "Guest Services." The attendant will verify your reservation and ask you to go ahead and pay. Once paid, you will receive a ticket to show the maitre d' on entering the showroom. This arrangement eliminates any requirement for paying the tab at your table (unless drinks are not included), thus simplifying service once you are seated. The ticket does not reserve you any specific seat; you still need to see the maitre d' about that. Also, the ticket does not include gratuities for your server in the showroom unless specifically stated.

As discussed earlier, a growing number of showrooms have discarded maitre d' seating in favor of "box office" or "hard" seating. At the Mirage, the MGM Grand, the Luxor, Treasure Island, Monte Carlo, the Excalibur, the Stardust, Bally's, the Las Vegas Hilton, and Caesars Palace, specific reserved-seat assignments are designated on each ticket sold, as at a football game or on Broadway.

Most showrooms that issue hard (reserved-seat) tickets will allow you to charge your tickets over the phone using your credit card. If you charge your tickets over the phone, however, the quality of your seat assignments is at the mercy of the box office. On the other hand, if you take the trouble to buy your tickets in person at the hotel box office, you can review the seating chart and pick your seats from all seats available.

Where to Sit

When it comes to show seating, there are two primary considerations: visibility and comfort. The best accommodations in most showrooms are the plush, roomy booths, which provide an unencumbered view of the

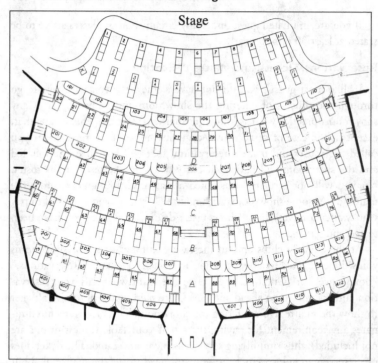

A good example of the alternating configuration of tables and booths
found in most Las Vegas showrooms.

show. The vast majority of seats in many showrooms, however, and all in
some, will be at banquet tables—a euphemism for very long, narrow tables
where a dozen or more guests are squeezed together so tightly they can
hardly move. When the show starts, guests seated at the banquet tables
must turn their chairs around in order to see. This requires no small degree
of timing and cooperation, since every person on the same side of the table
must move in unison.

Showrooms generally will have banquet table seating right in front of
the stage. Next, on a tier that rises a step or two, will be a row of plush
booths. These booths are often reserved for the casino's best customers
(and sometimes for big tippers). Many maitre d's would rather see these
booths go unoccupied than have high rollers come to the door at the last
minute and not be able to give them good seats. Behind the booths but on
the same level will be more banquet tables. Moving away from the stage
and up additional levels, the configuration of booths and banquet tables is
repeated on each tier.

For a big production show on a wide stage like *Jubilee!, Siegfried & Roy,* the *Folies Bergere, EFX!,* or *Enter the Night,* you want to sit in the middle and back a little. Being too close makes it difficult to see everything without wagging your head back and forth as if you were at a tennis match. Likewise, at a concert by a band or musical celebrity headliner (Tom Jones, Al Jarreau, Pointer Sisters, etc.), partway back and in the center is best. This positioning provides good visibility and removes you from the direct line of fire of amplifiers and lights. This advice, of course, does not apply to avid fans who want to fling their underwear or room keys at the star.

For smaller production shows on medium-sized stages (*Country Tonite, Lance Burton, Legends in Concert,* etc.), right up front is great. This is also true for headliners like Bill Cosby, Jerry Seinfeld, and David Copperfield. For female impersonators (*La Cage,* etc.), the illusion is more effective if you are back a little bit.

At comedy clubs and smaller shows, there are really no bad seats, though the *Comedy Stop* at the Tropicana has some columns in the showroom you want to avoid. Finally, be aware that comedians often single out guests sitting down front for harassment, or worse, incorporate them into the act.

Getting a Good Seat at Showrooms with Maitre d' Seating

1. Arrive early No maitre d' can assign you a seat that's already taken. This is particularly important for Friday and Saturday shows. We have seen comped invited guests (the casino's better customers) get lousy seats because they waited until the last minute to show up.

2. Try to go on an off night, i.e., Sunday through Thursday Your chances of getting a good seat are always better on weeknights when there is less demand. If a citywide convention is in town, weekdays may also be crowded.

3. Try to know where (as precisely as possible) you would like to sit In showrooms with maitre d' seating, it is always to your advantage to specifically state your seating preferences.

4. Understand your tipping alternatives Basically, you have three options:

- Don't tip

- Tip the maitre d'

- Tip the captain (instead of the maitre d')

Don't tip   Politely request a good seat instead of tipping. This option actually works better than you would imagine in all but a few showrooms, particularly Sunday through Thursday. If the showroom is not sold out and you arrive early, simply request a seat in a certain area. Tell the maitre d', "We would like something down front in the center." Then allow the captain (the showroom staff person who actually takes you to your seat) to show you the seats the maitre d' has assigned. If the assigned seat is not to your liking, ask to be seated somewhere else of your choosing. The captain almost always has the authority to make the seat assignment change without consulting the maitre d'.

On slower nights, the maitre d' will often "dress the showroom." This means that the maitre d', not expecting a full house, will distribute patrons pretty equally throughout the showroom, especially nearer the stage. This procedure, which makes the audience look larger than it really is, is done for the morale of the performers and for various practical reasons, such as ensuring a near-equal number of guests at each server station. On these nights, you have a pretty good shot at getting the seats you want simply by asking.

Tip the maitre d'   When you tip the maitre d' it is helpful to know who you are dealing with. First, the maitre d' is the man or woman in charge of the showroom. The showrooms are their domain, and they rule as surely as battalion commanders. Maitre d's in the better showrooms are powerful and wealthy people, with some maitre d's taking in as much as $1,650 a night. Even though these tips are pooled and shared in some proportion with the captains, it's still a lot of money.

When you tip a maitre d', especially in the better showrooms, you can assume it will take a fairly hefty tip to impress him, especially on a busy night. The bottom line, however, is that you are not out to impress anyone; you just want a good seat. Somebody has to sit in the good seats, and those who do not tip, or tip small, have to be seated regardless. So, if you arrive early and tip $15–20 (for a couple) in the major showrooms, and $5–10 in the smaller rooms, you should get decent seats. If it is a weekend or you know the show is extremely popular or sold out, bump the tip up a little. If you arrive late on a busy night, ask the maitre d' if there are any good seats left before you proffer the tip.

Have your tip in hand when you reach the maitre d'. Don't fool around with your wallet or purse as if you are buying hotdogs at the ball park. Fold the money and hold it in the palm of your hand, arranged so that the maitre d' can see exactly how big the tip is without unfolding and counting the bills. State your preference for seating at the same time you inconspicuously place the bills in the palm of his hand. If you think all this protocol is pretty ridiculous, I agree. But style counts, and observing the local customs may help get you a better seat.

A variation is to tip with some appropriate denomination of the casino's own chips. Chips are as good as currency to the maitre d' and implicitly suggest that you have been gambling with that denomination of chips in his casino. This single gesture, which costs you nothing more than your cash tip, makes you an insider and a more valued customer in the eyes of the maitre d'.

Many maitre d's are warm and friendly and treat you in a way that shows they appreciate your business. These maitre d's are approachable and reasonable and will go out of their way to make you comfortable. There are also a number of maitre d's and captains, unfortunately, who are extremely cold, formal, and arrogant. Mostly older men dressed in tuxedoes, they usually have gray hair and a military bearing and can seem rather imposing or hostile. Do not be awed or intimidated. Be forthright and, if necessary, assertive; you will usually be accommodated.

Tip the captain   Using this strategy, tell the maitre d' where you would like to sit but do not offer a tip. Then follow the captain to your assigned seats. If your seats are good, you have not spent an extra nickel. If the assigned seats are less than satisfactory, slip the captain a tip and ask if there might be something better. If you see seats you would like to have that are unoccupied, point them out to the captain. Remember, however, that the first row of booths is usually held in reserve.

Before the Show Begins

For years, the admission price to cocktail shows has included two drinks. Recently, however, this policy has been subject to experimentation, resulting in a confusing and constantly changing variety of drink inclusions and exclusions. While many showrooms continue to offer two drinks with admission, others have gone to either one drink or no drinks included.

The inclusion of drinks is not what makes Las Vegas shows a good entertainment value, but the absence of any standard practice in this regard certainly creates enough ill will and confusion to bias the customer's perception of value. From a consumer perspective, a package that includes drinks is straightforward, understandable, and a lot easier to administer in the showroom.

Some of the variations you will encounter are as follows: At the Sahara, there will be a cash bar and no table service; if you want a drink before the show, you walk to the bar and buy it. At *La Cage,* the *Comedy Club,* and *Crazy Girls* at the Riviera, and the *Comedy Stop* at the Tropicana, drinks are included but there is no table service. You take a receipt stub to the bar and exchange it for drinks.

In most other showrooms there is table service where you can obtain drinks from a server. If drinks are included, some slip of paper, a receipt stub, or other type of documentation will be deposited at your place by the captain when you are seated. This scrap of paper will alert your server that you have some drinks coming. When the server takes your order or, alternatively, when the drinks are delivered, he or she will remove the paper. If drinks are not included, there will usually be a small table sign or drink menu with prices listed.

In showrooms where there is table service, the servers run around like crazy trying to get everybody served before the show. Since all of the people at a given table are not necessarily seated at the same time, the server responsible for that table may make five or more passes before everyone is taken care of. If your party is one of the last to be seated at a table, stay cool. You *will* be noticed and you *will* be served.

Servers in showrooms are generally well organized and have their own way of getting things done. You can depend on your waiter or waitress to advise you when it is time to settle your tab. Until then, just relax. Do not try to offer the server a gratuity until the final bill is brought. Normally your server will collect for any drinks not included (and for your show admission in some showrooms with maitre d' seating) just before the performance begins. On busy nights in large showrooms, the tab might not be presented until after the curtain has gone up. Most showrooms accept major credit cards and traveler's checks in addition to cash.

If you have prepaid for admission and drinks, your gratuity may have been included in your prepayment. If drinks and admission are prepaid, but not the gratuity, you should tip the server when your drinks are delivered (a dollar or two per person served is about right). If you are not sure whether drinks, gratuities, or anything else is included, ask.

Bladder Matters   Be forewarned that in most showrooms there is no rest room, and that the nearest rest room is invariably a long way off, reachable only via a convoluted trail through the casino. Since the majority of show-goers arrive early and consume drinks, it is not uncommon to start feeling a little pressure on the bladder minutes before show time. If you assume that you can slip out to the rest room and come right back, think again. If you are at the Las Vegas Hilton, Caesars, or the Tropicana, give yourself more than ten minutes for the round trip, and prepare for a quest. If you get to the can and back without getting lost, consider yourself lucky.

At most other showrooms, rest rooms are somewhat closer but certainly not convenient. The Riviera, the Imperial Palace, Harrah's, the MGM Grand, Stratosphere, and the Mirage, however, seem to have considered that show guests may not wish to combine emptying their bladders with a five-mile hike. Showrooms in these casinos are situated in close and much-appreciated proximity to the rest rooms.

Selecting a Show

Selecting a Las Vegas show is a matter of timing, budget, taste, and schedule. Celebrity headliners are booked long in advance but may play only for a couple of days or weeks. If seeing Tom Jones, Cher, or Frank Sinatra in concert is a big priority for your Las Vegas trip, you will have to schedule your visit to coincide with their appearances. If the timing of your visit is not flexible, as in the case of conventioneers, you will be relegated to picking from those stars playing when you are in town. To find out which shows and headliners are playing before you leave home, call the Las Vegas Convention and Visitors Authority at (702) 892-7576 and ask them to mail you a Las Vegas *Showguide*.

Older visitors are often more affluent than younger visitors. It is no accident that most celebrity headliners are chosen, and most production shows created, to appeal to the 40-year-old-and-over crowd. If we say a Las Vegas production show is designed for a mature audience, we mean that the theme, music, variety acts, and humor appeal primarily to older guests. Most Las Vegas production shows target patrons 40–50 years old and up, while a few appeal to audiences 55 years of age and older.

As the post–World War II baby boomers have moved into middle age and comparative affluence, they have become a primary market for Las Vegas. Stars from the "golden days" of rock and roll, as well as folk singers from the '60s, are turning up in the main showrooms of the Hard Rock, Desert Inn, and Bally's with great regularity. Not too long ago, Paul Revere and the Raiders, the Four Seasons, the Mamas and the Papas, the Temptations, the Four Tops, B. J. Thomas, and Arlo Guthrie were playing in different showrooms on the same night.

If you are younger than 35 you will still enjoy the Las Vegas production shows, though for you their cultural orientation (and usually their music) will seem a generation or two removed. Several production shows, however, have broken the mold, in the process achieving a more youthful presentation while maintaining the loyalty of older patrons. *Splash II* (Riviera) is a youthful, high-energy show—intensity, action, and volume personified. *Cirque du Soleil* (Treasure Island) is an uproarious yet poignant odyssey in the European tradition, brimming over with unforgettable characters. *Spellbound* (Harrah's), *Lance Burton* (Monte Carlo), and *Country*

Tonite (Aladdin) are smaller productions but are extremely creative and work well for all ages. And, again, the comedy clubs have a more youthful orientation.

■ Las Vegas Shows for the Under-21 Crowd ■

An ever-increasing number of showrooms offer productions appropriate for younger viewers. Circus Circus provides complimentary, high-quality circus acts about once every half hour, and *King Arthur's Tournament* at the Excalibur is a family dinner show featuring jousting and other benign medieval entertainments. Other family candidates include *Country Tonite,* a rollicking music show at the Aladdin; *Legends in Concert,* a celebrity impersonation show at the Imperial Palace; the magic-illusion shows *Siegfried & Roy* at the Mirage, *Spellbound* at Harrah's, and *Lance Burton* at the Monte Carlo; the *Cirque du Soleil's Mystere* at Treasure Island; the hard-hitting roller-skating musical *Starlight Express* at the Las Vegas Hilton; and *EFX!* at the MGM Grand.

Many of the celebrity headliner shows are fine for children, and a few of the production shows offer a covered early show to accommodate families. Of the topless production shows, some operate on the basis of parental discretion while others do not admit anyone under 21. Comedy clubs and comedy theater usually will admit teenage children accompanied by an adult. All continuously running shows are profiled later in this section. The profile of each show will tell you whether the show is topless or particularly racy. If you have a question about a given showroom's policy for those under 21, call the showroom's reservation and information number listed in the profile.

The Best Shows in Town:
Celebrity Headliners

Choosing which celebrity headliner to see is a matter of personal taste, though stars like Wayne Newton and Engelbert Humperdink seem to have the ability to rev up any audience. We talked to people who, under duress, were essentially dragged along by a friend or family member to see Wayne Newton. Many of these folks walked into the showroom prepared to hate Wayne Newton. Yet despite their negative attitude, Newton delighted and amazed them.

My point is not to hype Wayne Newton but to suggest that the talent, presence, drive, and showmanship of many Las Vegas headliners often exceed all expectations, and that adhering to the limitations of your preferences may prevent you from seeing many truly extraordinary performers. Las Vegas is about gambling, after all. Do not be reluctant to take a chance on a headliner who is not readily familiar to you.

Most of the major headliners play at a relatively small number of showrooms. A profile of the major celebrity showrooms and their regular headliners follows. The list is not intended to be all-inclusive but rather to give you an idea of where to call if you are interested in a certain headliner. Remember to check the "dark" entry to see when the showroom is closed.

Aladdin Theater for the Performing Arts

Reservations and Information: 736-0240

Frequent Headliners: The Theater for the Performing Arts features celebrity headliners, short-run production shows, and concerts.

Usual Show Times: Varies with show and performer

Approximate Admission Price: $9–150

Drinks Included: None

Showroom Size: 7,000 persons   *Smoking Allowed:* No

Description and Comments   An enormous concert hall with seats arranged in a crescent configuration rising from the stage, the theater hosts special community events in addition to serving as a mega-showroom for the Aladdin. Most seats afford a good view of the stage.

Consumer Tips   For events at the theater, use the Aladdin's rear parking lot (accessible from Harmon Avenue and South Audrie Street). Support columns in the theater partially limit the view of patrons sitting in the last 30 or so rows. Advanced, reserved-seat tickets for performances at the theater can be purchased at the box office, located in the long hall connecting the theater to the casino. Tickets can also be purchased at all Ticketmaster outlets (474-4000).

Bally's Celebrity Room

Reservations and Information: 739-4567 or (800) 237-SHOW

Frequent Headliners: George Carlin, Andrew Dice Clay, Al Jarreau, Louis Anderson, Engelbert Humperdink, Barbara Mandrell, Anne Murray, Bernadette Peters, Liza Minnelli

Usual Show Times: 9 p.m.   *Dark:* Varies

Approximate Admission Price: $25–77

Drinks Included: None

Showroom Size: 1,450 persons   *Smoking Allowed:* No

Description and Comments   The Celebrity Room, one of Las Vegas's larger theaters, hosts a variety of big-name headliners. Show times vary with each performer, and the length of engagement for most headliners is short— usually from three to six days, but occasionally as long as two weeks.

Consumer Tips   For most Celebrity Room shows, simply make reservations by calling in advance and charging your reserved seats on your credit card. Most shows begin selling tickets six weeks in advance of show date. You may then pick up your tickets at Will-Call anytime after 5 p.m. and up to one hour before curtain time. You can also buy tickets in person at the hotel box office. Either way, you will be given a seat assignment. Booth seating is usually available if you call well in advance. Admission and taxes are included in the ticket price. The tab for drinks will be collected at the table. Children accompanied by an adult are usually admitted, but the policy varies according to the show. Be aware that Bally's is a big meeting and convention hotel, and shows at Bally's are almost as likely to sell out on a weekday as on a weekend.

Caesars Palace Circus Maximus Showroom

Reservations and Information: 731-7333 or (800) 445-4544

Frequent Headliners: Julio Iglesias, Jay Leno, David Copperfield, Reba McEntire, Johnny Mathis, Jerry Seinfeld, Natalie Cole, Ray Charles

Usual Show Times: Varies with performer   *Dark:* Varies

Approximate Admission Price: $55–75 plus a $2.50 surcharge
  per ticket

Drinks Included: None

Showroom Size: 1,200 persons   *Smoking Allowed:* No

Description and Comments   The Circus Maximus is a large showroom with four levels and generally excellent visibility, though some seats are somewhat distant from the stage. Banquet table seating is extremely crowded, with narrow tables and very little foot or elbowroom. Most headliners work Caesars for one- or two-week engagements, and appear several times each year.

Consumer Tips   Reserved seats can be purchased with a credit card at the box offices or over the phone throughout the year for any show scheduled that season. Ticket price includes admission and taxes. Box offices are open daily from 8 a.m. to 10 p.m. Phone purchases can be made between 8 a.m. and 10 p.m. All beverages in the showroom are extra and are paid for at the table. If you use Caesars's self-parking lot, give yourself about ten extra minutes for the long walk to the showroom. Be forewarned that the rest rooms closest to the showroom are a long way off and hard to find.

Debbie Reynolds Hollywood Hotel—Debbie's Star Theater

Reservations and Information: 733-2243 or (800) 633-1777

Frequent Headliners: Debbie Reynolds

Usual Show Times: 7:30 p.m.   *Dark:* Saturday and Sunday

Approximate Admission Price: $35, tax and tip included

Drinks Included: 2

Showroom Size: 500 persons   *Smoking Allowed:* No

Description and Comments   Debbie's Star Theater is modeled after the Crystal Room at the Desert Inn, and thus affords good acoustics and visibility as well as reasonable comfort. In addition to producing her own show, Debbie Reynolds hosts various headliners, most with a Hollywood connection, for short- to medium-run engagements.

Consumer Tips   Debbie's Star Theater is a medium-sized showroom that works well for headliners and musicians. Seats are assigned by the maitre d'. Reservations can be made by phone with your credit card one month in advance. Pick up tickets before the show at the box office. Price includes tax, gratuity, and two drinks. For most shows, children five and older accompanied by an adult are allowed.

Desert Inn Crystal Room

Reservations and Information: 733-4566
Frequent Headliners: Buddy Hackett and Gordon Lightfoot
Usual Show Times: 9 p.m.   *Dark:* Monday
Approximate Admission Price: $41–53, tax included
Drinks Included: None
Showroom Size: 636 persons   *Smoking Allowed:* No

Description and Comments   The Desert Inn is experimenting with some new entertainment concepts, alternating veteran Las Vegas performers with oldies rock stars, contemporary country stars, and short- to medium-run production shows.

Consumer Tips   The Crystal Room is a comfortable, medium-sized showroom, with an unusually low stage best suited to celebrity headliners and musical groups. Reservations can be made in advance by phone. Seats are assigned by the maitre d'. Payment for admission is collected tableside before the show. For most shows, children five and older accompanied by an adult are allowed.

Hard Rock Hotel—The Joint

Reservations and Information: 693-5066
Frequent Headliners: Top current and oldies rock stars
Usual Show Times: 8 p.m.
Approximate Admission Price: $35–125
Drinks Included: None
Showroom Size: 1,400 persons   *Smoking Allowed:* Yes

Description and Comments   Have you ever been to a major rock concert in a facility so large that you needed binoculars to see the band? And did you wish that just once you could enjoy that band in a smaller, more intimate setting? Hard Rock Hotel's The Joint is that setting, a medium-sized two-level venue for rock and roll concerts, hosting the likes of Bob Dylan, the Black Crowes, Melissa Etheridge, the Eagles, and Seal. True, seeing Bob Dylan in a 1,400-person showroom is not as cozy as having him in your living room, but it sure beats Yankee Stadium. Because most performers playing The Joint are booked for short, limited engagements, each show is a special event.

On the floor, the tightly packed audience sits on folding chairs and barstools around small tables; there are 1,000 of these reserved seats. The stage is high and the floor is on an incline, so visibility is good. Acoustics are excellent, especially in the middle of the floor and the front of the balcony.

Consumer Tips   When the reserved seats are sold out (or if someone *wants* to stand), 400 or so "standing-room" tickets are sold. These entitle patrons to a spot toward the back of the floor (by the bar), the back of the balcony, or in "the pit." Visibility from a standing-room position on the balcony is limited (except from the first few rows, which are reserved). And stageside at The Joint, be prepared for ear-splitting, head-pounding, bone-quaking acoustics, not to mention being hemmed in by the crowd. If you don't want to be put in balcony Siberia where you can hear well enough but see nothing, or pinned against the stage for the whole show by a crush of sweaty rowdies, don't buy standing-room tickets. Book early for reserved seating—or shrug and say, "Oh well."

The Hard Rock Hotel box office sells reserved seats to shows at The Joint. You can purchase tickets via phone using your credit card or in person at the box office. Shows at The Joint are hot tickets in Las Vegas and sell out quickly, so buy your tickets as far in advance as possible.

Las Vegas Hilton—Showroom

Before the four-year run of the *Starlight Express* production show, the Las Vegas Hilton operated one of the most prestigous celebrity headliner rooms in town. Frequent performers included Elvis, Bill Cosby, and Wayne Newton, among others. As we went to press the Hilton was considering a return to celebrity headliner entertainment. If the change is made, *Starlight Express* will likely continue until the end of 1997, after which time the showroom will be closed for a month or two while it is reconfigured for headliners.

MGM Grand—Garden Arena

Reservations and Information: 891-7777 or (800) 646-7787
Frequent Headliners: Barbra Streisand, The Rolling Stones, Elton John, Neil Diamond, Bette Midler, Billy Joel, Rod Stewart, Sting, Reba McEntire, and sports celebrities such as Mike Tyson, George Foreman, and Andre Agassi
Usual Show Times: Varies   *Dark:* Varies
Approximate Admission Price: Varies
Drinks Included: None
Showroom Size: 15,200   *Smoking Allowed:* No

Description and Comments   This 275,000-square-foot special events center is designed to accommodate everything from sporting events and concerts to major trade exhibitions. The venue also offers auxiliary meeting rooms and ballrooms adjacent to the entertainment center. Barbra Streisand christened this venue with her first concert in more than 20 years on New Year's Eve, 1993. Championship boxing events, such as George Foreman vs. Michael Moorer (heavyweight championship of the world) and Mike Tyson's return to boxing, are favorite attractions at the Grand Garden Arena, as are the many big-name musical concerts.

Consumer Tips   Reserved-seat tickets can be purchased one to two months in advance with your credit card by calling the MGM Grand main reservations number or Ticketmaster outlets (474-4000). If you are not staying at the MGM Grand, either arrive by cab or give yourself plenty of extra time to park and make your way to the arena.

MGM Grand—Hollywood Theater

Reservations and Information: 891-7777

Frequent Headliners: Frank Sinatra, Righteous Brothers,
  Liza Minnelli, Sheena Easton, Tom Jones, Don Rickles

Usual Show Times: Varies   *Dark:* Varies

Approximate Admission Price: Varies

Drinks Included: None

Showroom Size: 630 persons   *Smoking Allowed:* No

Description and Comments   A modern and comfortable showroom, with all front-facing seats, the Hollywood Theater hosts a wide range of musical and celebrity headliner productions for one- to three-week engagements.

Consumer Tips   Reserved-seat show tickets can be purchased one to two months in advance with your credit card by calling the MGM Grand's main reservations number. Children are allowed at most presentations. If you are not staying at the MGM Grand, either arrive by cab or give yourself plenty of extra time to park and make your way to the showroom.

Mirage—Theatre Mirage

Reservations and Information: 792-7777

Frequent Headliners: Siegfried and Roy, Bill Cosby, Kenny Rogers

Usual Show Times: Varies with performer, 7:30 and 11 p.m. for Siegfried
  and Roy

Dark: Wednesday and Thursday (for Siegfried and Roy)

Approximate Admission Price: $90

Drinks Included: 2 (taxes and gratuities also included)

Showroom Size: 1,500 persons   *Smoking Allowed:* No

Description and Comments   The *Siegfried & Roy* illusion and production show is featured at the Theatre Mirage the vast majority of the year. When Siegfried and Roy are off, other headliners are brought in for one- or two-week stands. The Theatre Mirage is one of the most modern showrooms in Las Vegas, with good visibility from every seat. All seats are reserved and preassigned.

Consumer Tips   Although it's assigned seating, no reservations are taken for any show in the Theatre Mirage. You must purchase tickets one to three days in advance of the performance at the Mirage box office. The only exception is for hotel guests at the Mirage, who are permitted to charge show tickets to their room. For more on obtaining tickets, see Consumer Tips under *Siegfried & Roy*.

Production Shows

■ Las Vegas Premier Production Shows: ■ Comparing Apples and Oranges

While we acknowledge that Las Vegas production shows are difficult to compare and that audiences of differing tastes and ages have different preferences, we have nevertheless ranked the continuously running shows to give you an idea of our favorites. This is definitely an apples-and-oranges comparison (how can you compare *Siegfried & Roy* to *An Evening at La Cage*?), but one based on each show's impact, vitality, originality, pace, continuity, crescendo, and ability to entertain.

We would hasten to add that even the continuously running shows change acts and revise their focus periodically. Expect our list, therefore, to change from year to year. Also, be comforted by the knowledge that while some shows are better than others, there aren't any real dogs. The quality of entertainment among the continuously running production shows is exceptional. By way of analogy, we could rank baseball players according to their performance in a given All-Star game, but the entire list, from top to bottom, would still be All-Stars. You get the idea.

Production Show Hit Parade

Here's how we rank the Las Vegas production shows. Excluded from the list are short-run engagements (i.e., comedy clubs, comedy theater, and celebrity headliners) and afternoon-only shows. In addition to ranking the shows, we also have assigned each show a Value Rating as follows:

A Exceptional value, a real bargain

B Good value

C Absolutely fair, you get exactly what you pay for

D Somewhat overpriced

F Significantly overpriced

Show prices increased again during 1997, resulting in fewer bargains than in previous years.

Production Show Hit Parade

Rank	Show	Location	Value Rating
1.	*Cirque du Soleil's Mystere*	Treasure Island	B
2.	*EFX!*	MGM Grand	C
3.	*Siegfried & Roy*	Mirage	F
4.	*Danny Gans*	Rio	B
5.	*Caesars Magical Empire*	Caesars Palace	B
6.	*Lance Burton*	Monte Carlo	C
7.	*Legends in Concert*	Imperial Palace	B
8.	*Country Fever*	Golden Nugget	A
9.	*Starlight Express*	Las Vegas Hilton	B
10.	*Forever Plaid*	Flamingo	A
11.	*Country Tonite*	Aladdin	A
12.	*Enter the Night*	Stardust	B
13.	*Jubilee!*	Bally's	C
14.	*The Great Radio City Music Hall Spectacular*	Flamingo	C
15.	*American Superstars*	Stratosphere	B
16.	*Debbie Reynolds*	Debbie Reynolds Hollywood Hotel	C
17.	*Folies Bergere*	Tropicana	C
18.	*Spellbound*	Harrah's	C
19.	*Splash II*	Riviera	D
20.	*King Arthur's Tournament*	Excalibur	A
21.	*La Cage/Kenny Kerr Show*	Riviera/Debbie Reynolds	B
22.	*Crazy Girls*	Riviera	D
23.	*MADhattan*	New York–New York	D

A Word about Small Showrooms

During the past couple of years, we have seen a number of casinos convert their lounge into a small showroom. Though the stage in these showrooms is routinely about the size of a beach towel, productions are mounted that include complex choreography, animal acts, and, in one notable case, an illusionist catching bullets in his teeth. In the case of musical revues, as many as four very thin or three average hula dancers can fit comfortably on the stage at one time. If the Mamas and the Papas performed in one of these showrooms, Mama Cass would have to join in from the hall.

A real problem with some smaller shows is that they often cost as much as productions in Las Vegas's major showrooms. We once reviewed *Hell on Heels* at the Maxim, for instance, and paid about $21 including tax and tip. Though *Hell on Heels* was a decent show and professionally performed, it could not compare in scope, talent, and spectacle to the lavish *Folies Bergere* at the Tropicana, available for only a few extra dollars.

Another problem is that small shows often play to even smaller crowds. We saw a performance of *That's Magic* at O'Sheas where the cast outnumbered the audience. Though the show featured talented illusionists, a good ventriloquist, and some dancers, the small facility made the production seem amateurish. It was heartrending to see professional entertainers work so hard for such a tiny audience. We felt self-conscious and uncomfortable ourselves, as well as embarrassed for the performers.

When it comes to smaller showrooms, simpler is better. That's why *Forever Plaid* and *Crazy Girls* work so well: both shows take a minimalist approach. Additionally, both shows play in casinos large enough to draw an audience. Little showrooms in smaller casinos that attempt to mount big productions create only parody and end up looking foolish. Better that they revert to offering lounge shows, like those at the Four Queens or Arizona Charlie's.

We have abandoned trying to cover the productions that play these small showrooms, mostly because the shows are very short-lived. If a small showroom production is exceptionally good and demonstrates staying power, however, we sometimes review it right along with the full-scale shows. In this edition, for example, we provide full reviews of *Crazy Girls* and *An Evening at La Cage* at the Riviera, and *Forever Plaid* at the Flamingo. Two other small room shows, not profiled but worthy of your attention, are *Showgirls of Magic* at the San Remo and *The Original Unknown Comic* at the Holiday Inn Boardwalk. Both shows are well produced, fast paced, and use the intimacy of a small showroom to their advantage. This discussion, by the way, does not apply to comedy clubs, which work best in small rooms.

■ Production Show Profiles ■

Following is a profile of each of the continuously running production shows, listed alphabetically by the name of the show. If you are not sure of the name of a show, consult the previous section. Comedy clubs and celebrity headliner showrooms are profiled in separate sections. Prices are approximate and fluctuate about as often as you brush your teeth.

American Superstars

Type of Show: Celebrity impersonator production show

Host Casino and Showroom: Stratosphere—Broadway Showroom

Reservations and Information: 382-4446 (reservations necessary)

Admission Cost with Taxes: $25.50

Cast Size: Approximately 24

Nights of Lowest Attendance: Sunday, Monday

Usual Show Times: 7 and 10 p.m.   *Dark:* Thursday

Special Comments: Much enhanced on the larger stage

Topless: No   *Smoking Allowed:* Yes

Author's Rating: ★★★½

Overall Appeal by Age Group:

Under 21	21–37	38–50	51 and older
★★★	★★★ ½	★★★★	★★★ ½

Duration of Presentation: An hour and 30 minutes

Description and Comments   *American Superstars* is a celebrity-impersonator show similar to *Legends in Concert* (Imperial Palace). Impersonated stars, which change from time to time, include Madonna, Michael Jackson, Gloria Estefan, and the ever-present Elvis. The impersonators, who do their own singing, are supported by a live band and (frequently upstaged) by an energetic troupe of dancers.

American Superstars is a fun, upbeat show. While the impersonations are, in general, not as crisp or realistic as those of *Legends in Concert,* the show exhibits a lot of drive and is a great night's entertainment.

Consumer Tips   *American Superstars* now plays in the Stratosphere's main showroom, a change of venue that has allowed the production to improve and become truly competitive with *Legends in Concert.* Though tickets must be purchased in advance, seat assignment is at the discretion of the maitre d'. Drinks are not included, but can be purchased at a bar outside the showroom. The showroom is situated at the end of the shopping arcade near the elevator bank for the Stratosphere Tower.

Caesars Magical Empire

Type of Show: Magic and illusion dinner show

Host Casino and Showroom: Caesars Palace—Caesars Magical Empire

Reservations and Information: 731-7333 or (800) 445-4544 (reservations necessary)

Admission Cost with Taxes: $75 adults; $37.50 children (ages 5–10)

Cast Size: Approximately 20
Nights of Lowest Attendance: Monday, Tuesday
Usual Show Times: Continuous daily from 4:30 p.m.
Special Comments: Best dinner show food in town
Topless: No   *Smoking Allowed:* No
Author's Rating: ★★★★
Overall Appeal by Age Group:

Under 21	21–37	38–50	51 and older
★★★★	★★★★	★★★★	★★★★

Duration of Presentation: About 3–3½ hours to eat and see everything

Description and Comments   The best dinner entertainment package in Las Vegas is Caesars Magical Empire at Caesars Palace. Unusual and unique, even by Las Vegas standards, Caesars Magical Empire is part restaurant, part attraction, and part stage show. Diners are first led down into a subterranean network of tunnels and chambers where a nicely prepared meal is served while a magician performs tableside. The dining chamber is mysterious and intimate, imparting a feeling of exclusivity totally absent at other dinner shows or dinner theaters. Diners choose from several main courses, all quite a cut above what you would expect at a dinner show. After the meal, diners join other guests in a vast underground rotunda where they can explore, relax, and sip a drink while awaiting the invitation to enter one of two adjacent theaters. A smaller theater features sleight-of-hand performed literally in the midst of the audience. The other theater is large and offers eye-popping, prop-dependent illusions of the David Copperfield and *Siegfried & Roy* ilk. All of the performers are extremely accomplished, and the shows avoid much of the redundancy that plagues most Las Vegas magic and illusion productions. After guests have seen both shows, they can stick around and enjoy the exotic surroundings or exit back into the casino.

Consumer Tips   The magic and illusion at Caesars Magical Empire are as good as any you are likely to see in Las Vegas. When you include the knock-out atmosphere and the intimate performance venues, it's one of the best evenings of entertainment available. When you consider that Caesars Magical Empire costs $15 less than *Siegfried & Roy and* includes an excellent dinner with wine, it's hard to beat. Reservations with advance payment are necessary and can be made at the Caesars box office or by calling (702) 731-7333 or (800) 445-4544. The package price is $75 per adult (11 years and older) and $37.50 for children ages 5 through 10. Open from 4:30 p.m. on, discounts of $10 per person are available to those willing to dine extra early or extra late. The menu includes salad, bread, choice of main course, accompanying side dishes, and dessert. Wine and soft drinks come with the meal. Mixed drinks can be purchased at one of two bars in the rotunda. The dining is not rushed, but is not particularly leisurely either. Everything is on a schedule, and there are no cocktails before dinner or much lingering over coffee after the meal.

Cirque du Soleil's Mystere

Type of Show: Circus as theater
Host Casino and Showroom: Treasure Island—*Cirque du Soleil* Showroom
Reservations and Information: 894-7722 or (800) 392-1999
Admission Cost with Taxes: $65 adults; $33 children
Cast Size: 75
Nights of Lowest Attendance: Thursday
Usual Show Times: 7:30 and 10:30 p.m.   *Dark:* Monday and Tuesday
Special Comments: No table service (no tables!)
Topless: No   *Smoking Allowed:* No
Author's Rating: ★★★★½
Overall Appeal by Age Group:

Under 21	21–37	38–50	51 and older
★★★★	★★★★★	★★★★★	★★★★½

Duration of Presentation: An hour and a half

Description and Comments   Chalk up another first for Steve Wynn. *Mystere* is a far cry from a traditional circus but retains all of the fun and excitement. It is whimsical, mystical, and sophisticated, yet pleasing to all ages. The action takes place on an elaborate stage that incorporates almost every part of the theater. The original musical score is exotic, like the show.

Note: In the following paragraph, I get into how the show *feels* and why it's special. If you don't care how it feels, or if you are not up to slogging through a boxcar of adjectives, the bottom line is simple: *Mystere* is great. See it.

Mystere is the most difficult show in Las Vegas to describe. To categorize it as a circus does not begin to cover its depth, though its performers could perform with distinction in any circus on earth. *Cirque du Soleil* is more, much more, than a circus. It combines elements of classic Greek theater, mime, the English morality play, Dali surrealism, Fellini characterization, and Chaplin comedy. *Mystere* is at once an odyssey, a symphony, and an exploration of human emotions. The show pivots on its humor, which is sometimes black, and engages the audience with its unforgettable characters. Though light and uplifting, it is also poignant and dark. Simple in its presentation, it is at the same time extraordinarily intricate, always operating on multiple levels of meaning. As you laugh and watch the amazingly talented cast, you become aware that your mind has entered a dimension seldom encountered in a waking state. The presentation begins to register in your consciousness more as a seamless dream than as a stage production. You are moved, lulled, and soothed as well as excited and entertained. The sensitive, the imaginative, the literate, and those who love good theater and art will find no show in Las Vegas that compares with *Mystere*.

Consumer Tips   Be forewarned that the audience is an integral part of *Mystere* and that at almost any time you might be plucked from your seat to participate. Our advice is to loosen up and roll with it. If you are too rigid, repressed, hungover, or whatever to get involved, politely but firmly decline to be conscripted.

Because *Mystere* is presented in its own customized showroom, there are no tables and, consequently, no drink service. In keeping with the show's circus theme, however, spectators can purchase refreshments at nearby concession stands. Tickets for reserved seats can be purchased seven days in advance at the Cirque's box office or over the phone using your credit card.

Country Fever

Type of Show: Country music and dance show
Host Casino and Showroom: Golden Nugget—Cabaret Theatre
Reservations and Information: 386-8100 or (800) 634-3454
Admission Cost with Taxes: $25, tip not included
Cast Size: 24
Nights of Lowest Attendance: Sunday
Usual Show Times: 7 and 9:45 p.m.   *Dark:* Friday
Special Comments: Hors d'oeuvres with 2 nonalcoholic drinks or beers at
   both shows
Topless: No   *Smoking Allowed:* No
Author's Rating: ★★★★
Overall Appeal by Age Group:

Under 21	21–37	38–50	51 and older
★★★★	★★★★	★★★★	★★★★

Duration of Presentation: An hour and 15 minutes

Description and Comments   Country Fever is to a musical revue what neon is to an electric sign: bright, versatile, sizzling. Neon cacti, saguaro, and bullheads grace the showroom entrance and walls (the closest you'll come to neon lights anywhere in town), and neon best describes the energy level onstage. This show *glows.* And it's not only the nine-piece band (complete with violin, pedal-steel guitar, harmonica, saxophone, and congas), nor the sextet of gospel singers, quintet of dancers, three performers, and comedian. It's the synergy among them, the seamless integration of music, dance, and comedy that makes *Country Fever* one of the hottest shows to hit Las Vegas for years. From the very first note the band broils, the dancers dazzle, and the show smokes for the next 75 minutes. The musicians were "discovered" in bands from Nashville to Los Angeles, and every one is an all-star. The arrangements go way beyond "country"—incorporating pop, blues, gospel, soul, and some screaming rock licks.

Consumer Tips   The Cabaret at the Golden Nugget is a small showroom, which feels considerably smaller with 500+ people inside. Almost all of the seating is at banquet tables, and conditions are quite cramped. On the plus side, most seats are fairly close to the stage. Seating is by maitre d'. Children over ten years old are welcome but must pay the adult admission charge. Reservations may be made up to five days in advance; payment is made at the table.

Country Tonite

Type of Show: Country music and dance show
Host Casino and Showroom: Aladdin—Country Tonite Showroom
Reservations and Information: 736-0240 or (800) 637-8133
Admission Cost with Taxes: $22 adults; $15 children (under 12)
Cast Size: Approximately 22
Nights of Lowest Attendance: Thursday
Usual Show Times: 7:15 and 10 p.m.   *Dark:* Tuesday
Special Comments: Show with buffet offered costing $27 for adults, $19
   for children (ages 11 and under), tax included; gratuity is extra.
Topless: No   *Smoking Allowed:* Yes
Author's Rating: ★★★★
Overall Appeal by Age Group:

Under 21	21–37	38–50	51 and older
★★★★	★★★★	★★★★	★★★★

Duration of Presentation: An hour and 20 minutes

Description and Comments   If you think you can survive an evening without feathers and bare breasts, *Country Tonite* is one hot show. As the name suggests, the show is about country music and that is exactly what it delivers, everything from traditional country music to this week's big hit. As the curtain rises, the stage is aswarm with musicians, much in the style of Nashville's Grand Ole Opry. And as at the Opry, everything is upbeat and informal. *Country Tonite* is a show where you immediately feel comfortable, where the audience and the performers coalesce almost instantly into one roof-raising crowd. Clapping and footstomping are encouraged, and even the maitre d' and captains have difficulty maintaining decorum.

While it is unlikely that you will have heard of any of the musicians, they are indeed talented and keep the production moving at a furious clip. For additional zip, the music is augmented by the energetic efforts of Appalachian cloggers.

Consumer Tips   *Country Tonite* is a robust, spirit-lifting family show and one of the few productions in town with real appeal to guests of all ages (provided you enjoy country music). At $22 for adults and $15 for children, it is also a real bargain. Reservations can be made up to two weeks in advance, and advance tickets are available at the box office. Payment is made at the table. Seating is by the maitre d'.

Crazy Girls

Type of Show: Erotic dance and adult comedy
Host Casino and Showroom: Riviera—Mardi Gras Showrooms, second floor
Reservations and Information: 794-9433 or (800) 634-3420
Admission Cost with Taxes: $23 general admission, $28 VIP (includes 2 drinks and gratuity)
Cast Size: 8
Nights of Lowest Attendance: Wednesday, Thursday
Usual Show Times: 8:30 and 10:30 p.m., with a midnight show on Saturdays
Dark: Monday
Topless: Yes   *Smoking Allowed:* No
Author's Rating: ★★★½
Overall Appeal by Age Group:

Under 21	21–37	38–50	51 and older
N/A	★★★½	★★★½	★★★½

Duration of Presentation: An hour and 10 minutes

Description and Comments *Crazy Girls* gets right to the point. This is a no-nonsense show for men who do not want to sit through jugglers, magicians, and half the score from *Oklahoma!* before they see naked women. The focus is on eight engaging, talented, and athletically built young ladies who bump and grind through an hour of exotic dance and comedy. The choreography (for anyone who cares) is pretty creative, and the whole performance is highly charged and quickly paced. The dancers are supported by a zany comedienne who, though funny, usurps more than her share of stage time.

Consumer Tips The show is not really as dirty as the Riviera would lead you to believe, and the nudity does not go beyond topless and G-strings (how could it?). While designed for men, there is not much of anything in the show that would make women or couples uncomfortable. Men looking for total nudity should try the Palomino Club in North Las Vegas.

   Ticket and box office information is the same as for *La Cage* (see Consumer Tips under *An Evening at La Cage,* page 191). The VIP, up-close seating for old poots who forgot their eyeglasses includes a line pass.

Danny Gans: "The Man of Many Voices"

Type of Show: Impressions and variety
Host Casino and Showroom: Rio—Copacabana Entertainment Complex
Reservations and Information: 252-7776 or (800) PLAY-RIO
Admission Cost with Taxes: $35, includes tax and 2 drinks
Cast Size: Approximately 4
Nights of Lowest Attendance: Thursday
Usual Show Times: 8 p.m.   *Dark:* Monday and Tuesday
Topless: No   *Smoking Allowed:* No
Author's Rating: ★★★★
Overall Appeal by Age Group:

Under 21	21–37	38–50	51 and older
★★★★	★★★★	★★★★	★★★★

Duration of Presentation: One hour and 25 minutes

Description and Comments Danny Gans was well on his way to a promising career in major league baseball when he suffered a career-ending injury. Baseball's loss is Las Vegas entertainment's gain. This "man of many voices" is a monster talent. He does upwards of a hundred impressions during the show: Michael Jackson; Willie Nelson; James Stewart; Kermit the Frog; Pee

Wee Herman; John Travolta; Peter Falk; Garth Brooks; Sammy, Frank, and Dino; Walter Cronkite with Presidents Clinton, Bush, Reagan, Carter, and Ford; Billy Joel; Bruce Springsteen; Stevie Wonder; Ray Charles; Sylvester Stallone and Homer and Marge Simpson talking to Dr. Ruth's answering machine; Henry Fonda and Katharine Hepburn doing *On Golden Pond;* Paul Lynde; Wayne Newton; Neil Diamond; Sammy Davis Jr.; Natalie and Nat King Cole; Sarah Vaughan; The Artist Formerly Known as Prince; Bill Cosby; and, of course, Elvis. And that's a *short* list. At the end, he even does Danny Gans.

Gans not only does impressions, but also expressions. He captures his characters' faces, postures, and moves; he gets maximum effect from minimal props; he even plays a mean trumpet (for the Louis Armstrong bit). But that's not all. Gans's brand of comedy, especially its pace, is reminiscent of Robin Williams's style—cerebral, sophisticated, hilarious. This is perhaps the most intelligent show in Las Vegas. It's also probably the tightest. Gans, his three-piece band (drums, guitar, keyboards), and the lighting are in perfect sync every note of the night. *Danny Gans: "The Man of Many Voices"* is great for the Rio *and* for Las Vegas. Tough luck for baseball.

Consumer Tips   The Copacabana Entertainment Complex is one of the best designed and most comfortable showrooms in Las Vegas. Though some seats are a bit distant, the line of sight is uniformly excellent. In any event, the show is more of an auditory than a visual experience, and the sound system is awesome.

Debbie Reynolds

Type of Show: Musical revue
Host Casino and Showroom: Debbie Reynolds Hollywood Hotel—
   Debbie's Star Theater
Reservations and Information: 733-2243 or (800) 633-1777
Admission Cost with Taxes: $39.95, includes 2 drinks, tax, and gratuity
Cast Size: Approximately 6
Nights of Lowest Attendance: Wednesday, Thursday
Usual Show Times: 7:30 p.m.   *Dark:* Saturday and Sunday
Topless: No   *Smoking Allowed:* No
Author's Rating: ★★★½
Overall Appeal by Age Group:

Under 21	21–37	38–50	51 and older
★★★	★★★½	★★★★	★★★★

Duration of Presentation: An hour and 30 minutes

Description and Comments   When film stars cut back on their workload or retire from the cinema, we forget very quickly what it was that propelled them to the top of the heap. If you take in a performance of Debbie Reynolds's modest production revue, however, you will quickly be reminded of the extraordinary talent that made this diminutive and feisty woman one of Hollywood's most beloved stars. The Reynolds revue is a tour de force, a showcase for Reynolds's singing, dancing, and robust spirit. With a small cast and a simple production, the focus is on Debbie Reynolds. And Reynolds delivers.

Consumer Tips   Debbie Reynolds serves up a good night's entertainment for patrons of all ages, and in fact takes great delight in teasing members of the audience too young to be familiar with her film credits. It must be said, however, that those who grew up watching Debbie Reynolds movies will have a greatly enhanced appreciation of this show and will be much more moved by the intrepid spirit of its star. Debbie's Star Theater is a medium-sized showroom that works well for headliners and musicians. Admission can be purchased via phone with your credit card or at the hotel box office one week in advance. Seats are assigned by the maitre d'. Admission includes two drinks, tax, and tip. For most shows, children are allowed if accompanied by an adult.

EFX!

Type of Show: Grand-scale musical production show
Host Casino and Showroom: MGM Grand—Grand Theater
Reservations and Information: 891-7777 or (800) 929-1111
Admission Cost with Taxes: $49.50 general admission; $70 preferred admission
Cast Size: 70
Nights of Lowest Attendance: Sunday
Usual Show Times: 7:30 and 10:30 p.m.
Dark: Sunday and Monday
Special Comments: Children's admission is $35 Tuesday–Thursday.
Topless: No   *Smoking Allowed:* No
Author's Rating: ★★★★½
Overall Appeal by Age Group:

Under 21	21–37	38–50	51 and older
★★★	★★★★½	★★★★½	★★★★

Duration of Presentation: An hour and a half

Description and Comments   *EFX!*, pronounced "Effects," is the MGM

Grand's entry into the Las Vegas megashow competition. With a cast of 70 and a backstage support crew of 80, *EFX!* is designed to overwhelm. The production recently switched stars, losing a phantom (Michael Crawford, best-known as Broadway's original "Phantom of the Opera") and gaining a partridge (David Cassidy of Partridge Family fame). David Cassidy is excellent. Like Michael Crawford before him, he brings his considerable talents to bear with infinite precision so that he complements the production instead of monopolizing or overwhelming it.

In *EFX!* Cassidy guides the audience through an animatronic (robotic) and technological odyssey that is reported to have cost $30 million to produce. Broadway talent and aesthetics are integrated with cutting-edge, Hollywood special effects as Cassidy takes the audience on a journey through time and space, appearing in the process as Merlin, H. G. Wells, P. T. Barnum, and Houdini.

We were surprised by how beautiful and aesthetically grounded *EFX!* is, and also by its delightful humor. Far from another Las Vegas monument to excess, the spectacle of *EFX!* fits its theme and operates in context. *EFX!* is a stunning and sensitive show that makes excellent use of its technology rather than being a numbing parade of special effects. There is nothing of the tail wagging the dog about *EFX!* The technology artfully augments the overall production and is integrated in a most unobtrusive way. *EFX!*, like *Cirque du Soleil's Mystere,* is most of all human, and like *Mystere,* it operates on multiple levels and engages many emotions. The score is lilting and uplifting and the choreography flawless. While the costumes and sets are staggering, they serve to create a theatrical environment that totally envelops the audience. The audience is one with the cast, and there are no feelings of boundaries or separation.

Consumer Tips   We think *EFX!* has a stupid and misleading name that conveys none of its depth or artistry. *EFX!* is a must-see, ranking second only to *Cirque du Soleil's Mystere* as the best production show in Las Vegas. If *EFX!* has a shortcoming, it is that its technology is so complex that malfunctions have been common. We expect that these technical problems will be resolved over time.

While guests on the highest tiers are pretty far away from the stage, the only bad seats are those right up front where guests are periodically enveloped in fake fog. The better seats for *EFX!* are back about four tiers from the front and in the center. Reserved-seat tickets can be purchased over the phone with your credit card approximately six weeks in advance or in person at the Grand Theater box office. We recommend booking your seats a couple of weeks in advance. Children over five years old are welcome but must pay the stiff adult price. On the night of the show, give yourself an extra 20–30 minutes if you plan to use MGM Grand valet parking or self-parking.

Enter the Night

Type of Show: Music, dance, and variety production show

Host Casino and Showroom: Stardust—Stardust Theatre

Reservations and Information: 732-6111 or (800) 824-6033

Admission Cost with Taxes: $30 general seating; $35 booth seating

Cast Size: Approximately 72

Nights of Lowest Attendance: Thursday, Sunday

Usual Show Times: 7:30 and 10:30 p.m., Tuesday–Thursday, Saturday; 8 p.m., Sunday and Monday

Dark: Friday

Special Comments: Includes tax, 2 drinks, and gratuity

Topless: Yes   *Smoking Allowed:* No

Author's Rating: ★★★★

Overall Appeal by Age Group:

Under 21	21–37	38–50	51 and older
N/A	★★★½	★★★★	★★★★

Duration of Presentation: An hour and a half

Description and Comments   *Enter the Night* opened in July of 1991, replacing the long-running and extremely successful *Lido de Paris*. *Enter the Night* is a modern yet timeless, sophisticated, and elegant show. The production plays like a nocturnal fantasy, a dream both fluid and continually changing. *Enter the Night* is soothing and compelling, sometimes exciting, but always just beyond reality. The show draws upon night's mystery, reverie, sultriness, and eroticism to provide ephemeral sequences of dance and haunting music. *Enter the Night* is, without question, a model of integration and continuity, flowing so well you don't notice the transitions.

The well-choreographed production numbers cover such disparate elements as erotic dance, tap dance, and chorus. Specialty acts are blended gracefully into the production and enhance the dream-fantasy theme. The most beautiful and arresting act in the show is a sequence in which dancers appear out of lasers and the complex laser patterns create a setting for their dance. In a show town gone mad with special effects, it is a welcome surprise to see lasers used with such artfulness and subtlety.

The costuming for *Enter the Night* may be the best designed in Las Vegas. Not only are the costumes tasteful and elegant, but they also flatter the performers. Not one costume in this show diminishes the wearer or makes her or him look silly. Considering most Las Vegas production shows, that's saying a lot.

Enter the Night might seem a little slow to Jeff Kutash *(Splash II)* fans, and may not offer enough variety to please the *Jubilee!* crowd, but it provides a production show alternative distinct in its sophistication and unique in its beauty and tone.

Consumer Tips   Visitors over 35 years old, on average, will appreciate *Enter the Night* more than younger folks. Individuals who appreciate subtlety, as well as spectacle, will also like this show.

All seats to *Enter the Night* are reserved. While you can reserve tickets over the phone up to two weeks in advance, you must come to the box office to pay for and pick up your tickets any time prior to two hours before show time. A great value, the cost of admission includes the show, taxes, gratuities, and two drinks. *Enter the Night* is limited strictly to persons 21 years and older. If you drive to the Stardust, give yourself a little extra time to park and make your way to the showroom.

An Evening at La Cage

Type of Show: Female-impersonator revue

Host Casino and Showroom: Riviera—Mardi Gras Showrooms, third floor

Reservations and Information: 794-9433 or (800) 634-3420

Admission Cost with Taxes: $26 general admission; $32 VIP (includes 2 drinks and gratuity)

Cast Size: Approximately 20

Nights of Lowest Attendance: Sunday, Monday

Usual Show Times: 7:30 and 9:30 p.m., with an 11:15 p.m. show on Wednesdays

Dark: Tuesday

Topless: No   *Smoking Allowed:* No

Author's Rating: ★★★

Overall Appeal by Age Group:

Under 21	21–37	38–50	51 and older
N/A	★★★½	★★★	★★★

Duration of Presentation: An hour and 15 minutes

Description and Comments   *La Cage* re-creates the unique female-imper-sonator revue made famous by productions of the same name in New York and Los Angeles. A high-tempo show with a great sense of humor, *La Cage* is at once outrageous, lusty, weird, and sensitive. All of the per-formers, of course, are men. Celebrities impersonated include Joan Rivers, Tina Turner, Cher, Carol Channing, Shirley MacLaine, Bette Midler, and Madonna. A crew of dancers (also men impersonating women) give the presentation the feel of a quirky production show.

Some of the impersonators are convincing and pretty enough to fool just about anyone. Their costumes reveal slender, feminine arms and legs and hourglass figures. Others, however, look just like what they are—men in drag. The cast performs with great self-effacement and gives the impres-sion that nobody is expected to take things too seriously. As one imperson-ator quipped, "This is a hell of a way for a 40-year-old man to be earning a living."

La Cage is kinky yet solid entertainment. It is also very popular and plays to appreciative heterosexual audiences. If you are curious, broad-minded, and looking for something different, give it a try. If the idea of a bunch of guys traipsing around in fishnet stockings and feather boas gives you the willies, opt for something more conventional.

Consumer Tips   In addition, you can see the production show *Splash II,* which plays off the main casino in the Versailles Theatre (see page 208). Shows can be purchased in conjunction with a meal, usually the buffet. The food on the show-dinner combos won't knock you out, but is a pretty good deal for the money. Also, it's quick and convenient. There is usually plenty of time to eat between shows.

Tickets for *La Cage* and the other Mardi Gras shows may be reserved up to 21 days in advance at the Riviera box office, or over the phone using your credit card up to 10 days in advance. Two cocktails are included in your admission. Seating is by the maitre d'. Once seated, you fetch your own drinks from the bar using your ticket stub as a voucher. The VIP, up-close seating for $28 includes a line pass, which allows you priority seating through the maitre d' and prevents a long wait in the general admission line.

Folies Bergere

Type of Show: Music, dance, and variety production show
Host Casino and Showroom: Tropicana—Tiffany Theater
Reservations and Information: 739-2411 or (800) 634-4000
Admission Cost with Taxes: $45–55

Cast Size: Approximately 90

Nights of Lowest Attendance: Monday, Tuesday, Sunday

Usual Show Times: 8 and 10:30 p.m.   *Dark:* Thursday

Special Comments: No cocktails available at early show

Topless: Yes   *Smoking Allowed:* No

Author's Rating: ★★★

Overall Appeal by Age Group:

Under 21	21–37	38–50	51 and older
★★	★★★	★★★	★★★★

Duration of Presentation: An hour and a half

Description and Comments   The *Folies Bergere,* a Las Vegas tradition modeled on the bawdy Parisian revue of the same name, has been playing at the Tropicana on and off since 1959. The show, which changes almost every year, is a classy dance and musical variety production with a large cast.

The *Folies Bergere* is pretty much what you would expect: exotically clad (or unclad) showgirls and cancan dancers, chorus lines, singers, and music with a turn-of-the-century French cabaret feel. The show runs through 14 different scenes, celebrating the music and dance traditions of Paris, Hollywood, and Las Vegas from the 1860s to the 1960s. The *Folies Bergere* is elaborate and colorful but not particularly compelling. The singing and dancing are competent and professional but, with one or two exceptions, not creative or exciting. The *Folies* has been successful for more than 30 years, so it is understandable that the producers would be reluctant to tamper with the formula. The ante for competing in the big leagues, however, has gone up. The production innovations of *Siegfried & Roy* and the energy of *EFX!* have established new standards for action, tempo, and creativity in Las Vegas production shows. The *Folies Bergere* has failed to keep pace, and an extremely talented cast has been relegated to plugging its way through a staid and dated format.

In fairness, the latest edition of the *Folies* has cranked up the energy quota a notch, with some cross-stage acrobatics and gymnastics in the cancan extraordinaire, an interesting striptease under black light, a hot modern street dance, and the frantic juggling comedy of Charlie Frye & Company, who have delighted Las Vegas audiences on many different stages for years.

Given the music and style of the *Folies*, you will be more likely to appreciate the production if you are over 50. Younger patrons will fail to identify with the nostalgic music and dance of *la belle epoque,* or find much spontaneity in the overall *Folies* theme; the "Lion King" finale, for example, is strange and overwrought. But imaginative sets and costumes, elaborate staging, a diverse soundtrack, and the contemporary choreography that revs up near the end give this show some pop.

Consumer Tips   The *Folies* is presented on a wide stage in the nicely designed Tiffany Theater. There is a lot more booth seating than in most showrooms and a good view from practically every seat in the house. Dinner is no longer offered in the showroom, though there's a buffet show package for an extra $12. No drinks come with the price of the show. If you need to use the distant rest room before the show, allow yourself plenty of time.

Reservations can be made up to a month in advance, and all seats are reserved, so you can show up five minutes prior to show time and your seats will be waiting.

Forever Plaid

Type of Show: Fifties musical nostalgia

Host Casino and Showroom: Flamingo—Bugsy's Theater

Reservations and Information: 733-3333 or (800) 221-7299

Admission Cost with Taxes: $22

Cast Size: 6

Nights of Lowest Attendance: Wednesday–Thursday

Usual Show Times: 7:30 and 10 p.m.   *Dark:* Monday

Special Comments: Drinks not included

Topless: No   *Smoking Allowed:* No

Author's Rating: ★★★½

Overall Appeal by Age Group:

Under 21	21–37	38–50	51 and older
★★	★★★	★★★½	★★★★

Duration of Presentation: An hour and 30 minutes

Description and Comments   As we approach the new millennium, living through an age in which elephants disappear, robotic dragons battle, and showgirls do water ballet in a 65,000-gallon tank on stages around Las Vegas, it's refreshing to sit back in a Strip showroom and be entertained by a quirky, clever, and small-stage revue pulled off by four crooners, two musicians, and little else.

Forever Plaid is the story of the Four Plaids, a quartet modeled after the Four Freshmen, the Four Aces, the Lettermen, and other four-part guy groups that had a brief heyday in the late '50s and early '60s. The Plaids are killed in a car crash on the way to their first big gig; 20 years later, through a series of cosmic and harmonic convergences, Sparky, Smudge, Jinx, and Frankie are given one chance to return to life and perform their career-launching concert.

The show is held together by song and dance, clever shtick, and engaging characterizations having to do with the young Plaids' life and death. The stage is tiny, with simple sets but effective use of props, such as toilet-plunger mike stands and telescoping palm trees. Plaid tablecloths decorate the showroom. But it's the music that has earned *Forever Plaid* its rave reviews. The Plaids do part or all of 30 golden favorites, such as "Catch a Falling Star," "Love Is a Many Splendored Thing," "Sixteen Tons," "Three Coins in the Fountain," and "Cry." A particularly rousing version of "Matilda" gets the audience belting out the chorus. The Plaids also present a tribute to Perry Como (and his golden cardigan) and perform a frantic three-minute compression of a full hour of the "Ed Sullivan Show."

In short, the Four Plaids return to Earth to send the audience's over-50 crowd to nostalgia heaven.

Consumer Tips Every seat in the intimate 200-seat showroom is adequate, though the casino is right on the other side of the door (a bit distracting during quieter moments). Tickets may be purchased one week in advance via phone or in person at the box office. Seating is conducted by the maitre d' at all shows. Since drinks are extra ($2–$3.50), you might want to carry a fresh one in from the casino. Don't sit up front unless you want to be fair game to be dragged up on stage to play the top piano part of "Heart and Soul" and join in an impromptu chorus line with the cast.

Jubilee!

Type of Show: Grand-scale musical and variety production show

Host Casino and Showroom: Bally's—The Jubilee Theater

Reservations and Information: 739-4567 or (800) 237-show

Admission Cost with Taxes: $49.50–66 ($2 extra on credit card purchase)

Cast Size: 100

Nights of Lowest Attendance: Sunday, Monday

Usual Show Times: 8 and 11 p.m.; Sunday and Monday feature
   8 p.m. show only

Dark: Friday

Topless: Yes   *Smoking Allowed:* No

Author's Rating: ★★★★

Overall Appeal by Age Group:

Under 21	21–37	38–50	51 and older
★★★	★★★	★★★½	★★★★

Duration of Presentation: An hour and 58 minutes

Description and Comments   Jubilee! is the quintessential, traditional Las Vegas production show. Faithfully following a successful decades-old formula, *Jubilee!* has elaborate musical production numbers, extravagant sets, beautiful topless showgirls, and quality variety acts. In *Jubilee!* you get what you expect—and then some.

With a cast of 100, an enormous stage, and some of the most colossal and extraordinary sets found in theater anywhere, *Jubilee!* is much larger than life. Running almost two hours each performance, the show is lavish, very sexy, and well performed, but redundant to the point of numbing.

Two multiscene production extravaganzas top the list of *Jubilee!* highlights. The first is the sultry saga of Samson and Delilah, climaxing with Samson's destruction of the temple. Not exactly biblical, but certainly awe-inspiring. The second super-drama is the story of the *Titanic*, from launch to sinking. Once again, sets and special effects on a grand scale combine with nicely integrated music and choreography to provide an incredible spectacle.

In June 1997, *Jubilee!* unveiled a new $3 million, 16-minute opening act, based on a popular song by Jerry Herman, "Hundreds of Girls," and featuring 75 singers, dancers, and showgirls multiplied by gargantuan mirrors. The above-average specialty acts include an illusionist executing big-stage tricks, a juggler-acrobat couple whose main prop is a giant aluminum cube, and a strongman who performs mostly upside-down. The production concludes with "The Jubilee Walk," a parade of elaborately costumed showgirls patterned after the grand finale of the *Ziegfeld Follies.*

Consumer Tips   The 1,035-seat Jubilee Theater, with its high, wide stage and multitiered auditorium, is one of the best-designed showrooms in town. The Jubilee underwent a complete $2.5 million renovation in mid-1997. It now consists of seating at banquet tables at the foot of the stage ($60; too close and cramped); one row of booths above the tables ($66 and worth it); and 789 theater-style seats ($55 in the middle of the room and $49.50 at the back). The table and booth seats come with cocktail service; the theater-seat audience has to carry in their own drinks.

Reserved seats for *Jubilee!* can be purchased over the phone with a credit card up to six weeks in advance. Tickets can also be purchased in person at the Bally's box office. The price of a ticket covers admission and taxes.

Kenny Kerr Show

Type of Show: Female-impersonator production show

Host Casino and Showroom: Debbie Reynolds Hollywood Hotel— Debbie's Star Theater

Reservations and Information: 733-2243 or (800) 633-1777

Admission Cost with Taxes: $25 including tax

Cast Size: Approximately 15

Nights of Lowest Attendance: Monday

Usual Show Times: 10:30 p.m. *Dark:* Sunday

Topless: No *Smoking Allowed:* No

Author's Rating: ★★★

Overall Appeal by Age Group:

Under 21	21–37	38–50	51 and older
N/A	★★★	★★★	★★★

Duration of Presentation: An hour and 20 minutes

Description and Comments The *Kenny Kerr Show* (formerly *Boy-lesque*) is Las Vegas's oldest continuously running female-impersonator show. Since 1976 the production starring Kenny Kerr has operated successfully at the Silver Slipper, the Sahara, the Stardust, and the Plaza. With grace, wit, and good-natured self-effacement, the all-male cast impersonates a number of famous celebs, including Diana Ross, Cher, Tina Turner, Barbra Streisand, and Dolly Parton. Some of the impersonators achieve an incredible likeness; it is often difficult to believe the cast is all-male. Like most Las Vegas shows, the *Kenny Kerr Show* features dancing (males in tights with wigs) and specialty acts. The production is robust, fast-paced, and performed with a great deal of humor.

Consumer Tips The *Kenny Kerr Show*, along with *An Evening at La Cage* (Riviera), is an excellent show and plays primarily to heterosexual audiences. Though well performed by an exceptional cast, the *Kenny Kerr Show* is basically a curiosity, drawing more on its cross-dressing notoriety than on the strength of the production. If you are open-minded and have a sense of the absurd, the *Kenny Kerr Show* will more than provide a good night's entertainment. If, on the other hand, your stomach does a flip when you contemplate men dancing around in lace panties and bras, you may want to consider some other show. The *Kenny Kerr Show* and *La Cage* are very similar in both content and quality. If you see one, it would be redundant to see the other. If you are trying to choose, *La Cage* is probably a better value for the dollar. Tickets can be purchased one month in advance through the box office or in person. Seating is assigned by the maitre d'.

King Arthur's Tournament

Type of Show: Jousting and medieval pageant

Host Casino and Showroom: Excalibur—King Arthur's Arena

Reservations and Information: 597-7600 or (800) 637-8133

Admission Cost with Taxes: $30 includes dinner, tax, and gratuity

Cast Size: Approximately 100

Nights of Lowest Attendance: Tuesday, Wednesday, Thursday

Usual Show Times: 6 and 8:30 p.m.

Special Comments: Reserved seating for dinner shows only

Topless: No   *Smoking Allowed:* No

Author's Rating: ★★★

Overall Appeal by Age Group:

Under 21	21–37	38–50	51 and older
★★★★	★★★★	★★★★	★★★★

Duration of Presentation: An hour and a half

Description and Comments   *King Arthur's Tournament* is dinner theater on a grand scale. The idea is that you are the guest of the king and queen for a feast and jousting tournament. Guests overlook the arena from dinner tables divided into sections; a knight is designated to represent each section in the competition. Serving girls and lads double as cheerleaders, doing their best to whip the audience into a frenzy cheering for their section's knight. The audience, which does not seem to require much encouragement, responds by caterwauling, hooting, and pounding incessantly on the dinner tables.

The tournament is barely under way, however, when an uninvited guest, an evil knight, arrives to challenge King Arthur's finest. The response is predictable, and there is a great deal of jousting, sword fighting, and dastardly tricks on the part of the evil knight before he is ultimately vanquished. The prevailing good knight wins the princess in marriage, setting the stage for a wedding ceremony with attendant festivities that include equestrian acrobats, tumblers, and jugglers.

King Arthur's Tournament is patterned after the successful *Medieval Times* attractions imported to this country from Spain in the mid-1980s, but it operates on a more superficial level. While *Medieval Times* develops its presentation in a historical and cultural context, elaborating on the customs of the times, *King Arthur's Tournament* is more like big-time wrestling. Everything is very simple: there is a bad guy, there are some good guys, and there is a lot of fighting.

At *King Arthur's Tournament* the jousting and sword fighting are exciting and well executed, even though the outcome is never in doubt. The undoing of the evil knight, curiously, comes about midway through the show, rendering the subsequent festivities somewhat anticlimactic. There is a surprise at the end, but the production never regains the momentum of the combat sequence.

Consumer Tips   One of the few Las Vegas shows suitable for the entire family, *King Arthur's Tournament* enjoys great popularity and often plays to a full house. Reserved seats can be purchased with a credit card up to six days in advance by calling the number listed above. Tickets can also be bought up to six days in advance by going in person to the Excalibur's box office, which opens each morning at 8 a.m.

All seating is computer-assigned, and admission includes dinner, tax, and gratuities. Because all seating is reserved, there is no need to tip the maitre d' or other showroom personnel. The arena is well designed, providing an unobstructed view of the show from every table.

Since dinner is served without utensils and eaten with the hands, guests might want to wash up before entering the showroom. The meal consists of soup, a Cornish hen, an incredibly stingy portion of potatoes and broccoli, a roll, and a dessert turnover. Beverages include your choice of coffee or soft drink, all served from large pitchers. Service is spotty. Never, on any of several visits, did we receive anything to drink until five minutes or more after our meal had been served. In addition, we asked for, but were never brought, water.

A few words of caution: Very loud fireworks unexpectedly go off as part of the show while dinner is being served. The explosions are sufficiently powerful to make you flinch or jump. We saw several people wind up with soup in their laps. The servers are familiar with the timing of the fireworks and will put their fingers in their ears at the right moment. This should be a cue for you to do the same. A second warning concerns banging on the tabletops when cheering the good knights. This pounding causes many drinks to be spilled. If and when you engage in this hammering, keep your eye on your drink and on those of the people next to you.

Lance Burton: Master Magician

Type of Show: Magical illusion with dancing and specialty acts
Host Casino and Showroom: Monte Carlo—Lance Burton Theatre
Reservations and Information: 730-7000 or (800) 311-8999
Admission Cost with Taxes: $35 balcony seating; $40 main-floor seating

Cast Size: 14

Nights of Lowest Attendance: Thursday, Friday

Usual Show Times: 7:30 and 10:30 p.m. *Dark:* Sunday and Monday

Special Comments: No drinks included

Topless: No   *Smoking Allowed:* No

Author's Rating: ★★★★

Overall Appeal by Age Group:

Under 21	21–37	38–50	51 and older
★★★★	★★★★	★★★★	★★★★

Duration of Presentation: An hour and a half

Description and Comments   In a brand new showroom designed especially for him, Lance Burton stars in an innovative and iconoclastic magic show, the only magic production show in town to escape the curse of redundancy (see *Siegfried & Roy*). Performing in tight-fitting clothing with rolled-up sleeves (nothing can be concealed), Burton displays some extraordinary sleight of hand in a repertoire of illusions that cannot be seen in other showrooms. Augmented by comely assistants and a talented dance troupe, Lance Burton delivers quality entertainment. If you've never seen Lance Burton before, you will be very pleased.

For repeat visitors, however, the show is a bit of a letdown. For starters, the production fails to take advantage of the large and beautifully designed Lance Burton Theatre. The show seems too modest for its grand setting, and Burton's close-up work is lost to those seated farther back. Then there's Burton's penchant for gratuitous and distracting small talk. We've encountered this problem with previous Lance Burton shows: in short, he seems to go through periodic gabby phases. Finally, for the Burton fan, there's nothing really different about the new show. It's good, excellent in many respects, but we expected more.

Consumer Tips   The Lance Burton Theatre is an opulent imitation of a Parisian opera house and is both beautiful and comfortable. Theater seats ensure that no one gets wedged sideways at cramped banquet tables. On the down side, the venue is so large that it's hard to appreciate Burton's exquisite and subtle sleight of hand if you are seated in the boonies. Also, some illusions are difficult to see from the balcony seats. Try to get seats on the main floor close to the stage.

Legends in Concert

Type of Show: Celebrity-impersonator musical production show

Host Casino and Showroom: Imperial Palace—Imperial Theatre

Reservations and Information: 794-3261

Admission Cost with Taxes: $30 includes tax, 2 drinks, and tip

Cast Size: Approximately 20

Nights of Lowest Attendance: Wednesday, Thursday

Usual Show Times: 7:30 and 10:30 p.m.   *Dark:* Sunday

Topless: No   *Smoking Allowed:* No

Author's Rating: ★★★★

Overall Appeal by Age Group:

Under 21	21–37	38–50	51 and older
★★★★	★★★★	★★★★	★★★★

Duration of Presentation: An hour and a half

Description and Comments *Legends in Concert* is a musical production show featuring a highly talented cast of impersonators who re-create the stage performances of such celebrities as Elvis, Madonna, Liberace, Marilyn Monroe, Cher, Neil Diamond, the Blues Brothers, Buddy Holly, Michael Jackson, Roy Orbison, and Sammy Davis Jr. Impersonators actually sing and/or play their own instruments, so there's no lip-syncing or faking. In addition to the Las Vegas production, *Legends in Concert* also fields a road show. The second show makes possible a continuing exchange of performers between the productions, so that the shows are always changing. In addition to the impersonators, *Legends* features an unusually hot and creative company of dancers, much in the style of TV's Solid Gold Dancers. There are no variety acts.

The show is a barn-burner and possibly, minute-for-minute, the fastest-moving show in town. The impersonations are extremely effective, replicating the physical appearances, costumes, mannerisms, and voices of the celebrities with remarkable likeness. While each show features the work of about eight stars, with a roster that ensures something for patrons of every age, certain celebrities (most notably Elvis) are always included. Regardless of the stars impersonated, *Legends in Concert* is fun, happy, and upbeat. It's a show that establishes rapport with the audience—a show that makes you feel good.

Consumer Tips Admission includes two drinks. Payment must be made at the box office any time prior to the show. Arrive 40 minutes before show time for seating by the maitre d'. If you drive to the Imperial Palace and intend to use the self-parking, give yourself a little extra time. Since *Legends* is very popular and almost always plays to a full house on weekends, be sure to make your reservations early.

MADhattan

Type of Show: Music, dance, and variety production show
Host Casino and Showroom: New York–New York—MADhattan Theatre
Reservations and Information: 740-6815
Admission Cost with Taxes: $44 at box office; $47 over the phone
Cast Size: 32
Nights of Lowest Attendance: Monday, Tuesday
Usual Show Times: 7:30 and 10 p.m.
Dark: Wednesday, Thursday
Topless: No   *Smoking Allowed:* No
Author's Rating: ★★½
Overall Appeal by Age Group:

Under 21	21–37	28–50	51 and older
★★★½	★★★	★★½	★★

Duration of Presentation: An hour and a half

Description and Comments   *MADhattan* is by far the most authentic fea-ture of New York–New York and a significant departure from what's come to be called Las Vegas–style entertainment. The cast consists of trans-planted performers who were discovered on the street corners, in the sub-way stations, and at the train terminals of the "Big Apple." They were re-cruited, relocated to Las Vegas, rehearsed, and readied for show time—and they never changed their clothes.

The clothes are key, because you can take a performer off the street, but in this case, you can't take the street out of the performer. *MADhattan* is an eclectic collection of stray artists and odd talents set in a sanitized metro-politan landscape; the "costumes," such as they are, tend toward jogging suits, jerseys, and T-shirts—everyday street clothes. Most of the perfor-mances also tend toward the everyday.

The show opens with a song from a street-corner quartet, then moves quickly through some reggae into one of the strongest segments—a drum-mer playing a motley, but well-tuned, accumulation of pots and pans. That energy is advanced by a capable troupe of hip-hop and break dancers. From there, however, *MADhattan* starts to bog down. A manic-and-mime comedy duo is annoyingly over the top; a solo vocalist and songstress trio sing in the subway (for good reason); a unicyclist goes through the mo-tions; and the hip-hoppers come back for more of the same. Three tap dancers pick up the pace for a bit, and a free-form, large-easel painter uses a broom, his hands, and his hips to evoke some surprising images. A gospel finale ends the show on a tepid note, and when the performers circulate through the theater, you can barely tell the cast from the audience.

MADhattan would be much more effective in a small showroom at about half the price.

Consumer Tips   The showroom itself is large and comfortable. It seats 850 on the floor and 350 in a steeply ranked balcony. The chairs, complete with drink holders, are the cushiest in Las Vegas. There's a bar in the lobby; drinks average $4. You can reserve seats 60 days in advance; the box office personnel will help you make the best seat selection from what's available. Since all tickets are the same price (so far), go for anything on the floor and avoid the balcony, which is too far from the stage.

The Great Radio City Music Hall Spectacular

Type of Show: Broadway-oriented musical variety show
Host Casino and Showroom: Flamingo Hilton—Flamingo Showroom
Reservations and Information: 733-3333 or (800) 221-7299
Admission Cost with Taxes: $54 to $64 dinner; $47 cocktail
Cast Size: Approximately 30
Nights of Lowest Attendance: Wednesday, Thursday
Usual Show Times: 7:45 and 10:30 p.m.   *Dark:* Friday
Special Comments: Early show is dinner or cocktail.
Topless: No   *Smoking Allowed:* No
Author's Rating: ★★★½
Overall Appeal by Age Group:

Under 21	21–37	38–50	51 and older
N/A	★★★½	★★★★	★★★★

Duration of Presentation: An hour and a half

Description and Comments   Our big question about this show was whether a production starring the Radio City Music Hall Rockettes could escape redundancy. How many variations on a theme can a line of high-kicking chorus girls achieve? As it turns out, quite a few. Precision dancing, we discovered, covers a lot of territory. The statuesque Rockettes, aided competently by four male dancers, treat the audience to a choreographic clinic. From tap to cancan to a typical Las Vegas finale, the Rockettes stay crisp and fresh.

The show opens with a little historic retro-perspective on the Radio City Music Hall and the Rockettes and then gets down to business. The most compelling numbers include the Rockettes' signature "Parade of the

Wooden Soldiers," traditionally performed at Christmas at Radio City, and a riveting dance dramatization of Ravel's "Bolero."

The Rockettes are supported by Paige O'Hara (vocal star of *Beauty and the Beast*), who serves as both master of ceremonies and lead vocalist. Specialty acts include the magic of Tim Kole and Jenny-Lynn.

The Great Radio City Music Hall Spectacular's tone and choice of music is more likely to be appreciated by older audiences. At times the production is elegant, and it is consistently professional. While mostly devoid of surprises, the show moves at a fast pace and maintains excellent continuity.

Consumer Tips   Reservations can be made at the number listed above. You can pay two weeks in advance with your credit card or at the box office prior to the show. Seats are assigned by the maitre d'. Dinner is available at the early show, with a 5:45 p.m. seating. Cocktail admission is optional for the early show, with seating at 7:15 p.m. The late show has cocktails only, with seating beginning around 9:45 p.m. Cocktail admission for either show includes two drinks. Dinner entrees, at varying prices, include chicken, salmon, prime rib, and New York steak. Cost of a dinner show ranges from $7 to $17 more than the cocktail admission, depending on choice of entree.

Siegfried & Roy

Type of Show: Production magic and illusion show with choreography and great spectacle

Host Casino and Showroom: Mirage—Siegfried & Roy Theatre

Reservations and Information: 792-7777 or (800) 456-4564

Admission Cost with Taxes: $90 (includes 2 drinks, gratuity, and souvenir program)

Cast Size: Approximately 75

Nights of Lowest Attendance: Sunday, Monday

Usual Show Times: 7:30 and 11 p.m.   *Dark:* Wednesday and Thursday

Special Comments: All gratuities included in admission price

Topless: No   *Smoking Allowed:* No

Author's Rating: ★★★★

Overall Appeal by Age Group:

Under 21	21–37	38–50	51 and older
★★★★★	★★★★★	★★★★★	★★★★★

Duration of Presentation: An hour and 40 minutes

Description and Comments   This show has revolutionized Las Vegas production shows, paving the way for *Cirque du Soleil's Mystere, EFX!,* and

Starlight Express. Staged in a modern 1,500-person theater with good visibility from all seats, *Siegfried & Roy* delivers a great deal more than magic and illusion. With a cast of approximately 75, extraordinary costuming, and special effects comparable to those in *EFX!*, this Kenneth Feld production establishes new definitions for spectacle, impact, and energy.

A fantasy depicting archetypal good and evil provides story-line continuity to the varied illusions of *Siegfried & Roy.* The illusions involve (among other things) white tigers, elephants, and even mechanical dragons. Most illusions are incorporated into elaborate productions, with choreography and often an original score augmenting the skill of the illusionists. At the end of the show the fantasy is discarded to provide a glimpse of Siegfried and Roy as individuals and to showcase their famous white tigers. The production maintains continuity, pace, and focus throughout. Unlike most production shows, this one has no variety acts, no intrusions on the central theme.

The sets and special effects in this show are beyond belief, even overwhelming, with their rich profusion of color, shape, and image. But the presentation is still tasteful and sophisticated.

If there is a problem with *Siegfried & Roy,* it is the same problem that plagues most Las Vegas magic-illusion shows: redundancy. How many variations of making something in a box disappear can performers parade before a single audience without losing their impact? Does it really matter that the boxes and animals keep getting larger? Isn't it still the same illusion?

Siegfried & Roy is visually impressive. But are we drawn in and truly delighted or are we simply staggered by its size and scope? For most of us, it's a bit of both.

We recommend *Siegfried & Roy* as a landmark Las Vegas production show, as an example of what can be accomplished when a talented producer with extensive resources and advanced technology pulls out all the stops. Regardless of how you feel about the substance of the illusions, you will have witnessed in *Siegfried & Roy* a vision that established a new standard for Las Vegas production shows.

People in Las Vegas are peculiar about money. The same man who drops $500 in an hour at the craps table will canvas the entire city for the best $2 breakfast. The big question concerning *Siegfried & Roy* is whether the show is worth the hefty $90 admission. Because this show has moved its genre ahead a quantum leap, it deserves attention. *Mystere* (Treasure Island) and *EFX!* (MGM Grand), however, deliver comparable spectacle at $25 and $20 less, respectively, while *Lance Burton* and *David Copperfield* offer better illusion at half the price. When *Siegfried & Roy* was the only super-show in town (1992), it was easier to swallow the big price tag (then

$67). But now, the quality of the competition suggests that *Siegfried & Roy* is significantly overpriced.

Consumer Tips   Even at $90 a pop in a theater with 1,500 seats, *Siegfried & Roy* sells out almost every night. No reservations are accepted, and the only way to get a ticket (for those not staying at the Mirage) is to line up at the Mirage box office one to three days in advance. Though reserved seats are issued by computer, patrons can, to a limited degree, specify their seating preferences.

The best way to see *Siegfried & Roy* on short notice with the least hassle is to set your sights for the late show on a Sunday, Monday, or Tuesday. Try the box office between 2:30 and 5 p.m. On many days advance ticket buyers will not buy out both shows, and some same-day seats will be available. Obviously you will not have first choice of seats, but there really are no bad seats in this well-designed theater.

A second, but riskier, same-day strategy is to try the box office during the half hour before show time. With 1,500 seats it is almost invariable that there will be a small (sometimes very small) number of cancellations and no-shows. Additionally, the Siegfried & Roy Theatre, like all Las Vegas showrooms, reserves a number of seats for casino high rollers. Sometimes, and always at the last minute, some of these seats may be made available to paying guests.

Since all seats are reserved, you do not have to tip the maitre d' or the captains. You also do not have to arrive an hour in advance. The showroom is well staffed, and guests are ushered to their assigned seats efficiently and usually without any waiting. We recommend entering the theater 25 to 30 minutes before show time. This will allow you plenty of time to get settled in and order the two drinks per person included in your admission. If you drive to the Mirage and use the self-parking, give yourself an extra 10 to 15 minutes for the long hike in from the parking lot.

If you are staying at the Mirage, you can call the box office from your room and reserve tickets. You may have the tickets charged to your hotel bill. Tickets for hotel guests can be picked up and paid for at the guest service window to the right of the box office at the theater entrance. If you fail to pick up your tickets, you will still be charged.

Several other showrooms (the Las Vegas Hilton, Bally's, the Stardust, Caesars Palace, etc.) have introduced reserved-seat, box office ticketing without insisting that customers purchase tickets in person. At every box office except the Mirage, customers can buy reserved seats over the phone with their credit card (sometimes up to 30 days in advance) and pick the tickets up at a Will-Call office just prior to show time.

If you really enjoy magic and illusion but are unwilling to put up with the expense and hassle of buying a ticket to *Siegfried & Roy*, try *David Copperfield* or *Lance Burton*. Though they lack the elaborate production component of *Siegfried & Roy*, these magicians perform comparable, if not superior, illusions, and with a great deal less redundancy. Another very good show that features illusion is *Spellbound* at Harrah's. Though not in the same league with *Siegfried & Roy*, it is nevertheless a first-class show, available at a fair price with no hassle.

Spellbound

Type of Show: Musical production show with emphasis on magic

Host Casino and Showroom: Harrah's—Commander's Theatre

Reservations and Information: 369-5111 or (800) 392-9002

Admission Cost with Taxes: $40 (includes tax, tip, and 1 drink)

Cast Size: Approximately 25

Nights of Lowest Attendance: Thursday

Usual Show Times: 7:30 and 10 p.m.   *Dark:* Sunday

Special Comments: One of the most beautiful and comfortable showrooms in town

Topless: No   *Smoking Allowed:* No

Author's Rating: ★★★½

Overall Appeal by Age Group:

Under 21	21–37	38–50	51 and older
★★★½	★★★½	★★★½	★★★½

Duration of Presentation: An hour and 20 minutes

Description and Comments   Revised and updated in 1997, *Spellbound* is one in an ever-increasing number of Las Vegas production shows that feature magic and illusion. Sensual without nudity, and tastefully produced, the show features a number of first-rate illusions. Between the illusions, *Spellbound* offers energetic street-dance choreography professionally executed by a handsome and talented troupe of dancers. The dancers and magicians are augmented by Human Design, gymnasts who contort and leverage themselves into incredible and statuesque poses. Sets are straightforward and simple but are artfully augmented by imaginative lighting and laser effects.

Consumer Tips   While *Spellbound* is a solid production, it does not break any new ground in terms of magic or illusion. Like most Las Vegas illusion shows, *Spellbound* is somewhat redundant. It does not achieve the creativity of *David Copperfield* or the spectacle of *Siegfried & Roy,* but does make for a great night's entertainment in a beautiful showroom at a good price. You can pay for reserved-seat admission via phone with your credit card or before the show at the box office. Children over five years old are welcome but must pay the adult ticket price.

Splash II

Type of Show: Musical variety aquacade show

Host Casino and Showroom: Riviera—Versailles Theater

Reservations and Information: 794-9301 or (800) 634-3420

Admission Cost with Taxes: $57 VIP; $46 general

Cast Size: Approximately 50

Nights of Lowest Attendance: Sunday, Tuesday, Wednesday

Usual Show Times: 7:30 and 10:30 p.m.

Special Comments: Price includes 1 drink and gratuity

Topless: Late show only   *Smoking Allowed:* No

Author's Rating: ★★★

Overall Appeal by Age Group:

Under 21	21–37	38–50	51 and older
★★★	★★★½	★★★½	★★★

Duration of Presentation: One hour and 30 minutes

Description and Comments   When *Splash* first rolled into Las Vegas in 1985, it was like a peppy young jet-ski revue buzzing among ponderous cruise-ship extravaganzas. Though the ride was a bit bumpy—the show alternated frenetic production numbers with bizarre variety acts and you walked away with a mild case of whiplash—*Splash* managed to stay afloat for nearly ten years on rock and roll, great dancing, and pure exuberance. Meanwhile, however, a new wave of contemporary entertainment (*Siegfried & Roy, Mystere,* and *EFX!,* to name three) churned into town and left *Splash* bobbing in the wake. So producer Jeff Kutash remade the show into *Splash II.*

The anticipation starts building as soon as you walk into the showroom, which is incorporated into the "supersubmarine" set, with ceiling misters, ushers and usherettes in nautical costumes, and a horseshoe-shaped runway with a metal-mesh grill, through which fountains and veritable walls of water are sure to drain.

And then it starts, and it turns out that the new *Splash* is a lot like the old *Splash,* only more so. The show is held together by a thin thread: the super-submarine visits the North Pole, the Bermuda Triangle, and Atlantis. On the way, though, it pauses at so many ports—four rip-roaring production numbers and a good dozen gimmicks and variety acts—that you wonder if anyone is steering the thing. The title and credits, to begin with, are displayed in 3-D. And then the performers come on like at a circus: an ice-skating duo, performing pigeons and parrots, the world's only "pre-recorded" comic (all body shtick, with the comedian riffing off of laser images, song snippets, and show sound bites), interactive laser tag with the VIP section of the audience, motorcycle daredevils, a juggler, the water ballet in *Splash*'s trademark 20,000-gallon tank, and finally a trained sea lion act!

Two performances are standouts. There's a break dancing and gangsta segment by the four Dragon Masters, who spin on every appendage (except one) and do some eye-popping acrobatics. And the juggler, Wally Eastwood, is so fast and funny that he saves the day. When he juggles with stainless-steel bowling pins that reflect the multicolored spotlights and plays classical music on an oversized keyboard by juggling rubber balls on the keys, he provides the only transcendent moments in the show.

When it's all over, a few in the audience look a little disoriented, like they somehow missed the boat, and others seem to be suffering from culture shock, like they'll never use that travel agent again. But for most people, this is exactly the kind of entertainment they expect out of a Las Vegas extravaganza.

Consumer Tips   All seats are reserved and assigned in the order in which the reservations are received; the earlier you buy, the better your seats will be. Tickets may be purchased up to ten days in advance over the phone or up to one month in advance in person at the box office. Tickets may be picked up at the box office prior to the show. The VIP tickets are for the first five rows of the front center section, which are theater-style seats that come with vibrating bass speakers and the laser guns. The Versailles Theater has been remodeled, and though it's still big and the back seats are as far away as ever, the VIP section has replaced the dreaded banquet tables (except for one row of four-seaters directly behind the VIPs)—in short, everyone in the audience has an unobstructed view.

Splash II is four-walled (meaning the producer gets the "gate" or proceeds from the ticket sales, and leases the showroom from the hotel), and it seems the producer and the hotel weren't able to get together over the drink situation. One drink is included in the price of the ticket but is not available in the showroom. Glassware is not allowed in the showroom. You must carry in your own fluid refreshments in plastic cups. There's a bar just outside the theater entrance that will provide you with the complimentary drink. Meal deals at the Riviera's Mardi Gras Food Court are often bundled with the show. See local visitor magazines for money-saving coupons.

Starlight Express

Type of Show: Roller skating musical production show

Host Casino and Showroom: Las Vegas Hilton—Starlight Express Theater

Reservations and Information: 732-5755 or (800) 222-5361

Admission Cost with Taxes: $22–50 (varies with quality of seat)

Cast Size: Approximately 38

Nights of Lowest Attendance: Varies

Usual Show Times: 7:30 and 10:30 p.m., Tuesday, Thursday, and Saturday; 7:30 p.m., Monday and Wednesday

Dark: Friday

Special Comments: This show may be cancelled at the end of 1997

Topless: No   *Smoking Allowed:* No

Author's Rating: ★★★★

Overall Appeal by Age Group:

Under 21	21–37	38–50	51 and older
★★★★	★★★★½	★★★★	★★★★

Duration of Presentation: An hour and a half

Description and Comments   *Starlight Express* has been playing in New York, London, and a number of other cities for some time. It is legitimate theater, with music by Andrew Lloyd Weber of *Cats* and *Phantom of the Opera* fame. *Starlight Express* may not be the best musical to have played Broadway, or the work for which Weber will ultimately be remembered, but it does introduce a new genre of theater to the all-too-homogeneous Las Vegas entertainment scene. *Starlight Express* has a plot, the unlikely story of a train race, complete with heroes, villains, and lovers. Most of all, it has continuity and integrity. It is much more than the usual Las Vegas amalgamation of choreography, song, and specialty acts loosely tied to a theme.

As musicals go, *Starlight Express* fits Las Vegas extremely well. The production is fast-paced, gimmicky, and high-tech, and it employs a vast array of laser, pyrotechnic, and other special effects. The costumes are extremely exotic (without feathers or nudity). Each character is a train engine or railroad car and rumbles around on roller skates. The diesel engine is swaggering and arrogant, while the electric engine, which runs on either AC or DC current, is bisexual. The steam locomotive is stolid and dependable; the switch engine is lumbering and strong. The railroad cars, from the red caboose to the luxurious passenger observation car, are likewise imbued with a personality consistent with their car's function. The action takes place on ramps that circle around and through the audience and on a broad open stage.

The musical score of *Starlight Express* is both compelling and clever, and helps shore up a minimalist plot that is predictable from the start. The choreography is excellent. *Starlight Express* costumes are a knockout, making the apparition of roller skaters masquerading as trains almost credible. There is a lot of redundancy in the sing-a-song then race-around-the-track pattern of the show, but not enough to blunt the overall impact. On balance, *Starlight Express* is an excellent addition to the Las Vegas production show lineup and a fine night's entertainment.

Consumer Tips With tax, a ticket to *Starlight Express* ranges from about $22 for a side view, upwards to $50 for main floor and balcony seats. For children ages 4–12, admission is $22 regardless of seating. No drinks are included. While this is an expensive ticket for Las Vegas, the show is unusual and distinctive and the price is in line with what you would pay to see a comparable production on Broadway. Tickets may be purchased three months in advance by phone or at the box office. Seat assignments for *Starlight Express* are computer-generated and are printed on your admission tickets. The best way to get a good seat is to stop by the Las Vegas Hilton box office well in advance and check out available seats using the seating chart. Because of convention traffic, weekday shows are sold out as often as weekend shows. If no big convention is at the hotel, the most lightly attended performances are the late shows on Sunday and Tuesday.

The Hilton spent over $11 million renovating their showroom for *Starlight Express,* including the installation of some of the most comfortable seats in town. Unfortunately, they failed to adequately elevate the rows of seats in the rear of the theater. The view from these rows is seriously restricted. Amazingly, however, the cheapest seats (in the "Grandstand Cheering Section") offer a good view and are an incredible bargain as well. There is a cash bar located just outside the showroom. Drinks range from an expensive $2.50 to over $4 and cannot be taken back into the theater after the show begins.

Finally, the Las Vegas Hilton is leaning toward replacing *Starlight Express* with celebrity headliners in the first quarter of 1998.

Comedy Clubs

There is a lot of stand-up comedy in Las Vegas and several of the large production shows feature comedians as specialty acts. In addition, there is usually at least one comedy headliner playing in town. Big names who regularly play Las Vegas include Bill Cosby, Rodney Dangerfield, the Smothers Brothers, Joan Rivers, Andrew Dice Clay, George Carlin, Yakov Smirnoff, Don Rickles, and Rich Little. Finally, there are the comedy clubs.

A comedy club is usually a smaller showroom with a simple stage and two to five stand-up comics. In most of the Las Vegas comedy showrooms, a new show with different comedians rotates in each week. There are five bona fide Las Vegas comedy clubs:

MGM Grand	*Catch a Rising Star*
Harrah's	*An Evening at the Improv*
Maxim	*Comedy Max*
Riviera	*Comedy Club*
Tropicana	*Comedy Stop*

The comedy clubs, unlike the production showrooms, are never dark. There are two shows each night, seven days a week (except at the Riviera, where there are three performances nightly). The humor at the comedy clubs, as well as the audience, tends to be young and irreverent. A favorite and affordable entertainment for locals as well as for tourists, comedy clubs enjoy great popularity in Las Vegas.

The comedy club format is simple and straightforward. Comedians perform sequentially, and what you get depends on who is performing. The range of humor runs from slapstick to obscene to ethnic to topical to just about anything. Some comics are better than others, but all of the talent is solid and professional. There is no way to predict which club will have the best show in a given week. In fact, there may not be a "best" show, since response to comedy is a matter of individual sense of humor.

Catch a Rising Star

Type of Show: Stand-up comedy
Host Casino and Showroom: MGM Grand—Center Stage Cabaret

Reservations and Information: 891-7777

Admission Cost with Taxes: $16–18

Cast Size: 2 to 4 comedians

Nights of Lowest Attendance: Sunday, Monday

Usual Show Times: 8 and 10:30 p.m.

Special Comments: No drinks included

Topless: No   *Smoking Allowed:* No

Description and Comments   Advance reservations can be made by phone with your credit card with a $2 service charge per ticket or before the show at the Grand Theater box office. Drinks are not included in your admission but can be purchased from a server after you are seated. If you use MGM Grand valet or self-parking, give yourself an extra 15 minutes or so to get to the showroom. Seating is by the maitre d'.

Comedy Max

Type of Show: Stand-up comedy

Host Casino and Showroom: Maxim—Cabaret Showroom

Reservations and Information: 731-4300 or (800) 634-6787

Admission Cost with Taxes: $18.75 includes tax and 2 drinks

Cast Size: Usually 3 comedians

Nights of Lowest Attendance: Wednesday, Thursday

Usual Show Times: 7 and 9 p.m.

Special Comments: Show and buffet combo at $21.95

Topless: No   *Smoking Allowed:* No

Description and Comments   Reservations may be made by phone or in person in advance, or tickets may be purchased with a credit card up to one month in advance at (800) 634-6787. Admission must be prepaid at the *Comedy Max* box office near the entrance to the showroom. After being seated by the maitre d', patrons turn in their ticket stubs to waiters for two drinks. The Cabaret Showroom is a comfortable and intimate room where patrons sit grouped around small tables. Visibility is good from almost all seats. The best place to park is in the Maxim's garage, situated on Flamingo just east of the hotel.

Comedy Stop

Type of Show: Stand-up comedy

Host Casino and Showroom: Tropicana—Comedy Stop Showroom

Reservations and Information: 739-2714

Admission Cost with Taxes: $16 with 2 drinks and gratuity

Cast Size: Usually 3 comedians

Nights of Lowest Attendance: Monday–Wednesday

Usual Show Times: 8 and 10:30 p.m.

Special Comments: Admission includes 2 drinks

Topless: No   *Smoking Allowed:* Only at late show

Duration of Presentation: An hour and a half

Description and Comments   To reach the Comedy Stop Showroom take the elevator (between the main casino and the shopping arcade) up one floor. The 400-person showroom is rectangular, with the stage on the long side. All seating is at banquet tables. Tickets may be purchased up to two weeks in advance by phone with a credit card, or admission can be prepaid at the *Comedy Stop* guest desk near the entrance to the showroom. After being seated by the maitre d', patrons turn in their ticket stubs at a self-service bar for two drinks. If you use the Trop's self-parking lot, give yourself an extra ten minutes to get to the showroom.

An Evening at the Improv

Type of Show: Stand-up comedy

Host Casino and Showroom: Harrah's—The Improv

Reservations and Information: 369-5111

Admission Cost with Taxes: $17

Cast Size: 3 to 4 comedians

Nights of Lowest Attendance: Wednesday, Thursday

Usual Show Times: 8 and 10:30 p.m.   *Dark:* Monday

Topless: No   *Smoking Allowed:* No

Description and Comments   Drinks are not included, but there is a self-serve cash bar. The showroom is located on the second floor at the top of the escalator from the main casino. Reserved seats may be purchased by phone or in person up to 30 days in advance.

Riviera Comedy Club

Type of Show: Stand-up comedy

Host Casino and Showroom: Riviera—Mardi Gras Showrooms, second floor

Reservations and Information: 794-9433

Admission Cost with Taxes: $19 general admission; $25 VIP (includes tax, tip, and 2 drinks)

Cast Size: Approximately 4

Nights of Lowest Attendance: Sunday–Wednesday

Usual Show Times: 8, 10, and Friday and Saturday only at 11:45 p.m.

Topless: No   *Smoking Allowed:* No

Description and Comments   Three shows—*Riviera Comedy Club, Crazy Girls,* and *La Cage*—are staged on the second and third floors above the Riviera casino in what are called the Mardi Gras Showrooms. In addition, the production show *Splash II* plays off of the main casino in the Versailles Theater. It is not possible to schedule different shows back to back unless there is a minimum of an hour and a half between performances.

Show tickets can also be purchased as a package with the Riviera's buffet. The food with the show-dinner combo is a good deal for the money but is not exactly a culinary breakthrough. The buffet is fast and convenient, however, and there is usually plenty of time to eat between shows.

Tickets for the *Comedy Club* may be purchased 21 days in advance at the Riviera box office located in the front center of the casino or by phone with a credit card. Seating is by the maitre d'. There is no table service. After you are seated, proceed to the bar and turn in your ticket stub for drinks. Drinks are included even with the dinner combos.

Las Vegas Night Life

When it comes to nightspots, visitors and locals tend to go in different directions. With the exception of patronizing the comedy clubs, locals stay away from the Strip; visitors, conversely, almost never leave it. Both groups are missing out on some great night life.

Happily, lounges and clubs all over town are friendly and open, welcoming anyone who walks through the door. Visitors can feel comfortable in places primarily frequented by locals and vice versa. This kind of acceptance allows for a wide range of choices when it comes to night life.

Since you don't have to worry about feeling unwanted or out of place, you can select your nighttime entertainment on the basis of personal taste. Listed alphabetically below are profiles of the better nightspots in town. Celebrity headliner shows, production shows, and comedy clubs are detailed in the preceding section. Striptease shows (for men and women) are also described in the following chapter, "Las Vegas below the Belt."

THE BEACH

Dance music of the '70s, '80s, and '90s

Who Goes There: 21–40+; locals, visitors,
conventioneers (cosmopolitan mix)

356 Convention Center (corner of Paradise and Convention Center,
across from the Convention Center) 731-1925   Strip Zone 1

Hours: Varies according to entertainment. Sports bar and book: open 24 hours; dance bar opens at 10 p.m.

Cover: Varies; usually $10 for out-of-state guests on weekends; ladies are never charged.

Minimum: None

Mixed drinks: $2.50 and up

Wine: $2.50 and up

Beer: $2.50 and up

Dress: Casual to stylish (dress code enforced)

Specials: Friday is martini night with a buffet; call for concert information.

Food available: Typical pub fare and daily plate specials

What goes on: These beach lovers don't miss the sand or the surf because all the action is indoors. On the main floor, singles, couples, and new friends alike dance, drink, eat, and laugh the night away in this "local's favorite" party club. The fun is so contagious that even the bartenders and cocktail waitresses join in the dancing. From the second-floor sports bar, patrons watch games on over 35 TVs; play slots, video poker, or arcade games; and view the action on the main floor. The Beach is an unpretentious and fun-loving spot that radiates positive energy and vibes.

Setting & atmosphere: Neon beer lights, palm fronds, coconuts, surfboards, and brightly painted murals give the club a beach flavor without adding salt or sand. The wood walls offer excellent acoustics for live performances and the deejay's taped music. The main floor has four bars, high-table seating, and a dance area. Adjacent to the upstairs sports bar is a separate room available for private parties or extra party space. ATM machines are on each floor.

If you go: Long lines begin at 9 p.m. and continue well past 2 a.m. on weekends. Even with an attached four-level garage, parking is quite limited. Plan to arrive very early or take a cab. Smoke can be heavy in some corners of the club. Women on their own can expect to find company. Call ahead for special events information.

CLUB PARADISE

Upscale topless bar

Who Goes There: Men 21–65; professionals and conventioneers

4416 Paradise Road
734-7990   Strip Zone 1

Hours: Open 6 p.m. to 6 a.m.
Cover: $10
Minimum: 2 drinks
Mixed drinks: $5 and up
Wine: $4.50 and up

Beer: $4.50 and up
Dress: Casual to dressy
Specials: None
Food available: Salty snacks and light
   hors d'oeuvres

What goes on: Club Paradise is a very plush, upscale topless bar featuring more than 100 dancers in a setting designed to make executives feel at ease. Featured dancers perform on an elevated stage, while others dance at patrons' tables. A live jazz group provides accompaniment to the dancing most evenings. There is a special VIP section that has its own small dance stage. To sit in the VIP section you must commit to purchasing a minimum of $50 in drinks per person during the course of the evening, in addition to the cover charge.

Setting & atmosphere: The club is tastefully decorated with upholstered armchairs, dark carpet, erotic wall art, and elegant fixtures.

If you go: Parking is valet only. Seating is by the maitre d'. Though Club Paradise bills itself as a gentleman's club, women patrons are welcome. Be sure to eat dinner before you go.

CLUB RIO

Nightclub—Top 40 music

Who Goes There: 25–35 professionals; locals and visitors

3700 W. Flamingo (Rio Hotel)
252-7777   Strip Zone 1

Hours: Wednesday–Saturday,
   10:30 p.m.–4:30 a.m.
Cover: Ladies, free; men, $10; out-
   of-state ladies, $5
Minimum: None
Mixed drinks: $4.50 and up
Wine: $4 and up

Beer: $3.50 and up
Dress: Collared shirts for men; no
   jeans, shorts, or sandals
Specials: None
Food available: Restaurants on
   property

(Club Rio)

What goes on: Sexy and stylish, Club Rio is the hottest nightclub for successful singles and the chic well-to-do. Dancers fill the spacious dance floor and the limited area on the curtained stage. Couples snuggle in the showroom's comfy booths, while others mingle with potential partners. Although the music is loud and pulsating, there's little trouble conversing with new friends or ordering drinks from the attractive cocktail waitresses.

Setting & atmosphere: After the last show, the Copacabana showroom is transformed into a cosmopolitan nightclub with table lamps, tuxedoed bartenders, mosaic laser lights, and giant video panels. Selected sections of booth seating are reserved for casino players. The sound system is clean and clear, loud but not deafening.

If you go: Arrive early to avoid the long lines after 11 p.m. The dress code encourages stylish attire (jackets for the men and dresses for the women). Watch your step along the showroom's terraced levels as you make your way to and from the dance floor. The club is located off the new Masquerade Village.

THE DRINK

Top 40 blended with taped '70s and '80s music

Who Goes There: 25–40; locals, visitors, and college students

Corner of Harmon & Kovall
796-5519   Strip Zone I

Hours: 8 p.m.–3 a.m.,
  Tuesday–Saturday
Cover: $5 after 10 p.m.; no cover,
  Tuesday and Wednesday
Minimum: None
Mixed drinks: $3–5
Wine: $3

Beer: $3–3.75
Dress: No sleeveless shirts for men;
  casual to dressy
Specials: '70s band on Thursday
  night; foam night, Tuesday
Food available: Pasta, burgers, salads,
  steak, ribs, and appetizers

What goes on: This latest hip and happening nightspot prides itself on old-fashioned fun—eat, drink, be merry, and smoke cigars. Couples and friends enjoy the salads, sandwiches, soups, steaks, pasta, and pizza before joining the crowd on the dance floors. Guys act cool smoking the long cigars, and gals act like the guys don't impress them.

Setting & atmosphere: Imagine an old pirate fortress first redecorated by hippies, then discovered by Generation X, and you have The Drink. Mod colors and flowers adorn the rough walls and exposed rebar and air-conditioning ducts. With six party rooms, three themed bars, and three dance areas, there's elbowroom for everyone. The enclosed courtyard serves as the main dance floor and concert venue. Libations vary from martinis to vodka infusions to microbrews and imports. Select your favorite stogy from the humidor in the VIP room.

If you go: While the dress style is eclectic, you'll feel best when dressed to impress. Because the club comes to life at midnight, arrive early to avoid long lines and congested parking. People who do not appreciate cigars will enjoy their evening more at another club.

DYLAN'S SALOON & DANCE HALL

Recorded country music

Who Goes There: 25–40; urban and rodeo cowboys

4660 S. Boulder Hwy.
451-4006   Southeast Zone 5

Hours: 7 p.m. until, Wednesday–Saturday	Beer: $1.75 and up
	Dress: Jeans and cowboy hats
Cover: None	Specials: Happy hour, 7–9 p.m., with 50 cent beer; line dance
Minimum: None	
Mixed drinks: $2 and up	lessons, 7:30–9 p.m.
Wine: $2.25 and up	Food available: Typical bar fare

What goes on: Whether it's doing the two-step, shooting a game of pool, or enjoying a summer evening on the covered patio, the young and lively crowd whoops it up on the weekends. From ballads to rockabilly, the deejay mixes the music to the crowd's delight. Seating at the railing is at a premium as singles look to meet new partners. In a recent poll, Dylan's was voted best country bar.

Setting & atmosphere: This small dance hall has a spacious, 2,400-square-foot, silky smooth dance floor, two bars, friendly folks, and the usual rodeo decor. The party flows onto the patio and, on busy nights, the chain-linked, flood-lit, dirt area adjacent to the parking lot. As the night parties on, the odors of beer and cigarette smoke get thicker.

If you go: The attitude is looser and hipper than Sam's Town Dance Hall. Arrive early for good seating. Because the parking lot is quite dark in areas, women on their own are advised to ask for an escort to their car.

FINAL SCORE SPORTS BAR

Sports bar

Who Goes There: 21–35; locals, Air Force personnel, college crowd, visitors

---

5111 Boulder Hwy. (Sam's Town Hotel & Gambling Hall)
   456-7777   Southeast Zone 5

Hours: 10 a.m.–1 a.m. or later, Monday–Thursday; 24 hours, Friday–Sunday
Cover: None
Minimum: None
Mixed drinks: $2 and up
Wine: $1.50 and up

Beer: $1–2
Dress: Casual
Specials: Happy hour, 2 a.m.–10 a.m., Friday–Sunday, with 75 cent drafts and $1.50 drinks
Food available: Hamburgers, wings, bar fare

What goes on: Whether it's shooting the hoops, spiking the volleyball, or making the corner pocket, the sports enthusiast can find it all at this hands-on sports bar. In addition to the indoor games, the bar also hosts football parties, special events, exhibitions, and tournaments. Friday and Saturday nights are the busiest, offering the solo guest a great chance to meet new friends.

Setting & atmosphere: Besides the usual assortment of sports memorabilia, photos, and equipment, the bar offers excellent amusements—regulation-size basketball key court for two players, five pool tables, electric dart boards, pop-a-shots, video slots, pinball, interactive TV games, over 25 TVs, VH1 music videos, a sand volleyball pit in the outdoor recreation area, and more. Harking back to the golden days of baseball, the bar is made from mahogany wood and has a checkered floor, hand-painted wall murals, domestic and imported beer on tap, and good menu fare.

If you go: Because it's located in the indoor park, use valet parking for easy access. Call ahead for special event information.

FRENCH QUARTER

Live jazz, folk, vintage rock

Who Goes There: 35–65; tourists, locals

Four Queens, 202 Fremont
385-4011 Downtown Zone 2

Hours: 8 p.m.–midnight, Tuesday–Friday; 8 p.m.–1 a.m., Saturday	Wine: $3.50 and up
	Beer: $1.25 and up
Cover: None	Dress: Casual to dressy
Minimum: $4	Specials: None
Mixed drinks: $1.25 and up	Food available: In casino

What goes on: People of all ages and backgrounds pack this New Orleans–themed club. A variety of jazz artists and others entertain nightly. On Monday night, host Alan Grant tapes his popular public radio show. Nearby casino patrons gamble in time to the music.

Setting & atmosphere: If the lounge wasn't open to the casino, you could imagine yourself enjoying a spring evening in a Southern courtyard. An 1800s New Orleans facade provides the backdrop. A few tables are dotted about the room, making space for more seating.

If you go: Reservations are strongly suggested anytime. The price per drink is steep, but the entertainment is first rate. Dress comfortably or stylishly for a night of live music. Call ahead for specific information.

GOLD COAST DANCE HALL & SALOON

Country, ballroom, rock and roll

Who Goes There: 25–40 for country-western; 35–50 for rock; 40+ for ballroom dancing; real and urban cowboys; locals and tourists

---

4000 W. Flamingo Rd.
367-7111 Strip Zone 3

Hours: Varies according to the entertainment; generally noon–3 a.m., Sunday–Thursday; noon–4 a.m., Friday and Saturday	Cover: $5
	Minimum: None
	Mixed drinks: $1.50 and up
	Wine: $1.50 and up

(Gold Coast Dance Hall & Saloon)

Beer: $1.50 and up
Dress: Jeans and boots for country; casual for rock; semi-dressy to dressy for ballroom dancing

Specials: Gold Coast Orchestra (8 weeks during the year)
Food available: In casino

What goes on: A locals' top-rated dance hall, tourists join in for a fun night of country, rock, salsa, or big band sounds. Silver-haired waltzers take over on big band nights. Live music notwithstanding, conversation is possible, especially at the bars toward the rear of the dance hall.

Setting & atmosphere: The Gold Coast Dance Hall could hold three tractor-trailers and a herd of buffalo. The oval-shaped dance floor is the largest in Las Vegas. Wood-grained walls and wrought-iron chandeliers give the place a touch of Old California elegance.

If you go: Whether it's country, rock, or the special Gold Coast Orchestra engagements, the entertainment is set on a weekly basis. Call for the current schedule. The pluses are the spacious dance floor and discreet hotel security. Those under 35, however, might find the crowd too conservative. For more excitement, try Dylan's or The Drink.

MONTE CARLO PUB & BREWERY

Comedy and music

Who Goes There: 25–50; tourists, conventioneers, and microbrew lovers

Monte Carlo Casino
3770 Las Vegas Blvd., S. 730-7777 Strip Zone 1

Hours: Sunday–Thursday, 11–2 a.m.; Friday and Saturday, 11–4 a.m.; entertainment starts at 9 p.m.
Cover: None
Minimum: None
Mixed drinks: $3 and up

Wine: $2.75 and up
Beer: $2.95–9.50 (logo glass)
Dress: Casual
Specials: Nightly dinner specials and seasonal brews
Food available: Burgers, appetizers, pizza, and other bar fare.

What goes on: The pub fills up quickly with hungry folk looking for fresh pub food, brews, and rollicking comedy and music. The room reverberates with conversation, laughter, and sing-alongs. The staff quickly serves up hamburgers, pizzas, and more, while the cocktail waitresses offer after-dinner drinks and cigars.

(Monte Carlo Pub & Brewery)

Setting & atmosphere: While the concrete floors, copper pipes, and steel catwalks help create the brewery atmosphere, they do little to absorb the room's noise. Conversation is strained. Watch the antics of the comedic musicians on one of the 35+ monitors scattered throughout the room. Two small patios overlook the Parisian promenade.

If you go: Dress is casual. Lines are short and fast moving. If you don't want to fight traffic on the Strip to get to the Monte Carlo, try the easy-access Triple Seven Brewpub at downtown's Main Street Station.

THE NIGHTCLUB

Top 40/show combination

Who Goes There: 30–50; visitors, locals, convention-goers/businesspeople

Las Vegas Hilton, 3000 Paradise Road
   732-5755 or 732-5422   Strip Zone 1

Hours: 8 p.m.–2 a.m., nightly	Dress: Upscale casual
Cover: None	Specials: Two regular alternating
Minimum: One drink per set	performers, with guest performers
Mixed drinks: $3.75–5.75	on Thursday night
Wine: $3.75	Food available: None
Beer: $2.50	

What goes on: Couples and friends boogie to good live renditions of pop music on the small, curvy dance floor. Others are content to watch the leather-clad dancers on stage cavorting with the musicians. Meanwhile, onlookers admire the whole scene. Singles can either sit back and enjoy the show or meet new friends.

Setting & atmosphere: A combination of a Las Vegas showroom and a New York dance club, The Nightclub is a trendy art deco hot spot. The bar, situated in the rear of the 450-seat lounge, serves up libations and hosts more intimate conversation. On the wall to the left of the stage is a mutely painted mural of an art deco cityscape. The second floor provides a bird's-eye view of the band and offers a bit more seating space.

If you go: Arrive early for choice seating. Cocktail service tends to be relaxed in this no-pressure environment. Because of the long hike from the public parking areas, take a cab or use valet for convenience. Dress is upscale yet casual.

OLYMPIC GARDEN

Topless bar

Who Goes There: Men 21–65; locals, visitors, and conventioneers

1531 Las Vegas Blvd., S.
385-8987   Strip Zone 1

Hours: Open 2 p.m.–6 a.m.	Beer: $4.75
Cover: $15, includes 2 drinks	Dress: Casual
Minimum: 2 drinks, after 8 p.m.	Specials: None
Mixed drinks: $4.50	Food available: Snack-bar subs, fries,
Wine: $4.75–6	wings, and fingers; $3–5

What goes on: Connoisseurs consider Olympic Garden the finest topless joint in Las Vegas. It's not the classiest club in town, but it is one of the most relaxed and least aggressive. And the women are top of the line. At any given time, 50 of the most eye-popping strippers in varying degrees of undress are on display. Four dancers in bikini bottoms or t-backs occupy the four center stages, playing the stageside audiences for tips, with some very explicit moves. Other showgirl-quality women gyrate in laps, walk to and from the dressing rooms, or just hang around the main entrance. You won't have any trouble getting entertained at Olympic Garden. Most nights there's a male strip show on the second floor for local and visiting ladies (men must be accompanied by a woman to watch).

Setting & atmosphere: Olympic Garden is basically a large, dimly lit room with booths against the walls and tables on the floor. Near the front door is a clothing shop with a large selection of lingerie. There's a video poker bar in the back.

If you go: Parking is free in the large, well-lit lot (usually crowded); valet parking is also available. Seating is by the cocktail waitress.

PALOMINO CLUB

Totally nude dance club

Who Goes There: Men 21–65; tourists, locals, conventioneers

1848 Las Vegas Boulevard, N.
642-2984   North Las Vegas Zone 4

Hours: Open 1:30 p.m. to 4 a.m.	Minimum: Two drinks
Cover: $10	Mixed drinks: $6

(Palomino Club)

Wine: $6   Specials: None
Beer: $6   Food available: None
Dress: Casual

What goes on: Because it is situated in North Las Vegas, in a different jurisdiction from the Strip, the Palomino can offer both nude dancing and alcoholic beverages. On the Strip and downtown, clubs can offer either total nudity or alcohol, but not both. Go figure. Anyway, about nine professionals and an equal number of so-called amateurs strip completely nude each night. A stand-up comic spells the dancers from time to time and provides the patrons with a good excuse to increase their alcohol consumption.

Setting & atmosphere: Unpretentious but comfortable, the emphasis at the Palomino is definitely on the performers, not the decor.

If you go: The Palomino has its own lighted self-parking lot. Seating is by the maitre d'. Once you have paid the cover charge and ordered your two drinks, you can stay all night as long as you are well behaved. For what it's worth, women are welcome.

PEPPERMILL INN'S FIRESIDE LOUNGE

Romantic and quiet

Who Goes There: 25–45; locals and tourists

2985 Las Vegas Blvd., S.
   (across from the Stardust, between Silver City Casino and La Concha)
   Restaurant, 735-4177; Lounge, 735-7635   Strip Zone 1

Hours: Open 24 hours   Beer: $2.25 and up
Cover: None   Dress: Casual
Minimum: None   Specials: None
Mixed drinks: $3.50 and up   Food available: Appetizers available;
Wine: $3.50 and up   restaurant adjacent

What goes on: The Peppermill has been a longtime favorite of the locals. Couples and friends relax on plush, circular sofas while enjoying conversation and munchies. The peacefulness of the Fireside Lounge is a great escape from the frantic pace of the casinos.

Setting & atmosphere: One doesn't expect a lounge like this in a 24-hour coffee shop. It's inviting, quiet, and even tranquil. Tropical greenery creates secluded alcoves of privacy. A unique fireplace with gas flames dancing upon a small pool of water can be hypnotizing! Taped soft rock and popular music play over a modest sound system.

If you go: Be warned—Las Vegas Boulevard car traffic is congested on weekends, making it preferable to walk or let a cabbie fight the traffic for you. Drinks are a bit pricey and vary in quality depending on the bartender. Service can be as relaxed as the atmosphere. If you really need to unwind, order your first drink from the bartender.

SAM'S TOWN DANCE HALL

DJ country-western music

Who Goes There: 25–40 weekends, 25–60 during the week; locals, tourists, cowboys

Sam's Town Hotel, 5111 Boulder Hwy.
456-7777   Southeast Zone 5

Hours: Monday–Saturday,
  7 p.m.–3 a.m.; Sunday, 7 p.m.–3
  a.m. (deejay)
Cover: None
Minimum: None
Mixed drinks: $1.75 and up
Wine: $1.75 and up
Beer: $1.50 and up
Dress: Casual and Western wear
Specials: Happy hour, 7–9 p.m., well
drinks and domestic beer $1; special events and parties throughout the year; karaoke, Sundays; Ladies' Night, Mondays, domestic beer or well drinks $1 all night; Cowboy Beer Night, Tuesdays, 22-ounce beer; dance lessons nightly
Food available: In casino

What goes on: City slickers rub elbows with real cowboys of all ages and kick up their heels to some of the best country music bands in Las Vegas. Newcomers, singles, and couples attend free dance lessons to pick up the latest line and swing steps. Monday through Saturday, at 9 p.m., the party gets started. On Sundays, croon to your favorite songs during karaoke time.

Setting & atmosphere: The cozy dance hall has high ceilings and a smooth wooden dance floor. Booths line the stuccoed walls, and additional tables are huddled in back next to the bar. Men and women looking for a partner sit at the railing. Neon beer signs, cowboy pictures, branding irons, and buffalo heads enhance the Western ambiance. The bar is service-oriented and has no seating or slots.

(Sam's Town Dance Hall)

If you go: Put on your fancy boots for a hot night of dancing. Be aware that the dance hall can get quite smoky. The music is loud, so if you want to talk it's best to step outside the dance hall. Hotel security discreetly keeps an eye out for unruliness. Women can expect to be asked to dance. Parking is scattered around the property at Sam's Town. Your best bet is to park in the "Nellis parking barn" connected to the casino.

SAND DOLLAR BLUES LOUNGE

Rhythm and blues

Who Goes There: Bikers to yuppies

3355 Spring Mountain Rd. (at Polaris)
    871-6651   Southwest Zone 3

Hours: Open 24 hours; music starts at 9:30 p.m.	**Beer:** $2.50 and up
	Dress: Casual
Cover: $3–5, Wednesday–Saturday	**Specials:** Drink specials and prices depend on the event.
Minimum: None	
Mixed drinks: $2.50 and up	**Food available:** Packaged snack food; no kitchen
Wine: $2.50 and up	

What goes on: Everyone from attorneys to bikers sits back for an evening full of moody and marvelous blues by popular Las Vegas or out-of-town bands. It's standing-room only on Friday, Saturday, and special-event nights. Strip musicians gather for various jam sessions. In the back, pool players croon to the blues.

Setting & atmosphere: The exterior is nondescript. Both the interior and the patrons are earthy and full of character. The low ceiling keeps the lounge quite smoky. The U-shaped bar separates the dance floor from the pool tables. Nautical rope, worn wood pilings, small fishing nets, and sand dollars add to the bar's salty character. Neon beer signs and handwritten flyers dot the walls.

If you go: The club's unshaven appearance may deter some solo ladies from experiencing a night of great blues. The regulars make sure everything stays cool. The Sand Dollar is hard to spot at night, so arrive early or come by cab.

TOMMY ROCKER'S CANTINA AND CAFE

Top 40 and Jimmy Buffett–style music

Who Goes There: 25–30; professionals and career starters

4275 S. Industrial Road
  261-6688   Strip Zone 1

Hours: Open 24 hours
Cover: None
Minimum: None
Mixed drinks: $1.50–3.25;
  wide selection of tequilas and
  rums
Wine: $2.75
Beer: $1.50–3; many microbrew
draft selections
Dress: Casual to sporty
Specials: Happy hour 4–7 p.m. and
  4–7 a.m. with $1 off all drinks
  and appetizers; they are also the
  official Jimmy Buffett fan club
  location—call for special event
  information.

What goes on: Singles and couples gather to check out the music and witty repartee of Tommy Rocker, the club's owner and professional musician when he's in town. Otherwise, they enjoy meeting new friends, singing Jimmy Buffett songs, shooting a friendly game of pool, cheering their favorite team on the big-screen TV, and indulging in the tasty libations and food fare.

Setting & atmosphere: An eclectic mix of Indian petroglyph images, palm trees, parrots, and neon gives Tommy Rocker's Cantina and Cafe a refreshing twist to the beach-style bar scene. In addition to the big-screen TV and two pool tables, the club offers a small dance floor, a nonsmoking party area, patio seating, and a standard center bar complete with progressive slot machines and a palm cabana roof.

If you go: Voted best singles bar in a local survey, Tommy Rocker's offers plenty of parking, friendly yet professional security, and a great attitude. The music is loud but not deafening, allowing for good conversation. Come early for best seating.

TRIPLE SEVEN BREWPUB

Brewpub

Who Goes There: 25–45; locals and visitors

Main Street Station, 200 N. Main Street
  387-1896   Downtown Zone 2

Hours: Open 24 hours
Cover: None
Minimum: None
Mixed drinks: $1.75 and up
Wine: $2.50 and up
Beer: $1.75 and up
Dress: Casual
Specials: The late-night 16 oz.
microbrew for $1; the 40 oz. beer glass (with logo) for $5; and seasonal brews
Food available: 24-hour kitchen with regular menu offered weekdays from 11–2 a.m., weekends until 3 a.m.

What goes on: The emphasis is on fresh microbrews, creative food, and entertainment. Locals and visitors alike enjoy an evening of relaxed frivolity. Singles hang out at the counter seating, while couples and friends fill up the tables.

Setting & atmosphere: Finely detailed mahogany bar counters, high pressed-tin ceilings, crystal wall lamps, and mirrors give the room a Victorian touch, and the brewery's serving tanks can be viewed through the room's windows.

If you go: Valet service is friendly and fast, just like the brewpub on weekends. While Triple Seven Brewpub serves up excellent beer and food, skip the so-so sushi and California rolls. Call ahead for special events.

VOODOO CAFE AND LOUNGE

Restaurant and lounge with live entertainment

Who Goes There: 25+; upscale visitors and locals

Rio Hotel, 3700 W. Flamingo Rd.
  257-7777, ext. 8090   Southwest Zone 3

Hours: 11–3 a.m.
Lunch: 11:30 a.m.–3 p.m.
Dinner: 5–11 p.m.
Entertainment: 9 p.m.–2 a.m. (dark Monday)
Cover: None
Minimum: None
Mixed drinks: $3 and up
Wine: $2.75 and up
Beer: $2 and up

(VooDoo Cafe and Lounge)

Dress: Casual to dressy; no hats, T-shirts, sport sandals, tank tops, tennis shoes, jean shorts, or torn/baggy jeans.
Specials: None

Food available: Creole/Cajun- and Louisiana-style soups, salads, and entrees in restaurant. Lunch prices: $5.95–13.95; dinner prices: $10.95–32.95

What goes on: Sweethearts, friends, and colleagues enjoy conversation, delicious regional cuisine, and live music. The lounge crowd grows as the evening approaches midnight and the VooDoo Cafe diners and late-night party-goers ascend to the 51st floor. Music lovers relax and enjoy the jazz and blues beat in the lounge. Adventurous souls party on the open-air patio, amazed at the electrifying view of the famous Strip and the surrounding Las Vegas valley.

Setting & atmosphere: The trendy decor is complete with black ceilings, mysterious paintings illuminated by black light, and animal-skin chair furnishings. Both the 50th-floor restaurant and the 51st-floor lounge are surrounded by glass windows and connected by a center staircase. The restaurant's menu includes such delectable items as shrimp Creole, seafood gumbo, soft-shell crab Lafayette, veal Oscar, and lobster thermidor. The staff is friendly, attentive, and knowledgeable about the menu. At the centralized bar, bartenders offer little conversation, as they efficiently serve the packed crowd. Conversation can be strained due to the ambient noise and entertainment.

If you go: While gusty desert winds are normal in Las Vegas, expect stronger winds in the spring and fall months and during weather changes. If the weather is questionable, call ahead to confirm that the patio will be open. After 10 p.m. on Friday and Saturday, expect a long line at the VooDoo elevators (managed by a humorless staff). Park in the "Masquerade Village" parking garage for easy access. If your evening plans include dancing, go to Club Rio.

Las Vegas below the Belt

■ Don't Worry, Be Happy ■

In many ways, Las Vegas is a bastion of hedonism. Just being there contributes to a lessening of inhibitions and a partial discarding of the rules that apply at home. Las Vegas exults in its permissiveness and makes every effort to live up to its image and to give its visitors freedom to have fun. Las Vegas has a steaminess, a sophisticated cosmopolitan excitement born of excess, an aura of risk and reward, a sense of freedom. The rules are different here; it's all right to let go.

Behind the illusion, however, is a community, and more particularly, a police department that puts a lot of effort into making it safe for visitors to experience the liberation of Las Vegas. It is hard to imagine another city where travelers can carry such large sums of money so safely. A tourist can get robbed or worked over in Las Vegas, but it is comparatively rare, and more often than not is due to the tourist's own stupidity. The Strip and downtown, especially, are well patrolled, and most hotels have very professional in-house security forces.

In general a tourist who stays either on the Strip or downtown will be very safe. Police patrol in cars, on foot, and, interestingly, on mountain bikes. The bikes allow the police to quickly catch pickpockets or purse snatchers attempting to make their escape down sidewalks or through parking lots. Streets that connect the Strip with Paradise Road and the Las Vegas Convention Center are also lighted and safe. When tourists get robbed, they are commonly far from downtown or the Strip, and often are trying to buy drugs.

■ Organized Crime and Cheating ■

Very few visitors walk through a casino without wondering if the games are rigged or the place is owned by the mafia. During the early days of legalized gambling, few people outside of organized crime had any real experience in managing gaming operations. Hence a fair number of characters fresh from Eastern gangs and crime families came to work in Nevada. Since they constituted the resource pool for experienced gambling operators, the state suffered their presence as a necessary evil. In 1950, Tennessee senator

Estes Kefauver initiated an attack on organized crime that led (indirectly) to the formation of the Nevada Gaming Commission and the State Gaming Control Board. These agencies, in conjunction with federal efforts, were ultimately able to purge organized crime from Las Vegas. This ouster, coupled with the Nevada Corporate Gaming Acts of 1967 and 1969 (allowing publicly held corporations such as Hilton, Holiday Inn, Bally, and MGM to own casinos), at last brought a mantle of respectability to Las Vegas gambling.

Today the Gaming Control Board oversees the activities of all Nevada gaming establishments, maintaining tight control through frequent unannounced inspections of gambling personnel and equipment. If you ever have reason to doubt the activity or clout of the Gaming Control Board, try walking around the Strip or downtown in a dark business suit and plain black shoes. You will attract more attention from the casino management than if you entered with a parrot on your head.

Cheating exists in Las Vegas gambling to a limited degree but is seldom perpetrated by the house itself. In fact, most cheating is done at the expense of the house, though honest players at the cheater's table may also get burned. Sometimes a dealer, working alone or with an accomplice (posing as a player), will cheat, and there are always con artists ready to take advantage of the house and legitimate players.

Skin Games—Sex in Las Vegas   Though nudity, prostitution, and pornography are regulated more tightly in Las Vegas than in many Bible Belt cities, the town exudes an air of sexual freedom and promiscuity. Las Vegas offers a near-perfect environment for marketing sex. Over 50% of all visitors are men, most between the ages of 21 and 59. Some come to party, and many, particularly convention-goers, are lonely. Almost all have time and money on their hands.

Las Vegas evolved as a gambling man's city, proudly projecting the image of a trail town where a man could be comfortable and just about anything could be had for a price. It was not until strong competition developed for the gambling dollar that hotels sought to enlarge their market by targeting women and families. Today, though there is something for everyone in Las Vegas, its male orientation remains unusually strong.

Las Vegas, perhaps more than any other American city, has objectified women. A number of Las Vegas production shows continue to feature topless showgirls and erotic dance, even though audiences are mostly couples. Lounge servers and keno runners are almost exclusively women, invariably attired in revealing outfits. Showroom comedians, after 30 years, persist in describing Las Vegas as an adult Disneyland.

Stripping on the Strip Compared to the live adult entertainment in many cities, "girlie" (and "boy") shows in Las Vegas, both downtown and on the Las Vegas Strip, are fairly tame. In some of the larger showrooms, this is an accommodation to the ever-growing percentage of women in the audience. More often, however, it is a matter of economics rather than taste, the result of a curious City of Las Vegas law which stipulates that you can offer totally nude entertainment or you can serve alcoholic beverages, but not both.

More often than not, topless showgirls are a mere embellishment to a production that features song, dance, and variety acts. For the most part, the partial nudity is incidental and unimportant. While half a dozen continuously running shows include a steamy, highly erotic dance number, these acts are not the focal point. Las Vegas entertainment is slowly moving away from nudity and eroticism, though for the moment, the genre is in no imminent danger of extinction. Some shows have de-emphasized bare breasts, and a few shows offer both a topless and a "covered" performance.

If you want to see stunning topless showgirls and dancers, the most erotic of the continuously running productions are *Crazy Girls* at the Riviera, followed by *Enter the Night* at the Stardust. *Crazy Girls* is a topless, all-girl revue. The other show is a production spectacular that has prettier-than-average showgirls and sultrier-than-average dance numbers.

Male Strippers Economics and the market have begun to redress (or undress) the inequality of women's erotic entertainment in Las Vegas. Spearheaded by the now-extinct Dunes, which featured (Chippendales) male strippers for lengthy engagements, and empowered by the ever-growing number of professional women visiting Las Vegas for trade shows and conventions, the rules for sexual objectification are being rewritten. Today in Las Vegas, if watching a young stud flex his buns is a woman's idea of a good time, that experience is usually available (see the Olympic Garden in the Night Life section on page 225).

Expensive Voyeurism Just off the Strip are a number of adult entertainment nightspots that feature total nudity. The Can Can Room, located on Industrial Road, bills itself as the "only totally nude show in Las Vegas" and promises to "leave nothing to your imagination." Its claim is justified when it comes to the girls; they are indeed beautiful, young, and plentiful. What is left to the imagination, however, is the alcohol in your drink—there isn't any! And beyond your imagination is the price tag on these nonalcoholic concoctions. Never again will you have the opportunity to pay so much for a glass of fruit punch.

As expensive as the Can Can Room is, there are other Las Vegas nude nightspots that can be far more expensive, not to mention embarrassing. Most of the clientele is funneled to these places by cab drivers who get a kickback for every customer delivered. Usually, as the scenario goes, a lonely tourist or businessman asks the cabbie about places where he can pick up a girl, or, more explicitly, find a prostitute. For a hefty tip the naive fellow is delivered to a nightclub which the cabbie describes as a "swinger's club: the hottest place in town—just what you are looking for." Inside the lights are low and there are a number of alluring young women, some nude, and some clad in negligees or other scanty attire. On the walls, barely readable in the dim light, are signs that state, "Prostitution Is Illegal in Las Vegas," and "No Alcoholic Beverages Shall Be Served or Consumed on These Premises."

There is no entertainment other than taped music or perhaps a jukebox; no dancers, no performers, no show. After paying a cover charge of up to $50 and being seated, the customer is invariably joined by a woman who gives every impression that she is prepared to have sex with him. In getting acquainted, she encourages him to buy her a drink, once again some astronomically priced nonalcoholic potion. If the fellow consents, she strings him along, ordering more drinks and promising great things to come. Later, she suggests that he buy a bottle of champagne (nonalcoholic), and they retire to a private back room.

In the back room she continues to come on to him and play him for additional bottles of champagne. This continues as long as he is willing to keep buying. Should he become impatient and demanding, insist on sex or refuse to buy more champagne, she will excuse herself on the pretext of using the rest room. Moments later, one or more bouncers enter the private room and forcibly eject the fellow from the club. Because of his complicity in soliciting the services of a prostitute, the customer has no legal recourse without incriminating or at least embarrassing himself.

The Palomino Club   While the Can Can Room claims to have the only totally nude show in Las Vegas, this is only true in a narrowly defined geographic sense. In North Las Vegas, a separate jurisdiction, there is no prohibition against nude entertainment and alcoholic beverages under the same roof. At the Palomino Club, four minutes from downtown, the customer can have it all.

The Palomino Club is not inexpensive, but at least they're up front about what they're selling, and best of all, you do not have to drink Shirley Temples all night. There is a $10 cover charge and a two-drink minimum, at six bucks a drink, for $22 total. To get one of the better seats, you should arrive before 10 p.m. and tip the maitre d'. Once you have purchased your two drinks, you can stay as long as you can stand it—all night if you wish.

An average of nine professionals dance every night, performing in rotation and stripping completely nude. The pros are supplemented by five or more alleged amateurs who compete for prize money and tips in a strip contest held nightly at 11 p.m. All of the women, both pro and amateur, are attractive, well-built, and athletic. A stand-up comic rounds out the entertainment.

The Palomino is without pretense. It delivers some of the best erotic dancing in town for about the same cost as a production show on the Strip. Conventioneers and tourists are the usual clientele.

Topless Bars   The main difference between a topless bar and a totally nude nightclub (aside from the alcohol regulations) is a G-string. Unless you're a gynecology intern, you might be satisfied with a topless bar. The topless bars aren't less expensive than the Palomino but are often more conveniently located. Downtown, on Fremont Street, is the Girls of Glitter Gulch. There's no cover charge, but drinks average a stiff (no pun intended) $5.75 each, with a two-drink minimum. A U-shaped stage/runway ensures a good view from most seats.

A very upscale and elegant topless bar is Club Paradise at 4416 Paradise Road, not far from the Strip. Catering to a professional clientele, high rollers, and conventioneers, Club Paradise is the Rolls Royce of topless bars. The cover charge is $10 and there is a two-drink minimum, unless you elect to sit in the VIP section, where you are obligated to consume at least 80 dollars' worth of drinks. Fortunately, because drinks go for $4.50 and up, this is not difficult.

Another plush topless bar is Cheetah's, at 2112 Western Avenue. Cover is $5, and drink prices start at about four bucks. A less upscale venue is the Olympic Garden at 1531 South Las Vegas Boulevard. Considered by locals and connoisseurs to be the best topless club in town, the Olympic Garden is the only club that also features male strippers for its female customers (in a separate showroom). The cover for either showroom is $15 and includes two drinks. The Palomino, Club Paradise, and the Olympic Garden are profiled in the Night Life section of this guide.

▪ Prostitution: Now You See It, Now You Don't ▪

The people of Nevada have always maintained a practical and essentially laissez-faire attitude toward prostitution. For years prostitution was allowed to flourish and was accorded an implicit legal status by a body of some 50 statutes enacted to regulate it. The circumstances were similar to an equally confusing situation on Mississippi's Gulf Coast 35 years ago.

Mississippi was a dry state, but along the coast there were bars everywhere, recognized as a necessary adjunct to the developing tourist industry. It was laughable to watch the local police attempt to structure and regulate an illegal industry. How do you make rules for something that is against the law?

The history of prostitution in Nevada is essentially the same story. Prostitution was against the law, yet was administered as conscientiously as tax collection. Nevadans, while of conservative, principled, pioneer origins, always accepted prostitution as a practical reality, something as predictable and inevitable as cactus in the desert. Prostitution both filled a need and, by way of payoffs, augmented the meager income of law enforcement officials, county commissioners, and others. Prostitution was making great strides as a growth industry in Nevada, moving rapidly in the direction of total legalization, until it had a head-on collision with another growth industry—gambling.

At first glance, prostitution and gambling looked like a perfect team. The legalization of gambling perpetuated the Wild West, mining-town atmosphere of Nevada cities. There had always been women to take care of the prospectors, the speculators, the railroad workers, and later the dam builders and soldiers. It seemed the most natural thing in the world, completely in keeping with the state's robust, pragmatic Western image, for gambling and prostitution to work hand in glove to stimulate the burgeoning tourism industry.

The gaming czars, however, saw it differently. They were trying to get gambling out of the back room and install it as a respectable form of recreation (like bowling or shuffleboard, only more lucrative). Elderly ladies, married couples, and even Episcopal priests could enjoy a little innocent gambling, but prostitution was a different story. There was no way to make prostitution innocent, no way to separate it from infidelity, syphilis, and gonorrhea.

On the practical side, casino owners recognized that legal or illegal, prostitution was a fact of life (if not an out-and-out necessity) in every major convention and tourist city in the United States. The owners also realized that the wild, "anything goes" Western tradition (the thematic foundation of all Nevada tourism) demanded that sex be a part of the gambling-town product mix. The real question, as the gaming industry perceived it, was, how do you impart a little sexual sauciness to your operation without actually providing for the satisfaction of appetites aroused? In other words, what were you going to do with 5,000 conventioneers who had been fed a steady diet of topless showgirls and provocatively clad lounge waitresses and keno runners? Gambling and sex were like Siamese twins, an unfortunate pairing that defied separation. Reid and Demaris did not mince words in their classic *Green Felt Jungle* when they wrote, "Money mysteriously breeds prostitutes the way decaying flesh breeds maggots. Where there's easy money there's whores; it's that basic. And where there's gambling, there's easy money."

The uneasy conclusion was that prostitution had to be illegal, yet available. Gambling, with its newfound respectability, had to distance itself from prostitution without precipitating its demise. Las Vegas, in particular, had to have the best, most efficient prostitution system in the world while appearing as wholesome as Disneyland. When it came to sex, part of the market needed to be assured that Las Vegas was not pure form with no underlying substance. Another part of the market needed to believe that Vegas was a clean resort town, that gambling was a legitimate form of recreation, and that the tourism industry and the police were doing their best to stamp out prostitution.

This paradox was reconciled, incredibly, through a curious combination of legislation and role-playing. The casinos and the convention authority came down on prostitution with the righteous wrath of the Moral Majority. Joined by the conservative, largely Mormon local population, they used their combined clout to have prostitution outlawed in counties with a census of over 250,000 residents. In addition, the gaming commission was persuaded to further accentuate the difference between wholesome recreational gambling and the carnality of whoring by denying gambling licenses to hotels or other properties that engaged in or supported prostitution. Later, with the election of John Moran as Clark County sheriff in the early '80s, the streetwalkers were effectively run off the Strip.

As intended, prostitution remained alive and healthy. So-called legal prostitution, symbolized by the large brothels, was just chased over the county line into Nye County where it was allowed to operate under stringent state regulation, but basically without interference. In Las Vegas and Clark County (where prostitution was declared illegal), the world's oldest profession simply switched to an entrepreneurial base. Where hotels and casinos previously had a virtual oligopoly in procuring women, they now stepped aside to permit a broad free-lance trade to develop. A quintessential case of having your cake and eating it too, prostitution had been removed from sight without otherwise being harmed.

The flaw in the plan, predictably, was that the ever-increasing corps of sexual entrepreneurs could not be controlled. Part of the original procurement business devolved from hotel top management to any number of bellmen, pitmen, and other small operatives who kept male guests as happy as ever but did it quietly and discreetly, with nothing required of the host property. It was the other players, the small prostitution rings, the free-lancers, and the "weekend warriors," who managed to unsettle the status quo.

Unlike the bellmen and other hotel personnel, who worked without fanfare from a private list of known and highly recommended professional courtesans, the free-lancers were as visible as a Kmart grand opening, taking out ads in the Las Vegas Yellow Pages and distributing free "adult entertainment" magazines up and down the Strip. Las Vegas was again becoming a Sodom and Gomorrah, with gambling looking less all-American as a function of guilt by association.

What's in a Name?

Since it is against the law to promote and advertise prostitution in Las Vegas, the inventive carnal entrepreneurs started off by listing themselves as massage parlors. This, of course, outraged legitimate professional masseurs ("We don't do genitals"), who forced the state to pass standards and licensing legislation. Unable to meet the standards, the free-lancers reappeared as escort or dating services. Once again, stringent licensing standards were applied, and the free-lancers disappeared temporarily from sight. When they next surfaced, they were private dancers, entertainers, or party services. This most recent, and highly visible, reincarnation continues to this day. The Las Vegas Yellow Pages are chock-full of lurid ads.

Sensuous XXX Rated Dancers
Let Us Explore Your Fantasies . . .
Nude Strippers Direct to Your Room
24 Hours—Most Major Credit Cards Accepted

For tourists who do not sit around reading the Yellow Pages, adult entertainment newsprint tabloids, with the same ads, are distributed gratis up and down the Strip.

A couple of visiting businessmen, slightly inebriated and in high spirits, decided to call a number from one of the ads and have a stripper sent over. Both men, being married and absolutely terrified of sexually transmitted disease, had no intention of having intercourse. They simply wanted, as the ad promised, "sizzling hot erotic dancing, direct to your room." What they expected was a naughtier-than-average version of the wholesome young ladies, available in every city, who perform tasteful striptease at yuppie birthday parties. What they got was a sullen prostitute who made it abundantly clear (the ad notwithstanding) that if they wanted to see dancing, they could "march right over and buy a ticket to the *Folies Bergere.*"

In a similar situation, three unsophisticated conventioneers from Little Rock phoned a private dancer service and requested information and prices. What the callers understood was that they could buy an hour of private dancing for $125, payable in advance with cash or credit card. What they were told, however, quite deliberately, was that the fee was $125 for "up to an hour" of private dancing. When the prostitute arrived and discovered, to her amazement, that these guys really wanted dancing, she obligingly took their money and launched into a perfunctory disrobing, without music or other artistic embellishment. In five minutes she was gone with the $125.

The most recent variation on the theme, taking advantage of growing consumer outrage, is "adult entertainment information services." These operations, ostensibly consultation services that "assist you in getting what you want without being ripped off," are nothing more than referral services, owned and operated by the prostitution agencies. It's only a matter of time, of course, before the authorities force prostitution into yet another metamorphosis, perhaps "Plumbing by the Hour" or "Gynecology Made Easy."

Writer Deke Castleman speculates that in future phone books, we may find prostitutes variously listed as "Bedroom Accessories, or Temporary Services, or even All-Purpose Rentals." The possibilities are endless.

Who's on First?

The cast of players in the Las Vegas prostitution game is a little confusing. At the top of the caste are select call girls with a small, but extremely lucrative, regular clientele. Another population of respected, highly recommended professionals work quietly on an on-call basis at the request of bell captains, pit bosses, and maitre d's. Next come a cadre of seasoned and novice, but less exclusive, prostitutes whose services are marketed by cab drivers, bartenders, and even convenience store clerks. Tied with these are the entertainers, the contingent that forms the stable of the private dancers and other operations that deal directly with customers. At the bottom of the heap are the streetwalkers, often past their prime, diseased, or drug-addicted. Driven off the streets by the law, streetwalkers work out of lounges, lobbies, transportation terminals, and hotel shopping arcades, but only rarely on the street.

A final category that defies any ranking is that of the weekend warriors. These are working girls and professional women (teachers, nurses, sales clerks) from Utah, Southern California, and Arizona who augment their income by turning tricks in Las Vegas on weekends. While some of these women develop connections with specific procurers, most work alone and free-lance out of casino lounges and singles bars. Nicely dressed and usually intelligent, they have a style more like that of a single woman cruising than that of a prostitute soliciting business. When it comes to striking a deal, however, they play hardball as well as their full-time sisters. There are no free samples.

Pay Now, Pay Again Later

All prostitutes plying their trade in Las Vegas and Clark County operate illegally. Regardless of their exclusivity or clientele, these women are not regulated by the standards applied to prostitutes working for the legal brothels in less-populated counties. Women of this latter group are checked weekly by a physician for communicable disease and work under very strict guidelines on the premises of their employer.

In Las Vegas, sexually transmitted diseases, including syphilis, gonorrhea, genital herpes, and AIDS, are routinely passed from prostitute to client; customers of streetwalkers are most at risk. Las Vegas police work incessantly to identify disease-carrying prostitutes and get them off the street, but it's like excavating a bottomless pit. At the time this book went to press, the police were tracking 68 prostitutes known to have AIDS.

Be forewarned that it is just as illegal in Las Vegas for you to solicit the services of a prostitute as it is for them to solicit you, and that sometimes policewomen work undercover. If you are determined to have a sexual adventure, you had better drive to the lawful Nye County brothels.

Deadly Games People Play

Not all of the sex games played in Las Vegas involve prostitution. In Las Vegas, as in any resort town, many men and women keep their eyes open for a little romance. Frequently lonely and vulnerable, these tourists fall prey to any number of deceptions.

Women who allow themselves to come under the influence of an unknown male risk the possibility of being robbed and/or raped. Sometimes the crime is premeditated, but more often it is a variation of date rape, where the man, rejected, refuses to take no for an answer. To many men, tourists and locals alike, the Las Vegas female stereotype is a bimbo showgirl, good only for sex and decoration. If a woman looking for companionship hooks up with a guy who subscribes to this myth, she might well be in for a rough time.

Interestingly, middle-aged men are the most common victims of sex scams in Las Vegas. In an oft-played scenario, a comely, well-dressed woman will make eye contact with a middle-aged man at the gaming tables. Always subtle, she may favor him with a smile when he wins or an expression of consolation when he loses. Working slowly and deliberately, sharing the moment and perhaps exchanging a few innocent words, she becomes an unintroduced friend. She does not push or direct, but instead allows the man to take the initiative. He likes her, invites her to grab a bite to eat or have a drink. They talk about their jobs, music, food, and all the other things people discuss when getting acquainted. If things proceed as she hopes, he finally asks her to his room for a drink. Making all the pro forma protestations, she ultimately pretends to be persuaded. Once in the room, he makes drinks. Talking and passing the time, she waits until he uses the rest room, then takes advantage of his absence to slip a powerful, quick-acting drug into his drink. A half hour later he is in dreamland. Usually with a male accomplice, the woman searches the room as the victim slumbers. Everything of value is stolen. The victim of this drug-induced trick roll commonly sleeps anywhere from 8 to 20 hours. Occasionally, if the victim is hypersensitive to the drug or has a medical condition, he dies.

How Felons Choose Their Victims   Felons choose their marks by observing a potential victim's attire and behavior. Wearing lots of jewelry and flaunting big bills is a sure way to attract attention. Stupid bets suggest inexperience, and excessive drinking lowers inhibitions and defenses. Playing without friends suggests that you are a solitary business traveler or on vacation and perhaps hungry for companionship.

If you meet somebody interesting, resist the urge to rush the relationship. In Las Vegas, as in any city, you should exercise caution. Proceed slowly with your new friendship. No matter what, keep the drinking under control and do not go anywhere to be alone. If you have a nice evening in the casino or over drinks or dinner, you can arrange to meet again tomorrow.

In the behavior department, learn the table games before you play, and make sensible bets. Go light on glitzy jewelry and refrain from flaunting your bankroll. Limit your alcohol intake and do not drink on an empty stomach. Beware of loners of either sex. Do not divulge your room number. Do not extend an invitation to come to your room or accept an invitation to go to the other party's room. If you are traveling alone, keep that to yourself.

PART THREE

Gambling

The Way It Is

Gambling is the reason Las Vegas (in its modern metamorphosis) exists. It is the industry that fuels the local economy, paves the roads, and gives the city its identity. To visitors and tourists, gambling may be a game. To those who derive their livelihood from gambling, however, it is serious business.

There is an extraordinary and interesting dichotomy in the ways gambling is perceived. To the tourist and the gambler, gambling is all about luck. To those in the business, gambling is about mathematics. To the visitor, gambling is a few hours a day, while to the casinos, gambling is 24 hours a day, all day, every day. The gambler *hopes* to walk away with a fortune, but the casinos *know* that in the long run that fortune will belong to the house. To visitors, gambling is recreation combined with risk and chance. To the casinos, gambling is business combined with near certainty.

The casino takes no risk in the games themselves. In the long run the house will always win. The games, the odds, and the payoffs are all carefully designed to ensure this outcome. Yet the casino does take a chance and is at risk. The casino's bet is this: that it can entice enough people to play.

Imagine a casino costing millions of dollars, with a staff numbering in the hundreds. Before a nickel of profit can be set aside, all the bills must be paid and the payroll must be met. Regardless of the house's overwhelming advantage at the tables, it cannot stay in business unless a lot of people come to play. Ten players, 20 players, even 30 are not enough; the larger the casino, the more gamblers are required. If the casino can fill the tables with players, the operation will succeed and be profitable, perhaps incredibly so. On the other hand, if the tables go empty, the casino will fail.

The casino business is competition personified. Every owner knows how absolutely critical it is to get customers (gamblers) through the door. It is literally the sine qua non: no players, no profit. The casinos are aggressive and creative when it comes to luring customers, offering low-cost buffets, dollar shrimp cocktails, stage shows, lounge entertainment, free drinks, gambling tournaments, and slot clubs.

The most recent tactic for getting customers through the door is to package the casino as a tourist attraction in its own right. Take the Mirage, for example. There are exploding volcanoes in the front yard, white tigers in the entrance hall, palm trees in the living room, and live sharks in the parlor. Who, after all, wants to sip their free drink in a dingy, red Naugahyde-upholstered catacomb when they could be luxuriating in such a resplendent tropical atrium?

The Short Run

If you ask a mathematician or a casino owner if you can win gambling in a casino, the truthful answer is yes, but only in the short run. The longer you play, the more certain it is that you will lose.

I learned about the short run (and the long run) on a road trip when I was in the fifth grade. My family lived in Kentucky, and every year we were fortunate enough to take a vacation to Florida. This particular year I was permitted to invite a schoolmate to come along.

As the long drive progressed, we became fidgety and bored. To pass the time, we began counting cars traveling in the opposite direction. Before many miles had passed, our counting evolved into a betting game. We each selected a color and counted the cars of that color. Whoever counted the most cars of his chosen color would win.

My friend chose blue as his color. I was considering red (my favorite) when I recalled a conversation between my mother and a car salesman. The salesman told my mother that white was by far the most popular color "these days." If this were true, I reasoned, there should be more white cars on the road than blue cars. I chose white.

As we rumbled through the hilly Kentucky countryside between Elizabethtown and Bowling Green my friend edged ahead. This puzzled me and I began to doubt the word of the car salesman. By the time we made Bowling Green, my friend Glenn was ahead by seven cars. Because I was losing, I offered to call it quits and pay up (a nickel for each car he was ahead). Glenn, not unexpectedly, was having a high time and insisted we continue playing.

By the time we crossed the Tennessee line I had pulled even. Once again I suggested we quit. Glenn would have none of it. Gloating enormously, he regained a three-car lead halfway to Nashville. Slowly, however, I overtook him, and by Nashville I was ahead by four cars. Tired of the game, I tried once more to end it. Since he was behind, Glenn adamantly demanded that we play all the way to Atlanta. We did, and by the time we got there Glenn owed me almost $4.

After a night in Atlanta and a great deal of sulking on Glenn's part, we resumed our travels. To my amazement, Glenn insisted—demanded, in fact—the opportunity to win back his previous day's losses. There would be one great "do-or-die battle, blues against whites," he said, all the way to our destination (St. Augustine, Florida). As we drove south, I went ahead by a couple of cars, and then Glenn regained the lead by a small margin. By the time we made St. Augustine, however, Glenn owed me another $5.40.

Outraged (and broke), Glenn exercised the only option remaining—he complained to my parents. Shaking his head, my father said, "Give Glenn his money back. Everybody knows that there are more white cars than blue cars." Not so. Glenn didn't.

While Glenn's behavior is not particularly unusual for a preadolescent, you would assume that adults have better sense. Everybody knows there are more white cars than blue cars, remember? In Las Vegas, however, the casinos are full of Glenns, all over 21, and all betting on blue cars.

I nailed Glenn on the cars because I knew something that he didn't. In casino games, patrons either do not understand what they are up against, or alternatively (and more intelligently), they do understand, but chalk up their losses as a fair price to pay for an evening's entertainment. Besides, in the short run, there's a chance they might actually win.

Glenn's actions on our trip mirrored almost exactly the behavior of many unfortunate casino gamblers:

1. He did not understand that the game was biased against him.

2. He did not take his winnings and quit when he was ahead in the short run.

3. On losing, he continued playing and redoubled his efforts to pull even or win, ultimately (in the long run) compounding his losses.

Eagles and Robins

If on our drive I had said, "Let's count birds. You take eagles and I'll take robins," Glenn would have laughed in my face, instantly recognizing that the likelihood of spotting an eagle was insanely remote. While the casinos will not offer a fair game (like betting even money on the flip of a coin), they do offer something a bit more equitable than eagles and robins.

I had another friend growing up who was big for his age. Whenever I went to his house to play, he would beat me up. I was not a masochist, so I finally stopped going to his house. After a few days, however, he asked me to come back, offering me ice cream and other incentives. After righteously spurning his overtures for a time, I gave in and resumed playing at his house. True to his word, he gave me ice cream and generously shared his best toys, and from that time forward he beat me up only once a week.

This is exactly how the casinos operate, and why they give you a better deal than eagles vs. robins. The casinos know that if they hammer you every time you come to play, sooner or later you will quit coming. Better to offer you little incentives and let you win every once in a while. Like with my big friend, they still get to beat you up, but not as often.

The Battle and the War

In casino gambling, the short run is like a battle, and either player or casino can win. However, the casino always wins the war. The American Indians never had a chance against the continuing encroachment of white settlers. There were just too many settlers and too few Indians for the outcome ever to be in doubt. Losing the war, however, did not keep the Indians from winning a few big battles. So it goes in casino gambling. The player struggles in the face of overwhelming odds. If he keeps slugging it out, he is certain to lose. If, on the other hand, he hits and runs, he may come away a winner. It's like a commando raid: the gambler must get in, do some damage, and get out. Hanging around too long in the presence of superior force can be fatal.

To say that this takes discipline is an understatement. It's hard to withdraw when you are winning, and maybe even harder to call it quits when you are losing. Glenn couldn't do either, and a lot of gamblers are just like Glenn.

■ The House Advantage ■

If casinos did engage in fair bets, they would win about half the bets and lose about half the bets. In other words, the casino (and you), on average, would break even, or at least come close to breaking even. While this arrangement would be more equitable, it would not, as a rule, generate enough money for the casino to pay its mortgage, much less foot the bill for the white tigers, pirate battles, lounge shows, $2 steaks, and free drinks.

To ensure sufficient income to meet their obligations and show a profit, casinos establish rules and payoffs for each game to give the house an advantage. While the house advantage is not strictly fair, it is what makes bargain rates on guest rooms, meals, and entertainment possible.

There are three basic ways that the house establishes its advantage:

1. The rules of the game are tailored to the house's advantage   In blackjack, for instance, the dealer by rule always plays his own hand last. If any player busts (attains a point total over 21), the dealer wins by default without having to play out his hand.

2. The house pays off at less than the actual odds   Imagine a carnival wheel with ten numbers. When the wheel is spun, each number has an equal chance of coming up. If you bet a dollar on number six, there is a one in ten chance that you will win and a nine in ten chance that you will lose. Gamblers express odds by comparing the likelihood of losing to the likelihood of winning. In this case, nine chances to lose and one to win, or nine to one. If the game paid off at the correct odds, you would get $9 every time you won (plus the dollar you bet). Each time you lost you would lose a dollar.

Let's say you start with $10 and do not win until your tenth try, betting your last dollar. If the game paid off at the correct odds, you would break even. Starting with $10, you would lose a dollar on each of your first nine attempts. In other words, you would be down $9. Betting your one remaining dollar, you win. At nine to one, you would receive $9 and get to keep the dollar you bet. You would have exactly the $10 you started with.

As we have seen, there is no way for a casino to play you even-up and still pay the bills. If, therefore, a casino owner decided to install a wheel with ten numbers, he would decrease the payoff. Instead of paying at the correct odds (nine to one), he might pay at eight to one. If you won on your last bet and got paid at eight to one (instead of nine to one), you would have lost a dollar overall. Starting with $10, you lose your first nine bets (so you are out $9) and on your last winning bet you receive $8 and get to keep the dollar you bet. Having played ten times at the eight-to-one payoff, you have $9 left, for a total loss of $1. Thus the house's advantage in this game is 10% (one-tenth).

The house advantage for actual casino games ranges from less than 1% for certain betting situations in blackjack to in excess of 27% on keno and some slots. Although 1% doesn't sound like much of an advantage, it will get you if you play long enough. Plus, for the house it adds up.

Because of variations in game rules, the house advantage for a particular game in one casino may be greater than the house advantage for the same game in another casino. In most Las Vegas casinos, for instance, the house has a 5.26% advantage in roulette. At Sam's Town, however, because of the elimination of 00 (double zero) on certain roulette wheels, the house advantage is pared down to about 2.7%.

Rule variations in blackjack swing the house advantage from almost zero in single-deck games (surrender, doubling on any number of cards, dealer stands on soft 17, etc.), to more than 6% in multiple-deck games with draconian rules. Quite a few mathematicians have taken a crack at computing the house's advantage in blackjack. Some suggest that the player can actually gain an advantage over the house in single-deck games by keeping track of cards played. Others claim that without counting cards, a player utilizing a decision guide known as "basic strategy" can play the house nearly even. The reality for 95% of all blackjack players, however, is a house advantage of between 0.5% and 5.9%, depending on rule variations and the number of decks used.

Getting to the meat of the matter: blackjack played competently, baccarat, and certain bets in craps minimize the house advantage and give the player the best opportunity to win. Keno and wheel of fortune are outright sucker games. Slots, video poker, and roulette are not much better.

How the house advantage works in practice causes much misunderstanding. In most roulette bets, for example, the house holds a 5.26% advantage. If you place a dollar on black each time the wheel is spun, the house advantage predicts that, on average, you will lose 5.26 cents per dollar bet. Now, in actual play you will either lose one whole dollar or win one whole dollar, so it's not like somebody is making small change or keeping track of fractional losses. The longer you play, however, the greater the likelihood that the percentage of your losses will approximate the house advantage. If you played for a couple of hours and bet $1,000, your expected loss would be about $53.

House Advantages	
Baccarat	1.17% on bank bets, 1.36% on player bets
Blackjack	0.5% to 5.9% for most games
Craps	1.4% to almost 17%, depending on the bet
Keno	20% to 35%
Roulette	5.26% to 7.89%, depending on the bet
Slots	2% to 25% (average 4% to 14%)
Video poker	1% to 12% (average 4% to 8%)
Wheel of fortune	11% to 24%

All right, you think, that doesn't sound too bad. Plus, you're thinking: I would never bet as much as $1,000. Oh, yeah? If you approach the table with $200 and make 20 consecutive $10 bets, it is not very likely that you will lose every bet. When you take money from your winning bets and wager it, you are adding to your original stake. This is known as "action" in gambling parlance, and it is very different from bankroll. Money that you win is just as much yours as the stake with which you began. When you choose to risk your winnings in additional betting, you are giving the house a crack at a much larger amount than your original $200. If you start with $200, win some and lose some, and keep playing your winnings in addition to your original stake until you have lost everything, you will have given the house (on average) about $3,800 worth of action. You may want to believe you only lost $200, but every penny of that $3,800 was yours.

3. The house takes a commission   In all casino poker games and in certain betting situations in table games, the house will collect a commission on a player's winnings.

Sometimes the house combines its various advantages. In baccarat, for instance, rules favor the house; payoffs are less than the true odds; and in certain betting situations, the house collects a commission on the player's winnings.

▪ Games of Chance and the Law of Averages ▪

People get funny ideas about the way gambling works. In casinos there are games of chance (roulette, craps, keno, bingo, wheel of fortune, slots, baccarat) and games of chance *and* skill (poker and blackjack).

A game of chance is like flipping a coin or spinning a wheel with ten numbers. What happens is what happens. A player can guess what the outcome will be but cannot influence it. Games of chance operate according to the law of averages. If you have a fair coin and flip it ten times, the law of averages leads you to expect that approximately half of the tosses will come up heads and the other half tails. If a roulette wheel has 38 slots, the law of averages suggests that the ball will fall into a particular slot one time in 38 spins.

The coin, the roulette ball, and the dice, however, have no memory. They just keep plugging along doing their thing. If I toss a coin and come up with heads nine times in a row, what are my chances of getting heads on the tenth toss? The answer is 50%, the same chance as getting heads on any toss. Each toss is completely independent of any other toss. When the coin goes up in the air that tenth time, it doesn't know that tails has not come up for a while, and certainly has no obligation to try to get the law of averages back into whack.

Though most gamblers are familiar with the law of averages, not all of them understand how it works. The operative word, as it turns out, is "averages," not "law." If you flip a coin a million times, there is nothing that says you will get 500,000 heads and 500,000 tails, no more than there is any assurance you will get five heads and five tails if you flip a coin ten times. What the law of averages *does* say is that, *in percentage terms,* the more times you toss the coin, the closer you will come to approximating the predicted average.

If you tossed a coin ten times, for example, you would not be surprised to get six tails and four heads. Six tails is only one flip off the five tails and five heads that the law of averages tells you is the probable outcome. By percentage, however, tails came up 60% (six of ten) of the time, while heads only came up 40% (four of ten) of the time. If you continued flipping the coin for a million tries, would you be surprised to get 503,750 tails and only 496,250 heads, a difference of 7,500 more tails than heads? The law of averages stipulates that the more we toss (and a million tosses are certainly a lot more than ten tosses) the closer we should come to approximating the average, but here we are with a huge difference of 7,500 more tails. What went wrong?

Nothing went wrong. True, after ten flips, we had only two more tails than heads, while after a million flips we had 7,500 more tails than heads. But in terms of percentage, 503,750 tails is 50.375% of one million, only about one-third of a measly percent from what the law of averages predicts. The law of averages is about percentages. Gambling is about dollars out of your pocket. If you had bet a dollar on heads each toss, you would have lost $2 after ten flips. After a million flips you would have lost $7,500. The law of averages behaved just as mathematical theory predicted, but that's probably not much consolation for going home broke.

Games of Chance and Skill

Blackjack and poker are games of chance and skill, meaning that the knowledge, experience, and skill of the player can have some influence on the outcome. All avid poker players or bridge players can recall nights when they played for hours without being dealt a good hand. That's the chance part. In order to win (especially in blackjack, where there is no bluffing), you need good cards. There is usually not much you can do if you are dealt a bad hand. As the Nevada mule drivers say, "You can't polish a turd."

If you are dealt something to work with, however, you can bring your

The Intelligence Test

If you have been paying attention, here is what you should understand by now:

1. That all gambling games are designed to favor the house, and that in the long run the house will always win.

2. That it costs a lot to build, staff, and operate a casino, and that a casino must attract many players in order to pay the bills and still make a profit.

3. That casinos compete fiercely for available customers and offer incentives ranging from 50-cent hot dogs to free guest rooms to get the right customers to their gaming tables.

Question: Given the above, what kind of customer gets the best deal?

Answer: The person who takes advantage of all the incentives without gambling.

Question: What kind of customer gets the next best deal?

Answer: The customer who sees gambling as recreation, gambles knowledgeably, makes sensible bets, sets limits on the amount he or she is prepared to wager, and enjoys all of the perks and amenities, but stays in control.

Question: What kind of customer gets the worst deal?

Answer: The person who thinks he or she can win. This person will foot the bill for everyone else.

skill into play and try to make your good hand even better. In casino poker, players compete against each other in the same way they do at Uncle Bert's house back home. The only difference is that, in the casino, the house takes a small percentage of each winning pot as compensation for hosting the game (are you listening, Uncle Bert?). Although not every casino poker player is an expert, your chances of coming up against an expert in a particular game are good. Our advice on casino poker: if you are not a tough fish, better not try to swim with the sharks.

Blackjack likewise combines chance and skill. In blackjack, however, players compete against the house (the dealer). Players have certain choices and options in blackjack, but the dealer's play is completely bound by rules. Much has been written about winning at blackjack. It's been said that by keeping track of cards played (and thereby knowing which cards remain undealt in the deck), a player can raise his or her bets when the deck contains a higher-than-usual percentage of aces, tens, and picture cards. In practice, however, the casino confounds efforts to count cards by combining several decks together, "burning" cards (removing undisclosed cards from play), and keeping the game moving at a fast pace. If an experienced gambler with extraordinary memory and power of concentration is able to overcome these obstacles, the casino will simply throw this person out.

In blackjack, as in every other casino game, it is ludicrous to suggest that the house is going to surrender its advantage. Incidentally, a super-gambler playing flawlessly in a single-deck game and keeping track of every card will gain only a nominal and temporary advantage over the house. On top of playing perfectly and being dealt good cards, the super-gambler must also disguise his play and camouflage his betting so the house won't know what he's up to. If you really want to make money on blackjack, write a book about it.

Playing It Smart

Experienced, noncompulsive, recreational gamblers typically play in a very disciplined and structured manner. Here's what they recommend:

1. *Never gamble when you are tired, depressed, or sick.* Also, watch the drinking. Alcohol impairs judgment and lessens inhibitions.

2. *Set a limit before you leave home on the total amount you are willing to lose gambling.* No matter what happens, do not exceed this limit.

3. *Decide which game(s) interest you and get the rules down before you play.* If you are a first-timer at craps or baccarat, take lessons (offered free at the casinos most days). If you are a virgin blackjack player, buy a good book and learn basic strategy. For all three games, spend an hour or two observing games in progress before buying in. Stay away from games like keno and wheel of fortune, in which the house advantage is overwhelming.

4. *Decide how long you want to play and work out a gambling itinerary consistent with the funds you set aside for wagering.* Let's say you plan to be in Las Vegas for two days and want to play about five hours each day. If you have $500 gambling money available

for the trip, that's $250 a day. Dividing the $250 a day by five hours, you come up with $50 an hour.

Now, forget time. Think of your gambling in terms of playing individual sessions instead of hours. You are going to play five sessions a day with $50 available to wager at each session.

5. *Observe a strategy for winning and losing.* On buying in, place your session allocation by your left hand. Play your allotted session money only once during a given session. Any time you win, return your original bet to the session-allocation stack (left hand), and place your winnings in a stack by your right hand. Never play any chips or coins you have won. When you have gone through your original allocation once, pick up the chips or coins in your winning stack (right hand) and quit. The difference between your original allocation and what you walk away with is your net win or loss for the session.

During the session, bet consistently. If you have been making $1 bets and have lost $10, do not chase your losses by upping your bets to $10 in an effort to get even in a hurry.

If you were fortunate and doubled your allocated stake during the session (in this case, walked away with $100 or more), take everything in excess of $100 and put it aside as winnings, not to be touched for the remainder of your trip. If you won, but did not double your money, or if you had a net loss (quit with less than $50 in your win stack), use this money in your next playing session.

6. *Take a break between sessions.* Relax for a while after each session. Grab a bite to eat, enjoy a nap, or go for a swim.

7. *When you complete the number of sessions scheduled for the day, stop gambling.* Period.

■ Indecent Expectations ■

Each month the *Las Vegas Advisor* (a newsletter published by Huntington Press—(702) 252-0655) runs a feature on gambling. The following article from a past issue will give you an idea what gamblers talk about at cocktail parties.

"The Odds against Woody Harrelson and Demi Moore"

By now, you've probably heard the basis of the plot of the hit movie *Indecent Proposal.* A young couple (Woody Harrelson and Demi Moore) find themselves desperate for money, and head to Las Vegas. There, they meet up with a "billionaire" gambler played by Robert Redford. Redford offers Moore a million dollars, and all she has to do is spend the night with him. Moore and Harrelson decide to accept the offer. The talk-show circuit went wild with discussions about morality and relationships, but we were more intrigued by an interesting and pertinent gambling question buried within the plotline. Namely: What are the chances of turning a little money into a lot by gambling?

In the movie, the couple takes a $5,000 stake to Las Vegas in an attempt to turn it into $50,000. What were the odds against their achieving their goal? By applying an optimal strategy of "bold" play at craps (line bets) or baccarat, the odds would have been about 9.5 to 1 against them. Bold play requires betting the entire $5,000 on a single coup, then rebetting the original wager, plus winnings, until either reaching the $50,000 goal or going broke (see chart). Any departure from this strategy raises the odds against success. Unfortunately for our heroes, they departed dramatically. Though it cannot be determined from the movie what the exact wagers were, it appears that the couple split their stake and made multiple wagers of $300–$400 per coup, a decision that doomed their chances. Given this method, the odds against their winning the $50,000 were greater than *one million to one!*

The analysis above deals with a concept known as "gambler's ruin" and has implications for virtually all recreational gamblers, who find that they must choose between (1) optimizing their chances of winning and (2) getting in playing time at their game of choice.

There's a clearly defined trade-off. Assuming you want to win a specific

---

BOLD-PLAY STRATEGY

Bet entire $5,000.

If lose, go home; if win, bet $10,000.

If lose, go home; if win, bet $20,000.

If lose, go home; if win, bet $10,000 (of $40,000 total).

If win, succeed; if lose, bet $20,000 (of $30,000 total).

If win, succeed; if lose, begin again betting entire $10,000.

amount of money, your best strategy is to bet as much as you can on as few wagers as possible until you reach your goal. You'll either go broke or reach your win figure—quickly. The first outcome is obviously undesirable. But so is the second (for most), since this strategy dictates that you now refrain from gambling any more.

If you divide your stake and make smaller bets, you are assured of gambling longer, but your chances of winning are diminished. Faced with this dilemma, most turn to the mystical idea of money management. Unfortunately, no system of money management can earn a profit (long-term) in a negative expectation game. In fact, most money-management systems require that you divide your stake into many units, and we've already seen that this leads to ultimate doom.

So, you have two choices:

1. Play only positive expectation games—certain blackjack (for expert card counters) and video poker games, promotions, coupons, the things we tell you about in the *LVA*. Dividing your stake is desirable when you have the advantage.

2. Accept the fact that you gamble for entertainment value and are destined to pay a fee (your losses) for "admission," just as surely as you must pay to see a concert or a sporting event.

In a sidebar to the *Las Vegas Advisor* article, mathematician and gambling author Peter Griffin had this to add:

The best the couple [Woody and Demi] could have done is apply a complicated combination of bold play and a betting method that utilizes 10 × odds [at a craps table]. This betting method is "99 and 44/100% pure," i.e., it gives .09944 chance of success (only about 9–1 against, which are the lowest odds achievable given Las Vegas's negative expectation gambling options).

What about blackjack at a casino like the Frontier where favorable rules afford a basic strategy player [with perfect play] a slight edge?

The couple needed $50,000 quickly, else they might have gone to work and saved (probably ruled out by the Hollywood media elite since they don't want to encourage such values). This also rules out playing blackjack. Playing $1 per hand (perfect basic strategy),

they would be virtually assured of turning their $5,000 into
$50,000. However, it would take about 30 million hands. At 1,000
hands per day, both playing, that's about 40 years. At $5 per hand,
they would reach their goal about 97% of the time, and it would
take about 6 million hands or about 8 years. Plus, they'd win Frontier free-room tokens redeemable for nearly 30,000 nights.

■ Gaming Instruction and Resources ■

Most casino games are actually fairly simple once you know what's going on. A great way to replace inexperience and awkwardness with knowledge and confidence is to take advantage of the free gaming lessons offered
by the casinos. Friendly, upbeat, and fun, the lessons introduce you not
only to the rules but also to the customs and etiquette of the respective
games. Going slow and easy, the instructors take you step-by-step through
the play and the betting without your actually wagering any money.
Many casinos feature low-minimum-bet "live games" following the instruction. We also recommend the lessons to nonplaying companions of
gamblers. For folks who usually spend a fair amount of time spectating,
casino games, like all other games, are more interesting if you know what is
going on.

No matter how many books you have read, take a lesson in craps before
you try to play in a casino. You don't need to know much to play baccarat,
but *understanding* it is a different story. Once again, we strongly recommend lessons. Though you can learn to play blackjack by reading a book
and practicing at home, lessons will make you feel more comfortable.

When "new games" are added to the traditional selection, casinos often
offer instruction for a limited time. The latest rages are Red Dog poker
and, owing to the increasing number of Asian gamblers, Pai Gow and Pai
Gow poker. Lessons are also available in traditional poker. The San Remo
offers regularly scheduled gaming lessons in Japanese.

Written References and the Gambler's Book Club   Most libraries and
bookstores offer basic reference works on casino gambling. If you cannot
find what you need at home, call the Gambler's Book Club at (800) 634-
6243 for a free catalog. If you would like to stop in and browse while you
are in Las Vegas, the club's store is located at 630 South 11th Street, just off
East Charleston Boulevard. The local phone is 382-7555. Before you buy,
check our list of recommended reading on pages 504–506. Gambler's
Book Club, incidentally, sells single issues of the *Las Vegas Advisor,* quoted
above.

Where to Go for Lessons

Baccarat

Aladdin
Bally's
Caesars Palace
Fiesta
Luxor
MGM Grand

Blackjack

Aladdin
Bally's
Boomtown
Caesars Palace
Circus Circus
Excalibur
Fiesta
Harrah's
   Imperial
   Palace
Las Vegas
   Hilton
Luxor
Maxim
MGM Grand

Riviera
Sahara
Stardust

Caribbean Stud

Harrah's
MGM Grand
Stardust

Craps

Aladdin
Bally's
Caesars Palace
Circus Circus
Excalibur
Fiesta
Flamingo
Harrah's
   Imperial
   Palace
Lady Luck
Las Vegas
   Hilton

Luxor
Maxim
MGM Grand
Riviera
Sahara
Sam's Town
Stardust

Let It Ride

Harrah's
MGM Grand
Monte Carlo
Stardust

Pai Gow and Pai Gow Poker

Caesars Palace
Circus Circus
Fiesta
Harrah's
Las Vegas
   Hilton

Luxor
MGM Grand

Poker

Fiesta
Luxor
MGM Grand
Monte Carlo
Sam's Town

Roulette

Aladdin
Bally's
Caesars Palace
Circus Circus
Excalibur
Fiesta
Harrah's
Las Vegas
   Hilton
Luxor
MGM Grand
Sahara

Funbooks, Matchplay, and Understanding the Marquees

Casino games, not unexpectedly, are entrenched in jargon. Most of the terminology you can figure out intuitively, and much of the rest is useless in any event. The terms below, however, keep popping up in ads, in coupons, and on marquees, and manage to confuse a lot of people.

Crapless Craps   In crapless craps, dice totals of 2, 3, 11, and 12 count as point numbers. For information on the rules of craps, see page 285.

Double Exposure 21   A version of blackjack in which both of the dealer's cards are dealt face up.

Double Odds   The option in craps of making an odds bet twice the size of your line bet. See craps, page 285.

Funbooks   Little booklets of coupons available without charge from certain casinos. The coupons in funbooks vary widely from casino to casino but usually include coupons for souvenir gifts, discount show tickets, discount meals, two-for-one or free drinks, and matchplay (see below). Some funbooks offer exceptional value, while others are nothing more than a hustle. Coupons for keno and slots, for example, are practically worthless, while matchplay coupons for table games can be valuable. On balance, coupon books are worth checking out.

Loose Slots   Slot machines that are programmed to pay off more frequently. The term is usually applied to machines with a return rate of 94% or higher, meaning that the house advantage is 6% or less.

Matchplay Coupons   Coupons from funbooks or print ads that can be redeemed for matchplay chips. The matchplay chips must be combined with an equal amount of your own money on certain table game bets. If you win, you are paid off for the entire bet in real money. If you bet $5 in matchplay chips and $5 of your bankroll on the color black in roulette, you will win $10 of real money if the ball lands in a black slot. When you are paid off, the dealer collects your matchplay chips, which can only be used once, but you keep the $5 in real money you bet. If you lose, of course, the dealer will take both the real money and the matchplay chips.

Megabucks Slots   A statewide progressive slot machine network with grand jackpots in excess of $3 million. For additional information on progressive slot systems, see page 264.

Single-Deck Blackjack   Blackjack dealt from a single deck as opposed to two or more decks shuffled together.

Triple Odds   The option in craps of making an odds bet three times the size of your line bet. See craps, page 285.

▪ Where To Play ▪

We receive a lot of mail from readers asking which casino has the loosest slots, the most favorable rules for blackjack, and the best odds on craps. We directed the questions to veteran gambler and tournament player Anthony Curtis, publisher of the *Las Vegas Advisor.* Here's Anthony's reply:

Where's the best casino in Las Vegas to play blackjack, video poker, and the rest of the gambling games? It could be almost anyplace on any given day due to spot promotions and changing management philosophies. A few casinos, however, have established reliable track records in specific areas. Absent a special promotion or change in policy, I recommend the following casinos as the best places to play each of the games listed:

Blackjack
Binion's Horseshoe

Low-minimum single decks. Great cocktail service and low-end comps (coffee shop) for $5 action.

Quarter Slots
Fitzgeralds

Competes hard for quarter slot players. You'll be treated well for 25-cent play.

Dollar Slots
Treasure Island

All the latest machines and a great atmosphere. The fantastic slot club might make the return percentage higher than the Stratosphere's guaranteed 98% payback.

Craps
Binion's Horseshoe

Legendary dice house. Low minimums. Recently has allowed up to 100× odds on $1 pass line bets.

Quarter Video Poker
Orleans

Several machines return 100%+ for expert play. Frequent double- and triple-point slot club promotions.

Dollar Video Poker
Fiesta

Excellent opportunities for skilled players and a good slot club.

Roulette
Monte Carlo

The only Las Vegas casino with single-zero on all tables. The absence of the usual double-zero lowers the casino's edge from 5.26% to 2.7% here.

Baccarat
Binion's Horseshoe

This recommendation stems from the fact that the mini-baccarat tables on the first floor charge a 4% commission on winning bank bets as compared to the standard 5%. This concession lowers the house edge from 1.06% to 0.6%.

Keno
Gold Coast

A comparison of keno return percentages shows casinos that target locals offer the best chance of winning.

Bingo
Showboat

Most elegant and airy bingo room in Las Vegas.

Race and Sports Betting Mirage	Big, bustling NASA-esque room covering all the major events.
Let It Ride Holiday Inn Boardwalk	Consistent $3 minimum.
Caribbean Stud Binion's Horseshoe	High reset on progressive with low minimums.
Pai Gow Poker Stardust	7-5 coupon in funbook.

■ Changes in Attitude, Changes in Latitude ■

Most people who love to gamble are not motivated by greed. Usually it is the tension, excitement, and anticipation of the game that they enjoy. Misunderstanding this reality has led many naive and innocent people into the nightmare of addictive gambling.

Ed was attending a convention on his first visit to Las Vegas. One evening, he decided to try his luck at roulette. Approaching the table, Ed expected to lose ("I'm not stupid, after all"). His intentions were typical. He wanted to "try" gambling while in Nevada, and he was looking for an adventure, a new experience. What Ed never anticipated was the emotional impact gambling would have on him. It transcended winning and losing. In fact, it wasn't about winning or losing at all. It was the *playing* that mattered. The "action" made him feel alive, involved, and terribly sophisticated. It also made him crazy.

The "high" described by the compulsive gambler closely parallels the experience of drug or alcohol abusers. In fact, there is a tendency for chemical addiction and gambling compulsion to overlap. The compulsive gambler attempts to use "the action" as a cure for a variety of ills, in much the same way that people use alcohol and drugs to lift them out of depression, stem anxiety or boredom, and make them feel more "in control."

Some people cannot handle gambling, just as some people cannot handle alcohol. The problem, unfortunately, is compounded by the attitude of our society. As we profess to admire the drinker who can "hold his liquor," we likewise reinforce the gambler who beats the odds in Las Vegas. By glamorizing these behaviors we enable afflicted individuals to remain in denial about the destructive nature of their problem.

The compulsive gambler blames circumstances and other people for the suffering occasioned by his or her affliction. One may hear excuses like: "I didn't get enough sleep; I couldn't concentrate with all the noise; I lost track of the time; I'm jinxed at this casino."

If this sounds like you or someone you love, get help. In Las Vegas there is a meeting of Gamblers Anonymous almost every night. Call 385-7732. To have a schedule faxed to you, call 438-6311. If, like Ed, you catch something in Las Vegas and take it home with you, Gamblers Anonymous is listed in your local White Pages.

Rules of the Games

■ **Slot Machines** ■

Slot machines, including video poker, have eclipsed the table games in patron popularity. There are few casinos remaining that have not allocated more than half of their available floor space to various types of slot machines.

The popularity of slots is not difficult to understand. First, slots allow a person to enjoy casino gambling at low or high stakes. In downtown Las Vegas at the Nevada and the Gold Spike, for instance, you can play the slots for a penny a pop. Nickel slots, meanwhile, can be found in virtually every casino in town. Quarter slots are the most popular and the most common. Higher-stakes players can find machines that accept bets of $1 to $500 (high-stakes slots use special tokens instead of coins).

Second, many people like the slots because no human interaction is required. Absent in slot play is the formal, adversarial atmosphere of the table games. Machines are much less intimidating, or at least more neutral, than dealers and pit bosses. Once appropriate change is obtained, a patron can sit down at a machine for as long as his stamina and money last and never be bothered by a soul.

Finally, slot machines are simple, or at least ostensibly so. Although there are a number of things you should know before you play the slots, the only thing you have to know is to put a coin in the slot and pull the handle.

What You Need to Know before You Play Slot Machines

For the moment we will confine our discussion to traditional slot machines, the so-called one-armed bandits. Later we will take a look at video poker.

Starting at the beginning: All slot machines have a slot for inserting coins, a handle to pull (or button to push) to activate the machine, a visual display where you can see the reels spin and stop on each play, and a coin tray that you hope some winnings will drop into.

While most slot machines have three reels, some have as many as eight. Each reel will have some number of "stops," positions where the reel can come to rest. Reels with 20, 25, or 32 stops are the most common. On

Modern multiple-coin, multiple-pay-line (nonprogressive) slot machine. (Courtesy of Las Vegas News Bureau)

each reel at each stop (or resting position) is a single slot symbol (a cherry, a plum, an orange, etc.). What you hope will happen (when the reels stop spinning) is that three of the same symbol will line up on the pay line. If this happens, you win.

In addition to three of the same symbol on a line, many machines will pay for single cherries in the far left or far right position, two cherries together side by side, or two bells or two oranges side by side with a bar on the end.

With the old slot machines things were pretty simple. There was one coin slot, one handle to pull, and a display with one pay line. Symbols either lined up on that line or they didn't. Modern machines are much more complex. Almost all modern machines accept more than one coin per play (usually three to five). No matter how many coins the machine will take, it only requires one to play.

If you put in additional coins (bet more), you will buy one of the following benefits:

1. Payoff schedules On a certain type of machine, two, three, four, or five different payoff schedules are posted on the front of the machine above the reel display. If you study these schedules you will notice that by playing extra coins you can increase your payoff should you win. Usually the increase is straightforward. If you play two coins, you will win twice as much as if you play one coin. If you play three coins, you will win three times as much as if you play one coin, and so on. Some machines, however, have a grand jackpot that will pay off only if you have played the maximum number of coins. If you line up the symbols for the grand jackpot but have not played the maximum number of coins, you will not win. Always read the payoff schedule for a machine before you play and make sure you understand it. If you do not, ask an attendant or find a simpler machine.

Though most casino slot machines are kept in good working order, watch to make sure a section of the payoff schedule lights up for every coin you play. If you are playing a machine with four payoff schedules, the schedules should light up, one at a time, as you put in your coins. On machines where the payoff schedules do not illuminate, there will ordinarily be a light (or lights) above or below the reel display that will verify that the machine has accepted your coins. If you put in multiple coins without the appropriate lights coming on, do not play until you check things out with an attendant.

2. Multiple pay lines When you play your first coin, you buy the usual pay line, right in the center of the display. By playing more coins, you can buy additional pay lines.

Each pay line you purchase gives you another way of winning. Instead of being limited to the center line, the machine will pay off on the top, center, or bottom lines, and five-coin machines will pay winners on diagonal lines. If you play machines with multiple pay lines, make sure that each pay line you buy is acknowledged by a light before you pull the handle.

An irritating feature of many multiple-line machines are "blanks" or "ghosts." A blank is nothing more than an empty stop on the reel—a place where you would expect a symbol to be but where there is nothing. As you have probably surmised, you cannot hit a winner by lining up blanks.

Nonprogressive vs. Progressive Slot Machines Nonprogressive slot machines have fixed payoffs. You can read the payoff schedules posted on

Slot Machine Reels

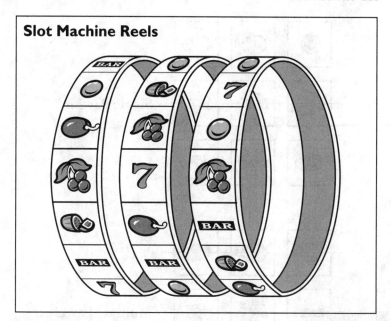

the machine and determine exactly how much you will get for each winning combination for any number of coins played.

A second type of machine, known as a progressive, has a grand jackpot that grows and grows until somebody hits it. After the grand jackpot has been won, a new jackpot is established and starts to grow. While individual machines can offer modest progressive grand jackpots, the really big jackpots (several thousand to several million dollars) are possible only on machines linked in a system to other machines. Sometimes an "island," "carousel," or "bank" of machines in a given casino is hooked up to create a progressive system. The more these machines are played, the faster the progressive grand jackpot grows. The largest progressive jackpots, however, come from huge multicasino systems that sometimes cover the entire state. Players have won up to $11 million by hitting these jackpots.

While nothing is certain in slot play, it is generally accepted that non-progressives will pay more small jackpots. Progressives, on the other hand, offer an opportunity to really strike it rich, but they give up fewer intermediate wins. Each type of machine targets a certain player. The nonprogressive machine appeals to the player who likes plenty of action, who gets bored when coins aren't clanking into the tray every four or five pulls. The progressive machine is for the player who is willing to forgo frequent small payouts for the chance of hitting a really big one.

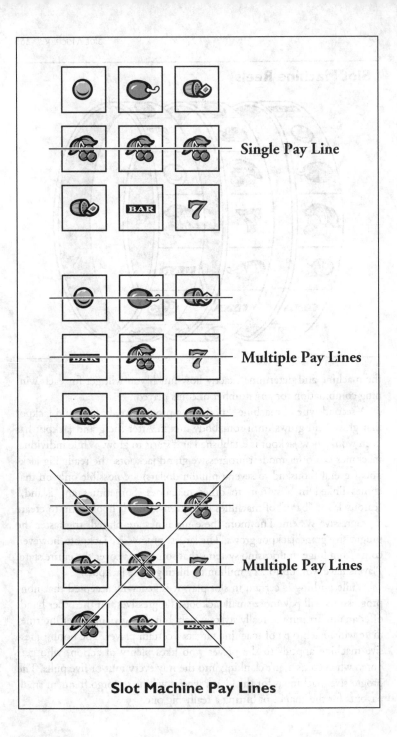

Slot Machine Pay Lines

How Slot Machines Work

Almost all slot machines used in casinos today are controlled by microprocessors. This means the machines can be programmed and are more like computers than mechanical boxes composed of gears and wheels. During the evolution of the modern slot machine, manufacturers took a whack at eliminating the traditional spinning reels in favor of a video display, and replacing the pull handle with a button. The public rejected these innovations, however, and the spinning reels and pull handles have been retained. In a modern slot machine there is a device that computer people call a "random number generator" and that we refer to as a "black box." What the black box does is spit out hundreds of numbers each second, selected randomly (i.e., in no predetermined sequence). The black box has about four billion different numbers to choose from, so it's very unusual (but not impossible) for the same number to come up twice in a short time.

The numbers the black box selects are programmed to trigger a certain set of symbols on the display, determining where the reels stop. What most players don't realize, however, is that the black box pumps out numbers continuously, regardless of whether the machine is being played or not. If you are playing a machine, the black box will call up hundreds or thousands of numbers in the few seconds between plays while you sip your drink, put some money in the slot, and pull the handle.

Why is this important? Try this scenario: Mary has played the same quarter machine for two hours, pumping an untold amount of money into it. While she turns for a moment to buy gum from a cigarette girl, a man walks up to Mary's machine and wins the grand jackpot. Mary is livid. "That's my jackpot," she screams. Not so. While Mary bought her gum, thousands of numbers and possible symbol combinations were generated by the black box. The only way Mary could have won the grand jackpot (even if the man had not come along) would have been to activate the machine at that same exact moment in time, right down to a fraction of a millisecond.

There is no such thing as a machine that is "overdue to hit." Each spin of the reels on a slot machine is an independent event, just like flipping a coin. The only way to hit a jackpot is to activate the machine at the exact moment that the black box randomly coughs up a winning number. If you play a slot machine as fast as you can, jamming in coins and pumping the handle like a maniac, the black box will still spew out more numbers (and possible jackpots) between each try than you will have pulls in a whole day of playing.

Cherry, Cherry, Orange   The house advantage is known for every casino game except slots. With slot machines, the house advantage is whatever the casino wants it to be. In Atlantic City the maximum legal house advantage is 17%. There is no limit in Nevada. In theory a casino could program a machine to keep 50% of all the coins played. Interviews with ex–casino employees suggest, however, that the house advantage on casino slots in Las Vegas ranges from about 2.5 to 25%, with most machines giving the house an edge of between 4 and 14%.

Casinos advertise their slots in terms of payout or return rate. If a casino states that its slots return up to 97%, that's just another way of saying that the house has a 3% advantage. Some casinos advertise machines that pay up to 98%, and one casino even claims to offer slots paying 101%! We're skeptical about the 98% machines, and as for the 101% machine . . . well, if you ever find it, drop us a line. Incidentally, the operative terminology is "up to," not "98%." In most casinos, only a few slots will be programmed to return in excess of 92%.

Slot Quest   A slot machine that withholds only a small percentage of the money played is referred to as "loose," while a machine that retains most of the coins it takes in is called "tight." "Loose" and "tight" are figurative descriptions and have nothing to do with the mechanical condition of the machine. Because return rates vary from casino to casino, and because machines in a given casino are programmed to withhold vastly differing percentages of the coins played, slot players devote much time and energy to finding the best casinos and the loosest machines. Exactly how to go about this is the subject of much discussion.

In terms of choosing a casino, there are several theories which have at least a marginal ring of truth. Competition among casinos is often a general indicator for finding loose slots. Some say that smaller casinos such as Slots-A-Fun and Silver City, which compete against large neighbors (the Riviera, Circus Circus, and the Stardust), must program their slots to provide a higher return. Alternatively, some folks will play slots only in casinos patronized predominantly by locals (Gold Coast, Palace Station, Boulder Station, Fiesta, Texas Station, El Cortez, Gold Spike, Showboat, Sam's Town, Arizona Charlie's, Santa Fe). The reasoning here is that these casinos vie for regular customers on a continuing basis and must therefore offer extremely competitive win rates. Downtown Las Vegas is likewise cast in the "we try harder" role because smaller downtown casinos must go head to head with the Strip to attract patrons.

Extending the logic, machines located in supermarkets, restaurants, convenience stores, airports, and lounges are purported to be very tight. In these places, some argue, there is little incentive for management to provide good returns because the patrons will play regardless (out of boredom or simply because the machine is there).

Veteran slot players have a lot of theories when it comes to finding the loose machines in a particular casino. Some will tell you to play the machines by the door or in the waiting area outside the showroom. By placing the loose machines in these locations, the theory goes, the casino can demonstrate to passersby and show patrons that the house has loose slots. A more labor-intensive suggestion for sniffing out the loose machines is to hang around the casino during the wee hours of the morning when the machines are being emptied. Supposedly machines with the least number of coins in the hopper have been paying off more frequently. Or maybe these machines have just been played less often.

Of the theories for finding the loose machines in a specific casino, the suggestion that makes the most sense is to select a casino and play there long enough to develop a relationship with the slot attendants. Not as difficult as it sounds, this means being friendly and engaging the attendants in pleasant conversation. If the casino has a slot club, join up and use the club card so the slot personnel will regard you as a regular. If the attendants are responsive and kind, and particularly if you win, give them a tip. After a couple of hours, the attendants will begin to take an interest in you. Ask them candidly and forthrightly to point out a good (i.e., loose) machine. Tip them for the information and tip again if you do well on the machine. If the machine is not hitting for you, don't blame the attendant. Continue to be positive and build the relationship. In the long run, it is in your best interest, as well as in the best interest of the attendant and of the house, for the relationship to prosper. If the attendant turns you on to the loosest machine in Las Vegas, the house is still going to make money in the long run. If the force is with you, however, you might rack up a nice short-term win or at least get more play for your money.

I have had a slot manager admit to me that his nickel machines are tighter than his quarter machines and that his dollar and five-dollar machines are the loosest of all. Tight or loose, however, all slots are programmed to give the casino a certain profit over the long run. It is very unlikely, in any event, that you will play a machine long enough to experience the theoretical payoff rate. What you are concerned about is the short run. In the short run anything can happen, including winning.

Maximizing Your Chances of Winning on the Slots In any multiple-coin slot machine, as we have seen, you have a higher expectation of winning if you play the maximum number of coins. If what you actually desire to bet is 25 cents per play, you will probably be better off putting five nickels into a multiple-coin nickel slot than one quarter into a multiple-coin quarter slot. Likewise, if you are up for wagering a dollar a play, go with four coins in the quarter slot rather than one dollar in the dollar slot. Never play a progressive machine unless you are betting the maximum number of coins. If you play less than the maximum on a progressive, you are simply contributing to a jackpot that you have no chance of winning. If you don't want to place a maximum bet, play a nonprogressive machine.

Slot Machine Etiquette and Common Sense

Regardless of whether you are playing a one-armed bandit, a video poker machine, or any other type of coin-operated slot machine, there are some things you need to know:

1. Obtain your change before you select a machine.

2. Realize that avid slot players sometimes play more than one machine at a time. Do not assume that a machine is not in use simply because nobody is standing or sitting in front of it. Slot players can be fanatically territorial.

3. Before you start to play, check out the people around you. Do you feel safe and comfortable among them?

4. Read and understand the payout schedule of any machine you play.

5. Check to see if the machine automatically pays coins into the tray or whether your winnings are registered on a credit meter. If your machine has a credit meter, be sure to cash out your credits before you abandon the machine.

6. If the casino has a slot club, join (this usually takes less than five minutes on-site, but can be accomplished through the mail prior to your trip). Use the club card whenever you play. When you quit, don't forget to take your club card with you.

7. Never play more machines than you can watch carefully. Be particularly vigilant when playing machines near exits and corridors. If you are asleep at the switch, a thief can dip into your coin tray or bucket and be out the door in seconds.

8. Keep your purse and your money in sight at all times. Never put your purse on the floor behind you or to the side. Leave unopened rolls of coins in your purse or pocket.

9. If you line up a winner and nothing happens, don't leave the machine. Sometimes large jackpots exceed the coin capacity of the

machine and must be paid directly by the casino cashier. Call immediately for an attendant but do not wander off looking for one. While you wait, refrain from further play on the machine in question. When the attendant arrives, check his casino employee identification.

10. If the appropriate payout sections or pay lines fail to illuminate when playing multiple coins, do not leave or activate the machine (pull the handle) until you have consulted an attendant.

Slot Clubs and Frequent-Player Clubs

Most Las Vegas casinos now have slot or frequent-player clubs. The purpose of these clubs is to foster increased customer loyalty among gambling patrons by providing incentives.

You can join a club by signing up at the casino or (at some casinos) by applying through the mail. There is neither a direct cost associated with joining nor any dues. You are given a plastic membership card that very much resembles a credit card. This card can be inserted into a receptacle on certain quarter and dollar slots (including video poker machines). As long as your card is in the receptacle, you are credited for the amount of action you give that machine. Programs at different casinos vary, but in general, you are awarded "points" based on how long you play and how much you wager. Some clubs award points for both slot and table play, while other clubs confine their program to slots. As in an airline frequent-flyer program, accumulated points can ultimately be redeemed for awards. Awards range from casino logo apparel to discounts (or comps) on meals, shows, and rooms.

The good thing about slot clubs is that they provide a mechanism for slot players to obtain some of the comps, perks, and extras that have always been available to table players. The bad thing about a slot club is that it confines your play. In other words, you must give most of your business to one or two casinos in order to accumulate award points. If you are a footloose player and enjoy gambling all around town, you may never accrue enough points in any one casino to redeem a prize.

Even if you never redeem any points, however, it's still a good idea to join. Joining a club gets you identified as a gambler on the casino's mailing list. Just for joining, and without gambling that first quarter, you will be offered discounts on rooms and a variety of other special deals. If you travel to Las Vegas regularly on business, join your hotel's slot club. Membership might make you eligible for deals on rooms and food that would otherwise not be available to you.

▪ Video Poker ▪

Never in the history of casino gambling has a new game become so popular so quickly. All across Nevada, casinos are reallocating game-table and slot space to video poker machines. More people are familiar with poker than with any other casino game. The video version affords average folks an opportunity to play a game of chance and skill without going up against professional gamblers.

In video poker you are not playing against anyone. Rather, you are trying to make the best possible five-card-draw poker hand. In the most common rendition, you insert your coin(s) and push a button marked "deal." Your original five cards are displayed on the screen. Below the screen and under each of the cards pictured are "hold" buttons. After evaluating your hand and planning your strategy, designate the cards you want to keep by pressing the appropriate hold button(s). If you hit the wrong button or change your mind, most machines have an "error" or "erase" button, which will allow you to revise your choices before you draw. If you do not want to draw any cards (you like your hand as dealt), press all five hold buttons. When you press the hold button for a particular card, the word "hold" will appear over or under that card on the display. Always double-check the screen to make certain the cards you intend to hold are marked before proceeding to the draw.

When you are ready, press the button marked "draw" (on many machines it is the same button as the deal button). Any cards you have not designated to be held will be replaced. As in live draw poker, the five cards in your possession after the draw are your final hand. If the hand is a winner (a pair of jacks or better on most quarter machines and dollar machines), you will be credited the appropriate winnings on a credit meter on the video display. These are actual winnings that can be retrieved in coins by pressing the "cash-out" button. If you choose to leave your winnings on the credit meter, you may use them to bet, eliminating the need to physically insert coins in the machine. When you are ready to quit, simply press the cash-out button and collect your coins from the tray.

You do not have to know much about poker to play video poker. All of the winning hands with their respective payoffs are posted on or above the video display. As with other slot machines, you can increase your payoffs and become eligible for bonus jackpots by playing the maximum number of coins. Note that some machines have jackpots listed in dollars, while others are specified in coins. Obviously, there is a big difference between $4,000 and 4,000 nickels.

Quarter and dollar video poker machines come in progressive and nonprogressive models. Nonprogressive machines will pay more on a full house (nine coins) and a flush (six coins) than will progressives (eight and five coins respectively). Progressives feature a grand jackpot that continues to build until somebody hits it. Nonprogressives usually feature a bonus jackpot for hitting a royal flush when playing the maximum number of coins.

In popular jargon, video poker machines are labeled according to these different payoffs as "nine/six" or "eight/five" machines. Never play a progressive (eight/five) machine unless you are playing the number of coins required to win the grand jackpot. By playing less than the maximum number of coins, you disqualify yourself for the grand jackpot while subsidizing the jackpot's growth. Plus, you get a lower return rate than you would on a nonprogressive (nine/six). Also be aware that the grand jackpot for maximum coin play on a nonprogressive can sometimes be larger than the grand jackpot on a progressive. Always scout around before you play.

It should be noted that some casinos (Luxor, Bally's, Las Vegas Hilton, Main Street Station, Stratosphere) have begun to experiment with progressive and nonprogressive ten/six and nine/seven machines. The expected value of perfect play on these machines exceeds 100%.

In addition to straight draw poker, games with jokers or deuces wild are also available at many casinos. Jokers wild machines normally pay on a pair of kings or better, while deuces wild programs pay on three-of-a-kind and up. Casinos clean up on the wild card machines because very few players understand the basic strategy of proper play.

With flawless play, the house advantage on nine/six quarter and dollar machines ranges up from about ½% (0.5%), and for eight/five machines and wild card programs, from about 3%. On nickel video poker machines, the house advantage is about 5–10%.

Video Poker Strategy

Each deal in a video poker game is dealt from a fresh 52-card deck. Each hand consists of ten cards, with a random number generator or "black box" selecting the cards dealt. When you hit the deal button, the first five cards are displayed face up on the screen. Cards six through ten are held in reserve to be dealt as replacements for cards you discard when you draw. Each replacement card is dealt in order off the top of the electronic deck. The microprocessor "shuffles" the deck for each new game. Thus on the next play, you will be dealt five new and randomly selected initial cards, and five new and randomly selected draw cards to back them up. In other words, you will not be dealt any unused cards from the previous hand.

The Power of the Royal Flush   In video poker, the biggest payout is usually for a royal flush. This fact influences strategy for playing the game.

Simply put, you play differently than you would in a live poker game. If in video poker you are dealt:

A♣   Q♣   10♣   A♠   J♣

you would discard the ace of spades (giving up a sure winner) to go for the royal flush. Likewise, if you are dealt:

5♠   A♠   K♠   Q♠   J♠

you would discard the 5 of spades (sacrificing a sure spade flush) in an attempt to make the royal by drawing the 10 of spades. If you are dealt:

J♥   Q♥   K♥   4♥   6♣

draw two cards for the royal flush as opposed to one card for the flush. If you are initially dealt the following straight:

7♣   8♣   9♣   10♣   J♦

keep it on a nine/six or eight/five quarter or dollar machine. This particular hand occasions much debate among video poker veterans. The 6 of clubs or the jack of clubs would give you a straight flush, while any other club would give you a flush. Your chances of improving this hand are 9 in 47, with a 5 in 47 chance of recapturing your straight with a drawn non-club 6 or jack. It's a close call, but keeping the sure straight gets the nod (with an expected win of four coins for standing versus two and three-fourths coins for drawing). If the same situation comes up on a nickel machine, however, take the gamble and draw.

The payoff for the royal flush is so great that it is worth risking a sure winning hand. The payoff for a straight flush, however, does not warrant risking a pat flush or straight.

Other Situations   If you are dealt:

Q♦   A♣   4♥   J♠   4♣

hold the small pair except when you have a chance at making a royal flush by drawing one or two cards.

But, if you are dealt:

K♦   A♣   4♥   J♣   3♠

hold the ace of clubs and the jack of clubs to give yourself a long shot at a royal flush. Similarly, if you are dealt:

K♣   A♣   4♥   J♣   3♠

hold the ace of clubs, king of clubs, and jack of clubs.

Straight Poker   If you are playing straight poker (no wild cards), with a pair of jacks or better required to win, observe the following:

1. Hold a jacks-or-better pair, even if you pass up the chance of drawing to an open-end straight or to a flush. If you have:

    Q♣   4♠   6♠   2♠   Q♠

    or

    Q♥   9♦   10♣   J♠   Q♣

    in each case, keep the pair of queens and draw three cards.

2. Split a low pair to go for a flush. If you are dealt:

    2♦   4♣   4♦   8♦   10♦

    discard the 4 of clubs and draw one card to try and make the flush.

3. Hold a low pair rather than drawing to an inside or open-end straight.

4. A "kicker" is a face card or an ace you might be tempted to hang onto along with a high pair, low pair, or three-of-a-kind. If you are dealt, for example:

    5♣   5♦   8♠   10♠   A♥

    or

    J♣   J♠   8♣   7♥   A♦

    or

    2♣   2♠   2♥   8♠   A♥

    hold the pair or the three-of-a-kind, but discard the kicker (the ace).

■ Blackjack ■

Many books have been published about the game of blackjack. The serious gamblers who write these books will tell you that blackjack is a game of skill and chance in which a player's ability can actually turn the odds of winning in his favor. While we want to believe that, we also know the casinos wouldn't keep the tables open if they were taking a beating.

The methods of playing blackjack skillfully involve being able to count all the cards played and flawlessly manage your own hand, while mentally blocking the bustle and distraction of the casino. The ability to master the prerequisite tactics and to play under casino conditions is so far beyond the average (never mind beginning) player that any attempt to track cards is, practically speaking, exhausting and futile.

This doesn't mean that you should not try blackjack. It is a fun, fast-paced game that is easy to understand, and you can play at low-minimum-wager tables without feeling intimidated by the level of play. Moreover, most people already have an understanding of the game from playing "21" at home. The casino version is largely the same, only with more bells and whistles.

In a game of blackjack, the number cards are worth their spots* (a 2 of clubs is worth two points). All face cards are worth ten points. The ace, on the other hand, is worth either 1 point or 11, whichever you choose. In this manner, an ace and a 5 could be worth 6 points (hard count) or 16 (soft count). The object of the game is to get as close to 21 points as you can without going over (called "busting"). You play only against the dealer, and the hand closest to 21 points wins the game.

The dealer will deal you a two-card hand, then give you the option of taking another card (called a "hit") or stopping with the two cards you have been dealt (called "standing"). For example, if your first two cards are a 10 and a 3, your total would be 13, and you would normally ask for another card to get more points. If the next card dealt to you was a 7, you would have a total of 20 points and you would "stand" with 20 (i.e., not ask for another card).

It makes no difference what the other players are dealt, or what they choose to do with their hands. Your hand will win or lose only in comparison to the hand that the dealer holds.

The dealer plays his hand last. This is his biggest advantage. All the players that go over 21 points, or bust, will immediately lose their cards and their bet before the dealer's turn to play. What this means in terms of casino advantage is that while the player has to play to win, the only thing the dealer has to do is not lose. Every time you bust, the casino wins. This sequence of play ensures a profit for the casino from the blackjack tables.

We recommend that you take the time to observe a few hands before you play. This will give you the opportunity to find a personable, friendly dealer and to check out the minimum-bet signs posted at each table. They will say something like: "Minimum bet $2–500." This means that the minimum wager is $2, and the maximum wager is $500. If you sit down at a blackjack table and begin to bet with insufficient cash or the wrong denomination chip, the dealer will inform you of the correct minimum wager, whereupon you may either conform or excuse yourself.

*The correct term for the spots on playing cards is "pips."

A blackjack table is shaped like a half circle, with the dealer inside the circle and room for five to seven players around the outside. Facing the dealer, the chair on the far right is called "first base." The chair on the far left is called "third base." The dealer deals the cards from first base to third, and each player plays out his hand in the same order.

The best possible position is at third base or as close to it as you can get. This gives you the advantage of watching the other players play out their hands before you play.*

To buy in, find an empty seat at a table with an agreeable minimum wager and wait until the hand in progress is concluded. Though you can bet cash, most players prefer to convert their currency to chips. This is done by placing your money on the table *above* the bettor's box. Because blackjack is one of the many games in the casino in which the dealer is allowed to accept cash bets, he will assume that any money placed *in* the bettor's box is a wager.

Your dealer will take the cash, count out your chips, and push the money through a slot cut in the top of the table. Because he cannot give you change in cash, the total amount you place on the table will be converted to chips. You may at any time, however, redeem your chips for cash

---

*For beginning gamblers, a seat at third base can sometimes lead to an unpleasant experience. In simplest terms, the third base player, because he plays just before the dealer, can really screw things up for knowledgeable (basic strategy) bettors if he makes a dumb move. Let's say that the dealer has a 6 as his up card. An experienced player would bet that the dealer had a 10-value down card, for a total count of 16. Because the rules force the dealer to hit a count of 16, there is a high probability that the dealer will bust. Given this logic, a basic strategy player would stand on a count of 12 or higher.

A friend described the following confrontation evolving from a similar set of circumstances. A novice was seated at third base when a serious player (seated at the novice's immediate right) elected to stand with a count of 13 against the dealer's up card of 6. The novice at third base had a jack (ten count) and a 4, for a total of 14. The correct play for the novice was to stand and hope that the dealer busted. Unfortunately, however, the novice elected to take a hit, drew a 10, and busted. The dealer subsequently drew a 4 to his initial deal of a queen and a 6, and won with a total count of 20. If the novice had stood with 14 as smart play dictates, the dealer (instead of the novice) would have drawn the 10 and busted. The serious player, enraged that the novice's bad play had also caused him to lose, pounded the table, cursed the novice roundly, and told him "to take some lessons before playing with the grown-ups." The object lesson of this rather lengthy tale is not to sit at third base unless you really know what you are doing.

from the casino cashier. Once you have been given chips and have bet, you will be included in the next deal.

To confound a player attempting to count cards, many casinos deal blackjack with two to six decks shuffled together. This huge stack of cards is rendered manageable by dealing from a special container known as a shoe.

The dealer will shuffle the decks and may offer the cards to you to cut. Don't get fancy. Simply take off the top half of the deck and lay it beside the other half. Do this with one hand and never conceal the deck from the dealer. If you are playing with a large multiple deck, the dealer may offer you a plastic card stop. Place the card stop halfway or so into the deck, leaving the stop sticking out. The dealer will cut the deck at that point and put it into the shoe.

After he cuts a single deck, or puts the multiple deck into the shoe, the dealer will "burn" one or more cards by taking them off the top and putting them into the discard pile. This is yet another tactic to inhibit players from keeping track of cards dealt. Also to the advantage of the casino is the dealer's right to shuffle the cards whenever he pleases. Usually the dealer will deal from the shoe until he reaches the plastic stop card and then he will "break the deck," which means reshuffle and recut before dealing the next hand. In a single-deck game, the dealer will usually reshuffle about three-quarters through the deck.

Because the dealer always plays his hand last, you must develop your strategy by comparing your card count to what you assume (based on his visible card) the dealer has. The rule of thumb for most situations is to play your hand as if you know the dealer's down card has a value of ten. The principles governing when or when not to take a hit are known as "basic strategy" (summarized below in a chart). If you elect to take a hit and go over 21 (bust), you lose. If you stand with your original two cards or take a number of hits without going over 21, you can sit back and relax for a few seconds while the dealer continues on around the table, repeating the same process with the other players. When the other players finish, the dealer exposes his "down" card and plays out his hand according to strict rules. He must take a hit on any total of 16 or less, and he must stand on any total of 17 or more. When he finishes his hand, the dealer goes from third base to first, paying off each winning player and collecting chips from the losers who didn't bust.

If you have more points than the dealer, then you win. If he has more points (or if you busted), then he wins. If there is a tie, neither hand wins. When you tie, the dealer will knock on the table above your bet to indicate that the hand is a tie, or a "push." You may leave your bet on the table for the next hand, or change it.

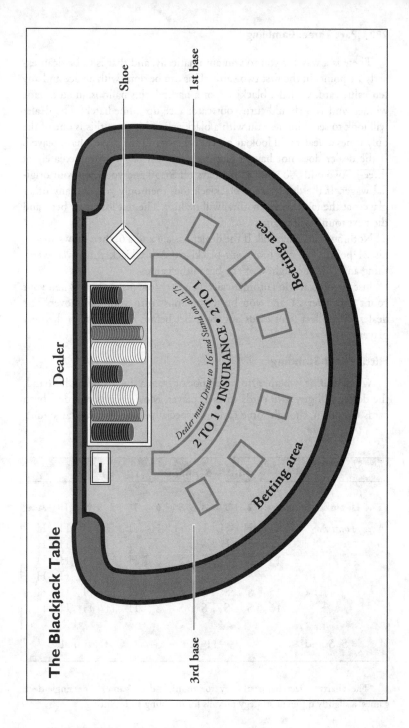

The Blackjack Table

Shoe

1st base

Betting area

Dealer

Dealer must Draw to 16 and Stand on all 17s

2 TO 1 • INSURANCE • 2 TO 1

Betting area

3rd base

There is a way for you to win automatically, and that is to be dealt exactly 21 points in the first two cards. This can be done with an ace and any ten-value card. Called a blackjack, or a natural, this hand is an automatic winner, and you should turn your cards face up immediately. The dealer will look to see if he ties you with a blackjack of his own; this is one of the only times a dealer will look at his cards before all the players have played. If the dealer does not have a blackjack, he will pay you immediately at three-to-two odds, so your $5 bet pays off $7.50 and you keep your original wager. If the dealer has a blackjack too, then only you and any other players at the table with a natural will tie him. The rest lose their bets, and the next round will begin.

Nothing beats a natural. If the dealer has a 4 and a 6, then draws an ace, his 21 points will not beat your blackjack. A blackjack wins over everything and pays the highest of any bet in the game.

Just as you can win automatically, you may lose just as fast. When your count goes over 21 and you bust, you must turn your cards over. The dealer will collect your cards and your bet before moving on to the next player.

Hitting and Standing

When dealing, whether from the shoe or from a single deck in his hand, the dealer will give two cards to each player. Most casinos will deal both cards facedown, though some casinos, especially those that use large mul-

BASIC STRATEGY *									
The Dealer is Showing: 2	**3**	**4**	**5**	**6**	**7**	**8**	**9**	**10**	**Ace**
Your Total is: 4–11 H	H	H	H	H	H	H	H	H	H
12 H	H	S	S	S	H	H	H	H	H
13 S	S	S	S	S	H	H	H	H	H
14 S	S	S	S	S	H	H	H	H	H
15 S	S	S	S	S	H	H	H	H	H
16 S	S	S	S	S	H	H	H	H	H
S=Stand		H=Hit			O=Optional				

*The charts reflect basic strategy for multiple-deck games. For single-deck games, a slightly different strategy prevails for doubling and splitting.

tiple decks, will deal both cards faceup. There is no advantage to either method. Most players are more comfortable with the secrecy of the face-down deal, but the outcome will not be affected either way. Starting with the player at first base, the dealer will give you cards to play out your hand. After the initial deal, you have two basic options: either stand or take a hit.

If you are satisfied with your deal, then you elect to stand. If your cards were dealt facedown, slide them under the chips in the bettor's box with one hand, being careful not to touch your chips or conceal them from the dealer. If the cards were dealt faceup, wave your hand over the top, palm down, in a negative fashion, to signal the dealer not to give you another card.

Sometimes you will improve your hand by asking for another card. You signal for a hit by scratching the bottom of your cards toward you on the felt surface of the table. In a faceup game, scratch your fingers toward you in the same fashion. You may say, "Hit me," or "I'll take a hit," depending on the mood at your table but use the hand gestures also. Because of noise and distractions, the dealer may misinterpret your verbal request.

The card you request will be dealt faceup and you may take as many hits as you like. When you want to show that you do not want another card, use the signals for standing. If you bust, turn your cards faceup right away so the dealer can collect your cards and chips. He will then go to the next player.

SOFT HAND STRATEGY *									
The Dealer is Showing: 2	3	4	5	6	7	8	9	10	**Ace**
You Have: Ace, 9 S	S	S	S	S	S	S	S	S	S, H
Ace, 8 S	S	S	S	S	S	S	S	S	
Ace, 7 S	D	D	D	D	S	S	H	H	S
Ace, 6 H	D	D	D	D	S	H	H	H	H
Ace, 5 H	H	D	D	D	H	H	H	H	H
Ace, 4 H	H	D	D	D	H	H	H	H	H
Ace, 3 H	H	H	D	D	H	H	H	H	H
Ace, 2 H	H	H	D	D	H	H	H	H	H
S=Stand			**H=Hit**				**D=Double Down**		

*The charts reflect basic strategy for multiple-deck games. For single-deck games, a slightly different strategy prevails for doubling and splitting.

There are times when the dealer stands a good chance of busting. At these times, it is a good idea to stand on your first two cards even though the total in points may seem very low. The accompanying basic strategy chart shows when to stand and when to take a hit. It is easy to follow and simple to memorize. The decision to stand or take a hit is made on the value of your hand and, once again, the dealer's up card, and is based on the probability of his busting. Although following basic strategy won't win every hand, it will improve your odds and take the guesswork out of some confusing situations.

Basic strategy is effective because the dealer is bound by the rules of the game. He must take a hit on 16 and stand on 17. These rules are printed right on the table so that there can be no misunderstanding. Even if you are the only player at the table and stand with a total of 14 points, the dealer with what would be a winning hand of 16 points *must* take another card.

There is one exception to the rule: Some casinos require a dealer to take a hit on a hand with an ace and a 6 (called "soft 17"). Because the ace can become a 1, it is to the casino's advantage for the dealer to be allowed to hit a soft 17.

Bells and Whistles

Now that you understand the basic game, let's look at a few rules in the casino version of blackjack that are probably different from the way you play at home.

Doubling Down   When you have received two cards and think that they will win with the addition of one and *only* one more card, then double your bet. This "doubling down" bet should be made if your two-card total is 11, since drawing the highest possible card, a 10, will not push your total over 21 points. In some casinos you may double down on ten points, and some places will let you double down on any two-card hand.

DOUBLING DOWN										
The Dealer is Showing:	**2**	**3**	**4**	**5**	**6**	**7**	**8**	**9**	**10**	**Ace**
Your Total is: 11	D	D	D	D	D	D	D	D	D	H
10	D	D	D	D	D	D	D	D	H	H
9	H	D	D	D	D	H	H	H	H	H
H=Hit					**D=Double Down**					

To show the dealer that you want to double down, place your two cards touching each other faceup on the dealer's side of the betting box. Then place enough in the box to equal your original bet. Now, as at all other times, don't touch your chips once the bet is made.

Splitting   Any time you are dealt two cards of the same value, you may split the cards and start two separate hands. Even aces may be split, though when you play them, they will each be dealt only one additional card. If you should happen to get a blackjack after splitting aces, it will be treated as 21 points; that is, paid off at one to one and not three to two.

Any other pair is played exactly as you would if you were playing two consecutive hands, and all the rules will apply. Place the two cards *apart from each other* and above the betting box, so the dealer won't confuse this with doubling down. Then add a stack of chips equal to the original bet to cover the additional hand. Your two hands will be played out one at a time, cards dealt faceup.

You will be allowed to split a third card if it is the same as the first two, but not if it shows up as a later hit. Always split a pair of eights, since they total 16 points, a terrible point total. *Never* split two face cards or tens, since they total 20 and are probably a winning hand.

Some casinos will let you double down after splitting a hand, but if you're unsure, ask the dealer. Not all blackjack rules are posted, and they can vary from casino to casino, and even from table to table in the same casino.

SPLITTING STRATEGY										
The Dealer is Showing:	**2**	**3**	**4**	**5**	**6**	**7**	**8**	**9**	**10**	**Ace**
You Have: 2, 2	H	H	SP	SP	SP	SP	H	H	H	H
3, 3	H	H	SP	SP	SP	SP	H	H	H	H
4, 4	H	H	H	H	H	H	H	H	H	H
5, 5	D	D	D	D	D	D	D	D	H	H
6, 6	H	SP	SP	SP	SP	H	H	H	H	H
7, 7	SP	SP	SP	SP	SP	SP	H	H	H	H
8, 8	SP	SP	SP	SP	SP	SP	SP	SP	SP	SP
9, 9	SP	SP	SP	SP	SP	S	SP	SP	S	S
10, 10	S	S	S	S	S	S	S	S	S	S
Ace, Ace	SP	SP	SP	SP	SP	SP	SP	SP	SP	SP

S=Stand   H=Hit   SP=Split   D=Double Down

Insurance   When the dealer deals himself an ace as his second, faceup card, he will stop play and ask, "Insurance, anyone?" Don't be fooled. You're not insuring anything. All he's asking for is a side bet that he will have a natural. He must make the insurance bets before he can look at his cards, so he doesn't know if he has won or not when he asks for your insurance bets.

The insurance wager can be up to half the amount of your original bet. Place the chips in the large semicircle marked "insurance." Just as it says, it pays off two to one. If your original bet was $10 and you bet $5 that the dealer had a natural, you would be paid $10 if he actually did. Depending on your cards, you would probably lose your original $10 bet but break even on the hand. If the dealer does not have a ten-value card, you lose your $5 insurance bet, but your $10 bet still has a chance of winning.

This sounds deceptively easy. Insurance is always a bad move for the basic strategy player because the odds are against the dealer actually having a natural. You will lose this bet more often than you will win it, though the dealer may suggest it to you as a smart move. The dealer might also tell you to insure your own blackjack, though this should never be done. The odds are always against the insurance bet. When you insure your blackjack you can be paid off for it at one to one, as if it were 21 points, instead of the three to two that you would normally be paid for the blackjack. Even though you may occasionally tie with the dealer, you will more than make up for it with the three-to-two payoffs on the blackjacks you don't insure.

Avoiding Common Pitfalls

1. Always check the minimum bets allowed at your table *before* you sit down. Flipping a $5 chip into a $25-minimum game can be humiliating. If you make this mistake, simply excuse yourself and leave. It happens all the time.

2. Keep your bet in a neat stack, with the largest value chips on the bottom and the smallest on top. A mess of chips can be confusing should you want to double down, and your dealer will get huffy if he has to ask you to stack your chips.

3. Never touch the chips once the bet is down. Cheaters do this, and your dealer may assume you're cheating. It's too easy for a player to secretly up his bet once he's seen his cards or lower it if the cards are bad. Do not stack a double-down bet or split bets on top of the original bet. Place them beside the original bet and then keep your hands away.

4. Along the same lines, don't touch a hand if the cards are dealt faceup. Use the hand signals to tell the dealer that you stand or that you want a hit. *Never* move your cards below the level of the table, where the dealer can't see them. When you brush your cards for a hit, do so lightly so that the dealer won't think that you are trying to mark them by bending them.

5. Take your time and count your points correctly. The pace of the game in the casino can pick up to a speed that is difficult for a beginner. It's perfectly all right to take your time and recount after a hit. One hint: Count aces as 1 first, then add 10 to your total. An ace and a 4 is equal to 5 or 15. Once you have this notion in your head, you won't make a mistake and refrain from hitting a soft hand. If you throw down an ace, a 10, and a 9 in disgust, for example, many dealers will simply pick up your cards and your bet, even though your 20 might have been a winning hand. If you are confused about your point total, do not be embarrassed to ask for help.

6. Know the denomination of the chips that you are betting. Stack them according to denomination, and read the face value every play until you know for sure which chips are which color. Otherwise you might think you are betting $5 when you are actually throwing out a $25 chip on every hand.

7. Be obvious with your hand signals to the dealer. The casinos are loud and busy, and the dealer may be distracted with a player. Don't leave any room for misinterpretation.

8. If cards fly off the table during the deal, pick them up slowly using two fingers. See number four, above.

9. Tip the dealer at your discretion if he or she has been friendly and helpful. One of the better ways to tip the dealer is to bet a chip for him on your next hand and say, "This one is for you." If you win, so does he. Never tip when a dealer has been rude or cost you money by being uncooperative. Then you should finish your hand and leave. Period.

■ Craps ■

Of all the games offered in casinos, craps is by far the fastest and, to many, the most exciting. It is a game in which large amounts of money can be won or lost in a short amount of time. The craps table is a circus of sound and movement. Yelling and screaming are allowed—even encouraged—here, and the frenetic betting is bewildering to the uninitiated. Don't be intimidated, however: the basic game of craps is easy to understand. The confusion and insanity of craps have more to do with the pace of the game and the amazing number of betting possibilities than with the complexity of the game itself.

The Basic Game

Because it is so easy to become confused at a crowded and noisy craps table, we highly recommend that beginning players take advantage of the free lessons offered by most of the casinos. Once you understand the game, you will be able to make the most favorable bets and ignore the rest.

In craps, one player at a time controls the dice, but all players will eventually have an opportunity to roll or refuse the dice. Players take turns in a clockwise rotation. If you don't want the dice, shake your head, and the dealer will offer them to the next player.

All the players around the table are wagering either with or against the shooter, so the numbers he throws will determine the amount won or lost by every other player. The casino is covering all bets, and the players are not allowed to bet among themselves. Four casino employees run the craps table. The boxman in the middle is in charge of the game. His job is to oversee the other dealers, monitor the play, and examine the dice if they are thrown off the table.

There are two dealers, one placed on each side of the boxman. They pay off the winners and collect the chips from the losers. Each dealer is in charge of half of the table.

The fourth employee is the stickman, so called because of a flexible stick he uses after each roll to retrieve the dice. His job, among other things, is to supply dice to the shooter and to regulate the pace of the game. When all bets are down, the stickman pushes several sets of dice toward the shooter. The shooter selects two dice, and the stickman removes the others from the table. From time to time, the stickman checks the dice for signs of tampering.

The shooter then throws the dice hard enough to cause them to bounce off the wall at the far end of the table. This bounce ensures that each number on each die has an equal probability of coming up.

The Play   When it is your turn to throw the dice, pick out two and return the other to the stickman. After making a bet (required), you may throw the dice. You retain control of the dice until you throw a seven ("seven out") or relinquish the dice voluntarily.

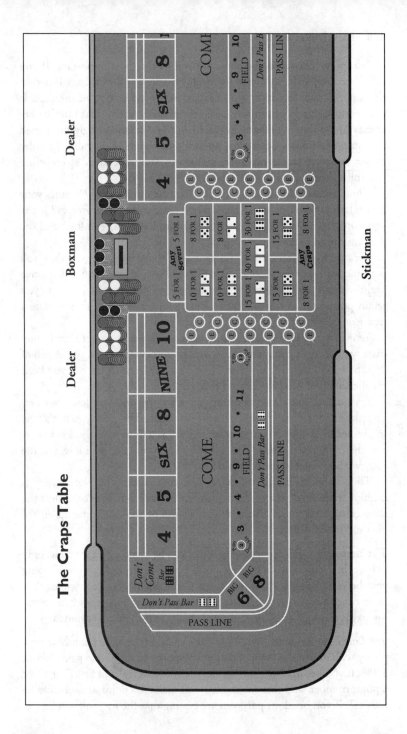

The Craps Table

Your first roll, called the come-out roll, is the most important. If you roll a 7 or an 11 on your come-out roll, you are an immediate winner. In this case, you collect your winnings and retain possession of the dice. If your come-out roll is a four, five, six, eight, nine, or ten, that number becomes "the point." A marker is placed in the correspondingly numbered box on the layout to identify the point for all players at the table. In order to win the game, this number (the point) will have to be rolled again before you roll a seven.

Thus, if you roll a five on your first roll, the number five becomes your point. It doesn't matter how long it takes you to roll another five, as long as you don't roll a seven first. As soon as you roll a seven, you lose, and the dice are passed to another player.

Let's say five is your point, and your second roll is a four, your third roll is a nine, and then you roll another five. You win because you rolled a five again without rolling a seven. Because you have not yet rolled a seven, you retain possession of the dice, and after making a bet, you may initiate a new game.

Your next roll is, once again, a come-out roll. Just as 7 or 11 are immediate winners on a come-out roll, there are immediate losers, too. A roll of 2, 3, or 12 (all called "craps") will lose. You lose your chips, but you keep the dice because you have not yet rolled a seven.

If your first roll is two, for example, it's craps, and you lose your bet. You place another bet and roll to come-out again. This time you roll a five, so five becomes your point. Your second roll is a four, your third is a nine, and then you roll a seven. The roll of seven means that you lose and the dice will be passed to the next player.

This is the basic game of craps. The confounding blur of activity is nothing more than players placing various types of bets with or against the shooter, or betting that a certain number will or will not come up on the next roll of the dice.

The Betting   Of the dozens of bets that can be made at a craps table, only two or three should even be considered by a novice craps player. Keeping your bets simple makes it easier to understand what's going on, while at the same time minimizing the house advantage. Exotic, long-shot bets, offering payoffs as high as 30 to 1, are sucker bets and should be avoided.

The Line Bets: Pass and Don't Pass   Pass and don't pass bets combine simplicity with one of the smallest house advantages of any casino game, about 1.4%. If you bet pass, you are betting that the first roll will be a 7 or 11 or a point number, and that the shooter will make the point again before he rolls a 7. If you bet don't pass, you are betting that the first roll will be a 2,

3, or 12, or, if a point is established, that the shooter will seven out and throw a 7 before he rolls his point number again. The two and three are immediate losers, and the casino will collect the chips of anyone betting pass. A roll of 12, however, is considered a standoff where the shooter "craps out" but no chips change hands for the "don't" bettor. Almost 90% of casino craps players confine their betting to the pass and don't pass line.

Come and Don't Come   Come and don't come bets are just like pass and don't pass bets, except that they are placed *after* the point has been established on the come-out roll. Pass and don't pass bets must be placed before the first roll of the dice, but come and don't come bets may be placed before any roll of the dice *except* come-out rolls. On his come-out roll, let's say that the shooter rolls a nine. Nine becomes the shooter's point. If at this time you place your chips in the come box on the table, the next roll of the dice will determine your "come number." If the shooter throws a six, for example, your chips are placed in the box marked with the large six. The dealer will move your chips and will keep track of your bet. If the shooter rolls another six before he rolls a seven, your bet pays off. If the shooter sevens out before he rolls a six, then you lose. If the shooter makes his point (i.e., rolls another nine), your come bet is retained on the layout.

If you win a come bet, the dealer will place your chips from the numbered box back into the come space and set your winnings beside it. You may leave your chips there for the next roll or you may remove them entirely. If you fail to remove your winnings before the next roll, they may become a bet that you didn't want to make.

Don't come bets are the opposite of come bets. A 7 or 11 loses, and a 2 or 3 wins. The 12 is again a standoff. The don't come bettor puts his chips in the don't come space on the table and waits for the next roll to determine his number. His chips are placed *above* the numbered box to differentiate it from a come bet. If the shooter rolls his point number before he rolls your number, your don't come bet is retained on the layout. You are betting against the shooter; that is, that he will roll a seven first. When he rolls seven, you win. If he rolls your don't come number before he sevens out, you lose.

The come and don't come bets have a house advantage of about 1.4% and are among the better bets in craps once you understand them.

Odds Bets   When you bet the pass/don't pass, or the come/don't come area, you may place an odds bet *in addition* to your original bet.

Once it is established that the come-out roll is not a 7 or 11, or craps, the bettor may place a bet that will be paid off according to the actual odds of a particular number being thrown.

ACTUAL ODDS CHART		
Number	**Ways to Roll**	**Odds against Repeat**
4	3	2–1
5	4	3–2
6	5	6–5
8	5	6–5
9	4	3–2
10	3	2–1

Note that the Actual Odds Chart shows the chances against a number made by two dice being thrown. For example, the odds of making a nine are three to two. If you place an odds bet (in addition to your original bet) on a come number of nine, your original come bet will pay off at even money, but your odds bet will pay off at three to two.

Because this would make a $7.50 payoff for a $5 bet, and the tables don't carry 50-cent chips, you are allowed to place a $6 bet as an odds bet. This is a very good bet to make, and betting the extra dollar is to your advantage.

To place an odds bet on a line bet, bet the pass line. When (and if) the point is established, put your additional bet behind the pass line and say, "Odds."

To place an odds bet on a come bet, wait for the dealer to move your chips to the come number box, then hand him more chips and say, "Odds." He will set these chips half on and half off the other pile so that he can see at a glance that it's an odds bet.

Craps Etiquette

When you arrive at a table, find an open space and put your money down in front of you. When the dealer sees it, he will pick it up and hand it to the boxman. The boxman will count out the correct chips and hand them to the dealer, who will pass them to you.

A craps table holds from 12 to 20 players and can get very crowded. Keep your place at the table. Your chips are in front of you, and it is your responsibility to watch them.

After you place your bets, your hands must come off the table. It is very bad form to leave your hands on the table when the dice are rolling.

Stick to the good bets listed here, and don't be tempted by bets that you don't understand. The box in the middle of the layout, for example, offers a number of sucker bets.

■ **Baccarat** ■

Originally an Italian card game, baccarat (bah-kah-rah) is the French pronunciation of the Italian word for zero. The name refers to the value of all the face cards in the game: zero.

Because baccarat involves no player decisions, it is an easy game to play, but a very difficult game to understand. Each player must decide to make a bet on either the bank or the player. That's it. There are no more decisions until the next hand is dealt. The rules of playing out the hands are ridiculously intricate, but beginning players need not concern themselves with them, because all plays are predetermined by the rules, and the dealer will tell you exactly what happened.

All cards, ace through 9, are worth their spots (the 3 of clubs is worth three points). The 10, jack, queen, and king are worth zero (0). The easiest way to count points is to add all points in the hand, then take only the number in the ones column.

BACCARAT RULES

Player

When First Two Cards Total:

1, 2, 3, 4, 5, or 10	Draws a Card
6 or 7	Stands
8 or 9	A Natural—Stands

Banker

Having:	*Draws When Player's Third Card Is:*	*Does Not Draw When Player's Third Card Is:*
3	1, 2, 3, 4, 5, 6, 7, 9, 10	8
4	2, 3, 4, 5, 6, 7	1, 8, 9, 10
5	4, 5, 6, 7,	1, 2, 3, 8, 9, 10
6	6, 7	1, 2, 3, 4, 5, 8, 9, 10
7	Stands	Stands
8 or 9	Stands	Stands

If you have been dealt a 6 and a 5, then your total is 11, and taking only the ones column, your hand is worth 1 point. If you hold a 10 and a king, your hand is worth zero. If you have an 8 and a 7, your point total is 15, and taking the ones column, your hand is worth 5. It doesn't get any simpler than this.

In baccarat, regardless of the number of bettors at the table, only two hands are dealt: one to the player and one to the bank. The object of the game is to be dealt or draw a hand worth nine points. If the first two cards dealt equal nine points (a 5 and a 4, for example), then you have a natural and an automatic winner. Two cards worth eight are the second best hand and will also be called a natural. If the other hand is not equal to or higher than eight, this hand wins automatically. Ties are standoffs, and neither bank nor player wins.

If the hands equal any total except nine or eight, the rules are consulted. These rules are printed and available at the baccarat table. The hands will be played out by the dealer whether you understand the rules or not.

The rules for the player's hand are simple. If a natural is not dealt to either hand, and if the player holds one, two, three, four, five, or ten (zero), he will always draw a card. He will stand on a total of six or seven. A total of eight or nine, of course, will be a natural.

The bank hand is more complicated and is partially determined by the third card drawn by the player's hand. Though the rules don't say so, the bank will always draw on zero, one, or two. When the hand is worth three or more, it is subject to the printed rules.

If you study a few hands, the method of play will be clear:

First Hand   The player's hand is worth three, and the bank's is worth four. The player always goes first. Looking at the rules for the player, we see that a hand worth three points draws a card. This time he draws a 9, for a new total of 12 points, which has a value of 2. The bank, having four points, must stand when a player draws a 9. The bank wins four to two.

Second Hand   The player's hand is worth six points, and the bank has two queens, for a total of zero. The player must stand with six points, while the bank must draw with zero. The bank gets another card, a 4. Player wins, six to four.

The Atmosphere

The casinos try to attract players by making baccarat seem Continental and sophisticated. The section is roped off from the main casino, and the dealers are often dressed in tuxedoes instead of the usual dealer's uniforms. Don't be put off by glamorous airs; everyone is welcome to play.

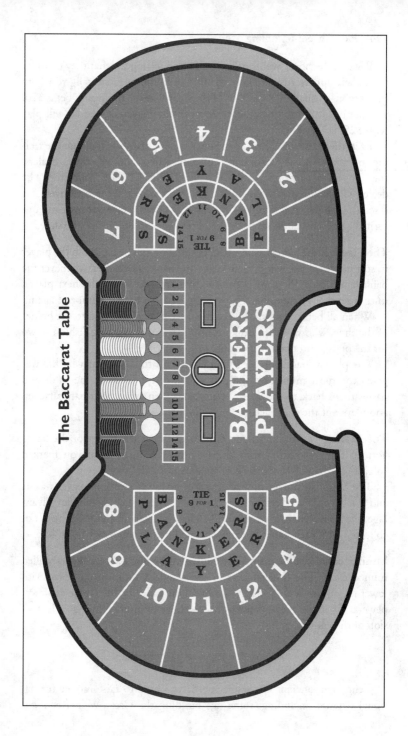

The Baccarat Table

Because the house wants baccarat to be appealing to what they consider to be their upper-crust clientele, the table minimums are usually very high in baccarat—usually $20–2,000. This means that the minimum bet is $20, and the maximum bet is $2,000. Most of the players, however, will play with $25 and $100 chips.

Even the shuffle and deal of the deck is designed to perpetuate the feeling of the exotic. Elaborately cut and mixed by all three dealers, the cards are cut by one player and marked with the plastic card stop. The dealer will then separate the cards at the stop, turn the top card over, and discard, or burn, the number of cards equal to the face value of the up-turned card. The cards are then placed in a large holder called the shoe.

The Play   If the game has just begun, the shoe will be passed to the player in seat number one, who is then called the bank. Thereafter, whenever the bank hand loses, the shoe is passed counterclockwise to the next player, until it reaches seat number 15, where it is passed to seat number 1 again.

When all bets are down, one of the three dealers will nod to the holder of the shoe, who will then deal out four cards in alternating fashion—two for the player and two for the bank.

The player's hand is passed (still facedown) to the bettor who has wagered the most money on the player's hand. He looks at the cards and passes them back to the dealer. The dealer then turns both hands faceup and plays out the game according to the rules.

The Betting   In baccarat, you must back either the player or the bank. You do this by putting your chips in the box in front of you marked "player" or "bank." Once the bets are down, the deal will begin.

The house advantage on baccarat is quite low: 1.36% on player wagers and 1.17% on bank bets. Because the bank bet has such an obvious advantage, the house extracts a commission when you win a bank bet. This is not collected with each hand, but must be paid before you leave the table.

Minibaccarat   Some casinos have installed smaller baccarat tables, called minibaccarat. The dealers dress in the standard uniform and play with lower minimum bets. The games move more quickly, since there are fewer players. If you feel intimidated by baccarat, we recommend the smaller version of the game.

■ **Keno** ■

Keno is an ancient Chinese game. It was used to raise money for national defense, including, some say, building the Great Wall. Keno was brought to America by the thousands of workers who came from the Far East to work on the railroads during the 1800s. It is one of the most popular games in the Nevada casinos, though it is outlawed in Atlantic City.

This game has a house advantage of between 20 and 35% or more, depending on the casino—higher than any other game in Las Vegas. Too high, in fact, for serious gamblers. So if you're down to your last dollar and you have to bet to save the ranch, don't go to the keno lounge.

While keno is similar to bingo, the betting options are reminiscent of exacta horse-race betting. It is like bingo in that a ticket, called a blank, is marked off and numbers are randomly selected to determine a winner. And it is similar to exacta betting because any number of fascinating betting combinations can be played in each game. The biggest difference between keno and bingo and exactas is that in the other two, there's always a winner. In keno, hours can go by before anyone wins a substantial amount. The main excitement in keno lies in the possibility that large amounts of money can be won on a small bet.

Playing the Game

In each casino there is a keno lounge that usually resembles a college lecture hall. The casino staff sit in front while players relax in chairs with writing tables built into the arms. It is not necessary to sit in the keno lounge to play. In fact, one of the best things about keno is that it can be played almost anywhere in the casino, including the bars and restaurants. As in bingo, it is acceptable to strike up a conversation with your neighbor during a game, and because the winning numbers are posted all over the place, keno also offers the opportunity to gamble while absent from the casino floor.

Keno is one of the easiest games to understand. The keno blank can be picked up almost anywhere in any Nevada casino. On the blank are two large boxes containing 80 numbers: the top box with 1–40, and the bottom box with 41–80. Simply use one of the crayons provided with the blanks to mark between 1 and 15 numbers on the blank, decide how much you want to bet, and turn the blank in to a keno writer. The keno writer records your wager, keeping your original, and gives you a duplicate, which *you* are responsible for checking. The keno writer can be found at the front of the keno lounge. The keno runner is even easier to spot: she is usually a woman in a short skirt with a hand full of blanks and crayons. She will place your bets, cash in your blanks, and bring you your winnings. Of course, you are expected to tip her for this service.

The drawing of the winning numbers takes place in the keno lounge. When the keno caller has determined that the bets are in for the current round, he will close the betting just like the steward does at the racetrack. Then the caller uses a machine similar to those employed by state lotteries: a blower with numbered Ping-Pong balls. Ten balls are blown into each of two tubes. These 20 balls bear the numbers that will be called for the current round. The numbers, as called out, are posted on electronic keno boards around the casino. If any of the lighted numbers are numbers that you marked on your card, you "caught" those numbers. Catching four or more numbers will usually win something, depending on how many numbers you marked on your card. The payoffs are complicated, but the more numbers you guess correctly and the more money you bet, the greater your jackpot. Suffice it to say, however, that you are not paid at anything even approaching true odds. If, by some amazing quirk of fate, you win, you must claim your winnings before the next round starts or forfeit.

The Odds   A "straight" or basic ticket is one where the player simply selects and marks a minimum of 1 number to a maximum of 8 to 15 numbers, depending on the casino. The ways to combine keno bets are endless and understandable only to astrophysicists. Any number can be played with any other number, making "combination" tickets. Groups of numbers can be combined with other groups of numbers, making "way" tickets. Individual numbers can be combined with groups of numbers, making "king" tickets. Then there is the "house" ticket, called different things at each casino, which offers a shot at the big jackpot for a smaller investment, though the odds won't be any better.

All of these options and the amounts that you are allowed to bet (usually from 70 cents up per ticket) will be listed in the keno brochures, which are almost as ubiquitous as the blanks. The payoffs will be listed for each type of bet and for the amount wagered. Keno runners and keno lounge personnel will show you how to mark your ticket if you are confused, but they cannot mark it for you. The only thing you really need to know about keno, however, is that the house has an unbeatable advantage.

The best strategy for winning at keno is to avoid it. If you want to play for fun (and that is the only rational reason to play), then understand that one bet is about as bad as another. Filling out a complicated combination ticket won't increase your chances of winning. If by some miracle you do win, accept the congratulations and the winnings, and then run, do not walk, to the nearest exit.

■ Roulette ■

A quiet game where winners merely smile over a big win and losers suffer in silence, roulette is very easy to understand. The dealer spins the

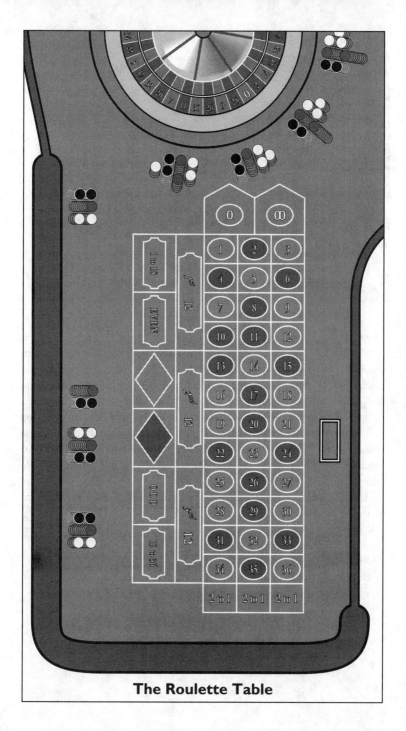

The Roulette Table

ROULETTE BET AND PAYOFF CHART

Bet	Payoff
Single number	35 to 1
Two numbers	17 to 1
Three numbers	11 to 1
Four numbers	8 to 1
Five numbers	6 to 1
Six numbers	5 to 1
12 numbers (column)	2 to 1
1st 12, 2nd 12, 3rd 12	2 to 1
1–18 or 19–36	1 to 1
Odd or Even	1 to 1
Red or Black	1 to 1

wheel, drops the ball, and waits for it to fall into one of the numbered slots on the wheel. The numbers run from zero to 36, with a double zero thrown in for good measure. You may bet on each individual number, on combinations of numbers, on all black numbers, all red numbers, and many more. All possible bets are laid out on the table.

Special chips are used for roulette, with each bettor at the table playing a different color. To buy in, convert cash or the casino's house chips to roulette chips. When you are ready to cash out, the dealer will convert your special roulette chips back to house chips. If you want cash, you must then take your house chips to a casino cashier.

To place a bet, put your chips inside a numbered square or choose one of the squares off to the side. A chip placed in "1st 12," for example, will pay off if the ball drops into any number from 1 to 12. The box marked "odd" is not for eccentrics—it pays when the ball drops into an odd-numbered slot.

Roulette is fun to play, but expect to pay! The house advantage on most bets is a whopping 5.26%, and on some wagers it can be as high as 7%.

PART FOUR

Exercise and Recreation

Working Out

Most of the folks on our *Unofficial Guide* research team work out routinely. Some bike; some run; some lift weights or do aerobics. Staying in hotels on the Strip and downtown, it didn't take them long to discover that working out in Las Vegas presents its own peculiar challenges.

The best months for outdoor exercise are October through April. The rest of the year it is extremely hot, though mornings and evenings are generally pleasant in September and May. During the scorching summer, particularly for visitors, we recommend working out indoors or, for bikers and runners, very early in the morning. If you do anything strenuous outside, any time of year, drink plenty of water. Dehydration and heat prostration can overtake you quickly and unexpectedly in Las Vegas's desert climate. For outdoor workouts in Las Vegas comparable to what you are used to at home, you will deplete your body's water at two to three times the usual rate.

■ Walking ■

Primarily flat, Las Vegas is made for walking and great people-watching. Security is very good both downtown and on the Strip, making for a safe walking environment at practically all hours of the day and night. Downtown, everything is concentrated in such a small area that you might be inclined to venture away from the casino center. While this is no more perilous than walking in any other city, the areas surrounding downtown are not particularly interesting or aesthetically compelling. If the downtown

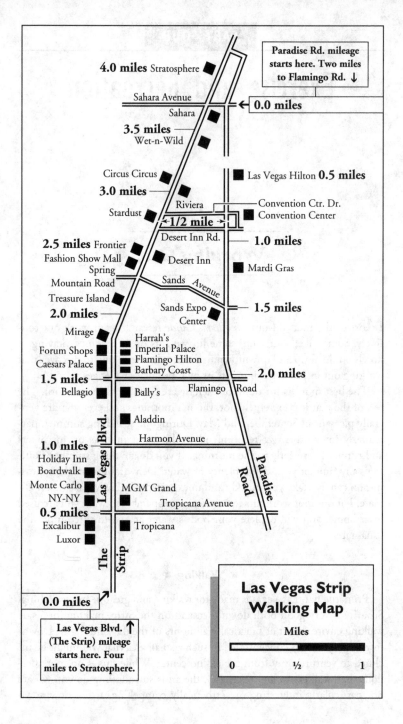

Paradise Rd. mileage starts here. Two miles to Flamingo Rd. ↓

4.0 miles Stratosphere

Sahara Avenue

← **0.0 miles**

Sahara

3.5 miles

Wet-n-Wild

Circus Circus

■ Las Vegas Hilton **0.5 miles**

3.0 miles

Riviera

Convention Ctr. Dr.
Convention Center

Stardust

←**1/2 mile**→

Desert Inn Rd. — **1.0 miles**

2.5 miles Frontier

Fashion Show Mall

Desert Inn

■ Mardi Gras

Spring

Mountain Road

Sands *Avenue*

Treasure Island

2.0 miles

Sands Expo
Center — **1.5 miles**

Mirage

Harrah's

Forum Shops

Imperial Palace

Caesars Palace

Flamingo Hilton

Barbary Coast

1.5 miles — — **2.0 miles**

Bellagio

Bally's

Flamingo   Road

Las Vegas Blvd.

Aladdin

Harmon Avenue

1.0 miles

Holiday Inn

Boardwalk

Monte Carlo

MGM Grand

Paradise   Road

NY-NY

Tropicana Avenue

0.5 miles

Excalibur

Tropicana

Luxor

The   Strip

0.0 miles

Las Vegas Blvd. ↑
(The Strip) mileage
starts here. Four
miles to Stratosphere.

Las Vegas Strip
Walking Map

Miles

0   ½   1

casino center is not large enough to accommodate your exercise needs, you are better off busing or cabbing to the Strip and doing your walking there.

If you are walking the Strip, it is about four miles from the old Hacienda site on the south end to the Stratosphere on the north end. Because the topography is so flat, however, it does not look that far. We met a number of people who set out on foot along the Strip and managed to overextend themselves. Check out our Strip walking distance map before you go, and bear in mind that even without hills, marching in the arid desert climate will take a lot out of you. Finally, carry enough money to buy refreshments en route and to take a cab or bus back to your hotel if you poop out or develop a blister.

▪ Running ▪

If you stay on the Strip, you will have more options than if you stay downtown. Those of us who are used to running on pavement ran on the broad sidewalks of Las Vegas Boulevard, South. These runs are great for people-watching also, but are frequently interrupted by long minutes of jogging in place at intersections, waiting for traffic lights to change. Our early risers would often run before 7:30 a.m. on the Desert Inn golf course. This was the best (and safest) running in town, with good footing, beautiful scenery, and no traffic. Suffice it to say, however, that course managers were less than overjoyed to see a small platoon of travel writers trotting off the 18th fairway. If you run on a golf course, stay off the greens and try to complete your run by 7:30 a.m. In addition, the Desert Inn has a small running track, and the Las Vegas Hilton has a half-mile jogging circuit.

If you stay downtown, you must either run on the sidewalks or drive to a more suitable venue. Sidewalks downtown are more congested than those on the Strip, and there are more intersections and traffic lights with which to contend. If you want to run downtown, particularly on Fremont Street, try to get your workout in before 10 a.m.

For those who dislike pounding the blacktop, sneaking onto golf courses, or exercising early in the morning, a convenient option is to run on the track at the university. Located about two miles east of the Strip on Harmon Avenue, UNLV offers both a regulation track and some large, grassy athletic fields. Park in the dirt lot near the tennis courts if you do not have a university parking sticker. For more information call (702) 895-3177.

A more expensive alternative is the posh Las Vegas Sporting House at 3025 Industrial Road, which has both an indoor and outdoor track. The charge is a hefty $15 a day, or $50 a week, but the fee includes the use of all club facilities. Call (702) 733-8999.

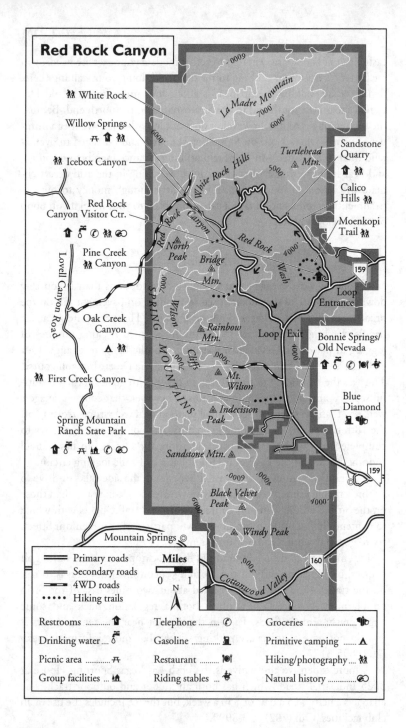

Red Rock Canyon

♙ White Rock

Willow Springs
ㅠ ⬆ ♙

♙ Icebox Canyon

La Madre Mountain
7000'
6000'

0009

Turtlehead
Mtn. △
5000'

Sandstone
Quarry
⬆ ♙

Calico
Hills ♙

Moenkopi
Trail ♙

Red Rock
Canyon Visitor Ctr.
⬆ ⚲ Ⓒ ♙ ∞

Pine Creek
♙ Canyon

North
Peak △

Bridge
Mtn. △

Red Rock Wash
4000'

159

Loop
Entrance

Lovell Canyon Road

Oak Creek
Canyon
▲ ♙

First Creek Canyon ♙

Spring Mountain
Ranch State Park
⬆ ⚲ ㅠ ♨ Ⓒ ∞

SPRING MOUNTAINS

Wilson Cliffs
7000'
5000'

Rainbow
Mtn. △

Mt.
Wilson △

Indecision
Peak △

Sandstone Mtn. △

Black Velvet
Peak △

Windy Peak △

Loop Exit

Bonnie Springs/
Old Nevada
⬆ ⚲ Ⓒ ⑩ ♨

Blue
Diamond
🖳 🍴

159

4000'

5000'

0009

0009

4000'

Mountain Springs ◎

160

Cottonwood Valley
5000'

Miles	
0	1

N ▲

─── Primary roads
─── Secondary roads
▬▬ 4WD roads
•••• Hiking trails

Restrooms	⬆	Telephone	Ⓒ	Groceries	🍴
Drinking water	⚲	Gasoline	🖳	Primitive camping	▲
Picnic area	ㅠ	Restaurant	⑩	Hiking/photography	♙
Group facilities	♨	Riding stables	♨	Natural history	∞

302

If you have a car and a little time, two of the better runs in the area are at Red Rock Canyon, out Charleston Avenue, 35 minutes west of town. Red Rock Canyon Conservation Area, managed by the U.S. Bureau of Land Management, is Western desert and canyon scenery at its best. Spectacular geology combined with the unique desert flora and fauna make Red Rock Canyon a truly memorable place. Maps and information can be obtained at the visitor center, on-site.

One two-mile round trip, the Moenkopi Loop, begins and ends at the visitor center. A three-mile circuit, the Willow Springs Trail, begins at the Willow Springs Picnic Area and circles around to Lost Creek Canyon. Both routes are moderately hilly, with generally good footing. The Moenkopi Loop is characterized by open desert and expansive vistas, while the Willow Springs Trail ventures into the canyons. The Willow Springs Trail is also distinguished by numerous Indian petroglyphs and other artifacts. Both trails, of course, are great for hiking as well as for running.

Finally, if you want to hook up with local runners, you can join the Las Vegas Track Club for a weekly run to Tule Springs (north of downtown on US 95) or many other area locations. For a current schedule or additional information call the Running Store at (702) 898-7866 or the Runner's Hotline at (702) 594-0970.

▪ Swimming and Sunbathing ▪

Swimming, during warm-weather months, is the most dependable and generally accessible form of exercise in Las Vegas. Most of the Strip hotels and a couple of the downtown hotels have nice pools. Sometimes the pools are too congested for swimming laps, but usually it is possible to stake out a lane.

If the pool at your hotel is a funny shape or too crowded for a workout, there are pools more conducive to serious swimming at the Las Vegas Sporting House on Industrial Road, at the Las Vegas Athletic Club on Flamingo Road, and in the McDermott Physical Education Complex of UNLV.

For those who want to work on their tans in style, the Mirage, Tropicana, Monte Carlo, MGM Grand, Treasure Island, Caesars Palace, Rio, Las Vegas and Flamingo Hiltons, Alexis Park, Hard Rock Hotel, and Desert Inn, among others, have particularly elegant facilities. Hotels with above-average pools include the Luxor, Frontier, Riviera, Harrah's, Imperial Palace, and Sahara. If you are staying in a place where the swimming is not very interesting, try the Wet 'n Wild water theme park near the Sahara on the Strip.

Be forewarned that sunbathing in Las Vegas can be dangerous. The climate is so arid that you will not feel yourself perspiring: perspiration evaporates as soon as it surfaces on your skin. If there is a breeze, particularly on a pleasant fall or spring day, you may never feel hot, sticky, or in any way uncomfortable until you come out of the sun and discover that you have been fried.

You can really get zapped in a hurry if you do not protect yourself properly, and even those who already have a good tan need to be extra careful. We recommend using twice the block you use in nondesert areas. If in Delaware, for example, you use a number four lotion, use at least a number eight in Las Vegas. Come out of the sun frequently to check yourself, and be careful not to fall asleep in the sun for an extended period.

If you overdo it somewhat, go to a nursery and buy an aloe plant. Slice the meaty tendrils lengthwise and rub the goop from the inside all over your skin. Repeat applications until you are tolerably comfortable. This treatment also works at home with minor kitchen burns.

■ Health Clubs ■

If you can get by with a Lifecycle, a Stairmaster, or a rowing machine, the fitness rooms of most major hotels should serve your needs. Fortunately, local health clubs welcome visitors for a daily ($10–20) or weekly ($25–50) fee. All of the clubs described here are coed.

The most luxurious (and expensive) club is the Las Vegas Sporting House, located close to the Strip at 3025 Industrial Road. Open 24 hours a day, the club offers racquetball, squash, tennis, basketball, volleyball, exercise equipment and weights, and aerobics. For information and rates call (702) 733-8999.

The Las Vegas Athletic Clubs, with five locations, offer much the same activities and services as the Sporting House, though not all features are provided at each location. The Las Vegas Athletic Clubs depend more on local patronage than on visitors; their facilities are commodious but less luxurious than those at the Sports Club, and fees are at the lower end of the range. While reasonably convenient to the Strip, only the West Sahara club is located within walking distance. For rates and additional information call:

Las Vegas Athletic Club
Spring Mountain Road at I-15
(702) 362-3720

Las Vegas Athletic Club
S. Maryland Parkway at Tropicana
(702) 795-2582

Las Vegas Athletic Club
E. Sahara at Maryland Parkway
(702) 733-1919

Las Vegas Athletic Club
E. Flamingo at Sandhill Road
(702) 451-2526

Las Vegas Athletic Club
W. Sahara and Decatur
(702) 364-5822

The 24 Hour Fitness centers, with three locations, run an excellent aerobics program and have an extensive weight and exercise facility. While the facilities are good and the use fees midrange, the locations are a little remote for most visitors staying on the Strip or downtown.

24 Hour Fitness	24 Hour Fitness	24 Hour Fitness
S. Eastern near Sahara	S. Valley View, half	Cheyenne and Rainbow
(702) 641-2222	mile south of Sahara	(702) 656-7777
	(702) 368-1111	

■ Aerobics ■

A number of health clubs offer coed aerobics on a daily basis. Daily or weekly rates are available. For additional information, see the preceding Health Club section.

■ Free Weights and Nautilus ■

Almost all of the major hotels have a spa or fitness room with weight-lifting equipment. Some properties have a single Universal machine, while others offer a wide range of free-weight and Nautilus equipment. Hotels with above-average facilities for pumping iron are the Las Vegas Hilton, the Desert Inn, Caesars Palace, the Golden Nugget, the Mirage, Monte Carlo, MGM Grand, Luxor, and Treasure Island.

For hardcore power lifters and body builders, try Gold's Gym at Sahara and Decatur, (702) 877-6966. Gold's offers daily and weekly rates for use of its Nautilus and free weights ($10 and $35 respectively). Gold's does not advertise that it is coed, but it is.

■ Racquetball, Squash, and Handball ■

The only hotel in Las Vegas with on-site courts is Caesars Palace. Visitors are welcome, however, at most local racquet and health clubs. Sports Club–Las Vegas and the Las Vegas Athletic Clubs, among others, provide good court facilities. For additional information see the preceding Health Club section.

Golf

Peak season for golf in Las Vegas is October through May. The other four months are considered prohibitively warm for most golfers, and green fees are reduced at most courses during the summer. Certain courses also have reduced rates for locals and for guests staying at hotels affiliated with the golf course. Morning tee times are always more difficult to arrange than afternoons. Call the starter one day before you wish to play. Same-day phone calls are discouraged. In summer, most courses and driving ranges stay open until at least 7:30 p.m. In winter and early spring, temperatures drop rapidly near sundown, so always bring a sweater or jacket. Las Vegas has an elevation of 2,000 feet and is considered high desert. Take this into account when making club selections.

Important Note: Two outstanding courses are not listed: Shadow Creek Country Club, privately owned by Mirage Resorts, Inc., and its chairman, Steve Wynn, is played only by Wynn's special guests. Built at a cost of nearly $40 million and looking more like a North Carolina layout bordered by cathedral pines than a traditional desert course, Shadow Creek was named by *Golf Digest* as the finest new course in the United States in

Golf Course Ratings		
Quality rating:	★★★	Championship, challenging
	★★	Playable, suitable for all caliber golfers
	★	Preferred by beginners and casual golfers
Value rating:	1	A good bargain
	2	A fair price
	3	Not a good bargain

Note: Quality and value ratings are abbreviated as *QV Rating* in the following listings.

1990. The ultimate accolade was bestowed when the same magazine listed Shadow Creek as the eighth best golf course in the United States, an unprecedented honor for a course less than five years old. The Tournament Players Club at Summerlin is strictly a private course and is currently the host course for both the Las Vegas Senior Classic and the Las Vegas Invitational. Other than La Costa Resort, this is the only course in the United States to host both men's professional tours. The Summerlin was designed by architect Bobby Weed with assistance from player/consultant Fuzzy Zoeller and is rated by both *Golf Digest* and *Golfweek* magazines as the second best course in Nevada, behind Shadow Creek. Many current professional athletes are members, including pitchers Duane Ward (Toronto Blue Jays), Mike Maddux (New York Mets), Greg Maddux (Atlanta Braves), and golfers Jim Colbert, Robert Gamez, and Bob May.

Angel Park Golf Club

Established: 1989

Address: 100 S. Rampart Blvd., Las Vegas NV 89128

Phone: (702) 254-4653

Status: Public/Municipal course

Tees:

Palm Course

Championship: 6,530 yards, par 70, USGA 70, slope 130.

Men's: 5,857 yards, par 70, USGA 70, slope 130.

Ladies': 4,570 yards, par 70, USGA 70, slope 110.

Mountain Course

Championship: 6,722 yards, par 71, slope 128.

Ladies': 5,164 yards, par 72, slope 119.

Fees: Palm Course and Mountain Course, $110 for 18 holes (carts included); Cloud 9 (par-three course), $22. No 9-hole rates available. Twilight rate (after 4 p.m.), $60. Club rentals, $25.

Facilities: Pro shop, night-lighted driving range and 18-hole putting course, putting green, restaurant, snack bar, bar, tennis courts, and walking track nearby.

QV Rating: ★★ 2

Comments Angel Park, a good, functional golf complex, is rapidly becoming one of the most successful public golf facilities in the United States. Its courses are well designed—by Arnold Palmer, no less—and the sophisticated 18-hole putting course, complete with night lighting, sand traps, rough, and water hazards, is a popular attraction even for nongolfers. In its eight-year existence, Angel Park has matured and become lush and attractive. Both courses are crowded year-round.

Black Mountain Golf and Country Club

Established: 1959

Address: 500 Greenway Rd., Henderson NV 89015

Phone: (702) 565-7933

Status: Semi-private

Tees:

   Championship: 6,550 yards, par 72, USGA 72, slope 123.

   Men's: 6,223 yards, par 72, USGA 72, slope 120.

   Ladies': 5,478 yards, par 73, USGA 73, slope 125.

Fees: Weekdays, $55 for 18 holes. Weekends, $50 for 18. Every day, $25 for 9. Seniors (over 63), $35 Tuesday and Thursday, excluding holidays. Carts mandatory on weekends and included in all fees. Club rentals, $13.

Facilities: Pro shop, clubhouse, driving range, putting green, restaurant, snack bar, and bar.

QV Rating: ★   1

Comments   Black Mountain is set amidst the Henderson hills, 20 minutes from the Strip. Many who prefer walking to riding play here, as it's one of the few area courses that don't require electric carts during the week. Many bunkers and unimproved areas off fairways make for tough recovery shots, but nobody said the game was supposed to be easy. A good course for beginning and intermediate golfers and juniors.

Boulder City Municipal Golf Course

Established: 1972; back nine completed 1986

Address: 1 Clubhouse Dr., Boulder City NV 89005

Phone: (702) 293-9236

Status: Public

Tees:

   Championship: 6,000 yards, par 72, USGA 70.2, slope 110.

   Men's: 6,132 yards, par 72, USGA 68.3, slope 103.

   Ladies': 5,566 yards, par 72, USGA 70.7, slope 113.

Fees: $36 for 18 holes, $27 to walk; $26 for 9 holes.

Facilities: Pro shop, driving range, putting green, restaurant, snack bar, and bar.

QV Rating: ★★ 1

Comments Just 20 minutes away from Las Vegas, in the one municipality in Nevada that forbids legalized gambling, this pleasant course is relaxing, accommodating to all level golfers, and just 10 minutes away from Hoover Dam. Walking is permitted.

Canyon Gate Country Club

Established: 1989

Address: 2001 Canyon Gate Dr., Las Vegas NV 89117

Phone: (702) 363-0481

Status: Private

Tees:

  Championship: 6,742 yards, par 72, USGA 72, slope 125.

  Men's: 6,259 yards, par 72, USGA 70.9, slope 121.

  Ladies': 5,141 yards, par 72, USGA 69.4, slope 121.

Fees: Must be a guest of a member to play. $75 for 18 holes (includes carts). Club rentals, $25.

Facilities: Clubhouse, pro shop, driving range, putting green, restaurant, snack bar, tennis courts, spa, steam room, weight room, and swimming pool.

QV Rating: ★★★ 2

Comments Canyon Gate was designed by noted architect Ted Robinson and is a championship golf course in every sense, with lush, narrow fairways, outstanding bent-grass greens, and an eclectic scattering of fairway bunkers and mounds. Management was taken over in 1992 by the elite company ClubCorp International (CCI). Frequently ranked as one of the top five courses in Nevada.

Craig Ranch Golf Course

Established: 1963

Address: 628 W. Craig Rd., North Las Vegas NV 89030

Phone: (702) 642-9700

Status: Public course

Tees:

  Men's: 6,000 yards, par 70, USGA 66.8, slope 105.

Ladies': 5,221 yards, par 70, USGA 69, slope 100.

Fees: $15 to walk 18 holes, $23 to ride. $9 to walk 9 holes, $13.50 to ride. Club rentals, $8 ($5 for 9 holes).

Facilities: Pro shop, driving range, putting green, and snack bar.

QV Rating: ★★ 1

Comments   A short public course with over 11,000 trees and perhaps the smallest greens in the state. A good course for beginning and intermediate golfers, with only one water hazard and three out-of-bounds holes.

Desert Pines Golf Club

Established: 1997

Address: 3415 E. Bonanza Rd., Las Vegas NV 89101

Phone: (702) 366-1616

Status: Public course

Tees:

Championship: 6,700 yards, par 71, USGA 70.4, slope 122.

Men's: 6,460 yards, par 71, USGA 66.8, slope 112.

Ladies': 5,870 yards, par 71, USGA not rated, slope not rated.

Fees: Nonresidents: $125 for 18 holes on weekdays, $145 on weekends and holidays (cart included).

Facilities: Pro shop, driving range, putting green, snack bar, and restaurant.

QV Rating: Not rated

Comments   Desert Pines is a new, 6,810-yard course located on Bonanza Road between Mohave and Pecos Roads. Inspired by the Pinehurst courses in North Carolina, Desert Pines' fairways and greens are flanked by trees, some already as tall as 40 feet. Instead of rough, developer Bill Walters laid down 45,000 bales of red pine needles imported from South Carolina.

Desert Rose Golf Course

Established: 1960

Address: 5483 Club House Dr., Las Vegas NV 89122

Phone: (702) 431-4653

Status: Public/Municipal course

Tees:

Championship: 6,600 yards, par 71, USGA 69.9, slope 117.

Men's: 6,100 yards, par 71, USGA 69.2, slope 114.

Ladies': 5,458 yards, par 71, USGA 69, slope 114.

Fees: Nonresidents: $65 for 18 holes on weekdays, $75 on weekends and holidays (cart included). After 2:30, $47. Nonresidents: $30 to walk 9 holes (before 7 a.m. or after 3:30 p.m.), $38 to ride 9 holes. Club rentals, $15.

Facilities: Pro shop, driving range, three putting/chipping greens, restaurant, banquet room, snack bar, and bar.

QV Rating: ★   2

Comments   With a name change (formerly it was Winterwood) and much moving of dirt, former PGA tour star Jim Colbert has created a functional public golf course that gets a lot of play year-round. A good course for recreational golfers, Desert Rose has fairly wide-open fairways with just a few out-of-bounds holes. Men must wear shirts with collars.

Highland Falls Golf Club

Established: 1992

Address: 10201 Sun City Blvd., Las Vegas NV 89134

Phone: (702) 254-7010

Status: Semi-private

Tees:

Championship: 6,512 yards, par 72, USGA 71.2, slope 126.

Men's: 6,017 yards, par 72, USGA 68.6, slope 116.

Gold: 5,579 yards, par 72, USGA 67.1, slope 112.

Ladies': 5,099 yards, par 72, USGA 68.8, slope 110.

Fees: Nonresidents of Sun City: $95 for 18 holes, $59 for 9. Sun City residents: $35 for 18 holes, $20 for 9. Carts included.

Facilities: Pro shop, driving range, one putting green, two chipping greens, luncheon area, patio for outside dining, and bar.

QV Rating: ★★   2

Comments   A testing layout designed by Hall of Famer Billy Casper's company, Casper-Nash Associates. Bent-grass greens with 328 Bermuda fairways overseeded with rye. More undulations than most desert courses, with several demanding holes. No one broke par for the first six months after opening.

Las Vegas Country Club

Established: 1967

Address: 3000 Joe W. Brown Dr., Las Vegas NV 89109

Phone: (702) 734-1122

Status: Private

Tees:

    Championship: 7,164 yards, par 72, USGA 72.8, slope 128.

    Men's: 6,718 yards, par 72, USGA 70.8, slope 123.

    Ladies': 5,581 yards, par 72, USGA 71.7, slope 121.

Fees: Not listed. Strictly private course for members and their guests only.

Facilities: Pro shop, driving range, putting green, restaurants, snack bar, tennis courts, swimming pool, and spas.

QV Rating: ★★★   N/A

Comments One of the host courses of the Las Vegas Invitational Men's PGA tournament. Beautifully conditioned, with recently planted bentgrass greens. Not available to the public, although a few tee times are reserved daily for high-rolling guests staying at the Las Vegas Hilton.

Las Vegas Golf Club

Established: 1949

Address: 4300 W. Washington Dr., Las Vegas NV 89108

Phone: (702) 646-3003

Status: Municipal course

Tees:

    Championship: 6,631 yards, par 72, USGA 71.8, slope 117.

    Men's: 6,337 yards, par 72, USGA 70.3, slope 114.

    Ladies': 5,715 yards, par 72, USGA 71.2, slope 113.

Fees: Residents: $10.50 for 18 holes, $19.50 to ride; $6.75 for 9 holes, $12.40 to ride. Nonresidents: $16.75 for 18 holes, $26 to ride; $10 for 9 holes, $16 to ride. Resident seniors, $5 (Monday, Wednesday–Friday). Club rentals, $25 for 18 holes, $15 for 9 holes. Twilight hours: residents, $6.75 to walk, $12.40 to ride; nonresidents, $10 to walk, $16 to ride. (Times vary.)

Facilities: Pro shop, night-lighted driving range, putting green, restaurant, snack bar, bar, and beverage-cart girls who patrol the course.

QV Rating: ★   1

Comments Popular public course and site of many local amateur tournaments. Formerly owned and managed by Senior PGA star Jim Colbert. A good course for recreational golfers, it offers fairly wide-open fairways and not a lot of trouble so play should move briskly. Tee times are always in great demand.

Las Vegas Hilton Country Club

Established: 1961

Address: 1911 E. Desert Inn Rd., Las Vegas NV 89109

Phone: (702) 796-0013 (tee-time service)

Status: Public course (privately owned)

Tees:
    Championship: 6,815 yards, par 71, USGA 72.1, slope 130.
    Men's: 6,418 yards, par 71, USGA 70.2, slope 121.
    Ladies': 5,741 yards, par 71, USGA 72.9, slope 127.

Fees: $131 weekdays, $158 weekends. Twilight golf (after 3 p.m.): $65 weekdays, $75 weekends.

Facilities: Pro shop, night-lighted driving range, putting green, snack bar, and bar.

QV Rating: ★★★   2

Comments   A championship course that has at one time co-hosted the Tournament of Champions, the Sahara Invitational, and the Ladies' Sahara Classic. Excellent variety of holes, with good bunkering and elevation changes uncharacteristic of a desert course. Better for intermediate and advanced golfers. No longer has any affiliation with the Sahara Hotel.

Las Vegas Paiute Resort

Established: 1995

Address: On Highway 95 between Kyle Canyon and Lee Canyon turn-off to Mount Charleston

Phone: (702) 658-1400

Status: Public

Tees:
    Snow Mountain
        Tournament: 7,158 yards, par 72, USGA 73.9, slope 125.
        Championship: 6,665 yards, par 72, USGA 71.2, slope 120.
        Men's: 6,035 yards, par 72, USGA 68.6, slope 112.
        Ladies' (red): 5,341 yards, par 72, USGA 70.4, slope 117.
    Sun Mountain
        Tournament: 7,112 yards, par 72, USGA 73.3, slope 130.
        Championship: 6,631 yards, par 72, USGA 70.9, slope 124.
        Men's: 6,074 yards, par 72, USGA 68.8, slope 116.
        Ladies': 5,465 yards, par 72, USGA 71, slope 123.

Fees: $100 weekdays and $110 weekends for 18 holes, includes cart and range balls. Spring and summer twilight hours (after 3 p.m.), $65 weekdays and $75 weekends.

Facilities: Pro shop, driving range, two putting greens, restaurant, snack bar, and bar with gaming.

QV Rating: ★★   2

Comments   The first of what is planned to be a 72-hole resort golf complex, the courses are Pete Dye designs, without the fangs. Director of Golf Johnny Pott, who enjoyed a fine career on the PGA tour, assures that all caliber golfers can enjoy the course and survive.

Legacy Golf Club

Established: 1989
Address: 130 Par Excellence Dr., Henderson NV 89014
Phone: (702) 897-2187
Status: Public course (privately owned)
Tees:

Championship: 7,233 yards, par 72, USGA 74.9, slope 136.
Men's: 6,744 yards, par 72, USGA 72.1, slope 128.
Ladies': 5,340 yards, par 72, USGA 71, slope 120.
Resort: 6,211 yards, par 72, USGA 69.1, slope 118.

Fees: All green fees include mandatory carts. $115 weekdays and $125 weekends for 18 holes, no 9-hole rate. Twilight rate (four hours before dark) is $65. Summer rates (June 15–September 19): $55 weekdays and $65 weekends for 18 holes; twilight rate is $35. Club rentals, $25.

Facilities: Clubhouse, pro shop, driving range, chipping facility, putting green, restaurant, snack bar, and bar.

QV Rating: ★★★   2

Comments   Legacy is a mixture of rolling fairways and target golf. Championship tees require long carry on tee-ball to clear desert mounding. Located at the southeastern tip of Las Vegas, Legacy has quickly become a favorite of intermediate and advanced golfers. Course plays host to a number of mini-tour professional events.

Los Prados Country Club

Established: 1985
Address: 5150 Los Prados Circle, Las Vegas NV 89130
Phone: (702) 645-5696
Status: Semi-private

Tees:

Championship: 5,358 yards, par 70, USGA 65, slope 107.
Men's: 4,937 yards, par 70, USGA 62.2, slope 101.
Ladies': 4,474 yards, par 70, USGA 64.4, slope 104.

Fees:

Nonhomeowners: $40 for 18 holes, $45 for weekends and holidays. Twilight golf (time varies) is $30 for 18 holes. Club rentals, $20.

Homeowners: weekdays, 9 holes for $11; weekends and holidays, $12 (includes cart). Walking 18 holes is $15, 9 holes $8. Weekends and holidays, walking 18 holes is $25, 9 holes $13. Club rentals, $20.

Nonhomeowners Associate Memberships and Homeowners Annual Memberships available through pro shop.

Facilities: Pro shop, putting green, restaurant, snack bar, and bar.

QV Rating: ★ 2

Comments Los Prados is a good course for beginners, intermediates, and families. Executive-length, with many short par-fours. Like most real estate developments in which golf is secondary to property values, the emphasis of the builders was on homesites rather than the design of the course. Not very accessible from the Strip, nearly a 25-minute drive.

Painted Desert

Established: 1987

Address: 5555 Painted Mirage Way, Las Vegas NV 89129

Phone: (702) 645-2568 (tee-time service); (702) 645-2880 (pro shop)

Status: Public course (privately owned)

Tees:

Championship: 6,840 yards, par 72, USGA 73.2, slope 136.
Men's: 6,323 yards, par 72, USGA 71, slope 128.
Ladies': 5,711 yards, par 72, USGA 72.7, slope 120.

Fees: Monday–Thursday, $95; twilight rate, $48. Friday–Sunday, $100; twilight rate, $53. Earlybird Back 9 Special (6:30–7:30 a.m.), $30. Regular club rentals, $25; deluxe clubs, $40.

Facilities: Pro shop, driving range, putting green, snack bar, and bar.

QV Rating: ★★ 2

Comments Target course designed by renowned architect Jay Morrish, Tom Weiskopf's partner. Lush fairway landing pads and well-manicured greens, but make certain you're on target. The rough is pure waste-area. Course gets heavy traffic, primarily from intermediate and advanced golfers. A sprinkling of beginners can really slow things down on this course.

Palm Valley Golf Club (formerly Sun City Summerlin)

Established: 1989

Address: 9201-B Del Webb Blvd., Las Vegas NV 89128

Phone: (702) 363-4373

Status: Semi-private

Tees:
> Championship: 6,849 yards, par 72, USGA 72.3, slope 127.
> Men's: 6,341 yards, par 72, USGA 69.8, slope 124.
> Ladies': 5,502 yards, par 72, USGA 71.5, slope 124.

Fees: Nonresidents of Sun City: $95 for 18 holes, $59 for 9. Sun City residents: $35 for 18 holes, $20 for 9. Carts included. Club rentals, $20. June through September, twilight fees are $50 before noon, $35 after noon.

Facilities: Pro shop, driving range, two putting greens, luncheon area, and bar. Additional facilities for members.

QV Rating: ★★ 2

Comments A demanding layout, situated in a retirement community. Rolling, wide-open terrain, heavy bunkering, and bent-grass greens. More than half of the 3,100 homes in this community have been bought, and the course will close to public play when membership fills.

Sheraton Desert Inn Country Club

Established: 1952

Address: 3145 Las Vegas Blvd., S., Las Vegas NV 89109

Phone: (702) 733-4290

Status: Resort course

Tees:
> Championship: 7,066 yards, par 72, USGA 73.9, slope 124.
> Men's: 6,685 yards, par 72, USGA 72.1, slope 121.
> Ladies': 5,791 yards, par 72, USGA 72.7, slope 121.
> Seniors': 6,270 yards, par 72, USGA 69.8, slope 118.

Fees: Nonguest: $195 for 18 holes. Guest: $120 Monday–Friday (includes cart), $145 Friday–Sunday and holidays. Club rentals, $40; shoe rentals, $6.

Facilities: Pro shop, driving range, putting green, snack bar on course, roving beverage carts, tennis courts, and world-class spa.

QV Rating: ★★★ 3

Comments   The most famous golf course in Las Vegas came under new ownership in 1993 when ITT–Sheraton purchased the hotel and golf course. The course reopened as the Sheraton Desert Inn Country Club in November 1994, and incorporated some design changes, including a switch from Bermuda to bent-grass greens.

Southshore Golf Club at Lake Las Vegas

Established: 1995

Address: 29 Grand Mediterra, Henderson NV 89011

Phone: (702) 558-0022

Status: Private

Tees:
   Tournament: 6,917 yards, par 71, USGA 72.8, slope 133.
   Championship: 6,524 yards, par 71, USGA 70.7, slope 130.
   Men's: 6,204 yards, par 71, USGA 69.2, slope 123.
   Seniors': 5,615 yards, par 71, USGA 66.7, slope 108.
   Ladies': 4,830 yards, par 71, USGA 66.5, slope 110.

Fees: Strictly private course for members and their guests only.

Facilities: Temporary clubhouse, pro shop, restaurant, bar, driving range, and putting green.

QV Rating: ★★★   N/A

Comments   Eventually, Lake Las Vegas will be a $3.8 billion residential community surrounding a private, 320-acre lake. The $19 million golf course was designed by Jack Nicklaus, and the hilly terrain includes a combination of manicured turf, Bermuda grass, bent-grass greens, and desert flowers, plants, and trees.

Spanish Trail Country Club

Established: 1984

Address: 5050 Spanish Trail Lane, Las Vegas NV 89113

Phone: (702) 364-0357

Status: Private

Tees: Based on longest 18-hole combination of 27-hole complex.
   Championship: 7,107 yards, par 72, USGA 73.8, slope 131.
   Men's: 6,516 yards, par 72, USGA 70.9, slope 126.
   Ladies': 5,727 yards, par 72, USGA 73.6, slope 128.

Fees: Not listed. Strictly private course for members and their guests only.

Facilities: Pro shop, driving range, putting green, restaurant, snack bar, and bar.

QV Rating: ★★★ N/A

Comments For six years Spanish Trail was a host of the Las Vegas Invitational PGA tournament. With undulating fairways, heavy bunkering, a number of water hazards, and fast, bent-grass greens, this course can play havoc with less-than-accomplished golfers. A 27-hole complex designed by Robert Trent Jones.

Sunrise Golf Club

Established: 1990

Address: 5000 E. Flamingo Rd., Las Vegas NV 89122

Phone: (702) 456-3160

Status: Private course

Tees:
  South Course
    Championship: 6,986 yards, par 72, USGA 71.7, slope 119.
    Men's: 6,493 yards, par 72, USGA 70, slope 115.
    Ladies': 5,523 yards, par 72, USGA 71.3, slope 121.
  North Course
    Championship: 7,005 yards, par 72, USGA 70.7, slope 113.
    Men's: 6,403 yards, par 72, USGA 67.3, slope 106.
    Ladies': 5,412 yards, par 72, USGA 68.8, slope 115.
  West Course
    Championship: 7,212 yards, par 72, USGA 73.6, slope 127.
    Men's: 6,519 yards, par 72, USGA 70.2, slope 121.
    Ladies': 5,465 yards, par 72, USGA 70.3, slope 118.

Fees: Not listed. Strictly private course for members and their guests.

Facilities: Pro shop, driving range, putting green, restaurant, snack bar, and bar.

QV Rating: ★★ N/A

Comments In just its second year of operation, Sunrise was a host course of the Las Vegas Invitational PGA tournament, and Chip Beck humbled it with a 59. It was only the second time in history a player had broken 60. With 54 holes and the city's largest driving range, Sunrise has become Las Vegas's most accommodating and affordable private club.

Wildhorse Golf Club

Established: 1961

Address: 2100 W. Warm Springs Rd., Henderson NV 89014

Phone: (702) 434-9000 or (702) 769-0013 (tee-time service)

Status: Resort course, open to the public

Tees:

    Championship: 7,041 yards, par 72, USGA 75.2, slope 135.

    Men's: 6,455 yards, par 72, USGA 72.2, slope 137.

    Ladies': 5,911 yards, par 72, USGA 69.7, slope 130.

Fees: Rates fluctuate and depend on time of day and day of week. Call for more specific fees. All green fees include mandatory carts. Discount cardholders: $45 for 18 holes, 7 days a week. Club rentals, $20; $40 for premium sets. Discount cards available to Clark County residents for $300.

Facilities: Pro shop, driving range, putting green, chipping green, practice traps, restaurant, snack bar, banquet facilities, and bar.

QV Rating: ★★★ 2

Comments This course has had more former names than Constantinople. The course and surrounding land were auctioned by the federal government for $16 million to the American Golf Company on April 28, 1994.

Outdoor Recreation

▪ Bicycling ▪

Ask any biker in Las Vegas about the on- and off-road riding nearby and you'll probably hear two kinds of comments. First, why pedaling in the desert is such a treat: excellent surface conditions; the option of pancake-flat or hilly riding; beautiful stark scenery any time of year, and cactus blossoms in March and April; the possibility of spying raptors or jack rabbits or wild burros as you pedal; the unbelievably colorful limestone and sandstone formations . . .

Unfortunately, newcomers to desert and high-elevation biking often recall only these comments and not the "Be sure to carry—" warnings, which fellow riders usually provide after they've gotten you all revved-up. So read the following and remember that bikers are subject to those very same conditions—heat and aridity—that make the desert so starkly beautiful.

Biking Essentials

1. Time of Day   Desert biking in late spring, summer, and early fall is best done early or late in the day. Know your seasons, listen to weather reports, and don't overestimate your speed and ability.

2. Clothing   Ever see someone perched on a camel? What was he wearing? Right, it wasn't a tank top and Lycra shorts. The point is protection—from the sun during the day, from the cold in the morning and evening. And if you don't use a helmet, wear a hat.

3. Sunscreen   In the desert, even well-tanned riders need this stuff.

4. Sunglasses   The glare will blind you without them.

5. Water   The first time we rode in the desert, we carried as much water as we would have used on a ride of comparable distance in the eastern United States. Big mistake. Our need for water was at least twice what it normally would be in New York or Alabama. We were thirsty the entire trip and might have gotten into serious trouble had we not cut our ride short.

You already know that you will need extra water, but how much? Well, a human working hard in 90° temperature requires ten quarts of fluid replenishment every day. Ten *quarts*. That's two and a half gallons—12 large water bottles, or 16 small ones. And with water weighing in at 8 pounds per gallon, a one-day supply comes to a whopping 20 pounds.

In other words, pack along two or three bottles even for the shortest rides. For longer rides, and particularly off-road, know ahead of time whether water is available along the way. If it is, unless it comes out of a tap, purify it. You can boil water for ten minutes and filter out the crud with a lightweight purifier (right!), or simply drop in a couple of effective, inexpensive tetraglycine hydroperiodide tablets. They're sold under the names of Potable Aqua, Globaline, Coughlan's, etc., and ought to be available at bike shops, but aren't. Check out a sporting goods store that specializes in backpacking equipment.

In the desert, the heat is dry and you do not notice much perspiration because your sweat evaporates as quickly as it surfaces. Combine the dry heat with a little wind and you can become extremely dehydrated before realizing it. Folks (like us) from the East tend to regard sweating as a barometer of our level of exertion (if you are not sweating much, in other words, you must not be exercising very hard). In the desert it doesn't work that way. You may never notice that you are sweating. In the desert you need to stay ahead of dehydration by drinking more frequently and more regularly and by consuming much more than the same amount of exercise would warrant in other climates. Desert days literally suck the water right out of you, even during the cooler times of the year.

6. Tools　Each rider has a personal "absolute minimum list," which usually includes most of the following:

tire levers	chain rivet tool
spare tube patch kit	spare chain link
air pump	spoke wrench
allen wrenches (3, 4, 5, and 6mm)	6-inch crescent (adjustable-end) wrench
small flat-blade screwdriver	

7. First Aid Kit　This too is a personal matter, usually including those items a rider has needed due to past mishaps. So, with the desert in mind, add a pair of tweezers (for close encounters of the cactus kind) and a snakebite kit. Most Las Vegas bikers have only seen snakes at the zoo or squashed on the highway, but you'll feel better if you pack one (the kit, that is) along.

Road Biking

Road biking on the Strip, downtown, or in any of Las Vegas's high-traffic areas is suicidal. Each year an astoundingly high number of bikers are injured or killed playing Russian roulette with Las Vegas motorists. If you want to bike, either confine yourself to sleepy subdivisions or get way out of town on a road with wide shoulders and little traffic.

There are a number of superb rides within a 30- to 40-minute drive from downtown or the Strip. The best is the Red Rock Canyon Scenic Loop ride, due west of town, which carves a 15.4-mile circuit through the canyon's massive, rust-colored, sandstone cliffs. The route is arduous, with a 1,000-foot elevation gain in the first six miles, followed by eight miles of downhill and flats with one more steep hill. One-way traffic on the scenic loop applies to cyclists and motorists alike. Although there is a fair amount of traffic on weekends, the road is wide and the speed limit is a conservative 35 miles per hour. If you park your car at the Red Rock Canyon Visitor Center, take careful note of when the area closes. If you are delayed on your ride and get back late, your car might be trapped behind locked gates.

A second ride in the same area follows State Route 159 from the town of Blue Diamond to the entrance of Red Rock Canyon Scenic Loop Drive and back again, approximately eight miles. From Blue Diamond the highway traverses undulating hills, with a net elevation gain of 193 feet on the outbound leg. In general, the ride offers gentle, long grades alternating with relatively flat stretches. Cliff walls and desert flora provide stunning vistas throughout. Traffic on NV 159 is a little heavy on weekends, but the road is plenty wide, with a good surface and wide shoulders. In the village of Blue Diamond there is a small store.

Another good out-and-back begins at Overton Beach on Lake Mead, northeast of Las Vegas, and ascends 867 feet in eight miles to the visitor center at the Valley of Fire State Park. (You can, of course, begin your round trip at the visitor center, but we always prefer to tackle the uphill leg first.) Geology in the park is spectacular, with the same red sandstone found in the cliffs and formations of the Grand Canyon. There are no shoulders, but traffic is light and the road surface is good. Since the route runs pretty much east-west, we like to schedule our ride in the afternoon so that we will have the setting sun at our back as we coast down to the lake on the return leg. Another good option is an early-morning ride with the sun at your back as you ascend and high in the sky as you return.

Dressing for a bike ride in the canyons and high country around Las Vegas is a challenge. In early December, when we rode the Red Rock loop, it was about 62° in town and about 10° cooler in the canyon. We started out in Lycra bike shorts and polypro long-sleeve windbreakers. By the time we completed the six-mile uphill, we were about to die of heat prostration. On the long, fast downhill, we froze.

Our recommendation is to layer on cooler days so that you can add or shuck clothing as conditions warrant. On warm days try to bike early in the morning or late in the afternoon and wear light clothing. Always wear a helmet and always, always carry lots of water. If you are not used to biking in arid climates, take twice as much water as you would carry at home, and drink *before* you get thirsty.

There is no place on any of these routes to get **help with a broken bike.** You should bring an extra tube and a pump and know how to fix flats and make other necessary adjustments and repairs. Water is available at Blue Diamond and at the Red Rock and Valley of Fire visitor centers, but no place else. Always replenish when you have the opportunity.

Mountain Biking

Most off-road biking in the Las Vegas area is done on jeep trails and dirt roads. In the Red Rock Canyon National Conservation Area, the Lake Mead National Recreation Area, the national forests, and the state parks, mountain bikes are not permitted (with one exception) on hiking trails. Fortunately, there are plenty of jeep trails and dirt roads.

There are several good rides in the Mount Potasi (POT-a-see) area southwest of Las Vegas, including a loop trail developed for mountain-bike racing, and a ride over the Potasi Pass to Potasi Spring and the Potasi mine. These are fairly challenging rides over dirt roads with some long pulls. In the same area is a ride from NV 160 to the old mining town of Goodsprings. This is one of the few rides in the Las Vegas area that covers mostly level terrain. Heat, wind, and dust can be a problem on all of these rides.

In Lee Canyon of the Toiyabe National Forest, bikes are allowed on the Bristlecone Pine Trail, a five-mile mountaintop loop through a ponderosa pine and white fir forest with a 700-foot rise and fall in elevation. Tough ride, but the air is cool and the scenery is great, with spectacular views down the canyon.

In addition to the foregoing, many mountain bikers ride the scenic loop (described under Road Biking) at Red Rock Canyon National Conservation Area. See the map on page 302.

Mountain bikes can be rented from Escape the City Streets! at 8221 W. Charleston on the way to Red Rock Canyon, (702) 596-BYKE. Rental fees include helmet, gloves, and water bottles. Escape the City Streets! is a good source of information on rides and provides guided tours and shuttles.

■ Hiking and Backpacking ■

Hiking or backpacking in the desert can be a very enjoyable experience. It can also be a hazardous adventure if you travel unprepared. Lake Mead ranger Debbie Savage suggests the following:

The best months for hiking are the cooler months of November through March. Hiking is not recommended in the summer when temperatures reach 120° in the shade. Never hike alone and always tell someone where you are going and when you plan to return. Carry plenty of water (at least a half gallon per person) and drink often.

Know your limits. Hiking the canyons and washes in the desert often means traveling over rough, steep terrain with frequent elevation changes. Try to pick a route that best suits your abilities. Distances in the desert are often deceiving. Be sure to check the weather forecast before departure. Sudden storms can cause flash flooding. Seek higher ground if thunderstorms threaten.

Essential equipment includes sturdy walking shoes and proper clothing. Long pants are suggested for protection from rocks and cactus. A hat, sunscreen, and sunglasses are also recommended. Carry a small daypack to hold such items as a first aid kit, lunch, water, a light jacket, and a flashlight.

Canyons and washes often contain an impressive diversity of plant life, most easily observed during the spring wildflower season. Desert springs are located in some of the canyons and support a unique community of plants and animals. They are often the only source of water for many miles around. Take care not to contaminate them with trash or other human wastes. Along similar lines, understand that desert soils are often very fragile and take a long time to recover if disturbed. These surfaces are recognizable by their comparatively darker appearance and should be avoided whenever possible.

Poisonous animals such as snakes, spiders, and scorpions are most active after dark and are not often seen during daylight hours by hikers. Speckled rattlesnakes are common but are not aggressive. Scorpion stings are no more harmful than a bee sting unless you are allergic. Black widow spiders are shy and secretive and are most often found around man-made structures. Watch where you place your hands and feet and don't disturb obvious hiding places.

The Las Vegas area offers quite a diversity of hiking options. Trips that include a choice of canyons, lakes, desert, mountains, or ponderosa pine forest can be found within an hour's drive of Las Vegas.

The Lake Mead National Recreation Area, an hour southeast of Las Vegas, offers a wide variety of hiking experiences, although there are few designated trails. Included within the NRA are Lakes Mead and Mohave, and part of the Mojave Desert. Ranger-guided hikes are offered during the winter months. The outings cover six to eight miles and are moderate to strenuous in difficulty. If you prefer to explore on your own, detailed maps and instructions to the most popular areas are available at the visitor centers. For information call (702) 293-8907.

The Red Rock Canyon National Conservation Area contains some of the most rugged rock formations in the West. Only 40 minutes from Las Vegas, Red Rock Canyon offers loop as well as out-and-back trails of varying lengths. (See map on page 302.) The short Moenkopi Loop originates at the visitor center, and it takes a little more than an hour to walk over undulating terrain in a broad desert valley. Other popular short hikes include out-and-backs to Lost Creek (three-tenths of a mile one-way), Icebox Canyon (one and three-tenths miles one-way), and Pine Creek Canyon (one mile one-way), leading to the ruins of a historic homestead near a running creek surrounded by large ponderosa pine trees. All the out-and-backs take you up canyons, so be prepared for some elevation gain. For additional information call (702) 363-1921.

The Toiyabe National Forest, high in the mountains 40 minutes northwest of Las Vegas, provides a totally different outdoor experience. The air is cool, and the trails run among stately forests of ponderosa pine, quaking aspen, white fir, and mountain mahogany. Hikes range in distance from one-tenth of a mile to 21 miles, and in difficulty from easy to very difficult. Most popular are the Cathedral Rock Trail (two miles round-trip), which climbs 900 feet to a stark summit overlooking Kyle Canyon, and Bristlecone, a five-mile loop that traverses the ridges above the Lee Canyon Ski Area. Longer, more difficult, but extremely scenic hikes include the 9-mile South Loop and the 11-mile North Loop. Though the distances of these loops are not great, the terrain is exceedingly rugged, and the hikes are not recommended for one-day outings unless you begin very early in the morning and are used to strenuous exercise at high elevations. For additional information call (702) 873-8800.

The Valley of Fire State Park, 45 minutes northeast of Las Vegas, rounds out the hiking picture. This park features rock formations similar to those found in the Grand Canyon, as well as a number of Indian petroglyphs. The *Las Vegas Advisor* compares hiking the Valley of Fire with being "beamed" onto another planet. Trails traverse desert terrain and vary from seven miles to a half mile in length. Visitors should check in at the visitor center before they begin hiking. For more information call (702) 397-2088.

■ Rock Climbing and Bouldering ■

The Red Rock Canyon National Conservation Area is one of the top rock-climbing resources in the United States. With over a thousand routes, abundant holds, and approaches ranging from roadside to remote wilderness, the area rivals Yosemite in scope and variety for climbers. Offering amazing diversity for every skill level amidst desert canyon scenery second to none, the area is less than a 40-minute drive from Las Vegas.

Though there is some granite and limestone, almost all of the climbing is done on sandstone. Overall, the rock is pretty solid, although there are some places where the sandstone gets a little crumbly, especially after a rain. Bolting is allowed but discouraged (local climbers have been systematically replacing bolts on some of the older routes with more modern bolts that blend with the rock). There are some great spots for bouldering, some of the best top-roping in the United States, a lifetime supply of big walls, and even some bivouac routes. Climbs range in difficulty from nonbelayed scrambles to 5.13 big-wall overhangs. You can climb year-round at Red Rock. Wind can be a problem, as can most of the other conditions that make a desert environment challenging. Having enough water can be a logistical nightmare on a long climb.

Red Rock Guide by Joanne Urioste describes a number of the older routes. Newer route descriptions can be obtained from Desert Rock Sports in Las Vegas, (702) 254-1143. Desert Rock Sports can also help you find camping and showers and tell you where the loose rock is. Offering climbing shoe rentals, the store is located at 8201 West Charleston, conveniently on the way to the canyon from Las Vegas. The Powerhouse Rock Gym is located next to Desert Rock Sports and offers excellent indoor climbing and showers. Guides and/or instruction are available from Desert Rock Sports or from Sky's the Limit Climbing School and Guide Service, (702) 363-4533 or (800) 733-7597. Sky's the Limit also teaches courses in winter mountaineering, avalanche awareness, and cross-country skiing. Most Sky's the Limit guides are UIAGM/IVBV/AMGA accredited and certified.

■ River Running ■

The Black Canyon of the Colorado River can be run year-round below Hoover Dam. The most popular trip is from the tailwaters of the dam to

Willow Beach. In this 11-mile section, canyon walls rise almost vertically from the water's edge, with scenery and wildlife very similar to that of the Colorado River in the Grand Canyon above Lake Mead. There are numerous warm springs and waterfalls on feeder streams, presenting the opportunity for good side-trip hikes. Bighorn sheep roam the bluffs, and wild burros can often be seen up the canyons. The water in the river, about 53° year-round, is drawn from the bottom of Lake Mead and released downstream through the Hoover Dam hydroelectric generators.

For the most part, the Black Canyon is a scenic flatwater float. There are some easy-to-avoid rocks below Boy Scout Canyon and Ring-bolt Rapids (Class II with sneak route on river left) three miles into the run. Less-experienced paddlers will probably have more difficulty with whirlpools and eddies than with rapids. Headwinds coming up the canyon pose a problem for all boaters. The Black Canyon is suitable for canoes, kayaks, and rafts. The trip takes about six hours in a canoe or kayak and about three hours in a *motorized* raft.

Private (noncommercial) parties must obtain a trip permit from:

Hoover Dam Canoe Lodge
P.O. Box 60400
Boulder City, NV 89006-0400
(702) 293-8204

Visitors can now fax the application to obtain a trip permit, and the Lodge will issue a permit two days in advance of the trip date. Only 30 private craft are allowed to launch daily, 15 at 8:30 a.m. and another 15 at 10 a.m., so apply for your trip permit early, if possible. Canoes and kayaks can be rented from Boulder City Watersport at (702) 293-7526.

A commercial outfitter, Black Canyon, Inc., (702) 293-3776, operates guided, motorized raft trips and can even arrange for guest transportation from Las Vegas.

The best seasons to run the Black Canyon are the spring and fall. There is little protection from the sun in the canyon, and temperatures can surpass 110° in the warmer months. Long-sleeve shirts, long pants, tennis shoes, and a hat are recommended minimum attire year-round. Be sure to take sunscreen and lots of drinking water.

■ **Snow Skiing** ■

The Lee Canyon Ski Area is a 45-minute drive from Las Vegas. Situated in a granite canyon in the Spring Mountain range, the resort provides three double chair lifts servicing ten runs. Though the mountain is small and the runs short by Western standards, the skiing is solid intermediate. Of the ten runs, seven are blue, two are black, and there is one short green. Base elevation of 8,510 feet notwithstanding, snow conditions are usually dependable only during January. Because of its southerly location and the proximity of the hot, arid desert, there is a lot of thawing and refreezing in Lee Canyon, and hence, frequently icy skiing conditions. If the snow is good, a day at Lee Canyon is a great outing. If the mountain is icy, do something else.

Snowmaking equipment allows the Lee Canyon Ski Area to operate from Thanksgiving to Easter. There is no lodging on-site and only a modest coffee shop and lounge. The parking lot is a fairly good hike from the base facility.

Skis can be rented at the ski area or from Las Vegas Ski and Snowboard Resort at the resort lodge. For information on lift tickets or snow conditions, call the ski area office at (702) 385-2SKI. If you do not have a car, bus service is available to the ski area. Call (702) 645-2754.

■ Horseback Riding ■

The best place for horseback riding is Kyle Canyon in the Toiyabe National Forest northwest of Las Vegas. Quarter horses with Western saddles can be rented spring through fall for one-, two-, and three-hour rides at $20, $40, and $55 respectively. All-day rides are available for $125 plus trailer fees. The scenery is spectacular, with mountain vistas, ponderosa pine forests, and 300,000 acres to explore. Guides are available. Advance payment and reservations are required. For information or reservations call Mount Charleston Riding Stables at (702) 872-5408.

■ Fishing ■

The Lake Mead National Recreation Area, twice the size of Rhode Island, offers some of the best fishing in the United States. Lake Mead is the largest lake, with Lake Mohave, downstream on the Colorado River, offering the most diverse fishery. Largemouth bass, striped bass, channel catfish, crappie, and bluegill are found in both lakes. Rainbow and cutthroat trout are present only in Lake Mohave. Remote and beautiful in its upmost reaches, with steep canyons reminiscent of the Grand Canyon, Lake Mohave is farther from Las Vegas but provides truly exceptional fishing. Bass and trout often run three pounds, and some trout weigh ten pounds or more. Willow Beach, near where the Colorado River enters the pool waters of Lake Mohave, is where many of the larger trout are taken.

Lake Mead, broader, more open, and much closer to Las Vegas, has be-

Lake Mead Bait and Tackle, Boat Rental, Fuel, and Supplies

Callville Bay Resort	(702) 565-8958
Echo Bay Resort	(702) 394-4000
Lake Mead Resort	(702) 293-3484 or (800) 752-9669 for reservations
Overton Beach Resort	(702) 394-4040
Temple Bar Resort (AZ)	(520) 767-3211

Lake Mohave Bait and Tackle, Boat Rental, Fuel, and Supplies

Cottonwood Cove Resort	(702) 297-1467
Lake Mohave Resort (AZ)	(520) 754-3245

come famous for its striper, with an occasional catch weighing in at over 40 pounds. Bass fishing is consistently good throughout Lake Mead. The Overton Arm (accessed from Echo Bay or Overton Beach) offers the best panfish and catfish action.

Because Lakes Mead and Mohave form the Arizona/Nevada state line, fishing license regulations are a little strange. If you are bank fishing, all you need is a license from the state you are in. If you fish from a boat, however, you need a fishing license from one state and a special use stamp from the other. Fortunately, all required stamps and licenses can be obtained from marinas and local bait and tackle shops in either state.

Nonresidents have the option of purchasing one- to ten-day fishing permits in lieu of a license. Permits range from about $12 for the one-day to $48 for the ten-day, and apply to the reciprocal waters of Lake Mead and Lake Mohave only. In addition to the permit, a special use stamp costing $3 is required for those fishing from a boat, and a $5 trout stamp is necessary to take trout. In addition, a $10 stamp is available for fishing with two rods. Youngsters 12 years and under in the company of a properly licensed, permitted, and stamped adult can fish without any sort of documentation. The best deal is an annual license, which costs $51 and includes the $3 stamp.

Sixteen-foot, aluminum, V-hulled fishing boats (seat five) can be rented on both lakes by the hour (about $20 with a two-hour minimum), by the half day (four hours for about $50), or by the day (about $100). Bass boats, houseboats, and pontoon craft are also available. Rods and reels rent for about $5 for four hours or less and about $12 a day.

■ Pleasure Boating, Sailing, Water Skiing, and Jet Skiing ■

Lake Mead and Lake Mohave are both excellent sites for pleasure boating, water skiing, and other activities. Both lakes are so large that it is easy to find a secluded spot for your favorite boating or swimming activity. Rock formations on the lakes are spectacular, and boaters can visit scenic canyons and coves that are inaccessible to those traveling by car. Boats, for example, can travel into the narrow, steep-walled gorge of Iceberg Canyon in Lake Mead or upstream into the Black Canyon from Lake Mohave.

First-timers, particularly on Lake Mead, frequently underestimate its vast size. It is not difficult to get lost on the open waters of Lake Mead or to get caught in bad weather. Winds can be severe on the lake, and waves of six feet sometimes arise during storms. In general, there is no shade on the lakes, and the steep rock formations along the shore do not make very hospitable emergency landing sites. When you boat on either lake, take plenty of water, be properly dressed and equipped, and be sure to tell someone where you are going and when you expect to return.

Most of the resorts listed under "Fishing" rent various types of pleasure craft and water skiing equipment, and two, the Overton Beach Resort on Lake Mead and the Callville Bay Resort, rent jet skis. In addition, at Callville Bay on Lake Mead and Cottonwood Cove on Lake Mohave, luxury houseboats are available for rental. The boats sleep up to ten adults and have fully equipped galleys and heads. For rates and other information concerning houseboats, call (800) 255-5561 or (800) 752-9669.

PART FIVE

Shopping and Seeing the Sights

Shopping in Las Vegas

The most interesting and diversified specialty shopping in Las Vegas is centered on the Strip at the Fashion Show Mall and at The Forum Shops. The Fashion Show Mall, located at the intersection of Las Vegas Boulevard and Spring Mountain Road, is anchored by Saks Fifth Avenue, May Company, Neiman Marcus, Macy's, and Dillard's, and contains 144 specialty shops, including 4 art galleries. The Forum Shops is an upscale shopping complex situated between Caesars Palace and the Mirage. Connected to the Olympic Casino in Caesars Palace, The Forum Shops offers a Roman market–themed shopping environment. Both shopping complexes have their own parking facilities and are within a half-mile walking distance of one another.

In fairness, it should be noted that The Forum Shops is not your average shopping center. The Roman market, an attraction in its own right, has been executed on a scale that is extraordinary even for Caesars. It is totally indoors, but clouds, sky, and celestial bodies are projected on the vaulted ceilings to simulate the actual time of day outside. Statuary in The Forum is magnificent; some is even animatronic. Regardless of your shopping inclinations (or lack thereof), a visit to The Forum Shops should be on your Las Vegas touring agenda. If you go, be forewarned that is much easier (via the moving walkway) to get into the arcade than it is to get out (a long hike through Caesars's casino and then 300 yards back to the street). Though it is not obvious and was not meant for pedestrian traffic, the easiest way out is to exit on foot through The Forum Shops' valet parking entrance.

You've probably heard of doubling down in blackjack. Well, now doubling has caught on with shopping centers. The Forum Shops doubled in size in 1997. New retailers include Fendi, FAO Schwarz, and Polo, among others. An Atlantis feature along with a giant aquarium provide some neat stuff to see for those who left all of their money in the casino. Not to be outdone, the Fashion Show Mall is also doubling in size. The project, scheduled to be completed in 2000, will make Fashion Show the largest mall in Nevada. Bloomingdales and Lord & Taylor will anchor the new development.

A third Strip shopping venue is the Showcase, adjacent to the MGM Grand. Although most of the 190,000-square-foot shopping and entertainment complex is devoted to theme restaurants, a Sega electronic games arcade, a Coca-Cola museum, and an eight-plex movie theater, there remains space for a number of retail specialty shops.

There are two large neighborhood malls in Las Vegas, the Boulevard Mall and the Meadows. The Boulevard Mall, with 122 stores anchored by Sears, Penney's, Marshalls, Dillard's, and Macy's, is located on Maryland Avenue, between Desert Inn Road and Flamingo Road. The Meadows, featuring the same department stores (except for Marshalls), offers 73 stores spread over two levels. The Meadows is situated between West Charleston Boulevard and the Las Vegas Expressway (US 95) on Valley View.

A large discount shopping venue has materialized about five miles south of Tropicana Avenue on Las Vegas Boulevard near the Blue Diamond Road exit off I-15. A mile or so south of Blue Diamond Road on Las Vegas Boulevard are the Las Vegas Factory Stores, with a total of 108 shops. Just north of Blue Diamond Road is a Belz Factory Outlet mall with 109 stores. Belz, like The Forum Shops, doubled its size in 1997. Promotional literature listing the individual shops at the three locations is available in almost all hotel brochure racks. The easiest way to reach the outlets is to drive south on I-15 to Exit 33, Blue Diamond Road. Proceed east on Blue Diamond to the intersection with Las Vegas Boulevard. Turn left on Las Vegas Boulevard to the Belz mall, or right to the Las Vegas Factory Stores. For those without transportation, Las Vegas Transit (LVT) operates a bus route that connects the various Strip and suburban shopping centers. Fare is $1.15 one-way. Service is provided daily (except Sunday) from 10:30 a.m. to 6:30 p.m. For more information on LVT, call (702) 384-3540.

Unique Shopping Opportunities

Wine & Liquor   Our favorite store for liquor and a decent bottle of wine is Town Pump Liquors, with five locations. In addition to a good selection of all spirits at competitive prices, Town Pump almost always offers a loss-leader bargain on good French, Italian, or California wines. The East Sahara Avenue store, in the Commercial Center, is the closest to the Strip. Though the address is listed as East Sahara, the easiest way to get there is via Karen Avenue.

Town Pump Liquors

953 E. Sahara Avenue	735-8515
3242 E. Desert Inn Road	737-7273
6040 W. Sahara Avenue	876-6615
1725 E. Warm Springs Road	897-9463
4410 W. Craig Road	645-9700

Art   Las Vegas is a great place to shop for contemporary and nontraditional art and sculpture, with galleries in both the Fashion Show Mall and The Forum Shops. Do not, however, expect any bargains.

Gambling Stuff   As you would expect, Las Vegas is a shopping mecca when it comes to anything having to do with gambling. If you are in the market for a roulette wheel, a blackjack table, or some personalized chips, try the Gamblers General Store at 800 South Main, (702) 382-9903, or (800) 322-CHIP outside Nevada. Another option is Paulson Dice and Card, 2121 Industrial Road, (702) 384-2425. For books and periodicals on gambling, we recommend the Gamblers Book Club store located near the intersection of South 11th Street and East Charleston, (702) 382-7555.

If you have always wanted a slot machine for your living room, you can buy one at Vintage Slot Machines, 3379 Industrial Road, (702) 369-2323. Possession of a slot machine (including video poker and blackjack) for personal use is legal in the following states:

Alaska	Minnesota	Texas
Arizona	Nevada	Utah
Arkansas	New Mexico	Virginia
Kentucky	Ohio	West Virginia
Maine	Rhode Island	

Another group of states will allow you to own a slot machine providing the machine is fairly old (how old depends on the state). In New Jersey, Pennsylvania, New York, and South Dakota, the machine must have been manufactured before 1941. In the following states and the District of Columbia, the required age falls somewhere between 20 and 42 years:

California	Kansas	New Hampshire	South Carolina
Colorado	Louisiana	New Jersey	South Dakota
Delaware	Maryland	New York	Vermont
Florida	Massachusetts	North Carolina	Washington
Georgia	Michigan	North Dakota	Washington, D.C.
Idaho	Mississippi	Oklahoma	Wisconsin
Illinois	Missouri	Oregon	Wyoming
Iowa	Montana	Pennsylvania	

In all other states the possession of any type of slot machine is illegal.

Head Rugs   The next time you go to a Las Vegas production show, pay attention to the showgirls' hair. You will notice that the same woman will have a different hairdo for every number. Having made this observation, you will not be surprised that the largest wig and hairpiece retailer in the United States is located in Las Vegas. At 953 E. Sahara Avenue about 5 minutes away from the Strip, Serge's Showgirl Wigs inventories over 7,000 hairpieces and wigs, made from both synthetic materials and human hair. In addition to serving the local showgirl population, Showgirl Wigs also specializes in assisting chemotherapy patients. A catalog and additional information can be obtained by calling (702) 732-1015.

Baseball Cards   Finally, in the "everyone has to be someplace" category, is Smokey's Sports Cards, possibly the largest buyer, seller, and auctioneer of sports trading cards in the United States. Open seven days a week, Smokey's is located at 3734 Las Vegas Boulevard, South (the Strip), (702) 739-0003. In addition to baseball cards, Smokey's also deals in football, basketball, and hockey cards.

Seeing the Sights

Residents of Las Vegas are justifiably proud of their city and are quick to point out that Las Vegas has much to offer besides gambling. Quality theater, college and professional sports, dance, concerts, art shows, museums, and film festivals contribute to making Las Vegas a truly great place to live. In addition, there is a diverse and colorful natural and historical heritage. What Las Vegas residents sometimes have a difficult time understanding, however, is that the average business and leisure traveler doesn't really give a big hoot. Until 1993 Las Vegas differed from Orlando and Southern California in that it did not have any bona fide tourist attractions except Hoover Dam. Nobody drove all the way to Las Vegas to take their children to visit the Guinness Book of Records exhibit. While there have always been some great places to detox from a long trade show or too many hours at the casino, they are totally peripheral in the minds of visitors. Las Vegas needed a legitimate, nongaming tourist draw, but the strange aggregation of little museums and factory tours was not it.

In 1993 the opening of the MGM Grand Hotel and Casino and Grand Adventures Theme Park brought Las Vegas a little closer to penetrating the consciousness of the nongambling traveler. During the same time period, Circus Circus opened a smaller theme park, Grand Slam Canyon, behind its main casino. For the most part, the new theme parks made little immediate impression on either the locals or the tourists. On the bright side, the battle toward entertainment diversification was finally joined.

The MGM Grand Adventures Theme Park

The MGM Grand Adventures Theme Park is the fourth amusement park in the United States to feature a movie theme. Unlike its predecessors (Universal Studios Hollywood, Universal Studios Florida, and the Disney-MGM Studios at Walt Disney World), however, the MGM Grand development does not include working motion picture and television production studios. For the record, the MGM Grand Adventures Theme Park is not related in any way to the Disney-MGM Studios theme park in Florida.

Though we, and just about everybody else, looked forward to the opening of the MGM Grand Adventures Theme Park with high hopes and great expectations, in the end we were sorely disappointed. As some wag once put it, "The mountain strained and groaned and issued forth a gnat." I can't remember who said this, but the MGM Grand people certainly put it into practice.

A couple of years ago, I was asked to be a consultant to a theme park being designed by a leading European architect. To my amazement, when I met with the architect and his staff, I learned that *none* of them had ever been to a theme park. Whether the MGM Grand Adventures Theme Park was planned by committee or entrusted to a single guiding hand, I don't know. What I do know is that whoever was responsible didn't have a clue about theme parks or the league they were trying to break into.

Think about it. Las Vegas's primary market is Southern California. To appeal to Southern Californians, a Las Vegas theme park must compete with Disneyland, Universal Studios Hollywood, Knott's Berry Farm, and Magic Mountain. The MGM Grand Adventures Theme Park doesn't even come close. In our 1994 edition we praised the MGM park's design and use of space. And, truth to tell, it did look good on paper, but a great deal was lost in the execution.

Disney sets the standard for theme parks in this country. Serious players in the theme-park big leagues understand this and manage to approximate, if not equal, the Disney standard. Included in this select group are all the Disney parks, Opryland, Universal Studios (Hollywood and Florida), and all of the Anheuser-Busch parks, including the Sea World parks. All of these parks are committed to quality and deliver a product that the entire family, regardless of age, can enjoy together. A rung down the ladder are a number of parks that feature midway thrill rides and roller coasters and target the young adult and youth market. These parks, which include the Paramount parks and the Six Flags parks, operate on a lower standard in terms of theme integrity, landscaping, attention to detail, and scale of attractions. They pursue a more local market and avoid attractions and developments that bring them into direct competition with the majors.

The MGM folks made two huge mistakes. First, they built a theme park that fell laughably short of the Disney standard, and then they promoted and hyped it as though it was the most wonderful theme park ever created. The deluge of media promotion led almost everyone to expect something way beyond MGM's ability to deliver. To express that differently, it was a first-class promotional campaign for a fifth-rate theme park.

Small by modern theme-park standards at 33 total acres (about one-third the size of the Magic Kingdom at Walt Disney World), the MGM Grand Adventures Theme Park features 9 separate themed areas containing 12 rides and 4 shows, as well as restaurants and shops. The theme areas are so small that the respective themes have little impact, and there is no sense of being in a self-contained or exotic environment. Along similar lines, there are a lot of mixed messages: inexplicably, we find the London Bridge at the Salem Waterfront, a Dutch windmill on the outskirts of Tumble-weed Gulch, and the Grand Canyon Rapids (instead of the Mississippi River) in New Orleans. And we wonder why American kids don't know squat about geography.

Lapses in providing themes could be forgiven if the attractions were top quality. Unfortunately, however, they are (or were) not. Four of the park's original eight rides were scrapped after only three years of operation. Included in this all-too-forgettable lineup were such wonders as the original Lightning Bolt roller coaster (a pitiful imitation of Disney's Space Mountain), the vacuous Haunted Mine, Deep Earth Exploration, and the Backlot River Tour (where you were supposed to be on a wild jungle stream and could wave to apartment residents on Koval Lane watching you from their windows). In addition to the rides, three of the four original theater presentations have been chucked as well.

In 1997, the original Lightning Bolt was replaced with a new, outdoor roller coaster, identified on the official handout park map as the "Exciting New Roller Coaster," and seven additional new rides were added. Pedalin' Paddleboats provide the opportunity to churn around a diminutive pond in pedal-powered boats like you might rent at a state park. The Zipper and Chaos are midway thrill rides that basically turn you upside down and spin you in circles. Three children's rides included the Grand Carrousel, a merry-go-round; Bumper Boats, a wet version of bumper cars; and the Red Baron, consisting of little airplanes circling a hub. Finally, to ensure the uniqueness of the MGM Grand Adventures theme park, a ferris wheel was tossed in.

Retained from the original lineup are the Grand Canyon Rapids (whitewater rafting), Parisian Taxis (bumper cars), and Over the edge (a flume ride). Over the Edge is described by MGM as "a journey through a nostalgic old saw mill with its quaint scenery and rustic charm." The quaint scenery consists of parking lots and the traffic on Harmon Avenue.

The only major attractions that live up to their press releases are the Grand Canyon Rapids and the SkyScreamer. The rapids ride is wet and zippy and, for the most part, maintains its theme's integrity. At least you are not staring over the park fence at parking lots, apartment buildings, or traffic. With the SkyScreamer, scenery is academic, because no one opens his or her eyes. Here, you are trussed into a harness, hoisted to the top of a 250-foot tower, and dropped. After 100 feet of free fall, you swing pendulum fashion to break the fall. Though the SkyScreamer is a truly thrilling experience (remember to put on your rubber underwear), it is not included in the price of admission to the park.

In addition to rides, there are four theater productions. The best of the lot is *Dueling Pirates,* a movie stunt show that plods along in fits and starts

MGM Grand Adventures Theme Park Ratings	
SkyScreamer	★★★★
Grand Canyon Rapids	★★★½
Chaos	★★★
Zipper	★★
Century Wheel	★★
Grand Carrousel	★★
Parisian Taxis	★★
Exciting New Roller Coaster	★★
Over the Edge	★★
Red Baron	★★
Les Bumper Boats	★★
Dueling Pirates	★★
Pedalin' Paddleboats	★½

with little realism, continuity, or even humor. Productions at the other theater venues vary, but almost always include some oldies music as in *Elvis, Shake It Up!* and *The Fab Four—A Live Tribute* to the Beatles. Magic, illusion, and acrobatics have also figured prominently in the park's theater presentations.

Getting There Located directly behind the MGM Grand Hotel at the intersection of the Strip and Tropicana Avenue, the theme park is accessed by passing through the MGM Grand Hotel and Casino. Pedestrians can reach the theme park through either the lion entrance on the Strip or the auto entrance off Tropicana. Vehicular traffic must approach the park by driving west on Tropicana and using the auto entrance. Both valet parking and self-parking are available. A monorail runs between Bally's and the MGM Grand. In addition, buses and Strip Trolleys service the MGM Grand.

Admissions Passing through the casino, guests work their way along the restaurant arcade to the complex's northeast corner, where the Rainbow Bridge connects the MGM Grand Hotel and Casino to the theme park. Ticket booths are located on both sides of the bridge from the casino. The cost of a single-day admission, which includes all attractions, has fluctuated wildly since the park opened. At the time of this publication, prices were about $17 (including tax) for guests ages 13 or older and about $12 for children ages 4 to 12. At last visit, guests were allowed into the theme park free to look around, eat, and shop. Strategically placed ticket kiosks sell ride and show passes to those who feel like they're missing something.

Arriving and Getting Oriented

Passing through the main-gate turnstiles, you enter Casablanca Plaza. Casablanca Plaza is to the MGM Grand Adventures Theme Park what Main Street U.S.A. is to Disneyland, i.e., the headquarters of the theme park and the location of most of its services. As you enter, a camera shop is on your left; it sells film and rents cameras. Stroller and wheelchair rentals, lockers, and the lost and found are on your right.

Guest Relations, also on the right, is the place to go for assistance and for information about live entertainment and special events in the park that day. As the park's communication center, it is also the place to report lost children (or lost adults), or to get help in the event of an emergency.

In addition to the services mentioned above, food and drink are available at Casablanca Plaza, along with sundries such as raingear, sunscreen, aspirin, baby supplies, feminine hygiene products, and tobacco.

The MGM Grand Adventures Theme Park is laid out in a convoluted but nevertheless generally circular configuration, with Casablanca Plaza situated outside the circle and serving as its entrance area. From Casablanca Plaza you enter the first themed area, New York Street. If you proceed around the park in a counterclockwise direction from New York Street (excluding a small cul-de-sac branching off New York Street to the right), you will encounter the following themed areas in order:

1. New York Street
2. Asian Street
3. French Street
4. Salem Waterfront
5. Tumbleweed Gulch
6. Rio Grande Cantina
7. New Orleans Street
8. Olde England Street

Most of the major attractions are situated on the outside of the circle and are distributed more or less equally around the park.

Grand Slam Canyon Theme Park

To further appeal to the family market targeted by the MGM Grand Adventures Theme Park, Circus Circus opened a small but innovative amusement park in the fall of 1993. Situated directly behind the main hotel and casino, the park goes by the name of Grand Slam Canyon. Architecturally compelling, the entire park is built two stories high atop the casino's parking structure and is totally enclosed by a huge glass dome. From the outside, the dome surface is reflective, mirroring its surroundings in hot tropical pink. Inside, however, the dome is transparent, allowing guests in the park to see out. Composed of a multilayer glass-and-plastic sandwich, the dome allows light in but blocks ultraviolet rays. The entire park is air-conditioned and climate-controlled 365 days a year.

As its name implies, the park is designed to resemble a classic Western desert canyon. From top to bottom, hand-painted artificial rock is sculpted into caverns, pinnacles, steep cliffs, and buttes. A stream runs through the stark landscape, cascading over a 90-foot falls into a rippling blue-green pool. Set among the rock structures are the attractions: a roller coaster, a flume ride, and some rides for small children. Embellishing the scene are several life-sized animatronic dinosaurs, a re-creation of an archeological dig, a fossil wall, and a replica of a Pueblo Indian cliff dwelling. There is also a small theater featuring magic and illusion. Finally, and inevitably, there is an electronic games arcade.

Grand Slam Canyon's premier attractions are the Canyon Blaster, the only indoor, double-loop, corkscrew roller coaster in the United States; and the Rim Runner, a three-and-one-half-minute water flume ride. Both rides wind in, around, and between the rocks and cliffs. The flume ride additionally passes under the snouts of the dinosaurs.

Guests can reach the theme park by proceeding through the rear of the main casino to the entrance and ticket plaza situated on the mezzanine level. Though Circus Circus has changed the admission policy so many times we have lost track, you can plan on spending about $12–17 a person. For exact admission prices on the day of your visit, call (702) 794-3939.

Luxor Attractions

The Luxor offers three high-tech, continuously running, gated (paid admission) attractions inside the pyramid on the level above the casino. Two attractions, which deal respectively with the past and present, were designed by Douglas Trumbull, creator of the Back to the Future ride at Universal Studios. The past, *In Search of the Obelisk* (in the Egyptian ruins), consists of a high-tech flight-simulation ride, while the present, *Luxor Live?*, showcases 3-D effects so advanced that audiences cannot differentiate illusion from reality. A new seven-story IMAX theater with a 15,000-watt sound system replaces *Theater of Time*. IMAX films run 24 hours a day and cost $7 or $8.50 for 3-D.

Technically, the attractions are quite advanced and much more sophisticated than anything offered at the MGM Grand Adventures or Grand Slam Canyon theme parks. The same cast of characters appear in the past and present attractions. While the story line is somewhat difficult to follow, the concept is basically that "you can't overcome the mysterious power of the obelisk." The obelisk is introduced in the first installment (the past) and is searched for, argued about, and fought over as the next segment unfolds.

Both presentations tend to be frenetic and disjointed. So much so, in fact, that some of the really wonderful, more subtle, touches are lost in the confusion. Overall, we like the Luxor attractions, but be forewarned that they are far from passive entertainment. They operate on several levels, so you have to be alert and make a real mental effort to stay connected through all of the system overload. For us, it was like trying to make a difficult chess move in the midst of a fire drill. By the time you have seen the past and present attractions, your brains are fried, but you will have seen some cutting-edge technology.

The IMAX presentations include a film about special effects in the movies and a 3-D flick about life on a giant space station. While both films are interesting, the 3-D presentation is pretty slow moving.

The Luxor attractions can be seen individually, with tickets purchased on an à la carte basis, or as a package for $19 with a couple of ancillary exhibits thrown in for good measure. If you plan to take in all three presentations, see the past and present before the IMAX show.

Las Vegas Hilton Attractions

In 1997, the Hilton launched an attraction called *Star Trek: The Experience*. Guests enter through a museum of *Star Trek* TV/movie memorabilia and props en route to boarding a four-minute space flight simulation ride. The Hilton ride differs from other simulation attractions in that the field of vision seemingly surrounds the guests. Upon returning from their heroic mission to far-flung reaches of the galaxy, guests are welcomed home at the gift shop. Besides the museum, the ride, and the gift shop, *Star Trek: The Experience* includes an electronic games arcade, a restaurant, and a lounge.

Stratosphere Attractions

The Stratosphere Tower stands 1,149 feet tall and offers an unparalleled view of Las Vegas, 24 hours a day. You can watch aircraft take off simultaneously from McCarran International Airport and Nellis Air Force Base. To the south, the entire Las Vegas Strip is visible. To the west, Red Rock Canyon seems practically within spitting distance. North of the tower, downtown glitters beneath the canopy of the Fremont Street Experience. By day, the rich geology of the Colorado basin and Spring Mountains merge in an earthtone and evergreen tapestry. At night, the dark desert circumscribes a blazing strand of twinkling neon.

A 12-level pod crowns the futuristic contours of 3 immense buttresses that form the tower's base. Level 12, the highest level, serves as the boarding area for the High Roller, a roller coaster, and the Big Shot, an acceleration/free-fall thrill ride. Levels 11 and 10 are not open to the public. An outdoor observation deck is situated on Level 9, with an indoor observation deck directly beneath it on Level 8. Level 7 features a 220-seat lounge, and Level 6 houses an upscale revolving restaurant. Levels 4 and 3 contain meeting rooms and wedding chapels respectively. The remaining levels, 1, 2, and 5, are not open to the public.

The view from the tower is so magnificent that we recommend experiencing it at different times of the day and night. Sunrise and sunset are particularly stunning, and a storm system rolling in over the mountains is a sight you won't quickly forget. Be sure to try both the indoor and outdoor observation decks.

The rides are a mixed bag. The roller coaster was such a snoozer that the Statosphere re-engineered it only two months after it opened and then closed it indefinitely because of "technical problems." When the coaster is working, it basically lumbers around the circumference of the pod. Visibility, the only thing this coaster has going for it, is limited by the tilt of the tracks, the safety restraints, and other people in the car. All sizzle and no steak, this ride only works in the press release.

Where the High Roller is hype at best, the Big Shot is cardiac arrest. Sixteen people at a time are seated at the base of the skyward projecting needle that tops the pod. The next thing you know, you are blasted 160 feet straight up in the air at 45 miles per hour and then allowed to partially free fall back down. At the apex of the ascent, it feels as if your seatbelt and restraint have mysteriously evaporated, leaving you momentarily hovering 100 plus stories up in the air. The ride lasts only about a half minute, but unless you're accustomed to being shot from a cannon, that's more than enough.

If you're having difficulty forming a mental image of the Big Shot, picture the carnival game where macho guys swing a sledgehammer, propelling a metal sphere up a vertical shaft. At the top of the shaft is a bell. If the macho man drives the sphere high enough to ring the bell, he wins a prize. Got the picture? OK, on the Big Shot, you are the metal sphere.

The elevators to the tower are located at the end of the shopping arcade on the second floor of the Stratosphere, above the casino. Tickets for the tower can be purchased at the elevator lobby (on the second floor) or at various places in the casino. The ticket line at the elevator lobby is usually shorter. Tower tickets cost about $5 for adults and $4 for children, seniors, active military, and Nevada residents (hey, what about one-legged cross-dressers or flamenco dancers?). Tickets for the rides sell for $5 per ride and are available at the same place.

Expect big crowds at the tower on weekends for the foreseeable future. Waits to board the elevator Friday through Sunday often surpass an hour. Once up top, the observation levels are congested, as are the lounge, snack bar, rest rooms, and gift shops. If you want to try the rides, expect to wait an additional 40–70 minutes for each on weekends. When you've had your fill of the tower and are ready to descend, you'll have another long wait to look forward to before boarding the elevator. However, if you walk down to the restaurant, you can catch the down elevator with virtually no wait at all. If you must see the tower on a weekend, go in the morning as soon as the tower opens.

Another way to see the tower without a long wait is to make a reservation for the Top of the World restaurant. To be safe, reservations should be made at least two weeks in advance. When you arrive, inform the greeter in the elevator lobby that you have a dinner reservation and give him your confirmation number. You will be ushered immediately into an express elevator. The restaurant is pricey, but the food is good and the view is a knockout, and you do not have to pay the $5 tower admission. If you want to try the Big Shot or the High Roller, purchase ride tickets before taking the elevator to the restaurant. Finally, be aware that most folks dress up to eat at the Top of the World.

On weekdays it is much easier to visit the Stratosphere Tower. Monday through Thursday, except at sunset, the wait to ascend is usually less than 15 minutes. Waits for the rides up top are also short.

Caesars Palace Attractions

Caesars Magical Empire offers an exotic setting so rich in detail that you could visit several times without exhausting the attraction's surprises. The attraction combines banquet dining and magic with an underground toga party to present one of Las Vegas's more unique dinner theaters. Twenty-four guests at a time enter the "Chamber of Destiny," where the history of Caesars Magical Empire is explained. Through an illusion similar to that of the "stretch room" at Disney's Haunted Mansion, you are then delivered to the 66,000-square-foot maze of catacombs that makes up the Magical Empire. Finally, you are ushered to one of ten cozy, vaulted-ceiling, stone banquet chambers and hosted by a sorcerer who entertains while you enjoy a three-course meal.

After the feast, you are free to stay as long as you like and explore the Empire. The cavernous Sanctum Secorum, the seven-story centerpiece of the complex, features an animatronic light and laser show. Two adjacent theaters offer additional performances of magic and illusion in intimate settings. Themed lounges offer refreshments between shows. For reservations or additional information, call (702) 731-7333.

Other attractions at Caesars Palace include the Omnimax Theater, where nature and travel documentaries are projected onto a six-story screen. At the adjacent Forum Shops you'll find the 3-D Cinema Ride, a simulation attraction featuring a haunted graveyard, a space flight, and (hold your hats!) a submarine race. This last segment is somewhat different from the submarine races my girlfriend and I enjoyed as teenagers, parked in a car on the banks of the Ohio.

Mirage and Treasure Island Attractions

Not only are the Mirage and Treasure Island attractions of top quality, they are also free. The two biggies are the pirate battle at Treasure Island and the exploding volcano at the Mirage. The pirate battle takes place every 90 minutes, weather permitting, beginning at 4 p.m., with the last performance at 10 p.m. (11:30 p.m. on warm-weather-month Fridays and Saturdays). As you face Treasure Island, the pirate ship is on your left and the British man o' war enters on the right. The best vantage points are on the rope rail facing the man o' war. If you want to relax with a drink before the show, try the terrace bar right behind where the British dock. On weekdays, claim your spot 15–20 minutes before show time. On weekends, make that 35–45 minutes. If you do not insist on having a *perfect* vantage point, you can see most everything just by joining the crowd at the last minute. If you are short, or have children in your party, it's probably worth the effort to arrive early and nail down a position by the rail.

The volcano at the Mirage goes off about every 15 minutes from 8 p.m. until midnight, if the weather is good and the winds are light. In the winter, when it gets dark earlier, the volcano starts popping off at 6 p.m. Usually, because of the frequency of performances (eruptions?), getting a good, rail-side vantage point is not too difficult. If you want to combine the volcano with dinner or a snack, grab a window table in the second-floor coffee shop of the Casino Royale across the street.

The Mirage also has some of *Siegfried & Roy*'s white tigers on display in a well-executed, natural habitat exhibit. In addition to the tigers, the Mirage maintains a nice dolphin exhibit open weekdays, 10 a.m.–5:30 p.m., and weekends, 11 a.m.–5:30 p.m. While the tigers are free, the dolphin exhibit costs $10. (Children 10 and under are free.)

A Word about Strip Roller Coasters

There are now four roller coasters on the Strip. The best of the lot is the Manhattan Express at New York–New York. After cranking 20 stories above the ground, the 16-seat coaster dives down a 75-foot drop to warm you up for the 55°, 144-foot fall that follows. Zipping in, out of, and among New York–New York's various buildings, the Express screams through a 360° loop, a "heartline twist and dive," a half curl, and a barrel roll. That's the good news. The bad news is that the Manhattan Express was shut down for "technical" reasons and nobody knows when, or if, it will reopen. If it is back in service when you visit, be sure to ride. You must be 46 inches tall. If you have any loose items on your person (hats, eyeglasses, wigs, pagers, purses, etc.), stow them in the handy lockers adjacent to the entrance.

The second best roller coaster on the Strip is the Canyon Blaster at Circus Circus's Grand Slam Canyon. The other two coasters, the High Roller at the Stratosphere and the "Exciting New Roller Coaster" at the MGM Grand Adventures Theme Park, are duds.

Other Area Attractions

The local visitor guides describe nearby attractions and sites pretty honestly. If you have children, try the **Scandia Family Fun Center** for miniature golf and the **Lied Discovery Museum** for a truly rewarding afternoon of exploration and enjoyable education. Right across the street from the Lied is the **Natural History Museum.** The **Wet 'n Wild** water theme park may be the best place in Las Vegas for teens and is also good for preschoolers. Look for Wet 'n Wild discount coupons in the local visitor guides.

Adults who wax nostalgic over vintage automobiles should check out the **Auto Collection at the Imperial Palace,** where more than 200 antique and historically significant vehicles are on display. Part of a much larger collection, these automobiles are rotated periodically to keep the exhibit fresh. Seeing the collection is well worth the admission price of $6.95, though discount coupons are readily available in the local visitor guides and at the Imperial Palace casino.

The **Liberace Museum** on East Tropicana Avenue is one of Las Vegas's most popular tourist attractions. Housed in multiple buildings connected by a parking lot, the exhibit chronicles the music, life, and excesses of Liberace. Though possibly the most professionally organized and well-presented celebrity museum in the United States, it's definitely more fun if you are a Liberace fan.

Debbie Reynolds Hollywood Motion Picture Museum is located on the first floor of the Debbie Reynolds Hollywood Hotel. Open Monday–Saturday, 10 a.m. to 10 p.m. and Sunday, 10 a.m.–6 p.m., the museum combines a screening of vintage Hollywood films with Reynolds's collection of movie memorabilia. Well conceived and nicely presented, the museum is a worthwhile two-hour diversion for movie buffs.

Adjacent to the MGM Grand is the **Showcase,** a new shopping, dining, and entertainment venue featuring a giant Sega electronic games arcade, an eight-screen movie complex, and the World of Coca-Cola with a 150-foot coke bottle housing two elevators and a Coca-Cola museum.

■ Natural Attractions near Las Vegas ■

In the Mexican Pavilion of Epcot at Walt Disney World, tourists rush obliviously past some of the most rare and valuable artifacts of the Spanish colonial period in order to take a short, uninspired boat ride. Many Las Vegas visitors, likewise, never look beyond the Strip. Like the Epcot tourists, they are missing something pretty special.

Las Vegas's geological and topographical diversity, in combination with its stellar outdoor resources, provides the best opportunities for worthwhile sight-seeing. So different and varied are the flora, fauna, and geology at each distinct level of elevation that traveling from the banks of Lake Mead to the high, ponderosa pine forests of Mount Charleston encompasses (in one and a half hours) as much environmental change as driving from Mexico to Alaska.

Red Rock Canyon, the Valley of Fire, the Mojave Desert, and the Black Canyon of the Colorado River are world-class, scenic attractions. In combination with the wet summits of the Spring Mountains, they comprise one of the most dramatically diversified natural areas on the North American continent. So excuse us if we leave coverage of the Guinness World of Records Museum to the local visitor's guides.

Driving Tours

For those who wish to sample the natural diversity of the Las Vegas area, we recommend the following driving tours. The trips begin and end in Las Vegas and take from two hours to all day, depending on the number of stops and side trips. The driving tours can very conveniently be combined with picnicking, hiking, horseback riding, and sight-seeing. If you have the bucks ($70–200 per person depending on the package), we also recommend taking one of the air/ground tours of the Grand Canyon.

1. Mount Charleston, Kyle Canyon, Lee Canyon, and the Toiyabe National Forest   *4 to 6 hours*

If you have had more than enough desert, this is the drive for you. Head north out of Las Vegas on US 95 and turn left on NV 157. Leave the desert and head into the pine and fir forest of the Spring Mountains. Continue up Kyle Canyon to the Mount Charleston Inn (a good place for lunch) and from there to the end of the canyon. Backtracking a few miles, take NV 158 over the Robbers Roost and into Lee Canyon. When you hit NV 156, turn left and proceed to the Lee Canyon Ski Area. For the return trip to Las Vegas, simply take NV 156 out of the mountains until it intersects US 95. Turn south (right) on US 95 to return to Las Vegas. If you start feeling your oats once you get into the mountains, there are some nice short hikes (less than a mile) to especially scenic overlooks. If you are so inclined, there is also horseback riding, and there are some great places for picnics.

2. Red Rock Canyon Scenic Loop   *2 ½ to 4 hours*

Red Rock Canyon is a stunningly beautiful desert canyonland only 40

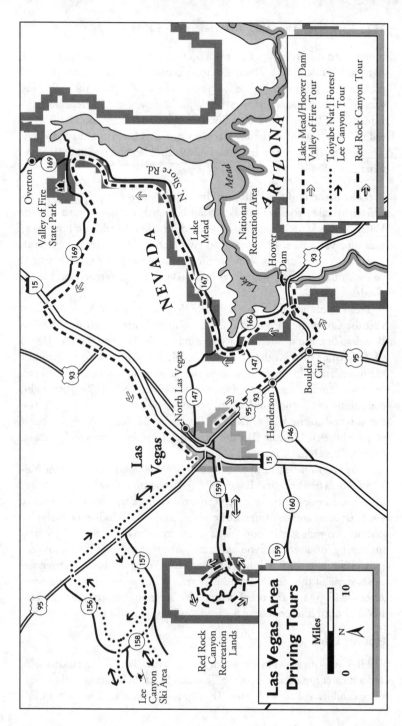

Las Vegas Area Driving Tours

Legend:
- Lake Mead/Hoover Dam/Valley of Fire Tour
- Toiyabe Nat'l Forest/Lee Canyon Tour
- Red Rock Canyon Tour

Overton

Valley of Fire State Park

NEVADA

Lake Mead

N. Shore Rd.

Lake Mead National Recreation Area

ARIZONA

Hoover Dam

Boulder City

Henderson

North Las Vegas

Las Vegas

Lee Canyon Ski Area

Red Rock Canyon Recreation Lands

Miles
0   10
N

minutes from Las Vegas. A scenic loop winds among imposing, rust-red, Aztec sandstone towers. There is a visitor center, as well as hiking trails and picnic areas. With very little effort you can walk to popular rock-climbing sites and watch the action. From Las Vegas head west on Charleston Boulevard (NV 159) directly to Red Rock Canyon. The scenic loop is 13 miles (all one-way), with numerous places to stop and enjoy the rugged vistas. The loop road brings you back to NV 159. Turn left and return to town via Charleston Boulevard.

3. Lake Mead and the Valley of Fire   *5 to 8 hours*

This drive takes you to the Lake Mead National Recreation Area and the Valley of Fire State Park. How long the drive takes depends on how many side trips you make. If you plan to visit Hoover Dam during your visit, it will be convenient to work it into this itinerary. The same is true if you wish to tour the Ethel M. (as in Mars) Chocolate Factory and Cactus Garden.

Head south out of Las Vegas on US 95 (detour west on Sunset Road to visit the Chocolate Factory and Cactus Garden), turning left on US 93 to Boulder City. From Boulder City continue to the Hoover Dam on US 93 (if desired) or turn on the Lakeshore Scenic Drive (NV 166) to continue the drive. Travel through the washes and canyons above the lake until you reach the Northshore Scenic Drive (NV 147 and NV 167). Turn right, continuing to the right on NV 167 when the routes split. If you wish, you can descend to the lake at Callville Bay, Echo Bay, or Overton Beach. If you are hungry, Callville Bay and Echo Bay have restaurants and lounges. Overton Beach has a snack bar.

Near Overton Beach, turn left to NV 169 and follow signs for the Valley of Fire State Park. Bear left on NV 169 away from Overton. The Valley of Fire features exceptional desert canyon scenery, a number of panoramic vistas, unusual and colorful sandstone formations, and Indian petroglyphs. A short two-mile scenic loop makes it easy to see many of the valley's most interesting formations. If you have time, take the road past the visitor center and climb to the Rainbow Vista overlook. From here a new highway accesses some of the most extraordinary terrain in the American Southwest. After the loop (and any other detours that interest you), continue west on NV 169 until it intersects I-15. Head south to return to Las Vegas.

Hoover Dam

Hoover Dam is definitely worth seeing. There is a film, a guided tour, and a theater presentation on the Colorado River drainage, as well as some static exhibits. All are well done. Try to go on a Monday, Thursday, or Friday. Arrive no later than 9 a.m., and do the tour first. After 9:30 or so, long lines form for the tour, especially on Tuesdays, Wednesdays, Saturdays, and Sundays.

Other than chauffeured transportation, there is no advantage in going to Hoover Dam on a bus tour. You will still have to wait in line for the tour of the dam and to see the other presentations. If you are the sort of person who tours quickly, you probably will have a lot of time to kill waiting for the rest of the folks to return to the bus.

The Canyons of the Southwest

Las Vegas tourist magazines continue to claim Bryce Canyon (400 miles round-trip) and Zion Canyon, Utah (350 miles round-trip), as well as the Grand Canyon, Arizona, as local attractions. We recommend all of the canyons if you are on an extended drive through the Southwest. If your time is limited, however, you might consider taking one of the air day tours that visit the canyons from Las Vegas. Running between $100 and $400 per passenger, the excursions follow one of two basic formats: air only, or air and ground combined. Some tour companies offer discounted fares for a second person if the first person pays full fare. Also, discount coupons are regularly available in *Today in Las Vegas,* distributed free of charge in most hotels.

Almost all canyon tours include a pass over Lake Mead and Hoover Dam. The trip involving the least commitment of time and money is a round-trip flyover of one or more of the canyons. A Grand Canyon flyover, for example, takeoff to touchdown, takes about two hours. While flying over any of the canyons is an exhilarating experience, air traffic restrictions over the Grand Canyon severely limit what air passengers can see. Flying over the other canyons is somewhat less restricted. If you want to get a real feel for the Grand Canyon particularly, go with one of the air/ground excursions. The Grand Canyon is many times more impressive from the ground than from the air.

The air/ground trips fly over the Grand Canyon and then land. Passengers are transferred to a bus that motors them along the rim of the canyon, stopping en route for lunch. Excursions sometimes include one or more of the other major canyons in addition to the Grand Canyon, and they last from seven to ten hours. Many flights offer multilingual translations of the tour narrative.

All of the aircraft used will feel very small to anyone accustomed to flying on big commercial jets. Most of the planes carry between 8 and 20 passengers. The captain often performs the duties of both flight attendant and pilot. Each passenger usually has a window, though some of the windows are pretty small. Cabin conditions for the most part are spartan, and there is not usually a toilet on board.

Because small aircraft sometimes get bounced around and buffeted by air currents, we recommend taking an over-the-counter motion-sickness medication if you think you might be adversely affected. The other thing you want to do for sure is to relieve your bladder *immediately* before boarding. If you go on an early-morning excursion, take it easy on the coffee and juice during breakfast.

PART SIX

Dining and Restaurants

Dining in Las Vegas

Las Vegas is a good restaurant town. It's not New York or San Francisco, but it offers respectable culinary and ethnic diversity, served dependably. Las Vegas hotel dining is relatively homogeneous in style and cuisine, while proprietary restaurants try hard to be different. The restaurant business in Las Vegas is as much a psychological as a culinary art, an exercise in perceived versus real value. In Las Vegas you can have the same meal in an astounding variety of environments for an unbelievable range of prices.

Left to its own devices, Las Vegas would be a meat-and-potatoes town. Owing to the expectations of its many visitors, however, Las Vegas restaurants put on the dog. There are dozens of designer restaurants—gourmet rooms, as they are known locally—where the pampered and the curious can pretend they are dining in an exclusive French or Continental restaurant while enjoying the food they like most: meat and potatoes. It is a town full of Ponderosas masquerading as Lutèce or The Four Seasons.

What has saved the day for discriminating diners is the increased presence of foreign visitors, particularly Asians. The needs of these visitors, in conjunction with their economic clout, have precipitated great growth and improvement among proprietary ethnic restaurants, which in turn have forced improvement among the more staid hotel-casino dining rooms. While many of the hotel gourmet rooms continue to be gastronomic and stylistic carbon copies, Las Vegas's proprietary restaurants have established distinct identities based on their creativity in the kitchen.

Subsidized Dining and the Free-Market Economy

There are two kinds of restaurants in Las Vegas: restaurants that are an integral part of a hotel-casino operation, and restaurants that must make it entirely on the merits of their food. Gourmet rooms in the hotels are usually associated with the casinos. Their mission is to pamper customers who are giving the house a lot of gambling action. At any given time, most of the folks in a hotel gourmet room are dining as guests of the casino. If you are a paying customer in the same restaurant, the astronomical prices you are charged help subsidize the feeding of all these comped guests. Every time you buy a meal in a gourmet room, you are helping to pay the tab of the strangers sitting at the next table.

This is not to say that the gourmet rooms do not serve excellent food. On the contrary, some of the best chefs in the country cook for hotel-casino gourmet rooms. The bottom line, however, if you are a paying guest, is that you are taking up space intended for high rollers, and the house is going to charge you a lot of rent.

Restaurants independent of casinos work at a considerable disadvantage. First, they do not have a captive audience of gamblers or convention-goers. Second, their operation is not subsidized by gaming, and third, they are not located where you will just stumble upon them. Finally, they not only compete with the casino gourmet rooms but also go head-to-head with the numerous buffets and bulk-loading meal-deals that casinos offer as loss-leaders to attract the less affluent gambler.

Successful proprietary restaurants in Las Vegas must offer something very distinct, very different, and very good at a competitive price, and must somehow communicate to you that they are offering it. Furthermore, their offer must be compelling enough to induce you to travel to their location, forsaking the convenience of dining in your hotel. Not easy.

All of this works to the consumer's advantage, of course. High rollers get comped in the gourmet rooms. Folks of more modest means can select from among the amazing steak, lobster, and prime rib deals offered by the casinos, or enjoy exceptional food at bargain prices at independent restaurants. People with hardly any money at all can gorge themselves on loss-leader buffets.

In many ways, Las Vegas restaurants are the culinary version of free-market economy. The casinos siphon off the customers who are willing to pay big bucks for food and feed them for free. This alters the target market for the independents and serves to keep a lid on their prices. Independents providing exceptional quality for such reasonable charges ensure in turn that buffets and meal-deals stay cheap. Ah, America, what a country!

So Many Restaurants, So Little Time

Dining options in Las Vegas, as noted above, have been shaped by the marketing strategies of the casinos. Before a gambler can wager any money, the casino has to get him through the front door. If what it takes are $3 steaks, buffets, and dollar shrimp cocktails, that's what the casino does. For those more attracted to eating than to gambling, this is a great boon to mankind.

While there are hundreds of restaurants in Las Vegas, you will be able to sample only a handful during your stay. But which ones? Our objective in this section is to point you to specific restaurants that meet your requirements in terms of quality, price, location, and environment. No beating around the bush.

■ **Buffets** ■

Buffets, used by the casinos to lure customers, have become a Las Vegas institution. Like everything else, they come and go, but on average there are around 40 to choose from. The majority of casinos operate their buffets at close to cost or at a slight loss. A few casinos, mostly those with a more captive clientele (like the Las Vegas Hilton, the Mirage, and Caesars Palace), probably make money on their buffets.

Buffet Speak	
Action Format	Food cooked to order in full view of the patrons
Gluttony	A Las Vegas buffet tradition that carries no moral stigma
Groaning Board	Synonym for a buffet; a table so full that it groans
Island	Individual serving area for a particular cuisine or specialty (salad island, dessert island, Mexican island, etc.)
Shovelizer	Diner who prefers quantity over quality
Fork Lift	A device used to remove shovelizers
Sneeze Guards	The glass/plastic barriers between you and the food

Almost all of the buffets serve breakfast, lunch, and dinner, changing their menus every day. Prices for breakfast range from under $3 to $8. Lunch goes for $5–10, with dinner ranging between $5 and $15. The Rio Village Seafood Buffet is in a class all its own with lunch at $14.95 and dinner at $18.95 (and worth every penny). Because most buffets operate as an extension of sales and marketing, there is not necessarily any relationship between price and quality.

At breakfast, relatively speaking, there is not much difference between one buffet and the next. If your hotel has a breakfast buffet, it is probably not worth the effort to go somewhere else. When it comes to lunch and dinner, however, some buffets do a significantly better job than others.

If you are looking for well-seasoned meats and vegetables, ethnic variety, and culinary creativity, choose from among our top seven buffets. If your taste runs more to roast beef, ham, fried chicken, and mashed potatoes (i.e., well-prepared simple foods), the remaining three buffets in our hit parade do an excellent job of serving traditional American fare.

With the opening of the Festival Buffet at the Fiesta and the Market Street Buffet at Texas Station (part of a continuing Coke-Pepsi rivalry between the two casinos), along with the Garden Court Buffet at Main Street Station, the buffet standings have changed dramatically and a new standard of buffet variety and creativity has emerged. The Fiesta has introduced wok cooking and a monster rotisserie for barbecuing a side of beef, chicken, pork, brisket, and ribs, along with a large selection of pizza and

Las Vegas's Ten Best Buffets		
Buffet	Quality Rating	Last Year's Ranking
1. Texas Station Market Street Buffet	96	1
2. Rio Carnival World Buffet	95	2
3. Fiesta Festival Buffet	94	3
4. Main Street Station Garden Court Buffet	93	Not ranked
5. Sunset Station—The Feast	92	Not ranked
6. Boulder Station—The Feast	91	4
7. Palace Station—The Feast	90	5
8. Bally's Big Kitchen	86	6
9. Mirage Buffet	83	7
10. Caesars Palace Palatium Buffet	82	8

Las Vegas's first and only coffee bar. Texas Station has introduced a chili station and fajitas, along with a level of food and beverage quality that has surpassed even the Rio, Las Vegas's buffet king for several years.

As a footnote, Main Street Station, the Flamingo, the Fremont, Caesars Palace, Monte Carlo, the Mirage, the Golden Nugget, Sunset Station, the MGM Grand, Boomtown, and Treasure Island provide the most attractive settings for their buffets. The buffets at the Rio, Fiesta, and Texas, Palace, and Boulder Stations are the favorites of Las Vegas locals. The Frontier Friday Seafood Extravaganza, which has a quality rating of 90, does not appear in the ranking because it is not served on a daily basis. If you are looking for an up-and-comer for next year's top ten, check out the new buffet at Harrah's. Also keep your eye on the French Market Buffet at Orleans.

A number of casinos have very acceptable, though not exceptional, buffets. Not worth a special trip if you are staying or playing elsewhere, these buffets are just fine if you happen to be at the hotel in question when you get the urge to go to the trough. Alphabetically, they are:

Aladdin Market Place Buffet

Circus Circus—Circus Buffet

Excalibur Round Table Buffet

Fitzgeralds—Molly's Country Kitchen and Buffet

Flamingo—Paradise Garden Buffet

Gold Coast Buffet

Golden Nugget—The Buffet

Harrah's Galley Buffet

Imperial Palace Emperor's & Imperial Buffets

Lady Luck Daily Buffet

Las Vegas Hilton Buffet of Champions

MGM Grand Oz Buffet

Maxim—Grand Evening Buffet

Orleans French Market Buffet

Riviera World's Fare Buffet

Sahara Buffet

Sam's Town Great Buffet

San Remo Ristorante del Flori Buffet

Santa Fe Lone Mountain Buffet

Showboat Captains Buffet

Stardust Warehouse Buffet

Treasure Island International Buffet

Tropicana Island Buffet

Seafood and Specialty Buffets

Several casinos feature seafood buffets on Friday and sometimes on other days. The best of the seafood buffets are the Rio's Village Seafood Buffet, Frontier's Friday Seafood Extravaganza, the Fremont's Seafood Fantasy, and the Texas Station Market Street Buffet.

The Rio's seafood buffet is the most expensive buffet, and one of the great bargain buffets of Las Vegas. How can it be both? The quality and variety of this piscatory repast far surpasses, in dollars and sense, a lone oceanic entree at any seafood restaurant you can name. Check it out: peel-and-eat shrimp, Dungeness crab legs, Manila steamers, and oysters on the half-shell; seafood salads, chowders, and Mongolian grill; plus Italian, Mexican, and Chinese dishes, along with fried, grilled, broiled, breaded, and barbequed preparations. And if you have even a millimeter of stomach space left after the main courses, the dessert selection is outstanding.

The Frontier puts on an excellent seafood buffet but manages to alien-ate patrons with a manipulative seating process. Because of the popularity of the Frontier's Friday buffet, guests start lining up between 4 and 5 p.m. Instead of simply serving the early arrivals, each person is given a number and dispatched into the casino to wait for that number to be called. Though this process is represented by the Frontier as a courtesy to guests, it is obviously a mechanism for holding diners captive in the casino. Re-gardless of how early you arrive, you will probably be sentenced to at least one hour, and more often two hours, in the casino. When you finally are seated, you will be surprised to discover that the dining room is only half full! The Fremont's Tuesday, Friday, and Sunday Seafood Fantasy approxi-mates the Frontier's buffet in choice and quality but can be enjoyed with a lot less hassle. Ditto for the Texas Station contender, which offers steamed clams and crawfish. The Lady Luck offers a seafood dinner buffet every day. None of the lot, however, come close to the seafood buffet at the Rio.

The pick of the specialty-buffet litter is the Rio's Carnival World, with its separate "serving islands" for American, Italian, Chinese, and Mexican cuisines and Mongolian barbecue. In addition, the Rio offers sushi, fish and chips, burgers and franks, and the best dessert selection in town. Texas Station serves flaming wok Chinese and Mexican cuisines, a selection of nine Texas chilis, and lots of pizza. The Fiesta features the monster rotis-serie, a Mongolian barbecue, Chinese and Cajun cuisines, and a coffee bar serving espresso, cappuccino, and latte. Main Street Station's buffet fea-tures the "action" format, with islands serving barbeque, Italian, Chinese, Mexican, pizza, ribs, and ample desserts. It's the largest buffet downtown, served in the most aesthetically pleasing buffet room in town. The Las Vegas Hilton buffet offers all-you-can-eat cold king crab legs and peel-and-eat shrimp. The Riviera buffet serves a different ethnic specialty nightly. Treasure Island, Palace and Boulder Stations, and Luxor routinely serve Italian, Chinese, Mexican, and other ethnic entrees.

Buffet Line Strategy

Popular buffets develop long lines. The best way to avoid the crowds is to go Sunday through Thursday and get in line before 6 p.m. or after 9 p.m. If you go to a buffet on a weekend, arrive extra early or extra late. If a large trade show or convention is in town, you will be better off any day hitting the buffets of casinos that do not do a big convention business. Good choices among the highly ranked buffets include Texas Station, Fiesta, Main Street Station, Palace Station, Boulder Station, Boomtown, Showboat, and the Fremont.

■ Champagne Brunches ■

Upscale, expensive Sunday champagne brunches with reserved tables, imported champagne, sushi, and seafood are making an impact on the local brunch scene. Although there are a plethora of value-priced champagne brunches, the big-ticket feasts attract diners who are happy to pay a higher tab for fancy food and service and reservations to avoid a wait. In general, the higher the price of the brunch, the better the champagne served. Bally's and the MGM serve decent French champagne; California sparkling wine is the norm at the others. Reservations are accepted at all of the following.

- **Sterling Brunch,** Bally's Steakhouse   739-4651
  The Sterling Brunch was the first of its kind. At $49.95 per person (plus tax), it's also the most costly, but there's no shortage of diners who love it, even at double its original price. The lavish selection of foods includes a host of breakfast items, freshly made sushi, real lobster salad, raw and cooked seafood, caviar, and French champagne. Pheasant and rack of lamb appear regularly. The dessert selection is awesome. Entree selections change weekly. Available: 9:30 a.m.–2:30 p.m.; reservations are required.

- **Grand Champagne Brunch at the Brown Derby,** MGM Grand 891-3110 (after 9 a.m.)
  A complete seafood bar, filet mignon, prime rib, and rack of lamb are regular features. Eggs Benedict and omelets are prepared to order. There are more than 50 items and desserts. Adults, $28.95 per person (includes tax); children 12 and under, $10.95; children under 5 dine free. Available: 9 a.m.–2 p.m. On Sundays call 891-7318 for reservations.

- **The Steak House,** Circus Circus   734-0410
  Elaborate ice carvings and decorative food displays are a tribute to the chef's cruise line background. Many breakfast items, steak and seafood, entrees and salads. Adults, $24.95 (all-inclusive); children 6–12 years, $14.95. Available: 10 a.m.–1:30 p.m.

- **Signature Brunch,** The Broiler at Boulder Station   432-7777

  An excellent price that includes the fine soup and salad bar, separate seafood bar, carving station, and omelet station. Entrees are served at the table. Diners can choose one dish from each of the entree categories—Benedicts, breakfast, shellfish, chicken, and lamb. Adults, $14.95 plus tax and gratuity. Available: 10 a.m.–2 p.m.

Bally's Sterling Brunch, though quite expensive, is by far the best brunch in town and, in our opinion, a fair value for the money ($49.95), if you are a big eater. The brunch at the Brown Derby at the MGM Grand charges $28.95 and is worth it, but there's an early-bird price from 9–10 a.m. for $20. The Tropicana and Circus Circus both have excellent Sunday brunches in the $25 range. Other good brunches include Boulder, Palace, and Sunset Stations (combining a buffet with entree selections from a menu), Caesars Palace (which often features Bananas Foster), the Fiesta (serving Mexican specialties and substituting margaritas for champagne to correspond with the Southwest theme), Santa Fe, and Golden Nugget.

■ Meal-Deals ■

In addition to buffets, many casinos offer special dining deals. These include New York strip and porterhouse steaks, prime rib, lobster, crab legs, shrimp cocktails, and various combinations of the foregoing, all available at give-away prices. There are also breakfast specials.

While the meal-deals generally deliver what they promise in the way of an entree, many of the extras that contribute to a quality dining experience are missing. With a couple of notable exceptions, the specials are served in big, bustling restaurants with the atmosphere of a high school cafeteria. Eating at closely packed formica tables under lighting bright enough for brain surgery, it is difficult to pretend that you are engaged in fine dining.

Our biggest complaint, however, concerns the lack of attention paid to the meal as a whole. We have had nice pieces of meat served with tired, droopy salads, stale bread, mealy microwaved potatoes, and unseasoned canned vegetables. How can you get excited about your prime rib when it is surrounded by the ruins of Pompeii?

Deke Castleman of the *Las Vegas Advisor* doesn't believe that discount dining is about food at all. He writes,

> *Of course you're entitled to your opinion, and I'll fight to the death for your right to express it. But 'quality dining experience' is not really what Las Vegas visitors, IMHO ('in my humble opinion,' in Netspeak),*

are looking for when they pursue a $3 steak, a $4.95 prime rib, or a $9.95 lobster. To me what they're after is twofold: a very cheap steak, prime rib, or lobster and damn the salad, vegetable, and Formica; and to take home a cool story about all the rock-bottom prices they paid for food.

Finally, it's hard to take advantage of many of the specials. They are offered only in the middle of the night, or alternatively you must stand in line for an hour waiting for a table, or eat your evening meal at 3:30 in the afternoon. In restaurants all over town, in and out of the casinos, there is plenty of good food, served in pleasant surroundings, at extremely reasonable prices. In our opinion, saving $5 on a meal is not worth all the hassle.

Because Las Vegas meal-deals come and go all the time, it is impossible to cover them adequately in a book that is revised annually. If you want to stay abreast of special dinner offerings, your best bet is to subscribe to the *Las Vegas Advisor,* a monthly newsletter that provides independent, critical evaluations of meal-deals, buffets, brunches, and drink specials. The *Las Vegas Advisor* can be purchased by calling (800) 244-2224. If you are already in town and want to pick up the latest edition, single copies are available at the Gamblers Book Club store at 630 South 11th Street, (702) 382-7555.

Steak Though specials constantly change, there are a few that have weathered the test of time. Our favorite is the 16-ounce porterhouse steak dinner at the Redwood Bar & Grill in the California. A complete dinner, including relish plate, soup or salad, and steak with excellent accompanying potatoes and vegetables, can be had for about $13 excluding drinks, taxes, and tips. What's more, it is served in one of the most attractive dining rooms in Las Vegas. The porterhouse special, incidentally, does not appear on the menu. You must ask for it.

Binion's Horseshoe offered a complete New York steak dinner for $2 for more than 20 years. The price was raised to $4 in January 1996 but then rolled back to $2 in April 1997. The steak is a 10-ounce New York strip, served with potato, roll, and salad. This is a good meal at an unbelievable price, but it is available only from midnight to 8 a.m. There is always a line from 11:15 p.m. until 2 or 3 a.m. To avoid the lines, play a little blackjack and ask the pit boss for a line pass. This meal has not only been the Las Vegas bargain icon for at least a decade, it's also a subculture all its own. If you're going to be up late in Vegas to begin with, why not have the unique experience of a complete steak dinner for $2 while you're at it?

There's a great 16-ounce T-bone served in the coffee shop of the Gold

Coast 24 hours a day for $8.95. This big slab is accompanied by soup or salad, potatoes, onion rings, baked beans, garlic bread, and a glass of draft beer. For $8.95 this would be a deal *without* the steak.

Some worthwhile on-again, off-again steak specials (if offered while you are in town) are: the filet mignon at Pasta Pirate in the California, the 16-ounce New York strip at the Sahara coffee shop, and the New York strip or filet mignon special at Pablo's Cafe in the Santa Fe.

Prime Rib The most readily accessible and one of the best prime rib specials in a town full of prime rib specials is available at the San Remo's Ristorante del Flori coffee shop. They offer a generous piece of meat, accompanied by good sides. The special is available 24 hours a day, and the restaurant is rarely crowded. The best prime rib deal in town, according to the *Las Vegas Advisor,* is served at the Lady Luck, downtown, where you can choose among cuts ranging from 8 to 24 ounces. Another great one is at the Frontier in Michelle's Cafe for $4. Portions of beef are massive, one and a half inches thick, and wonderfully seasoned. The meal is served with salad, bread, potato, and vegetables. As with the Frontier's Friday seafood buffet, however, it takes anywhere from 40 minutes to one and a half hours to get a table. On the bright side, the prime rib special is served from noon to midnight, so if you really want it, you can go at an off hour.

For $4 or $5 more you can dine in comparative luxury with much less effort at Sir Galahad's at the Excalibur. The prime rib is excellent and served tableside in huge slabs accompanied by fresh salad/soup and excellent side dishes, including Yorkshire pudding. There is no hassle about getting a table if you arrive by 6:30 p.m.

Other good prime rib specials, when available, are at Bally's (listed at $14.95 on the menu but only $9.95 on your bill) and downtown at the Horseshoe.

Lobster and Crab Legs Lobster and steak (surf & turf) combos and crab leg deals appear regularly on casino marquees around Las Vegas. Pasta Pirate at the California serves the best all-around shellfish specials. Unfortunately, they are on-again, off-again. When on, they alternately feature a steak and lobster combo, a lobster dinner, or a king crab dinner, all for $11–13, not including tax or gratuity. Entrees are served with soup or salad, pasta, veggies, garlic bread, and wine. The setting is relaxed and pleasant. Reservations are accepted.

In addition to the Pasta Pirate, excellent crab specials are routinely offered in the Mediterranean Room at the Gold Coast and the Plantation Room at the Showboat. The best deal in town, however, may be the king crab special served for $10 at Roberta's at El Cortez. Though El Cortez is not the fanciest joint in town, the total restaurant experience is not a drawback, either: Roberta's is the best bargain gourmet room in town.

The perennial favorite of the steak and lobster deals (which tend to be of lesser quality than steak, prime rib, and crab leg meal-deals) is found at Toucan Harry's at the Stardust ($8.95). The best whole Maine lobster deal in town is available 24 hours a day at the Poker Palace in North Las Vegas. Beware of buffets advertising lobster. Buffet lobsters have the consistency of rubber and have been known to leap tall buildings in a single bounce.

Shrimp Cocktails   Shrimp cocktails at nominal prices are frequently used to lure gamblers into the casinos. Usually the shrimp are small (popcorn shrimp) and are served pickled in cocktail sauce in an ice-cream sundae glass. The best and cheapest shrimp cocktail can be found at the Golden Gate, a small downtown casino. Other contenders (also downtown) are the Fremont, the Four Queens, and the Lady Luck.

Pasta and Pizza   The Pasta Palace at Palace Station regularly runs half-price specials on excellent pasta entrees, and the Pasta Pirate at the California offers some of the best designer pasta dishes in town. As far as pizza is concerned, our favorite is the on-again/off-again $5 pizza and beer combo at the Pasta Palace.

Breakfast Specials   Our favorite breakfast deal is the huge ham and eggs special at the Gold Coast. One of the best breakfasts you will ever eat, it would still be a bargain at five times the price. Other worthwhile breakfast deals include steak and eggs at the Frontier (11 p.m. to 11 a.m.), Arizona Charlie's, the San Remo (24 hours), and the ham and eggs breakfast at the Horseshoe.

■ New Restaurants ■

New entries in the ever-burgeoning dining race include many that are not profiled. These are just a little taste.

The Magnolia Room at Jerry's Nugget in North Las Vegas. Major reconstruction of the venerable Jerry's Nugget includes a lovely dining room with a fine value-priced menu. This total departure from the Nugget's usual restaurants has a creative female chef who is attracting the uptown crowd that knows a good deal when they eat one.

Cozymel's in the Howard Hughes Business Center on Paradise Road serves the seafood dishes of the Yucatán peninsula along with traditional

Mexican fare. Trendy and upscale, Cozymel's can be wonderful or just fair, depending on who's in the kitchen. No reservations.

The Lobster House on the Strip in the Epicenter Plaza north of the MGM Grand is a nautical-themed eatery with jumbo lobsters at fair prices. Like dining on a rich uncle's yacht.

Mama Marie's Cucina in the Rio is just one of many new restaurants in the Masquerade Village. Chef Italia cooks the dishes of her native Rome with the passion of a fine artist. Reasonable and delicious.

Wolfgang Puck's latest venture in the new addition to The Forum Shops is a two-story restaurant with two different themes. The lower level cafe offers moderately priced quick fare, including noodle dishes and stir-fries. The beautiful upstairs dining room has the foods and excitement of Puck's Chinoise on Main Street.

The Restaurants

■ **Our Favorite Las Vegas Restaurants** ■

We have developed detailed profiles for the best restaurants (in our opinion) in town. Each profile features an easily scanned heading that allows you, in just a second, to check out the restaurant's name, cuisine, Star Rating, cost, Quality Rating, and Value Rating.

Star Rating   The Star Rating is an overall rating that encompasses the entire dining experience, including style, service, and ambiance in addition to the taste, presentation, and quality of the food. Five stars is the highest rating possible and connotes the best of everything. Four-star restaurants are exceptional, and three-star restaurants are well above average. Two-star restaurants are good. One star is used to denote an average restaurant that demonstrates an unusual capability in some area of specialization—for example, an otherwise unmemorable place that has great barbecued chicken.

Cost   To the right of the Star Rating is an expense description that provides a comparative sense of how much a complete meal will cost. A complete meal for our purposes consists of an entree with vegetable or side dish, and choice of soup or salad. Appetizers, desserts, drinks, and tips are excluded.

Inexpensive	$14 and less per person
Moderate	$15–30 per person
Expensive	Over $30 per person

Quality Rating   On the far right of each heading appear a number and a letter. The number is a Quality Rating based on a scale of 0–100, with 100 being the highest (best) rating attainable. The Quality Rating is based expressly on the taste, freshness of ingredients, preparation, presentation, and creativity of food served. There is no consideration of price. If you are a person who wants the best food available, and cost is not an issue, you need look no further than the Quality Rating.

Value Rating   If, on the other hand, you are looking for both quality and value, then you should check the Value Rating, expressed in letters. The value ratings are defined as follows:

A   Exceptional value, a real bargain

B   Good value

C   Fair value, you get exactly what you pay for

D   Somewhat overpriced

F   Significantly overpriced

Location   Just below the address is a zone name and number. This zone will give you a general idea of where the restaurant described is located. For ease of use, we divide Las Vegas into five geographic zones:

Zone 1   The Strip and Environs

Zone 2   Downtown

Zone 3   Southwest Las Vegas

Zone 4   North Las Vegas

Zone 5   Southeast Las Vegas and the Boulder Highway

If you are staying downtown and intend to walk or take a cab to dinner, you may want to choose a restaurant from among those located in Zone 2. If you have a car, you might include restaurants from contiguous zones in your consideration. (See pages 12–17 for detailed zone maps.)

Other Information   If you like what you see at first glance when you scan a particular restaurant's heading and location, you might move on to read the rest of the profile for more detailed information.

■ Our Pick of the Best Las Vegas Restaurants ■

Because restaurants are opening and closing all the time in Las Vegas, we have tried to confine our list to establishments with a proven track record over a fairly long period of time. Newer restaurants (and older restaurants under new management) are listed but not profiled. Those newer or changed establishments that demonstrate staying power and consistency will be profiled in subsequent editions. Also, the list is highly selective. Noninclusion of a particular place does not necessarily indicate that the restaurant is not good, only that it was not ranked among the best in its genre. Note that some restaurants appear in more than one category.

The Best Las Vegas Restaurants

Name	Star Rating	Price Rating	Quality Rating	Value Rating
Adventures in Dining				
Emeril's (contemporary New Orleans)	★★★★★	Expensive	95	B
Bacchanal (Roman banquet)	★★★★	Expensive	94	B
Mamounia (Moroccan)	★★★½	Moderate	88	A
Marrakech (Moroccan)	★★★	Moderate	86	B
Yolie's (Brazilian steak)	★★★	Moderate	86	B
American				
Spago	★★★★★	Mod/Exp	94	C
Kokomo's	★★★★	Expensive	93	C
Neros	★★★★	Expensive	90	C
Brown Derby	★★★★	Mod/Exp	87	C
Diamond Lil's	★★★½	Moderate	89	B
DIVE!	★★★½	Moderate	89	B
Hugo's Cellar	★★★½	Expensive	89	B
Redwood Bar & Grill	★★★½	Moderate	87	A
Lawry's The Prime Rib	★★★½	Expensive	85	C
Top of the World	★★★½	Expensive	85	C
Wolfgang Puck Cafe	★★★½	Moderate	85	B
Kathy's Southern Cooking	★★★	Inexpensive	80	A
Philips Supper House	★★★	Moderate	80	A
Sadie's	★★★	Inexp/Mod	80	A
Poppa Gar's	★★½	Inexpensive	79	A
Barbecue				
T-Bone's Texas Barbecue	★★★½	Inexp/Mod	88	A
Sam Woo Bar-B-Q	★★★	Inexpensive	89	A
Brazilian				
Yolie's	★★★	Moderate	86	B
Brewpub				
Barley's	★★★	Inexpensive	86	A
Triple Seven Brewpub†				
California American				
Fog City Diner	★★★★	Mod/Exp	89	C

†No profile

The Best Las Vegas Restaurants (continued)

Name	Star Rating	Price Rating	Quality Rating	Value Rating
Chinese (see also Dim Sum)				
Chin's	★★★★½	Expensive	96	C
Lillie Langtry's	★★★★	Expensive	90	B
Chang's	★★★½	Moderate	88	B
Peking Market	★★★½	Moderate	87	B
Garden of the Dragon	★★★½	Expensive	85	C
Kim Tar	★★★	Inexp/Mod	89	B
Sam Woo Bar-B-Q	★★★	Inexpensive	89	A
Cathay House	★★★	Moderate	84	C
Chinese/French				
Mayflower Cuisinier	★★★★½	Mod/Exp	94	B
Continental/French				
Bistro Le Montrachet	★★★★★	Mod/Exp	98	C
Palace Court	★★★★★	Expensive	98	C
Napa	★★★★★	Expensive	95	C
Buccaneer Bay Club	★★★★½	Moderate	96	B
Monte Carlo	★★★★½	Expensive	95	C
Andre's	★★★★½	Expensive	90	D
Fiore	★★★★	Mod/Exp	95	B
Bistro	★★★★	Expensive	94	C
Michael's	★★★★	Expensive	93	D
Gatsby's	★★★★	Expensive	90	C
Isis	★★★★	Mod/Exp	90	B
Seasons	★★★★	Expensive	90	D
Swiss Cafe	★★★½	Moderate	89	B
Café Nicolle	★★★½	Moderate	88	B
Renata's	★★★½	Mod/Exp	88	B
Pamplemousse	★★★½	Expensive	87	D
Burgundy Room	★★★½	Mod/Exp	85	B
Café Michelle	★★★	Mod/Exp	85	B
Dim Sum (see also Chinese)				
Chang's	★★★½	Moderate	88	B
Cathay House	★★★	Moderate	84	C

The Best Las Vegas Restaurants (continued)

Name	Star Rating	Price Rating	Quality Rating	Value Rating
Greek				
Olympic Cafe	★★★½	Inexpensive	88	B
Tony's Greco Roman†	★★★	Moderate	81	B
Indian				
Shalimar	★★★½	Mod/Exp	86	C
Italian				
Piero's	★★★★½	Expensive	92	C
Stefano's	★★★★	Expensive	94	C
Ristorante Italiano	★★★★	Expensive	91	C
al Dente	★★★★	Moderate	90	C
Antonio's	★★★★	Mod/Exp	90	B
Mortoni's	★★★★	Mod/Exp	90	B
Tre Visi/La Scala	★★★½	Mod/Exp	94	B
Manhattan	★★★½	Mod/Exp	92	B
Anna Bella	★★★½	Inexp/Mod	89	A
Bootlegger	★★★½	Moderate	89	A
Cipriani	★★★½	Expensive	89	C
Ferraro's	★★★½	Moderate	89	B
North Beach Cafe	★★★½	Moderate	89	A
Bertolini's	★★★½	Moderate	88	B
Sfuzzi	★★★½	Moderate	88	B
Il Fornaio	★★★½	Mod/Exp	87	B
Alta Villa	★★★½	Moderate	85	A
Sergio's	★★★½	Mod/Exp	85	B
Venetian	★★★	Moderate	87	B
Café Milano	★★★	Moderate	84	C
Macaroni Grill	★★★	Moderate	82	B
Pasta Mia	★★★	Moderate	82	A
Carluccio's Tivoli Gardens	★★½	Moderate	78	A
Japanese (see also Sushi)				
Hakase	★★★★	Mod/Exp	90	B
Tokyo	★★★½	Moderate	85	B
Fuji	★★★	Moderate	84	B

†No profile

The Best Las Vegas Restaurants (continued)

Name	Star Rating	Price Rating	Quality Rating	Value Rating
Lobster				
Alan Alberts	★★★★	Expensive	89	C
Rosewood Grille	★★★½	Expensive	88	C
Mexican/Southwestern				
Coyote Cafe	★★★½	Mod/Exp	90	B
Garduno's Chili Packing Co.	★★★½	Inexp/Mod	89	B
Lindo Michoacan	★★★½	Moderate	86	A
Viva Mercado's	★★★½	Moderate	86	A
Ricardo's	★★★½	Moderate	85	B
Middle Eastern				
Habib's	★★★½	Moderate	88	C
Jerusalem (Kosher)†	★★½	Inexpensive	86	A
Moroccan				
Mamounia	★★★½	Moderate	88	A
Marrakech	★★★	Moderate	86	B
Persian				
Habib's	★★★½	Moderate	88	C
Polynesian				
Papyrus	★★★	Moderate	86	B
Prime Rib				
Sir Galahad's	★★★½	Moderate	89	A
Redwood Bar & Grill	★★★½	Moderate	87	A
Lawry's The Prime Rib	★★★½	Expensive	85	C
Golden Steer	★★★	Expensive	80	C
Philips Supper House	★★★	Moderate	80	A
Seafood				
Buzios	★★★★	Mod/Exp	93	A
Kokomo's	★★★★	Expensive	93	C
The Broiler	★★★½	Moderate	89	A
The Tillerman	★★★½	Mod/Exp	87	C
Pasta Pirate	★★★	Moderate	86	A

†No profile

The Best Las Vegas Restaurants (continued)

Name	Star Rating	Price Rating	Quality Rating	Value Rating
Steak				
Ruth's Chris Steak House	★★★★	Expensive	94	C
Kokomo's	★★★★	Expensive	93	C
The Palm	★★★★	Expensive	90	C
Alan Alberts	★★★★	Expensive	89	C
The Broiler	★★★½	Moderate	89	A
Morton's	★★★½	Expensive	89	C
Outback Steakhouse	★★★½	Moderate	88	B
Rosewood Grille	★★★½	Expensive	88	C
Redwood Bar & Grill	★★★½	Moderate	87	A
The Steak House	★★★½	Moderate	86	C
Billy Bob's Steakhouse	★★★	Moderate	88	A
Yolie's	★★★	Moderate	86	B
Embers	★★★	Moderate	84	B
Binion's Ranch Steakhouse	★★★	Moderate	82	B
Golden Steer	★★★	Expensive	80	C
Lone Star Steakhouse	★★½	Moderate	83	B
Sushi (see also Japanese)				
Hakase	★★★★	Mod/Exp	90	B
Teru Sushi	★★★½	Mod/Exp	89	C
Tokyo	★★★½	Moderate	85	B
Hamada of Japan†	★★★	Mod/Exp	84	C
San Remo Sushi Bar†	★★★	Expensive	84	C
Thai				
Lotus of Siam	★★★	Moderate	85	A
Vietnamese				
Saigon	★★★	Inexpensive	83	A
Rooms with a View				
Top of the World (American)	★★★½	Expensive	85	C
Cathay House (Chinese)	★★★	Moderate	84	C

†No profile

■ More Recommendations ■

The Best Bagels

Bonjour Bagels   2600 West Sahara (across from Palace Station) 220-7887
Excellent bagels and muffins baked fresh hourly.

Bagel Oasis   9134 West Sahara Avenue 363-0811
The best bagels in town, New York–style; baked fresh daily; large selection.

Harrie's Bagelmania   855 East Twain Avenue (at Swenson) 369-3322
Baked on the premises; garlic and onion among the choices.

The Best Bakeries

Great Buns   3270 East Tropicana Avenue (at Pecos) 898-0311
Commercial and retail; fragrant rosemary bread, sticky buns, and apple loaf are good choices. Regularly add new items.

Rancho Bakery   850 South Rancho Dr. (at Charleston) 870-6449
Ethnic specialties and party cakes; good selection of breads and fancy cookies.

Samuel's   2744 North Green Valley Parkway 454-0565
Full-service bakery. Bagels are chewy delights. Many Jewish-style specialties. Recently added gourmet coffee bean selection.

The Best Brewpubs

Barley's Casino and Brewing Company   4500 East Sunset Road, Suite 30, Henderson 458-2739
Reminiscent of old Las Vegas, Barley's features a small casino, attractive decor, and comfort foods galore.

Gordon Biersch Brewpub
1303 West Sunset Road, Henderson 312-2337
3987 Paradise Road (Hughes Center) 312-5247
These are upbeat brewery restaurants with contemporary menus and surprisingly good food.

Holy Cow!   2423 Las Vegas Boulevard, South 732-2697
A trilevel barn-styled bar with comical cow decor. They also feature 24-hour food service.

Monte Carlo Pub & Brewery   Monte Carlo 730-7777
Located adjacent to the pool area in a faux-warehouse setting, this new

brewpub offers six different beers and affordable food options. The beer is brewed right on the premises. Eighteen different pizzas are available, as well as sandwiches, pastas, and more.

Triple Seven Brewpub   200 North Main Street (Main Street Station) 387-1896
Late-night happy hour with bargain brews and food specials. Open 24 hours.

The Best Burgers

Kilroy's   1021 South Buffalo Dr. (at West Charleston) 363-4933
Half-pound burgers, choice of 15 toppings.

Lone Star
   1290 East Flamingo Road 893-0348
   1611 South Decatur Boulevard 259-0105
Cheese, Bubba, Texas, Mexi, or Willie half-pounders on a toasted onion bun.

Champagne Cafe   3557 South Maryland Parkway 737-1699
Classic half-pounder with creative toppings.

Sneakers   2250 East Tropicana Avenue (at Eastern) 798-0272
Enjoy a hefty burger and watch your favorite sports on TV.

Tommy's Hamburgers   2635 East Tropicana Avenue 458-2533
Good eat-in or carry-out burgers.

Fog City Diner   325 Hughes Center Drive 737-0200
Large, hand-crafted burger on a delicious bun.

The Best Delis

Celebrity Deli   4055 South Maryland Parkway (at Flamingo) 733-7827
Full-service New York–style deli.

Max C's   603 Las Vegas Boulevard, South 382-6292
The owner dispenses advice, philosophy, and Philadelphia-style sky-high sandwiches.

Siena Deli   2250 East Tropicana Avenue (at Eastern) 736-8424
Italian spoken here: everything Italian and homemade. Excellent bread baked fresh every morning. Siena bakes bread for many of the area's Italian restaurants. Local favorite for Italian grocery items.

Stage Deli   The Forum Shops at Caesars 893-4045
Las Vegas branch of New York's famous pastrami palace; enormous menu
runs gamut of Jewish specialties, including triple-decker sandwiches
named for celebrities, and 26 desserts. Open wide—the sandwiches are
skyscrapers.

Samuel's Deli   2744 North Green Valley Parkway, Henderson
454-0565
Full-service deli, bakery, and restaurant. Excellent breads, bagels, and
smoked fish.

The Best Espresso & Dessert

Café Nicolle   4760 West Sahara Avenue (at Decatur) 870-7675
Sidewalk café west; cooling mist in summer.

Coffee Pub   2800 West Sahara Avenue 367-1913
Great breakfast and lunch location, imaginative menu.

Java Centrale   2295 North Green Valley Parkway 434-3112
Soups, sandwiches, chocolate-raspberry-bash pie, English scones.

Jitters Gourmet Coffee
2457 East Tropicana Avenue (at Eastern) 898-0056
8441 West Lake Mead Boulevard (Summerlin location) 256-1902
Many varieties of coffees; homemade muffins; sandwiches, brownies,
truffles. Popular local hangout.

La Piazza   Caesars Palace 731-7110
Caesars's bakers create pies, cakes, and cookies to eat in or take out.

Spago   The Forum Shops at Caesars 369-6300
Wolfgang Puck's pastry chef creates imaginative and sinful creations.
Available all day in café only.

Starbucks Coffee Houses   Many area locations.

The Best Oyster & Clam Bars

Buzios   Rio 252-7697
Oyster stews, cioppino, shellfish, and pan roasts. Table service or oyster
bar.

The Best Pizza

Bootlegger   5025 South Eastern Avenue (at Tropicana) 736-4939 or
736-8661 (laugh line)
Great selection; crispy, tender, homemade crust.

California Pizza Kitchen
Mirage 791-7111
Golden Nugget 385-7111
Trendy—even offers low-cal versions without cheese. No take-out service.

Metro Pizza
4001 South Decatur Boulevard (at Flamingo) 362-7896
3870 East Flamingo Road (at Sandhill) 458-4769
2250 East Tropicana Avenue (at Eastern) 736-1955
Fast service, generous with the cheese. Try the Old New York with thick-sliced mozzarella, plum tomatoes, and basil. Thick Ragu-style tomato sauce topping.

Spago   The Forum Shops at Caesars 369-6300
Wolfgang Puck's regular specials include spicy shrimp, duck sausage, and smoked salmon with dill cream and golden caviar. Other toppings change frequently.

Venetian   3713 West Sahara Avenue 876-4190
Old-time Las Vegas favorite; pizza with greens and olive oil (no cheese) is a popular item.

The Best Soup & Salad Bars

Paradise Garden Cafe   Flamingo Hilton 733-3111
A magnificent display at lunch; a large choice of seafood added at dinner.

Souper Salad
2059 North Rainbow 631-2604
4022 South Maryland Parkway 792-8555
4712 West Sahara Avenue 870-1444
Moderate prices, many combinations, shiny clean, and inexpensive.

Restaurants with a View

Voodoo   Rio Hotel and Casino 252-5777
At the top of the new Rio tower, Voodoo offers the mystique of New Orleans, a complete view of the city, Cajun/Creole cooking, and an $18.95 seafood buffet for lunch and dinner.

ALAN ALBERTS

			QUALITY
Steak/Lobster	★★★★	Expensive	89
			VALUE
			C+

Epicenter Plaza, North of the MGM Grand
  740-4421   Strip Zone I

Customers: Tourists, locals
Reservations: Suggested
When to go: Any time
Entree range: $15–market price
Payment: VISA, MC, AMEX, DC, CB,
  JCB
Service rating: ★★★★★

Friendliness rating: ★★★★★
Parking: Lot
Bar: Full service
Wine selection: Excellent
Dress: Business attire, informal
Disabled access: Ground floor

Dinner: Every day, 5–11:30 p.m.

Setting & atmosphere: This self-named "vintage steakhouse" features beveled glass, fine wood paneling, and photo walls showcasing celebrities and stars of the glory days of Old Las Vegas. The dining room has comfortable, easy-to-get-into booths and expert, flattering lighting.

House specialties: Prime Angus steaks and jumbo lobsters; a flavorful culotte steak seldom found elsewhere; crab cakes; osso buco; a 26-ounce rib-eye; veal and lamb chops.

Other recommendations: Grilled salmon on garlic spinach; oysters Rockefeller; delectable desserts, especially the tiramisu.

Summary & comments: Tucked away in the corner of a strip mall, Alan Alberts is a pleasant surprise. Lobsters are fairly-priced—choose one from the live tank. Average weight is $2^{1}/_{2}$ pounds. Portions are generous. A meal could be made from a combination of appetizers.

AL DENTE

			QUALITY
Italian	★★★★	Moderate	90
			VALUE
			C

Bally's
  739-4656   Strip Zone I

Customers: Tourists, locals
Reservations: Important
When to go: Any time
Entree range: $12–30
Payment: VISA, MC, AMEX, DC, D
Service rating: ★★★★

Friendliness rating: ★★★★
Parking: Valet, hotel lot
Bar: Full service
Wine selection: Excellent
Dress: Informal
Disabled access: Ground floor

(al Dente)

Dinner: Thursday–Monday, 6–10:30 p.m.; Tuesday and Wednesday, closed.

Setting & atmosphere: Stylish, contemporary decor with bright, colorful appointments. The comfortable bar is a fine meeting place for drinks before or after dinner.

House specialties: Roast chicken on a bed of caramelized onions is a perennial favorite; pastas are freshly made, lightly sauced; al Dente's chef creates imaginative daily specials using seasonal foods; flavored olive oil in lieu of butter; thin-crusted, plate-size pizzas; tomato- and herb-topped bruschetta—the savory toast is addictive; salmon-filled tortellini. The tiramisu and the pear poached in red wine and honey, served in a stem balloon glass with vanilla ice cream and chocolate sauce, are sweet conclusions.

Summary & comments: Al Dente is a busy, busy restaurant. Reservations are a must, especially during conventions. If it is not too busy, the chef will honor requests for dishes not on the menu, but not on weekends.

ALTA VILLA

Italian	★★★½	Moderate	QUALITY 85
			VALUE A

Flamingo Hilton
733-3434   Strip Zone I

Customers: Tourists, locals
Reservations: Required
When to go: Any time
Entree range: $9.50–21.95
Payment: VISA, MC, AMEX, DC, D
Service rating: ★★★½
Friendliness rating: ★★★★
Parking: Self, valet

Bar: Full service
Wine selection: Small selection listed on label of wine bottle on table. Good selection of wine by the glass.
Dress: Casual
Disabled access: Ground floor

Dinner: Friday–Tuesday, 5:30–10:30 p.m.

Setting & atmosphere: Vine-covered piazza faces the main dining room and gives the illusion of al fresco dining. Many live plants and antique wine bottles; stone and wood decor.

House specialties: Minestrone soup served from a large copper kettle at the front of the room. Pizza oven in the room bakes the pies and the complimentary garlic bread served with all entrees. Pizza comes in two sizes and can be ordered as appetizer or main course. Variety of pastas and risottos; broiled filet mignon Alta Villa.

Summary & comments: Over-sized natural wood tables make for comfortable dining. There are no tablecloths in this room, just the warmth of the polished wood. The roomy woven leather chairs have a wicker look. Alta Villa's exclusive china pattern imitates the design of the Spanish tile on the walls. The strolling guitarist adds to the restaurant's charm.

ANDRE'S

Continental/French	★★★★½	Expensive	QUALITY 90
			VALUE D

401 South 6th Street
  385-5016   Downtown Zone 2

Monte Carlo Hotel
  798-7151   Strip Zone 1

Customers: Tourists, locals	Friendliness rating: ★★★½
Reservations: Necessary	Parking: Street, valet
When to go: Early or late	Bar: Full service
Entree range: $19.75–33.50	Wine selection: Excellent
Payment: VISA, MC, AMEX, DC	Dress: Sport coat, dressy
Service rating: ★★★★	Disabled access: Ramps

Dinner: Every day, 6–10 p.m.

Setting & atmosphere: Country French decor in a converted former residence in a historic part of the city.

House specialties: Menu changes with the seasons. Sea scallops with duck foie gras, black truffle, and port wine en papillote; marinated salmon tartare with cucumber salad; Maryland blue crab cakes with citrus beurre blanc, escargot garlic butter; rabbit loin with spinach fettuccini Dijon; pavé of veal sautéed with morel mushrooms; variety of unusual fresh fish with imaginative sauces; filet of pork tenderloin stuffed with sun-dried fruit and nuts, served with apricot sauce. Soufflés and pastries.

Other recommendations: Ask if you can tour Andre's extensive wine cellar; vintages date back to 1830. The daily specials, especially the fish.

Summary & comments: Owner-chef Andre Rochat is in the kitchen but makes frequent forays into the dining room to visit with guests. He honors special requests if given 24-hour notice. Spectacular winemakers' dinners (Thursday nights) several times a year. Ask to be put on the mailing list. Downtown location is closed the month of July.

Honors & awards: *Wine Spectator* Award of Excellence; *Travel/Holiday* magazine award for many years; Ambassador Award of Excellence through 1987 (discontinued); DiRoNA Award.

ANNA BELLA			
			QUALITY
Italian	★★★½	Inexpensive/Moderate	**89**
			VALUE
			A

3310 Sandhill Road at Desert Inn
  434-2537   Southeast Zone 5

Customers: Locals	Friendliness rating: ★★★★★
Reservations: Suggested on weekends	Parking: Shopping-center lot
When to go: Any time	Bar: Full service
Entree range: $7.95–21.95	Wine selection: Modest
Payment: VISA, MC, AMEX, DC	Dress: Casual
Service rating: ★★★★	Disabled access: Ground floor

Dinner: Tuesday–Sunday, 4:30–10:30 p.m.

Setting & atmosphere: A charming neighborhood restaurant with flower-bedecked booths, pink tablecloths, soft lighting, and a caring staff.

House specialties: The hot panini (Italian sandwiches) served at lunchtime; homemade ravioli filled with wild mushrooms (not on the menu, but frequently available); fettuccine with fresh salmon in vodka sauce; cannelloni alla Romano; pollo alla Tony; osso buco; capellini gamberi puglia.

Other recommendations: The flavorful homemade soups; a generous bowl or a green salad comes with entrees. Veal marsala; linguini with clams in a red or white sauce (try the pink sauce made from a mix of both); the classic angelhair pasta with fresh tomato sauce, garlic, basil, and olive oil.

Summary & comments: Anna Bella is a real find. The owners are always there, the service is friendly and caring, and the food is affordable for even modest budgets. Daily specials allow the chef to offer seasonal seafood and higher-end Italian dishes. Service can be slow at times, but be patient. The wait staff is small, and most of the delicious food is cooked to order.

ANTONIO'S

			QUALITY
Italian	★★★★	Moderate/Expensive	**90**
			VALUE
			B

Rio, 3700 West Flamingo Road
  252-7777   Strip Zone I

Customers: Locals, tourists
Reservations: Suggested
When to go: Any time
Entree range: $17–48
Payment: VISA, MC, AMEX, D, DC
Service rating: ★★★★★
Friendliness rating: ★★★★★

Parking: Lot, valet, garage
Bar: Full service
Wine selection: Excellent
Dress: Informal, slacks and collared
  shirts for men
Disabled access: Through casino

Dinner: Every day, 5–11 p.m.

Setting & atmosphere: Marble accents, fresh flowers, elegant table appointments, and expert lighting highlight the comfortable dining room; domed ceiling replicates the sky.

House specialties: The chef's appetizer of the day; vitello al marsala, veal scallops with porcini mushrooms and marsala wine, a superior version of the classic dish; osso buco, the traditional braised veal shank, is presented à la the Rio chef. Daily specials such as oven-roasted pork loin with apricot port wine demi-glacé.

Other recommendations: Lobster sautéed with delicate lobster sauce over capellini; pollo all'aglio e rosmarino. There's a small patio outside with its own moderately priced menu of soups, salads, and a dozen pastas. Cioppino. Tiramisu, the classic mascarpone cheese–based dessert.

Entertainment & amenities: Enjoy drinks and Italian coffees before or after dinner in the comfortable lounge.

Summary & comments: There are nice touches at Antonio's. A fruity olive oil for dunking is offered instead of butter—the imported breadsticks are habit-forming; a complimentary liqueur is offered "to thank you for dining at Antonio's." A small private dining room for up to 12 is available. This attractive restaurant is a local favorite.

BACCHANAL

			QUALITY
Roman banquet	★★★★	Expensive	**94**
			VALUE
			B

Caesars Palace
731-7731   Strip Zone 1

Customers: Tourists, a few locals

Reservations: Required, but house guests come first

When to go: Weekdays

Entree range: Fixed price, $69.50 per person (plus tax and gratuity)

Payment: VISA, MC, AMEX, DC, CB, D

Service rating: ★★★★★

Friendliness rating: ★★★★

Parking: Indoor garage, valet

Bar: Full service

Wine selection: Included with dinner

Dress: Casual (no jeans or tennis shoes)

Disabled access: Via kitchen

Dinner: Tuesday–Friday, seatings at 6–6:30 p.m. and 9–9:30 p.m.; Saturday, 5:30–6 p.m. and 8:30–9 p.m.; Sunday and Monday, closed.

Setting & atmosphere: Roman garden with fountains. The sound system creates such special effects as thunder and lightning, and Zeus and Venus speaking from above. Wait staff in Roman costume, wine servers in goddess gowns.

House specialties: Seven-course fixed-price dinner; entree choices include steaks, chops, seafood, and veal. Menu changes with the seasons.

Entertainment & amenities: Belly dancers perform by the pool. Caesar and Cleopatra, as well as other notables from the Roman past, make an appearance. Wine goddesses not only pour wine but also provide neck massages to male diners at their bidding. No such service, as yet, provided for females.

Summary & comments: Be aware that à la carte appetizers such as Beluga caviar or imported smoked salmon can add substantially to your check. More for fun than food, but the food is surprisingly good.

Honors & awards: *Travel/Holiday* award eight years; East-West Network four-star award; *Esquire, Food Times* magazine awards.

BARLEY'S

			QUALITY
Brewpub	★★★	Inexpensive	**86**

	VALUE
	A

Town Center, 4500 East Sunset, Green Valley
  458-2739   Southeast Zone 5

Customers: Locals, tourists
Reservations: No
When to go: Any time
Entree range: $5.95–18.95
Payment: VISA, MC, AMEX, DC, D
Service rating: ★★★½

Friendliness rating: ★★★★★
Parking: Town Center lot
Bar: Full service
Wine selection: Fair
Dress: Casual
Disabled access: Ramp, ground floor

Open: *Brewer's Cafe:* 24 hours, breakfast served 7–11 a.m.;
Pizza Parlor: Sunday–Thursday, 11 a.m.–11 p.m.;
Bar menu: 24 hours, breakfast served 11 p.m.–7 a.m.

Setting & atmosphere: Housed in the trendy Town Center in upscale Green Valley, Barley's is reminiscent of Old Las Vegas. With a small casino as the anchor, Barley's offers popular foods at modest prices. The brewery is the high point of the casino with gleaming stainless steel tanks. You can enter directly into the Brewer's Cafe without going into the casino. Dine on the outdoor patio facing one of the center's most popular attractions, the interactive fountain—it's wonderful entertainment. The decor features an open ceiling, wood floors, and attractive, comfortable seating.

House specialties: Comfort foods galore. Breakfast potato patties (home fries) filled with everything from eggs to green chiles—diner's choice; grilled vegetable lasagna in a rich marinara sauce; wood-roasted chicken breast; charbroiled, honey-glazed pork chops; man-sized sandwiches with great steak fries; large soft pretzels with lager mustard and pepper Jack cheese sauce; Barley's barley soup; smoked barbecued brisket sandwich in the bar.

Summary & comments: Generous amounts of food for the money. Entrees include endless trips to the small soup and salad bar; it costs an additional $2.95 with sandwiches and other items. The Pizza Parlor also serves sausage and meatball heros. Barley's regularly runs out of the popular brews, so plans are under way to increase the capacity for brewing the frothy drink. Pastas are sometimes overcooked; ask for them al dente. On Thursdays, this casual eatery dons tablecloths and candlelight. Even the servers dress up for this weekly bit of gastronomy. Gourmet specials change weekly. Dinner prices are moderate.

BERTOLINI'S

			QUALITY
Italian	★★★½	Moderate	**88**
			VALUE
			B

The Forum Shops at Caesars
735-4663   Strip Zone I

Customers: Tourists, locals
Reservations: Not accepted
When to go: Always busy, especially
  Friday and Saturday evenings
Entree range: $9.95–19.95
Payment: VISA, MC, AMEX, DC, JCB
Service rating: ★★★

Friendliness rating: ★★★★
Parking: Hotel garage, valet
Bar: Full service
Wine selection: Good
Dress: Informal, casual
Disabled access: Ground floor

Lunch & dinner: Sunday–Thursday, 11 a.m.–midnight;
Friday–Saturday, 11 a.m.–1 a.m.

Setting & atmosphere: The beautifully decorated interior of the restaurant offers peaceful respite from the lively action of the dining patio. A colorful mural decorates one wall. There is a display of antipasto, a mesquite-fired pizza oven, an open kitchen, and a gelateria. Butcher paper–covered tables and crayons for doodling.

House specialties: Focaccia and pizza made in a wood-burning oven. Carpaccio di manza; insalata di pollo con pasta; four-cheese pizza with roasted tomatoes and pesto; rigatoni with sausage ragout, tomato sauce, and mozzarella; angelhair pomodoro. Homemade ice cream as well as cakes, espresso, and cappuccino in the gelateria.

Other recommendations: Salad with homemade mozzarella, tomatoes, and basil oil; prosciutto and smoked mozzarella with fig jam crostini and sun-dried tomato vinaigrette; roasted garlic, fresh spinach, béchamel, and mozzarella pizza; lasagna. Any of the new dishes, especially crusted chicken Romano with gorgonzola sauce and the fazzoletto con funghi—a "handkerchief" of pasta enfolding spinach and ricotta cheese in a delicate wild mushroom sauce. Cappuccino crème brûlée.

Summary & comments: The Sidewalk Cafe outside Bertolini's overlooks the Forum's bustling scene. Table turnover is good, but even with a busy day's wait, time goes quickly.

BILLY BOB'S STEAKHOUSE & SALOON

| Steak | ★★★ | Moderate | QUALITY 88 |
| | | | VALUE A |

Sam's Town, Boulder Highway
456-7777   Southeast Zone 5

Customers: Locals, tourists
Reservations: Suggested
When to go: Any time
Entree range: $15.95–52
Payment: VISA, MC, AMEX, DC, D
Service rating: ★★★★

Friendliness rating: ★★★★
Parking: Valet, lot, garage
Bar: Full service
Wine selection: Good
Dress: Come as you are
Disabled access: Through casino

Dinner: Every day, 4:30–10 p.m.

Setting & atmosphere: Stroll through the lovely climate-controlled park to Billy Bob's. The critters that chirp and peep are lifelike robotics; the trees and lush foliage are real. Mosey into the Western-themed Billy Bob's for a taste of the Old West and some mighty fine grub.

House specialties: Beef is king at Billy Bob's: steaks, prime rib, and barbecued brisket. The 28-ounce rib-eye is a huge favorite. Entree prices include soup or salad and a selection from the potato bar. One of the few places to offer that macho specialty, Rocky Mountain Oysters. "Western Roundup," for two or more, includes pork ribs, barbecued chicken and brisket, seafood kabob, sautéed mushrooms, cole slaw, baked beans, salad, and a choice of potato. Desserts serve four to six. The Grand Canyon chocolate cake could serve a small army. The foot-long eclair is a dessert lover's fantasy.

Summary & comments: Prepare to eat as if you were heading out for a day on the range. The setting and the prices make Billy Bob's a popular choice. At prime times, even with a reservation, there might be a wait. Have a drink in the saloon.

BINION'S RANCH STEAKHOUSE

| Steak | ★★★ | Moderate | QUALITY 82 |
| | | | VALUE B |

Binion's Horseshoe Hotel
382-1600   Downtown Zone 2

Customers: Locals, tourists
Reservations: Required
When to go: Avoid late-night crowds
  for steak special

Entree range: $24–40
Payment: VISA, MC, AMEX, DC, CB, D
Service rating: ★★★★

(Binion's Ranch Steakhouse)

Friendliness rating: ★★★★   Wine selection: Good
Parking: Garage, valet   Dress: Casual
Bar: Full service   Disabled access: Elevator

Dinner: Every day, 6–11 p.m.

Setting & atmosphere: Western decor, friendly service, and large portions. Ten-gallon hats, fancy boots, and Levis are very much in evidence.

House specialties: Prime rib roasted in rock salt; 20-ounce porterhouse. Entrees are accompanied by soup or salad and ample servings of rice pilaf or baked potato.

Other recommendations: Prime New York steak; half chicken with honey Dijon sauce; broiled spring lamb chop.

Entertainment & amenities: Dramatic panoramic view from top floor of hotel.

Summary & comments: The late Benny Binion believed in good food and large portions. The restaurant maintains his philosophy. One of the best buys in town.

BISTRO			
			QUALITY
Continental	★★★★	Expensive	**94**
			VALUE
			C

The Mirage
791-7111   Strip Zone 1

Customers: Tourists   Friendliness rating: ★★★★
Reservations: Required; high rollers and hotel guests get preference   Parking: Free covered parking garage, valet
When to go: Caters to tourists   Bar: Full service
Entree range: $24–36   Wine selection: Very good
Payment: VISA, MC, AMEX, DC, D   Dress: Informal
Service rating: ★★★★★   Disabled access: Ground floor

Dinner: Every day, 5:30–11 p.m.

Setting & atmosphere: Decor reflects the times of the French Impressionists; colorful and warm, beautiful art, plants, and flowers.

House specialties: House-baked lavosh and breadsticks served with the colorful menus. Escargot baked in garlic, shallots, and white wine; rack of lamb roasted with English mustard and honey and encrusted with pecans; prawns St. Tropez. Crème brûlée; warm chocolate cake pudding.

Other recommendations: Venison tenderloin chasseur; breast of duck au poivre; grilled salmon Monte Carlo.

Summary & comments: This lively boîte, bistro in name only, is located on a cobblestone street in the center of the hotel. The elegant dishes and service belie the earthy appellation, so don't expect the classic bistro dishes, just fine food with style.

BISTRO LE MONTRACHET

Contemporary French ★★★★★ Moderate/Expensive		**QUALITY**	**98**
		VALUE	**C**

Las Vegas Hilton
   732-5111   Strip Zone 1

Customers: Tourists, some locals
Reservations: Recommended
When to go: Nonconvention times
Entree range: Bistro, $14–29;
   dining room, $23.50–35
Payment: VISA, MC, AMEX, DC, CB, D
Service rating: ★★★★★

Friendliness rating: ★★★★½
Parking: Lot, valet, garage
Bar: Full service
Wine selection: Excellent
Dress: Bistro, casual; dining room,
   sport coat, dressy
Disabled access: Ramp access

Dinner: *Bistro,* 5–10:30 p.m.; *dining room,* 6–10:30 p.m. (closes on variable nights during low-occupancy times; call ahead)

Setting & atmosphere: Bistro Le Montrachet combines the relaxed ambiance of a contemporary bistro with the elegance of a fine dining room. The informal bistro is filled with colorful art and decorative touches; enter Le Montrachet through the glass-enclosed wine cellar. Soft lights, elegant appointments, and luxurious seating are the hallmarks of this fine restaurant.

House specialties: The bistro features six entrees, which change frequently. A recent menu offered a tower of grilled, rare Ahi tuna with a beautifully dressed salad of greens, artichoke hearts, tomatoes, and olives; and sautéed scallops layered with fresh spinach and waffled potatoes—a delicious combination. Presentation is gorgeous. A separate dessert menu offers exquisite desserts created by award-winning pastry chef Stanton Ho. The Sun, the Moon, and the Stars is a work of art. Le Montrachet is known for the quality of the venison; the selection of fresh fish; the roast guinea hen served with a tart of potatoes, leeks, and truffles; and the delicate foie gras appetizer. Equally renowned is the classic lobster bisque.

(Bistro Le Montrachet)

Summary & comments: The addition of the bistro to the fine dining has given new life to this formerly formal dining room. Each dish is still a work of art, but the new surroundings are lighter and more lively.

BOOTLEGGER			

Italian	★★★½	Moderate	QUALITY 89
			VALUE A

5025 South Eastern Avenue at Tropicana
  736-4939 or 736-8661 (laugh line)   Southeast Zone 5

Customers: Locals, some tourists	**Friendliness rating:** ★★★★★
Reservations: Accepted	**Parking:** Shopping-center lot
When to go: Any time	**Bar:** Full service
Entree range: $7.95–42	**Wine selection:** Large
Payment: VISA, MC, AMEX, DC, D	**Dress:** Informal
Service rating: ★★★★	**Disabled access:** Ground floor

Lunch: Tuesday–Saturday, 11:30 a.m.–3:30 p.m.; Sunday and Monday, closed.
Dinner: Tuesday–Saturday, 11:30 a.m.–10 p.m.; Sunday, 3:30–9 p.m.; Monday, closed.

Setting & atmosphere: Turn-of-the-century decor, Italian style. Wonderful ancestral portraits decorate the walls. The full bar overlooks an informal dining room with fireplace. Two additional dining rooms offer comfortable banquettes.

House specialties: Complimentary homemade appetizer panettis (small bread puffs) tossed with garlic, oregano, and oil, served with tomato-basil sauce. Homemade breads. Seafood diavolo; veal saltimbocca à la Blackie; and veal Lorraine with fresh mushrooms in a cream and wine sauce, named for the owners. Varied pasta menu; vegetarian menu; pizzas; and calzones. Biscuit tortoni and tartufo.

Other recommendations: The seafood dishes are very good. The restaurant is a participant in the national Project Lean program and offers a good selection of tasty reduced-fat, lower-calorie pasta dishes such as angelhair pomodoro and linguini with clam, shrimp, or calamari sauce.

Summary & comments: One of the oldest Italian restaurants in town, it is still run by chef Maria Perri and her family. Hearty portions and consistent quality make the Bootlegger a popular local dining spot.

THE BROILER

Steak/Seafood	★★★½	Moderate	QUALITY **89**
			VALUE **A**

Boulder Station, Boulder Highway and Desert Inn Road
    432-7777   Southeast Zone 5

Customers: Locals, tourists	Friendliness rating: ★★★★★
Reservations: Suggested	Parking: Valet, lot
When to go: Any time	Bar: Full service
Entree range: $12.95–26.95	Wine selection: Fair
Payment: VISA, MC, AMEX, DC, D	Dress: Casual
Service rating: ★★★★	Disabled access: Through casino

Brunch: Sunday, 10 a.m.–2:30 p.m.
Dinner: Monday–Saturday, 5–10:30 p.m.; Sunday, 5–9 p.m.

Setting & atmosphere: Comfortable, relaxed dining room with greenery, an exhibition kitchen, and a handsome soup and salad bar. Desert decor with style. A refrigerated showcase at the entrance displays the day's fresh fish and meat selection.

House specialties: Fresh seafood, steaks, and prime rib. All entrees include the soup and salad bar, a choice of potatoes or rice, and vegetable or cole slaw. Fish selections are mesquite-grilled or broiled, baked, or sautéed. Most earn the American Heart Association heart symbol for being low cholesterol. Nonfat dressings and sour cream are available, too. Chicken, marinated in herbs and garlic, cooked on the rotisserie. Sunday brunch is a fine value. Included for $13.95 are the soup and salad bar, the seafood bar, the dessert bar, and table service for the entrees.

Summary & comments: Reservations should be made for dinner and Sunday brunch.

BROWN DERBY

American	★★★★	Moderate/Expensive	QUALITY **87**
			VALUE **C**

MGM Grand
    891-7300   Strip Zone 1

Customers: Tourists, locals	Payment: VISA, MC, AMEX, DC, CB,
Reservations: Requested	JCB, D
When to go: Any time except con-	Service rating: ★★★★★
certs or boxing matches	Friendliness rating: ★★★★★
Entree range: $25–50	Parking: Valet, garage

(Brown Derby)

Bar: Full service
Wine selection: Very good

Dress: Casual
Disabled access: Ground floor

Dinner: Every day, 5:30–10:30 p.m.

Setting & atmosphere: A reincarnation of the original Brown Derby, a Hollywood icon of the elite of filmdom since the 1920s. MGM Grand bought the name, photographs, artifacts, and recipes from the owner, who was the consultant for the restaurant. There's a good bit of nostalgia and many memories of Hollywood, in the days when it was HOLLYWOOD and the only things known about a star's private life were the stories concocted by the studio flacks.

House specialties: The Brown Derby mixed grill; the original Cobb salad; Mr. Derby beef Wellington; chateaubriand or rack of lamb for two; Montana buffalo sirloin steak; fennel-crusted sea bass.

Other recommendations: Brown Derby–style Caesar salad; lump crab meat cakes; the iced seafood assortment appetizer; "Meet Me at the Derby" ice cream cake; the old-fashioned baked apple dumpling redolent with cinnamon and brown sugar.

Summary & comments: Sit in the Oscar room with its marvelous photographs and feel like a star. Most of the Brown Derby recipes have been adapted well. The acclaimed grapefruit cake still needs work, but this throwback to the Hollywood that was is a fine dining choice.

BUCCANEER BAY CLUB

Continental	★★★★½	Moderate	QUALITY
			96

	VALUE
Treasure Island	**B**

894-7111   Strip Zone 1

Customers: Tourists, locals; hotel guests get preference
Reservations: Accepted 7 days in advance
When to go: Avoid peak hours
Entree range: $16.95–26.50, higher for lobster
Payment: VISA, MC, AMEX, DC, JCB, D

Service rating: ★★★★
Friendliness rating: ★★★★★
Parking: Garage, valet
Bar: Full service
Wine selection: Small, but good
Dress: Sport jacket, informal
Disabled access: Elevator

(Buccaneer Bay Club)

Dinner: Every day, 5–10:30 p.m.

Setting & atmosphere: Exotic decor and accessories gathered from all parts of the world. Restaurant overlooks the Pirates Village and Buccaneer Bay, scene of the "fight to the finish" sea battles between the British ship *Britannia* and the pirates' *Hispaniola*. It's a fierce, colorful encounter with dialogue to match.

House specialties: Pyramid of fresh salmon fillets atop a mound of mashed potatoes and fresh vegetables; Buccaneer clams casino; oysters (topped with smoked salmon and hollandaise); lobster bisque under a puff-pastry dome. Bay Club combination—filet mignon au poivre, breast of chicken Oscar. Pirate's Plunder—chocolate treasure chest filled with coconut rum mousse, white chocolate treasure map, and devil's rock cake. Menu changes seasonally.

Other recommendations: Smoked salmon Napoleon; lobster ravioli; escargot in brioche; osso buco; veal Florentine; prime rib; Chilean sea bass with fruit salsa. Chocolate Frigate—pair of chocolate ships filled with frozen chocolate and walnut parfaits topped with coconut cookie sails.

Summary & comments: The menu is geared to the pirate theme. The rousing sea battle takes place every hour and a half from 4 to 11:30 p.m. Diners experience the fun without the din and smoke. Request a window table for best view. Who wins the battle? It's a surprise, mateys!

BURGUNDY ROOM

Continental	★★★½	Moderate/Expensive	QUALITY
			85
			VALUE
			B

Lady Luck Hotel
  477-3000   Downtown Zone 2

Customers: Locals, tourists
Reservations: Suggested
When to go: Any time
Entree range: $14.95–44.95
  (chateaubriand for two)
Payment: VISA, MC, AMEX, DC, CB, D
Service rating: ★★★★

Friendliness rating: ★★★★★
Parking: Valet, garage, and lot
Bar: Full service
Wine selection: Good
Dress: Informal
Disabled access: Ground floor

Dinner: Every day, 5–10:30 p.m.

Setting & atmosphere: Plush and intimate; sculptures add to the decor of this attractive dining room.

(Burgundy Room)

House specialties: Filet of beef Wellington; veal Oscar; double-cut lamb chops. Chateaubriand and rack of lamb for two carved tableside. Porterhouse. Excellent prime rib.

Other recommendations: Salmon Monte Carlo; supreme of chicken angelo; veal picante; flaming desserts.

Summary & comments: A modestly priced gourmet room with a good selection of entrees and fine service in downtown Las Vegas. Overflow diners are seated in the adjacent dining room. The service and food are the same.

BUZIOS		

Seafood ★★★★	Moderate/Expensive	**QUALITY** 93
Rio		**VALUE** A
252-7697 Strip Zone I		

Customers: Locals, tourists	**Friendliness rating:** ★★★★
Reservations: Accepted for dinner	**Parking:** Valet, lot, covered garage
When to go: Any time	**Bar:** Full service
Entree range: $10–52	**Wine selection:** Very good
Payment: VISA, MC, AMEX, DC, D	**Dress:** Casual
Service rating: ★★★★	**Disabled access:** Through casino

Lunch & Dinner: Every day, 11 a.m.–11 p.m.

Setting & atmosphere: This popular seafood restaurant recently doubled in size and has a smashing new entrance. The new section has been cleverly added so that the original ambiance is intact. The decor includes massive alabaster chandeliers and flowering plants suspended from the canvastented ceiling. Walls of glass allow a beautiful view of the sandy beach and pool. A comfortable counter à la Grand Central Station attracts diners who like to watch the seafood being prepared in the individual high-pressure steam kettles. An exhibition kitchen provides a view of the chefs at work.

House specialties: Buzios offers a selection of fresh oysters from Canada, Maine, and Washington State; clams; shrimp; and many hot seafood appetizers. Fish soups and stews such as bouillabaisse and cioppino; huge bowls filled with a savory assortment of denizens of the deep. Rockefeller-style prawns, clams, or oysters; lobsters from Japan, Finland, Great Britain, Germany, Iceland, and the Netherlands; a selection of fresh fish flown in daily. The irresistible Rio breads, baked in their own bakery in a European open-hearth oven, accompany all dishes. They're wonderful when used to mop up the broth from the fish soups and stews. Endless baskets are provided.

Other recommendations: Seafood salads and Louis; pastas with seafood; the chicken and shrimp combination glazed with a tarragon and honey sauce; any preparation with Chilean sea bass.

Summary & comments: Buzios, named for a small Portuguese fishing village, is the Rio's version. All entrees include a choice of salad or soup. On weekends and during conventions, even with reservations, there is sometimes a short wait for a table. Don't fret. For seafood aficionados Buzios is worth a brief delay.

CAFÉ MILANO

Italian	★★★	Moderate	QUALITY
			84

	VALUE
	C

3900 Paradise Road
732-2777   Strip Zone I

Customers: Locals, conventioneers	Friendliness rating: ★★★★
Reservations: Suggested	Parking: Shopping-center lot
When to go: Any time	Bar: Wine and beer only
Entree range: $9.75–21.95	Wine selection: Limited
Payment: VISA, MC, AMEX, DC, D	Dress: Informal
Service rating: ★★★	Disabled access: Ground floor

Lunch: Monday–Friday, 11 a.m.–3 p.m.
Dinner: Monday–Saturday, 5–10 p.m.; Sunday, closed, except during large conventions.

Setting & atmosphere: Café Milano's walls are covered with original art painted by the owner. The small storefront restaurant is smartly done in black and white. A large refrigerated case displays antipasti and desserts flown in from Italy.

House specialties: Nightly specials; penne arrabbiata or Milano; veal alla Siciliana with eggplant, mozzarella, and marinara sauce; orange roughy Calabrese or Fiorentina; scampi. Any of the lunch specials or Italian sandwiches. Pastas are prepared al dente.

Summary & comments: Italian spoken by most of the staff. Special requests are honored with advance notice.

CAFÉ NICOLLE

Continental	★★★½	Moderate	QUALITY
			88

			VALUE
4760 West Sahara Avenue			**B**

870-7675   Southwest Zone 3

Customers: Locals	**Friendliness rating:** ★★★★
Reservations: Strongly suggested	**Parking:** Shopping-center lot
When to go: Any time	**Bar:** Full service
Entree range: $6.95–21.95	**Wine selection:** Excellent
Payment: VISA, MC, AMEX	**Dress:** Informal, casual
Service rating: ★★★★	**Disabled access:** Ground floor

Lunch & dinner: Monday–Saturday, 11 a.m.–11 p.m.; Sunday, closed.

Setting & atmosphere: Restaurant and European-style outdoor café with cooling overhead mist in summer and heat lamps in winter. Bright, cheerful interior on two levels, with cozy corners for intimate dining.

House specialties: Spinach pie; variety of egg dishes; calamari appetizer; osso buco with wine sauce; blue crab cakes; Atlantic salmon cakes. Scallops Nicolle baked with white wine, paprika, and light butter sauce; lamb chops à la grecque; filet mignon with béarnaise sauce. Same menu all day and evening, plus lunch and dinner specials on blackboard.

Other recommendations: Selection of salads including garlicky Caesar with garlic bread. Selection of pastas such as penne arrabbiata. Variety of fresh seafood. Spicy veal stew with fettuccini; chicken française; daily specials. Entree and dessert crêpes; tiramisu; pecan pie. Cappuccino; espresso; caffe latte.

Entertainment & amenities: Live entertainment nightly except Sunday in the bar-lounge area.

Summary & comments: Owner Manny Messologitis was one of the founders of Café Michelle and has included a number of Café Michelle dishes such as quiches and crêpes on his new menu. Strong local following.

CARLUCCIO'S TIVOLI GARDENS

			QUALITY
Southern Italian	★★½	Moderate	**78**

VALUE
A

1775 East Tropicana Avenue
   795-3236   Southeast Zone 5

Customers: Locals, some tourists
Reservations: Not taken
  (except for parties of 8 or more)
When to go: Any time
Entree range: $6.95–16
Payment: VISA, MC, AMEX
Service rating: ★★★★

Friendliness rating: ★★★★
Parking: Large lot
Bar: Full service
Wine selection: Good
Dress: Informal, casual
Disabled access: Ramps

Dinner: Tuesday–Sunday, 4:30–10 p.m.; Monday, closed.

Setting & atmosphere: The owners acquired the glittering restaurant from the Liberace estate. The decor is intact, but the excitement of Liberace's constant presence and culinary expertise, alas, is no more.

House specialties: Crab-stuffed shrimp; seafood diablo; chicken Florentine. Hearty basket of garlic bread.

Other recommendations: Veal Milanese; chicken angelo; zuppa di clams; linguini with red or white clam sauce.

Entertainment & amenities: Take time to explore the unique restaurant decor, as well as the museum next door, and see memorabilia from Liberace's career.

Summary & comments: A popular family restaurant featuring hearty portions and moderate prices. Always busy; has a strong local following.

CATHAY HOUSE

			QUALITY
Cantonese/Dim Sum	★★★	Moderate	**84**

VALUE
C

5300 Spring Mountain Road
   876-3838   Southwest Zone 3

Customers: Locals, Asian community
Reservations: Suggested
When to go: Late lunch
Entree range: $7–26
Payment: VISA, MC, AMEX, DC, D
Service rating: ★★★

Friendliness rating: ★★★
Parking: Large lot
Bar: Full service
Wine selection: Good
Dress: Casual
Disabled access: Ground floor

(Cathay House)

Lunch: Every day, 11 a.m.–2:30 p.m.
Dinner: Every day, 3–10:30 p.m.

Setting & atmosphere: Large picture windows overlook the Strip. Circular seating in the center is packed with dim sum diners for lunch.

House specialties: Sautéed crystal shrimp; assorted meats in a crisp basket; seafood worbar; orange-flavored beef; strawberry chicken; Peking duck.

Other recommendations: Moo shu shrimp; scallops with cashew nuts; garlic chicken; Szechuan shredded pork; braised shark's fin soup. Live Maine lobster at market price. Luncheon specials Monday through Friday from 11 a.m. to 2:30 p.m.

Entertainment & amenities: Karaoke for banquets. Request a table with a view.

Summary & comments: A good selection of dim sum from traditional carts. You don't have to be Asian to dine at Cathay House, but if it's busy you'll get better service if you are. Tasty food does not excuse the sometimes brusque service. Request a window booth at night—the view is spectacular.

CHANG'S

Chinese/Dim Sum	★★★½	Moderate	QUALITY 88
			VALUE B

Gold Key Shopping Center, Strip and Convention Center Drive
   731-3388   Strip Zone 1

Bally's
   739-4656   Strip Zone 1

Customers: Locals, tourists
Reservations: Suggested
When to go: Any time
Entree range: $7.95–36
Payment: VISA, MC, AMEX
Service rating: ★★★★

Friendliness rating: ★★★★★
Parking: Shopping-center lot
Bar: Full service
Wine selection: Fair
Dress: Casual
Disabled access: Ground floor

Lunch: Monday–Friday (except holidays), 11 a.m.–3 p.m.
Full menu: Every day, 10 a.m.–2 a.m.
Dim Sum: Every day, 10 a.m.–3 p.m.

(Chang's)

Setting & atmosphere: Chang's is filled with Chinese art and artifacts, artistic sand-blasted glass, live plants, comfortable booths, and many lazy Susan tables for large parties.

House specialties: Excellent assortment of dim sum, including the seldom-seen-here Chinese cruller. The sizable dim sum menu offers items not available elsewhere such as the large, steamed shark's fin dumpling served in a bowl. Bite into it over the bowl, for the delicious dumpling contains not only bits of seafood and mushrooms, but also shark's fin soup. New dumplings include sweet rice enclosed in a steamed bun and piquant Chinese sausage spiral-wrapped in flaky pastry. Peking-style pork cutlet (called Mandarin here); jumbo crystal prawns; half or whole steamed chicken with ginger sauce; crispy beef—a spicy dish of shredded beef; and eggplant Szechuan cooked with ground pork and red chili peppers are all fine choices.

Summary & comments: Chang's shines during the day when owner Hing is on the premises. She is friendly and helpful and never minds answering questions, even when the restaurant is busy. Service in the evening is friendly, but reserved. Special dishes are always available for Chang's Asian customers. Adventurous eaters are welcome to ask what's available. Chang's at Bally's is an attractive dining room with a smaller menu.

CHIN'S		

			QUALITY
Chinese	★★★★½	Expensive	**96**
			VALUE
			C

3200 Las Vegas Boulevard, South (Fashion Show Mall)
 733-8899   Strip Zone I

Charlie Chin's at Arizona Charlie's, 740 South Decatur Boulevard
 258-5200   Strip Zone I

Customers: Locals, tourists	Friendliness rating: ★★★★★
Reservations: Suggested	Parking: Underground in mall, valet
When to go: Any time	Bar: Full service
Entree range: $10–28;	Wine selection: Good
more for special dishes	Dress: Casual
Payment: VISA, MC, AMEX	Disabled access: Elevator
Service rating: ★★★★★	

Lunch & dinner: Monday–Saturday, 11:30 a.m.–9:30 p.m.;
 Sunday, noon–9:30 p.m. (Charlie Chin's closed, Monday).

(Chin's)

Setting & atmosphere: The Fashion Show location is a modern, spacious dining room with handsome architectural effects; the traditional Chinese decor at Charlie Chin's in Arizona Charlie's includes authentic Chinese artifacts and art. A private dining room is available at the Fashion Show location.

House specialties: Chin's is known for its original dishes. Attempts to copy them by other restaurants don't quite make it. Chin's beef; strawberry chicken; steamed scallops with black beans on baby abalone shells; pepper roughy; and shredded chicken salad. Glazed bananas or crispy pudding are for traditionalists; try one of the gorgeous flaming desserts prepared tableside. The lunch menu features a dim sum plate and many specials at reasonable prices. Some crossover dishes fuse East and West in a bit of reverse daring. Charlie Chin's is a much lower priced restaurant with a simple, value-priced menu.

Entertainment & amenities: Piano player, Wednesday to Sunday, in lounge.

Summary & comments: Owner Tola Chin will prepare a special menu upon request. Prices are more than fair for the multicourse repasts. Because so many restaurants "adopt" Chin's favorite recipes, he's kept busy developing new ones.

CIPRIANI

Italian	★★★½	Expensive	QUALITY 89
			VALUE C

2790 East Flamingo Road
369-6711   Southeast Zone 5

Customers: Locals, tourists	Friendliness rating: ★★★★
Reservations: Suggested	Parking: Convenient lot
When to go: Any time	Bar: Full service
Entree range: $10.95–24	Wine selection: Good
Payment: VISA, MC, AMEX, DC	Dress: Informal, dressy
Service rating: ★★★★	Disabled access: Ground floor

Lunch: Monday–Friday, 11:30 a.m.–2 p.m.; Saturday and Sunday, closed.
Dinner: Monday–Saturday, 5:30–10:30 p.m.; Sunday, closed.

Setting & atmosphere: Contemporary Italian tables, chairs, and soft decor make an attractive, comfortable setting for dinner. The exhibition kitchen offers a view of the cooking.

(Cipriani)

House specialties: Escargot and steamed clams in herbs, shallots, and garlic; pasta e fagioli; capellini pomodoro e basilico; breast of chicken Frascati with artichokes, mushrooms, black olives, and fresh herbs; veal scallopini Boscaiola; Oregon lamb chops with wild mushrooms.

Other recommendations: Buffalo mozzarella with sliced tomatoes and fresh basil; imaginative salads, pastas, and specials for lunch and dinner; fettuccini with fresh salmon and caviar with a light cream sauce; gnocchi casalinga; sautéed sea scallops with armagnac dill cream sauce. Tiramisu; crème caramel; chocolate mousse.

Entertainment & amenities: Skilled chefs cut, chop, broil, and bake in the open kitchen. Lots of exchange between kitchen and tables nearby. Accordionist Tuesday through Saturday evenings.

Summary & comments: This deservedly popular Italian restaurant offers many dishes not available elsewhere.

COYOTE CAFE

			QUALITY
Southwestern	★★★½	Moderate/Expensive	**90**
			VALUE
			B

MGM Grand
891-7349   Strip Zone 1

Customers: Tourists	Friendliness rating: ★★★★
Reservations: Suggested in Coyote's Grill Room	Parking: Valet, garage, lot
	Bar: Full service
When to go: Any time	Wine selection: Excellent
Entree range: Cafe, $10–20; Grill Room, $17–32	Dress: Cafe, casual; Grill Room, informal
Payment: VISA, MC, AMEX, DC, D	Disabled access: Ground floor
Service rating: ★★★★	

Open: Every day, 8 a.m.–11 p.m

Setting & atmosphere: Mark Miller's original Southwestern decor. Two dining rooms: one is an all-day cafe; the Grill Room is for dinner only. Paintings of corn, beans, squash, and chiles cover the walls.

House specialties: Sweet corn soup with poblano chiles and cilantro; grilled buttermilk corn cakes; spicy crab cake with tomato-basil salsa; coriander-rubbed Ahi tuna; "cowboy" Angus rib chop with fire-roasted salsa, black beans, and spicy onion rings. Sour lemon bread pudding with fresh berries; chocolate truffle cake with bittersweet chocolate sauce.

(Coyote Cafe)

Other recommendations: Chilled yellow tomato gazpacho; cold poached Maine lobster; Coyote's vegetarian plate; Texas Hill Country lemon-crusted venison with ragout of lima beans, artichokes, and roasted tomatoes. Entrees change seasonally. Desserts change seasonally, too. All are imaginative and scrumptious.

Summary & comments: Mark Miller has defined Southwestern cuisine in his own expert style. He uses blue corn, a variety of hot and sweet peppers, and spices to greatest advantage. None of the dishes are palate searing. Those who like a lighter touch of heat should tell the server. The moderately priced cafe has a new margarita bar and menu. Both are value priced.

DIAMOND LIL'S

American	★★★½	Moderate	QUALITY 89
			VALUE B

Sam's Town, Boulder Highway at Flamingo Road
   456-7777   Southeast Zone 5

Customers: Locals, some tourists	**Friendliness rating:** ★★★★★
Reservations: Suggested	**Parking:** Large lot, garage, valet
When to go: Any time	**Bar:** Full service
Entree range: $15.95–52;	**Wine selection:** Good
seafood at market price	**Dress:** Casual
Payment: VISA, MC, AMEX, DC, CB, D	**Disabled access:** Ground floor
Service rating: ★★★½	

Dinner: Friday and Saturday, 5:30–11 p.m.; Sunday, 5:30–10 p.m.; Monday–Thursday, closed.

Setting & atmosphere: Turn of the century. Dark red brocade booths, simulated gas lights. Cozy alcoves.

House specialties: Toasted thin-sliced bagels with cream cheese and jalapeño jelly served as soon as guests are seated. Lil's grilled oysters with mild salsa and mozzarella; grilled and chilled shrimp cocktail. Whole roasted chicken; chicken Dijon and piccata; barbecued baby back pork ribs; half rack of lamb. Baked, broiled, or blackened fresh fish with pistachio, Cajun pecan, or ginger lime butter.

Other recommendations: Escargot maitre d'; rib-eye steak; prime rib; filet mignon with jalapeño hollandaise; veal dishes. Death by chocolate and peach schnapps cake.

(Diamond Lil's)

Summary & comments: Entree price includes romaine salad with cherry tomatoes, sliced mushrooms, and bay shrimp or a soup such as cream of banana, crab corn chowder, seafood bisque, or wild rice duck. Fine dining at moderate prices.

DIVE!

American	★★★½	Moderate	QUALITY
			89
			VALUE
Fashion Show Mall			**B**
369-3483 Strip Zone 1			

Customers: Tourists, some locals	**Friendliness rating:** ★★★★
Reservations: For parties of 8 or more	**Parking:** Valet, lot, garage
	Bar: Full service
When to go: Any time	**Wine selection:** Limited
Entree range: $7.95–15.95	**Dress:** Casual
Payment: VISA, MC, AMEX, DC, D	**Disabled access:** Ramps, elevator
Service rating: ★★★★	

Lunch & dinner: Sunday–Thursday, 11:30 a.m.–10 p.m.; Friday and Saturday, 11:30 a.m.–11 p.m.

Setting & atmosphere: Steven Spielberg's Hollywood version of a submarine-themed restaurant is a fanciful mélange of special effects, electronics, and periscopes that can scan the Strip or a neighbor's table. Tables with portholes give a watery view as you dine. When the captain signals dive time, you almost believe him. The briny effects are a child's delight, especially when the order is given to submerge and the entrance wall is awash with water or when the "depth charges" go off. Even the bathrooms (heads) have special effects.

House specialties: Super DIVE! french fries served in a wrought-iron holder with a choice of two dips; portholes, DIVE!-style pizzas; savory Dungeness crab cake appetizer with Cajun mayonnaise; meal-size salads— the Chinese chicken salad is large enough to share; DIVE!'s signature submarine sandwiches served on special rolls; seafood pasta, a savory mix of mussels, clams, and salmon in a wine-garlic sauce over linguini; wood-roasted entrees. Sublime desserts—Lemon Bar Explosion; unctuous, rich crème brûlée; cappuccino ice cream with toffee nuggets, billows of whipped cream, and chocolate sauce; warm cookie sundae (warm chocolate chunk cookie, white chocolate ice cream, hot fudge, whipped cream, and trimmings); it's a deadly delight.

(DIVE!)

Summary & comments: DIVE! offers a good selection of draft and bottled beers and colorful, frozen tropical-type mixed drinks (they can be ordered without the alcohol). The realistic sound effects can get noisy at times. DIVE! specializes in children's and grown-up parties and corporate events. A DIVE! Gear retail store adjacent to the restaurant sells high-quality logo items. New items are added regularly to the menu.

EMBERS			
Steak	★★★	Moderate	**QUALITY** 84
			VALUE B

Imperial Palace
731-3311   Strip Zone I

Customers: Tourists, locals	**Friendliness rating:** ★★★★
Reservations: Suggested	**Parking:** Garage, valet
When to go: Any time	**Bar:** Full service
Entree range: $14–49.99	**Wine selection:** Excellent
Payment: VISA, MC, AMEX, DC, CB, D	**Dress:** Informal
Service rating: ★★★★	**Disabled access:** Elevator

Dinner: Wednesday–Sunday, 5–11 p.m.; Monday and Tuesday, closed.

Setting & atmosphere: Burgundy striped wallpaper. Attractive wine cabinets with leaded glass doors at entrance. Service friendly and efficient.

House specialties: Oysters Embers with spinach and hollandaise; roast Long Island duck with lingonberries and wild rice; tournedos Rossini with foie gras and marchand de vin sauce. Flambé desserts. Cappuccino Royal.

Other recommendations: Shrimp scampi; lobster bisque; spinach and Caesar salads prepared tableside; orange roughy sautéed with macadamia nuts; petit filet mignon with lobster tail.

Summary & comments: Well-priced classic hotel dishes in pleasant surroundings. Pass on the tiramisu.

EMERIL'S NEW ORLEANS FISH HOUSE

			QUALITY
Contemporary New Orleans	★★★★★	Expensive	95
			VALUE
			B

MGM Grand
891-7374   Strip Zone 1

Customers: Locals, tourists
Reservations: Strongly suggested
When to go: Nonconvention times
Entree range: $18–38
Payment: MC, VISA, AMEX, DC, D
Service rating: ★★★★★

Friendliness rating: ★★★★★
Parking: Valet, lot, covered garage
Bar: Full service
Wine selection: Excellent
Dress: Upscale casual
Disabled access: Through casino

Lunch: Every day, 11 a.m.–2:30 p.m.
Dinner: Every day, 5:30–10:30 p.m.
Oyster Bar/Cafe: Every day, 11 a.m.–10:30 p.m.

Setting & atmosphere: "A bit of New Orleans" is the way award-winning chef-owner Emeril Lagasse describes his beautiful restaurant. The main restaurant is comfortable and handsome with fine appointments and accessories. The separate courtyard dining room is French Quarter pretty with a faux balcony and louvered shutters. Masses of real plants and a stone floor complete the illusion.

House specialties: The five- to eight-course "tasting" dinner is a fine way to sample small portions of many dishes; some are special recipes being considered for the menu. Emeril's lobster cheesecake with Creole-spiced tomato coulis; the house Louisiana Choupiquet caviar; the "lobster dome," a whole lobster shelled and served with roasted potatoes, onion marmalade, and lobster sauce and covered with a baked puff pastry dome; Louisiana campfire steak served on a cedar plank on a bed of country-style mashed potatoes and drizzled with warm rémoulade and Emeril's homemade Worcestershire sauce.

Summary & comments: Emeril's is an exciting restaurant that personifies the "new Las Vegas." The food and service are a tribute to Emeril's concern for his diners. He is in town often and is very accessible to his patrons, visiting with them in the dining room.

Honors & awards: Emeril's is the recipient of many dining awards including: "Best Southeast Regional Chef"—The James Beard Foundation; "One of the Top 25 Chefs in the Country"—*Food & Wine* magazine; "American Express Fine Dining Hall of Fame"—*Nation's Restaurant News*.

FERRARO'S RESTAURANT & LOUNGE

Italian	★★★½	Moderate	QUALITY
			89
			VALUE
			B

5900 West Flamingo Road
    364-5300   Southwest Zone 3

Stratosphere
    380-7777   Strip Zone 1

Customers: Locals
Reservations: Suggested, required
    on weekends
When to go: Any time
Entree range: $12.95–28
Payment: VISA, MC, AMEX, DC, D
Service rating: ★★★★

Friendliness rating: ★★★★★
Parking: Lot
Bar: Friendly, fully stocked
Wine selection: Good
Dress: Informal, casual
Disabled access: Two-level dining

Dinner: Every day, 5–10:30 p.m.

Setting & atmosphere: Classic Roman-style dining room with white walls, columns, and recessed lighting. Handsome black carpeting has pink highlights that are reflected in the table appointments.

House specialties: Panzerotti, a family recipe (potato croquettes with roasted peppers), and Manila clams in tomato-sauce appetizers. Penne amatriciana; osso buco in burgundy sauce with fettuccini; fresh seafood; linguini Portofino; Rosalba's tiramisu and Godiva passion liqueur desserts. Bread made daily in the pizza oven. Plate-size pizzas are available at Stratosphere.

Other recommendations: Light menu includes chicken with honey-mustard sauce and bow-tie pasta; shrimp with risotto; bow-tie pomodoro; grilled halibut; plus rustica salad, a meal in itself. Carciofo ripieno (artichoke stuffed with seasoned bread crumbs, garlic, butter, and wine); pasta e fagioli; veal and lamb chops. Pistachio passion dessert.

Entertainment & amenities: A musician plays the piano in the lounge and strolls with a guitar.

Summary & comments: While Rosalba Ferraro is usually at the Flamingo location, Gino Ferraro divides his time between the two locations. Southern Italian cooking, with some northern Italian specialties. Pizza is available only at the Stratosphere location.

FIORE

			QUALITY
Continental	★★★★	Moderate/Expensive	**95**
			VALUE
			B

Rio, 3700 West Flamingo Road
  252-7777   Strip Zone 1

Customers: Tourists, locals
Reservations: Suggested
When to go: Any time except during
  conventions
Entree range: $26–48
Payment: VISA, MC, AMEX, DC, D
Service rating: ★★★★½

Friendliness rating: ★★★★★
Parking: Lot, garage, valet
Bar: Full service
Wine selection: Excellent
Dress: Dressy, informal
Disabled access: Ground floor

Dinner: Every day, 5–11 p.m.

Setting & atmosphere: Handsome exhibition kitchen filled with cookware. Elegant table appointments. Climate-controlled cigar terrace for smokers. A fine selection of cigars.

House specialties: Dill- and grappa-cured salmon with tye blinis; limestone lettuce with marinated shiitake mushrooms, lemon avocado oil; charred tuna carpaccio; Dungeness crab cake with diablo sauce; breast of quail salad; Moroccan-spiced chicken in phyllo; pheasant ravioli with prosciutto and sage cream sauce. The menu changes every seven to ten days, so specialties are always changing.

Other recommendations: Pizzas from the wood-burning ovens; any of the nightly rotisserie offerings, including roast lamb; hand-carved New York strip; duck or chicken; whole salmon (portioned). Different woods used for grilling include cherrywood, almond, olive, and mesquite. Edible flowers garnish dishes; Dom Perignon tops sorbets (doused tableside by captain). Twenty fine wine selections by the glass.

Summary & comments: Fiore is a departure from the Rio's usual moderately priced restaurants. There is much that's new and exciting here, with constant changes.

FOG CITY DINER

California American	★★★★	Moderate/Expensive	**QUALITY**
			89

VALUE
C

325 Hughes Center Drive, Flamingo and Paradise Roads
737-0200   Strip Zone 1

Customers: Locals, tourists	Friendliness rating: ★★★★
Reservations: Suggested	Parking: Large lot
When to go: Any time	Bar: Full service
Entree range: $10.50–16.95	Wine selection: Good
Payment: VISA, MC, DC, D, CB	Dress: Casual
Service rating: ★★★	Disabled access: Ground floor

Lunch & dinner: Sunday–Thursday, 11:30 a.m.–10 p.m.;
Friday and Saturday, 11:30 a.m.–11 p.m.

Setting & atmosphere: Beautiful woods, spacious comfortable booths, and fine appointments set Fog City apart from the usual diner—but, not too far. The classic counter faces the kitchen where diners in search of a quick meal can watch the chefs as they cook it. A separate dining room in the rear of the diner has seating at tables for those who prefer chairs to booths.

House specialties: Any of the daily specials, chosen for freshness and season. Outside of a very good hamburger and some diner-style platters (large plates), Fog City's menu is a tribute to California cuisine. Red curry mussel stew, Manila clam chowder, and a zesty sirloin-and-black-bean chili are meals in a bowl. "Small plates" are small portions for small appetites or can be starters; crab cakes with ancho chile succotash, moo shu pork burritos, whiskey chicken wings, and seared rare Ahi tuna with red tomato chow chow are favorites. "Large plate" specials (think blue plate) include grilled turkey breast with pappardelle noodles, grilled pork chops, pot roast with horseradish potato pancake, and slivered calf's liver and caramelized onions over polenta. One salad is a tribute to yesterday's diner fare—a huge wedge of iceberg lettuce is smothered with blue cheese or crab Louis dressing. Desserts are scrumptious, and the milk shakes are real. Menu items change regularly, but the most requested remain. Fog City offers some of the freshest, plumpest oysters. Don't miss the Fanny Bay.

Summary & comments: Fog City Diner is filled with imagination and innovation, but it ain't perfect. If you want bread with your meal you'll have to ask for it, but don't expect to get the jalapeño corn sticks, Dutch crunch rolls, or delicious garlic, leek, and basil loaf.

FUJI

			QUALITY
Japanese	★★★	Moderate	**84**

	VALUE
3430 East Tropicana Avenue	**B**
435-8838 Southeast Zone 5	

Customers: Locals	Friendliness rating: ★★★★
Reservations: Accepted	Parking: Large lot
When to go: Any time	Bar: Beer and wine only
Entree range: $7.50–16.50	Wine selection: Fair
Payment: VISA, MC, JCB, DC	Dress: Informal, casual
Service rating: ★★★★	Disabled access: Ground floor

Open: Every day, 4:30–10:30 p.m.; Monday, sushi bar only.

Setting & atmosphere: Small family-style restaurant with two teppan tables, booths, and traditional seating.

House specialties: All the basic Japanese fare is available: sushi, tempura, sukiyaki, teriyaki. Combination dinners also available.

Other recommendations: Tall or large diners will find a table more comfortable than the small booths.

Summary & comments: Moderate prices, a caring staff, and good food make Fuji a popular local dining option. Children are treated like honored guests.

GARDEN OF THE DRAGON

			QUALITY
Chinese	★★★½	Expensive	**85**

	VALUE
Las Vegas Hilton	**C**
732-5111 Strip Zone 1	

Customers: Tourists, high rollers	Friendliness rating: ★★★★
Reservations: Accepted	Parking: Large lot, valet
When to go: During week	Bar: Full service
Entree range: $12–36	Wine selection: Excellent
Payment: VISA, MC, AMEX, DC, CB, D	Dress: Informal to casual
Service rating: ★★★★	Disabled access: Ground floor

Dinner: Every day, 6–10:30 p.m.

Setting & atmosphere: Serene elegance and comfort are highlights of the decor in the newly revamped Garden of the Dragon—cherrywood chairs and tables and marble, brass, and etched-glass appointments. A wall has been placed in front of the formerly open kitchen to baffle the noise; glass dividers between booths give the effect of private dining. A luxurious private dining room in the back includes etched-gold wall coverings and distinctive wood-framed windows. Lazy-Susan tables large enough for ten allow for good conversation. The room divides to accommodate small or large parties.

House specialties: Peking-style roast pork; bird's nest and shark's fin soups; Garden Dragon chicken; orange beef; steamed whole flounder; Szechuan shrimp in a noodle nest; Hong Kong–style house chow mein; fresh vegetable dishes.

Other recommendations: Family-style dinners for two to five diners; pot stickers; whole Peking duck; Mongolian beef; Peking-style pork chop; sizzling lamb; lobster in curry sauce.

Summary & comments: Garden of the Dragon is now totally separate from its adjacent neighbor, Benihana Village. The noise level from the light show and other Benihana entertainment is now subdued and acceptable, yet the show still can be seen through the low, dragon-etched glass divider.

GARDUNO'S CHILI PACKING CO.

Mexican	★★★½	Inexpensive/Moderate	QUALITY
			89
			VALUE
			B

Fiesta Hotel, 2400 North Rancho Drive
631-7000   Northwest Zone 4

Customers: Locals, tourists	Friendliness rating: ★★★★
Reservations: Not accepted	Parking: Valet, lot
When to go: Any time	Bar: Full service
Entree range: $6.95–12.95	Wine selection: Good
Payment: VISA, MC, AMEX, DC, D	Dress: Informal
Service rating: ★★★★	Disabled access: Ground floor

Brunch: Sunday, 11 a.m.–3 p.m.
Lunch & dinner: Sunday–Thursday, 11 a.m.–10 p.m.; Friday and Saturday, 11 a.m.–11 p.m.

Setting & atmosphere: Colorful, appealing Mexican decor with many plants and beautiful artifacts. This large restaurant has been cleverly divided, making it more intimate.

House specialties: Hatch chiles, grown only in the Mesa Valley of New Mexico, are used exclusively. Baskets of fresh sopaipillas accompany entrees. The honey on the table is for pouring over the puffy pillows of dough. Spicy chili verde served in a huge bowl. Guacamole prepared table-side; fresh avocadoes are mashed, then lime juice, spices, chiles, and seasonings are added to your taste. Tortillas are handmade the old-fashioned way. Posole soup rich with hominy, pork, and red chiles. Any of the fajitas. The red snapper served with adobe corn cake.

Summary & comments: This is the first venture out of New Mexico for the Garduno restaurant family. The food is authentic and good. Daily lunch specials are large enough to be an early dinner. The Sunday margarita brunch is a fine value and a good way to get to know the Garduno style of Mexican cooking.

GATSBY'S

French/California-style	★★★★	Expensive	QUALITY 90
			VALUE C

MGM Grand
891-7337   Strip Zone 1

Customers: Tourists, locals	Friendliness rating: ★★★★★
Reservations: Requested	Parking: Valet, garage
When to go: Any time but concert and prizefight dates	Bar: Full service
	Wine selection: Outstanding
Entree range: $35–39.95	Dress: Casual elegance
Payment: VISA, MC, AMEX, DC, D	Disabled access: Ground floor
Service rating: ★★★★	

Dinner: Every day, 5:30–10 p.m.

Setting & atmosphere: Dine in the splendor that was formerly Charlie Trotter's. Some minor changes have been made; a new, more visible entrance has been added. Appointments and furnishings are gorgeous.

House specialties: Seasonal terrines; a Japanese-inspired fish plate appetizer; sweetbreads with fresh Hudson Valley foie gras; lobster and sweet corn bisque; farm-raised abalone; grilled ostrich with wild mushroom risotto; genuine Kobe beef from Japan (market price); Chilean sea bass, Asian-style. Gatsby's sinful signature desserts.

Other recommendations: Gatsby's price-fixed three-, four-, and five-course dinners, priced at $62, $70, and $95 per person. The combination dinner and *EFX!* show with David Cassidy package. At $115 for everything it's a good deal. Included are a multicourse dinner and a preferred seat for the show.

(Gatsby's)

Summary & comments: It took a while for Gatsby's to find its identity, but it has finally found its niche. It's pricey, for sure, but it's a posh dining experience.

GOLDEN STEER			

Prime Rib/Steak	★★★	Expensive	QUALITY 80
			VALUE C

308 West Sahara Avenue
384-4470   Strip Zone 1

Customers: Mostly tourists, some locals	**Service rating:** ★★★★
	Friendliness rating: ★★★★
Reservations: Suggested	**Parking:** Valet
When to go: Avoid convention periods	**Bar:** Full service
	Wine selection: Extensive
Entree range: $17–35	**Dress:** Informal
Payment: VISA, MC, AMEX, DC, D	**Disabled access:** Ground floor

Dinner: Every day, 4:30–11:30 p.m.

Setting & atmosphere: Large, rambling Old West atmosphere. Number of intimate dining rooms. Decorated with Western art.

House specialties: Prime rib in gigantic portions; charcoal-broiled steaks; veal; lamb chops; quail; pastas. Wine list is worth a second look; moderate prices and good choices.

Other recommendations: Seafood selections run from trout to lobster.

Summary & comments: Because of its close-to-the-Strip location, generous portions, and male-appeal food, the restaurant is packed during every convention. Seating 300, the Golden Steer often handles up to 1,000 a night. During off-convention periods, the restaurant offers the same food and service. Beef dishes are the best choices.

HABIB'S

			QUALITY
Persian/Middle Eastern	★★★½	Moderate	88
			VALUE
			C

4750 West Sahara Avenue, Sahara Pavilion
  870-0860   Southwest Zone 3

Customers: Locals, tourists
Reservations: Accepted
When to go: Any time
Entree range: $8.50–15.95
Payment: MC, VISA, AMEX
Service rating: ★★★

Friendliness rating: ★★★★
Parking: Shopping-center lot
Bar: Beer and wine
Wine selection: Poor
Dress: Casual
Disabled access: Ground level

Lunch: Monday–Saturday, 11:30 a.m.–3 p.m.
Dinner: Monday–Saturday, 5–10 p.m.

Setting & atmosphere: Located in the restaurant corridor of a popular neighborhood shopping center, this attractive, small restaurant has gained a loyal local following. A mist-controlled outdoor patio allows for al fresco dining even in warm weather. The area is filled with beautiful plants.

House specialties: Middle Eastern appetizers and salads; chicken, ground beef, and beefsteak kabobs; many Persian specialties.

Other recommendations: Tabbouleh salad, so fresh the parsley tastes just-picked; the eggplant appetizer, borani; hummus; torshi, a mixture of pickled, aged vegetables; zereshk polo, a seasoned chicken breast kabob prepared with barberries and fragrant spices that are then mixed with rice.

Summary & comments: Habib's menu is not large, but it is filled with exotic, delicious dishes that, except for the Middle Eastern starters and salads, have unfamiliar names. The wait staff is happy to explain the food to the best of their ability. At least two of the special Persian dishes listed separately on the menu are available each day. Habib's is the only Persian restaurant in Las Vegas; the Middle Eastern dishes are a concession to his sizable following of Middle Eastern customers. Photos of the dishes are included with the menu, enabling diners unfamiliar with the cuisine to see what the finished dish looks like.

HAKASE

			QUALITY
Japanese/Sushi	★★★★	Moderate/Expensive	**90**
			VALUE
			B

3900 Paradise Road
796-1234   Strip Zone I

Customers: Locals, some tourists
Reservations: A must at dinner
When to go: Lunch, early or late dinner
Entree range: $10.95–25, regular menu; $16.75–25, teppanyaki dinners
Payment: VISA, MC, AMEX, DC, JCB
Service rating: ★★★★

Friendliness rating: ★★★★
Parking: Large lot, additional parking in back
Bar: None
Wine selection: Limited domestic selections, plus saké, Japanese beers, plum wine
Dress: Informal, casual
Disabled access: Ground floor

Lunch: Tuesday–Friday, noon–2:30 p.m.
Dinner: Sunday–Saturday, 5–10:30 p.m.; Monday, closed except during conventions.

Setting & atmosphere: Contemporary Japanese decor. The small but attractive dining room includes a good-sized tatami room and a colorful sushi bar in addition to standard seating.

House specialties: The combination dinner Hakase Bento, served from a "box," includes sashimi, fried shrimp, broiled fish and beef, and Japanese boiled vegetables for $14.95. Shabu shabu (thin-sliced beef and vegetables in broth) and Hakase's special seafood and vegetable broth, which, for an extra charge, your waiter or waitress will cook at a table of two or more diners.

Other recommendations: Anything from the sushi bar—Hakase offers some of the freshest, most skillfully made sushi in the city. Also, good appetizers such as caviar with radish, sunomono with octopus, grated mountain potato with tuna, and soft-shelled crab. Sukiyaki; combination dinners.

Summary & comments: Unless you're Japanese there is a language barrier here. The menu clearly states the dishes, but attempts at getting further descriptions of the more exotic dishes can be frustrating. During the busiest hours service can be brusque, so come early or late for the most relaxed dining.

HUGO'S CELLAR

			QUALITY
American	★★★½	Expensive	**89**
			VALUE
			B

Four Queens Hotel
385-4011   Downtown Zone 2

Customers: Locals, tourists
Reservations: Strongly recommended
When to go: Any time but Friday
  and Saturday
Entree range: $25–49
Payment: VISA, MC, AMEX, DC, D
Service rating: ★★★★

Friendliness rating: ★★★★★
Parking: Indoor garage, valet
Bar: Full service
Wine selection: Very good wine list
Dress: Informal, tie and jacket
  suggested
Disabled access: Elevator to cellar

Dinner: Every day, 5:30–10:30 p.m.

Setting & atmosphere: Unique cellar location, comfortable lounge, warm bar, and gracious hostess. Booths provide privacy; noise at minimum. Cozy cocktail lounge serves pâté, cheese, crackers, and very large drinks.

House specialties: Variety of breads including lavosh crackers, warm French bread. Waiter creates salad of choice from selection on the cart wheeled to your table. Steaks and prime rib; duck flambé anise; snapper en papillote with shallots and white wine; medallions of lobster with white wine, crushed red pepper, sun-dried tomatoes, and mushrooms.

Other recommendations: Appetizer for two of beef tenderloin medallions; marinated swordfish, breast of chicken, and jumbo shrimp cooked at the table on sizzling granite slab. Imaginative preparations of veal and chicken; rack of lamb Indonesian.

Entertainment & amenities: Hostess presents a fresh rose to female guests. Sorbet is served in a miniature cone. Chocolate-dipped fruits with whipped cream are presented before dessert order is taken.

Summary & comments: A most popular downtown restaurant. On weekends the Cellar is packed. Expert wine steward to assist you with selection. Don't let the little cone of sherbet served between courses throw you—it's a house signature. A consistent local favorite.

IL FORNAIO

Italian ★★★½	Moderate/Moderately Expensive	QUALITY
		87
		VALUE
		B

New York–New York
740-6403   Strip Zone 1

Customers: Tourists, locals
Reservations: Suggested for dinner
When to go: Any time
Entree range: $9.50–$22.50
Payment: VISA, MC, AMEX, D, CB, JCB
Service rating: ★★★★

Friendliness rating: ★★★★★
Parking: Valet, garage
Bar: Full service
Wine selection: Small, but good
Dress: Informal
Disabled access: Ground floor

Lunch & dinner: Sunday–Thursday, 11:30 a.m.–midnight; Friday and Saturday, 11:30 a.m.–1 a.m.

Setting & atmosphere: Upscale, upbeat contemporary decor. Rich woods and natural stone and marble accents. Dine on the outdoor patio with a view of the flowing brook and people-watch as you dine. Faux trees add an almost real touch of nature.

House specialties: Carpaccio with shavings of Italian cheese, capers, and baby arugula; Tuscan tomato and bread soup; the meal-sized salad of mixed greens, rotisserie chicken, apple wood-smoked bacon, and shaved Parmesan; the selection of thin-crusted pizzas baked in the wood-fired oven. Eat at the bar and watch as they're assembled and baked. The herbed chicken roasted on the wood-burning rotisserie and served with vegetables and roasted potatoes; the 22-ounce certified Angus porterhouse marinated in olive oil and rosemary, served with Tuscan white beans and sautéed spinach; the remarkable breads, baked on the premises, served with all meals.

Other recommendations: Any of the homemade pastas, especially the ravioli filled with spinach, Swiss chard, pine nuts, and basil, with baby artichokes; grilled fresh salmon; veal scallopini with baby artichokes and lemon; elbow macaroni with chicken breast, fresh broccoli, and sun-dried tomatoes.

Summary & comments: The success of New York–New York has brought an enormous amount of business to Il Fornaio. Dine during off hours for the most relaxing experience. Patio dining is the most requested. It can be noisy, so opt to dine in the lovely dining room. Take home the remarkable Il Fornaio European breads. They're sold in Il Fornaio's retail bakery/coffee house just a few doors from the restaurant.

ISIS

Continental	★★★★	Moderate/Expensive	QUALITY
			90
			VALUE
			B

Luxor
262-4773   Strip Zone I

Customers: Tourists, locals
Reservations: Suggested
When to go: Any time
Entree range: $24–45
Payment: VISA, MC, AMEX, DC, JCB, D
Service rating: ★★★★★

Friendliness rating: ★★★★★
Parking: Lot, valet
Bar: Full service
Wine selection: Excellent
Dress: Dressy, informal
Disabled access: Elevator

Dinner: Every day, 6–11 p.m.

Setting & atmosphere: Exact replicas of the statues guarding the entrance to the pharaohs' tombs dramatically flank the entrance to Isis. Glass-enclosed Egyptian artifacts separate the comfortable booths. A statue of Isis is the focal point of this lovely dining room.

House specialties: Poached oysters over creamed spinach with a touch of pernod; baked shrimp filled with crab and mushroom duxelle; Sonoma greens with warm goat cheese and walnut dressing; beef Wellington; lobster tail en croute with seafood mousse and white zinfandel sauce. Baked Egypt (pyramid-shaped baked Alaska); specialty coffees, Ramses' Torch and Flaming Sceptor.

Other recommendations: Grenadine of veal loin sautéed with sorrel and dry vermouth sauce; Red Sea sesame chicken with lobster tahini; seafood ravioli in chive and lobster sauce. Dahibeyeh Delight (barge-shaped chocolate mousse with raspberry filling).

Entertainment & amenities: Romantic harpist performs at restaurant's entrance.

Summary & comments: Unusual menu cover decorated with illustrations of Egyptian stone carvings is just one of the original touches at Isis.

KATHY'S SOUTHERN COOKING

			QUALITY
American	★★★	Inexpensive	**80**

	VALUE
	A

6407 Mountain Vista Street
   433-1005   Southeast Zone 5

Customers: Locals
Reservations: Suggested, especially
  for groups of 6 or more
When to go: Any time
Entree range: $7.99–19.99
Payment: VISA, MC, D, AMEX
Service rating: ★★★★

Friendliness rating: ★★★★
Parking: Shopping-center lot
Bar: Wine and beer only
Wine selection: Limited (house
  wine)
Dress: Informal
Disabled access: Ground floor

Lunch & dinner: Tuesday–Thursday, 11 a.m.–9 p.m.; Friday and Saturday, 11 a.m.–10 p.m.; Sunday, 1–8 p.m.; Monday, closed. Same menu day and evening.

Setting & atmosphere: Casual, down-home dining room with 46 seats. One wall is painted with a mural of a paddle wheeler on the Mississippi River.

House specialties: Gumbo; catfish; "gravy dinners"—smothered pork chop, steak, or chicken with rice or mashed potatoes, slabs of cornbread, and a side dish from a selection of black-eyed peas, red beans and rice, greens, and more.

Other recommendations: Oxtails; shrimp Creole; barbecued beef and spareribs; étouffé, sweet-potato pie. Kathy's spareribs are huge, with a zesty sauce that will make you tingle. Hearty, wholesome fare.

Summary & comments: The owners of this family operation, Kathy and Felix Black, present authentic selections from Mississippi and Louisiana kitchens "like Mama used to make." Comfortable, with a "you all" kind of friendliness. Park in shopping center and walk through to Mountain Vista Street (no access from shopping center).

KIM TAR

QUALITY	**89**
VALUE	**B**

Chinese ★★★ Inexpensive/Moderate

4215 West Spring Mountain Road (upstairs)
227-3588 Southwest Zone 3

Customers: Asian community, locals, and tourists
Reservations: Not necessary
When to go: Any time
Entree range: $5.50–13.50
Payment: VISA, MC, AMEX, D
Service rating: ★★★★

Friendliness rating: ★★★★½
Parking: Self, large lot
Bar: Beer and wine only
Wine selection: Fair
Dress: Anything goes
Disabled access: Elevator

Lunch & dinner: Every day, 10 a.m.–11 p.m.; same menu all day with some lunch specials.

Setting & atmosphere: The live fish tank as you enter gives the promise of the food to come. Unpretentious, but pleasant decor.

House specialties: Seafood and fresh fish, especially fresh-from-the-tank lobsters and Dungeness crabs prepared with a variety of sauces; steamed whole fish with black bean sauce; jumbo shrimp with heads, steamed and served with a spicy dipping sauce; warm, braised goose, served with cold pickled vegetables; meal-size soups; any of the sizzling dishes.

Summary & comments: This modest eatery, located in the new Chinatown mall, serves some of the best seafood in town, along with a large selection of Chinese dishes. The cooking is Chiu Chow style and is very good. Language can be a problem, but the manager and a few of the wait staff have enough English to answer questions. Small parties are sometimes seated at large tables, but no one minds if you rearrange the seating to make it cozier. Lobster prices change according to market price. Ask before you order to avoid surprises.

KOKOMO'S

QUALITY	**93**
VALUE	**C**

Seafood/Steak ★★★★ Expensive

The Mirage
791-7111 Strip Zone 1

Customers: Tourists
Reservations: Required; high rollers and hotel guests get preference.

When to go: Any time
Entree range: $24–45
Payment: VISA, MC, AMEX, DC, D

(Kokomo's)

Service rating: ★★★★★
Friendliness rating: ★★★★
Parking: Lot (long walk), valet
Bar: Full service

Wine selection: Good choices
Dress: Casual
Disabled access: Ramp

Breakfast: Thursday–Sunday, 8–10:30 a.m.
Lunch: Every day, 11 a.m.–2:30 p.m.
Dinner: Every day, 5:30–11 p.m.

Setting & atmosphere: Magnificent tropical decor. Waterfalls, streams, lush foliage, orchids and other exotic flowers. South Pacific on the Strip. Tables well spaced for privacy.

House specialties: Red onion soup with Monterey Jack and Parmesan cheeses. Shaved fried onions; steaks; chops and ribs; grilled rib-eye with sautéed red onions and tricolor pepper sauce. Crème brûlée; peanut butter cheesecake; chocolate mousse; and bread pudding.

Other recommendations: Orange roughy caprice; veal and salmon combo; baked oysters in a smoked-salmon crust; sea bass Montego; lobster Mediterranean-style; grilled Polynesian swordfish; broiled breast of chicken basted with honey mustard; extra-thick lamb chops. English trifle; marshmallow brownie cheesecake; apple torte with cinnamon ice cream; taco shell delight; raspberries with Grand Marnier crème; chocolate sinful pâté with pecan brandy sauce.

Summary & comments: Imaginative chefs and decor combine to create a memorable lunch or dinner in this romantic room. Peaceful and romantic: Kokomo's is a sleeper.

LAWRY'S THE PRIME RIB

American	★★★½	Expensive	QUALITY 85
			VALUE C

4043 Howard Hughes Parkway
893-2223   Strip Zone I

Customers: Locals, tourists
Reservations: Requested
When to go: Any time but convention times
Entree range: $18.95–29.95
Payment: VISA, MC, AMEX, CB DC, D
Service rating: ★★★★★

Friendliness rating: ★★★★★
Parking: Valet, lot
Bar: Full service
Wine selection: Good
Dress: Business attire
Disabled access: Ground floor

(Lawry's The Prime Rib)

Dinner: Sunday–Thursday, 5–10 p.m.; Friday and Saturday, 5–11 p.m.

Setting & atmosphere: Elegant but not intimidating, Lawry's reflects the founder's philosophy that a restaurant should be "believable, understandable and appeal to all." The dramatic "silver" carts brought to the table, so the beef can be carved as you watch, are actually made of hammered stainless steel. A handsome separate bar is a fine place for before- or after-dinner drinks.

House specialties: Prime rib, and not much else, has kept diners happy since the original Lawry's The Prime Rib opened in Beverly Hills, California, in 1938. All prime rib dinners include a spinning salad bowl, Yorkshire pudding, mashed potatoes, and whipped cream horseradish. Four cuts of prime rib are offered. Add twin lobster tails to a prime rib dinner for an additional $12.95.

Other recommendations: The fresh fish of the day—expertly prepared in the kitchen, accompanied by seasonal vegetables; the nostalgic creamed spinach or creamed corn. The selection of homespun desserts, especially the deep-dish apple pie with caramel sauce and the coconut banana cream pie.

Summary & comments: How can a restaurant survive that's devoted almost exclusively to prime rib in a town filled with inexpensive prime rib deals? Very well indeed. Lawry's Las Vegas opened with a rush that's never stopped. For prime rib devotees, it's the ultimate luxurious temple of beefdom.

LILLIE LANGTRY'S

Chinese	★★★★	Expensive	QUALITY
			90
Golden Nugget			VALUE
			B

385-7111   Downtown Zone 2

Customers: High rollers, some locals
Reservations: Recommended
When to go: Any time
Entree range: $10.50–26.50
Payment: VISA, MC, AMEX, D
Service rating: ★★★★★

Friendliness rating: ★★★★
Parking: Garage, valet
Bar: Complete service
Wine selection: Excellent
Dress: Informal
Disabled access: Elevator

Dinner: Every day, 5–11 p.m.

(Lillie Langtry's)

Setting & atmosphere: Cheerful, comfortable. Exquisite decor with bright mirrored walls and polished woods.

House specialties: The Great Combination Plate appetizer (four ribs, two fried shrimp, two egg rolls). Stir-fried shrimp with mixed vegetables; black pepper steak; moo goo gai pan. Dragon eye fruit.

Other recommendations: Lemon chicken; sliced beef with oyster sauce; shrimp Cantonese; Chinese broccoli with oyster sauce. Family-style dinners.

Summary & comments: Elaine's gourmet room converted into gourmet Chinese restaurant. Special high-roller menu not available to regular diners, features shark's fin soup, crab with black bean sauce, oyster sauce abalone. Asian kitchen staff well versed in exotic dishes.

LINDO MICHOACAN

Mexican	★★★½	Moderate	QUALITY 86
			VALUE A

2655 East Desert Inn Road
735-6828   Southeast Zone 5

Customers: Locals	**Friendliness rating:** ★★★★
Reservations: Suggested	**Parking:** Lot
When to go: Any time	**Bar:** Full service
Entree range: $8.95–17	**Wine selection:** Good
Payment: VISA, MC, AMEX, D	**Dress:** Casual
Service rating: ★★★★	**Disabled access:** Ground floor

Lunch & dinner: Monday–Thursday, 11 a.m.–10 p.m.; Friday and Saturday, 11 a.m.–11 p.m.; Sunday, 10 a.m.–10 p.m. Same menu day and evening with some lunch specials.

Setting & atmosphere: Cozy storefront, neighborhood cantina with wood-paneled walls and a brick bar. Decor includes Mexican wall hangings—a woven rug, guitar and serape, and posters of the picturesque (lindo) region of Michoacan on the southern coast of Mexico.

House specialties: Mexican cactus with onions, cilantro, tomatoes, and jalapeños; chicken broiled and served with cactus, or simmered in a Spanish orange sauce; large selection of seafood. Menudo (tripe soup) is served on Saturday and Sunday. Milanesa con papa (breaded steak with potatoes). Flan Tio Raul.

(Lindo Michoacan)

Other recommendations: Monday–Friday, $5.25 lunch buffet, served until 3 p.m.; Saturday and Sunday, $5.95 brunch buffet, served from 11 a.m. to 3 p.m.; margarita with Cointreau; combination platters.

Summary & comments: The entrance is not impressive, but the good food is. Lindo Michoacan presents an amazing variety of more than 100 appetizers and entrees, all authentic, a good bet for Mexican food enthusiasts. When busy, the chef is sometimes careless with food presentation, but it always tastes good.

LONE STAR STEAKHOUSE & SALOON

Steak	★★½	Moderate	QUALITY **83**
			VALUE **B**

1290 East Flamingo Road
   893-0348   Strip Zone 1

1611 South Decatur Boulevard
   259-0105   Southwest Zone 3

3131 North Rainbow Boulevard
   656-7125   Southwest Zone 3

210 North Nellis
   453-7827   North Zone 4

Customers: Locals
Reservations: Not accepted
When to go: Any time but prime hours
Entree range: $9.45–19.95
Payment: VISA, MC, AMEX, DC, CB, D
Service rating: ★★★½

Friendliness rating: ★★★★★
Parking: Lot
Bar: Full service
Wine selection: Limited
Dress: Casual
Disabled access: Ramp

Lunch & dinner: Sunday–Thursday, 11 a.m.–10 p.m.; Friday and Saturday, 11 a.m.–11 p.m.

Setting & atmosphere: Wild West, with buckets of peanuts to nosh while waiting for a table. Throw the shells on the floor; kids love to do it. Wait staff in Western garb. Taped Western music. Every now and then, depending on how busy the place is, the sound is turned up and everybody sings.

House specialties: Texas tumbleweed, a huge flower-shaped, batter-dipped, fried onion; Amarillo cheese fries, enough calories and cholesterol for a month; chili; Texas rib-eye; baby back ribs.

(Lone Star Steakhouse & Saloon)

Summary & comments: Informal, fun "Texas roadhouse" ambiance. Shucks, pardner, the food's fine for what it is—fairly priced, family-pleasin' victuals.

LOTUS OF SIAM

Thai	★★★	Moderate	QUALITY 85
			VALUE A

953 East Sahara Avenue (Commercial Center)
735-3033   Strip Zone 1

Customers: Locals	Friendliness rating: ★★★★
Reservations: Accepted	Parking: Large lot
When to go: Any time	Bar: Limited service
Entree range: $6.95–15.95	Wine selection: Fair
Payment: VISA, MC, AMEX, D	Dress: Casual
Service rating: ★★★★	Disabled access: Ground floor

Lunch: Monday–Friday buffet, 11:30 a.m.–2:30 p.m.
Dinner: Every day, 4:30–10 p.m.

Setting & atmosphere: Calm and peaceful. Traditional Thai decor.

House specialties: Mee krob, the delightful Thai rice stick appetizer; pad thai, the national rice noodle dish, a hot and spicy entree made with chicken, beef, or seafood.

Summary & comments: The staff will be happy to explain the menu. All dishes can be ordered mild, medium, or hot. A complete vegetarian menu is available. Small but charming Thai dining room.

MACARONI GRILL

Italian	★★★	Inexpensive/Moderate	QUALITY 82
			VALUE B

2400 West Sahara Avenue
248-9500   Strip Zone 1

Customers: Locals, tourists	Friendliness rating: ★★★★★
Reservations: Not accepted	Parking: Large lot
When to go: Any time	Bar: Full service
Entree range: Lunch, $4.95–8.95;	Wine selection: Good
dinner, $6.75–19.95	Dress: Casual
Payment: VISA, MC, AMEX, DC, D	Disabled access: Ground floor
Service rating: ★★★★★	

(Macaroni Grill)

Lunch & dinner: Sunday–Thursday, 11 a.m.–10 p.m.; Friday and Saturday, 11 a.m.–11 p.m.

Setting & atmosphere: Handsome Italian country decor. Spacious dining rooms with high ceilings and many decorative touches. Fresh flowers fill the counters. A display case at the entrance showcases fresh produce and coils of fresh pasta. An exhibition kitchen.

House specialties: Fresh-from-the-oven focaccia bread redolent with herbs and dribbles of good olive oil; grilled items; marinated, grilled chicken breast with roasted vegetables and potatoes.

Summary & comments: If only the food matched the excellent service. Some of it does, but the same kitchen that produces the grilled chicken breast and the wonderful focaccia bread also produces gluey risotto and, sometimes, overcooked pasta. Accept Macaroni Grill for value and ambiance and you won't be disappointed.

MAMOUNIA			
			QUALITY
Moroccan	★★★½	Moderate	88
			VALUE
4632 South Maryland Parkway			A
597-0092 Strip Zone 1			

Customers: Tourists, locals	**Friendliness rating:** ★★★★
Reservations: Suggested	**Parking:** Lot
When to go: Any time	**Bar:** Full service
Entree range: $12.95–15.95; complete feast, $22.95	**Wine selection:** Good, but limited
Payment: VISA, MC, AMEX, D	**Dress:** Informal, casual
Service rating: ★★★★	**Disabled access:** Ground floor

Dinner: Every day, 5–11 p.m.

Setting & atmosphere: Guests sit on low upholstered benches or colorful pillows. Simulated Middle Eastern desert tent with servers in native garb.

House specialties: Hummus; kefta; shrimp scampi; tabbouleh; briouats (pastry filled with feta cheese or ground beef); and cacik (yogurt dip made with cucumber served with pita bread). Shish kabobs; whole Cornish hen; couscous; and pastilla.

Other recommendations: Moroccan feast includes harira (lentil soup), assorted salads, lamb, chicken or beef kabob, couscous with vegetables, Cornish hen, and, for dessert, chicken, seafood, or vegetable pastilla.

(Mamounia)

Entertainment & amenities: Undulating belly dancers perform the traditional steps and encourage guests to try their hand (hips?) at the sensual art.

Summary & comments: Guests enjoy an authentic Moroccan dinner starting with the traditional hand-washing and the serving of home-baked bread and fresh mint tea. Most dishes are served in the traditional style, without silverware, but utensils are yours for the asking. Most courses are cooked to order. Allow about two hours when ordering the feast. A la carte dishes are also available.

MANHATTAN			
Italian ★★★½	Moderate/Expensive	**QUALITY**	92
2600 E. Flamingo Road		**VALUE**	B
737-5000 Strip Zone I			

Customers: Locals, tourists	**Friendliness rating:** ★★★★★
Reservations: Suggested for dining room	**Parking:** Valet, large lot
	Bar: Full service
When to go: Any time	**Wine selection:** Good
Entree range: $11.95–49.95	**Dress:** Informal
Payment: VISA, MC, AMEX, DC, CB, D	**Disabled access:** Ground floor
Service rating: ★★★★★	

Dinner: Every day, 5 p.m.–1 a.m. (dining room); every day, 4 p.m.– 2 a.m. (bar-lounge).

Setting & atmosphere: Manhattan carries on the tradition of Old Las Vegas with tuxedoed captains, deep booths that afford privacy, and personal service. The entrance is highlighted with an etched-mirrored wall portraying the Manhattan, New York skyline, a vaulted ceiling, and other designer touches. Lighting is designed to make everyone look their best. The music of Frank Sinatra, Tony Bennett, Nat King Cole, and Ella Fitzgerald is kept at a soothing, nonintrusive level.

House specialties: Scampi P.J.; carpaccio of salmon; salad Caprese served country-style on a bed of roasted peppers; pasta alla Mary Macaluso (the owner's mother's recipe); the pastas with seafood; New York steak Florentine; the 22-ounce, double-cut, fully trimmed veal chop; rib-eye steak with garlic mashed potatoes and portobello mushrooms.

Other recommendations: The antipasto Manhattan, a selection of marinated and grilled vegetables, assorted meats and cheeses, and a wonderful chunky homemade caponato; the rich homemade ice cream served almost soft—have it with seasonal berries.

Summary & comments: A separate bar and lounge features a late-night menu with appetizers, hamburgers, steak sandwiches, and other casual fare. The dining room menu is also available. The food is always good, but it's at its best when chef/owner P.J. is in the kitchen. Dining hours are flexible. If reservations warrant, the staff will accommodate by remaining open later, so call ahead. In spite of the tuxedoed captains, Manhattan is, like its management, casual and relaxed.

MARRAKECH			
			QUALITY
Moroccan	★★★	Moderate	**86**
			VALUE
3900 Paradise Road			**B**
737-5611 Strip Zone 1			

Customers: Tourists, locals

Reservations: Suggested; required on weekends

When to go: After 7 p.m. for belly dancers; busy during conventions

Entree range: 3-course, $14.95; complete dinner, $23.95

Payment: VISA, MC, AMEX, DC, CB, D

Service rating: ★★★★

Friendliness rating: ★★★★

Parking: Shopping-center lot

Bar: Full service

Wine selection: A Moroccan red and French white by the glass or bottle; Mondavi and Jordan, plus imported wines

Dress: Informal, casual

Disabled access: Ground floor

Dinner: Sunday–Thursday, 5:30–9 p.m.; Friday and Saturday, 5:30–11 p.m.

Setting & atmosphere: Simulated desert tent with servers in native garb. Brass tables, floor pillows, and benches for seating maintain the illusion. Diners eat with their hands.

House specialties: Shrimp scampi; harira soup; Moroccan-style chicken in light lemon sauce; flambé lamb brochette. Multicourse fixed-price dinner, which does not include couscous. Pastilla, a flaky chicken pie, is not served for dessert in Morocco, but it is at Marrakech.

Entertainment & amenities: Belly dancers undulate and undulate, pausing only to have greenbacks thrust into their costumes.

Summary & comments: Moroccan food in an Arabian Nights setting. Belly dancing is competent but often intrusive.

MAYFLOWER CUISINIER

Chinese/French	★★★★½	Moderate/Expensive	QUALITY
			94
			VALUE
			B

4750 West Sahara Avenue
870-8432   Southwest Zone 3

Customers: Locals, some tourists
Reservations: Suggested
When to go: Any time
Entree range: $12.95–21.95
Payment: VISA, MC, AMEX, DC, D
Service rating: ★★★★

Friendliness rating: ★★★★½
Parking: Shopping-center lot
Bar: Full service
Wine selection: Upscale
Dress: Casual to semi-dressy
Disabled access: Ground floor

Lunch: Monday–Friday, 11 a.m.–2:30 p.m.
Dinner: Monday–Thursday, 5–9:30 p.m.; Friday and Saturday, 5–10:30 p.m.; Sunday, closed.

Setting & atmosphere: Two-level, 100-seat dining room; tastefully decorated in pink with contemporary black lacquer accents and handsome wall hangings. Choose from the main-level dining room or the more private mezzanine, or dine on the mist-cooled patio.

House specialties: Roast duck salad with plum vinaigrette; roast duck and goat cheese quesadilla with salsa topping; chicken pot-stickers with peanut-basil sauce; grilled lemongrass chicken salad; Cornish game hen à la chinoise; grilled tenderloin of beef with Mongolian sauce; Mayflower shrimp in pineapple-apricot sauce with scallion noodles. New dishes are added regularly.

Other recommendations: Ginger chicken ravioli with scallion-Szechuan sauce; hot and sour soup; Mongolian grilled lamb chops with cilantro-mint sauce; grilled Ahi tuna with Dijon-lime sauce; stir-fried chicken in plum wine with lychee nuts. Imaginative desserts that change seasonally.

Summary & comments: Owner-chef Ming See Woo and manager Theresa, her daughter, created this fine cross-cultural restaurant. The new bar is ideal for a pre-dinner drink.

MICHAEL'S

			QUALITY
Continental	★★★★	Expensive	**93**
			VALUE
			D

Barbary Coast Hotel
 737-7111   Strip Zone I

Customers: Tourists, locals	**Service rating:** ★★★★★
Reservations: Difficult, but starts taking reservations at 3:30 p.m.	**Friendliness rating:** ★★★★★
	Parking: Parking garage, valet
When to go: Whenever you can get a reservation	**Bar:** Full service
	Wine selection: Excellent
Entree range: $45–70	**Dress:** Sport coat, dressy
Payment: VISA, MC, AMEX, DC, CB, D	**Disabled access:** Small staircase

Dinner: Every day, four seatings at 6, 6:30, 9, and 9:30 p.m.

Setting & atmosphere: Comfortable chairs in intimate table settings. Deep carpeting and romantic lighting create a luxurious room in the rococo style of early Las Vegas.

House specialties: Rack of lamb bouquetière; live Maine lobster; veal chop Florentine; fresh Dover sole.

Other recommendations: Shrimp cocktail served atop an igloo of ice, illuminated from within. All meats are prime.

Entertainment & amenities: Complimentary petits fours, chocolate-dipped fruits, and fancy fresh fruits are presented after dinner.

Summary & comments: If you're staying at a Strip hotel, the casino can help with a reservation. Early diners have a better chance of securing a table than those who like to dine at prime time. The menu (strictly à la carte) is a view of the Las Vegas of yesteryear.

MONTE CARLO

			QUALITY
Continental	★★★★½	Expensive	**95**
			VALUE
			C

Desert Inn
 733-4444   Strip Zone I

Customers: Tourists, locals	**Friendliness rating:** ★★★★
Reservations: A must	**Parking:** Large lot, valet
When to go: Nonconvention times	**Bar:** Full service
Entree range: $38–65	**Wine selection:** Excellent
Payment: VISA, MC, AMEX, DC, CB, D	**Dress:** Sport coat, dressy
Service rating: ★★★★★	**Disabled access:** Elevators

(Monte Carlo)

Dinner: Thursday–Monday, 6–11 p.m.; Tuesday and Wednesday, closed.

Setting & atmosphere: Garden atmosphere, oil paintings on walls, tables set dramatically with lots of crystal and lace.

House specialties: Duck liver terrine with truffled brioche; lobster bisque; salad of grilled lobster; classic Caesar's salad prepared tableside; veal chop with morel sauce.

Other recommendations: Roasted salmon in a potato crust; coq au vin; chateaubriand or rack of lamb for two; flaming desserts including such classics as crêpes suzette and cherries jubilee; warm dessert soufflés.

Summary & comments: A beautiful, romantic room. Waiters make a major production when serving flaming dishes tableside. Allow at least three hours to enjoy a complete meal. Some seasonal menu changes.

Honors & awards: Mobil four-star award.

MORTONI'S			
			QUALITY
Italian, California-style ★★★★ Moderate/Expensive			90
			VALUE
Hard Rock Hotel, Harmon Avenue and Paradise Road			B
693-5000 Strip Zone I			

Customers: Hotel guests, tourists, locals

Reservations: Recommended

When to go: Any time but concert time

Entree range: $13–29.95

Payment: VISA, MC, AMEX, DC, D

Service rating: ★★★★

Friendliness rating: ★★★★

Parking: Valet, lot

Bar: Full service

Wine selection: Good

Dress: Casual chic

Disabled access: Ground floor

Dinner: Sunday–Thursday, 6–10:30 p.m.; Friday and Saturday, 6–11 p.m.

Setting & atmosphere: Enter through a massive door that is a work of art; the decor is understated and elegant. Lighting is soft and subdued, enhancing both the food and the diner. In a hotel with a music theme, of course there is music in the dining room. Be assured that it is not intrusive and is not hard rock.

House specialties: Bisteca con funghi, a 20-ounce rib-eye with a bone that would have satisfied Elvis; clams and mussels steamed in wine with garlic; double-cut pork chops; veal Milanese, a chop pounded wafer-thin, breaded, and fried; pasta and risotto selection includes choices ideal for vegetarians; plate-size pizzas; chocolate paradise, fresh berries with mascarpone cheese, tiramisu, or the fine cookie selection for dessert. All entrees include generous portions of roasted potatoes and fresh vegetables, along with arugula salad—the spicy green is so perfect it looks just-picked. The steaks are first marked on the grill, then finished in the high heat of the wood-burning oven.

Summary & comments: Only natural ingredients and organic produce are used at Mortoni's. The menu is small but choice, offering a full selection of dishes. The Hard Rock Hotel transcends generations; it should be experienced by everyone, regardless of age.

MORTON'S

Steak	★★★½	Expensive	QUALITY 89
			VALUE C

3200 Las Vegas Boulevard, South (Fashion Show Mall)
  893-0703   Strip Zone I

Customers: Tourists, locals	Parking: Shopping-center lot,
Reservations: Recommended,	garage, valet
especially during conventions	Bar: Attractive, full service
When to go: Any time	Wine selection: Excellent
Entree range: $16.95–29.95	Dress: Informal
Payment: VISA, MC, AMEX, DC, CB	Disabled access: Same level as park-
Service rating: ★★★★	ing lot
Friendliness rating: ★★★★	

Dinner: Monday–Saturday, 5:30–11 p.m.; Sunday, 5:30–10 p.m.

Setting & atmosphere: Men's club atmosphere, with paneled boardroom (for large parties), polished oak barroom, and comfortable booths.

House specialties: Black bean soup. Whole onion bread brought to table. Porterhouse steak; New York sirloin steak; rib-eye steak; double filet mignon; whole Maine lobster; shrimp Alexander. Huge strawberries with sabayon sauce.

Other recommendations: Appetizer of broiled sea scallops wrapped in bacon, apricot chutney; double-cut prime rib; lamb chops; swordfish steak; lemon-oregano chicken. Shrimp Alexander as an appetizer.

Entertainment & amenities: Storage lockers for regular guests' wines.

Summary & comments: Branch of Chicago-based steakhouse. Entrance from outside Fashion Show Mall. Appetizers, salads, entrees, desserts all served in large portions. Everything à la carte, including side dishes. The dessert soufflés are a specialty but are disappointing. Stick to selections from the pastry tray or the gorgeous fresh berries. Cigar smoking is encouraged.

NAPA				
Contemporary French Cuisine	★★★★★	Expensive	**QUALITY**	
			95	
Rio Suites Hotel Valley View & Flamingo			**VALUE**	
252-7777 Strip Zone I			**C**	

Customers: Locals, tourists
Reservations: Requested
When to go: Any time
Entree range: $28–53
Payment: VISA, AMEX, MC, DC, D
Service rating: ★★★★★

Friendliness rating: ★★★★★
Parking: Valet, garage, lot
Bar: Full service
Wine selection: Outstanding
Dress: Business attire
Disabled access: Elevator

Dinner: Wednesday–Sunday, 6–11 p.m.

Setting & atmosphere: Napa has an enlightened mission, one wholeheartedly endorsed by Rio founder Tony Marnell and the mostly male executive staff: to create an ambiance specifically for women. The enchanting dining room is elegantly appointed and filled with art. Men enjoy the inviting room as much as the women.

House specialties: Maryland lump crab cake appetizer; Maui onion soup with truffle dumplings, served in a Maui onion; Maine diver scallops with black truffles; wood-grilled Maine monkfish, studded with garlic; marinated breast of chicken roasted in a salt crust.

Other recommendations: A large baked potato filled with Louisiana crayfish and lobster coral sauce; wood-grilled veal chop with truffled potato gnocchi; chicken pot pie; the selection of desserts.

Summary & comments: Celebrity chef Jean-Louis Palladin, formerly of the Watergate restaurant in Washington, D.C., works in an exhibition kitchen that can be viewed from the front tables. Napa's wine list includes 250 wines by the glass. A grand circular staircase joins Napa to the superb Wine Cellar Tasting Room. A grand tasting adventure at modest prices.

NEROS

	QUALITY
Contemporary American Cuisine ★★★★ Expensive	**90**
	VALUE
	C+

Caesars Palace Hotel
  731-7110   Strip Zone 1

Customers: Tourists, locals
Reservations: Requested
When to go: Any time except convention times
Entree range: $26–49
Payment: VISA, MC, AMEX, DC, CB, D
Service rating: ★★★★★

Friendliness rating: ★★★★★
Parking: Valet, garage, lot
Bar: Full service
Wine selection: Excellent
Dress: Business attire
Disabled access: Ground floor

Dinner: Sunday–Thursday, 5:30–10 p.m.; Friday and Saturday, 5:30–10:30 p.m.

Setting & atmosphere: Softly lit, with comfortable booths and tables, Neros is a fine example of understated elegance.

House specialties: Cut-to-order steak tartare with toasted brioche, waffled potato chips, and a garnish of pansies; pan-seared foie gras with 100-year-old balsamic vinegar; roasted beet and wild green salad; smoky vidalia onion soup with herbed goat cheese crouton; glazed, whole roasted Sonoma squab with parsnip puree; grilled swordfish with pan-fried risotto cakes.

Other recommendations: Pan-roasted free-range chicken atop truffled mashed potatoes; rack of Colorado lamb with creamy Parmesan polenta; grilled Pacific salmon with French de Puy lentils; chef Mario's splendid desserts, especially the delectable fallen chocolate soufflé.

Summary & comments: This one-time steak house has taken on new life under Chef Mario Capone, formerly of Biba restaurant in Boston. He is one of the bright young chefs who are fast making Las Vegas a culinary destination.

NORTH BEACH CAFE

			QUALITY
Italian	★★★½	Moderate	**89**
			VALUE
			A

2605 South Decatur Boulevard
  247-9530   Southwest Zone 3

Customers: Locals
Reservations: 6 or more
When to go: Any time
Entree range: $9.95–22.95
Payment: VISA, MC, AMEX, DC, CB, D
Service rating: ★★★★
Friendliness rating: ★★★★★

Parking: Lot
Bar: Full service
Wine selection: Good choices,
  including wines from South
  America
Dress: Informal to casual
Disabled access: Ground floor

Lunch: Monday–Saturday, 11:30 a.m.–4:30 p.m.
Dinner: Sunday–Friday, 5–10 p.m.; Saturday, 5–10:30 p.m.

Setting & atmosphere: Cheerful; walls are decorated with bold paintings by owner's cousin. Patio service.

House specialties: Empanadas Argentinas created by owner's Spanish mother; linguini pesto alla Genovese; agnolatti alla crema or pomodoro; linguini with grilled chicken breast, eggplant, zucchini, and a touch of tomato sauce; chicken cognac; zuppa Inglese.

Other recommendations: Lunch specialties including linguini with fresh clams; eggplant parmigiana; roasted chicken alla Veneziana with bell peppers; and Joey Special (penne with spinach, broccoli, grilled chicken breast, mozzarella, and light tomato sauce). Linguini with fresh mussels, calamari, or scallops; rigatoni with meat sauce; swordfish livornese; chicken angelo. Tiramisu della casa.

Entertainment & amenities: Violinist performs Friday and Saturday nights.

Summary & comments: Empanadas Argentinas are an unusual appetizer for an Italian restaurant. Created with ground beef, eggs, olives, and raisins, they are one of many nice touches here.

OLYMPIC CAFE

			QUALITY
Greek	★★★½	Inexpensive	88
			VALUE
			B

4023 Spring Mountain Road
  876-7900   Southwest Zone 3

Customers: Mostly locals, a favorite for Greeks
Reservations: Recommended
When to go: Any time
Entree range: $10.95–18.95
Payment: VISA, MC, AMEX
Service rating: ★★★★

Friendliness rating: ★★★★★
Parking: Lot
Bar: Full service
Wine selection: Mostly Greek
Dress: Casual
Disabled access: Ground floor

Lunch: Monday–Saturday, 11 a.m.–2:30 p.m.
Dinner: Every day, 5–10 p.m.

Setting & atmosphere: Greek garden decor, blue and white tablecloths, cozy atmosphere; small quarters.

House specialties: Saganaki (sautéed imported cheese flamed with metaxa at table); skordalia (garlic dip); dolmades; spanakopita; souvlaki. Galaktobouriko (Greek custard baked in phyllo dough).

Other recommendations: Greek combination plate; moussaka; gyros platter; broiled shrimp with lemon sauce; shish kabob; lamb chops à la grecque. Baklava.

Summary & comments: Belly dancers perform one Saturday a month. Call to confirm.

OUTBACK STEAKHOUSE

			QUALITY
Steak	★★★½	Moderate	**88**
			VALUE
			B

3685 West Flamingo Road
   253-1020   Strip Zone 1

1950 North Rainbow Boulevard
   647-1035   North Zone 4

8671 West Sahara Avenue
   228-1088   Southwest Zone 3

4141 South Pecos Road at Flamingo Road
   898-3801   Southeast Zone 5

4423 East Sunset (Green Valley, Henderson)
   451-7808   Southeast Zone 5

Customers: Locals, tourists
Reservations: Not accepted
When to go: Any time
Entree range: $9.95–17.95
Payment: VISA, MC, AMEX, DC, D
Service rating: ★★★★
Friendliness rating: ★★★★★

Parking: Lot
Bar: Full service
Wine selection: Good
Dress: Casual
Disabled access: Ground floor and ramp

Dinner: Sunday–Thursday, 4–10:30 p.m.; Friday and Saturday, 4–11:30 p.m. Sunset and Sahara locations: Sunday, noon–9 p.m.

Setting & atmosphere: Boomerangs, surfboards, maps, flags, and other Aussie memorabilia decorate the walls of these comfortable, busy, ranch-themed restaurants.

House specialties: Center-cut Jackeroo pork chops; grilled shrimp, yes, on the barbie; a variety of steaks; bloomin' onions, battered and fried; Aussie cheese fries; barbecued ribs and chicken; Sydney's sinful sundae; chocolate thunder from Down Under.

Summary & comments: The owners are well on their way to having six Outbacks in Las Vegas. A cut above other moderately priced formula steak houses. Friendly, caring service. Expect a wait, sometimes a long one, if you dine at prime times. Beat the crowds—dine early or late. Other locations at 1950 North Rainbow (647-1035) and 4423 East Sunset (451-7808).

PALACE COURT

			QUALITY
Continental	★★★★★	Expensive	**98**

	VALUE
Caesars Palace	**C**

731-7110   Strip Zone I

Customers: Tourists, locals
Reservations: A must
When to go: Avoid conventions
Entree range: $33–65
Payment: VISA, MC, AMEX, DC, CB, D
Service rating: ★★★★★

Friendliness rating: ★★★★★
Parking: Garage, valet
Bar: Full service
Wine selection: Excellent
Dress: Jacket required
Disabled access: Elevator

Dinner: Every day, seatings every half-hour beginning at 6 p.m., with the last seating at 10 p.m.

Setting & atmosphere: A magnificent stained-glass dome is the focal point in the dining room. Statuary, seasonal flowers, and greenery adorn the room. Early diners can watch the sunset. A new, young, French chef has awakened this sleeping beauty.

House specialties: The turbot, flown in from France; appetizers of any kind, especially the foie gras; any of the chef's suggestions, including the tasting dinners, of four or more courses; veal and beef dishes.

Other recommendations: Lobster bisque flamed in armagnac; onion soup baked with Gruyère cheese and served in jumbo onion; a tasting dinner of four or more courses. Desserts—crème brûlée and chocolate, raspberry, and Grand Marnier soufflés with vanilla sabayon.

Entertainment & amenities: Relaxing piano music in the romantic lounge bar.

Summary & comments: Superb dining in elegant surroundings.

Honors & awards: Winner of Mobil four-star award since 1978; *Wine Spectator* Award of Excellence; DiRoNA Award.

THE PALM

			QUALITY
Steak	★★★★	Expensive	**90**
			VALUE
The Forum Shops at Caesars			**C**
732-7256 Strip Zone 1			

Customers: Tourists, locals
Reservations: Recommended
When to go: Any time
Entree range: $19–60
Payment: VISA, MC, AMEX, DC, CB, D
Service rating: ★★★★

Friendliness rating: ★★★★★
Parking: Parking garage, valet
Bar: Extensive, full service
Wine selection: Very good
Dress: Informal
Disabled access: Ground floor

Lunch: Every day, 11:30 a.m.–4 p.m.
Dinner: Every day, 11:30 a.m.–11 p.m.

Setting & atmosphere: Colorful caricatures of local notables as well as nationally known entertainers cover walls. Antique wall boasts reproductions of some of the original '20s artwork from the first Palm in New York.

House specialties: Monday Night Salad, named for football fans who frequent the Palm Too in New York (lettuces, onion, pimento, tomato, and anchovy); Raju salad. Jumbo lobsters; clams and shrimp Posillipo; cottage fries and fried onions. The 38- to 40-ounce New York strip for two can easily serve three. Steak à la Stone; veal martini; outstanding lump-meat crab cakes—broiled, not fried. Excellent hash brown potatoes.

Other recommendations: Veal; lamb and pork chops; pastas; blackened breast of chicken.

Entertainment & amenities: Celebrity-watching is the entertainment.

Summary & comments: Caters to celebrities, with drawings of many entertainers and local movers and shakers on the walls. The Palm suffers from the "good news, bad news" Las Vegas malady—too much business. Avoid the banquet room in back. It's noisy and drab; the service is careless. Stick to your guns and insist on a table in the dining room.

PAMPLEMOUSSE

			QUALITY
Continental/French	★★★½	Expensive	**87**

	VALUE
400 East Sahara Avenue	**D**

733-2066   Strip Zone I

Customers: Locals, tourists
Reservations: Required
When to go: Any time a reservation
  is available
Entree range: $17–26
Payment: VISA, MC, AMEX, DC, D
Service rating: ★★★★★

Friendliness rating: ★★★★★
Parking: Street, lot
Bar: Beer and wine only
Wine selection: Excellent
Dress: Upscale casual
Disabled access: Ground floor

Dinner: Tuesday–Sunday, 6–9:30 p.m.; Monday, closed.

Setting & atmosphere: Country French. Attractive wine cellar at entrance to dining room. Restaurant has no menu; waiters recite the day's offerings and describe each dish.

House specialties: Duckling dishes; medallions of veal prepared with baked apples; special seafood dishes in season—mussels, monkfish, salmon; assorted desserts, all delicious.

Other recommendations: Dinner begins with a fine assortment of fresh vegetables (crudités) served from a handsome basket with an individual crock of house vinaigrette.

Summary & comments: Waiters will give prices when reciting menu only if asked. Ask, so there are no surprises when the check arrives.

PAPYRUS

			QUALITY
Polynesian	★★★	Moderate	**86**

	VALUE
Luxor	**B**

262-4774   Strip Zone I

Customers: Tourists
Reservations: Accepted
When to go: Any time
Entree range: $15.95–34.95
Payment: VISA, MC, AMEX, DC, D, CB
Service rating: ★★★★

Friendliness rating: ★★★★★
Parking: Lot, valet
Bar: Full service
Wine selection: Fair
Dress: Informal, casual
Disabled access: Ramp

Dinner: Every day, 5–11 p.m.

Setting & atmosphere: Romantic Polynesian decor with grass-hut booths and hanging blowfish. Many alcoves give cozy appearance to 240-seat room. New York skyline looms over Pacific Island atmosphere.

House specialties: Otemanu hot rock sampler—Luxor's version of Pacific Basin hot rock grilling at your table—a chicken, beef, shrimp, and julienne vegetables appetizer. Ahi tuna tartare in soy-chile sauce (East-West version of sashimi). Papyrus eight-treasure fried rice. Mandarin chocolate cake.

Other recommendations: Shrimp and bay scallop chow mein; wok-seared rare salmon; pork loin with Mandarin sauce; Paniola steak, named after famous Hawaiian cowboys; grilled Korean-style short ribs with basil mashed potatoes and tempura vegetable garnish; Thai charred lemongrass chicken breast with sweet chile sauce.

Summary & comments: Unusual appetizers are a highlight. Exotic tropical drinks are beautifully depicted on their own colorful menu.

PASTA MIA

Italian	★★★	Moderate	QUALITY 82
			VALUE A

2585 East Flamingo Road
  733-0091 Southeast Zone 5

4455 West Flamingo Road
  251-8871 Southwest Zone 3

Customers: Locals, tourists	**Parking:** Lot
Reservations: Not accepted	**Bar:** Wine and beer
When to go: Any time	**Wine selection:** Good choice of
Entree range: $8.50–14	moderately priced Italian and
Payment: VISA, MC, D	domestic
(AMEX at West Flamingo)	**Dress:** Informal, casual
Service rating: ★★★★	**Disabled access:** Ground floor
Friendliness rating: ★★★★★	

Lunch: Monday–Friday, 11:30 a.m.–5 p.m.

Dinner: Every day, 5–9:30 p.m. Hours vary slightly for the West Flamingo location.

Setting & atmosphere: Checked tablecloths, booths, round family-style tables. The aroma of garlic greets guests. Sinatra tapes provide musical background. Casual, friendly place.

(Pasta Mia)

House specialties: Penne broccoli and spinach; angelhair with tomato and basil; linguini with fresh mussels, shrimp, clams, or scallops. Pasta e fagioli or romaine salad with garlic dressing and garlic bread included with all entrees. Roasted chicken with peppers and onions. Piero's cheesecake.

Other recommendations: Tortellini bolognese; penne arrabbiata; chicken angelo; salmon meunière; orange roughy française. Antipasto including roasted peppers and marinated eggplant; stuffed artichoke.

Summary & comments: A longtime chef founded the restaurants and developed the menu. His wife and daughter run Pasta Mia East. Family atmosphere. Extra-large portions—take-home boxes are a way of life. Garlic permeates everything except the desserts.

PASTA PIRATE

Seafood/Pasta	★★★	Moderate	QUALITY 86
			VALUE A

California Hotel, 12 Ogden Avenue
385-1222   Downtown Zone 2

Customers: Locals, tourists
Reservations: Suggested
When to go: Any time
Entree range: $7.95–23.95
Payment: VISA, MC, AMEX, DC, D
Service rating: ★★★★

Friendliness rating: ★★★★
Parking: Garage, valet
Bar: Full service
Wine selection: Adequate
Dress: Casual
Disabled access: Ground floor

Dinner: Every day, 5:30–11 p.m.

Setting & atmosphere: Small restaurant with waterfront motif featuring tin walls, a brick floor, fishnets, neon signs, and an open kitchen.

House specialties: Pasta and seafood; Alaskan king crab legs; scampi; baby lobster tails; marinated sesame lobster brochettes. A glass of wine is included with all entrees.

Other recommendations: Filet mignon with prawns; live Maine lobster; rigatoni Romano; cavatelli with broccoli; penne Diana; Cajun tuna.

Entertainment & amenities: Piano player, 6–11 p.m.

Summary & comments: The Pasta Pirate offers an imaginative menu at moderate prices. It's a fine value.

PEKING MARKET

Chinese	★★★½	Moderate	QUALITY
			87
			VALUE
			B

Flamingo Hilton Hotel
  733-3111   Strip Zone 1

Customers: Tourists, locals	Friendliness rating: ★★★★★
Reservations: Suggested	Parking: Valet, garage
When to go: Any time	Bar: Full service
Entree range: $10–30	Wine selection: Good
Payment: VISA, MC, AMEX, CB, DC, D	Dress: Informal
Service rating: ★★★★★	Disabled access: Ground floor

Dinner: Every day, 5:30–10:30 p.m.

Setting & atmosphere: Contemporary Chinese decor with traditional, authentic art and antiques. Each dining area is a treasure with teakwood walls, silk fabric accents, and other decorative enhancements. The upholstered booths are plush and comfortable. Table linens are moire embossed. A captivating saltwater aquarium is on view at the entrance.

House specialties: Seafood dishes with shrimp, lobster, and crab; orange peel beef; Peking duck, available without advance notice; lop chung fried rice; five-spice monkfish; Peking Market chow mein with tender pieces of squid.

Other recommendations: Well-priced family-style dinners for two or more diners; Chinese chicken salad; pot stickers; Peking Market's signature flambéed dessert, prepared tableside—warm, crispy pudding topped with vanilla ice cream and a heady sauce made from caramelized sugar, coconut and pineapple juice, and Triple Sec.

Summary & comments: Peking Market has been completely refurbished, but in spite of the large amount spent on the re-do, menu prices have been reduced. With all its posh new decor and expanded staff, Peking Market is an excellent value.

PHILIPS SUPPER HOUSE

			QUALITY
American/Prime Rib	★★★	Moderate	80
			VALUE
			A

4545 West Sahara Avenue
  873-5222   Southwest Zone 3

Customers: Locals, tourists
Reservations: Accepted
When to go: Any time
Entree range: $14.95–32.95
  (complete dinner); lobster at mar-
  ket price
Payment: VISA, MC, AMEX, DC, D

Service rating: ★★★★
Friendliness rating: ★★★★
Parking: Lot
Bar: Full service
Wine selection: Ample
Dress: Casual
Disabled access: Ground floor

Dinner: Every day, 4:30–11 p.m.

Setting & atmosphere: Victorian bay-windowed home. Comfortable dining rooms and many small rooms create a homey atmosphere.

House specialties: Fresh baked loaf of bread; hearty soups; variety of seafood dishes, broiled, baked, fried; Black Angus New York steak. Twilight menu Sunday through Friday: choice of 11 entrees from $8.95 to $14.95, including soup or salad, and potato or pasta, from 4:30 to 6 p.m.

Other recommendations: Blackened scampi; scalone (abalone and scallops); steamed clams; broiled lamb chops; sand dabs; Italian chicken and veal dishes.

Summary & comments: Hearty full-course dinners. Select lighter soups and vegetables for better enjoyment of entree, or take home a "person" bag. A good getaway from the Strip; only a ten-minute cab ride from most hotels. Philips is a longtime local favorite.

PIERO'S

			QUALITY
Italian	★★★★½	Expensive	92
			VALUE
			C

355 Convention Center Drive
  369-2305   Strip Zone 1

Customers: Locals, tourists,
  conventioneers
Reservations: Required
When to go: Any time
Payment: VISA, MC, AMEX, DC, D

Service rating: ★★★★½
Friendliness rating: ★★★★½
Parking: Valet, lot
Bar: Full service
Wine selection: Excellent

(Piero's)

Entree range: $17–32
  (higher for lobster)

Dress: Informal
Disabled access: Ground floor

Dinner: Every day, 5:30–9:30 p.m.

Setting & atmosphere: Many softly lit booths and alcoves for guests desiring privacy. Excellent wait staff. Old World service.

House specialties: Osso buco Piero; zuppa di pesce, a seafood "soup" filled with lobster, clams, mussels, shrimp, calamari, and scallops; whole roasted kosher chicken as good or better than Mama used to make; any dish with Provimi veal; the Italian pastas with French-influenced sauces; the 25-ounce New York steak; stone crab claws or cakes of Maryland blue crab, in season.

Summary & comments: Piero's has just completed a major renovation. The main dining room is unchanged, but there are now two private dining rooms for 12 to 20 people; a banquet room that can accommodate up to 250; a piano bar; and a much larger kitchen. Celebrities and sports figures always make their way to Piero's, as do Las Vegas power brokers, who consistently dine here. Dom Perignon, Cristal, Grand Cordon champagnes and $400 bottles of Montrachet are the norm at Piero's.

POPPA GAR'S

American	★★½	Inexpensive	QUALITY
			79
			VALUE
			A

1624 West Oakey Boulevard
  384-4513   Downtown Zone 2

Customers: Locals, politicians
Reservations: Accepted
When to go: Avoid noon–2 p.m.
Entree range: $7.25–14.95
Payment: Check with bank guarantee or cash
Service rating: ★★★★

Friendliness rating: ★★★★★
Parking: Large lot
Bar: Beer and wine only
Wine selection: Fair
Dress: Come as you are
Disabled access: Ground floor

Open: Monday–Friday, 5 a.m.–9 p.m.; Saturday, 5 a.m.–2 p.m.; Sunday, closed.

Setting & atmosphere: Hunting, fishing, and political memorabilia. Lunch counter–cum–museum: walls covered with pictures, mounted animals, and fish. Prepare for some of the tallest hunting and fishing stories in town. Spotting local celebrities is a popular luncheon pastime.

(Poppa Gar's)

House specialties: Brace of quail; pan-fried mountain trout; home-baked bread and pastries.

Other recommendations: Rib-eye steak; buffalo hamburgers. Old-fashioned desserts such as grapenut custard and hot fudge nut cake. Breakfast—Philadelphia scrapple and Reuben omelets.

Summary & comments: Owner Garland Miner has been serving locals for over 29 years. Just about every dish is homemade and hearty. Reminiscent of a '30s diner serving home-cooked foods. Same menu for breakfast, lunch, and dinner. A favorite local hangout that's a throwback to Old Las Vegas.

REDWOOD BAR & GRILL

American/Prime Rib	★★★½	Moderate	QUALITY 87
			VALUE A

California Hotel, 12 Ogden Avenue
385-1222   Downtown Zone 2

Customers: Tourists, locals	Friendliness rating: ★★★★★
Reservations: Suggested	Parking: Hotel lot and valet
When to go: Early evening	Bar: Full service
Entree range: $12.95–29.95	Wine selection: Good
Payment: VISA, MC, AMEX, DC, D	Dress: Informal
Service rating: ★★★★	Disabled access: Ground floor

Dinner: Every day, 5:30–11 p.m.

Setting & atmosphere: Country English furnishings and fireplace make for comfortable dining. A quiet room where service is efficient and gracious.

House specialties: Caesar salad; steak Diane; chicken with apricot sauce. Porterhouse steak special: 16 ounces for $12.95 includes soup or salad, potatoes, vegetable, dessert.

Other recommendations: Soup du jour such as seafood chowder; Australian lobster tail; fresh fish; roast prime rib; veal Oscar; steak and lobster. Macadamia nut tartufo.

Entertainment & amenities: Piano music nightly.

Summary & comments: Excellent value. Prime rib portion is very generous, cooked as ordered. Although part of a locally owned group of five hotels, the Redwood Bar & Grill maintains its cozy individuality in both decor and service.

RENATA'S

			QUALITY
Continental	★★★½	Moderate/Expensive	**88**
			VALUE
			B

4451 East Sunset Road (Green Valley, Henderson)
  435-4000   Southeast Zone 5

Customers: Locals, some tourists
Reservations: Suggested
When to go: Any time
Entree range: $9.50–35
  (Chinese specialties: $8.95–18.50)
Payment: VISA, MC, AMEX, D
Service rating: ★★★★

Friendliness rating: ★★★★★
Parking: Shopping-center lot
Bar: Full service
Wine selection: Very good
Dress: Informal, casual
Disabled access: Ground floor

Dinner: Tuesday–Saturday, 5–11 p.m.; 24-hour bar and lounge menu, every day.

Setting & atmosphere: Attractive pale-green and salmon decor, with booths around dining room. Bright and cheerful by day, dimly lit and cozy by night. Large bar/lounge area open 24 hours.

House specialties: Caesar salad with grilled chicken or bay shrimp; grilled prawn salad with enoki mushrooms and dill vinaigrette. Angelhair with fresh tomato, roasted garlic, and basil; broiled salmon fillet with golden lentil salsa; vol-au-vent of chicken for lunch; crab puffs Rangoon; imaginative pastas; swordfish piquant; tournedos Rossini; flambéed desserts.

Other recommendations: Renata's meat loaf with mashed potatoes, caramelized onions, and cabernet demi-glacé; spinach fettuccini with broiled chicken breast and tequila cream for lunch. Chilled abalone appetizer; rack of lamb Sumatra; chicken Santa Fe; steak au poivre for dinner; plus nightly specials. Sunday champagne brunch.

Entertainment & amenities: Strolling trio—violin, bass, guitar. Monthly (Wednesday nights) wine-maker dinners.

Summary & comments: This suburban Green Valley dining room features an ambitious menu. The combination of an Asian food-and-beverage director and a French chef makes for an interesting selection of dishes. A new wine-themed dining room with a separate menu features French cuisine.

RICARDO'S

			QUALITY
Mexican	★★★½	Moderate	**85**
			VALUE
			B

4930 West Flamingo Road
  871-7119   Southwest Zone 3

2380 East Tropicana Avenue
  798-4515   Southeast Zone 5

Meadows Mall
  870-1088   North Zone 4

Customers: Locals
Reservations: Accepted
When to go: Any time
Entree range: $5.95–12.95
Payment: VISA, MC, AMEX, DC, D, CB
Service rating: ★★★

Friendliness rating: ★★★★
Parking: Lots at all locations
Bar: Full service
Wine selection: Good
Dress: Informal, casual
Disabled access: At all locations

Lunch & dinner: Same menu day and evening, all locations.
At West Flamingo Road: Friday and Saturday, 11 a.m.–11 p.m.; Sunday–Thursday, 11 a.m.–10 p.m.
At East Tropicana Avenue: Sunday–Thursday, 11 a.m.–10 p.m.; Friday and Saturday, 11 a.m.–11 p.m.
At Meadows Mall: Monday–Saturday, 11 a.m.–10 p.m.; Sunday, 11 a.m.–9 p.m.

Setting & atmosphere: Attractive Mexican decor at each location.

House specialties: Good selection of appetizers to complement margaritas. Chimichanga ranchera; enchiladas rancheras; chicken picado; sizzling camarones al diablo; steak cilantro verde.

Other recommendations: Albondigas soup, thick with vegetables; enchilada-taco combinations; chili Colorado; chile relleno; burritos. Lunch buffet at West Flamingo and East Tropicana locations Monday through Saturday from 11 a.m. to 2 p.m.—all you can eat for $6.75.

Summary & comments: Although all the restaurants are operated by the same owners, each restaurant has its own distinctive flavor and specials.

RISTORANTE ITALIANO

			QUALITY
Italian	★★★★	Expensive	**91**

	VALUE
	C

Riviera Hotel
  734-5110   Strip Zone 1

Customers: Tourists, some locals
Reservations: Recommended
When to go: Any time
Entree range: $9.95–38
Payment: VISA, MC, AMEX, DC, D, CB
Service rating: ★★★★
Friendliness rating: ★★★★

Parking: Garage lot, valet
Bar: Full service
Wine selection: Good choice of reds
  and whites
Dress: Informal
Disabled access: Casino level

Dinner: Wednesday–Sunday, 5:30–10 p.m.; Monday and Tuesday, closed.

Setting & atmosphere: Soft lighting highlights Italian Mediterranean murals. Richly upholstered booths line the walls.

House specialties: Pasta rolls with ricotta cheese, spinach, prosciutto, and mozzarella baked in a mushroom cream sauce; vermicelli salsa bella vista; melanzane al caprino; costolete di vitello and gorgonzola. Ristorante special dessert—grilled eggplant stuffed with mascarpone cheese, rolled in pistachio nuts, heated and topped with liqueur-flavored sauce.

Other recommendations: Squid-ink lasagna layered with salmon mousse and scallop mousse, spinach, and ricotta served in creamy pink sauce; rack of lamb roasted with fresh garlic, rosemary, and mustard; breast of chicken saltimbocca; sautéed swordfish on a bed of fettuccini with olives, sun-dried tomatoes, capers, and white wine sauce with herbs; vermicelli tutto di mare alla ristorante.

Summary & comments: Opened in 1975, the Ristorante is a favorite of many of the stars who have appeared at the hotel. Menu includes contemporary dishes as well as a good classic Italian selection. A new private dining room, which is warm and inviting, is available for small parties.

ROSEWOOD GRILLE

			QUALITY
Lobster/Steak	★★★½	Expensive	88
			VALUE
			C

3339 Las Vegas Boulevard, South
  792-9099   Strip Zone 1

Customers: Tourists/locals
Reservations: Strongly recommended
When to go: Any time
Entree range: $19.50–29.50, higher for lobster and stone crab
Payment: VISA, MC, AMEX, DC, D, JCB

Service rating: ★★★★
Friendliness rating: ★★★★
Parking: Lot behind restaurant
Bar: Full service
Wine selection: Excellent
Dress: Informal
Disabled access: Ground floor

Dinner: Every day, 4:30–11:30 p.m.

Setting & atmosphere: Muted lighting, large booths, seating for 200. This always-busy restaurant still retains its Old World charm.

House specialties: Live Maine lobster in humongous sizes.

Other recommendations: Lobster and steak combination; beef chop; beef-eaters brochette; scampi; stone crabs; broiled salmon Charlotte; tournedos Scandia; lobster ravioli; chicken with strawberries in Cointreau. Strawberries with Dom Perignon for two; café Mozart.

Summary & comments: Restaurant stocks a week's supply of large and extra-large lobsters (up to 16 pounds). Price (three-pound minimum) changes with the market. Make certain you know price of lobster to avoid surprise when bill arrives.

RUTH'S CHRIS STEAK HOUSE

			QUALITY
Steak	★★★★	Expensive	94
			VALUE
			C

3900 Paradise Road
  791-7011   Strip Zone 1

4561 West Flamingo Road
  248-7011   Southwest Zone 5

Customers: Tourists, locals
Reservations: A must
When to go: Nonconvention times
Entree range: $18.95–53.95
Payment: VISA, MC, AMEX, DC, D
Service rating: ★★★★★

Friendliness rating: ★★★★★
Parking: Lot
Bar: Full service
Wine selection: Excellent
Dress: Informal
Disabled access: Ground floor

(Ruth's Chris Steak House)

Lunch: *Paradise:* Monday–Friday, 11 a.m.–4:30 p.m.

Dinner: *Paradise:* Every day, 4:30–10:30 p.m. *Flamingo:* 4:30 p.m.– 3 a.m.

Setting & atmosphere: Plush with dark cherry woods and beveled glass windows. Comfortable cocktail lounge.

House specialties: Prime steak, cooked to order and served sizzling with butter (steaks may be ordered dry).

Other recommendations: Besides excellent steaks, the restaurant offers veal chops, lamb chops, fresh salmon, and an outstanding variety of potatoes and vegetables. The Lyonnais and hash brown potatoes are addictive.

Summary & comments: Wine selection includes Dom Perignon and Louis Roederer Cristal, in the $100- to $300-per-bottle category. Ruth's Chris serves only prime beef. The check for two, however, can be steep; everything is à la carte, but portions are large enough to be shared. There is no service charge for sharing. The new Proprietor's Reserve private dining room can seat up to 45. Visit the new, choice wine cellar. There's a new, attractive garden room at the Paradise location. A lunch and late-night supper menu is available at the Flamingo location.

SADIE'S

American/Southern ★★★	Inexpensive/Moderate	QUALITY
		80
		VALUE
		A

505 East Twain Avenue
796-4177   Strip Zone I

Customers: Locals, some tourists	**Friendliness rating:** ★★★
Reservations: Accepted	**Parking:** Lot
When to go: Any time	**Bar:** None
Entree range: $6.95–20.95	**Wine selection:** None
Payment: VISA, MC	**Dress:** Casual
Service rating: ★★★	**Disabled access:** Ground floor

Lunch & dinner: Tuesday–Saturday, 11 a.m.–9:30 p.m.; Sunday, noon–7:30 p.m.; Monday, closed. Same menu day and evening.

Setting & atmosphere: Chintz and charm—Sadie's has the grace of the South, with its down-home cooking. Enjoy the comfort of the tall wingback chairs.

House specialties: Red beans and rice with ham hocks; ham hocks with lima beans, served with jalapeño and plain cornbread muffins. Grilled lemon-herb chicken served among sandwich specials (11 a.m. to 3 p.m.), in a salad, and as an entree. Catfish prepared crisp without a trace of grease. This is fried food as it should be.

Other recommendations: Chitterlings as an appetizer and, on Saturdays and Sundays, as an entree; fried or smothered chicken or pork chops; side orders (two included with entree) such as collard greens, cabbage, rice, yams, macaroni and cheese. Sweet potato pie and fruit cobbler à la mode.

Summary & comments: Authentic Southern cooking. Service matches leisurely Deep South lifestyle, so expect a short wait for cooked-to-order dishes.

SAIGON

			QUALITY
Vietnamese	★★★	Inexpensive	**83**
			VALUE
			A

4251 West Sahara Avenue
   362-9978   Southwest Zone 3

Customers: Mostly local Vietnamese
Reservations: Accepted
When to go: Any time
Entree range: $5–9
Payment: VISA, MC, AMEX, DC, D
Service rating: ★★★★★

Friendliness rating: ★★★★★
Parking: Small lot in front
Bar: Wine and beer
Wine selection: Fair
Dress: Casual
Disabled access: Ground floor

Lunch & dinner: Every day, 10 a.m.–10 p.m.; lunch specials, 10 a.m.– 3 p.m.

Setting & atmosphere: Seats about 40. Long, narrow dining room with minimal decor and no frills.

House specialties: Beef noodle soup. Clay-pot cooking; especially good are the chicken risotto, spicy shrimp with bamboo shoots, and chicken in coconut curry.

Other recommendations: Hot sautéed beef with lemongrass; barbecued pork.

Summary & comments: This popular restaurant is the Vietnamese head-quarters of Las Vegas. The staff is friendly and helpful. Prices are modest. Food is interesting. Watch out for the hot peppers! Staff changes have not improved the food quality—it's sometimes inconsistent, but at such modest prices, it's worth a try.

SAM WOO BAR-B-Q

				QUALITY
Chinese Barbecue	★★★	Inexpensive	**89**

	VALUE
	A

Chinatown Mall, 4215 Spring Mountain Road
368-7628   Southwest Zone 3

Customers: Asian community,
  locals, tourists
Reservations: No
When to go: Any time
Entree range: $4.50–8.95
Payment: Cash only
Service rating: ★★★½

Friendliness rating: ★★★½
Parking: Large lot
Bar: None
Wine selection: None
Dress: Anything goes
Disabled access: Ground floor

Lunch & dinner: Every day, 10 a.m.–5 a.m. Take-out barbecue shop:
  every day, 10 a.m.–10 p.m.

Setting & atmosphere: Enter Sam Woo and enjoy the sights of meats and
whole ducks hanging from hooks in the glass holding case. To the left is
the popular take-out barbecue counter; to the right, a spacious good-sized
restaurant. No frills, but pleasant.

House specialties: Any of the barbecued foods—roast pork, spareribs,
duck, and chicken; the Sam Woo combination plate is an exceptional
value—the large platter is heaped high with roast and barbecued pork,
roast duck, and chicken. Be aware that the noodle-like threads surrounding the meats are cold jellyfish. If this authentic touch is a bit much, tell
the server to omit it. Vegetable dishes are outstanding and inexpensive. The
extensive menu is filled with an interesting selection of dishes, including
hot pots that are cooked at the table.

Summary & comments: Very little English is spoken here, but the menu
is in English. Service is good but can be brusque when the restaurant is
busy. Take it in stride. Sam Woo is one of the best values in a town filled
with them.

SEASONS

				QUALITY
Continental	★★★★	Expensive	**90**

	VALUE
	D

Bally's
739-4111   Strip Zone 1

Customers: Tourists
Reservations: Required

When to go: Any time
Entree range: $24.95–49.95

Payment: VISA, MC, AMEX, DC, D	Bar: Full service
Service rating: ★★★★★	Wine selection: Excellent
Friendliness rating: ★★★★★	Dress: Sport coat, dressy
Parking: Valet, hotel lot	Disabled access: Ramps

Dinner: Tuesday–Saturday, 6–11 p.m.; Sunday and Monday, closed.

Setting & atmosphere: Marie Antoinette would have been at home in this exquisite room.

House specialties: Fresh fish prepared in imaginative ways; roast duckling Grand Marnier; lobster in light crayfish sauce with smoked salmon mousse.

Other recommendations: Seasonal appetizers such as sea scallops on a bed of spinach with pine nuts and pear vinegar. Grilled chicken breast in hazelnut sauce; chateaubriand bordelaise for two with cabernet sauvignon sauce and potato soufflés. Strawberries Romanoff; crème brûlée; seasonal coffees.

Summary & comments: Bally's featured gourmet room. Menu reflects today's demand for lighter, healthier dining. Menu changes four times a year to include seasonal specialties.

SERGIO'S			
Southern Italian	★★★½	Moderate/Expensive	**QUALITY** 85
1955 East Tropicana Avenue			**VALUE** B
739-1544 Southeast Zone 5			

Customers: Locals	Friendliness rating: ★★★★
Reservations: Suggested	Parking: Private lot
When to go: Any time	Bar: Full service
Entree range: $9.95–28.50	Wine selection: Good
Payment: VISA, MC, AMEX, DC, JCB	Dress: Informal, casual
Service rating: ★★★	Disabled access: Ground floor

Dinner: Every day, 5:30–11 p.m.

Setting & atmosphere: Charming Italian garden with Roman columns and silk flowers. Patio for additional seating in mild weather.

House specialties: Calamari alla Siciliana; Belgium endive salad with mixed greens, black olives, hearts of palm, and orange pieces. Capelli d'angelo in salsa cruda and farfalle alla vedova nera; chicken with mushrooms and capers; sautéed veal chop with porcini mushrooms and sun-dried tomatoes, flamed with cognac in demi-glacé sauce; filet mignon Rossini. Tiramisu; flan.

Other recommendations: Fettuccini Monte Bianco; fettuccini paglia e fieno con scampi e calpesante; ziti alla Piemontese. Fagotti di vitello alla Romana; zuppa di pesce alla Mediterranea; specials such as osso buco.

Summary & comments: Owner speaks only Italian; his attractive wife interprets requests. Banquet room available.

SFUZZI LAS VEGAS

Italian	★★★½	Moderate	QUALITY
			88
			VALUE
			B

Fashion Show Mall
699-5777   Strip Zone I

Customers: Tourists, locals	**Friendliness rating:** ★★★★★
Reservations: Recommended	**Parking:** Valet, lot, covered garage
When to go: Any time	**Bar:** Full service
Entree range: $10–26	**Wine selection:** Very good
Payment: VISA, MC, AMEX, DC	**Dress:** Casual
Service rating: ★★★★	**Disabled access:** Ground floor

Brunch: Sunday, 11 a.m.–4 p.m.
Lunch: Monday–Saturday, 11:30 a.m.–4 p.m.
Dinner: Sunday–Thursday, 4–10 p.m.; Friday and Saturday, 4–11 p.m.

Setting & atmosphere: Sfuzzi (sfoo-zee—slang for fun food) considers itself an Italian bistro, but with such an elegant design it's a bistro like no other. In spite of the spectacular Romanesque decor with arches, stone floors, and fine appointments, Sfuzzi is not the least bit intimidating; it is comfortable and fun. Walls of windows give diners a fine view for people-watching.

House specialties: Pastas; plate-size pizzas from the wood-burning oven; roasted portobello mushroom salad; Romano-crusted chicken breast; mixed seafood grill with spinach; grilled tenderloin with garlic mashed potatoes and black pepper Chianti sauce; seasonal daily specials; frozen Bellinis—the champagne/white wine and peach juice drink never tasted better.

Other recommendations: Crisp calamari appetizer with spicy marinara sauce and garlicky aïoli; wild mushroom ravioli with asparagus, mushrooms, and tomato herb broth; the smoked chicken, goat cheese, and caramelized onion pizza; grilled chicken with green beans and garlic mashed potatoes; any of the scrumptious desserts listed on the separate menu; dessert coffees, dessert wines, and fiery grappas available after dinner.

Summary & comments: Sfuzzi was recently acquired by Coco Pazzo. Don't be dismayed if the name has changed; the food is still great. Dining on the patio at an umbrella-topped table is a delight. This popular eatery is always busy. They do accept walk-ins, but sometimes there's a wait.

SHALIMAR

			QUALITY
Indian	★★★½	Moderate/Expensive	**86**
			VALUE
			C

3900 Paradise Road
796-0302   Strip Zone I
2605 South Decatur Boulevard
252-8320   Southwest Zone 3

Customers: Locals, tourists
Reservations: Accepted
When to go: Any time
Entree range: $8.95–15.95
Payment: VISA, MC, AMEX, DC, D
Service rating: ★★★★

Friendliness rating: ★★★★
Parking: Shopping-center lot
Bar: Full service
Wine selection: Good
Dress: Informal, casual
Disabled access: Ground floor

Lunch: Monday–Friday buffet, 11:30 a.m.–2:30 p.m.;
Saturday and Sunday, closed.
Dinner: Every day, 5:30–10:30 p.m.

Setting & atmosphere: Pleasant Indian decor with brass lamps and large tandoori oven.

House specialties: Indian appetizers—samosas, pakoras. Lamb Shalimar with fresh vegetables; tandoori chicken. Large variety of lamb, chicken, and seafood curries spiced according to diner's taste. $5.95 buffet lunch featuring chicken tandoori, seekh kebab, lamb balls, a lu gobi, vegetable jalfrazie, chana marsala, rice, salad, naan bread, and rice pudding.

Other recommendations: Naan (bread) with onion, chicken, lamb, garlic, or potatoes. Any dish from the tandoori oven. Complete vegetarian dinners with eggplant, cauliflower, okra, spinach, and tomatoes. Everything à la carte at dinner. Ask server to describe desserts.

(Shalimar)

Summary & comments: The tandoori oven turns out a variety of delicious Indian breads and skinless tandoori chicken in minutes. Restaurant attracts large numbers of Indian nationals. The restaurant has been enlarged to accommodate private parties and banquets.

SIR GALAHAD'S			

			QUALITY
Prime Rib	★★★½	Moderate	**89**
			VALUE
			A

Excalibur
   597-7777   Strip Zone 1

Customers: Tourists, locals	Friendliness rating: ★★★★
Reservations: Suggested	Parking: Large lot, valet, garage
When to go: Less crowded weekdays	Bar: Full service
Entree range: $12.95–19.95	Wine selection: Good
Payment: VISA, MC, AMEX, DC, D	Dress: Casual
Service rating: ★★★★	Disabled access: Elevators

Dinner: Sunday–Thursday, 5–10 p.m.; Friday, Saturday, and holidays, 5–11 p.m.

Setting & atmosphere: English castle; wait staff in costume of days of King Arthur.

House specialties: Prime rib, prime rib, and prime rib served with beef barley soup or a garden salad, plus mashed potatoes, creamed spinach, and whipped cream horseradish.

Other recommendations: Appetizers such as mushrooms Cliffs of Dover. Chicken à la reine; fresh fish of the day.

Entertainment & amenities: Prime rib served from large, gleaming steel and copper cart. Sliced to order by skilled carvers tableside.

Summary & comments: Prime rib with Yorkshire pudding, creamed spinach, mashed potatoes, and beef barley soup or green salad is a very hearty meal. Top it off, if you can, with English trifle or mud pie.

SPAGO

			QUALITY
American ★★★★★	Moderate/Expensive		**94**
			VALUE
			C

The Forum Shops at Caesars
369-6300   Strip Zone 1

Customers: Tourists, locals
Reservations: Recommended for dinner; not accepted for lunch
When to go: Any time except during busy conventions
Entree range: $12–20 in the café; $18–30 in the dining room
Payment: VISA, MC, AMEX, DC, D

Service rating: ★★★★
Friendliness rating: ★★★★★
Parking: Garage, valet
Bar: Full service
Wine selection: Excellent
Dress: Informal, casual
Disabled access: Ground floor

Lunch & dinner: *Café:* Sunday–Thursday, 11 a.m.–11 p.m.; Friday and Saturday, 11 a.m.–midnight.
Dinner: *Restaurant:* Monday–Thursday, 6–10 p.m.; Friday–Sunday, 5:30–10:30 p.m.

Setting & atmosphere: There are two separate dining rooms. The casual café offers a fine bird's-eye view of The Forum Shops from the comfort of a European-styled sidewalk setting. The restaurant inside is an eclectic mix of modern art, wrought iron, and contemporary tables and chairs and booths.

House specialties: *Café:* Wolfgang Puck's signature pizzas; imaginative sandwiches on homemade bread; salads; pastas; and frequently, a super-tasty meat loaf with port wine sauce, grilled onions, and garlic potato purée. *Restaurant:* exquisite appetizers; pastas; grilled veal chop with dried cherry-wild rice and sage hollandaise; big-eye tuna with couscous; salmon encrusted with almonds and ginger. Menus in the café and restaurant change daily. Desserts are sensational.

Entertainment & amenities: Each Sunday in the café from about 2:30 to 6:30 p.m., a jazz band entertains. A private banquet room is available for parties up to 100. A small private room within the restaurant can seat up to 20.

Summary & comments: Wolfgang Puck's first venture outside California is an instant success. Puck surrounds himself with the best staff, the best ingredients, the best of everything. One caveat—on very busy nights the dining room noise level can make conversation difficult, but the people-watching is terrific.

THE STEAK HOUSE

			QUALITY
Steak	★★★½	Moderate	**86**
			VALUE
			C

Circus Circus
  734-0410   Strip Zone 1

Customers: Locals, tourists
Reservations: Required
When to go: Weekdays
Entree range: $15.95–39.95
Payment: VISA, MC, AMEX, DC, CB, D
Service rating: ★★★★

Friendliness rating: ★★★★
Parking: Garage, lot, valet
Bar: Full service
Wine selection: Good
Dress: Informal
Disabled access: Ramps

Dinner: Every day, 5 p.m.–midnight.

Setting & atmosphere: Wood-paneled rooms. Small dining room decorated like manor-house library. Mesquite-fired broiler in center of main room creates cozy atmosphere. Glass refrigerator case displays over 3,000 pounds of aging meat.

House specialties: Thick steaks; black bean soup; giant baked potato.

Other recommendations: Shrimp, crab, and lobster cocktails; Caesar salad; grilled chicken.

Summary & comments: The Circus Circus Hotel and Casino is an unusual place for a steak house. Don't be fooled by the children running around the lobby. Inside the Steak House, the atmosphere is adult and the food is wonderful. Plan ahead to dine here.

STEFANO'S

			QUALITY
Southern Italian	★★★★	Expensive	**94**
			VALUE
			C

Golden Nugget
  385-7111   Downtown Zone 2

Customers: Tourists, locals·
Reservations: Required
When to go: Nonconvention times
Entree range: $11.50–29
Payment: VISA, MC, AMEX, DC, CB, D
Service rating: ★★★★

Friendliness rating: ★★★★
Parking: Garage, valet
Bar: Full service
Wine selection: Very good
Dress: Sport coat
Disabled access: Elevators

Dinner: Sunday–Thursday, 6–11 p.m.; Friday and Saturday, 5:30–11 p.m.

Setting & atmosphere: A bright, cheerful room decorated with custom tile and hand-decorated cabinetry. Venetian chandeliers. Murals of Italy grace the walls.

House specialties: Agnolotti, fresh mussels; veal scallopini Stefano (with prosciutto, asparagus, and mozzarella); chicken Sorrentino; osso buco; veal chop with porcini mushrooms and mascarpone cheese.

Other recommendations: Roasted peppers; carpaccio; cioppino; capellini frutti di mare; fresh fish; daily specials. Chocolate pasta with vanilla ice cream, almonds, strawberries, and honey sauce; crème brûlée; tiramisu.

Entertainment & amenities: The staff breaks into classical Italian songs throughout the meal. You will, too.

Summary & comments: Dishes presented with flair. A happy dining experience.

SWISS CAFE

European	★★★½	Moderate	QUALITY 89
			VALUE B

3175 East Tropicana Avenue
454-2270   Southeast Zone 5

Customers: Locals, conventioneers
Reservations: A must at dinner, not accepted for lunch
When to go: Early lunch; weeknights, dinner
Entree range: $9.95–23.95
Payment: VISA, MC, AMEX

Service rating: ★★★
Friendliness rating: ★★★★★
Parking: Shopping-center lot
Bar: Full service
Wine selection: Fair
Dress: Informal
Disabled access: Ground floor

Lunch: Monday–Friday, 11 a.m.–2:30 p.m.
Dinner: Monday–Saturday, 6–10 p.m.

Setting & atmosphere: Swiss collectibles fill the restaurant; pepper mills, antique kitchenware, and plants make for a charming Old World setting.

House specialties: Duck salad; schnitzel; a variety of veal dishes; nightly specials; Veal Zurich, scallopini with herb sauce; steak Diane prepared with a New York strip; tournedos in the style of the Cafe de Paris; duck with orange or raspberry sauce. Sauces are well seasoned. Entree price includes salad and a vegetable medley; handmade apple strudel, baked by a Viennese friend of the owners.

Other recommendations: The newly added steaks, pork chops, and veal chops.

(Swiss Cafe)

Summary & comments: Chef-owner Wolfgang and his wife-partner, Mary, welcome everyone. The affable couple have a devoted local following. Specials change daily and are listed on a blackboard.

T-BONE'S TEXAS BARBECUE		

		QUALITY
Barbecue ★★★½	Inexpensive/Moderate	**89**
		VALUE
4734 East Flamingo		**C**
456-9898 Southeast Zone 5		

Customers: Locals	Friendliness rating: ★★★★½
Reservations: Suggested for parties over 6	Parking: Shopping-center lot
	Bar: Beer and wine only
When to go: Any time	Wine selection: Very limited
Entree range: $5–15	Dress: Casual
Payment: VISA, MC	Disabled access: Ground floor
Service rating: ★★★★½	

Open: Monday–Saturday, 10 a.m.–10 p.m.; Sunday 11 a.m.–9 p.m. Same menu all day.

Setting & atmosphere: This small, modest eatery located in a no-frills neighborhood shopping center is not much to look at, but the food is good, plentiful, and value-priced. The decor is strictly down-home—red-and-white checkered cloths cover the tables. A wooden divider separates the diners from those waiting for take-out. It's as basic as it gets.

House specialties: Country-style hearty breakfasts; beef and pork ribs cooked long and slow until the meat falls easily from the bone; T-Bone's hearty steak sandwich with grilled onions, peppers, mushrooms, and cheese—served with a side of french fries; the barbecue sampler plate piled high with brisket, baby back ribs, and beef ribs, served with corn muffin, barbecue beans, and a choice of homemade potato salad or cole slaw; mile-high sandwiches—barbecue pork, brisket, ham, or hot link sausage slow-cooked in T-Bone's zesty, thin barbecue sauce and accompanied by the restaurant's signature french fries.

Other recommendations: The "Feast for Two" that can easily feed three. Items included are two barbecued chicken halves, three large, meaty beef ribs, six pork ribs, eight ounces of brisket, one pint of cole slaw or potato salad, a pint of barbecued beans, and corn muffins.

(T-Bone's Texas Barbecue)

Summary & comments: In a town noted for good food values T-Bone's funky, small restaurant gives a lot of bang for the buck. The servers are friendly, caring, and remember your name when you return; just like in Old Las Vegas.

TERU SUSHI			
			QUALITY
Sushi	★★★½	Moderate/Expensive	**89**
			VALUE
700 East Sahara Avenue			**C**
734-6655 Strip Zone 1			

Customers: Asian community, locals, tourists
Reservations: Not necessary
When to go: Any time
Entree range: $6–30
Payment: VISA, MC, AMEX
Service rating: ★★★½

Friendliness rating: ★★★½
Parking: Street and lot
Bar: None
Wine selection: Minimal
Dress: Casual
Disabled access: Ground floor

Dinner: Monday–Saturday, 5–11 p.m.; Sunday, closed.

Setting & atmosphere: Small storefront restaurant with a large sushi bar. A restaurant in the true tradition of sushi. Servers are kimono-clad. Japanese screens and art add a little bit of color.

House specialties: Sushi is king. Everything from sea urchin to flying fish–egg sushi is available. With the small dishes and combination plates and a side of tempura or chicken teriyaki, diners can create a traditional Japanese meal. Two sushi combination plates and a beautiful sashimi combination. Teru Sushi specializes in seasonal fresh fish and vegetable dishes. The soft-shelled crab is a delight. Udon or soba noodles, usually eaten at the end of the meal.

Summary & comments: Sushi-quality fish is the best, and here it is priced accordingly. Portions are Japanese-style—small. It takes many dishes to satisfy hearty appetites and can be costly. The selection at Teru Sushi is excellent.

THE TILLERMAN

Seafood	★★★½	Moderate/Expensive	QUALITY 87
			VALUE C

2245 East Flamingo Road
731-4036   Southeast Zone 5

Customers: Tourists, locals
Reservations: Not taken
When to go: Early evening
Entree range: $18–37
Payment: VISA, MC, AMEX, DC, D
Service rating: ★★★★

Friendliness rating: ★★★★
Parking: Lot
Bar: Full service
Wine selection: Excellent
Dress: Informal, casual
Disabled access: Ramp

Dinner: Every day, 5–11 p.m.

Setting & atmosphere: Attractive, airy main dining room with balcony seating. Hanging plants, wood paneling, beautiful live trees.

House specialties: Seafood fresh from California, the Gulf of Mexico, the Atlantic, and the rest of the world—Pacific salmon, Chilean sea bass, Florida snapper.

Other recommendations: Prime steaks; Tillerman pasta Portofino. Fresh homemade pastries.

Entertainment & amenities: Menu presented on scroll. Servers memorize orders without taking any notes. Lazy-Susan salad bar brought to each table so you can eat your fill. Ten to 15 fresh fish listed daily.

Summary & comments: One of the most popular Las Vegas seafood restaurants. Will take reservations only for groups of eight or more; however, seating for 250-plus makes for short waiting time.

Honors & awards: *Wine Spectator* Award of Excellence for many years.

TOKYO

Japanese/Sushi	★★★½	Moderate	QUALITY 85
			VALUE B

953 East Sahara Avenue (Commercial Center)
735-7070   Strip Zone 1

Customers: Locals, tourists
Reservations: Accepted
When to go: Any time
Entree range: $8.95–24.95

Payment: VISA, MC, AMEX, DC,
JCB, D
Service rating: ★★★★
Friendliness rating: ★★★★

(Tokyo)

Parking: Large lot
Bar: Full service
Wine selection: Fair

Dress: Informal, casual
Disabled access: Ground floor

Dinner: Every day, 5–10 p.m.

Setting & atmosphere: Newly decorated Japanese interior—tatami room, sushi bar.

House specialties: Small hibachi grills for those who wish to cook their own dinner. Shabu shabu also available.

Other recommendations: Combination, special, and deluxe dinners, all modestly priced, offer a wide selection.

Summary & comments: A family-run restaurant—very popular with the locals. Tokyo has been enlarged to include party and catering facilities.

TOP OF THE WORLD

American	★★★½	Expensive	QUALITY 85
			VALUE C

Stratosphere Tower, 2000 South Las Vegas Boulevard
380-7711   Strip Zone 1

Customers: Tourists, locals	Friendliness rating: ★★★★
Reservations: Required	Parking: Valet, garage, and lot
When to go: Any time	Bar: Full service
Entree range: $22–market price	Wine selection: Excellent
Payment: VISA, MC, AMEX, DC, D	Dress: Dressy casual
Service rating: ★★★★★	Disabled access: Elevator

Dinner: Sunday–Thursday, 5–11 p.m.; Friday and Saturday, 5 p.m.–midnight

Setting & atmosphere: Without question, Top of the World offers the most beautiful view of the city. The restaurant revolves as you dine, giving a panoramic spectacle of the surrounding mountains. The dining room is handsomely designed with inlaid tables, fine woods and brass, and copper accents. There are no bad tables.

House specialties: San Francisco–style cioppino; chicken quesadilla soup; char-broiled portobello mushrooms with marsala demi-glacé; Sonoma Valley rack of lamb; Santa Fe–style rotisserie chicken.

Other recommendations: Tequila-lime shrimp, served on a bed of linguini; almond-crusted salmon; the towering vacherin dessert; the signature bread pudding made with egg bread.

Summaries & comments: The food is secondary to the view, which is simply spectacular. Arrive before sunset and watch one of the best free shows. The fine service and the view make up for any inconsistencies in the food. The wine list received the *Wine Spectator* 1996 Award of Excellence.

TRE VISI/LA SCALA

Italian	★★★½	Moderate/Expensive	QUALITY 94
MGM Grand			VALUE B
891-1111 Strip Zone 1			

Customers: Tourists, locals
Reservations: Suggested for La Scala
When to go: Nonconvention times
Entree range: Tre Visi, $15–28; La Scala, $25–55
Payment: VISA, MC, AMEX, DC, D
Service rating: ★★★★

Friendliness rating: ★★★★
Parking: Valet, lot, covered garage
Bar: Full service
Wine selection: Excellent
Dress: Tre Visi, casual; La Scala, upscale casual
Disabled access: Through casino

Lunch & dinner: *Tre Visi:* every day, 11 a.m.–1 a.m.
Dinner: *La Scala:* every day, 5:30–11 p.m. (Hours extended when warranted.)

Setting & atmosphere: As the name says, Tre Visi has three faces. First is the gracious dining patio overlooking the MGM restaurant corridor. The patio flows into a handsome dining room. And between the two is an elegant bar. Adjacent is the La Scala dining room with posh appointments; La Scala's booths are designed to emulate the boxes at the namesake La Scala opera house in Milan.

House specialties: The casual patio features pizzas with special toppings, sandwiches, and the Tre Visi menu. Tre Visi also offers daily additions of antipasti and soups; risotto; veal, fish, and pastas. Dishes change with frequency—orecchiette with eggplant, roasted peppers, olives, and tomato sauce; risotto with braised lamb shanks; baked sausage served with cannellini and grilled polenta have all been featured. La Scala has its own à la carte menu that changes daily. The dishes are highly original and made with the finest seasonal products by a chef who puts his own spin on the classic dishes of Northern and Southern Italy.

(Tre Visi/La Scala)

Summary & comments: Tre Visi's wine list is exceptional. More than 1,000 bottles are in the wine cellar. The surroundings are a tribute to good taste. In spite of its size, Tre Visi maintains the highest fine-dining standards. Tre Visi owner Francho Nuschese also owns the noted Cafe Milano restaurant in Georgetown, Washington, D.C.

VENETIAN			
Italian	★★★	Moderate	**QUALITY** 87
			VALUE B

3713 West Sahara Avenue
 876-4190   Southwest Zone 3

Customers: Locals, tourists	Friendliness rating: ★★★★★
Reservations: Accepted	Parking: Large lot
When to go: Any time	Bar: Full service
Entree range: $9.95–29.95	Wine selection: Outstanding
Payment: VISA, MC, AMEX, D	Dress: Casual, informal
Service rating: ★★★★★	Disabled access: Ground floor

Open: Every day, 24 hours (dinner starts at 3 p.m.).

Setting & atmosphere: This landmark eatery recently changed owners. They've lightened the decor.

House specialties: Specialty homemade breads such as tomato and mozzarella, bruschetta, garlic. Hearty dinners with a good selection of pastas. The grilled veal chop is a favorite. Unique to the Venetian, and very popular, are the sautéed greens and the pork neckbones marinated in wine. Chilled roasted eggplant; pasta with cream sauce and lemon zest.

Other recommendations: The baked halibut, shrimp à la pizzaiola, and shrimp à la bianca are excellent, as are the veal scallopini picante, pizzaiola, marsala, chicken cacciatore, and chicken breast dore. The early dining menu, served nightly from 4 to 6 p.m., is extensive and moderately priced.

Summary & comments: Portions are generous, and the menu is extensive. Longtime diners are hoping it remains that way. Some changes in the menu, but nothing major. All the favorite dishes and longtime staff remain.

VIVA MERCADO'S

			QUALITY
Mexican	★★★½	Moderate	**86**
			VALUE
			A

6182 West Flamingo Road
  871-8826   Southwest Zone 3
Town Center (adjacent to Barley's Sunset)
  435-6200   Southeast Zone 5

Customers: Locals
Reservations: Accepted
When to go: Any time; the lunch
  hour is very busy.
Entree range: $7.95–17.95
Payment: VISA, MC, AMEX, D
Service rating: ★★★★★

Friendliness rating: ★★★★★
Parking: Shopping-center lot
Bar: Full service
Wine selection: Good
Dress: Casual
Disabled access: Ground floor

Lunch & dinner: Sunday–Thursday, 11 a.m.–10 p.m.;
  Friday and Saturday, 11 a.m.–11 p.m. Same menu day and evening.

Setting & atmosphere: Friendly, cozy restaurant. The decor is wall-to-wall Mexican, with hats, serapes, and posters everywhere.

House specialties: Chile relleno—roasted, peeled peppers filled with Monterey Jack cheese; turf and surf (tierra y mare). Carnitas; carne asada; and a fillet of roughy à la Mexicana. Lunch specials from 11 a.m. to 2 p.m., $5.25; Saturday and Sunday sangria brunch from 11 a.m. to 3 p.m.

Other recommendations: Broiled breast of chicken in a variety of styles; New York steak with stir-fried cactus, onion, garlic, cilantro, and chile verde strips. Siesta Dining, 2–5 p.m., Monday through Friday, when the chef prepares a number of items such as enchiladas, burritos, tacos, tostadas, tamales, and chiles rellenos for $6.95, and invites diners to create their own combinations from any two of the above; served with sopa de fideo (angelhair pasta in a chicken broth), rice, and refried beans.

Summary & comments: The owner created a number of the entrees. In keeping with today's healthier lifestyle, he cooks exclusively with canola oil. Upon request, cheese can be eliminated from any dish.

WOLFGANG PUCK CAFE

American	★★★½	Moderate	QUALITY
			85

			VALUE
MGM Grand			**B**
891-3019	Strip Zone 1		

Customers: Tourists, locals
Reservations: Not accepted
When to go: Any time
Entree range: $9.95–20
Payment: VISA, MC, AMEX, DC
Service rating: ★★★

Friendliness rating: ★★★★
Parking: Hotel lot, valet, garage
Bar: Full service
Wine selection: Excellent
Dress: Casual
Disabled access: Ramp

Lunch & dinner: Sunday–Thursday, 8 a.m.–11 p.m.; Friday and Saturday, 8 a.m.–midnight.

Setting & atmosphere: Designed by Wolf's partner-wife, designer Barbara Lazaroff. Cheerful, attractive, with posters, tiled walls, and an open kitchen.

House specialties: Appetizers such as Chinois chicken salad with spicy honey-mustard dressing; roasted corn chowder with jalapeño cream. A variety of pizzas, including barbecued chicken with tomatoes and julienned red onion; smoked salmon with red onion and fresh dill cream; Barbara's fettuccini with shrimp, fresh vegetables, and tomato curry sauce; Grandma Puck's linguini with chicken bolognese; Wolf's meat loaf with port wine sauce and garlic mashed potatoes. Apple tarte tatin (caramelized apples on puff pastry with whipped or ice cream).

Other recommendations: Mixed green salad with herb and goat cheese crostini; vegetable spring rolls with orange cabernet glaze; fried calamari with cilantro aïoli. Calzone with mozzarella, sweet roasted peppers, sautéed spinach, wild mushrooms, roasted garlic, and thyme; rotisserie barbecued chicken with garlic mashed potatoes, french fries, or Caesar salad. Vanilla or chocolate crème brûlée.

Summary & comments: When busy, as it usually is, service can be slow. Sidewalk café design allows diners to watch people in the MGM Grand's casino.

YOLIE'S

			QUALITY
Brazilian	★★★	Moderate	86
			VALUE
			B

3900 Paradise Road
794-0700   Strip Zone 1

Customers: Tourists, locals
Reservations: Accepted for lunch
  and dinner
When to go: Cocktail hour is lively
Entree range: $14.95–22.95
Payment: VISA, MC, AMEX, DC, D
Service rating: ★★★★

Friendliness rating: ★★★★
Parking: Shopping-center lot
Bar: Full service
Wine selection: Leans toward reds,
  some Brazilian
Dress: Informal
Disabled access: Elevator

Lunch: Monday–Friday, 11 a.m.–3 p.m.; Saturday and Sunday, closed.
Dinner: Monday–Saturday, 5–11 p.m.; Sunday, 5–10 p.m.

Setting & atmosphere: Large wood-fired, glass-enclosed rotisserie cooks a variety of meats in view of diners. High ceiling and balconies.

House specialties: Meat of many different kinds: steak, chops, lamb, turkey, brisket of beef, spring chicken, and sausage. Fixed-price dinner includes salad or black bean soup and a taste of all the meats cooked in the pit, sliced from a skewer to your plate. Side dishes include polenta, fried bananas, vegetable of the day, rice à la Rio, farofa, and baked red-skinned potatoes. Sunday through Wednesday, 4–7 p.m., $12.95 mini-grill with all of the above.

Other recommendations: Feijoada (black bean stew), the national dish of Brazil. A la carte house special scampi; sautéed orange roughy; catch of the day. Desserts such as Romeo and Juliet (guava marmalade and cheese), Brazilian flan, chocolate mousse cake. Yolie's café especial.

Entertainment & amenities: Live piano music on occasional weekends.

Summary & comments: A complete Brazilian dining experience; fixed-price dinner is $20.95, $10.95 at lunch. Carnivores will have a ball. Forget about cholesterol and calories.

Hotel Information Chart

■ How to Use This Chart ■

The following 32 pages contain the information necessary to evaluate the suitability of a given hotel or motel. The chart is ordered alphabetically, with the entry for any specific hotel appearing in the same position on the page for eight consecutive pages as follows:

In general the listings are self-explanatory and are designed to allow you to access desired information quickly. For example, does the hotel you are considering offer golf? A quick scan of the "Golf" column will provide the answer. A checkmark is an affirmative. If the hotel you are considering has a checkmark under "Room Service," then room service is available. Conversely, a blank space indicates that the feature or service is unavailable.

Star Ratings apply to the quality of a property's standard rooms, as discussed on page 134. The more stars, the better the rooms.

The Nonsmoking entry applies to hotel guest rooms. "Floors" means that the hotel reserves entire floors for nonsmokers.

The Rack Rate is how much the hotel charges for a nondiscounted standard guest room. Each dollar sign ($) equals $30. $$$, for example, indicates an average rack rate of $90 per night. The charge may be somewhat less on weekdays and somewhat more on weekends.

The Room Rating gives a numerical value to the quality of the standard guest rooms and allows for a meaningful comparison between hotels with the same Star Rating. Once again, 100 is the best, and 0 is the worst. Room Ratings are explained in detail on page 133.

The **Value Rating,** also on a scale of 0 to 100, rates how much value you are getting for the dollar. The higher the rating, the better the deal. A list of the top 30 best hotel deals appears on page 139.

Fine Dining/Type of Food tells you how many full-service restaurants are operated by a particular hotel, and what the culinary specialty of each restaurant is. For example:

③ Italian, Mexican, Steak

means that the hotel offers three nice restaurants: an Italian restaurant, a Mexican restaurant, and a steak house. "No" under Fine Dining does not mean that the hotel is completely without food service but that its restaurants are more informal: coffee shops, cafés, buffets, or delis (listed separately).

Showroom Entertainment entries are defined on pages 170–176.

Movie Theater indicates the presence of a public movie theater on the premises.

Sauna/Steam Whirlpool indicates the availability of a common facility where these amenities are offered.

Hotel	Room Star Rating	Zone	Street Address
Aladdin	★★½/ ★★★½*	1	3667 Las Vegas Blvd., South Las Vegas, 89109
Alexis Park	★★★★½	1	375 East Harmon Avenue Las Vegas, 89109
Arizona Charlie's	★★/ ★★★*	3	740 South Decatur Blvd. Las Vegas, 89107
Bally's	★★★★	1	3645 Las Vegas Blvd., South Las Vegas, 89109
Barbary Coast	★★★½	1	3595 Las Vegas Blvd., South Las Vegas, 89109
Best Western Mardi Gras Inn	★★★	1	3500 Paradise Road Las Vegas, 89109
Best Western McCarran Inn	★★½	1	4970 Paradise Road Las Vegas, 89119
Boomtown	★★★	3	3333 Blue Diamond Road Las Vegas, 89139
Boulder Station	★★★	5	4111 Boulder Highway Las Vegas, 89121
Bourbon Street	★★★	1	120 East Flamingo Road Las Vegas, 89109
Caesars Palace	★★★★★	1	3570 Las Vegas Blvd., South Las Vegas, 89109
California	★★★½	2	12 East Ogden Avenue Las Vegas, 89101
Casino Royale	★★½	1	3411 Las Vegas Blvd., South Las Vegas, 89109
Circus Circus	★★½/ ★★★	1	2880 Las Vegas Blvd., South Las Vegas, 89109
Comfort Inn South	★★★	1	5075 Koval Lane Las Vegas, 89109
Continental	★★	1	4100 Paradise Road Las Vegas, 89109
Courtyard by Marriott	★★★½	1	3275 Paradise Road Las Vegas, 89109
Crowne Plaza	★★★★	1	4255 Paradise Road Las Vegas, 89109
Days Inn	★★★	2	707 East Fremont Street Las Vegas, 89101
Days Inn Town Hall Casino	★★½	1	4155 Koval Lane Las Vegas, 89109

* garden rooms / tower rooms

Local Phone	Fax	800 Reservations	Discount Available	Number of Rooms
(702) 736-0111	(702) 734-3583	(800) 634-3424		1,095
(702) 796-3300	(702) 796-3354	(800) 582-2228	Government, military	500
(702) 258-5111	(702) 258-5192	(800) 342-2695	Government	260
(702) 739-4111	(702) 739-4405	(800) 634-3434		2,814
(702) 737-7111	(702) 894-9954	(888) BARBARY		200
(702) 731-2020	(702) 733-6994	(800) 634-6501	Senior, military	315
(702) 798-5530	(702) 798-7627	(800) 626-7575	Senior, military	99
(702) 263-7777	(702) 896-5635	(800) 588-7711		300
(702) 432-7777	(702) 432-7744	(800) 683-7777		306
(702) 737-7200	(702) 734-3490	(800) 634-6956	Senior	166
(702) 731-7110	(702) 731-6636	(800) 634-6661	Senior, military, government	1,509
(702) 385-1222	(702) 388-2670	(800) 634-6255		781
(702) 737-3500	(702) 650-4643	(800) 854-7666		153
(702) 734-0410	(702) 734-5897	(800) 444-2472		3,746
(702) 736-3600	(702) 736-0726	(800) 221-2222	Senior, military	106
(702) 737-5555	(702) 737-9276	(800) 634-6641	Senior, military	370
(702) 791-3600	(702) 796-7981	(800 321-2211	Government, military	149
(702) 369-4400	(702) 369-3770	(800) 2-CROWNE	Senior	20
(702) 388-1400	(702) 388-9622	(800) 325-2344	Senior, military	146
(702) 731-2111	(702) 731-1113	(800) 634-6541	Senior, government, military	360

Hotel	Ck. Out Time	Non-Smoking	Rack Rate	Room Quality Rating	Room Value Rating
Aladdin	Noon	Floors	$$$–/ $$$$+*	62/75*	38/44*
Alexis Park	Noon	✓	$$$$$–	94	64
Arizona Charlie's	11 a.m.	✓	$+/$$–*	52/74*	57/97*
Bally's	11 a.m.	Floors	$$$$+	88	70
Barbary Coast	Noon	✓	$$$–	78	64
Best Western Mardi Gras Inn	Noon	✓	$$$–	67	47
Best Western McCarran Inn	Noon	✓	$$$–	61	36
Boomtown	Noon	✓	$$+	67	60
Boulder Station	Noon	✓	$$$$–	67	39
Bourbon Street	Noon	✓	$$+	71	65
Caesars Palace	Noon	Floors	$$$$$$$–	96	51
California	Noon	✓	$$+	77	81
Casino Royale	Noon	✓	$$$–	59	36
Circus Circus	11 a.m.	✓	$$$–/ $$$+**	63/70*	42/45
Comfort Inn South	11 a.m.	✓	$$$–	72	57
Continental	Noon		$$$–	54	30
Courtyard by Marriott	Noon	✓	$$$+	79	59
Crowne Plaza	Noon	✓	$$$$$–	85	49
Days Inn	Noon	✓	$$$–	66	52
Days Inn Town Hall Casino Hotel	Noon	✓	$$+	58	47

 * garden rooms / tower rooms

** manor rooms / tower rooms

Con-cierge	Convention Facilities	Meeting Rooms	Valet Parking	RV Park	Room Service	Free Breakfast
✓	✓	✓	✓		✓	
✓	✓	✓	✓		✓	Coffee
	✓	✓	✓			
✓	✓	✓	✓		✓	
			✓		✓	
		✓				
					✓	
	✓	✓	✓	✓		
✓	✓	✓	✓		✓	
		✓				
✓	✓	✓	✓		✓	
		✓	✓	✓	Breakfast	
✓		✓	✓	✓	Limited	
						✓
					✓	
		✓			Breakfast, Dinner	
✓		✓			✓	Coffee

Hotel	Fine Dining/ Type of Food	Coffee Shop	24-hr. Café	Buffet	Deli
Aladdin	② Steak, Seafood	✓	✓	✓	✓
Alexis Park	① Continental/ Italian	✓			
Arizona Charlie's	② Chinese, Steak	✓	✓	✓	✓
Bally's	③ Continental, Steak, Italian	✓	✓	✓	✓
Barbary Coast	② Continental, Chinese	✓	✓		
Best Western Mardi Gras Inn	No	✓			
Best Western McCarran Inn	No				
Boomtown	① Steak	✓	✓	✓	✓
Boulder Station	④ Steak/Seafood, Italian, Mexican, Chinese	✓	✓	✓	✓
Bourbon Street	No				
Caesars Palace	⑥ Oriental, French, Italian, Japanese, Steak, Continental	✓	✓	✓	✓
California	② Pasta/Seafood, Steak/Seafood	✓	✓	Breakfast	
Casino Royale	No	✓	✓		
Circus Circus	② Steak, Italian	✓	✓	✓	✓
Comfort Inn South	No	Adjacent			
Continental	No	✓	✓	✓	
Courtyard by Marriott	No	✓			
Crowne Plaza		✓			
Days Inn	① Continental	✓			
Days Inn Town Hall Casino Hotel	No	✓	✓		

	Casino	24-hour Bar	Lounge	Showroom Entertainment	Gift Shop Drugs/News	Hair Salon
	✓	✓	✓	Country music show	✓	✓
			✓		✓	✓
	✓	✓	Headliner	Headliner	✓	
	✓	✓	✓	Production show, celebrity headliners	✓	✓
	✓	✓			✓	
	✓	✓	✓		✓	✓
	✓	✓	✓	Country music concert once a month	✓	
	✓	✓	✓	Country-western performers	✓	
					✓	
	✓	✓	✓	Celebrity headliner	✓	✓
	✓	✓			✓	
	✓	✓	✓		✓	
	✓	✓	✓	Circus acts	✓	✓
	✓	✓			✓	
			✓			
			✓		✓	
	✓	✓	✓		✓	

Hotel	Pool	Youth Activities	Exercise Rooms	Tennis & Racket Games
Aladdin	✓			Tennis
Alexis Park	✓ heated		✓	
Arizona Charlie's	✓			
Bally's	✓		Health Spa	Tennis
Barbary Coast	✓			
Best Western Mardi Gras Inn	✓			
Best Western McCarran Inn	✓			
Boomtown	✓			
Boulder Station	✓	✓		
Bourbon Street	Privileges			
Caesars Palace	✓ heated	✓	Health Spa	
California	✓			
Casino Royale	✓ heated			
Circus Circus	✓ heated	✓		
Comfort Inn South	✓			
Continental	✓			
Courtyard by Marriott	✓ heated		✓	Tennis
Crowne Plaza	✓ heated		✓	
Days Inn	✓			
Days Inn Town Hall Casino Hotel	✓ heated			

Golf	Other	Movie Theater	Sauna/Steam Whirlpool	Shopping Arcade	Elec. Games Arcade
				✓	✓
Putting	Privileges,Wedding Gazebo		✓		
			✓		✓
	Privileges Monorail		✓	✓	
	Privileges				✓
			✓		✓
	Pan for gold		✓		✓
		✓			✓
					✓
	Privileges	✓	✓	✓	✓
					✓
	Grand Slam Canyon, Wedding chapel		At RV Park	✓	✓
			✓		
	Privileges		✓		
			✓		

Hotel	Room Star Rating	Zone	Street Address
Debbie Reynolds Hollywood Hotel	★★★	1	305 Convention Center Drive Las Vegas, 89109
Desert Inn	★★★★★	1	3145 Las Vegas Blvd., South Las Vegas, 89109
El Cortez	★★¹/₂	2	600 East Fremont Street Las Vegas, 89101
Excalibur	★★★	1	3850 Las Vegas Blvd., South Las Vegas, 89109
Fiesta	★★¹/₂	3	2400 North Rancho Drive Las Vegas, 89130
Fitzgeralds	★★¹/₂	2	301 Fremont Street Las Vegas, 89101
Flamingo Hilton	★★★¹/₂	1	3555 Las Vegas Blvd., South Las Vegas, 89109
Four Queens	★★¹/₂	2	202 Fremont Street Las Vegas, 89101
Fremont	★★¹/₂	2	200 East Fremont Street Las Vegas, 89101
Frontier	★★★¹/₂	1	3120 Las Vegas Blvd., South Las Vegas, 89109
Gold Coast	★★¹/₂	1	4000 West Flamingo Road Las Vegas, 89103
Golden Nugget	★★★★	2	129 East Fremont Street Las Vegas, 89101
Hard Rock Hotel	★★★★	1	4455 Paradise Road Las Vegas, 89109
Harrah's	★★★¹/₂/ ★★★★*	1	3475 Las Vegas Blvd., South Las Vegas, 89109
Holiday Inn Boardwalk	★★★	1	3750 Las Vegas Blvd., South Las Vegas, 89109
Holiday Inn Emerald Springs	★★★¹/₂	1	325 East Flamingo Road Las Vegas, 89109
Horseshoe	★★★	2	128 East Fremont Street Las Vegas, 89101
Howard Johnson	★★★	1	3111 West Tropicana Avenue Las Vegas, 89103
Howard Johnson Airport	★★¹/₂	1	5100 Paradise Road Las Vegas, 89119
Imperial Palace	★★★	1	3535 Las Vegas Blvd., South Las Vegas, 89109

* Mardi Gras Tower rooms / Carnival Tower rooms

Local Phone	Fax	800 Reservations	Discount Available	Number of Rooms
(702) 734-0711	(702) 734-7548	(800) 633-1777		203
(702) 733-4444	(702) 733-4676	(800) 634-6906	Military	714
(702) 385-5200	(702) 385-1554	(800) 634-6703		401
(702) 597-7777	(702) 597-7009	(800) 937-7777		4,008
(702) 631-7000	(702) 631-6588	(800) 731-7333		100
(702) 388-2400	(702) 388-2181	(800) 274-LUCK	Senior	638
(702) 733-3111	(702) 733-3528	(800) 732-2111	AAA	3,642
(702) 385-4011	(702) 387-5133	(800) 634-6045	Military, government	670
(702) 385-3232	(702) 385-6270	(800) 634-6182		452
(702) 794-8200	(702) 794-8326	(800) 421-7806		1,000
(702) 367-7111	(702) 251-3590	(888) 402-6278	Senior, military	750
(702) 385-7111	(702) 386-8362	(800) 634-3454		1,907
(702) 693-5000	(702) 693-5010	(800) 693-ROCK		340
(702) 369-5000	(702) 369-6014	(800) HARRAHS		2,700
(702) 735-2400	(702) 739-8152	(800) HOLIDAY	Senior, military, AAA, government	654
(702) 732-9100	(702) 731-9784	(800) HOLIDAY	Senior, AAA government	150
(702) 382-1600	(702) 384-1574	(800) 622-6468		354
(702) 798-1111	(702) 798-7138	(800) 654-2000	Senior, military, AAA	150
(702) 798-2777	(702) 736-8295	(800) 634-6439	Military, AAA senior	146
(702) 731-3311	(702) 735-8578	(800) 634-6441		2,700

Hotel	Ck. Out Time	Non-Smoking	Rack Rate	Room Quality Rating	Room Value Rating
Debbie Reynolds Hollywood Hotel	Noon	✓	$$$+	69	44
Desert Inn	Noon	✓	$$$$$+	97	66
El Cortez	11 a.m.	✓	$+	60	90
Excalibur	11 a.m.	✓	$$$$–	65	34
Fiesta	Noon	✓	$$$–	61	36
Fitzgeralds	Noon	✓	$$$–	62	38
Flamingo Hilton	Noon	Floors/ Portion of casino	$$$$$–	81	40
Four Queens	Noon	Floors	$$$$–	61	29
Fremont	Noon	Floors	$$$–	60	39
Frontier	Noon	Suites	$$+	79	89
Gold Coast	Noon	✓	$$$$–	56	27
Golden Nugget	Noon	✓	$$$+	87	74
Hard Rock Hotel	Noon	✓	$$$$$$+	87	44
Harrah's	Noon	Floors/ Part of casino	$$$$$$+/ $$$$$$–*	78/ 83*	30/33
Holiday Inn Boardwalk	Noon	✓	$$$+	70	45
Holiday Inn Emerald Springs	Noon	✓	$$$–	75	62
Horseshoe	Noon		$$	73	77
Howard Johnson	11 a.m.	✓	$$$–	66	53
Howard Johnson Airport	Noon	✓	$$$–	60	37
Imperial Palace	Noon	✓	$$$–	67	47

* Mardi Gras Tower rooms / Carnival Tower rooms

Concierge	Convention Facilities	Meeting Rooms	Valet Parking	RV Park	Room Service	Free Breakfast
		✓			✓	
✓	✓	✓	✓		✓	
		✓	✓		✓	
	✓	✓	✓		Breakfast	
		✓	✓			
		✓	✓		✓	
	✓	✓	✓		✓	
✓		✓	✓		✓	
		✓	✓		Breakfast	
			✓		✓	
	✓	✓	✓		✓	
✓	✓	✓	✓		✓	
✓	✓	✓	✓		✓	
	✓	✓	✓		✓	
		✓	✓		✓	
		✓			✓	
			✓		✓	
	✓	✓			✓	Coffee
	✓	✓	✓		✓	

Hotel	Fine Dining/ Type of Food	Coffee Shop	24-hr. Cafe	Buffet	Deli
Debbie Reynolds Hollywood Hotel	No		✓		
Desert Inn	④ French, Italian, Chinese, Continental	✓	✓	✓	✓
El Cortez	① Family/Steak	✓	✓		
Excalibur	④ Continental, Italian, Prime Rib, Steak	✓	✓	✓	
Fiesta	② Mexican, Steak	✓	✓	✓	✓
Fitzgeralds	② Steak, Italian	✓	✓	✓	
Flamingo Hilton	⑤ Italian, Chinese, Gourmet, Continental, Japanese	✓	✓	✓	✓
Four Queens	① American	✓	✓		
Fremont	① Ribs	✓	✓	✓	
Frontier	② Seafood, Mexican	✓	✓	✓	
Gold Coast	③ Steak, Italian, Seafood	✓	✓	✓	✓
Golden Nugget	② Italian, Chinese	✓	✓	✓	
Hard Rock Hotel	② Italian, Continental	✓	✓		
Harrah's	③ Steak/Seafood, Italian, Chinese	✓	✓	✓	
Holiday Inn Boardwalk	No	✓	✓	✓	✓
Holiday Inn Emerald Springs	No	✓		Breakfast	
Horseshoe	② Steak, Chinese	✓	✓	✓	✓
Howard Johnson	No	✓	✓		
Howard Johnson Airport	No				✓
Imperial Palace	⑤ Steak, Seafood, Chinese, Ribs, Pizza	✓	✓	✓	

Casino	24-hr. Bar	Lounge	Showroom Entertainment	Gift Shop Drugs/News	Hair Salon
		✓	Celebrity headliner, production show	✓	
✓	✓	✓	Celebrity headliner	✓	✓
✓	✓			✓	✓
✓	✓	✓	Production show, King Arthur's Tournament	✓	✓
✓	✓	✓		✓	
✓	✓			✓	
✓	✓	✓	Production show, musical comedy	✓	✓
✓	✓		Comedy show	✓	
✓	✓			✓	
✓	✓			✓	✓
✓	✓	✓	Dancing	✓	✓
✓	✓	✓	Production show	✓	✓
✓	✓	✓	Live music	✓	
✓	✓	✓	Production show, comedy show	✓	
✓	✓	✓	Comedy show	✓	
		✓			
✓	✓			✓	
✓	✓	✓	Variety, changes nightly		
		✓		✓	
✓	✓	✓	Impersonator show	✓	✓

Hotel	Pool	Youth Activities	Exercise Rooms	Tennis & Racket Games
Debbie Reynolds Hollywood Hotel	✓			
Desert Inn	✓ heated		Health Spa	Tennis
El Cortez				
Excalibur	✓ heated			
Fiesta	✓heated			
Fitzgeralds				
Flamingo Hilton	✓ heated		Health spa	Tennis
Four Queens				
Fremont				
Frontier	✓heated			Tennis
Gold Coast	✓heated	✓		
Golden Nugget	✓ heated		Health spa	
Hard Rock Hotel	✓ heated		Health spa	
Harrah's	✓	✓	✓	
Holiday Inn Boardwalk	✓			
Holiday Inn Emerald Springs	✓ heated		Privileges	
Horseshoe	✓			
Howard Johnson	✓			
Howard Johnson Airport	✓			
Imperial Palace	✓		✓	

Golf	Other	Movie Theater	Sauna/Steam Whirlpool	Shopping Arcade	Elec. Games Arcade
	Hollywood movie museum		✓		
On-site			✓		
					✓
	Wedding chapel		✓	✓	✓
					✓
	Wedding chapel		✓		
	Wedding chapel		✓	✓	✓
					✓
			✓	✓	✓
	Bowling	✓			✓
			✓	✓	✓
	Rock music memorabilia		✓		✓
			✓		✓
				✓	✓
			✓		
			✓		✓
					✓
	Auto collection, wedding chapel		✓	✓	✓

Hotel	Room Star Rating	Zone	Street Address
King 8 Hotel	★★	1	3330 West Tropicana Avenue Las Vegas, 89103
La Concha	★¹/₂	1	2955 Las Vegas Blvd., South Las Vegas, 89109
La Quinta	★★¹/₂	1	3970 Paradise Road Las Vegas, 89109
Lady Luck	★★★	2	206 North Third Street Las Vegas, 89101
Las Vegas Club	★★★	2	18 East Fremont Street Las Vegas, 89101
Las Vegas Hilton	★★★★	1	3000 Paradise Road Las Vegas, 89109
Luxor	★★★¹/₂	1	3900 Las Vegas Blvd., South Las Vegas, 89119-1000
Main Street Station	★★★	2	200 North Main Street Las Vegas, 89109
Maxim	★★★	1	160 East Flamingo Road Las Vegas, 89109
MGM Grand	★★★★	1	3799 Las Vegas Blvd., South Las Vegas, 89109
Mirage	★★★★¹/₂	1	3400 Las Vegas Blvd., South Las Vegas, 89109
Monte Carlo	★★★¹/₂	1	3770 Las Vegas Blvd., South Las Vegas, 89109
Nevada Hotel	★	2	235 South Main Street Las Vegas, 89101
Nevada Palace	★★¹/₂	5	5255 Boulder Highway Las Vegas, 89122
New York–New York	★★★	1	3790 Las Vegas Blvd., South Las Vegas, 89109
Orleans	★★★¹/₂	3	4500 West Valley View Avenue Las Vegas, 89103
Palace Station	★★★¹/₂	1	2411 West Sahara Avenue Las Vegas, 89102
Plaza	★★★	2	One Main Street Las Vegas, 89101
Quality Inn	★★¹/₂	1	377 East Flamingo Road Las Vegas, 89109
Residence Inn by Marriott	★★★★	1	3225 Paradise Road Las Vegas, 89109

Local Phone	Fax	800 Reservations	Discount Available	Number of Rooms
(702) 736-8988	(702) 736-7106	(800) 634-3488	Senior, AAA	300
(702) 735-1255	(702) 369-0862	None		352
(702) 796-9000	(702) 796-3537	(800) NU-ROOMS	Senior	228
(702) 477-3000	(702) 477-7021	(800) LADY-LUCK		792
(702) 385-1664	(702) 387-6071	(800) 634-6532		415
(702) 732-5111	(702) 794-3611	(800) 732-7117	Senior, military, government	3,174
(702) 262-4000	(702) 262-4404	(800) 288-1000		4,474
(702) 387-1896	(702) 386-4421	(800) 465-0711		406
(702) 731-4300	(702) 735-3252	(800) 634-6987		800
(702) 891-1111	(702) 891-3036	(800) 929-1111		5,005
(702) 791-7111	(702) 791-7446	(800) 627-6667		3,049
(702) 730-7777	(702) 730-7200	(800) 311-8999		3,002
(702) 385-7311	(702) 385-1854	(800) 637-5777		160
(702) 458-8810	(702) 458-3361	(800) 634-6283		209
(702) 740-6969	(702) 740-6920	(800) NY-FOR-ME		2,035
(702) 365-7111	(702) 365-7599	(800) ORLEANS		840
(702) 367-2411	(702) 367-2748	(800) 634-3101	Senior	1,028
(702) 386-2110	(702) 382-8281	(800) 634-6575		1,052
(702) 733-7777	(702) 369-6911	(800) 634-6617	Senior	324
(702) 796-9300	(702) 796-9562	(800) 331-3131	Senior, military	192

Hotel	Ck. Out Time	Non-Smoking	Rack Rate	Room Quality Rating	Room Value Rating
King 8 Hotel	Noon	✓	$$–	47	36
La Concha	1 p.m.	✓	$$–	45	24
La Quinta	Noon	✓	$$$–	64	45
Lady Luck	Noon	✓	$$$–	67	47
Las Vegas Club	Noon	✓	$$–	69	76
Las Vegas Hilton	Noon	✓	$$$$–	88	64
Luxor	11 a.m.	✓	$$$$$–	81	40
Main Street Station	1 p.m.	✓	$$+	73	71
Maxim	Noon	✓	$$$–	70	50
MGM Grand	11 a.m.	✓	$$$$$$+	85	38
Mirage	Noon	✓	$$$$$$$$$–	92	34
Monte Carlo	11 a.m.	✓	$$$$$–	80	39
Nevada Hotel	Noon	✓	$$–	31	13
Nevada Palace	Noon	✓	$$–	63	60
New York–New York	11 a.m.	✓	$$$$$–	69	29
Orleans	Noon	✓	$$$+	81	60
Palace Station	Noon	✓	$$$$–	76	47
Plaza	11 a.m.	✓	$$$–	70	74
Quality Inn	Noon	✓	$$$–	63	42
Residence Inn by Marriott	Noon	✓	$$$$–	83	59

Con-cierge	Convention Facilities	Meeting Rooms	Valet Parking	RV Park	Room Service	Free Breakfast
		✓				✓
			✓		✓	
		✓	✓		✓	
	✓	✓	✓		✓	
✓	✓	✓	✓		✓	
			✓			
		✓	✓		✓	
✓	✓	✓	✓		✓	
✓	✓	✓	✓		✓	
✓	✓	✓	✓		✓	
	✓	✓		✓		
✓	✓	✓	✓			
	✓	✓	✓		✓	
✓	✓	✓	✓		✓	
	✓	✓	✓		✓	
		✓			✓	
		✓			Breakfast	✓

Hotel	Fine Dining/ Type of Food	Coffee Shop	24-hr. Cafe	Buffet	Deli
King 8 Hotel	No	✓	✓		
La Concha	① Oriental				
La Quinta	No				
Lady Luck	① Steak/Seafood	✓	✓	✓	
Las Vegas Club	① Steak/Seafood	✓	✓		✓
Las Vegas Hilton	≈ French, Oriental, Italian, American, Mexican, Japanese	✓	✓	✓	
Luxor	③ American, Seafood, Steak	✓	✓	✓	✓
Main Street Station	② Steak, Brewery	✓	✓	✓	
Maxim	① Italian/ Continental	✓	✓	✓	✓
MGM Grand	⑤ Steak, Italian, Chinese, American, Seafood	✓	✓	✓	✓
Mirage	⑤ French, Japanese, Steak/Seafood, Italian, Chinese	✓	✓	✓	
Monte Carlo	③ Steak, Chinese, Italian	✓	✓	✓	✓
Nevada Hotel	No				
Nevada Palace	① Italian/Steak/ Seafood	✓	✓	✓	✓
New York–New York	③ Steak, Chinese, Italian	✓	✓		✓
Orleans	③ Italian, Steak, Mexican	✓	✓	✓	
Palace Station	④ Seafood, Chinese, Mexican, Italian	✓	✓	✓	
Plaza	① American/ Continental	✓	✓		Snack bar
Quality Inn	No	✓	✓		
Residence Inn by Marriott	No				

Casino	24-hr. Bar	Lounge	Showroom Entertainment	Gift Shop Drugs/News	Hair Salon
✓	✓	✓		✓	
				✓	✓
✓	✓		Production show	✓	
✓	✓	✓		✓	
✓	✓	✓	Production show	✓	✓
✓	✓	✓	Live entertainment changes nightly	✓	✓
✓	✓			✓	
✓	✓	✓	Comedy show	✓	✓
✓	✓	✓	Production show, celebrity headliner	✓	✓
✓	✓	✓	Production show, celebrity headliner	✓	✓
✓	✓	✓	Production show celebrity headliner	✓	✓
✓	✓			✓	
✓	✓	✓	Production show	✓	✓
✓	✓	✓	Celebrity headliners	✓	✓
✓	✓	✓		✓	✓
✓	✓	✓	Production show	✓	✓
✓	✓	✓		✓	

Hotel	Pool	Youth Activities	Exercise Rooms	Tennis & Racket Games
King 8 Hotel	✓			
La Concha	✓			
La Quinta	✓ heated			
Lady Luck	✓			
Las Vegas Club				
Las Vegas Hilton	✓ heated		✓	Tennis
Luxor	✓ heated	✓	✓	
Main Street Station				
Maxim	✓ heated			
MGM Grand	✓ heated	✓	✓	✓
Mirage	✓ heated	✓	Health spa	
Monte Carlo	✓ heated		Health spa	✓
Nevada Hotel				
Nevada Palace	✓			
New York–New York	✓ heated	Family entertainment center	Health spa	
Orleans	✓ heated	✓		
Palace Station	✓ heated	✓		
Plaza	✓ heated			Tennis
Quality Inn	✓ heated			
Residence Inn by Marriott	✓ heated		Privileges	

Golf	Other	Movie Theater	Sauna/Steam Whirlpool	Shopping Arcade	Elec. Games Arcade
			✓		
			✓		
			✓		
Privileges	Gated attraction		✓	✓	✓
	Gated attractions	IMAX	✓	✓	✓
					✓
	Theme park, wedding chapel	✓	✓	✓	✓
			✓	✓	✓
	Microbrewery, wedding chapel		✓	✓	✓
			✓		
	Roller coaster, wedding chapel		✓	✓	✓
	Bowling Alley	✓	✓	✓	✓
			✓		✓
	Wedding chapel				✓
			✓		✓
	Grocery shopping service		✓		

Hotel	Room Star Rating	Zone	Street Address
Rio	★★★★	1	3700 West Flamingo Road Las Vegas, 89103
Riviera	★★★¹/₂	1	2901 Las Vegas Blvd., South Las Vegas, 89109
Royal Hotel	★★¹/₂	1	99 Convention Center Drive Las Vegas, 89109
Sahara	★★★	1	2535 Las Vegas Blvd., South Las Vegas, 89109
Sam's Town	★★★¹/₂	5	5111 Boulder Highway Las Vegas, 89122
San Remo	★★★¹/₂	1	115 East Tropicana Avenue Las Vegas, 89109
Santa Fe	★★★	4	4949 N. Rancho Drive Las Vegas, 89130
Showboat	★★★¹/₂	5	2800 East Fremont Street Las Vegas, 89104
St. Tropez	★★★★¹/₂	1	455 East Harmon Avenue Las Vegas, 89109
Stardust	★★¹/₂/ ★★★¹/₂*	1	3000 Las Vegas Blvd., South Las Vegas, 89109
Stratosphere	★★★¹/₂	1	2000 Las Vegas Blvd., South Las Vegas, 89104
Sunset Station	★★★¹/₂	5	1301 Sunset Road Las Vegas, 89014
Super 8	★★	1	4250 South Koval Lane Las Vegas, 89109
Texas Station	★★★	3	2101 Texas Star Lane Las Vegas, 89030
Travelodge Las Vegas Inn	★★	1	1501 West Sahara Las Vegas, 89102
Treasure Island	★★★¹/₂	1	3300 Las Vegas Blvd., South Las Vegas, 89109
Tropicana	★★★	1	3801 Las Vegas Blvd., South Las Vegas, 89109
Vacation Village	★★	1	6711 Las Vegas Blvd., South Las Vegas, 89119
Westward Ho	★★	1	2900 Las Vegas Blvd., South Las Vegas, 89109

*garden rooms / tower rooms
** under construction at press time

Local Phone	Fax	800 Reservations	Discount Available	Number of Rooms
(702) 252-7777	(702) 252-8909	(800) PLAYRIO		2,563
(702) 734-5110	(702) 794-9663	(800) 634-6753		2,075
(702) 735-6117	(702) 735-2546	(800) 634-6118		236
(702) 737-2111	(702) 737-1017	(888) 696-2121	Senior, military, government	1,758
(702) 456-7777	(702) 454-8014	(800) 634-6371		650
(702) 739-9000	(702) 736-1120	(800) 522-7366		711
(702) 658-4900	(702) 658-4919	(800) 872-6823	Military, government, corporate	200
(702) 385-9123	(702) 383-9238	(800) 826-2800	Government, military	450
(702) 369-5400	(702) 369-1150	(800) 666-5400	Senior, military, AAA	150
(702) 732-6111	(702) 732-6296	(800) 634-6757		2,431
(702) 380-7777	(702) 380-7732	(800) 99-TOWER		1,500
(702) 547-7777	(702) 547-7744	(888) 786-7369		448
(702) 794-0888	(702) 794-3504	(800) 800-8000	Senior, military	300
(702) 631-1000	(702) 631-8120	(800) 654-8888		200
(702) 733-0001	(702) 733-1571	(800) 554-4092	Senior, military, AAA	223
(702) 894-7111	(702) 894-7414	(800) 944-7444		2,900
(702) 739-2222	(702) 739-2469	(800) 634-4000	Military	1,874
(702) 897-1700	(702) 361-6726	(800) 388-0608		313
(702) 731-2900	(702) 731-6154	(800) 634-6803		800

Hotel	Ck. Out Time	Non-Smoking	Rack Rate	Room Quality Rating	Room Value Rating
Rio	Noon	✓	$$$$$–	88	50
Riviera	Noon	✓	$$$$–	82	51
Royal Hotel	Noon	✓	$$+	57	46
Sahara	Noon	✓	$$$–	70	52
Sam's Town	Noon	✓	$$$–	80	78
San Remo	Noon	✓	$$$$+	78	44
Santa Fe	Noon	✓	$$+	72	66
Showboat	Noon	✓	$$$–	76	63
St. Tropez	Noon	✓	$$$$$$–	93	53
Stardust	Noon	Floors	$$$–/ $$$$$*	58/76	41/37
Stratosphere	11 a.m.	✓	$$$$–	82	55
Sunset Station	Noon	✓	$$$$–	82	51
Super 8	Noon	✓	$$–	48	34
Texas Station	Noon	✓	$$$–	70	50
Travelodge Las Vegas Inn	Noon	✓	$$–	49	35
Treasure Island	Noon	✓	$$$$+	80	46
Tropicana	Noon	✓	$$$$+	69	34
Vacation Village	Noon	✓	$$$–	49	27
Westward Ho	11 a.m.	✓	$$–	48	25

* garden rooms / tower rooms

Con- cierge	Convention Facilities	Meeting Rooms	Valet Parking	RV Park	Room Service	Free Breakfast
✓	✓	✓	✓		✓	Coffee
✓	✓	✓	✓		✓	
					✓	
	✓	✓	✓		✓	
✓	✓	✓	✓	✓	Breakfast	
	✓	✓	✓	✓	✓	
	✓	✓	✓			
	✓	✓	✓	✓	✓	
✓		✓			✓	✓
	✓	✓	✓		✓	
✓		✓	✓		✓	
✓	✓	✓	✓		✓	
		✓		✓		
✓			✓		✓	
		✓				
✓	✓	✓	✓		✓	
✓	✓	✓	✓		✓	
		✓			✓	
		✓				

Hotel	Fine Dining/ Type of Food	Coffee Shop	24-hr. Cafe	Buffet	Deli
Rio	Δ Italian, Oyster Bar, ✓ Chinese, Southwestern, New Orleans, and more	✓	✓	✓	
Riviera	③ Steak/Seafood, Chinese, Italian	✓	✓	✓	
Royal Hotel	① Chinese				
Sahara	② Steak, Mexican	✓	✓	✓	
Sam's Town	③ Steak, Italian, American	✓	✓	✓	✓
San Remo	③ Italian, Japanese, Steak/Seafood	✓	✓	✓	✓
Santa Fe	④ Mexican, Steak French, Italian	✓	✓	✓	✓
Showboat	② Italian, Steak/ Seafood	✓	✓	✓	
St. Tropez	Adjacent				✓
Stardust	③ Rib, Steak/Lobster, Mexican	✓	✓	✓	✓
Stratosphere	④ Continental, Steak, Italian, American	✓	✓	✓	
Sunset Station	④ American, Steak/ Seafood, Mexican, Italian	✓	✓	✓	✓
Super 8	No		Adjacent		
Texas Station	⑤ Seafood, Italian, Mexican, Steak, Chinese	✓	✓	✓	✓
Travelodge Las Vegas Inn	No				
Treasure Island	③ Seafood/Steak, American, Chinese	✓	✓	✓	✓
Tropicana	④ Steak, Chinese, Japanese, Italian	✓	✓	✓	✓
Vacation Village	② Chinese, Mexican/American	✓	✓		
Westward Ho	No	✓		✓	✓

Casino	24-hr. Bar	Lounge	Showroom Entertainment	Gift Shop Drugs/News	Hair Salon
✓	✓	✓	Live entertainment	✓	✓
✓	✓	✓	Production show, female impersonators, comedy club	✓	✓
✓	✓			✓	
✓	✓	✓	Production shows	✓	✓
✓	✓	✓	Western dance hall	✓	
✓	✓	✓	Production show	✓	
✓	✓	✓		✓	
✓	✓	✓		✓	✓
	✓	✓		Adjacent	
✓	✓	✓	Production show	✓	✓
✓	✓	✓	Production show	✓	
✓	✓	✓	Live entertainment	✓	
Adjacent	Adjacent	Adjacent			
✓	✓	✓		✓	
				✓	
✓	✓	✓	Production show	✓	✓
✓	✓	✓	Production show, comedy club	✓	✓
✓	✓	✓		✓	✓
✓	✓	✓	Production show	✓	

Hotel	Pool	Youth Activities	Exercise Rooms	Tennis & Racket Games
Rio	✓ heated		✓	
Riviera	✓ heated		✓	Tennis
Royal Hotel	✓			
Sahara	✓			
Sam's Town	✓	✓		
San Remo	✓ heated			
Santa Fe		Nursery		
Showboat	✓ heated	✓		
St. Tropez	✓ heated		✓	
Stardust	✓ heated			
Stratosphere	✓ heated	✓		
Sunset Station	✓	✓		
Super 8	✓			
Texas Station	✓			
Travelodge Las Vegas Inn	✓			
Treasure Island	✓ heated	✓	✓	
Tropicana	✓ heated		✓	
Vacation Village	✓			
Westward Ho	✓ heated			

Golf	Other	Movie Theater	Sauna/Steam Whirlpool	Shopping Arcade	Elec. Games Arcade
Privileges			✓	✓	✓
	Wedding chapel		✓	✓	✓
			✓	✓	✓
	Indoor park, 56-lane bowling center		✓		✓
					✓
	Bowling, ice skating				✓
	Bowling, shuttle to airport				✓
	Shuttle to the Strip & airport		✓		
			✓	✓	✓
	Big Shot (thrill ride), roller coaster, wedding chapels			✓	✓
		✓	✓		✓
			✓		
		✓ 12 screens	✓		✓
					✓
	Wedding chapels		✓	✓	✓
Privileges	Wedding chapel		✓	✓	✓
			✓		✓
			✓		

Other Books to Read

Anderson, Ian. *Turning the Tables on Las Vegas*. Vintage Books, 1976. This astute guide for aspiring card counters includes minute detail on playing and betting strategies, camouflage, handling casino personnel, and the winning attitude.

Bass, Thomas. *Eudaemonic Pie*. Houghton Mifflin, 1985. The fascinating story of physicists from the University of California–Santa Cruz who invent a computer to beat the casinos at the game of roulette. A hilarious, true-life adventure.

Castleman, Deke. *Las Vegas*. Compass American Guides, 1993. A well-written guide to Las Vegas and its environs. This book is long on anecdote and history. If you take only one other book to Las Vegas, take this one. A very enjoyable read. Castleman has also authored an excellent guide to the entire state of Nevada.

Dalton, Michael. *Blackjack, a Professional Reference*. Spur of the Moment Publishing, 1992. A sourcebook for professionals and serious recreational players.

Demaris, Ovid, and Ed Reid. *Green Felt Jungle*. Trident Press, 1963. When first published, this was a highly sensational exposé of Las Vegas—its mobsters, rackets, and prostitution. Lively reading. . . .

Humble, Land, and Carl Cooper. *The World's Greatest Blackjack Book*. Doubleday, 1980. A college-level crash course on one of the most popular games in Las Vegas. Everything you need to know—from card-counting strategies to spotting dealers who cheat. Includes many useful charts.

McGervey, John D. *Probabilities in Everyday Life*. Ballantine Books, 1986. Although this book covers much more than gambling, it also deals with the odds of winning at casino games. It identifies the faulty logic and misleading statistics that can lead to bad debts. Recommended reading.

Orkin, Mikael. *Can You Win?* W. H. Freeman and Company, 1991. A discussion of the real odds for casino gambling, sports betting, and lotteries, including winning strategies and computer odds.

Ortiz, Darwin. *On Casino Gambling*. Dodd, Mead & Company, 1986. Well written in a fluent and understandable style, this is a useful book for understanding the basics of casino games.

Rubin, Max. *CompCity: A Guide to Free Las Vegas Vacations.* Huntington Press, 1994. A practical and often hilarious guide to taking advantage of every possible comp and freebee.

Silberstang, Edwin. *The Winner's Guide to Casino Gambling.* Signet, 1980. The basic primer on casinos in simple, easy-to-understand language. A difficult subject made simple and fun.

Smith, John L. *No Limit: The Rise and Fall of Bob Stupak and Las Vegas' Stratosphere Tower.* Huntington Press, 1997. Well-researched, unauthorized biography of one of Las Vegas's most colorful characters.

Thompson, Hunter S. *Fear and Loathing in Las Vegas: A Savage Journey to the Heart of the American Dream.* Fawcett Popular Library, 1971. A now-famous account of Thompson's trip to Las Vegas to cover the Mint 400 Desert Race. The cast includes a 300-pound Samoan attorney, a red Cadillac, and enough psychedelic drugs to kill any normal human being.

Thorp, Dr. Edward O. *The Mathematics of Gambling.* Gambling Times, 1984. Thorp's book *Beat the Dealer* changed casino blackjack forever. In this book, he turns his attention to baccarat, roulette, and other games.

Vinson, Barney. *Las Vegas: Behind the Tables, Parts I and II.* Gollehon, 1986. These books are an entertaining look at gambling and casino management; they include amazing stories, tips, and trivia.

Vinson, Barney. *Casino Secrets.* Huntington Press, 1997. Breezy, entertaining, anecdotal gambling instruction and insider guide to Las Vegas casinos.

Vogliotti, Gabriel R. *The Girls of Nevada.* Citadel Press, 1975. One of the best books written about Nevada, this book focuses on prostitution—its sociological issues, advocates, and opponents. A truly unique history.

Whitney, Branch. *Hiking Las Vegas: 60 Hikes within 60 Minutes of the Strip.* Huntington Press, 1997. Details hikes in Red Rock Canyon, Mount Charleston, Lake Mead, and other areas with description, photos, and maps.

Index

1998 *Unofficial Guide* **Reader Survey**

If you would like to express your opinion about Las Vegas or this guidebook, complete the following survey and mail it to:

> *Unofficial Guide* Reader Survey
> P.O. Box 43059
> Birmingham, AL 35243

Inclusive dates of your visit _____

Members of your party:	Person 1	Person 2	Person 3	Person 4	Person 5
Gender (M or F)	_____	_____	_____	_____	_____
Age	_____	_____	_____	_____	_____

How many times have you been to Las Vegas? _____

On your most recent trip, where did you stay? _____

Concerning accommodations, on a scale with 100 best and 0 worst, how would you rate:

The quality of your room? _____ The value for the money? _____

The quietness of your room? _____ Check-in/checkout efficiency? _____

Shuttle service to the parks? _____ Swimming pool facilities? _____

Did you rent a car? _____ From whom? _____

Concerning your rental car, on a scale with 100 best and 0 worst, how would you rate:

Pickup processing efficiency? _____ Return processing efficiency? _____

Condition of the car? _____ Cleanliness of the car? _____

Airport shuttle efficiency? _____

Concerning your dining experiences:

How many restaurant meals (including fast food) did you average per day? _____

How much (approximately) did your party spend on meals per day? _____

Favorite restaurants in Las Vegas? _____

_____

Did you buy this guide: Before leaving? _____ While on your trip? _____

How did you hear about this guide?

Loaned or recommended by a friend _____ Radio or TV _____

Newspaper or magazine _____ Bookstore salesperson _____

Just picked it out on my own _____ Library _____

What other guidebooks did you use on this trip? _____

_____

On the 100 best and 0 worst scale, how would you rate them? _____

_____

Using the same scale, how would you rate the *Unofficial Guide?* _____

Are *Unofficial Guides* readily available in bookstores in your area? _____

Have you used other *Unofficial Guides?* _____ Which one(s)? _____

Comments about your Las Vegas trip or about the *Unofficial Guide:* _____

_____

_____

_____

_____

_____

_____

_____

_____

_____

_____